the woman who fell from the sky

AN AMERICAN

JOURNALIST

IN YEMEN

the woman who fell from the sky

JENNIFER STEIL

BROADWAY BOOKS · NEW YORK

BROADWAY

Published in the United States by Broadway Books, an imprint of the Crown Publishing Group, a division of Random House, Inc., New York.
www.crownpublishing.com

BROADWAY BOOKS and the Broadway Books colophon are trademarks of Random House, Inc.

Grateful acknowledgment is made to the following for permission to reprint previously published and unpublished material:

American Institute for Yemeni Studies for permission to reprint a poem from *The Book of Sana'a: Poetry of Abd al-Aziz al-Maqali,* translated by Bob Holman and Sam Liebhaber (2004). Reprinted by permission of the American Institute for Yemeni Studies.

Food and Agriculture Organization of the United Nations for permission to reprint excerpts of the locust recipes taken from their website. Reprinted by permission of the Food and Agriculture Organization of the United Nations, Viale delle Terme di Caracalla, 00153 Rome, Italy.

The *Yemen Observer* for permission to reprint excerpts of articles from the *Yemen Observer.* Reprinted by permission of Faris al-Sanabani and the *Yemen Observer.*

Zaid al-Alaya'a for permission to reprint an excerpt of his note and poem to Jennifer Steil. Reprinted by permission of Zaid al-Alaya'a.

Library of Congress Cataloging-in-Publication Data
Steil, Jennifer F.
The woman who fell from the sky : an American journalist in Yemen / Jennifer Steil.—1st ed.
p.   cm.
1. Steil, Jennifer—Travel—Yemen—San'a'. 2. San'a' (Yemen)—Description and travel.
3. Journalists—Yemen—San'a'—Biography. I. Title.
DS248.S26S74 2010
953.32—dc22   2009037172

ISBN 978-0-7679-3050-5

Printed in the United States of America

Design by ELINA D. NUDELMAN

10 9 8 7 6 5 4 3 2 1

First Edition

For Kawkab,
and all the other feisty Yemeni women
who give me hope for the country

she was a woman
who fell from the sky in robes
of dew
and became
a city

CONTENTS

ACKNOWLEDGMENTS

Nothing in this book or my life would be remotely possible without the entire staff, past and present, of the *Yemen Observer*. Thank you for working so very hard for me, despite my mercurial management style. I owe you all an infinite debt of gratitude.

I also owe bottomless thanks to:

Theo Padnos, for getting me here.

My friend Tom Zoellner, whose invaluable assistance and encouragement from the very beginning helped this book to get off the ground.

My agent, Brettne Bloom, for believing in this book, for her unflagging enthusiasm and support, and for her inspirational thoughts on my original proposal.

My editor Kris Puopolo and her assistant editor, Stephanie Bowen, for their wise counsel in shaping this book, their meticulous editing, and their patience with my frequent long-distance phone calls.

My editor Christine Pride, for guiding this book through its final stages of labor and birth and for so indefatigably championing it.

Faris al-Sanabani, for trusting me. Sometimes.

Sabri Saleem, for his warm friendship and for providing me with my first Yemeni home.

Sami al-Siyani, for being the best friend, neighbor, and guide to Old Sana'a I can imagine.

ACKNOWLEDGMENTS

My neighbors in the al-Wushali district of Old Sana'a for their infinite hospitality.

Muhoro Ndungu, for his tolerance of my moods during the darkest times, for his witch doctor skills, and for taking me in when I was homeless.

Bushra Nasr, for her generosity and friendship.

All of my Arabic teachers, but especially Fouad, for their patience with my erratic progress.

Mr. Jamal Hindi and the entire staff of Al Mankal restaurant, who always know exactly what I want for lunch.

The well-behaved taxi drivers who kept their hands on the wheel.

Harris Collingwood, for emotional and material support during difficult times.

Anne-Christine, Angelica, Carolyn, Koosje, and Jilles, housemates who turned my gingerbread house into a home.

Aida, without whom we would all have been wading through several feet of dust.

Rasheed, for showing me his Soqotra.

Anne Leewis, for helping me find a life outside work.

Phil Boyle, for making me laugh, feeding me curry, and granting me a pivotal interview with a British MP.

Don Lipinski, for the wine, movies, and loyal support, despite our political differences.

Marvin and Pearl, for the bootleg gin and Soqotra.

Tobias Lechtenfeld, for the lovely times in Sana'a, and for remaining a friend.

Peter Toth, for his phenomenal generosity, for his devoted friendship, and for Paris.

Chris and Peta Shute, for housing me as I wrote the first chapters of this book.

Lloyd, Dave, Colin, and the entire CP team, for keeping us all safe during the writing of this book and beyond.

Negesti, Alem, and Emebet, for taking such good care of us at home.

Cole and Ali, for keeping their senses of humor when I lost mine.

My classmates and professors from the Columbia University Graduate School of Journalism, for their assistance in creating my original training course.

My friends in New York and elsewhere in the world—too numerous to list here—whose love and e-mails help keep me sane.

My parents, who are always supportive, even when they doubt the wisdom of my career choices.

Timothy Achille Torlot, for reading this book more times than anyone should, and for loving me more than I thought anyone could.

ONE

fantasia in gingerbread

I didn't immediately see Zuhra when I walked into the bridal chamber. The room was dim, and she was curled over in prayer on the floor to my left, a mass of white satin with a black scarf over her head. Few people were allowed in the room with her—only sisters and dearest friends—and everyone was quiet. I stood still against a wall, watching her, waiting for her to finish. I hadn't thought I would see Zuhra until she began her slow, deliberate march down the catwalk that ran the length of the wedding hall. But her sisters had summoned me, pulling me by the hand into this back room. Zuhra looked tiny and vulnerable, solemnly whispering her prayers.

But all hint of gravity vanished as she finished and pulled the veil from her face to beam up at me. She stood, the silky scarf slithering from her bare shoulders, and came to let me kiss her. Above the white of her Brooklyn-bought dress, her arms, back, and clavicle were painted with curling flowery vines, rendered in *nagsh,* a black ink favored by Yemeni brides. We didn't speak at first but just stood smiling at each other.

"*Antee jameela,*" I said, touching her tiny waist. "Beautiful. Like a little doll bride."

"Really?" She turned this way and that, so I could admire all of her. Her thick black hair was piled on top of her head in fanciful hair-sprayed loops.

Her dark eyes were outlined in kohl, her face thickly powdered, and her lips colored a pale pomegranate.

"Really. I wish I could take a photo!" We had all been patted down at the door, to ensure none of us smuggled in a camera.

Zuhra pulled me down beside her on cushions at the end of the room, where we stayed for another hour waiting for her guests to finish their sunset prayers and work themselves into a frenzy of anticipation. Zuhra passed the time chatting with me and making calls on her mobile phone, mostly to her groom, who was (contrary to tradition) picking her up at the end of the night. "You are sure you haven't argued with anyone today?" she said into the receiver. "You sound like maybe you argued." She was worried that her husband had squabbled with her brother but was evidently reassured.

"Are you nervous?" I said. All the Yemeni brides I'd seen before had looked stricken with terror on their walks down the aisle. But unlike those brides, Zuhra knew her groom.

"No," she said, smiling placidly. "I am just happy."

Her two older sisters, clad in long, shiny ball gowns, popped in to tell us it was almost time.

I stood next to Zuhra, feeling tall and awkward in heels, which I rarely suffer for anyone. Outside the door, we heard the increasingly boisterous ululations of women, meant as encouragement for the bride. As this Arabic yodeling threatened to reach a crescendo, Zuhra suddenly looked panicked.

"My pill!" She grabbed her purse from a friend standing nearby and rummaged through the pockets of her wallet. She pulled out a blister pack of birth control pills, with all but four missing. We'd spent an entire afternoon picking out these pills, making sure they were the right combination of hormones and made by a legitimate pharmaceutical company.

Zuhra struggled with the package, unable to get the pill out with her fake nails. "Here," I said. "Let me." I popped one out and handed it to her. She washed it down with a swallow of water from someone's bottle and picked up her skirts.

"Jeez, Zuhra, just in time," I whispered as we started out the door.

I entered the room just ahead of her. The hundreds of black-cocooned women I had seen hurrying into the hall earlier that evening had transformed into gaudy miniskirted butterflies, coated with glitter and lipstick, tottering on three-inch heels. There were no men.

Zuhra's youngest sister thrust a basket of jasmine petals into my hand. "Here," she said. "Throw."

Zuhra stepped forward. The lights had been dimmed, and all of the younger women and girls were on the stage at the end of the catwalk, their hands over their heads, swaying like so many colored streamers. Music swelled from behind the screen, where the band was hidden. At first I couldn't quite believe the evidence of my ears. At a Yemeni wedding I expected Arabic music. But no, Zuhra was starting down the aisle toward her married life to Celine Dion's "My Heart Will Go On," from the soundtrack of *Titanic*.

☪

THERE IS AN OLD JOKE about Yemen, told to any traveler who sticks around long enough: "Noah came back to Earth recently, curious to see how it had evolved since his time. In a private jet on loan from God, he first flew over France and said, 'My! Look at France! How it has changed! What exciting new architecture! What amazing innovation!' He then flew over Germany. 'Incredible! I would hardly recognize it! So much new technology! Such thrilling industry!' And then he headed to southern Arabia. 'Ah, Yemen,' he said fondly. 'I'd know it anywhere. Hasn't changed a bit.'"

In many ways, it hasn't. Of course, I wasn't in Yemen back in the first millennium BC, when Noah's son Shem is said to have founded the capital city of Sana'a. But in many parts of the country, people are living exactly as their ancestors did thousands of years ago. They herd goats and cows; they grow wheat, pomegranates, and grapes; they travel long distances to fetch water. They live in simple square mud-brick homes. They paint themselves with *nagsh* for weddings. They pray.

The ancient landscape reveals little evidence of the passage of time. On a flyover today, Noah would find that erosion has run light fingers over the jagged mountains of the central highlands. Long stretches of empty beaches in the south are touched by the same tides that have washed them since the Flood. In the east, desert sands shift in barely perceptible ways. The green terraces carved into the Haraz mountains in the west or the hills around Ibb and Ta'iz to the south may have been there since the dawn of agriculture, cultivated by generation after generation of Yemeni farmers. The dense vegetation of the valleys suggests the whim of a playful god who, weary of the relentless beige of Arabian rock and sand, tossed a thick emerald quilt over Yemen's countryside, creating a fertile layer that has fed the Yemeni people for generations.

Noah would find the most familiar territory in the country's remotest places, such as the island of Soqotra, located 220 miles off Yemen's eastern coast. On Soqotra, there are few roads and fewer electric lights. The dominant structures are not the crumbling stone buildings (which blend so completely into the hillsides that you don't see them until you trip over a small child running out of one) but its fanciful dragon's blood trees, their tall, thousand-year-old trunks erupting into such a wild tangle of branches that they resemble a forest of umbrellas blown upward by the wind.

Many Soqotri people still live in caves, where they boil tea over fires in a corner to serve with goat milk still warm from their animals. Their dining rooms are thin woven mats spread outside their doors, where they eat fish stew with chewy flatbread under salty night skies. There are people on Soqotra who have no idea what happened on September 11, 2001, in America. There are no radio stations, and almost no one can read. Everything they know they have heard from neighbors, imams, or the occasional foreign aid worker. Britney Spears does not exist here. Hollywood is meaningless. Ice cream would not survive—there is almost no refrigeration.

Many of Yemen's mainland villages feel just as remote, tucked along a mountain ridge or at the edge of a stretch of desert. These villages get their news from state-controlled television or from the mosque. Only the elite would pick up a newspaper or read a book. But what use is news of the outside world to these people? Will it help their crops to grow? Will it keep their goats free from disease? Will it bring them closer to God? No? Well, then.

Yemen has not only kept herself looking much the same as she did in Noah's time, but she also wears the same perfume she did when she was young. Cruising at a lower altitude, Noah would smell frankincense, the fragrant resin that put Yemen on the map for traders four thousand years ago and is still burned as incense; the acrid sweat of laboring men and rayon-wrapped women; the purple-and-white jasmine flowers that proliferate in its lush lowlands; and the smoke of wood fires warming bread ovens. In her cities, these odors mingle with the smell of frying beans and jalapeños, fenugreek-flavored meat stews, tobacco smoke, and roasted lamb, while the countryside is fragrant with overtones of manure and ripening bananas, dates, and mangoes.

Following those scents earthward, Noah would soon glimpse clusters of boxy brown houses, their roofs strewn with airing carpets and drying laundry. Through the maze of streets hurry men on their way to mosque, women selling flat disks of bread, and children chasing a ball.

Sana'a is one of the oldest cities in the Arabian Peninsula—and in the world. Built at least 2,500 years ago, it was once home to Sabean kings and Himyarite rulers.

Islam arrived in the seventh century AD, rearranging the face of the city. Many of the buildings erected during the time of the Prophet Mohammed are still standing, though crumbling a bit around the edges. The Great Mosque of Sana'a was built under the instructions of the Prophet himself, according to local legend. It is not only the biggest but the most famous mosque in the Old City (Sana'a al-Qadeema). It contains a large library and a host of ancient manuscripts.

More than a hundred other mosques now populate the Old City, a fact that is particularly evident during the calls to prayer. No matter where you stand, you feel as if you are directly underneath a mosque loudspeaker. The muezzins drown out conversations and make it impossible to listen to music. Which of course is the point. Prayer is the only appropriate activity at these times. When Allah's messengers talk, you should be listening.

No modern buildings mar the ancient aesthetic of the Old City, which was declared a UNESCO World Heritage Site in 1984; it probably looks much the same as it did thousands of years ago. Noah would definitely recognize it.

This is Yemen yesterday, this is Yemen today.

☪

YET THERE ARE unmistakable signs of change, too. The city roofs are now dotted with satellite dishes. Billboards advertising GIRL brand ghee, the Islamic Bank of Yemen, cardamom and cinnamon toffees, and the fabulousness of President Ali Abdullah Saleh deface the sides of buildings. Women can be seen walking to jobs in government ministries. Men sport pinstriped Western suits or polo shirts. Brides march down the aisle to Celine Dion. A few silver Porsches can be spotted maneuvering down congested, Chinese-built roads. Even remote rural villages are now knee-high in modern detritus—plastic bags, candy wrappers, and soda cans.

And if Noah were zooming by in June 2006 and looked very, very closely, he might have seen me, clinging to the edge of a building in the center of Sana'a, terrified, exhausted, but bursting with wild hopes for changes of my own.

(☪

I WAS TEETERING on a ladder, under siege by my outfit. The long black skirt I'd bought back in Manhattan wrapped itself around my legs every time I took a step and the scarf kept slipping off my hair. Altogether too much material was swirling around me. I clung to the ladder with one hand and pulled at my drapery with the other.

I was standing between two roofs of a tall gingerbread house in Sana'a. It was my first morning in the country—my first morning in any Arab country, for that matter—and my first time attempting to dress like a Yemeni. The building I was climbing belonged to Sabri, the amiable director of the Yemen Language Center, and housed his apartment, a dozen or so students of Arabic, and, temporarily, me. I needed a place to stay while teaching a three-week journalism workshop to the staff of the *Yemen Observer,* and Sabri had kindly accommodated me.

Having landed in the middle of the night, I had no idea what Sana'a looked like. All I remembered from the hazy, nausea-inducing car ride from the airport was a series of bright storefronts, wheelbarrows brimming with mangoes, and *men*. Hundreds and hundreds of men. Men in long white robes (called *thobes*) with daggers dangling from ornate belts; men in Western suits; men in patterned *foutahs,* traditional Yemeni man-skirts.

There had been no other women on my flight, and I saw none at the airport. I found this most peculiar and striking. Yemen seemed to be a land without women.

Sabri was leading me up the side of his house to show me one of his favorite views of Sana'a. The bright early-summer sun sailing up the sky made me squint as I climbed, and I resisted looking down until I had managed to haul myself—and several yards of black fabric—up the last rung of the rickety ladder and staggered to Sabri's side. I was out of breath. Sana'a lies at 7,218 feet above sea level, and you can always tell who the foreigners are by who is panting on the stairs.

I stood next to Sabri on the flat, dusty rooftop and gazed around me. Sand-colored mountains rose from the plain in every direction. Having spent my formative years in Vermont, I have always found the sight of mountains enormously reassuring, and this morning was no exception. Below us stood the fantasia in gingerbread that is Sana'a's Old City, a cluster of tall, square, cookie-colored homes trimmed with what looked like white frosting, surrounded by thick, high walls. Sabri pointed out some of the more prominent of the city's hundreds of mosques, liberally sprinkled across the city in every direction, their slender minarets thrust perpetually toward God.

Sabri's house stood just outside of the Old City, on September Twenty-sixth Street, named for the date on which the Yemen Arab Republic was officially formed in 1962 (sparking civil war that lasted until 1970). As I stared silently at the improbable landscape, Sabri carried on, explaining to me which direction was north (toward Mecca) as well as the locations of various neighborhoods, hotels, and major streets. He also pointed out the antennas for his wireless Internet, on a roof below. He was particularly proud of these.

I was overcome with gratitude for Sabri. When I had shown up on his doorstep close to midnight the night before, reeling with disorientation, he had rushed downstairs to welcome me with the sprightliness of a woodland faun. In his early forties, Sabri was slim, dark eyed, curly-haired, and quick to dissolve into laughter. Even better, he seemed delighted to see me.

June was the busiest time of year for Sabri's school, and most of the rooms were full, so Sabri had given me a room in his personal quarters.

"I took a look at your face and in your eyes, and I decided I could trust

7

you," he said to me. "We make instant judgments, we Yemenis. And then we open ourselves completely. In New York, maybe you do not make such instant hospitality. But I could tell you were a good person, and I like your sense of humor. And also it is good that you are not young."

"Not young?" It's the jet lag, I wanted to say. Usually I look much, *much* younger.

"I mean, not twenty-two."

Well, that was true enough. I was thirty-seven, an age by which many Yemeni women are grandmothers.

Up about fourteen flights of uneven stone stairs, in my plain little white room near the top of the house, I was enormously relieved to find a wooden double bed, a desk, a closet, a chest of drawers—things I recognized. The bathroom, complete with a tub, was just across the hall. It looked like paradise. I don't know what kind of dwelling I had expected, perhaps a straw mat on a floor in a hut with no shower. But I hadn't expected this.

Sabri's quarters were palatial, particularly to a Manhattanite. The kitchen was about the size of my one-bedroom apartment, if not larger, and had all the modern conveniences, including a fancy espresso maker from Italy, a dishwasher, a microwave, and shockingly, even a wine collection. I had none of these things in New York. I didn't even own a toaster or a television. Next to the kitchen was a wide hallway hung with paintings by Sabri's German wife, from whom he was separated. Past that was his office. Between this floor and the floor where I was staying were Sabri's bedroom suite and his personal bathroom, which included a Jacuzzi. When I woke that morning, Sabri made me espresso, which we drank at his king-sized wooden dining table, the sun streaming in through the stained glass windows all around us. He had plants everywhere. Thick, leafy vines climbed around the whitewashed mud walls of the rooms in search of light.

Then he took me to his roof.

☪

THE SKY AROUND US was a clear, cloudless blue. Still wobbly from my twenty-four-hour journey, I inched slowly along the edge of the roof, letting my headscarf slide down and trail in the dust, and peered at the streets seven stories down. Tiny men in white below walked by in pairs, holding hands, as children in bright greens and pinks and yellows careened from side to side in the alleys, calling to each other.

Then I saw a woman. She was the first I had seen since my arrival. Completely shrouded in black, she looked like a dark ghost drifting by on the street below. The sight sent an unexpected shudder of fear and revulsion through me. Her features were utterly erased. She was invisible. I was immediately ashamed of my instinctive horror and relieved that I had seen her from the roof, where she could not sense my reaction. I said nothing to Sabri and took a steadying breath. The furnishings of his well-appointed house had felt so familiar, I had nearly forgotten I was in a place so utterly foreign.

☪

BEFORE I LEFT NEW YORK, several friends and colleagues had asked me if I would wear a *burqa* in Yemen. This is always one of the first things Americans ask me about Yemen. The various Eastern ways of swaddling women are perhaps the most perplexing and problematic part of Muslim culture for westerners.

"The women in Yemen do not wear *burqas,*" I said. This much I had learned. When westerners think of *burqas,* they generally envision the Afghan *burqa,* which is a one-piece garment that covers the entire body and has a grille over the face so the woman can peer out. Here, women instead wear a black *abaya* or *balto.* An *abaya* is a wider, fuller garment that is pulled on over the head, whereas the narrower *balto* has buttons down the front. Both garments are worn over clothing, like raincoats, and do not cover the head. Underneath, almost every Yemeni woman I would meet wore Western-style jeans and T-shirts.

In addition to these robes, almost all women wear a black headscarf called a *hijab* over their hair and a swath of black fabric called a *niqab,* which reveals just the eyes, over their faces. All of these terms—*abaya, niqab, hijab, burqa*—have shifting definitions depending on what country you're in. Some Muslims use the word *abaya* to mean a garment that includes the head covering, so that it is nearly interchangeable with the Iranian *chador.* And a *niqab* is also referred to as a *kheemaar.*

None of these garments is required by law in Yemen, which is one of the more (officially, anyway) liberal Muslim countries when it comes to the covering of women. Nor is the veiling of women mandated by the Holy Qur'an. Yet the social pressures to veil oneself are enormous. A Yemeni woman daring to venture out without cover is often harassed by men, who order her to cover herself, call her a shameful whore, and worse. Like many practices in Yemen, it is a cultural tradition dating back centuries rather than a religious rule. But the roles of culture and religion are often confused, by outsiders and Yemenis alike.

The tradition of veiling can be traced back to the Hadith of Sahih Bukhari. The Hadith is a document that contains the teachings of the prophet Mohammed, and Bukhari's interpretation is often considered the standard, although there are several others.

According to the Hadith, "My Lord agreed with me ('Umar) in three things . . . And as regards the veiling of women, I said 'O Allah's Apostle! I wish you ordered your wives to cover themselves from the men because good and bad ones talk to them.' So the verse of the veiling of the women was revealed" (Hadith, verse 1, book 8, *sunnah* 395).

Like many westerners, before I came to Yemen, I thought of the veil as an oppressive practice that kept women from being who they are. But the women I would meet in Yemen often told me the opposite was true. These women consider their coverings a statement of identity, an important defense against men, and a source of freedom.

The *hijab* is not to keep women from looking too alluring, one woman told me. "It is because I respect myself. And when the beauty is hidden, the more important things rise to the surface."

My initial reason for covering my head was simple: I wanted to fit in. I stood out enough, with my blue eyes and pale skin, and it didn't seem wise to call even more attention to myself by allowing my waist-length hair to fly about unfettered. I also wanted to demonstrate respect for my host culture, and the head scarf was a way of broadcasting that I knew how things were done here and that I was happy to play by the rules.

So I had arrived with a suitcase full of long black skirts, long black Indian blouses, and a black head scarf. My friend Nick coached me through these purchases, as I have a morbid fear of shopping. The head scarf we bought had actually been a dressing-room door in a small boutique, and Nick had talked the owner into selling it to me for $10. "It'll be just perfect," she said, holding up the length of dusty black cotton. "Once it's cleaned."

But while I planned to cover my head when I left the safety of Sabri's house, I had never considered covering my face. To have cloth over my nose and mouth gives me an intense feeling of claustrophobia. The thought of the heat of my breath being pushed back against my skin all day long made me queasy. I was already having enough trouble getting oxygen at this altitude.

And I had to wonder if there wasn't also a bit of vanity involved. I didn't know how to be *me* without my face. I suddenly felt terribly shallow. I wanted people to know what I looked like. It mattered to me. Perhaps these Yemeni women were simply more evolved than I was, not needing to flaunt their features. Imagine, though, going years on end without anyone outside of your nuclear family telling you that you looked pretty!

☪

VIEWING SANA'A from above is a wholly different (and much quieter) experience from living it on the ground. After we climbed down from the roof, Sabri announced that he wanted to prepare a special lunch to welcome me, and we set out on a shopping expedition. We couldn't head for the markets before two P.M., he said, or people would ask him why he wasn't at mosque on a Friday. So, just after two P.M., we went downstairs and stood in front of his black Mercedes as the two skinny boys who guarded the house opened the car doors. Inside, Sabri placed his thumb on the gearshift and the car thrummed to life.

As Sabri maneuvered through the crowded, labyrinthine streets toward the *souqs* (Arabian markets), I clung to my door handle. Yemenis are worse drivers than Bostonians. It doesn't seem to matter what side of the street one drives on, and traffic lights are mere suggestions. No one wears seat belts (except me, on the rare occasions they're available), although Sabri finally put his on when his car wouldn't stop beeping to remind him.

The honking was incessant. Yemenis, I noted, drive with one hand on the horn and the other on the wheel. In New York, drivers honk to warn of danger. In Vermont, they honk as a friendly greeting. In Yemen, people honk simply because they are driving.

The majority of the white-and-yellow taxis and other cars passing us appeared to be held together with duct tape and a prayer, belching clouds of black smoke. The absence of any semblance of emissions testing in Yemen has turned Sana'a's air into a soup of particulate matter.

The streets teemed with people, mostly men in white robes, hurrying home for the afternoon meal. Many carried long bunches of shiny green leaves tucked under their arms, which Sabri told me was *qat*, a plant whose stimulating leaves Yemenis chew for hours every day. I'd read about *qat* and was eager to try it, despite the fact that drugs don't usually interest me. But most of Yemen's social and political life revolves around ritualistic *qat* chews, and so if I were really going to learn about Yemeni culture, a chew was de rigueur.

As we hurtled on, I tried to decipher the Arabic writing scrawled on storefronts and mosques. I had taught myself the alphabet and a few phrases, and it was rather thrilling to see the graceful Arabic letters everywhere. On every sign! On every restaurant! I desperately desired to learn how to decode them. So far, I only recognized the occasional S sound and an article meaning "the."

We drove first to the fish markets in the old Jewish quarter, where rows of one-story buildings crowded around small squares packed with men pushing wheelbarrows of prickly palm fruits or cucumbers. Peddlers swiftly pared the skin away from their wares so that their customers could eat them right on the spot, dripping juice into the wheelbarrow. Men waiting at the fish stalls jostled and pushed each other to get to the front. There was no discernible line. Stepping over pools of water and fish blood, Sabri and I walked up two steps into a tiny, grimy storefront, where heaps of bloodied fish lay on the stone counter. A wall of smells accosted me: brine and decay and *fishiness*. My empty stomach began to seize, and I backed out into the street to wait for Sabri. Passing men turned to stare at me, wide-eyed. "Welcome to Yemen!" some said. How did they know I had just arrived? I wondered. (More than a year later, men would *still* be welcoming me to Yemen. While it was nice to feel wanted, the greeting irritated me. I *live* here, I wanted to say. I've been here *forever*.)

Sabri rejected all the fish in the first shop, and we moved on to the second. A man in a bloodied apron held up a medium-size *hammour* and opened the gills for Sabri's inspection. This fish passed muster and was placed in a plastic bag and handed over.

The next stop was a small, foul-smelling fish restaurant. We stepped through the doorway and Sabri handed our catch through a window to the kitchen, where it was split open, painted with red-orange spices, and shoved down into a deep, cylindrical oven. Men in stained aprons rushed platters back and forth to the small dining room, where tables of scrawny men (obesity was obviously not one of Yemen's problems) were tearing off strips of bread and fish with their hands and stuffing them into their mouths. In the kitchen, other men stirred chunks of fish into orange sauces or kneaded bread into large disks to be roasted. In the back room, Sabri directed a worker in the preparation of a salsa (called *zahawek*) for the fish. Garlic, tomatoes, peppers, and a slab of white cheese were pushed through what looked like a hamburger grinder, and the resulting sauce was poured into a plastic bag. I stood in a corner, watching, trying to stay out of everyone's way.

The white-clad, dagger-sporting men eating lunch stared at me, despite the fact that I was draped in black from head to toe, my hair covered. Their eyes made me feel like I had accidentally left the house in a sequined bikini. I had never felt quite so conspicuous. "Welcome to Yemen," each said when he first caught sight of my pale blue eyes. "Where are you from?"

One bearded man told me he had lived in New York for two years, but he left because there were too many drugs on the street. Another man told me he was a neighbor of Sabri's. A third man asked me if I had children and if I was married. They were so curious and excited to see me that you'd think Julia Roberts had walked in. Only these men probably had no idea who she was.

I said that I was married, and the men insisted that I have children. I promised to try. (Not only was I unmarried, but the thought of it terrified me. And at thirty-seven, I was still ambivalent about children.) Not a man in the place took his eyes off me until I turned to walk away. Maybe not even then.

Our fish at last was cooked, and Sabri collected it, along with bread and sauce. We headed out to a chorus of good-byes. *"Ma'a salaama!"* the men cried. "Welcome to our country!" Their attentions were flattering and sociable, but I was relieved to escape. There are no compunctions about staring in Yemen; none of the men are the least bit self-conscious about it. But for a woman to stare back was (I had read) ill-advised. This would be one of my greatest challenges. I am the kind of person who makes eye contact with strangers on the subway, flirts with men I meet on planes, and gives my phone number to random bus drivers. I can't *help* it. But now I would have to help it. Being too social a butterfly was likely to get my wings singed.

☪

BACK IN THE CAR, Sabri cranked up the air-conditioning although it didn't feel very hot. Sana'a is so high and dry that the heat never really gets unbearable. The car filled with the scents of cumin, roasted fish, and bread. We headed to the fruit market, where we picked out mangoes, skinny Yemeni apples, oranges, and cigar-sized bananas. Sabri split open a fresh fig and offered it to me. It tasted refreshingly like grass.

I was beguiled by the mounds of pomegranates, which didn't look anything like the small, red pomegranates I knew. These were enormous, yellow-green, and grapefruit sized, with just the faintest pink blush. I wanted to ask Sabri to get some but was afraid of looking greedy. Besides, pomegranates are terribly difficult to eat. The thought of peeling off all that tough skin and prying loose each little juicy seed was, at that particular moment, exhausting.

We stopped once more to pick up spiced saffron rice and headed home. I was relieved to return to the security of his First World quarters, where I could catch my breath and let all of the new sights and smells settle. We were setting the table when Theo arrived. Theo, my high school sweetheart and the reason I landed in Yemen, had already been living in Sana'a for nearly two years, doing research for a book and occasional work for the *Yemen Observer*. Frustrated with the chaos and lack of standards at the newspaper, he had summoned me to come instill a few basics in the heads of its reporters. He had no journalism training himself. I still wasn't sure why he had chosen me. Surely he knew other journalists. I couldn't help wondering if it could be, at least partly, a faint hope of rekindling our long-expired romance. It had been probably seventeen years since we'd been together, but I still felt naked in his presence—the kind of vulnerability only a first love can inflict. We still mattered a little too much to each other to be at ease. But I hadn't come here for romance. I came for the adventure of spreading the journalistic gospel in an utterly alien culture.

We had a massive amount of food. Sabri even broke out one of his best bottles of white wine, which we drank warm. Wine was a precious re-source in this dry country, where it was illegal to sell alcohol or to drink it in public. Non-Muslims caught drinking in public could be sentenced to up to six months in prison, while Muslims faced a year behind bars, plus (in theory) eighty lashes with a whip. So I was fortunate to be staying with one of the very few Yemenis with a wine cellar. Theo was impressed with Sabri's largesse and told me that I was being spoiled. "Don't get used to this," he said with a hint of warning.

We ate everything with our fingers from communal platters, ripping off pieces of chewy flatbread, using it to pull chunks off the blackened fish, and then dipping the bundles in the *zahawek*. It tasted of garlic and cumin. I loved it. The fish was sweet and tender, falling off the bones. All of the new foods preoccupied me, while Theo and Sabri talked about Faris, the mysterious founder and publisher of the *Yemen Observer,* whom I was to meet the next day.

I had examined several issues of the *Observer* online before my arrival and now listened carefully as Sabri and Theo enumerated the myriad faults of the paper. The biggest problem was management, said Theo. There wasn't any. Nothing seemed to come in on any real deadlines, and there were no procedures for getting story ideas approved. When I wrote for newspapers, things generally worked like this: Reporters ran around town talking to sources and coming up with ideas for stories. They pitched these ideas to their editor. The editor either approved, refined, or killed the ideas. The reporters then reported, wrote, and sent their stories to their editor. That editor checked the reporting and basic structure and sent it along to a copy editor, who checked solely for grammar and style. And then it was published. The *Yemen Observer* did none of this. According to Theo, people wrote what they wanted to write, and it went into the paper as is. Quality checks on either the reporting or the prose were non-existent.

This bit didn't bother me too much. It wasn't my problem. After all, I was there for only three weeks, to help the journalists hone their skills. I certainly wasn't going to muck about in management and I didn't have time for a revolution.

"And no one has any training," Theo said. "The whole staff is made up of English majors who have no background in journalism. They have no idea how to structure a story. Or how to report it. Oh—and you will have to convince them that it is wrong to plagiarize from the Internet."

I paused, a handful of fish midway to my mouth. "They *plagiarize?*"

"All the time."

"What about copyright law?"

"There is no copyright law in Yemen. Intellectual property rights don't really exist." He took a sip of wine.

"Oh."

"And they also write about advertisers all the time. Faris has them write about his friends and such."

"But that's unethical!" I protested. "You can't write stories about advertisers. It destroys credibility."

Theo shrugged. "Explain that to Faris."

Sabri, a friend of Faris's, smiled knowingly. "I've also noticed some mistakes in the reporting," he said.

"*Some* mistakes?" said Theo. "Anyway, that's why Jennifer is here." He turned to me. "And could you teach them how to do Internet research? And how to know which sources are valid? And, you know, they sometimes refuse to put bylines on stories. You should get them to do that."

I tried not to dissolve into a puddle of terror.

I'd been a journalist for more than ten years, but I had never taught a journalism course before, let alone in the Arab world. I was jellied with nerves. "You'll need to show them you are in command right away," said

Theo. "You will have to find some way to make them show up on time every day. Oh—and you will need to tell them you are married. No woman your age here is unmarried, and if they find out that you are single they will assume something is terribly wrong with you. You don't want to give them any reason to look for something wrong with you."

He had said this to me before I left New York, which is why I was wearing my divorced friend Ginger's wedding ring on my left hand. I don't normally wear jewelry, and it felt tight and uncomfortable on my finger.

Sabri was westernized enough to be able to handle the knowledge that I was unmarried. Earlier that morning, when he found out I was vegetarian (except for fish, a recent addition to my diet) he said, "Well! You would make someone a very cheap wife!"

Still, to be careful, I told him I had a boyfriend in the States, as a kind of insurance policy against any possible advances. It wasn't a lie; I did leave behind a romance. But it was complicated, like everything in New York.

☪

AFTER LUNCH, Theo and I left Sabri to his work and walked through Tahrir Square, the large plaza at the heart of Sana'a, to the walled Old City, weaving our way to his apartment.

As we walked, emaciated cats and children darted across our path. The streets were so narrow that if I stretched out my arms I could touch rough stone on either side. An earthy, damp smell wafted up from the ground. We passed men asleep in wheelbarrows, their legs dangling over the sides.

I was overwhelmed by the city's architectural beauty. I never could have dreamed up the edible-looking buildings. I wanted to take a bite out of their walls. It is almost impossible to see into the boxy tower houses; they have few windows on the lower floors, to keep men from spying the women within. The upper floors are adorned with elaborate stained glass windows often referred to as *qamaria* (although I was later informed that the word *qamaria* originally referred only to alabaster windows, which were used to soften the sun's rays and keep the interiors cool). I had never seen a lovelier city.

I quickly realized that a map would be utterly useless. Even as I followed Theo to his house, I knew I would not be able to find my way back easily. He had told me that there were no addresses in Yemen, and he was serious. The Old City is a labyrinth of seemingly unnamed streets and addressless buildings. While each neighborhood does have a name, I would eventually learn that even Sana'anis could rarely locate streets outside of their own neighborhood.

Tiny boys wearing tiny daggers in their belts ran after us as we passed, calling out, "Hello! I love you!" Theo spoke to a few of them in Arabic, and they laughed and scattered. A man in a white robe passed us carrying an enormous television on his shoulder.

Little girls were running around in pink satin princess dresses with puffy short sleeves. When I asked Theo if they were dressed this way for the holy day, he said, "They are dressed that way because they are princesses of the dust."

Theo's apartment, located at the top of a gingerbread building, was magnificent. We walked up a dozen flights of uneven stone steps—there is not a uniform set of stairs in the entire country—to a large metal door with three locks. Inside was a warren of rooms, including a large, airy *mafraj* filled with cushions and illuminated by a half dozen *qamaria*. The word *mafraj* literally means "a room with a view" and is usually the top floor of a Yemeni house. I was interested to learn that the word comes from the same root as an Arabic word for "vagina." In this room nearly all social activity takes place, from meals to *qat* chews. Theo had the top floor of his building and thus the only apartment with a true *mafraj*.

We settled there, on deep blue cushions, to talk about my class and finalize the plan for my first day. This had the effect of making me feel simultaneously more at ease and more apprehensive. "They will love you," he'd say. "Don't worry." And then a moment later he would add, "But you cannot show them any weakness. You cannot show them a flaw, or they will become completely disillusioned and lose faith in you."

After a few cups of tea, we climbed to his roof so I could take photographs before dark. The roofs around us were draped with carpets airing in the sun. I leaned over the walls, trying fruitlessly to see in the windows of other buildings. I was hoping to spot that elusive species, womankind. Already I missed them so much.

As evening fell, the stained glass windows in these buildings lighted up like gems, glowing from lamplight within and splashing color into the night. I couldn't take my eyes off of them. I felt as though I had caught sight of an extraordinary woman and was spellbound by the details of her face.

"Allaaaaaaahu Akbar!" a male voice suddenly blared through the speakers, which sounded as if they were set in Theo's windowsills. The sound jolted me, although I'd heard the call to prayer at least once before, that afternoon. And then Theo tossed me out of the nest.

"You haven't truly arrived until you've gotten lost in the Old City," Theo said. "So go, get lost."

Now, as independent a traveler as I am—I have nearly always traveled alone, usually without any concrete plans—I came very close to begging him to come with me. I had no idea how to find my way around this medieval city. It was getting dark. I was tired. I didn't speak Arabic. I was a little frightened. But hadn't I battled scorpions in the wilds of Costa Rica and prevailed? Hadn't I survived fainting in a San José brothel? Hadn't I driven a van full of theater sets over mountain passes in Montana during a blizzard? Hadn't I once arrived in Ireland with only $10 in my pocket and made it last two weeks? Surely I could handle a walk through an unfamiliar town. So I took a breath, tightened the black scarf around my hair, and headed out to take my first solitary steps through Sana'a.

I remained apprehensive as I headed up the alley toward the *souq,* having no idea where I was going. A clutch of black ghosts drifted by, their curious eyes following me. I imagined I could hear them whispering, "Who is *that?*"

"I don't know, but she obviously doesn't belong here. Her *hijab* is tied all wrong!"

As they brushed past me, I caught a whiff of musky incense rising off of their clothing. A man hurried by carrying a plastic bag of tomatoes and dragging a boy by the hand. Though I kept my eyes cast toward the ground, everyone I passed stared at me as though I were an escaped zoo animal. A Western, bare-faced, blue-eyed ocelot.

As soon as I had turned a corner, a small girl called out to me in English, "Hello, Bostonian!" and I laughed, feeling a little insulted. I may have been born in Boston, but I am a New Yorker to my bones. The laughter loosened the knot of fear in my chest. Another little girl in a tattered green taffeta dress followed me, saying, "What's yer name, what's yer name?" But when I finally answered her, she turned mute and ran away.

I quickened my pace, wanting to find the markets before it got too dark. But I was distracted by a flash of green on my right. I stopped and retraced my steps. A window was cut into the stone wall on the right side of the street. I stood on tiptoe to look through, into—a secret garden! Behind the wall was a lush oasis of palm trees and unidentifiable green crops that filled an area the size of several city blocks. Green! Bright, shiny green! Elated by the sight of something photosynthesizing in the midst of all of the urban brown, I carried on.

Emerging from a series of twisting alleys, I found myself in a wide plaza in front of a mosque. To the left was a tiny storefront restaurant with outside tables, where several men sat drinking tea from glass cups. Across from the mosque was a pharmacy, busy with both male and female customers. To the right were more gingerbread houses. A herd of mangy-looking goats trotted by me, followed by a boy with a stick and the faint scent of garbage. Children pushed wheelbarrows piled so high with produce they could not see where they were going.

I wasn't sure which way to turn, but a steady stream of people seemed to be heading down a street to the right, so I joined the flow.

Several men called out to me, "*Sadeeqa! Sadeeqa!* I love you!" But the women did not speak. They just followed me with their dark eyes, the only exposed part of their bodies.

At several points in my journey, I attracted a retinue of children, most of whom seemed to be completely unattended by adults. The girls were still in their fancy dresses, although many of them were smeared with dirt, while the boys wore suit jackets over their *thobes* and curved Yemeni daggers called *jambiyas*. They trotted after me, asking my name and where I came from, crying, "*Soura! Soura!*" I didn't learn until days later that *soura* was Arabic for "photograph." They wanted me to take their picture.

At last, I entered the maze of shops that made up the *souqs*. There are several different kinds of *souq*, arranged by type of merchandise. Hand-made jewelry is sold in the streets of the Silver Souq; cloves, cardamom, and cumin are found in the Spice Souq; and *jambiyas* are found in the—you guessed it—Jambiya Souq. There are also sections devoted entirely to woven shawls (mostly from Kashmir), livestock, *qat,* and coffee.

The shops were mostly tiny storefronts, with shelves behind the counters where men reclined on cushions with cheekfuls of *qat*. Some called out to me, gesturing to their wares, while others just chewed and stared. I didn't stop. This was reconnaissance work, not shopping.

The scents of cardamom and coriander overwhelmed the spice market. Piles of orange and yellow powder were teased into perfect pyramids that sat on tarps spread on the ground. How is it that they could make these perfectly uniform towers of spices, yet not create an even set of stairs? Another Yemeni mystery.

Raisins in an astonishing array of sizes and colors—green, yellow, black, blue, chartreuse—were also arranged in careful pyramids, next to bins of red pistachios, almonds, and cashews. Entire stalls were devoted to dates. Big, gluey, warm globs of dates under heating lamps. I'd never seen so many dates, or such *sticky* ones.

I walked on, past rows and rows of *jambiyas*. There were tiny *jambiyas* the length of my hand and giant ones as long as my thigh. They were made from silver, steel, wood, and rhinoceros horn. (It is officially illegal to sell rhinoceros-horn *jambiyas,* but that doesn't stop the traders in Old Sana'a.) The *jambiya* sellers were particularly keen to get my attention, waving me over to their stalls. I smiled but kept walking.

From a distance, even in the urban areas, it appeared as though everyone was dressed alike. The women were draped in black from head to toe, and the men in white. This was a world before color, before fashion, before the rise of the individual. Before God was declared deceased. The homogeneity of dress obscured the devastating poverty of most of Yemen's people. You could not tell a person's class or income bracket until you got close enough to see the embroidery along the wrists and collar of a woman's black *abaya* or the engraving on the *jambiya* dangling from a man's embroidered belt. Yemenis, of course, can size each other up in an instant, discerning by a few telling details a person's tribe, class, and level of devoutness. There are ways to tie a head scarf, for example, that indicate an especially pious nature, and a man demonstrates his wealth and prestige by flaunting a pricey rhinoceros-horn-handled *jambiya*.

The men looked so cool and comfortable—so much more comfortable than the women, swathed in their dark polyester. I wanted to trade outfits with them. I liked the daggers and their pretty sheaths. When I had asked

Sabri, earlier in the afternoon, why he didn't wear a dagger, he said, "You are my dagger." And laughed. I had no idea what he meant. Only weeks later would his comment make sense, when I learned how men appraised each other by the kind of dagger they wore. A cheap wooden-handled *jambiya* suggested a lowly social position, whereas a fancy ivory-handled *jambiya* conveyed the opposite. Strutting about town in the company of a Western woman, Sabri had implied, was another indicator of status. Only the most elite Yemenis spoke English and could therefore conduct business and socialize with foreigners.

☪

ENTIRE STREETS were full of shops flaunting brightly colored polyester prom dresses—lacy red floor-length confections, low-cut green satins, and flouncy pink ball gowns. This piqued my interest. I wondered if it were possible that women wore these scanty, frothy frocks under their black *abayas*. And where did they *go* decked out like that? I had to find out!

As I continued on, having no idea where I was headed, a teenage boy called out, "Hello, heavenly!" Which I have to say is somewhat of a step up from what I get called on the streets of New York.

I left the busiest part of the *souq* for quieter streets. I had no idea where I was or which direction was home. It got darker. Intrigue lurked in the shadows at every corner. The winding, dimly lighted cobblestone streets seemed ideally suited for a first kiss. And yet, this was a temptation to be resisted here, where a simple gesture of affection between a man and a woman could ruin their lives. The most romantic of atmospheres, squandered. Not, I reminded myself, that I was here for romance.

I felt my gait change as I walked farther and farther into the heart of the city. Gone was my confident New York swagger, gone was the flirtatious swing of my hips, gone was the dare in my eyes. Rather than holding my chin up and brazenly meeting the gaze of passersby, as I was accustomed to doing in New York and everywhere else, I kept my face cast downward. I became someone else.

TWO

reading, writing, and robbery

Eight pairs of dark eyes were fixed on me as I scribbled "THE ROLE OF THE PRESS" on the dry-erase board at the front of the classroom in large green letters. There were three women, all but their eyes obscured by black fabric, and five men, most in polo shirts and slacks. They sat around a long, rectangular table that took up most of the room. Across the hall from us was the newsroom, where these reporters had been busy at their computers before Theo and I had rounded them up.

So far I had managed to disguise my stark terror that I would be found out to be a charlatan. I was still waiting for one of these strangers in front of me to raise his or her voice in scorn and say, "And who are *you* to tell us what to do? Do you think you know better than us just because you are a *westerner?*" Who was I indeed? Just a smallish New Yorker dressed up like a poor facsimile of an Arab, who had no idea if she had anything of use to offer these people. I wished I had had more time to see the country, to read the Qur'an, to study Arabic, more time to sink into this baffling culture, before trying to teach something to its people. I was still off balance, dizzy with the thin air and unfamiliar scents.

It helped a little that I did not look like myself. I had braided my hair and pinned it up on my head, had left my face free of makeup, and wore a long loose black blouse over a black skirt, with a black shawl over that. I

23

felt like a spinster schoolteacher, someone sexless and dry. The costume was already altering my behavior; it is impossible to feel flirty with one's form obscured by yards of fabric.

My every affectionate impulse had been carefully handcuffed and tied to a chair. Yet I still fretted that I would accidentally smile flirtatiously at one of the men and instantly lay waste to my reputation. I couldn't, however, refrain from looking men in the eyes. Certainly not here, when I had to see their eyes to know if they had received what I was saying.

The classroom was plain but comfortable, like the building that housed it. While the three-story *Yemen Observer* office building, protected by high walls and a guard, was a less charming, more modern version of the Old City's gingerbread houses (factory-made *qamaria* instead of handcrafted windows, simple stone instead of mud bricks), it still managed to be pretty. Filigrees of white wrought iron shielded the dozen or so arched front windows, and the large, sunny courtyard was draped with a canopy of grapevines. Three marble steps led to a spacious central hallway, where Enass, the newspaper's zaftig secretary, served as gatekeeper. To the right was the newsroom, to the left the conference room I was using for my class. Upstairs was the office of the mysterious Faris al-Sanabani, whom I still hadn't met, as well as the office of *Arabia Felix,* the glossy magazine he owned in addition to the *Observer.*

"So, why do we have a press anyway?" I asked, turning to my class. "What kind of role do you think it should play in society? Why is it important?" The hand holding the marker trembled slightly, and I lowered my arm to hide it.

Silence. I could hear the sound of water running outside in the courtyard, where a tall man was spraying the rows of flowering plants with a hose. Finally, a small pillar of rayon piped up.

"Press is the consciousness of the public."

"Okay," I said, turning to her with relief. "How?"

She leaned forward, releasing a sudden torrent of words that tumbled over each other in their hurry to leave her lips. "It is a judge without a court; its authority comes from people. Therefore, people have to respond to journalists; otherwise they hide the truth. Press people know that they are the mouthpiece of people. People do not understand that we are like messengers; our mission is to deliver the message. If we deliver the message, without any faults, protecting the message from being changed during the way, and hand it over to the right people, in the right manner, we are doing the best favor to people and to those who sent the message."

She went on, without taking a breath, without even looking around her, the words flying out as if she had been waiting for someone to ask her this question for years. Her tiny hands stretched across the table, making rapid, birdlike gestures to give emphasis to her words.

"Life is a cycle. Each one of us has his or her part; if we are able to do that successfully, we will have a successful life. For example, how many nominees for the U.S. election fail because there are some journalists who reveal some truth about them? So, if there are not some good journalists, those people might win these posts and then make a damage to the country. Take the Abu Ghraib scandal as an example: If there were not good journalists to dig up the truth, no one would find out. After the journalists reveal that prison's scandals, the role of the NGOs and others follows. It is like the players at the opening ceremony of the Olympics: Each one gives the other the torch until they light up the biggest torch. If someone fails, there will not be the Olympic torch."

At last she took a breath, her eyes anxiously searching my face. For a moment, I was rendered speechless. Her classmates stared at her. Two of the men, Farouq and Qasim, began laughing.

"Hey," said Theo, who in high school would have been laughing alongside of them, "we have to respect everyone's opinion here if we're going to learn. If you want us to listen to you, you have to listen to everyone else."

"That's right." My mind was slightly eased by this reassurance that Theo was on my side. "Everyone's opinion is equally valuable to me. I want to hear what all of you have to say."

The men quieted down.

I turned to the woman I would quickly come to know as Zuhra and smiled at her. While it was difficult at first to tell the women apart, Zuhra was easy to identify by the silver-rimmed glasses perched between her *hijab* and *niqab*. And the fact that she pretty much never stopped talking.

She had been the only person in the newsroom when I arrived, so I had met her first. "This is Zuhra," Theo had said. "She should be running this place."

"That was a lovely definition. You are right in that by reporting something responsibly, by telling readers about the atrocities committed in Abu Ghraib and Guantánamo, we could possibly keep such things from happening again. And yes, the press is, in a way, the conscience of a people. You've obviously been thinking about this!" I copied a few of her comments to the board. "Thank you. What else?"

"It can help expose corruption?" This from a more sober Farouq.

"Yes, certainly! The press exists in a large sense to keep an eye on the government and let the people know what it's doing. So we know what our officials are up to with our money."

More men decided to join in the conversation. "The press can tell people about diseases," said Adel, the thin, solemn man who covered health and science.

"And about car accidents," added Qasim. Qasim wasn't a reporter at all, but was in charge of advertising for the newspaper. He wore a pinstriped suit and tie and reeked of cologne. He looked just like the advertising guys in the New York offices of *The Week* (where I worked), or advertising guys anywhere, really. Qasim never stopped smiling and had a high-pitched giggle that could be heard from any corner of the building. He looked better fed than the other men, who were painfully thin.

"Good. It can also get roads repaired, schools built, and presidents elected. It can help put criminals in jail and facilitate political change," I said. "It is a powerful tool. Which makes *you* powerful people. And when we are given that kind of power, we want to make sure that we use it ethically, to help people make informed decisions about their lives, their votes, and their investments."

The other women stayed silent, but Zuhra leaned forward again. "Sorry I am so talkative but there is so much I have to ask you! Could you please tell us, what is it that makes a journalist professional?"

I didn't have an immediate answer for her. Or rather, I had several. Professional journalists get paid? Professional journalists are accurate? "Professional journalists," I finally said, "are objective. This means that they keep their emotions out of their stories, that they keep their opinions to themselves, and that they report every side to a story."

"Why is that important?" Zuhra again.

"Well, because . . ." This was something we had taken for granted in graduate school as the crucial pillar of journalism. Wasn't it obvious why objectivity was important? "If you just report one side of a story, your reader is not going to trust you. He will think you are pushing some sort of personal agenda. If you accuse a politician of corruption, but then you do not call the politician for his side of the story, then you have failed to report the whole story and are not using your power responsibly. Also, that politician will decide you are a bad journalist and be afraid to talk to you in the future. More importantly, objectivity is the way to get closest to the truth."

"But how do you keep yourself from having feelings about a story?" Zuhra again, her pen poised over her notebook. Had I really worried that none of the women would speak up?

I had just begun to answer her—it's okay to have feelings, as long as they don't influence your work—when Theo leaped up from his chair.

"Give me my fifty dollars back," he said.

I stared at him. "What fifty dollars?"

"You took my money yesterday."

"No—I paid you back, remember? I changed money in the *souq* and gave it to you in *riyals*."

"You're lying!"

"I never lie! I'm a journalist!"

"You lie like a rug! You never gave me any *riyals*!"

"I cannot believe you would accuse me of such a thing! I thought we were friends!"

"Give me my money back or I'll take it."

"I don't owe you anything!" I glared at him, hands on my hips.

"Fine." He reached across the table, grabbed my big ugly black purse (bought especially so as not to attract attention in Yemen) from the table, and ran from the room.

"I'll get you for this!" I called after him, running to the door. "But I am not going to chase you! I refuse to interrupt my class!"

I turned back to my students, who were suddenly very alert, staring at me wide-eyed.

"How could Theo do this to you?" said one of the women. They had known Theo for months before I arrived; they liked and trusted him. They were shocked by his behavior toward a guest of honor—one whom he had invited, no less!

I had opened my mouth to answer her, trying very hard not to laugh, when Theo returned to the classroom, tossing my purse on the table, smiling broadly.

"You better check the contents," said one of the men.

"Yeah," concurred the others, getting excited about the prospect of drama. "You had better check!"

I looked inside. "Theo? Where's my camera?"

I couldn't help smiling a little, and the students caught on to our little performance. "Yes! Where is her camera, Theo?"

"What camera?" asked Theo.

"Okay," I said. "I want you to write me three paragraphs about what you just saw. What just happened here? Can you remember exactly what we said and did? Make sure you have a good lead, and turn it in to me by eight A.M. tomorrow." They scribbled furiously in their notebooks.

At one end of the table the three women—Zuhra, Radia, and Arwa—sat clustered together. At the other end were the men: Qasim, Farouq, Adel, Mohammed al-Matari (who went by al-Matari), and Theo. The women were all in their early twenties, as were Adel and Farouq. Qasim was a bit closer to my age, and al-Matari was at least a decade older. Theo was exactly my age. I had asked Theo not to participate, as his presence made me nervous, but he had insisted, promising to be supportive and to refrain from the kind of class-clown behavior that got him in trouble in high school. I didn't believe him, but if I had locked him out of the class-room, he would have simply climbed in the window. Theo had the obedience skills of your average housecat.

Before class, each of my student reporters had greeted me with passionate reverence. "We have been waiting so long for you," they told me, clutching my hand until my bones hurt. "We are so grateful you have come. We are so honored." Where was all that anti-American sentiment I had read so much about? Where were the bitter tirades against Western tyranny? The only times American newspapers ever wrote about Yemen were to report violence against Western interests. Yet so far, not one person in this country had been anything short of hospitable. My reporters fell upon me as though I were bestowing on them the greatest favor imaginable. I felt like Princess Diana. I felt like Seymour Hersh. I felt like a tribal sheikh. (Later, I would in fact be given the nickname Sheikah Jenny by the current editor of the paper, Mohammed al-Asaadi, who was curiously absent from my first class.)

There is quite a difference, however, between being an honored guest and being a boss. In these early days, it was impossible to imagine that one of these sweet, docile journalists, who treated me with such courtesy, would some months later try to tear up one of my editorials or storm out of my office. Just as it was impossible to imagine that I would ever raise my voice to them or threaten to dock their pay.

☪

I HAD BEGUN the class by introducing myself and telling them a few highlights of my ten-year journalism career so as to reassure them they were dealing with a professional. Not that anyone had questioned me. On Theo's advice, I had explained to them that this was a training course designed for professionals, to alleviate their fears of being patronized with a beginners' course (though Theo told me this was what they desperately needed).

I had planned to start by saying, "I am not here to teach you the American way of journalism. I am here to teach you the reporting and writing techniques that have served me over the past ten years." But Theo had vetoed this. "They *want* to learn the American way," he said. "They *dream* of going to America!"

We began by discussing the role of newspapers, the definition of news, kinds of stories, and how to cover a beat, but I ended up talking about a much wider variety of subjects than I had planned, because they had so many questions. Shyness and modesty are prized in Yemeni women, so Theo had warned me the girls might not be as vocal. Yet Zuhra was one of my most avid interrogators. "What do you think of anonymous sources?

Do we have to put a byline on a story if we worry it could get us killed? What's the difference between news and features?" She was relentless. She was, in short, a true journalist.

But I didn't want my class to be all talk, theory without practice. "I want to get all of you out of this office and onto the streets," I told them. "News doesn't happen in this building."

"How do you find stories on the streets?" they asked. They told me they left the office mainly to go to press conferences. It didn't occur to them that their corner grocer or a taxi driver or the local midwife might give them an idea for a story. Only press spokesmen and politicians were deemed worthy of quoting. Yet I knew from long experience that PR people and those in power were the least likely to have a good story. I would have to explain to my reporters how to wire a beat, how to cultivate sources, and how to convince people to trust them. I added these to my list of essential things to teach them, which was growing longer by the minute. I was starting to sweat.

And then the women told me that they weren't really allowed to approach men on the streets. And that they couldn't ride in cars with men. This meant that if a woman went out to report a story, she had to take a separate taxi from the photographer (all of whom were male).

"What are your other major barriers to getting stories?" I asked, curious.

"Well, no one wants to talk to reporters," said Farouq. "Or give us their name."

"That *is* a problem." It seemed it wasn't just this group of reporters who needed to know the various ways the press could serve society, it was the entire society itself. Almost all of Yemen's newspapers were blatantly partisan, and so anyone interviewed would of course assume a reporter had an agenda other than the truth.

I planned to assign them stories that they could publish in the paper, coaching them along the way. I wanted everything I taught them to contribute to the betterment of the *Yemen Observer*. There was much that needed bettering, starting with the English. For example: "The security source denied any dead incidents happened during the riots." Or, from another reporter, "Nemah Yahia, an elderly lady, said that they went to a mill in Raid, have an hour takes them, to crash the cereal." I suppose that "crash the cereal" isn't all that inappropriate a phrase to describe what occurs at a mill. But still.

Then there was the utter lack of structure to the stories, the dearth of legitimate sources, the three-paragraph-long sentences, and the nonsensical headlines. One notorious headline in the *Observer*, before my time, accidentally referred to the Ministry of Tourism as the Ministry of Terrorism. The folks at the U.S. embassy were so entertained by this that they pinned the story to their bulletin board. It was hard to know where to begin, but I figured I couldn't go wrong by starting with the country's biggest news story.

"There's a presidential election coming up in September," I said. "What role do you think a newspaper can play in the months before the elections? What are its obligations to its readers? In other words, how does the press contribute to the creation of a true democracy?"

The mention of democracy immediately perked them all up. The Yemeni government is officially quite keen on democracy and forever issuing statements about the glorious progress of its march toward such a political system. Yet at the moment, true democracy is but a speck on the horizon. Yemen has existed as a unified country only since 1990. After the end of Turkish occupation in 1918, the North was ruled as a quasi-monarchy by a series of politico-religious leaders called imams. In 1962, a civil war in the North resulted in the overthrow of the imamate and the establishment of the Yemen Arab Republic.

South Yemen was under British rule from 1839 to 1967, when the last British forces withdrew from Aden and the country became the People's Republic of South Yemen (renamed the People's Democratic Republic of Yemen in 1970), the only Arab Marxist state in history. After the Soviet Union began to dissolve in 1989, North and South Yemen began talking seriously about unification. They unified formally on May 22, 1990, though a bloody civil war erupted in 1994 between the (still unmerged) northern and southern armed forces.

Yemen has had the same president for more than thirty years. Well, technically President Ali Abdullah Saleh has only been president of all of Yemen since unification. But before that he ruled North Yemen for twelve years. While grumbling about President Saleh's leadership is a popular national pastime, the Yemeni people have not experienced a peaceful transfer of power in their lifetime and thus struggle to imagine such a thing.

Still, this year, for the first time, Yemen has a real opposition candidate. In 1999, when the country held its first direct presidential election, Saleh handily defeated a candidate from his own party with a majority of 96 percent. Now, opposition candidate Faisal bin Shamlan is providing the press with the thrilling opportunity to write about someone other than Saleh and about a political party other than the ruling party, the General People's Congress. My reporters were bursting with pride about their country's democratic efforts. They seemed to feel that this transition could finally earn Yemen the respect it deserved. Even so, no one really doubted that Saleh would win reelection.

"But the press has an obligation to report impartially about *both* candidates," I told my class. "And to give voters as much information as they can, so that they can make informed choices." No easy task when it's against the law to directly criticize the president in the paper. And when the owner of the paper actually works for that president. Theo had explained to me that the *Yemen Observer* was just one of Faris's many enterprises. His main job was working as the president's media adviser. He also owned a security franchise, campaigned against corruption, helped organize investment conferences, and had his industrious fingers in many other ventures. While I found it clearly unethical for the owner of a newspaper to work for the president, it seemed best to keep my thoughts to myself. I was there for only three weeks. I would just have to try to get my reporters to report as fairly as possible and hope Faris wouldn't meddle too much.

The *concept* of even-handed reporting seemed to be going over remarkably well with my students, who said they wanted their stories to read like those in the *New York Times*. It remained to be seen how well they could execute this. They gave me several different ideas for kinds of election stories they could write: candidate profiles, issue-specific stories (on the eradication of weapons, say, or fighting corruption), and news stories about the direction of the candidates' campaigns. Farouq, the paper's main political reporter, was already working on a story about the opposition party's threatened boycott of the election.

I ended class by giving them each an assignment related to their beat, due at six P.M. This would help me learn more about Yemen as well as more about what my reporters considered news.

Arwa, for example, wanted to do a story about an all-women sports club, but I had trouble getting her to tell me what was *new* about it.

"We need a reason that we are writing about it *today*," I told her. "Tell me what is *new*. Did it just open? Is it the first club for women?"

"No . . ."

"Did it just introduce some new kind of sport? Or is it part of a growing trend? Are more women than ever before doing sports?"

"Yes!" she said to the last one. "More women are doing it."

"Good," I said. "So that is the information we lead with."

I kept referring to it as a health club, and she kept correcting me. "Not health! Sports!"

Adel went off to report on the recent Guantánamo suicide, Radia to write about street children, and little Zuhra to write about the new respect hairstylists were getting in Yemen.

After class, a tall, chubby man with greenish eyes and a shiny round face lingered in the classroom with visible anxiety. He had arrived halfway through class, just before my staged fight with Theo. "I am so sorry for being late," he said. "I had to take my wife to the hospital. She had surgery on her eye, and now there is something wrong with her—" He glanced at Theo, who was standing with us.

"Cornea," Theo supplied.

"Yes. Cornea. And she will need another surgery."

This was Zaid. I expressed my sympathy and sat down with him to go over everything he had missed. I liked him immediately. He was obviously bright, joked with me, and told me he had just won a scholarship to study next year in Britain. He was frothing with excitement.

I was beginning to sag with the relief that the first class had finished without catastrophe when Theo reminded me that I still had a hurdle ahead (other than the 1,001 new challenges I had just uncovered): I had to impress the Boss. He gave me a minute to take a breath and collect my papers, and led me upstairs to meet Faris.

FARIS AL-SANABANI was tall, dark, and handsome, with just about the worst case of attention deficit disorder I've ever seen. He did nothing in real time. He moved in fast-forward, spoke in fast-forward, and demanded an equally speedy response. A conference with Faris was an aerobic workout.

Faris was educated in the United States at Eastern Michigan University. Michigan is home to the largest population of expatriate Yemenis. Because Faris was elected the university's homecoming king—the first minority ever to win that honor—he was invited to many events held by campus organizations. One of these was a talk at a black fraternity on the theme of giving back to the ghetto. The speaker, Faris told me, said something like this: "You are at a good university. You have good lives, good educations. I want you to reach out to where you came from. I want you to let them see you. Not just as a basketball player or a singer. But as a successful educated person in another field."

And Faris sat there, thinking. He had been planning to accept a lucrative job in the United States as soon as he finished school. He had no intention of returning to Yemen. He was married to an American woman.

"But I realized that Yemen is my ghetto," he told me. "If everybody leaves the ghetto, dresses nice, and marries a nice white lady, then they in the ghetto will have nothing. They will have no hope. So I said, 'I am going back to Yemen. I have to go to my people.'"

He gave up the job offer and moved back to Yemen, where he took work as a translator, development worker, and government employee before deciding to launch the *Yemen Observer*.

Until then, there was just one English-language newspaper, the *Yemen Times*. But Faris felt that this paper was too relentlessly critical of his country. How was Yemen ever going to attract tourists if all they ever read about the country was negative? He decided that starting his own newspaper would be the best way to contribute to Yemen's development. An English-language paper would be most effective, he thought, because he wanted foreigners—especially Americans, because he had lived there—to be able to read about Yemen.

His American wife helped him write and edit the paper on their one computer. One thousand copies were printed of his first issue, which he delivered himself on foot, by bicycle, and through friends. That was more than a decade ago, in 1996. Faris had since divorced his American wife, who hadn't taken to life in Yemen, and married a Yemeni woman.

By the time Theo summoned me, the paper was printing about five thousand copies of each issue. It still lost money, but it was important enough to Faris that he continued to personally fund it. Besides, Faris was a wealthy man. Profits from his business ventures—not government money—funded the *Yemen Observer,* Faris was quick to tell me. This was his way of claiming the paper was independent, despite his lofty connections. After all, serving as the president's media adviser (and later his secretary) was not an ideal position for someone who owned a newspaper struggling to be seen as objective. But it was a perfect position for a driven, passionate man with infinite ambitions for his country.

When I arrived in Faris's office, he was seated behind an enormous desk, fiddling with his computer. He stood up to shake my hand. Only briefly did his eyes meet mine before darting around the room, as if making sure I hadn't arrived with a retinue of spies. Faris's eyes were always moving. I introduced myself and explained what I hoped to do with my class. He seemed properly impressed and expressed deep gratitude for my presence. I expressed deep gratitude for the opportunity to assist him. I gave him a copy of *The Week,* the magazine for which I write science, health, theatre, travel, and art pages, which he flipped through so quickly the pages blurred. I suddenly panicked as I realized I'd given him the copy with a cover story on gay marriage. The minimum punishment for homosexuality in Yemen is death. I stammered an explanation, but Faris didn't seem concerned.

"Of course we understand," he said. "Things are different there."

Before I left, he handed me a stack of thirty issues of the *Yemen Observer.* "Read these and tell me how to make it better," he said. "What sections are good, what sections to get rid of, and also, please read this interview I wrote and tell me what you think of it and how I can do better interviews in the future."

Staggering under the tower of newsprint, I took the papers to an empty office downstairs and read until my eyes dried out. I had managed only about an hour of sleep the night before. I can't remember ever having had such terrible insomnia, a combination of jet lag, nervousness about teaching, and the wild euphoria of travel. I was in rough shape.

Despite this, the excitement I felt about my class carried me along, and I managed to take about thirty pages of notes on the back issues of the *Yemen Observer*.

Reporters kept popping in to see me. "About that argument with Theo," said Adel. "Has he ever lied to you about money before?"

I was impressed—I had thought that none of them would think to interview either Theo or myself. Bravo, Adel! Then al-Matari popped in to ask me several questions about his story and journalism in general. Several small boys visited me periodically to bring me silver cups of water. I had no idea where they came from. Several men stopped in my doorway simply to stare at me.

During our meeting, Faris had asked me if I had any special needs during my stay, and I had told him that I would like to go for a swim if at all possible. I am hopelessly addicted to exercise. So after I had a quick falafel lunch with Theo, Faris sent one of his drivers to fetch me and drive me to the Sheraton, which has one of the only lap pools women can use. (All sports clubs in Yemen are sex-segregated, but the biggest hotels—the Sheraton and the Mövenpick—have coed pools.)

Water is my second home, and the emotional relief submersion brought was instantaneous. Stripped of my Yemeni drapery, I was exhilarated to feel the water and sun on my skin. I was Jennifer again. I recognized myself. As my elbows began their rhythmic rise and fall, the anxieties of the morning dispersed, rising through my body and out my fingertips, dissolving in the chlorine.

I swam for an hour, despite the best efforts of the small boys playing at the end of the pool to thwart me. At first, they just liked to get in my way and dodge me at the last minute, but then they began to imitate my stroke, splashing clumsily after me. I outlasted them, and finally they pulled their shivering grayish-brown bodies out of the pool and wrapped themselves in blanket-size towels, staring reproachfully at me as I serenely continued my laps.

When I arrived back at the *Observer,* revivified and still damp (it wasn't until nearly a year later that a Yemeni friend informed me that going about with wet hair was frowned upon, as it suggested one had just emerged from a bedroom romp—Yemenis shower after sex), I met with Faris and a new reporter named Hakim, a Detroit-born Yemeni. Hakim had joined us from the rival *Yemen Times,* where he and the editor had mutually decided to part ways. Faris had great hopes for him, as his English was better than that of most of our reporters and he had a modicum of journalism training. They peppered me with questions about the paper's format, and I told them exactly what I thought should be on every single page. After slaving away for other people for ten years, I was filled with the heady satisfaction of being treated like an authority. I was surprised by the things I knew and by how certain I felt that my suggestions were right.

By eight P.M., I thought I might swoon from exhaustion. But just when I feared I would be there all night, Faris invited me to dinner with him and three Tunisian models for *Arabia Felix.* So, at nearly eight thirty, after more than twelve hours of work, we headed out of the office.

Faris escorted us to a Chinese restaurant, where he ordered for all of us. Thirty dishes must have arrived, heaped with vegetables and fish and meats and rice and spring rolls. As soon as we were seated, the three stunning Tunisian women leaned back in their chairs and lighted their cigarettes in unison. They smoked through most of the meal. The chubbiest girl (still devastatingly beautiful) ate nothing but a few grains of rice, smoking cigarette after cigarette. Refusing an offer of food from a Yemeni is a major slight, so I ate twice as much to make up for her rudeness. But Faris was rude right back to her.

"You are not eating much but you are a big girl," he said. "Will you go eat when we are not watching?"

The girls spent most of the meal complaining about Yemen in various tongues. They had so much *fun* in Tunisia. In Tunisia, women don't have to cover their bodies. In Tunisia, the food is much better than Chinese food. Yet their contracts as flight attendants with Yemenia Airways would keep them in Yemen for the next three years. God help the Yemenis.

"Tunisia is a dictatorship," Faris told me. "But the dictator is liberal— he had all of the women remove their *hijabs,* and now they are free. But if Tunisia were to become a democracy, the Islamists would win an election in a landslide, and women would be sent back centuries." This fascinated me. "In Algeria, this happened," said Faris. "It used to be fairly liberal until it became a democracy, and the Islamists swept elections. They are still fighting there."

I wondered if the same could happen here. Yemen was moving toward democracy. Would that result in an even more conservative and restrictive culture? Faris didn't seem to think so. Saleh was almost guaranteed re-election, and Yemen was already an Islamic country.

When we left the restaurant at around ten P.M., Faris invited me to watch the World Cup with him and his friend Jalal, who had joined us, but I begged off. "If I don't get to bed I will be useless to you tomorrow!"

So Faris had Salem drive me home. I was asleep three seconds after I crawled into bed, although I woke briefly at three thirty to hear *"Al-laaaaahhhu Akbar!"* wail through loudspeakers across the city. A sound that would become as familiar to me as the rumble and blare of Manhattan traffic.

☪

IF I HAD THOUGHT that things would slow down after that marathon first day, I was seriously mistaken. Every day I accumulated new students, every day more of my reporters dragged me off after class to edit their stories, every day Faris would think up some new thing he wanted from me. In addition, I began studying Arabic for an hour a day with a tutor. I almost never slept.

But while I had never worked so hard in my life, I had never felt so useful or so motivated to get to the office. Letting down this group of reporters who had so willingly handed me their trust was unthinkable. They really thought I could turn them into professional journalists. I had to live up to their hopes. Besides, I kept telling myself, it's only three weeks. I can go flat out for three weeks. There will be time for sleep when I get home.

Still, there were moments when the size of the task overwhelmed me. I was expected to achieve something lasting during my short stay, but when I saw the stories my reporters wrote about my staged fight with Theo, that suddenly seemed impossible. Almost all lacked a coherent first sentence. Most got the facts wrong. And not one of them used anything approaching proper English. This last problem was not something I could fix. No matter how dedicated I was, I could not perfect the English of fifteen reporters in a few weeks. So I focused on what I could change: structure, reporting, and accuracy.

We began our second class by reading these pieces aloud. Here is Zaid's, in its exuberant entirety.

> It was very surprising for everybody to see Theo acting that way. The exchange that people heard between the two, Theo and Jennifer is anything but understood. Theo talking to Jennifer or let's say quarreling with her over a fifty dollars that she owed him or he give it to her, we don't exactly know. The quarrel heated a little and we all saw Theo snatching Jennifer's purse and rushed outside after asking for her camera. What did he do with her purse outside we all didn't know if really did something from her purse.
>
> I myself was perplexed as I have never seen Theo in this manner especially with a nice woman like Jennifer. We all knew Theo very well. To him money is no object and will never quarrel over it with anybody especially those who are very close to him. Probably Jennifer is the last person who would quarrel with over it. She is the one who responded to his call and came to Yemen in order to train us. She left a dying grandfather and rushed to middle of a place she never knew about. She can never ever be treated this way. It was more of a joke I reckoned in second thought.
>
> But when I looked deeply inside the eyes of the two I saw chemistry. I learned that they both were together in grade 11 and 12 and very competitive. So the whole thing happened between the two is Theo recollection of the memories that he terribly missed back in his school days that were brought back to his mind with the presence of Jennifer. Jennifer brought back all the sweet memories and things that Theo was craving. One could see that from the way he talks and the active attitude he took since the arrival of Jennifer.

Theo and I were laughing too hard to talk at first. "So," I finally managed. "I see you've written an opinion piece. Or was that news analysis?"

After all, I had not told them what *kind* of news story to write. I wasn't quite sure where to start.

"Um, Zaid, I guess I wasn't looking for quite so much *interpretation*. I want to see all of you write a straightforward news lead, with that who, what, where, when, and how that we talked about. Tell us what happened without your personal views interfering with the action."

Zaid nodded and wrote something down in his flowered notebook. (Yemeni men were quite comfortable carrying around notebooks festooned with flowers, hearts, or cartoon characters, something that charmed and amused me, given how macho their culture seemed from the outside.) I noticed a tape recorder on the table in front of him, its red light flashing.

"Zaid? Are you tape-recording me?"

"Yes!" He smiled. "I am going to memorize everything you tell us. I need to have it to refer to."

"I see." I was flattered, but now I'd have to watch what I said.

"Okay then, who is next? Let's look at Arwa's story."

Arwa had written a newsier piece. "In her first class as a trainer in *Yemen Observer,* Jennifer's camera is taken by Theo Panderos who work also as an editor of *Arabia Felix* magazine," her story began.

This illustrated a few more of my challenges. Where did I start with prose like this? Grammar? The importance of spelling names correctly? (Theo's surname is Padnos.) The use of the passive voice?

Arwa continued: "The accident happened after a cute an argument between them . . . Eyewitnesses said that Theo burst in anger shut the windows close, picked up her bag from meeting table before he pushed out of the room, neglecting all her attempts to explain. 'Don't attend my class again, Theo,' Jennifer said."

Most of this was patently untrue. So we had a little chat about factual reporting and the unreliability of eyewitnesses. "Many people who witness the exact same event will remember it in different ways," I said. "As you have seen. Even people who believe they are telling you the truth may not be telling you what actually happened. Each person is telling you her *version* of what happened. You need to be aware of this.

"I am unclear, however, whether this is what Arwa believes she actually *saw* or if she was merely trying to heighten the drama of the whole incident. Which is something we should try to avoid if possible. Let the facts be enough. Okay, next?"

Arwa bowed her head and I couldn't see her eyes. I hoped I had not embarrassed her. I couldn't bear the thought of hurting any of the women or giving the men something to tease them about. I was still a little afraid of the women, afraid to intrude on their carefully drawn boundaries.

While my reporters would often laugh at each other and openly criticize their colleagues' work, they never questioned my authority. My status as a westerner who had written for national magazines and newspapers in the United States granted me their automatic respect and immunity from criticism. I was surprised that the men were so deferential right from the start. I had expected them to challenge me, or to refuse to take me seriously, because I was female. But this was far from the case. The men were almost obsequious, falling over each other to try to please me. My education, career, and foreignness, it seemed, trumped my sex.

This passive attitude in the classroom wasn't unusual. The Yemeni education system does not encourage critical thinking. Children learn almost entirely by rote, and corporal punishment is common. Teachers are never, ever questioned, and school is largely a grim, daunting place. I have never heard Yemenis speak with fond nostalgia about their early school days.

After all the stories had been read, I took a marker out and walked to the board. "I notice a few things missing from all of these stories," I said. "First, no one, except Adel, interviewed me, and no one interviewed Theo. Yet the story was about *us*. Didn't you want to know if Theo had a history of stealing things from me, or if maybe we had had another fight before, if there might be other reasons we are angry at each other?"

We went over what else they should have done to get this story right—interview their fellow classmates and witnesses, ask to inspect my purse, and spell our names correctly.

For homework, I passed out a *Wall Street Journal* story with a textbook-perfect anecdotal lead and a BBC news story with a direct lead, so we could spend the entire next class on leads. My reporters were unclear on the concept. Every single story in the *Yemen Observer* began with a lengthy attribution. For example: "The Ministry of Arabian Absurdity spokesperson said in all his glorious wisdom today June 11 that . . ." Or "The Minister of Myopia announced in a beautiful way today that on June 17 they will plan a meeting to deal with the issues of the opposition party signing a contract about the election with the dignitaries of the Party of the

Usual Insanity, affirmed Ali al-Mallinguality . . ." That isn't much of an exaggeration.

So, in our next class, I taught them what I call the "Hey, Jolyon!" rule, which I developed at *The Week*. Jolyon used to write the art pages at *The Week* and sat next to me. Whenever I saw a really interesting story, I'd swing away from my computer and say, "Hey, Jolyon! Listen to this!"

I told them to write the leads of their stories as if they were telling their story to their own Jolyons. "Look away from your notes, your sources, your lists of names, and simply tell me what the story is about. In one sentence. So that when a Yemeni man, for example, reads the paper, he will turn to his wife and say, 'Hey, Arwa! Listen to this!'"

☪

AS THE DAYS PASSED, my relationships with my students grew warmer. When I arrived at work on my third day, Zaid met me at the door, wearing a long white *thobe* and *jambiya,* with a flash drive dangling from his neck. "Look, Jennifer!" he said, pointing to the *jambiya* and the flash drive. "I am both old-world and new-world!" He then followed me into the newsroom and bombarded me with questions about word definitions and how things were done in the West until my lesson began.

Now that we had all grown at ease with each other, I had no trouble getting anyone to speak up in class. They were so eager to tell me what they knew that they were continually interrupting each other.

The men often behaved like schoolboys, hiding each other's shoes in wastebaskets, stealing each other's chairs, and trying to one-up each other. They asked me things like "My lead was better than Zaid's though, right? Mine was the best? Jennifer! Tell us who is the *best!*"

One morning, Qasim and Farouq would not stop taunting each other. Qasim dialed Farouq on his cell phone while holding it under the table, just to get Farouq in trouble for having his phone on in class—which I had strictly forbidden.

"That's it," I said, extending my open palm. "Hand them over." Both men sheepishly handed me their phones, which I tucked into my purse. The women gazed at me in awe.

Qasim also handed me a television remote control that was lying on the table. "Great idea," I said. "Now you can only talk if I am pointing this at you!"

This helped enormously.

Theo, to my surprise, turned out to be one of my most enthusiastic cheerleaders. Not only did he help me to steer classroom discussions in constructive directions, he also cooked me dinner most evenings and helped me to plan out my days. Life outside the *Yemen Observer* offices (what little there was) was rarely more relaxing than life inside them, given how unfamiliar everything remained. I had to negotiate fares with taxi drivers in Arabic several times a day, for one thing. Grocery shopping was still beyond me and I never saw women eating alone in restaurants, so I ate only when either Sabri or Theo fed me. There was no time for me to meet people outside of work. I wondered how single foreigners survived the seeming dearth of romantic possibilities.

☾

AFTER CLASS ONE DAY, Zuhra, who was showing herself to be the most passionate of my reporters, asked me to sit and go through yet another story line by line. There were many corrections to be made, but she was learning quickly. Her questions had no end. She was a starving little plant and she thought I was the rain.

The office was empty; everyone else had gone home for lunch and a couple hours of *qat*-chewing. When we were finally finished, at close to three P.M. (too late for me to get to the pool before the evening class), she grasped my arm with both of her tiny hands and fixed me with fierce brown eyes. "Jennifer. You have to tell me. Please. Do you think I can do it? Can I be a journalist? A *real* journalist? I want to know, because this is the career I have chosen for myself and I want you to tell me if you think I can do it. So I am not wasting my time. I do not want to delude myself."

"Zuhra. I have no question that you can do it. But—"

"But?" Her eyes grew anxious.

"I don't know," I said truthfully. "I don't understand yet enough about you, enough about Yemen, to know your particular challenges. As a woman, I mean. Aren't there things you are not allowed to do? Like, could you interview a man?"

"Not alone. My family would be upset. Maybe in a group?"

"Okay." I thought. "Could you interview a man on the phone and over e-mail?"

"Yes." There was no hesitation. "But I cannot go out at night."

"So you can work a day shift. This is something that can be worked around. Men can cover things going on at night. Can you run around town interviewing women?"

"Yes!"

"Well, that's half the population, after all," I said. "That gives you something to work with. You could certainly find plenty to write about women and children." My brain was already at work, churning out story ideas for her. She could write about what was being done to combat the illiteracy of 70 percent of Yemen's women. Or the astronomical maternal mortality rate. Or the polio epidemic that continued to cripple children. Or . . .

She nodded. "So?"

"We can find a way for you to do this."

"But you think *I* can do it? Jennifer, I want this so much; I have chosen this. I need you to help me." *Tell me you believe in me.*

"Zuhra. If this is really what you want, you absolutely can do this. And I will help you every way I can."

She squeezed my hands even more tightly. "I won't let you down," she said. "I want to make you proud of me. Just as long as I have your help."

"You do, you do!" But my stomach twisted. I had no idea how much I could really help her. How, I wondered, was I ever going to be able to tell her everything she needed to know in three inadequate weeks?

I should have known then. I couldn't.

(*

THE NEXT DAY, I ducked into my classroom for a minute to fetch something and discovered the women having their lunch. Somehow I had failed to notice that the women were never with us when I ate with the men outside in the courtyard. Faris had always invited me to eat with the men as an honorary member of the sex. We ate standing up, dipping Yemeni baguettes called *roti* into a communal pot of stewed beans called *ful*. How could I have forgotten the women? Of course they couldn't lift their veils to eat among the men!

Now the women were laughing at the surprise on my face. Wait a minute, I could *see them laughing.* They had mouths and noses and white teeth! They had lifted their veils. It had taken me a moment to realize this.

"You have never seen us before!" they cried out gleefully. It took me a minute to figure out who they were. I didn't recognize them without their *niqabs!* I had to start with the eyes, the only part of them I knew. The long lashes belonged to Arwa, the large round eyes to Enass, and the smiling, almond-shaped eyes were Radia's.

"Come, eat with us," said Arwa.

"I'd love to!" I said. I was trying not to stare too hard at them, for fear of making them shy. I had not yet been alone with the women, not yet been privy to this secret society. I wanted to memorize their faces before they disappeared again.

They were so much easier with me away from the men. They laughed more often, spoke more freely, and teased each other. Every time a knock came on the door, they hastily flipped down their veils.

Enass, the paper's secretary, said that all the men tell her how smart I am. That I am the smartest woman they have ever met.

"Really?" I said, elated.

"They say this," she replied.

One of the other girls said something to her in Arabic and they argued for a minute. "Oh!" Enass said, turning back to me. "I didn't mean smart. I meant pretty! I got confused."

"Oh." My face fell. "I think I'd rather they thought I was smart."

I was disappointed that Zuhra wasn't with us. I didn't know if she had gone home for lunch or already eaten. But then, just as I opened the door to leave, she flew toward it from outside. Clutching my arm, she dragged me back into the conference room.

"You haven't seen me!" she said. She pulled me past the door and closed it tightly behind us. Then, as we stood facing each other just inside the doorway, she drew back her *niqab.* Unlike the other women, she yanked off her *hijab* as well, loosing thick ink-black hair that tumbled to her waist.

"Why, you're *adorable!*" I couldn't help myself. She really was, with chubby brown cheeks, dimples, and flashing black eyes. She glowed with pride, laughing, as she turned this way and that to let me admire her.

I can't express how thrilling this was. They had let me into their world; they had trusted me with their faces.

"People have the wrong idea about the *hijab*," said Zuhra with a toss of her glossy hair. "I wear it because I respect myself. And when the beauty is hidden the more important things rise to the surface."

"So people can appreciate you for your brains and not your beauty?" I said.

She laughed. "Yes. But there is more. I can talk to you for hours about the *hijab* if you would like."

"I would!"

"Careful!" said Arwa. "She can talk to you *forever* about the *hijab*!"

"She can talk to you forever about *anything*," said Enass.

"That's okay," I said. "There's an awful lot I need to know."

THREE

an invitation

Faris summoned me to his office a few days later. He had given me a copy of a
long, dull, and confusing interview he did with a man from USAID and
wanted me to critique it. I hardly knew where to begin; there was so little clarity or interest in the piece. I would never have let it run.

I dragged my feet up the stairs. Sleep deprivation and information
overload were sapping my strength. Little pieces of cultural knowledge
and news and Arabic were continually escaping from my head and scattering about me on the ground. I was exhausted from constantly trying to
pick them all up and stuff them back in. It's only three weeks, I told myself. It's not forever.

I staggered into Faris's office, where he welcomed me with a broad
smile, waving me to a chair. "Tell me," he said without preamble. "Tell me
what you think of this interview."

I perched on the edge of my chair and pressed my palms against his
desktop. "Now, it's okay for me to be totally honest with you?" Exhaustion
tends to vaporize my ability to speak anything but the naked truth. I didn't
have the energy to coddle him.

He spread out his arms again. "Totally honest. This is what I want."

I took a breath. Why was I scared? It wasn't like he was really my boss
or anything. He wasn't even paying me! "Your lead . . ." I pointed it out on

the paper spread between us. "It says *nothing*." And we went on from there. I had nearly twenty pages of notes and took his story apart piece by piece and told him how to make it better. To his credit, he never got defensive and expressed deep gratitude for my help, so I relaxed as we carried on.

The interview really contained several stories, so we talked about how the information could be better reported and organized. He nodded and said he understood. But every time I explained anything to my students, they would say the same thing, regardless of whether they truly got it. But I was grateful for the chance to spend time with Faris so that he could get an idea of the kinds of things I was telling his staff and perhaps help to carry on my ideas after I left.

Looking back, it's incredible that I was ever that naïve.

☪

THEO RESCUED ME from work that night and took me to the British Club, a bar next door to the British ambassador's residence in the upscale Hadda neighborhood, where most diplomats live. I'd hardly been anywhere outside of the *Yemen Observer* offices, and the mere prospect of encountering a pint glass and perhaps a native English speaker filled me with wild euphoria. We caught a cab down a long dusty road past neon-lighted supermarkets, travel agencies, furniture stores, spice markets, and bright windows displaying pyramids of honey jars.

The taxi turned left at an anomalous Baskin-Robbins creamery and dropped us off at a black-and-yellow-striped concrete barrier. Men in blue army fatigues clutching AK-47s stood around on street corners and at the gates of walled mansions along the street. Just beyond the British Club, I could see the Union Jack flying over a massive green building. As we approached the large black gates on our left, a small window flew open and a Yemeni man peered out. Theo flashed his membership card and the gate swung open to admit us to—a miracle!—a bar.

The warm scent of stale beer and fried food greeted me as we walked in, and I inhaled deeply. I love bars, everything about them. Though I am not a big drinker, I love the community, the chance for unexpected encounters, the eclectic mix of people. In New York, I spent nearly every

Sunday night at my local Irish pub, doing the *New York Times* Sunday cross-word puzzle and talking with Tommy, my favorite bartender in the world. For the first time since I arrived in this ancient city, I was completely at ease, in a place I recognized.

Operated by the British Embassy, the British Club draws an assortment of expats—diplomats, oil workers, development workers, teachers, and the odd journalist—desirous of escaping Yemeni prohibitions. It was relatively empty when we arrived. The World Cup was playing on television screens at either end of the room, and a scattering of Brits sat at the small tables with pints of forbidden beer. Beyond a long porch out back was a tennis court and a pool hidden by a row of shrubs.

Theo introduced me to the bartender, a slim, smiling Yemeni-Vietnamese man named Abdullah. My first—and likely only—Yemeni bartender! Theo ordered us a couple of Carlsbergs, which we had only just tasted when his French friends Sebastian and Alain arrived. Theo promptly abandoned me to go play tennis with them.

I didn't care. I was just happy to sip my beer and amuse myself with strangers. The beer made me tipsy nearly immediately—a combination of the altitude and the fact that I hadn't had time to eat. There were two men next to me at the bar, so I turned and asked them what they were doing in Yemen—thrilled to be able to talk to strange men without the risk of being thought a shameless harlot. Well, with slightly *less* of a risk of being thought a shameless harlot.

"Construction," the man next to me said. "Embassy specialists."

The two of them told me about the British embassies they'd built all over the world. We traded stories about our travels and love affairs. One man wore a wedding ring but was not married. The other was married but not wearing a ring. The ring wearer explained to me that a long time ago his Norwegian girlfriend gave him a wedding ring as a gift. When he left her and moved to Amsterdam, his jealous Dutch girlfriend bought him a second ring. And when he moved back to Britain, his British girl-friend bought him a third. He lost that one, so she bought a replacement ring, the one he still wore although he'd just broken up with her and sent her back to England. This is why I love bars. Maybe living here wouldn't be so difficult after all, if there were oases like this one.

After a second beer, I joined Theo and his friends. The night was delicious, cool and breezy. Stars flickered on over the tennis courts. We ordered another round of beers and some fish curry. As we talked, it occurred to me that the last time Theo and I had spoken French together was in 1986, in a small classroom on the top of a hill in Vermont. And that if I had not been on that Vermont hilltop in 1986, I would not have been in Yemen some twenty years later. Interesting where one teenage romance can lead. Eventually the Frenchmen left, and I sat talking with Theo until long after dark.

I was surprised by Theo's unabashed enthusiasm for my class. "They love you, you know," he said. "Zaid told me, 'Jennifer is the best American in the world.'"

"Really?"

"I was interviewing him for the article I wrote about you, and I wanted to move on to another subject, but he said, 'No! I want to talk more about Jennifer!' He asked me if he could marry you."

"Isn't Zaid already married?"

"Yes, but he wants to marry you too."

"I don't think I could get around the teeth." Zaid's teeth, like those of most Yemeni men I met, are stained dark brown with *qat* and tea and tobacco. Many Yemenis do not brush their teeth at all, though some chew on a stick called *miswaak* to clean their teeth. As a dental hygiene fetishist, I was horrified by the crumbling, putrid teeth and rotting mouths.

"Well, he loves you. They all love you. And it's funny how the girls have taken you in. You're like their leader now."

"I love them, too."

"I can't tell you how happy they are with your work, how happy I am with what you are doing. I don't know what I am going to do when you leave."

This was a historic first. Theo had never, to my recollection, praised anything I had done, and certainly never with this kind of passion. I glowed with a sense of accomplishment that dimmed anything I had ever felt writing my science pages at *The Week*. Maybe I really could make a difference here after all.

☾

THE NEXT MORNING I met yet another new student. Shaima worked for the World Bank and had called Faris looking for a place to improve her writing. Faris recommended my class.

Shaima smiled. She was very pretty, with a narrow face, long doe-like eyelashes, and full lips. She wore a *balto* and *hijab* but left her face bare. It was a terrific relief to speak face-to-face with a Yemeni woman for more than a few fleeting seconds. We sat down in the conference room, and I ran through everything we had covered so far. She asked what else she could do to improve her writing, and I told her to read something in English every day. "It doesn't matter what—read something you enjoy. But make sure it's written by a native English speaker." I wrote her a list of newspapers and websites.

Shaima had had an unusually privileged life for a Yemeni. She received a full scholarship to the American University in Cairo, although her mother forced her to turn it down because she was too worried that Shaima would come into contact with drugs and alcohol. But Shaima did manage to go to university and then graduate school—in Jordan. Though she was thirty, she still lived with her parents, in the upscale neighborhood of Hadda. "We are stuck to our families until we are married," she told me.

I enjoyed talking with her and sensed that she could become a real friend. Worldlier and more independent than my reporters, she could move about with greater freedom. She also was the only Yemeni woman I knew who owned a car—a Mercedes.

When I was through with Shaima, the women took me to one of the back offices, where they had spread out newspapers on the floor. They locked the door and lifted their veils, smiling at me.

"You don't think it's wrong?" Enass asked me. "To sit on newspapers, since that is your work?"

"Oh no," I said. "We line gerbil cages with them."

Three of the four girls hiked their black *abayas* up to their waists in order to sit comfortably. All were wearing blue jeans.

They handed me a rolled Jordanian sandwich of pickles and falafel and watched closely as I took a bite. "Do you find it delicious?" Arwa asked anxiously. I assured her that I did.

Zuhra then launched into one of her high-speed monologues, telling me about her seven brothers and sisters, her hopes for her future, and her criteria for a husband.

"I expect never to marry," she told me. "I expect that. Because I will never compromise my career. And I will only marry a man who will support my career. But he must also be religious. There are very few Yemeni men like this."

Zuhra and I were the last to finish our sandwiches. "Because you never stop talking!" said one of the other girls.

☾

A PILE OF WORK awaited me the next morning. Faris had asked me to go over the most recent issue in detail and critique it for the whole staff. I spread out the paper on Sabri's dining room table and, for three solid hours, read and took notes on every page, every story, every line. I was becoming obsessed with my students' stories. I thought about them when I was lying in bed. I mentally corrected them while riding in cabs. I found myself thinking of a crucial prepositional phrase that would make Zuhra's beauty parlor story perfect as I swam laps at the Sheraton.

By the time I finished writing my critique and covering the paper with circles, cross-outs, and blue ballpoint scrawl, I was zinging with energy. It was Thursday, which most Yemenis have off, as Thursday and Friday are the weekend. The *Yemen Observer* staff, however, worked every day except Friday.

I arrived at the office early, anxious to speak with Hakim before class. Faris seemed to have special hopes for him, thinking he could help revolutionize the paper. But so far he had done little to distinguish himself, other than to argue with me in class, rarely in constructive ways. He claimed that we didn't need to use the word "said" in attributions, because *Time* magazine doesn't. This was not only untrue but considerably unhelpful when I was trying to teach my reporters plain, straightforward language. They were hopelessly dependent on the words "affirmed" and "confirmed," which they generally used when quoting someone who didn't have the authority to affirm or confirm anything. They *needed* the word "said." I wanted to explain to Hakim, as diplomatically as possible, how helpful it would be to everyone if he supported my authority and followed the same rules as everyone else.

Hakim was late, however, so I had no chance to speak to him. Instead, I cornered editor in chief Mohammed al-Asaadi, who had only made it to one previous class, and asked him sweetly if he wouldn't mind joining us for an hour. He was the person I most needed to reach, but Theo had told me he felt threatened by my presence. Apparently he didn't believe his journalism skills needed improving, which was disappointing. I wanted him to be able to reinforce what I was teaching and carry on some of this work after I left.

Once Hakim and al-Asaadi were both settled amidst my other reporters, I launched into my critique. To my delight, both al-Asaadi and Hakim (and the rest of the class) were quite receptive. I got through everything I wanted to say with minimal disruption. I began with praise, saying how much I liked the layout of the front page, some of the front headlines, and most of the story ideas. Baiting the hook.

I especially praised Adel, the paper's health reporter, because his was one of the better pages. "Poor Adel," Theo often said. "He is the lowest-caste person on staff, and the rest of them treat him like an animal, even though he is one of the best journalists they have." Yemen is divided into several social strata, including *bedouin* (desert nomads), *fellahin* (villagers), *hadarrin* (townspeople), and *akhdam* (literally "servants"), which include Adel's family. So I told everyone what wonderful stories Adel had picked for his page, in the probably vain hope of boosting his status.

Then I reviewed some things that needed to be done more consistently. Every story should have a byline, I told them. (Often, the stories just said "Observer staff.")

"You all work hard on these stories," I said. "You deserve credit for them. I want you to be proud of your work. Putting your name on your story tells your readers that you stand behind your reporting. It enhances your credibility. And it keeps you accountable. If you are ashamed to put your name on a piece of work, it does not belong in the paper."

Theo raised his hand. "What if you are writing a story that could get you killed? So if you put your name on it, someone will come after you?"

"Well, in that case, we can make an exception. I don't want to get any of you killed. If you are quite sure that someone will come after you with a gun or any other weapon for a story you are writing, you have my permission to withhold your byline. However, every single one of the stories in this issue should be able to safely have a byline without getting anyone killed."

Next, we talked about the importance of spelling. "The word 'conference' is misspelled in a front-page headline," I said. "As a reader, I see this and say, 'If they make mistakes about things as small as spelling, what other kinds of mistakes are they making?' You increase your credibility when your grammar and spelling are perfect. And you erode it when they are not."

They nodded and scribbled.

A new fellow joined us for the critique, a blond, blue-eyed Californian named Luke, who had been hired to help with the copyediting. He radiated goodwill, and I was happy to have someone else there to reinforce the proper use of the English language.

When everyone had finally dispersed, Theo looked at me. I was crumpled against the blackboard. "Worn out?"

"I feel like I've just run a marathon. My diaphragm hurts." I get so enthusiastic when I am talking that I wave my arms a lot and lunge back and forth from the dry-erase board to the table. My calisthenics seemed to worry my students, who kept offering me a chair. But they often had just as much trouble sitting still.

"I've only just realized this since you've come here," said Theo a few days later. "But this entire nation has ADD. This is their central problem; this is why nothing gets done."

☾*

THE NEXT DAY'S CLASS focused just on leads. I needed to do something small and focused with them; it was too difficult to fix entire stories. If they could get just that first sentence of the story right, the rest would follow—I hoped. We went over everyone's leads, critiquing and rewriting them until they were perfect. Or at least printable. I gave them the last fifteen minutes of class to interview me and told them their assignment was to write a lead and three paragraphs based on their interview. They'd been very curious about me and were thrilled to have permission to quiz me. They asked me where I lived, whether I was married, where I had worked before Yemen, what I thought of them, what I thought of Yemen, and who was the best student (this from Zaid). I warned them that I might lie and said that they should investigate me on the Internet, to make sure I really am who I say I am and have done the things I say I have done.

They proved a little too good at this. That night, as I was halfway through dinner, Theo texted me. Apparently my students had discovered (via Google's image search) scores of photos of me in cocktail dresses at New York media parties. It had not occurred to me that they might find things I would rather keep concealed. I immediately panicked, worried they would think less of me after having seen me in lipstick and a low-cut cocktail dress, holding a glass of wine. I rang Theo immediately after dinner, and he assured me that they still loved me.

"For my brains?" I asked fretfully.

"Of course for your brains," he said. "What else could they love?"

☾

WHEN I WALKED into the newsroom the next morning, Zaid was sitting there gazing at a photo of me that he had installed as his desktop. In it, I had an arm draped around my photographer friend David, and I was smiling through my hair, which was loose and tumbling down to my waist. I was relieved, however, to see that only David was holding a beer. I immediately apologized for my scanty outfit and the fact that I had an arm around a man, but Zaid said, "Jennifer, I lived with an American family for three years! You don't need to explain these things to me. We understand."

"I just don't want you to get a poor impression of me," I said.

"Never! We love you! We just think you are beautiful, these are beautiful," he said, gesturing to the photos.

The women, Zuhra and Arwa, said the same thing. I relaxed slightly.

☾

LATER THAT AFTERNOON, I was updating Faris on my activities with his staff when he asked if I would be willing to report on a conference on democracy in the Arab world at the Mövenpick Hotel across town. I could write a story about democratic progress in the region for *Arabia Felix,* he said. Before I had time to think about it, or suggest that perhaps democracy in the Arab world was a bit broad for one magazine piece, a van arrived to sweep me off to the hotel, along with Adel, who became my translator.

We spent six hours at the hotel, interviewing professors, writers, and politicians from Egypt, Pakistan, Iraq, the United Arab Emirates, and Saudi Arabia. Exhausted from sprinting after interviewees and translating my questions, Adel begged for a rest. "Not until we have enough for a story," I said. By the end of the day, we had plenty. I was most excited about interviewing Iraqi parliament member Safia al-Souhail, as I was curious to hear her views on the situation in Iraq.

"People think that it's the Americans who are foisting ideas of women's rights and human rights on Iraqis," she told me. "This is not true. Iraqi women have been fighting for these things for a generation. I have always dressed like this." She gestured to her yellow pantsuit.

She was surprisingly optimistic about Iraq's future. The turmoil and bloodshed there were to be expected after so many years of oppression, she said. (Several other attendees had expressed similar views.) "The people don't know how to be free," she said. "Iraq needs help from the U.S. and other countries right now. But as soon as Iraq is independent, it will waste no time throwing them all out of the country. Just not yet."

☾

I BEGAN CLASS the next day by asking Adel to describe our reporting process at the Mövenpick. We talked about how we tracked people down and about how much more efficient it had been to take notes than to use a tape recorder. My students always wanted to record their interviews, which forced them to spend hours transcribing. I loathe tape recorders and believe they should be used only as a backup, when interviewing someone who might sue the paper. I told my class how one Egyptian woman had shied away when Adel produced his tape recorder. "It can intimidate people and keep them from talking to you."

And then I showed them my notebooks. I had filled them front to back and then written on the back side of every page. "Reporters for daily papers go through one to three of these a day," I told them. Their eyes widened. From what I could tell, they'd been using the same notebooks since I got there.

This led to a discussion of interviewing techniques. We talked about how I interviewed people at the conference and went over the interviewing handout I'd given them. Then came the fun part. I asked them to interview each other in pairs in front of the class. Zaid and Adel volunteered to go first. I asked the class to critique them. Which they enthusiastically did. Nothing got them more excited than criticizing each other.

I wanted to involve the women, who had been shyer about speaking up, so I asked Arwa and Zuhra to go next. Arwa was resistant but with a little encouragement agreed to interview Zuhra. She was a much better interviewer than the men—more focused and quicker with her questions. She also had the good fortune to be interviewing someone who answered every question with a torrent of words.

Faris rang me that afternoon as I was leaving my Arabic lesson and invited me out to dinner. At eight thirty P.M., he arrived promptly on my doorstep, beautifully dressed, in a dark pinstriped suit. Clouds of cologne wafted off of him. We climbed into his Mercedes and drove to Hadda, where we ate at an Americanesque Greek restaurant called Zorba's. "It's a five-star restaurant," said Faris. "One of the best in Sana'a!"

This it most certainly wasn't. The food was very basic: burgers and fries, salads, fish, spaghetti. But the place was packed with foreigners and the Yemeni elite and was one of the few places where women and men could be found in somewhat equal numbers. Faris knew the owner, who waved us to one of the front tables overlooking the street.

On the way, Faris had given me a flattering speech about how incredibly grateful he was to me for the work I had done. He asked if I would write up a few of my pithy pieces of advice for my students so he could frame my words and hang them around the newsroom to remind his reporters of what I had taught them.

"You mean, things like 'This is a NEWSpaper, not an OLDSpaper; let's put some news in it'?" I asked.

"Yes! I want that one. And as many others as you have."

He also said he wanted me to see the countryside and promised to arrange a car to take me on a day trip to the villages of Kawkaban and Shibam on Friday. He would pay for me to eat at a restaurant there. Like so many of Faris's promises, these turned out to be as insubstantial as the Sana'ani air.

Faris also said he wanted to have a dinner in my honor on one of my last nights and present me with some gifts. "Don't buy any jewelry," he said. "I have plenty for you." The chances of me buying jewelry were slim to none, and slim just left town. I didn't wear any jewelry, save Ginger's wedding ring.

Then he offered me a job. "I will pay you one thousand dollars a month"—most journalists at the paper made $200 a month—"plane tickets back and forth to New York, and occasional three-day vacations in Beirut," he said, "if you will come to run the *Yemen Observer*."

"To *run* it?" I thought he must have been joking. I had no management experience, almost no Arabic, and Faris had never even seen my résumé. Theo had hinted that Faris might offer me some kind of job, but I hadn't expected to be handed the entire paper. Not one newspaper editor in the whole of the United States would have looked over my résumé and thought, "I want this woman to run my paper."

"You would have total control," Faris continued. I would? I wouldn't have to write flattering pieces about the president? Was this possible?

"I'd be the editor?" I fleetingly imagined my name at the top of a masthead.

"We'd have to make you managing editor or something. The editor in chief must by law be Yemeni. But you would be in charge." Hmmm. I wondered if the Yemeni staff would really let me be in charge if there was a Yemeni name above me on the masthead.

For a moment, I allowed myself to contemplate the heady thrill of being the boss. Then, almost reflexively, I declined. "I am still paying off American debts," I said. "I don't see how I could possibly live on that." I was making $60,000 in New York and could hardly manage to scrape by.

"Think about it," he said.

"I'll think."

"I could make it fifteen hundred dollars."

"Do you know what I make in New York?"

"It will be cheaper to live here."

I looked out the window at the darkness settling over the city's scores of minarets, the slow brightening of the colored glass *qamarias*. I watched the women hurrying to beat the darkness home, laden with sacks of food, and the men, their cheeks fat with *qat,* striding past in long white robes. I thought about the gray New York office where I had spent the last five years.

"I'll think," I said.

FOUR

things to chew on

A few days before my departure, I woke up at six A.M. in a blind panic. Was it possible I had so little time left? There was so much still to do! I hadn't taught my reporters how to do research on the Internet. I hadn't given them enough investigative skills. I hadn't talked with them about follow-up stories. They often wrote a breaking news story about something—a new kind of irrigation being introduced, for example—but then never wrote about the effects of the project. The paper was full of the launchings of brilliant new projects, but my reporters never bothered to find out whether they met their goals. Given that a large percentage of development projects worldwide fail, I felt that it was the press's job to monitor them and hold them accountable.

I also hadn't finished writing my democracy story for *Arabia Felix* or my overall report on the paper. Then, in class that day, something happened that made me forget how much I *hadn't* done.

On the dry-erase board, I wrote a list of facts: A murder was committed. Thabbit al-Saadyi, ninety-four, murdered Qasim al-Washari, forty-nine. (I let the students pick the names.) The murder happened in a casino. It was committed with an AK-47. On Saturday at three A.M. Qasim was found riddled with five bullet holes, with three thousand *riyals* in his pocket. Next to him were a bottle of vodka and two roses. (Again, details courtesy of my students.)

They then had fifteen minutes to write me a really good lead.

And—miracle of miracles—they *did*! Farouq read his lead first, and it was *perfect*. "Thabbit al-Saadyi, 94, killed Qasim al-Washari, 49, with an AK-47 at a casino Saturday at 3 A.M." He included the who, what, where, when, and how. He included a subject, verb, and object. And he used the correct style for the ages of the men! It may sound ridiculous, but I was so moved that my skin tingled and tears came to my eyes.

"That is so perfect," I told Farouq. "That is just what I've been looking for."

☪

THERE WAS ALSO so much of Yemen I had left to see. On Fridays, my days off, I immersed myself in Yemeni life—in what my life might be like if I lived there. Yemenis are quick with hospitable invitations, and a thin, professorial man I met one night at the National Museum, Dr. Mohammed Saleh al-Haj, immediately invited me to lunch with his family. This is how Yemenis are—they will invite you home to lunch five minutes after meeting you. And after you have gone once, they will then want you to have lunch with them *every* Friday.

We met in the morning and took a taxi together to the fish market to pick out lunch. A little nervous to be heading home with a complete stranger, but curious to get a glimpse of Yemeni home life, I wandered around taking photographs of children. I was fascinated by the little girls, the dirty little street princesses, their bright taffeta dresses streaked with grime.

Dr. al-Haj's brother-in-law Khaled, sister Leila, and niece Chulud fetched us from the market in their car, and we drove to Dr. al-Haj's home, a two-room apartment up a flight of stairs and across a rooftop. After we removed our shoes and stepped inside, Leila and Chulud immediately stripped off their *abayas,* emerging looking like two Western women. Chulud wore skintight blue jeans and a loose short-sleeved shirt over a black bra, like any American fifteen-year-old, while Leila wore a checked shirt over loose plaid pants. They took over the kitchen, while Dr. al-Haj settled me in the living room/dining area. The room was carpeted with oriental rugs and lined with sitting cushions. A TV hulked in the corner, blaring a Friday sermon. Khaled came in wearing his long white robe and switched the television to an American channel showing a swimsuit fashion show. *"Amreekee!"* he told me, smiling. I ought to have been grateful for some American television, so I smiled, though the reverse was true. I have never owned a television, I have no interest in fashion, and it made me uneasy to watch women in bathing suits in the company of Yemeni men. In fact, I'd become rather taken with this whole modesty thing. Why should I let a man who is not my lover see any part of me? I was getting used to hiding.

Dr. al-Haj disappeared for a moment and returned with a gift for me: a lovely woven bag stuffed with something soft. I opened it to find a long, silky *abaya* and matching scarf, with glittery flowers along the edges. I was overwhelmed by his generosity.

"So you will be safer," he said, though I was already covered from tip to toe in loose black, so much so that when Dr. al-Haj saw me that morning, he had said, "Ah, so you are Yemeni now!"

"If you don't like it you can throw it away," he said. "And if it's the wrong size I will buy you a new one."

"I would never throw it away! I love it. Thank you. *Shukrahn.*"

The neighbors heard that I was visiting and came by to take a look at me. First came a little girl, dressed up like royalty in a frothy green dress. She was shy at first, and then impish, stealing someone's cell phone and playing with it. Then three boys came in. Each one solemnly took my hand and greeted me, and then the third boy kissed me on each cheek and then once on the top of my head. If I lived here for a year, would I ever cease to be a curiosity? Or would I simply adjust to being an object of study?

When lunch was ready, Chulud carried each of the dishes into the room. "This is *salatah,*" she said. "This is *roz.* This is *chobes.* This is *samak.*" I nodded approvingly and repeated the Arabic words after her.

Dr. al-Haj took me to the kitchen to wash my hands, and then we began to eat. Yemenis are lightning-fast eaters, so it was hard for me to keep up. We started with the yogurt-drenched spongy bread called *shafoot,* pouring chopped salad and chili sauce on our little corners of it and picking up clumps with our hands. Then there were roasted vegetables, potatoes, flaky white fish (the best pieces of which were flung in front of me, the guest of honor), and *bint al-sahn*—"the daughter of the dish." This was my favorite. It resembled an enormous flaky pancake, made with flour and butter and drizzled with honey. I ate until I could eat no more, despite the urging of my hosts. All of this we washed down with tiny glass cups of gingery tea. I could live with eating meals like this one every week.

Now that our stomachs were lined with food—an important prerequisite to chewing bitter *qat*—Leila and Chulud took me to my first *qat* chew, a women-only session at a friend's house, not far from where I was staying. I had been waiting eagerly for this, curious about the drug and the ritual so essential to Yemeni life. We walked through a ground-floor courtyard where children were playing to the *mafraj* in the back. There, I was introduced to the five women already sitting in identical postures on the cushions around the room. When Yemenis lounge in a *mafraj,* they customarily sit with the right knee bent so that it points skyward, the foot pulled close to the body, and the left knee dropped out to the side, with the foot tucked under the right leg. My left leg constantly falls asleep in this position, so I keep adjusting my posture, sometimes pulling both knees up to my chin, always keeping the soles of my feet hidden, as it is impolite in Arab cultures to show anyone the bottoms of your feet.

Women continued to stream into the room, each one circling to kiss the others several times on the cheek. Some of them had a rhythm: two quick kisses, a beat, then three quick kisses. Each seemed to have a signature way of kissing hello.

The women spoke to each other and over each other in rapid-fire Arabic. Without Dr. al-Haj, I had no one to translate for me; no one else in the group spoke English. Communication was accomplished with my few Arabic words and scores of hand gestures. If I were to stay, I thought, I'd learn Arabic quickly, out of sheer necessity. Leila told me they were discussing democracy. I should have liked to hear that, particularly because I'd been told that Yemeni women rarely talked about anything other than babies and other domestic matters. This did not seem to be true in our group.

When everyone had arrived, the group consisted of about twelve or thirteen women in various states of *abaya.* All had their veils pulled back from their faces, and many had taken them off entirely. I sat with Leila on my left and a faux-blond woman on my right. The blonde did most of the talking. She asked me if I were married, pointing to my ring and to hers. I told her (and all the other women, who stared at me the entire time I was there, as if I'd just landed from Pluto) that I was indeed.

"Babies?"

I shook my head. "Not yet." Then, as an afterthought, I added, *"In-sha'allah"* ("if God is willing). At that, everyone smiled and nodded, and seemed to relax a bit. I wasn't so different then after all. Despite my uncertainty about children, it did occur to me that if I accepted Faris's offer, I would be spending one of my last fertile years in a country where there was little chance I would find romance, let alone a partner with whom to raise a child. Should I decide I wanted one.

A large elderly woman, who I believe was our hostess, passed around a tray of cups of sweet tea before preparing the enormous water pipe standing in the corner by placing glowing-hot lumps of tobacco atop it. A three-inch-thick hose snaked from it across the floor, so that the mouthpiece would reach even the woman sitting farthest away. The mouthpiece was passed from woman to woman, each keeping it for the space of approximately ten inhalations. *"Khamsa wa khamsa,"* Leila said to me. "Five and five." I was grateful that I had learned all of my numbers before I left New York.

When the water pipe came my way, Leila showed me how to smoke it—you don't inhale all of the way, just slightly. I accidentally took in too much and began to cough. My eyes widened and I touched my hand to my heart, which was enough to make the women take it away from me. When I couldn't stop coughing, the blonde whipped out a little vial of oil and rubbed some on the back of my hands. She and Leila both gestured that I should sniff it.

"Oxygen," said Leila in English. I wasn't sure why sniffing rose oil on my hands would increase my oxygen levels, but I wasn't about to debate the issue.

An African-looking woman pulled tinfoil-wrapped pie shapes from her bag and began passing them around. I thought perhaps they were little tarts, but they were cakes of strong homemade incense. Many Yemeni women make these. She sold one to Leila (images of Avon parties flashed through my head), who broke off a piece and burned it in a small ceramic burner. She turned to me and held the incense under each one of my pinned-up braids, until the sweet smoke had suffused my hair. Then she made me stand and held the incense burner underneath my skirts. The smoke was hot on my bare legs. The blond woman picked up my head scarf from the cushion behind me and handed it to Leila, who scented that as well. I now smelled strongly of 1968.

Several women took out their bags of *qat* and began to place the little green leaves in their mouths. Leila placed a handful of her *qat* on my lap. The blond woman on my right added a sprig. We began to chew. The goal is to keep the leaves in the left cheek, between the gums and the cheek, while gnawing on them to release the juices. They were bitter, as if I were chewing something slightly poisonous.

My initial impression was that *qat* was a very mild drug—less of an immediate jolt to the body than coffee. I had been chewing for nearly an hour before I felt anything at all other than nausea. Then the curtains of my mind began to slide open. The fog of exhaustion dissipated, and I felt lucid and sharp. My thoughts rang like crystal. I suddenly felt like running a marathon, writing a novel, or swimming the English Channel. If American journalists were to ever get ahold of *qat,* I am sure they would promptly deplete the supply.

But this is just the first phase of the drug. During this phase, chewers customarily banter with each other, trading barbs. In the second phase, the conversation becomes more focused, zeroing in on a topic. After that is Solomon's Hour, named for the Prophet Solomon, rumored to be fond of meditation. During this time, everyone slips into thoughtful trances and cannot be bothered to talk.

I didn't stay long enough at this chew to get to that stage.

By the time Dr. al-Haj called to check on me, I was ready to go. I couldn't sit *still* any longer. What I found most mysterious about *qat* chews is how people were able to sit for so long while ingesting a stimulant.

Dr. al-Haj walked me home, where I was hugely relieved to be alone again. It wasn't until I was standing in my room that I realized the monumental effort it had cost me to be someone other than myself for the hours of lunch and the chew. It was obviously easy to make Yemeni friends, but for how long could I pretend to be a virtuous married woman who had never had a lover? It seemed impossible that I could ever manage this feat on a daily basis for as long as a year. Concealing so much of myself made me lonely. It also felt dishonest. This is what made spending time with Yemeni people so exhausting—all the parts of me I had to hold back. Restraint has never been my strong suit.

Not that I was thinking about staying. Was I?

☪

BACK AT WORK, I finished my piece on Arab democracy for *Arabia Felix,* which I titled "Cultivating the Desert." (Faris subsequently lifted this title for a coffee-table book on the elections he published later that year.) My students claimed the rest of my time as I crammed as much as I could into my final lessons. For a class on Internet research, I herded my reporters to the computers. We began by examining a site that collects tax forms of international nonprofits; a site that gives profiles of every domain; and snopes.com, an urban legend–debunking site, which everyone loved. They wanted to look up all kinds of urban legends. I found it intriguing that the men wanted to look up urban legends about marriage, whereas the women wanted to look up stories about Hurricane Katrina and war. So much for gender stereotypes. I bet if Yemen had a *Cosmo*-like magazine, the men would devour it at least as enthusiastically as the women.

The point of this exercise was to show my students how to figure out which sites were reliable sources of information and which were sources of unfounded rumor. They had a remarkable inability to tell the two apart. They believed *everything* they read on the Web, which made for some interesting assertions in their stories. They did not question what they were told. If I could teach them just one thing, I decided, it would be skepticism.

☪

EVERYTHING I DID during my last few days in Yemen was suffused with curiosity about what would happen if I actually accepted Faris's job offer. What would I be like as an editor in chief? Could I keep up the exhausting pace Faris expected of me? And what if I gave up my life in New York to come here, made myself a home, and then failed? What if I couldn't get my reporters to meet deadlines? What if I couldn't actually get an entire issue organized and out in time twice a week?

(*

FORTY-FIVE PEOPLE showed up at the farewell banquet Faris threw for me on my second-to-last night at Shaibani, a fish restaurant. No one had ever thrown me such an extravaganza! Almost everyone I invited showed up: Dr. al-Haj, Shaima, Sabri, the entire staff of the *Yemen Observer*, other friends, and even a jazz band from New York, scheduled to play at the American Embassy the following night. But I didn't realize until we were all assembled that my women were missing. Where were Zuhra and Arwa and Radia and all the people I loved best? I was heartbroken. I had forgotten that they were not allowed out this late.

Faris stood up and gave a speech, saying how much I had changed the newspaper in just a few weeks, that his staff had demanded that I return, and that they all loved me. He showered me with gifts, which were stacked in a pyramid on the table in front of me: a whole set of silver jewelry in an enormous blue velvet box, two *jambiyas* with belts, seven baseball caps (one signed by the entire staff, telling me not to go), and five miniature Yemeni houses to bring home as gifts. He also handed me an envelope containing three crisp $100 bills.

Faris had hired two photographers to capture the event, and they took pictures of me nonstop throughout the dinner. I had paparazzi! I felt like Madonna. We ate Yemeni fish and bread and salsa and bananas with honey. The honey—for which Yemen is renowned—tasted of jasmine and God. It was that good.

I went home alone that night feeling weepy and confused, and lonely in that particular way one gets lonely when one is in between places, belonging nowhere. My heart sank at the prospect of going back to my New York routine. But could I possibly ever belong here?

On my last day in Yemen, I stopped once more at the office. My reporters threw themselves at me and begged me not to go. Zuhra pulled me aside in the hallway and pressed a purple alligator-skin wallet into my hands.

"It's not new," she apologized. "But it's my favorite thing I own and I love it. I wanted to give you something I love."

I was so moved by this I couldn't speak. I just took both her small hands in mine and squeezed them. If I come back, I thought, this will be why.

FIVE

you'll die over there!

*The most dispiriting thing about returning to work at **The Week** after a holi-*day was that no one wanted to hear about it. I'd traveled quite a lot in my five years at the magazine, and it never failed to irk me that no one ever asked questions about my journeys beyond a polite "Nice vacation?" Perhaps this was understandable when I had been to well-trodden places such as Paris, Barcelona, and Dublin. But now I had been to Yemen! Few people in the office had even been able to place it on a map before I headed off there, and so I thought perhaps its exoticness would prompt some curiosity. After all, my colleagues were journalists, whose job it was to be professionally curious. They would surely be interested in the lands beyond the shores of Manhattan.

I was wrong. No one wanted to hear about the *Yemen Observer,* my students, or daily life in Arabia. A couple people asked what I wore while I was there, but that was the extent of their interest. This baffled and wounded me. I couldn't help but take their lack of interest personally. I always spent my first few days back from holiday feeling irritated with the world. I wanted to share my experiences with the people with whom I spent eight hours a day. I wanted to be found interesting. Instead, I stared at my gray computer screen and began, with dread, the return to my tired routine.

After less than a week back in New York, I found I was tired of pretty much everything. I was tired of my morning rituals, tired of running in the same parks, tired of swimming in the same pools, tired of spending eight hours of every day in a drab midtown office, tired of the United States and our embarrassment of a president. I was tired of feeling underestimated by my boss and underutilized at the magazine. I was tired of the bleak cynicism of my coworkers. I was tired of media cocktail parties. I was even tired of my favorite fruit stand on Fortieth Street and Broadway, where the Afghan fruit seller who measured out my cherries and grapes took more of an interest in my Yemeni adventures than anyone in my office.

In New York I was always maniacally social and spent most of my evenings at art openings, parties, the theater, the opera, book readings, or simply drinking with friends. But now I found myself growing increasingly restless and malcontent. I craved novelty and the chance to spend my energy on something more personally meaningful than *The Week*. I had loved working for *The Week* for many years. I was one of the magazine's first hires and had started there as an associate editor before its launch. It had been thrilling to see it through from conception to adolescence.

Still, five and a half years was longer than I had ever spent at any job, and my work at *The Week* sapped my energy for other projects I wanted to finish—some short stories, a novel, my stalled acting career.

Back in New York, I felt the years dwindling away, with little to show for them other than a few weekly magazine pages. Something had to be done, and before I got a day older. There had never been a better time. I was single, child free, and almost rid of my student loan debts from my two graduate degrees. If it took a year in Yemen to launch me out of the predictable routine of my life, so be it.

It was this combination of panic and thirst for novelty that prompted me finally to take Faris up on his offer. This was my chance to take a place on the front lines of the struggle for democracy in the Arab world! After all, democracy cannot take root without a free press. Perhaps I could help to make Yemen's freer, just a bit, by loosening the tethers restraining my timid reporters.

My life would certainly feel more meaningful if I were helping my

Yemeni journalists learn what they so ached to learn. I imagined revolu-
tionizing the newspaper, breaking stories exposing government corruption, election fraud, and human rights abuses. I imagined writing pieces
that would trigger policy changes, reduce terrorism, and alter the role of
women in society. I imagined polishing the staff of the *Yemen Observer* into
a well-oiled machine that scarcely needed interference or line editing
from me. Oppressed peoples all over the world would beg me to come
and transform their own press! (It's difficult to write this now, years later,
without dissolving into hysterical laughter at my naïveté.) I also imagined
Zuhra, waiting for me to return.

☾✴

THE FIRST PERSON to tell was Bill, my editor at *The Week*. The entire
morning of July 13, 2006, I was a nervous wreck, waiting to talk to him.
I'd never worked anywhere for as long as I had worked at *The Week,* and I
had never walked away from a job for as uncertain a future. I was giving
up the highest salary I'd ever earned. I was kissing fantastic health insurance good-bye. I was turning my back on stability.

"So, what's on your mind, Nif?" said Bill, tipping back in his chair. He
was the only one in the office who used that particular nickname, which
was reserved for my closest friends.

I took a breath. "I've just accepted another job."

The front legs of his chair hit the ground with a bang. For once, I had
thrown him. "What are you going to do? Run off and work at a newspaper
in Yemen?" he joked.

"Actually . . . yes. I am going to be the editor of the *Yemen Observer*. I've
been offered a year's contract."

His response could hardly have been more satisfying. "*Holy fucking shit,*
are you *kidding* me? Are you out of your fucking mind? You're *crazy*! You'll
die over there! I can't believe you are seriously doing this! Why?"

This was a much more exciting reaction than I had expected. I had
never seen Bill lose his cool like this. He ranted for a while about my questionable sanity, but when I finally calmed him down and explained what I
was doing, he seemed to understand. He told me that it had been a swell
five years and that the magazine would miss me. "We'll hire someone to
do your job," he said. "But we'll never replace you."

The rest of the staff of *The Week* and most of my friends were just as surprised, although they expressed this in a slightly less dramatic fashion. Several people promptly sent me names of companies that provide kidnapping insurance. My parents, who know me fairly well, just said resignedly, "We thought something like this might happen." One friend, a journalist for the *Wall Street Journal*, forwarded me a cautionary note from a woman who worked for the Foreign Service.

Yemen's not too bad (beautiful country), as long as one stays in Sanaa. I wouldn't recommend traveling outside of town, as people will take pot shots at you (generally just small arms fire) in some parts of the country. Also, Yemenis tend to kidnap foreigners for ransom—the most recent was only a few months ago, so one has to be incredibly vigilant. Lots of unsavory characters have been known to move through there on their way to other places.

On the other hand, it is gorgeous, and it has the largest open air arms market in the world, which is pretty cool. And the history is absolutely amazing . . . [But] why Yemen? There are lots of English language newspapers in the world that need editors.

While this was less than encouraging, around this time I found the following article on the website of the Yemen Observer, which I had failed to notice before.

Professional Journalist Raises Yemen Observer's Standards
By Zuhra al-Ammari

Jul. 4, 2006

The American journalist who has been teaching at the Yemen Observe, Jennifer Steil, was presented with Jambia, necklace and various gifts at a farewell dinner on Sunday night in Al-Shaibani restaurant.

"We are paying farewell to a friend and to a teacher," said Faris Sanabani, the publisher of the *Yemen Observer* as he presented Ms. Steil with the jambia. He thanked her for making a change in the newspaper in term of technical writing, and appearence," he said.

Jennifer, "This is my first time in Yemen and the Middle, it has just been remarkable, you are the most open-hearted and friendly people ever, I love you guys and I

hope to come back and can be with you again. Thank for you again" Everyone feel satisfied to the noticeable progress in their performance.

However, they feel sad too to say "farewell" to her and hope that she comes back.
Adel, a journalist, said "I like this teacher for her spirit of volunteerism; she has been a
patient teacher. I benefited a lot from her experience. I learned how to better my writing. She is really a queen." Hassan, a journalist, said "Really, she is a smart journalist.
It is enough for me to listen to her experience in field of journalism. She taught us modern principles of editing news and how one could do his or her news professionally."

Arwa, a journalist, said "It was the first training course for me in English. I benefited
by learning how to write. She is one of the best journalists I have seen. I make sure to
attend all her classes. I benefited tremendously." Radia, a secretary, said "She is a perfect woman. She is like the candle, she burns to give light to the others. I benefited a
lot from her" Jennifer Steil has come from U.S.A to teach the Yemen Observer's journalists some of the press skills.

She was observing the progress of every journalist. She gave them the advices for
which they upgrade heir profession.

The funny thing is, Zuhra was not allowed to attend my farewell dinner. Yet she managed to somehow get an accurate account of the evening
and even a fairly accurate quote from me. Did she hire a stringer to take
notes for her? Naturally, I would have been even happier if the story were
grammatical, but that was one reason for going back, after all.

Knowing I was about to leave, I fell in love with my city all over again.
I fell in love with my book-crammed apartment, with my belly-dancing
neighbor downstairs, with my local pub, the Piper's Kilt. I fell in love with
the A train, the Harlem YMCA, Inwood Hill Park. I fell in love with each
of my friends and went out almost every night that wasn't spent packing
to soak them all up. I went to art galleries and the theater. I went to one
last ecstatic baseball game at Yankee Stadium, where I euphorically inhaled
beer, popcorn, Cracker Jacks, peanuts, and everything else they had for
sale, because I didn't know when I could do it again. The Yankees graciously made the night perfect by winning.

The last Sunday I was in town, my friends in the neighborhood gathered at the Piper's Kilt, which was holding its first karaoke night. My friend Tommy was bartending and shook his head at me. *"Yemen,"* he said, setting a gin in front of me and moving down the bar. "The next time I see you will be in a kidnap video."

I wore a tiny red dress and red lipstick. Who knew when I could dress like that again? What I remember most from that night (other than standing on the bar barefoot singing "Leaving on a Jet Plane") is that when I told Tommy I was heading home, he told me to wait a moment and came out from behind the bar. Tommy had *never* come out from behind the bar to say good-bye to me before any of my other trips abroad. He hugged me and kissed me on the cheek. "My god," I said, looking at his mournful face as I stepped out of his arms. "You really don't think I'm coming back, do you?"

My last morning, I went for a run through Inwood Hill and Fort Tryon parks in a torrential rainstorm. After five minutes, my shorts and shirt were plastered to my body, and my braids had glued themselves to my arms. I plunged on. A montage of memories of the countless mornings I've spent trotting past these lilies, these dripping trees, this gray river, accosted me. Jennifer Steil, I thought, this is your life. This *was* your life.

SIX

when, exactly, is insha'allah?

I arrive at the offices of the **Yemen Observer** *on September 2, 2006, to find* no one waiting for me. Faris is away, I presume with the president, who is madly campaigning for reelection despite the fact that there is little doubt of his victory; editor Mohammed al-Asaadi has vanished from his corner office; and the rest of the staff is nowhere in evidence. My heart sinks. Surely they haven't forgotten me? I don't have a phone yet, so I have not been able to call anyone to tell them I have arrived.

My footsteps echo on the marble floors as I walk through the empty office. I am amazed to find the entire building festooned with my quotes. It's a bit unnerving to see my own words, *framed,* in both English and Arabic adorning every wall.

"This is a NEWSpaper, not an OLDSpaper! Let's put some news in it!"

"When you think your story is perfect, read it again."

"Never, ever begin a story with an attribution."

"A lead must contain a subject, verb, and object!"

I feel a bit like Chairman Mao. At least I know I haven't been totally forgotten.

I'd overslept my alarm this morning at Sabri's house, where I was temporarily housed in student quarters, and woke in a panic. I couldn't be late on my first day as the boss! I skipped coffee, skipped my planned walk to work, and dashed through a quick shower and into a cab, breathless. To find that I apparently have not been missed.

But wait! There are noises in a back office. The door opens, and a tiny pillar of black rayon launches herself across the front foyer and into my arms. "I cannot believe I have you before me!" Zuhra says, stepping back to look at me, keeping hold of my hands. Her dark eyes sparkle. "I have waited so long for this day. I love you so much! And now, we are for the first time going to have a woman in charge. I am so very happy!"

"I am so happy too!" I say, though perhaps with less confidence. "Where is everybody?"

She tells me that Faris is indeed with the president, that al-Asaadi rarely appears this early, and that Farouq is out because his one-and-a-half-year-old daughter has just died of a mysterious illness. He hasn't been able to work, she says. He is overwhelmed with grief. I cannot imagine. I have no idea how anyone recovers from the death of a child. "And Arwa has quit," Zuhra goes on. "She went to find a different job. And Zaid of course just left for London. Hassan and Adel are both working for the EU observers until the election is over." Theo, who is still in Yemen, has left the paper, apparently burning some bridges behind him. I fell out with him myself after he sent me a series of bizarrely discouraging e-mails about my return. I think he rather resented the invasion of what he saw as his turf.

"Do we have anyone left?" I am beginning to panic. How can I transform a paper with no staff?

"Radia is here! And we have some new ones," she says. "Come, meet them."

Radia, who is officially Faris's receptionist and not a reporter, emerges from the back room, where the women have been breakfasting, to tell me how much she missed me and how pleased she is that I am back.

They take me to the newsroom, where we find two women and two men hunched over computers. Zuhra tugs me over by the hand.

"This is Noor. She is doing the culture page." Noor has thick, long eyelashes and eyes that crinkle when she smiles. Like Zuhra, she wears glasses, but unlike Zuhra, she ties her *hijab* in the back of her head. I make a mental note of this so I can identify her later.

Najma, Zuhra tells me, has been writing the health page. Najma shyly takes my hand and tells me how glad she is to meet me. Her eyes are wider and more frightened than Noor's.

The men, a tall, bespectacled man named Talha and a stouter, boyishly attractive man named Bashir, are equally polite and welcoming.

"How long have you been here?" I ask them. They hadn't been hired when I left Yemen two months ago.

"A month or so."

All four of the new hires are recent graduates of university. None has any journalism experience. I am dismayed. So many of the people I had already begun to train are gone. I will have to start all over again.

☪

ZUHRA SHOWS ME to al-Asaadi's office in the back of the first floor, where I sit and take notes on recent issues of the paper until al-Asaadi arrives, close to noon. I've forgotten how tiny he is; just a bit taller than my shoulders (and I am only 5'6"). He's handsome, with doll-like features and Bambi eyelashes. I would guess he weighs something approaching ninety pounds. He wears a suit jacket and slacks.

"*Ahlan wa sahlan!*" (Welcome!) he says, taking my hand and smiling warmly.

"*Ahlan wa sahlan!* I am sorry for invading your office. I wasn't sure where to go."

"My office is your office."

Theo had warned me, when I was last in Yemen, that al-Asaadi would prove my biggest challenge. He won't want to give up control, he said. He is used to being in charge.

So I am cautious. I don't want to wound his pride and jeopardize our relationship by throwing my weight around and acting like an Ugly, Imperialist American. I tell him how much I look forward to learning from him and how much I hope we can work as partners.

"It is I who will learn from you," he says. "Faris feels—and I feel the same way—that you are to be the captain of this paper. You are to run the entire show."

My knees begin to tremble. "*Shukrahn,*" I say. "But perhaps you could help me begin? Can you walk me through how things work now, what your deadlines are?" I have no idea where to start.

"Of course."

He and I sit down with Zuhra in the front conference room to come up with a tentative game plan. Al-Asaadi explains all of the deadlines (which he concedes are generally missed), and Zuhra gives me a printed sheet detailing which reporters write which pages. I tell them I would like to hold editorial meetings at the beginning of each publishing cycle, one at nine A.M. on Sunday, and one at nine A.M. on Wednesday, so that each reporter can tell me what stories they are reporting, who their sources are, and when they will be handing them in. My goal is to somehow streamline the copy flow so that all the pages aren't coming in to edit at the last minute. This will clearly take a miracle.

After our meeting, Zuhra walks me to the grocery store (I forgot that the bathrooms at the *Observer* never have toilet paper; Yemenis use water hoses to clean themselves, which means the bathroom floors are nearly always flooded with what my copy editor Luke often refers to as "poop juice") and then to the Jordanian sandwich shop for one of the rolled-up spicy vegetable sandwiches I love so. I haven't eaten anything all day, although Zuhra has fetched me several cups of sticky-sweet black tea. "You are the only one I would make tea for," she says. "No one else." Like me, Zuhra does not cook. Tea is one of the few things she knows how to make.

After lunch, she hands me a story by Talha. No other copy has yet been filed for the next issue. I spend nearly an hour going through his story, making edits. It has no coherent structure, no clear first sentence, and a dearth of sources. I sigh. I will have to teach him everything.

A second desk has been moved into al-Asaadi's office for me, although I can't use the drawers yet as they are locked. It's a plain office, white walls, gray carpet, with no decoration save for a map of Jerusalem on the wall near the door. Light floods in from the windows along two walls of the office. Outside, stray cats yowl in the yard.

I seem to have gone numb. All the panic and fear and grief of those last few days in New York have fallen away, but nothing has moved in to take their place. I probably should be feeling stark terror about the challenges of this job, but for some reason I feel bizarrely level.

☾

LATER THAT AFTERNOON, after a swim, I am happy to find Qasim, whose irrepressible high spirits I'd enjoyed in June. He was the rascal always stealing people's shoes and hiding them in the wastebaskets, the one making prank phone calls, the one most likely to be caught singing in the office. But he is in charge of advertising, not a reporter, and thus not really part of my staff.

I also find my copy editor Luke, the blond Californian surfer dude. I've no idea if he actually surfs, but he looks like he should. He's not entirely sure what he's doing in Yemen, he tells me. He and a friend are thinking about launching some sort of business. "Yemen is a great place to be because they have nothing," he says. "Everything is new to them. You can do anything. And it's easy to rise to the top here."

Still, he complains that Yemen is destroying his health. He hasn't exercised since he got here, and he smokes way too much.

"And drinking? Do you drink?"

"Not anymore!"

"Guess you picked the right country."

"Actually, I didn't come here to get away from alcohol," he says. "I came here to get closer to the *qat*."

I find Talha in the newsroom and pull him aside to go over his story on the hazards of buying prescription drugs in Yemen. Drugs sold in Yemen are often either contaminated with toxic substances or completely ineffective sugar pills. Talha is quiet, serious, and eager to hear my suggestions. I explain to him all about leads, and story structure, and why we *never* begin a sentence with an attribution!

Mohammed al-Asaadi gives me the last ten issues of the paper to read after work before handing me off to Salem, who drives me and Radia home after nine P.M. They insist I ride up front, while Radia perches on a stack of *Yemen Observer*s in the back of the van. I offer her my seat, but she refuses.

As we near Radia's house, she leans forward and touches my arm. "Come with me," she says. "Come to my home." I look at her. Does she mean now?

"Come to my house," she says again. "Come sleep with me?"

This is not quite as provocative an invitation as it would be in New York. I learned on my previous trip that girls often invite new friends to sleep at their homes. Still, it catches me off guard.

"Why, I would love to!" I say. "But not tonight. I have things I need to get from home. Books and things. Presents to take to the office tomorrow."

She nods. But when she gets out she asks again. "But you will come, another time?"

"I will."

Salem teaches me several new Arabic words on the way home. I am famished by the time I arrive, close to ten P.M., and polish off a yogurt and a peanut butter and raisin sandwich. Did I mention I don't cook? I read a few issues of the *Observer,* try not to despair, and slip into sleep.

☾

IT IS A HUGE RELIEF finally to begin working. The anticipation and anxiety that have been building up since I accepted this job were harder to bear than the work itself. I don't do well with leisure time or stillness. I had arrived in Sana'a just a day and a half before my first day of work, and that was more than enough downtime. I'm not type A, I'm type A-plus.

On my second day of work, I arrive hours before my staff. (I have a staff! Okay, I am a little excited.) Only Qasim is there, so I give him one of the Jacques Torres chocolate bars I brought as gifts (it is impossible to find good chocolate in Yemen) and three Hershey bars for his three kids (who aren't yet picky about chocolate). When Radia and Zuhra arrive, I give them embroidered silk Chinese purses, stuffed with soap and chocolate and hand-woven change purses. Accessories are important in Yemen, where the basic outfit doesn't alter much from day to day. Radia is shyly pleased, while Zuhra announces her gift to everyone in sight.

I hold my first staff meeting that morning. Everyone tells me which stories they are writing and when they will get them to me. It is difficult to pin down exact deadlines, because when I ask, for example, if Bashir can get me a story by one P.M., the answer is *"Insha'allah." If God is willing.* Never, in my entire year, would I be able to get a reporter to say to me,

"Yes, I will finish the story by one P.M." In Yemen, nothing happens unless Allah wills it. And as it turns out, Allah is no great respecter of newspaper deadlines.

"Insha'allah" is also murmured reflexively after almost anything stated in the future tense. It makes Yemenis nervous when you leave it out. If I were to say to a Yemeni man, for example, "I am traveling to France next week but will return to Yemen Thursday," he would automatically add *"insha'allah."*

Ibrahim, who writes front-page stories for each issue from his home office, joins us, expressing great joy over my arrival. He invites me to a *qat* chew, which surprises me because I didn't know that women could go to *qat* chews with men. But apparently Western women are treated as a third sex in Yemen and thus can wander back and forth from male to female worlds. Western men, on the other hand, do not have this advantage.

This explains why my male staff members offer me immediate deference. To them I am not really a woman; I am a giraffe. Something alien and thus unclassifiable in the familiar male/female cubbyholes. Were a Yemeni woman to take over the paper, most of the men would quit in protest. They do not treat their female colleagues with anything like the respect with which they treat me, and they'd rather die on the spot than ask a Yemeni woman for help or advice on a story. But oddly, they rarely mind deferring to me.

Al-Asaadi is the exception. It doesn't take long for me to figure out that he *does* mind deferring to me, though he makes an initial effort to disguise his resentment. He is always smiling and polite, but he never shows up at the office on time in the mornings, when all of the other reporters arrive. He often ignores my deadlines, filing his stories when he feels like filing them. These things tell me that I may be filling his shoes, but he is still his own boss. Thankfully, though, he does show up to the editorial meeting on my second day and is helpful in suggesting which reporters should work on which articles.

After I send everyone off to pursue their stories, I spend the bulk of the morning editing a health story Najma has written about the psychological impact of eating various foods. There isn't a single source in the entire piece. When I go to the newsroom to ask her to come talk with me about the story, her eyes widen in terror.

"This won't be painful!" I say, trying not to laugh. "I am just going to help you."

Zuhra rushes over to reassure her. "Do not be afraid," she says as I lead Najma toward the conference room. "There is no one more supportive."

I explain to the trembling Najma that we need to know where the information in her story comes from, so that our readers can judge its legitimacy. If we are to contend that Brazil nuts can elevate a person's mood, then we need to be able to quote a specific study from a university or a hospital that proves such a thing.

This is all new to her. It seems she had thought that the mere fact that the words would appear in newsprint would give them authority. This was a common mind-set. One of the greatest challenges I would have working with Yemeni journalists is that they are too trusting, too willing to believe whatever they are told. In a deeply religious society such as this one, children are raised to take everything on faith, unquestioningly. The flip side is that they often do not feel they have to prove their contentions. I have to undo years of conditioning.

I spend the rest of the day editing other health stories and election briefs, and fretting about the dearth of stories we have for the front page. Farouq is still out, and he's our main political reporter. There is no one to replace him. The new guys have none of his political contacts and no idea whom to call for story ideas or quotes, and the women are busy with culture and health.

Only late that evening, after running out through a rainstorm to cover a batik exhibit at the nearby German House, do I finally find Faris for the first time. I am happy, as I have a long list of requests for him, including reimbursement for my plane fare. I give him the dental floss he had requested from the States, and he is happy too. He gives me a warm little speech about how he now considers me family and that if I need anything at all, money or anything else, I am to come to him. He has VIP passes for me to cover election events, as well as hotel rooms, he says, which I hope means I will be traveling to cover the polls. (None of which comes to pass.) He also has a phone for me, but it is still charging, and no one is sure of the number, so I will get it from the office tomorrow. *Insha'allah.*

☾⋆

I GO BACK TO WORK after this meeting to edit an unreadable story of Hassan's. Despite the fact that Hassan was in my original class, every single paragraph of his story begins with an attribution. I call him on Luke's phone to tell him that this is no longer acceptable. "Before you hand in anything else, please make sure you are not starting all of your sentences with 'according to' or 'he said.'" Hassan, being the sweet and deferential man he is, thanks me enormously and says he hopes we can talk more about this problem of his.

My day began at eight A.M., and I don't leave the office until nearly eleven P.M. that night. Salem drives me home, where I finish editing a few more stories in my small suite in Sabri's dormitory over some carrots and hummus, the first real meal I've had all day. I've stumbled upon a foolproof diet plan: Take over a newspaper in a poor, semiliterate Islamic country, and watch the pounds just fall away.

☾⋆

THE NEXT DAY, my third day at work, we close my first issue. It takes nineteen hours. Yet I am not unhappy, even with the overwhelming amount of work to do. The thing about being at the top of the masthead is there is never any question of leaving early or leaving anything undone. I find something very comforting about succumbing to this total commitment; it eliminates all other choices. I'm going to make this a better paper or die trying. I have nothing else to distract me. I am free of an intimate relationship, having just ended a turbulent on-again, off-again romance in New York; I haven't time to socialize outside of work; and I have no other deadlines. I can give the paper everything. I will have to.

I wake at six A.M. and walk to work. Men stare at me as I pass—it's unusual to see a woman walking alone, particularly one with blue eyes and uncovered hair—but their comments are mostly benign. Everywhere I go, I am showered with "Welcome to Yemen!"s and "I love you!"s. I stopped covering my hair after I realized it made no difference in the amount of attention I attracted and because Yemenis kept asking me, "Why do you cover your hair? You're a westerner!" The morning is deliciously cool and crisp. Sana'anis are not early risers, so the streets don't get busy until close to eleven A.M.

When the women get in, I consult with Zuhra, who is fast becoming my right-hand woman, and send Najma and Noor to cover a Japanese flower-arranging demonstration. Hardly real news, but it's a nice easy way to break them in and get them used to reporting outside of the office. I have to send them together, so that neither has to travel alone in a car with a man. It can damage a woman's reputation to be seen alone in a taxi with a male driver. There is no *Yemen Observer* driver available, so I have to wheedle the taxi fare out of the Doctor, who vigorously resists all attempts to draw down his allotment of *riyals*.

The Doctor. Everyone lives in terror of this tall, bespectacled man, who is not actually a doctor but the person in charge of administration and finance. He doles out salaries, takes attendance each morning, and serves as Faris's iron fist of enforcement. The Doctor never speaks; he shouts. He shouts at Enass the secretary, he shouts at my reporters, and, inevitably, he shouts at me. Shouting in the newsroom does not always suggest displeasure, however. Many of the men shout as a matter of course. Often I run out of my office thinking I am overhearing a fierce argument, when really the men are saying to each other: "FANTASTIC NEW CAR YOU HAVE! WHERE DID YOU GET IT? HEY, DO YOU WANT SOME OF THIS *QAT*? IT'S DELICIOUS." But when the Doctor shouts, it generally means trouble.

So far he is trying to be nice to me, so I get the taxi money for the women. I have to talk to Faris about providing transportation for our reporters; they do not have enough money to pay for these things themselves. I am amazed that Faris fails to provide his staff with so many essentials. My reporters are not given business cards, telephones, or press IDs and are even required to buy their own notebooks and pens. But they cannot afford these things on their salaries of $100 to $200 per month. No wonder they make a notebook last for weeks. I buy a stack of notebooks for them. I would buy them phones too, but my salary does not stretch that far.

I spend the morning editing the Panorama page, a collection of editorials from other Yemeni papers, and Najma's article about a course that trains women to manage money. It's an interesting story, but she hasn't talked with any of the women at the workshop, other than the instructor. "You should have talked with a minimum of fifteen women who participated in the workshop," I say. "Their personal stories are what would really make this interesting." Too late for this issue. (I have to let a *lot* of things slide in this first issue.) But Najma seems to understand. So. It's a start.

I write and edit all day, with no break, save for the twenty minutes I spend walking to the Jordanian sandwich shop with Zuhra. "You need to take a breath," she says. Back at the office, Zuhra helps me figure out which pages are missing stories. Farouq still hasn't turned up, so we have nothing for the front or local pages. I try not to panic. I ring Ibrahim at his home office to ask him about the election page, and he sends over two stories, promising a third by noon. Al-Asaadi promises at least one front-page story. Clearly we need more staff.

Luke swings around my doorjamb toward lunch, flushed with excitement. "Did you hear?" he says. "The crocodile hunter died."

"No! Steve Irwin?"

"Yes."

"What killed him, a crocodile?"

"Stingray. Right through the heart."

"Jesus."

"So—front page?"

"Perfect. We have nothing else."

"It's definitely of global significance."

Luke pops into my office often, to chat or to trade stories. A half hour later, he walks in holding an enormous jar of amber liquid. "I just accidentally bought thirty dollars' worth of honey," he says.

"Accidentally?"

"Well, I was with al-Asaadi, and there was this guy he usually gets honey from, so I ordered some too, but I didn't realize it would be this big! Or that it would cost thirty dollars." He looks forlornly at the enormous jar in his hand. "I have enough honey to last me a year."

"Well," I say, "I guess you'd better learn to bake."

"You don't bake with Yemeni honey! It's too special for that."

"It can't be *really* good Yemeni honey," says Zuhra, who has just walked in. "If it were *really* good honey, it would have cost you eighty dollars. At least."

Later in the afternoon, al-Asaadi pops his head into our office. "How about we don't have a front page this issue? What do you think?"

I shrug. "I can live without it."

But the banter hides a growing panic. The later it gets, the more we shuffle stories from page to page. We don't have enough local stories, so I suggest we move a story on the back page to the local page and that I quickly write the story on the batik exhibit to replace the back page. It is infinitely easier to churn out a story myself than to rewrite one of theirs. I feel some guilt over this, but not much. It's just one story.

☪

ZUHRA LEAVES WORK around three P.M., as she and the other girls must be home before dark. She is distressed to leave me on my own, worried I will never survive without her.

"I'll be fine," I say with a complete lack of conviction. "We just might not have a front page."

She looks at me with concern.

"Do you maybe need to swim?" she says.

I laugh. "Not today," I say, gesturing toward the stack of pages waiting to be edited. "Tomorrow."

☪

AL-ASAADI RETURNS from a long lunch around four P.M. and throws a handful of *qat* next to my computer. "This will help," he says. My energy flagging, I follow his lead. The *qat* tastes extra bitter, and the shiny leaves are hard to chew. But I imagine that al-Asaadi knows where to buy the best *qat,* so I assume it is a good vintage. It must be, given how much I immediately perk up. With newfound vigor, I whip out a 955-word story on the batik exhibit in less than an hour. No wonder everyone loves this drug.

I file the story and run upstairs to choose photos with Mas, the paper's precocious nineteen-year-old photographer. When I return, a pile of new things to edit is waiting on my desk. Ibrahim's election stories are thin; everything I edit ends up half its original length. My reporters repeat themselves ad nauseam.

Around ten P.M., when I finally start to crash from the *qat,* dinner arrives. We all eat outside in the courtyard, standing around a table piled with *roti* (Yemeni baguettes) and plates of *fasooleah* (beans), eggs, *ful,* cheese, and tea. We fall upon the food like a pack of wolves. I am the last to leave the table, reluctantly, with a fistful of bread.

My energy is back. Good thing, too, given how much is still left to do. The flash-drive-passing between me and Luke accelerates. I edit the stories, then he edits them, then I see them again on the page, and then he sees them one last time. I don't take a step out of the building from the time I get there—eight thirty A.M.—until the time I leave, in the early hours of the following morning. Yet I am so busy that the day feels short. So many times in those first few weeks, when my reporters come to me with a question, I instinctively think I should run it by someone else. Someone in charge. But slowly, it begins to sink in that the only person responsible for these decisions is me.

☪

MIRACULOUSLY, BY THREE A.M. we have a front page. And a Local page. And an Election page, a Health page, a Reports page, and Panorama and Middle East and Op-Ed. In fact, we have an entire newspaper! We all high-ten each other and say, *"Mabrouk!"* (Congratulations!). I am briefly euphoric before a terrifying thought occurs to me: We have to do it all over again. Starting in about six hours.

SEVEN

my yemeni shadow

*Zuhra has adopted me. Never mind that she is twenty-three and I am techni-*cally old enough to be her mother. When she isn't out running after a story, Zuhra is chronically at my elbow, asking me what I need. A back-page story? The telephone number of the foreign minister? Lunch? She'll help me get it. When I head to the small grocery store at the end of our block in search of matches, milk, and peanuts, she won't let me go until she has written me a shopping list in Arabic—even though I have become quite capable of asking for what I want in Arabic.

"Zuhra, I already have a mother!" I protest. "Really, I can manage."

"Motherhood is a feeling," she says. "It is not an age."

When other people try to take me tea or walk me to the sandwich shop, she bristles. "You are *my* Jennifer," she says. "I want to be the one to take care of you."

All of my women must be home well before dark, and so their work day ends earlier than the men's, at one P.M. But this stretches later and later throughout the year, until the women only rarely leave before three P.M. and sometimes stay until five P.M. It makes Zuhra anxious that she has to leave me alone at night, especially when I am closing an issue. She wants to be there to help me. When I arrive at work the day after my first endless close, Zuhra is waiting. "I can stay with you until three P.M.!" she announces with as much excitement as someone who has just been awarded the Nobel Peace Prize.

It is a long time before I truly understand how much it means to Zuhra to be in the office of the *Yemen Observer* at all, a long time before I understand her improbable journey to me.

The other reporters tease her for her possessiveness and call her Jennifer's Shadow. She is certainly dressed for the role. Her sisters, she tells me later, also tease her about her newfound passion for work. "When are you and Jennifer getting married?" they ask. It takes Zuhra months to tell me this, because she is afraid I will think they are implying I am a lesbian and that I will be offended.

She is just as energetic about chasing stories as she is about following me around. While Noor and Najma are timid about leaving the office and cling to each other for support, Zuhra often waltzes off on her own. She takes the *dabaabs* (small buses) around town, walks, or cajoles a friend into giving her a ride. When I am at a loss for a back-page story, Zuhra always finds one. Rummaging around in the back alleys of Old Sana'a, she comes up with, say, a story on the demise of Yemeni lanterns called *fanous,* which are being replaced by electric lights. Zuhra's story-shopping in the *souqs* of Old Sana'a also results in pieces on jewelry and fashion fads, the persistence of the illegal trade in rhinoceros-horn *jambiyas,* and the increasing popularity of Indian goods over Yemeni products.

She is even better at finding front-page stories. I like to have a minimum of five on every front page, and this always involves a lot of last-minute scrambling. When I need hard news, Zuhra heads to the courts. Or to the streets. Or to anywhere she can find a bit of news to bring triumphantly back to me.

☪

I FIND OUT Zuhra's personal story gradually. Not until late fall, when she and I are curled up in my *mafraj* looking over her essays for an application to graduate school, do I finally piece together the general outline of her life. This is a different Zuhra than the little black shadow who trails me around the office. In an aqua jogging suit with her hair in a ponytail, she looks like any Western girl kicking back at home on a weekend afternoon.

I try not to stare. Though I've seen her a few times without the *abaya* and veil, I'm still not used to seeing the contours of her body, the strands of hair falling across her dark eyes.

We sit side by side on my red and gold cushions as the late afternoon sun streams through my jeweled windows, sending bits of colored light cavorting around the room. My laptop is propped in front of us, and slowly we read through her application. In her personal essay, she describes her long battle with her family to seek education and eventually a career. Her written English still confuses me, so we go through each line together as she explains how she came to work at the *Observer.*

"My father died when I was ten." This is the centerpiece of her story. It is the root of all of her pain, the beginning of her struggle, and the explanation for her loneliness. "I get depressed because I have an unbalanced life," she says. "I have no men in my life."

Her father, Sultan, lost his own father when he was twelve and took off alone for the southern port city of Aden, then part of South Yemen. He was a socialist, a revolutionary against the British, and a supporter of unification. In Aden, Zuhra told me, he arranged many secret meetings. Yet the details of this part of his life remain a mystery to her. After marrying and divorcing his cousin, Sultan met Zuhra's mother, Sadira, a young teenager known for her beauty, who hailed from his home village of Ammar in Ibb Governorate. They married. But she became increasingly worried about her husband's political activities and the safety of her family. After the first three children were born, the family moved north to Sana'a and Sultan took a job with the government water corporation.

Zuhra is the fifth of eight children, two of whom are dead. One was miscarried, and the other died in her first few years of life. The surviving six are tight. Zuhra worships her oldest brother, Fahmi, thirty-five, who lives in Brooklyn, and her sisters are her dearest friends. Their early life, Zuhra says, was idyllic. "My father treated us equally, girls and boys. He insisted that the younger respect the older, not that the girls have to respect the boys. Maybe for that we have some kind of problems in our life, because this was the way our father raised us. This is why we have trouble with the restrictions of society. He hates us to wear a veil."

Because Sultan never had the chance to finish his own schooling, it was deeply important to him that his children receive an education. "He was desperate to make all of us study," said Zuhra. "He wanted Fahmi to be a doctor. He was amazing. He really fight for us. To be educated. He was a very modern man."

Nearly all of Zuhra's siblings have a university education, except for Ghazal, who is still at school, and Shetha, who married young. But it was a condition of Shetha's marriage that she be allowed to finish her studies. Sultan refused many suitors who came calling for his daughters' hands. "He yelled at the suitors and said, 'Are you crazy? They are too young! They must finish school!'" said Zuhra. "He was so protective, but not authoritarian."

Everything fell apart when Sultan died from a heart attack while visiting his home village.

"He went to attend a funeral of my young cousin. Then he died there, alone," said Zuhra. "He went there alone, and for lack of treatment—his brothers never got him to the hospital—he died. They lied and said our aunt died and that we had to come to the village. Then when we got there, all of us knew it was our father who died. He died without anyone next to him, even his brothers. It was really horrible.

"My mom, for twenty days she didn't speak. She cried day and night. She did not sleep. We were all afraid that she will die. She knew that. She held on because she felt that the uncles might try to take the children, so she became strong. She and Fahmi."

When Yemeni women and girls have no father or husband, their lives are handed over to their uncles or brothers. Women cannot be trusted with the reins of their own lives. This Yemeni emphasis on controlling and defending women is a result of the importance of *sharaf* (honor) in society. Nothing is more important to a Yemeni tribesman than his honor. Honor is communal as well as individual; when one man is shamed, his whole tribe is shamed. An assault on honor is called *ayb,* meaning shame or disgrace. Honor is a vulnerable thing; a man's honor depends heavily on his wives and daughters. When a daughter misbehaves, particularly if that misbehavior is sexual, she damages her father's honor. It is wise, therefore, for men to keep a close eye on their women.

So without Sultan, and without her oldest brother, Fahmi, who had found work in the United States, Zuhra's fate was left to her uncles. When she reached seventeen, she told them she wanted to go to medical school. Impossible, they told her flatly. They convinced her second-oldest brother, Aziz, to forbid Zuhra to attend. Zuhra's theory is that her uncles were jealous of how clever she was and how well she performed in school, because their sons did not do as well. Even Zuhra's mother, Sadira, who had supported her daughter's education, acquiesced.

Not only did the uncles refuse to allow Zuhra to go to medical school, they would not let her attend any kind of university. "They claimed that an educated woman would not find a husband and would become rebellious. This is the fear of most Yemeni men," she says. "They say college will corrupt girls and they will not get married."

So she studied on the sly, hiding her schoolbooks in magazines so her family would not see that she was reading medical books. On the day of the exam, she veiled herself and sneaked out. Her heart pounding with the fear of discovery, she finished the exam. "I remember that while taking the exam, looking at my watch, I felt like Cinderella, afraid of being revealed." A few days later, she found that she was one of twenty-nine people admitted to medical school.

Her family was furious. Immediately, her brothers and paternal uncles forbade her to go. Zuhra was so desperate that she contemplated sneaking out to attend classes. But she knew that she would eventually be caught, and her motives for her clandestine outings could easily have been misconstrued.

Thus began her darkest days. She was so angry with her family she decided to stop speaking. "I was locked up at home for an entire year. I waged a silent battle against them and refused to talk to them. I became ill and was close to death, making many more people support me. These people knew that if my father were alive, he would support me.

"During this period of my life, I have realized lots of things and built lots of things. And lost lots of things. One of the things I built is that I know how to be strong. And that sometimes in your life you will be alone and nobody next to you," she said. "And then I felt how horrible my father's death was, because if he were alive this wouldn't happen. So I learned how to be strong and not emotionally dependent on anybody in this world."

One of the things Zuhra lost during this time was belief and confidence in herself. To this day, insecurity plagues her.

"I feel I am a second-class human, that I am not important. Because no one cared about my priorities, which really hurts," she told me. "I know it's not my fault that I can't study, but I start to blame myself."

Soon, Zuhra had stopped doing any of her normal activities. She wasn't allowed to go to work. She began to believe that she was a horrible person.

"It was almost a prison. When you are an active person and smart and have many things in life waiting for you, but then you are stopped like a machine . . .

"I still remember one day, I was taking some garbage outside the home. I saw my friends that day, they were going to their college, and then I felt it is the worst feeling ever when you really feel pathetic to yourself. I felt how horrible it was—I knew I was smarter than all of them, and there I was throwing garbage."

She became embarrassed to appear in society, worried that she would be thought pathetic and helpless. Because of this, she even lied sometimes and said that she didn't want to go to college, just so no one would think she was controlled by other people.

At her nadir, discouraged and friendless, she became religious, but in a different way than she had been before.

"I established a new relationship with my God. I was praying alone. I started to feel like there was someone next to me, and that is what makes me strong. I started to feel I am not alone. Felt there was someone in this world loves me. I felt how important it was to have faith. One day, the room was dark and I was so hurt, it was close to my trauma, I started to pray and I felt something was going to happen. I remember that at the beginning I prayed all the people that hurt me to go to hell. Then I realized that I don't want this. I forgave all these people. I said this to God. All I want is to finish my education; the rest doesn't matter to me. I realized it wasn't my real battle, to pray against these people. Then, when I started to do that I felt that I am stronger."

One day, having noticed Zuhra's decline, one of her maternal uncles persuaded her other uncles to work together to convince Aziz to let Zuhra go to school. One of these uncles had consulted a religious scholar who had said that it was forbidden to stop her from an education if she wanted one.

At first, Aziz refused. He didn't want to admit he was wrong. By that time, Zuhra's health was in danger. She had lost weight, was often faint, and had developed eye problems and allergies. Her family was afraid for her.

Fear at last prompted Aziz to relent. "He said that it seemed like I was going to die, and he didn't want anything to happen to me."

Zuhra still wanted to study medicine, but her brother said that was out of the question. If she insisted on going to college, she would go to the College of Education, which was a more suitable place for girls.

Hardly daring to believe she had been reprieved, Zuhra began classes, majoring in English. But still she struggled, feeling that she was being forced to study at a place she did not freely choose. The only thing she chose was English. "I chose this field because I knew that the English language would empower me," she says. "Most of my diaries are in English, because I can speak freely. And through English I was exposed to another culture that I was curious to know."

Her college years were difficult socially. Many of her peers were more conservative than she was, with rigid ideas about how to dress, how to study, and how to express an opinion. But Zuhra refused to be cowed. She spoke often in class and was not afraid to debate the professor. She worked feverishly, constantly fearful that her brother would change his mind and pull her out of school.

Despite the fact that she was training to be a teacher, Zuhra had nightmares about joining the profession. "I remember after I graduated I was praying day and night not to be a teacher. But it was hard for me to look for another job."

When she was offered a teaching post at a school, she panicked and confessed her fears to her brother Fahmi. The school was run by religious zealots from the Islah (Reform) Party, she said. "They impose their opinions on others and I told Fahmi I hated that."

Her supportive older brother told her that it was okay to follow her heart. But she didn't know of an alternative to teaching. Her career choices were restricted by the fact that her family did not want her working with men.

Not knowing what to try, Zuhra put together the best résumé she could, adding a note at the bottom saying, "I know that I am not qualified, but I have what it takes to be successful." And she set out on a quest.

Clutching this piece of paper, Zuhra walked into the offices of the *Yemen Observer*. It was the first place she tried.

At reception, Enass took her résumé and said she would show it to al-Asaadi. "I waited. Al-Asaadi came in. You know him, he likes to show off. But I still remember that I was very confident and he was saying to me, what do you want to be? And I said I want to work as a journalist, if not, then as a translator."

Al-Asaadi told her that he would speak to Faris. Zuhra didn't hold out much hope. Not only was she inexperienced, but she was sure that her family would not allow her to be a journalist. "It was a huge fear. Exactly like when I go to my college. As important as that."

She was unaware of how much she had already impressed al-Asaadi, who saw her potential immediately. "Journalism isn't a job; it's a passion," he told me. "Zuhra had that passion. Even the first time I met her, I could tell how much she wanted to *work*." She was also unafraid to admit how much she didn't know, a rarity in the male reporters. Zuhra could kill you with questions—but they helped her to learn her job faster than anyone else.

When al-Asaadi told her she had the job but had to work evenings as well as mornings, her heart sank. She told him that she could not work nights. "He told me, you won't be a good journalist. And I thought he was right. I can't do work if I can't be available all the time."

But a week later two things happened. Al-Asaadi decided he could allow Zuhra to work only mornings, and Aziz realized how much it meant to Zuhra to have this job. "My brother said, 'I trust you like a blind person.'"

She began work. Her first hurdle was a fear of talking with men. Not because she was shy—not Zuhra!—but because she feared that the men would lose respect for her if they saw her speaking to other men. Never before had Zuhra mixed with men outside her family. "The nightmare of being a woman followed me when I started my career. Men do not say openly that we cannot do the job; they say it behind our backs and amongst themselves." I nod. I've seen the men do this.

"I felt like a cripple when I first started the job, since such weakness is expected of a Yemeni woman. Even more difficult was interviewing Yemeni men in such a conservative society. It was a hard time for me. I was fighting the many ideas of what constitutes a woman's role that were planted in me."

When Zuhra arrived at the *Observer*, she heard rumors about the women who worked there. "They are killing their reputation by working with men," people whispered. One girl in particular was derided for talking and laughing with men. "The men said she wasn't a good girl and she was having affairs outside of the job. That scares me," says Zuhra. She made herself strict rules to protect herself from gossip. She never laughed with men. She never gave out her phone number. She never got into cars with men. "I didn't want anyone to say anything bad about me," she says. "I lived in horror all the time."

Only slowly did her nervousness disappear. "When you came, I don't know what happens to me, but you take off some of this fear," she tells me. "I was asking you about objectivity. If you have belief in what you are doing it gives you more strength. Because I know what journalism can do and why it is there." She came to believe that it wasn't she who should feel ashamed—it was anyone who would give her a hard time for following a noble calling.

At the same time, Zuhra was grappling with the rudiments of journalism. "I had no real model. I didn't know what was good journalism," she tells me. "I got to know that when you come. Do you remember what I first told you? It was very eye-opening for me when you told me we had to be objective. When you said that, what made me believe was that you said [if you report objectively] then people will believe you."

Zuhra has an instinctive distrust of partisan media, because she loathes other people telling her what to feel or think or do. She would rather be presented with all of the facts in as balanced a way as possible and make up her own mind than read an editorial.

So when I began to define objective journalism for her, she was immediately attracted to the idea. "It seems the highest way of thinking," she said. "I met you, started thinking about going to the Columbia University Graduate School of Journalism, and my dreams started to have a face and legs."

EIGHT

kidnappings, stampedes, and suicide bombings

It is late on a Sunday afternoon when we hear about a kidnapping of French tourists in Shabwa Governorate. First we hear there are five hostages, then four. Then we hear that only two are French. Then we hear that three are French and one German. Such is the accuracy of reporting in Yemen.

We at least know who the kidnappers are: the al-Abdullah tribe. The kidnapping is a result of a long-running feud with the neighboring al-Riyad tribe. The al-Abdullah are the same tribe that kidnapped five Germans the previous December. Apparently, the government didn't keep the promises it made to get those Germans released, so tribesmen took a few French people to underscore their disappointment.

I'd heard a great deal about the kidnappings before I came to Yemen, as it was one of the few things westerners seemed to know about the place. "Aren't you worried you'll be kidnapped?" was one of the first things people asked me. That is, if they had heard of Yemen at all.

I wasn't worried that I would be kidnapped. Most kidnappings don't have anything to do with hostility toward foreigners. Tribesmen just see tourists as handy bargaining chips in their disputes with the government. Thus they sometimes capture a convoy or two to pressure the government to, say, build a school or improve the water system. (My parents, being parents, did worry I would get kidnapped. When I explained that my kidnappers would probably just want a mosque or a school in return for me, they fretted that they couldn't afford a whole building. "We could afford a stop sign," they said. "Tell them that.") Almost all of the approximately two hundred tourists kidnapped in Yemen in the past fifteen years have been treated kindly by their captors and released unharmed, though there are a few exceptions. In 1998, sixteen westerners were kidnapped by a group called the Aden-Abyan Islamic Army. Four were killed during a botched rescue attempt by the Yemeni government. Another tourist was killed in 2000, again as a result of a shootout between the government and the kidnappers. "If I ever get kidnapped," I say to al-Asaadi, "don't let the government try to rescue me."

Another reason I don't waste too much time worrying about kidnappings is that they very rarely happen to foreigners in Sana'a. Most attacks occur as tourists travel in conspicuous convoys through more remote parts of the country where there are active tribal conflicts.

Now that the al-Abdullah tribe has the government's attention, it is demanding that some of their incarcerated tribesmen be released in return for the French tourists. Al-Asaadi gives me ten stories he wrote about the kidnappings last year to get me up to speed. He also draws me a chart of the tribes and their various disputes, which started with the murder of some members of the al-Abdullah tribe years ago. My head reels.

Yemen is home to hundreds of tribes, which play an integral role in Yemeni politics and lives. Divisions among tribes are largely territorial. Before 1990, when Yemen was divided into North and South Yemen, both the British and the Communists in turn endeavored to weaken tribal allegiances in the South, in an effort to create a more cohesive society. But in the North, tribal ties remain strong.

President Saleh belongs to the Sanhan, a Hashid tribe from near Sana'a. The Hashid and Bakil tribal confederations are the most powerful in the country. But Saleh's control over tribesmen diminishes the farther one gets from Sana'a. Rural people are far more likely to turn to their tribal leaders, called sheikhs, than to the government to resolve disputes over land, grievances, or natural resources. Sheikhs serve as spokesmen for their tribes, arbitrating conflicts, helping parties agree on appropriate amends, and wielding political influence. For example, oil companies working in Yemen often must negotiate separate deals with the government and with the sheikhs of tribes upon whose land they are working. Otherwise they can find their buildings suddenly surrounded by angry, AK-47-wielding tribesmen.

Most Yemenis' first loyalty is to tribe and family rather than to their country. Whenever I get into a taxi with my reporters, the first thing they do is figure out what tribe our driver belongs to. Mohammed al-Matari, my elder-statesman reporter, is the most adept. He can find out the tribe, hometown, and family of a driver within the first three minutes of the journey. All of this has to be ascertained before conversation can continue.

☾

I CAN'T FIND ANYONE free to work on the kidnapping story, so when Farouq—the paper's main political reporter—walks into the office that day for the first time since my arrival, I nearly weep with joy. It is a struggle not to hug him; his face is pale with sorrow over the death of his daughter. The skin is pulled tight across his skull; Farouq is so skeletally thin that my first impulse every time I see him is to hand him a sandwich. "I am so sorry, Farouq," I say. "I am so sorry to hear of your tragedy."

He blinks back tears. "Yes, I had something very bad happen in my life," he says, unable to look at me.

"I am so, so sorry."

He shows me photos on his cell phone of the infant daughter he just lost and kisses the small screen. I ask if he needs more time off, but he says he wants to work. We go over what stories I need, and he says, "Do not worry about the front page. I will take care of the front page. It is my specialty."

There's a catch, of course. Farouq writes only in Arabic and requires translators for all of his stories. We have no good translators. Bashir and Talha struggle along, but often I cannot understand the results of their labor. I'll need to hire at least one translator in addition to several more reporters. If Faris will let me, that is.

Farouq asks me to call the French embassy, because I'm the only one in the office who speaks French. I speak to both the ambassador and the press attaché, but they have no new information. So Farouq taps his sources in the security department in the region and we get most of the story from them.

I end up writing the piece myself, based on Farouq's notes and al-Asaadi's background, and get it on the Web by ten fifteen P.M. the same day. This is thrilling, but I wish I could travel south to where the kidnappings happened to do some real reporting. It's tough to be stuck in the office, orchestrating coverage. None of my journalists can go either. No one has a car, enough money to get down there, or—most significantly—the drive to get the story in person. Not one of my reporters has expressed the slightest interest in trying to get face-to-face interviews. But how else can we get to the truth about what happened?

I'm learning that in Yemen the truth is a slippery thing. Two days after the kidnapping, fifty-one Yemenis are killed in a stampede at one of Saleh's election rallies at a stadium in Ibb, a city a couple hours south of Sana'a. As usual, the number of victims reported fluctuates throughout the day, from hundreds to dozens. Both the *Yemen Observer* and the *Yemen Times* report more than sixty dead, until the government news agency announces the official count as fifty-one.

The exact circumstances of the stampede depend on which newspaper you read. We report that the stampede was caused by overcrowding, as more than a hundred thousand people were crammed into a space meant to hold half that. Exits were poorly marked, and when people rushed out at the end of Saleh's speech, they trampled each other. The *Yemen Times* reports that two hundred thousand people were packed into a stadium with a capacity of ten thousand. People were crushed when fences installed to control the crowd's movement collapsed, trapping people underneath as the crowd swarmed over them. Still other reports say a hundred and fifty thousand people had been crammed into the stadium. The truth is elusive.

When Farouq asks the deputy security manager in Ibb how such tragedies could be prevented in the future, the man shrugs. "We don't have another rally," he says. "So it's not really a concern."

I am struck by the casual, fatalistic view Yemenis take of tragedy. Stampedes, car accidents, kidnappings, and terrorist attacks rarely seem overly to trouble anyone or trigger societal self-analysis. A stadium collapse and stampede in New York would provoke public outcry and a demand for improved safety standards and crowd control, but this doesn't happen in Yemen. Perhaps it is simply that they believe all catastrophes are Allah's will. For example, few Yemenis see any point in seat belts. If Allah decides it's time for you to go, it's time for you to go.

President Saleh issues a statement offering condolences and cash to the bereaved families, calling the deceased "martyrs of democracy." Opposition parties, eager to use the tragedy to their political advantage, rush to blame Saleh, decrying his shoddy security and criticizing him for busing groups of students from schools to the rally to support him, contributing to overcrowding and putting young people in danger.

This stampede followed a smaller one in Ta'iz, a hundred and fifty miles south of Sana'a, which killed four or five people. Several papers report a third stampede, rumored to have killed five or six people in Zinjibar in Abyan Governorate in the south, but government spokesmen vigorously deny this. An auto accident killed a few people, they say. Not a stampede.

The kidnappings and stampedes, happening right on top of each other, underscore the near-impossibility of squeezing facts out of the Yemeni government or any other sources, although perhaps this isn't surprising in a culture that values belief over empirical evidence.

Farouq keeps busy trying to sort out both tragedies. Big stories like these, I know from experience, are good at staving off grief. At least until deadline.

☾

ONE GOOD THING the kidnapping brings us is Karim, a Belgian-Tunisian photographer on freelance assignment for *Paris Match*. When I run up to Faris's office with a lengthy list of demands—a residency visa, more staff, business cards, toilet paper—I find Karim sitting there. Tall, with dark curling hair and mischievous eyes, he's possibly the most attractive person I've seen since arriving in Yemen. I am suddenly acutely aware of my untidy braids and spinsterish skirts.

Karim hopes to get photographs of the kidnapped tourists, so he'll be staying in Yemen until they are released. I immediately want to go with him, though Faris tells me in no uncertain terms that I am not to endanger myself. "Maybe you can do some reporting for us then," I say to Karim. No one seems to worry that any violence will befall the hostages. Farouq's source says that they are being fed well. Yemen will not attempt to use military might to get them back; a new sheikh has begun mediating.

I linger in the office until Faris invites me to join them for dinner. "Faris says he's taking me to some sort of five-star restaurant," says Karim.

I laugh. "That would be Zorba's."

☪

WE CHOOSE AN OUTSIDE TABLE, overlooking busy Hadda Street. Karim, I discover, has been everywhere. He has been embedded with the U.S. military in Afghanistan, traveled with the Taliban, covered the Iraq war, explored Iran, and written features on the nightlife of Beirut. Of all of the countries he has visited, Yemen is the most beautiful, he says. Karim's impressive résumé includes freelance work for the *New York Times, Time, Newsweek,* the *International Herald Tribune, Geo,* and various German magazines. He is planning to go back to Afghanistan next month to be embedded and then to go on a night raid against the Afghan National Army with the Taliban.

"That's just crazy," says Faris.

"That's just responsible journalism," says Karim.

I could use him on my staff. He tells me stories about smoking opium in the mountains with the Taliban. One morning, he woke up to find his socks missing, only to find out that the Taliban soldiers had washed them for him. I'm impressed by his fearlessness and a bit dispirited that I'll probably never have *my* socks washed by the Taliban.

Talk turns to the hostages down south. While the kidnappings don't make Faris worry about my personal safety in Yemen, he does fret that violence could break out around the upcoming elections and that westerners could be targeted. Yemen is home to myriad groups of extremists, among them al-Qaeda, which has been growing in strength in recent years.

"Jennifer," says Faris. "Do me a favor. Don't leave your house at the same time every morning." Predictable routines make one an easy target for terrorists. This is the same warning offered by the U.S. State Department website. Of course, if I believed everything I read on the State Department website, I would never leave home.

But I don't need encouragement to vary my route; boredom keeps me from ever walking the same streets two days in a row. This means that I often end up lost and add an extra half hour to my travel time just trying to get back to a major road. But at least I'm not predictable.

"Faris," I say as we stand to go, "are you worried al-Qaeda will come for me when they find out a New Yorker is editing the paper?"

He hesitates. "I don't *think* so."

☪

BUT AL-QAEDA HAS APPARENTLY set its sights on targets more strategic than me. It's a Friday, our only day off, when it next makes the news. Several oil installations have just been attacked by al-Qaeda operatives, and Faris wants the story on the website immediately. In the South, two terrorists drove car bombs at high speed toward oil storage tanks at al-Dhaba plant, Yemen's main export terminal on the Gulf of Aden. Guards managed to detonate the bombs before they reached their targets, but one security officer was killed in the explosions. Less than an hour later, two other cars loaded with explosives headed toward the oil-gathering and gas-oil separation plant in Ma'rib Governorate. Guards shot at the men, and only the attackers were killed when the car bombs exploded. Neither attack damaged facilities, but they are dramatic evidence that al-Qaeda has been resurrected.

Al-Qaeda in Yemen grew out of militant Islamic campaigns overseas. Yemenis flooded to Afghanistan in the 1980s to fight the Soviets, and many stayed through the 1990s to train. Others returned to Yemen to fight in the 1994 civil war against the "godless Socialists" in the South. Osama bin Laden, whose father was born in Yemen, recruited Yemenis to train in al-Qaeda's camps in Afghanistan. After the U.S. invasion of Iraq in 2003, large numbers of Yemenis traveled there to fight U.S. forces.

Until the late 1990s, Yemeni terrorists stuck to a deal they had made with the government: they would be allowed sanctuary and freedom of movement in Yemen in return for not staging attacks within Yemen's borders. But by the end of the decade, militant groups, frustrated with government negotiations with the United States for military basing rights in Yemen, opened training camps in the South and launched a campaign of attacks on government offices. And in October 2000, a group of al-Qaeda veterans launched a suicide attack on the USS *Cole* in Aden harbor, killing seventeen American seamen. The MV *Limburg,* a French ship, was hit two years later. These attacks prompted the government, with U.S. support, to crack down on terrorists. Nearly a hundred were arrested by 2003.

But al-Qaeda continued to grow, inside and outside Yemen. The September 11, 2001, attacks on the United States vaulted al-Qaeda into public consciousness. Before then, the terrorist organization was relatively obscure. But the massive publicity it received in the wake of the attacks suddenly made it a global brand. Afterward, any self-respecting terrorist group with Islamic credentials and aspirations to bring the West to its knees began claiming to be part of al-Qaeda.

In the Central Prison of the Political Security Organization (one of Yemen's domestic intelligence services), in Sana'a, several key al-Qaeda leaders continued to plot. On February 3, 2006, twenty-three prisoners, some of whom had participated in the *Cole* and *Limburg* attacks, escaped the maximum-security prison through a tunnel to the al-Awqaf Mosque. Since the prison break, al-Qaeda in Yemen has organized a series of terrorist attacks on Western and Yemeni government targets—the latest of which is today's assault on the oil installations. Al-Asaadi reports the story, and we get it online that evening.

It's only my second week at the paper, and already we've had kidnappings, stampedes, and suicide bombings. This is a news junkie's paradise.

NINE

the front lines of democracy

I'm still adjusting to my new role. One night at a party to celebrate Ethiopian New Year's, someone refers to me as Luke's girlfriend. Luke is quick to correct him. "She's not my girlfriend," he says. "She's my *boss*."

I like the sound of that. I've never been anyone's *boss*. That is, I like the sound of it until we get back later that night to the work I abandoned earlier on my desk.

Even without the recent catastrophes, we'd have no shortage of news. Hardly have I had time to learn the intricacies of Yemeni politics when I am plunged into orchestrating coverage of the September 20th presidential election. The elections are an excellent opportunity to drive home to my reporters the importance of fair and impartial journalism. Almost as important is that I am anxious to prove to our readers that the *Yemen Observer* is not a tool of the regime. Because of Faris's work with the president, many Yemenis assume the paper is simply a government mouthpiece.

Thus, in the days leading up to the election, I am careful to include coverage of all of the candidates. We split the front page equally between Saleh and bin Shamlan, the major contenders, but also include at least one story on each of the other candidates.

But while we are not short on news, we *are* short on people to write it. I don't have enough staff to cover the elections while still producing the regular Culture, Business, and Health and Science pages. Only Ibrahim and Farouq seem capable of writing political stories, but they can't fill the front page alone. How can I create a revolution without an army? If only I had arrived to find a full newsroom, what a world of difference that would have made! But Faris seems intent on running the paper with as few people as possible. This baffles me, because reporters' salaries cannot possibly be one of Faris's main expenses. My journalists earn between $100 and $200 per month and have no health insurance or any other benefits. How can a man who drives a Porsche and lives in a mansion with alabaster windows refuse to adequately staff his own paper for financial reasons?

I brainstorm with Luke and Zuhra for solutions to our dearth of staff. We decide to run an ad in the paper and to put up fliers in the university at the school of journalism. Al-Asaadi concurs with this decision but cautions me against hope. "The problem with hiring staff is that none of the graduates of the journalism school can write in English," he says. "And we can't hire translators for everyone. But if we hire people who can write in English, they have no journalism experience." I have no choice, really; I am going to have to train English majors. It irks me that Yemenis seem to believe that if they can write in English, they are qualified to be a reporter. It doesn't occur to them that other skills might be necessary for the job.

We also have copy-flow issues. I want to get reporters to file some stories on the first day of our three-day cycle, so not everything is coming in just before deadline. Ideally, the features pages would be filed to me Saturday; the Business, Panorama, and back pages would be filed Sunday; and only the front, Local, and Election pages—which need to contain the latest news—would be left to edit on Monday, a closing day. But this seems impossible. I'm lucky if I get any copy by midday on the second day of the cycle. This means I spend days worried sick that we won't have enough to fill the issue.

It bewilders me that al-Asaadi is unconcerned about the lack of a schedule. He seems perfectly happy to have everything come in at the last minute and to stay up all night closing each issue. In fact, he rarely bothers to come in before eight P.M., thus *ensuring* the lateness of our close. Our closing days continue to run from eight A.M. until three or four A.M.

the next day. I am exhausted, and the irregularity of my hours means that when I am home, I often cannot fall asleep. My body has no idea what time zone it is in. The irregular hours don't seem to bother any of my male staff—but then again, they're all on drugs. They chew *qat* every day. Like al-Asaadi, they are never in any rush to get home and seem to be quite content to spend all night in the office chewing with their friends.

"It doesn't speak highly of their wives that they never want to go home," I say to Luke.

"Well, if your wife was uneducated and illiterate, with no interest in politics and no conversational topics beyond the children and the next meal, would *you* be in a rush to get home?" he says.

☾

ONE FRIDAY, I have a chance to work on my delicate relationship with al-Asaadi and learn a bit more about Yemeni politics when he invites me to a journalists' *qat* chew. The focus is to be democracy and the imminent elections. This group of journalists chews together every week, in rotating locations. This week it is in the tented *mafraj* on the roof of the *Yemen Observer* building, which disappoints me as I am not anxious to spend any more time at work. Al-Asaadi picks me up at Sabri's, and we arrive at the office to find Faris's car outside.

"Great," I say. "He's going to try to make us work!"

I run up to the roof and take my seat next to al-Asaadi. Ten journalists are seated in the tent, all men. They work for a variety of media outlets, including al-Jazeera, several Yemeni Arabic-language papers, a Saudi paper, and the *Yemen Observer*. On the way there, I had asked al-Asaadi if the men would mind having a woman join the group. "They loooove having a woman join the group!" he said. Ibrahim, whom I've come to think of as Mr. Front Page because he reliably helps fill page one, sits on the other side of me. None of the other journalists speaks English, but al-Asaadi and Ibrahim translate things I don't understand.

Al-Asaadi has brought *qat* for me and shows me how to pick only the tenderest and prettiest leaves to chew. The big glossy leaves are too tough and hurt the gums.

Before the session, I run into Faris, who pulls me aside. "Jennifer, don't chew too much *qat*," he says, looking grim. "It isn't good for you. There are pesticides, and it's bad for your teeth."

"Don't worry," I reassure him. "I don't do too much of anything."

After some initial persiflage, the men fall into serious, focused discussions about the elections and *fatwahs* and democracy.

On paper, Yemen is a constitutional democracy, with executive, legislative, and judicial branches of its government. The president is head of state and the prime minister head of government. A 301-seat elected parliament and a 111-seat president-appointed Shura Council make up the legislative branch. Yemen has notional separation of powers. It has regular elections to the presidency, parliament, and local government. It has genuine pluralism. Any constitutional change requires a popular referendum. Which is more democracy than exists in any other country in the Arabian Peninsula.

But all is not quite as it seems.

While Yemen's government has many superficial resemblances to the checks and balances prevalent in developed Western democracies, in practice, parliament is little more than a tool of the executive. Saleh's party, the General People's Congress or al-Mu'tamar Party, wields nearly all of the power. Saleh uses parliament to stall legislation he doesn't want. The judiciary is corrupt and manipulated for political purposes by the regime. Big decisions are made by the president and not by ministers. A small ruling elite prevents decisions that are in the best interests of the country from being made, so as to protect their own vested interests. For example, costly fuel subsidies encourage oil smuggling, from which corrupt presidential allies benefit. Oil subsidies also help big *qat* producers, who include friends of the president, as diesel pumps are used for water to irrigate the crop.

There's no question Saleh will win reelection, though he is campaigning with the ruthlessness of an underdog. I'm amazed at the bitterness and viciousness of his attacks on his opponent. Does he truly believe negative campaigning is necessary when he has the election all but sewn up?

True, things are a bit tougher for him now than they were in the 1999 election. The second-most-important party, Islah, the Islamic reform party, has joined forces with the Yemen Socialist Party and other opposition parties to form the Joint Meeting Party. The JMP's presidential candidate is Faisal bin Shamlan, a former oil minister campaigning on an anti-corruption ticket. While no one thinks bin Shamlan has a chance, it would be a hopeful sign for Yemeni democracy if he could draw, say, 30 percent of the vote.

The journalists gnawing on their *qat* leaves are pessimistic about the chances of a completely fair election. Saleh has a near-monopoly on media time and resources. All broadcast media is government controlled and airs nonstop coverage of Saleh's rallies around the country. Even Sheikh Abdullah bin Hussein al-Ahmar, the head of the Hashids and the chairman of the Islah Party, endorses Saleh at the last minute. "Better the devil you know," he tells reporters.

Some Salafi clerics go so far as to contend that democracy is un-Islamic. The ultra-traditionalist Salafis believe that Islam has strayed from its roots since the Prophet Mohammed's day and desire a return to a "purer" version of the religion. "To compete with the ruler is an illegitimate act; this is un-Islamic," says scholar Abu al-Hassan al-Maribi at an election rally Naturally, the government broadcasts his speech.

In this last month before the election, there is hardly a surface in Sana'a that isn't plastered with Saleh's stern, mustached face. Posters paper the walls of the Old City, fill shop and car windows, and hang from bridges. I've begun to feel like I know the guy personally. My reporters tell me that the shopkeepers who put Saleh's face in their windows aren't necessarily supporters; they are merely trying to stay out of trouble with the ruling party.

The political talk at the chew eventually subsides and is followed by the inevitable Solomon's Hour of Zenlike quiet. I find myself feeling rather depressed as I stare into the carpet with nothing to say. I'm not sure Yemen is ready for true democracy. How can a largely illiterate people with no access to independent broadcast media make informed choices about their future? I wonder.

☪

AS PART OF MY EFFORTS to encourage impartial reporting, I am trying to keep the advertising department from telling my reporters what to cover.

When I say advertising department, I mean Qasim, whom I originally found so charming. He constantly steals one or two of my reporters and sends them off to cover one of his advertisers or stands in the newsroom trying to dictate a positive story about Saleh. He fails to grasp that the editorial and advertising departments of a newspaper must be discrete entities. I explain that what he is doing is unethical, that a thick wall must be maintained between editorial and advertising. "We lose all of our credibility if our readers think we are reporting something because advertisers are paying us to write about it," I tell him. "Besides, I am trying to teach my reporters how to do real reporting, and you are confusing them."

He nods and smiles, and then goes ahead and sends one of my reporters to cover a fund-raising event for one of President Saleh's charities.

☾

THESE TENSE DAYS have unpredictable moments of brightness. One night, I am scrambling to edit a couple of election stories before closing day when Luke comes running into my office. Luke never runs. "Jennifer," he says. "Come out and see the moon!"

I follow him outside, and we stand in the middle of the street, gazing up as the dark shadow of the sun creeps across the moon. A lunar eclipse! Farouq joins us and we all stand around with our faces to the sky and our mouths open. I run back in to fetch al-Asaadi. We stand in the courtyard breathing in the fragrance of jasmine and marveling.

"Call Mas," al-Asaadi says. "Tell him to get photos of it."

"Mas isn't here," I remind him. "He's traveling with the president."

"Jennifer," says al-Asaadi. "Tell me where is Mas that he cannot see the moon?"

☾

ON SEPTEMBER 11, I wake up in tears. I never anticipate how much the anniversary of the attacks on my city brings all the grief and horror back to the surface. Overwhelmed, I cry straight through my shower, coffee, and the walk to work. I am dressed all in white, in honor of the Ethiopian New Year (which falls on the same day) and because I am tired of dark colors and need to cheer myself up. I wear a floor-length white skirt, a white cotton Indian shirt, a white shawl, and, in a particularly daring move in this dusty city, white socks.

"You look like an angel!" Zuhra says when she sees me. Ha! Everyone comments on my outfit, even al-Asaadi, who tells me that white becomes me. Compliments from al-Asaadi are rare and precious things. Zuhra and I draw stares when we walk down the street for lunch, negative images of each other.

"Together, we're a penguin," I say. "Or a nun."

"Or I am your shadow!"

"That, we knew."

September 11 is a Monday, and thus a closing day, so work and its frustrations divert me from personal sorrow. I'm a wee bit exasperated with the three-and-a-half-hour lunch breaks my male reporters are taking. If they could cut their lunch break down to even an hour or two, we could get out of the office much earlier. However, I know I can never suggest this ridiculously American idea without a mutiny.

In an effort to help me with election coverage, al-Asaadi hands me a new intern, a tall, broad young man named Jabr. Jabr wears his hair slicked back and dreams of becoming a movie star. In the meantime, the *Yemen Observer* will do. He has no experience, but I can't afford to turn away able bodies.

I send Jabr out to poll people for our opinion poll column, in which four ordinary people answer a question such as "Can democracy work in Yemen?" "What is the first thing you want the new president to tackle?" or "Do you think the newly released bin Laden video is real?" This should take about half an hour, tops.

Jabr disappears before lunch and is gone for six hours. I'm wondering if maybe he has decided to quit when he returns to tell me he has quotes from only three people, and they are all men. I had told him explicitly that we must always interview two women and two men.

"Jabr," I say, "you've been gone from the office for *six hours,* and you're telling me you couldn't find four people to talk to? In all that time?"

"Some of the women wouldn't talk."

"So ask more of them."

"Where am I supposed to go?" He stands there looking large and helpless.

"Walk out to Algiers Street. Hundreds of people walk by every minute. Surely you can find *one* who will talk. And we need women. We *are* half of the population. And I would like to know what *both* halves of the population have to say." Representative democracy begins here.

He nods and backs out of the room.

Two hours later he comes back to tell me that he can't find anyone.

It would be generous to call Jabr a slow starter. Luke and I become so frustrated with his inability to perform even the simplest of tasks that we begin referring to him as the Missing Link. I can't fire him though; we're hardly paying him anything, and I suppose (though sometimes I have doubts about this) that having him around is better than having no one.

Adding to our woes, the Internet connection goes down regularly, usually on closing days, when we most need it. Ibrahim e-mails me his election stories from home on closing days, and all of the op-ed pieces and Middle Eastern news must be drawn from the wires. With the Internet connection down, we cannot finish an issue. No one seems to know what to do when this happens. Everyone stands around and complains, but no one *does* anything. The Doctor is supposed to help, but he is either out on a four-hour lunch break or useless. He will shout at people and then come tell me it's all taken care of, which it rarely is. Only one technician can help us with our Internet, Enass says. But often when we need him, his phone is off.

Faris has promised me an Arabic tutor, who has yet to materialize. I've taught myself enough to get around on my own, but here are a few phrases I'm desperate to know:

"None of the power outlets in my office is working. Can someone fix them?"

"Can you tell me when the toilet will be functional?"

"There is no water in the entire building."

"There will be no newspaper if something isn't done about the Internet."

"Am I ever going to get the key to open my desk drawers?"

☪

ON OUR NEXT CLOSING DAY, Zuhra finishes her stories before three P.M. and makes her reluctant departure. It occurs to me that *she* should be the person I train to take over the paper when I leave. This is one of my main goals: to train a successor to carry on my work when I leave. But Zuhra is a woman and thus cannot stay late in the office (or, probably, command the respect of the men). It's early to be thinking about my successor, but it could take the rest of the year to properly train someone.

At three A.M., we're still working, although I am having trouble reading the words on the page. I give the last of the front-page stories to our designer Samir and am about to call it a wrap and escape when I see al-Asaadi typing away on the pages I have already finished. "I'm just moving a few stories," he says. It turns out he has also rewritten several critical election headlines, none of which is grammatical. I am convinced he is only making these changes for the same reason a dog pees on lampposts. But I have no choice but to stay until he is done; my eyes *must* be the last to see the paper before it hits the printer. Sighing, I set down my bags and pick up the pages he has altered to do one last edit.

☾

THE PREELECTION DAYS turn quickly into newsprint. I am now beginning to realize the peril of trying to change everything at once. I've been trying to get the paper on a schedule, hire staff, train reporters, edit the entire paper, write some pieces of my own, and earn the respect of my staff all at the same time. But despite my growing awareness of the impossibility of this task, I haven't figured out yet how to do one thing at a time or what should come first.

I don't have enough time to sit with my reporters as I rewrite their pieces and explain to them how to do better. So I am happy when I get all three health and science stories early enough in the last preelection issue not only to edit them but to discuss with Najma, Bashir, and Talha what is missing from each of them. Bashir, for one, wrote about the accelerating melting of the Arctic ice without mentioning two major studies just conducted by NASA. I am trying to get my reporters to read all of the background stories on a subject before they begin reporting the news. But they resist and don't seem to understand why it is important. Farouq has flat-out refused, saying that he has his own reporting, so why does he need to know what everyone else is saying? When I explain that he can write a better story knowing the whole background, he simply tells me that I should read the background and fill it in myself.

Production has been slow this week, because every single staff member has had to take time off to care for a sick relative. Al-Asaadi's mother has a snakebite on her foot that has turned into a cyst that won't heal. Bashir's mother is ill. Farouq's brother is in the hospital. So is Hakim's wife, who has stomach problems.

We are also burdened by a love letter that the minister of health has written to President Saleh for our last preelection issue. Faris insists that we put it in the paper, saying it will encourage other officials to talk to us and write for us. He also insists that it be on the back page, which he considers prime real estate. This is all communicated to me by al-Asaadi.

"I won't do it," I say. "Opinion does not belong on the back page."

"*You* tell him that." Al-Asaadi is unwilling to argue with Faris over anything.

I run upstairs and explain to Faris that an opinion piece belongs on the Op-Ed page, which is widely considered the most powerful page in a newspaper.

"That is not true here," says Faris. "Here the back page is most important."

"Really?"

"Arabic is read right to left. So Arabs will naturally turn first to what for you is the back page."

This hadn't occurred to me. "But we're an English paper. And even if that is true, we lose legitimacy when we publish opinions in the regular pages," I say. "Opinions and news must be kept separate."

Finally, Faris suggests a compromise. "I will let you put it on the Op-Ed page," he said, "if you will put a mention in the banner on the front page, with a little photo."

"Done!" I say, greatly pleased.

I run back downstairs. "It's going on the Op-Ed page," I tell al-Asaadi, who looks at me in astonishment.

The minister's piece, it transpires, is utter garbage. Al-Asaadi gets stuck translating it and moans the entire time. "Jennifer," he says, "you know what it's like when you are forced to eat something that makes you gag? That is what I am doing." The heavily edited piece is then thrust upon Luke, who wrestles with it some more. And I still have to do further edits. It tortures all of us.

Faris stops by in the late afternoon with his friend Jalal. On their way to a *qat* chew, they're clad in long white robes. "Faris," I say with mock sternness, "you shouldn't chew too much *qat*. It has pesticides and isn't good for your teeth."

"But I am Yemeni!" he says in defense. "Whereas *you* are soft and tender."

"*Soft?*" I flex a bicep.

Faris pinches my arm and agrees that there is nothing soft about it. "It's just that when I see your face, I think of meditation and tranquility," he says. "You're like a calm angel."

Luke laughs so hard he almost chokes. "Come back and see her at two in the morning."

☪

ON ELECTION DAY, I walk to work, disregarding all warnings that it is unsafe for westerners to be outside. I just can't get through such a busy day without a bit of exercise. If I don't burn off some energy, I'll need to be peeled off the ceiling by noon. The streets are deserted. All of the shops are dark and shut with steel gates, except for a few juice places. Even the big Huda supermarket is closed. To keep a low profile, I wear all black, plus sunglasses to hide my blue eyes, but I'm conspicuous no matter what I do. This is driven home when just a few blocks from my office, a filthy man I pass on the sidewalk invites me to suck his cock. Who taught him this English?

I arrive at work to find the gates locked and no one there. I pound on the doors, trying to wake the guard, to no avail. Dear god, does everyone think this is a holiday? Our biggest reporting day of the year? I mean, it *is* a holiday for the rest of the country, but we work for a *newspaper!* Surely my staff knows that they must show up? It hasn't even occurred to me that this is something I needed to tell them.

Desperate, I ring al-Asaadi. He doesn't have keys but makes a few phone calls to try to find someone to let me in. In vain. "You shouldn't stand around in front of the newspaper," he tells me. "It isn't safe."

"Al-Asaadi, there is nowhere else to *go!*" I am so frustrated that I kick the gate in frustration, and to my great surprise, it swings open. Now I am in the courtyard but still can't get into the building. The welcome mat that usually hides the key is missing. So I pound on the door to the guard's hut until I finally rouse him. Rubbing his eyes, he stumbles out to open the building.

I worry that no one will show up. It is unusual for the women reporters not to be here at this hour. Enass is also missing from the reception desk and there's no sign of the Somali cleaning lady. So it is an enormous relief when I see Zuhra bustling into the courtyard. "Please call everyone else and tell them to get their butts to the office," I say.

Noor and Najma say that their families won't let them out of the house. "It's too dangerous." The usually reliable Hassan is spending the day working for the EU election observers. Talha, who has no phone, is MIA. We also have no secretary, Doctor, or drivers.

Trying not to panic, I send Zuhra out to the polls. As soon as she is gone, Farouq shows up. He promptly heads out to report from the Supreme Council for Elections and Referendum (SCER) and to visit other polling sites. Two reporters in action!

Jabr, the Missing Link, shows up an hour later, and I send him out to the polls as well. I hand him a notebook. "Don't come back until you fill this," I say. He looks terrified. I soften a bit. "Here, I will write you a list of questions to ask."

Luke arrives next, followed by Qasim, who waves his dark purple thumb—proof that he has voted. I beg him to take me to the polling sites. I don't want to sit in the office missing all of the action. He insists on calling Faris to get permission to take me out, and we finally head to the SCER. It's housed in a massive building filled with scores of hustling and bustling Yemeni officials and local and international reporters dashing about looking important and typing up stories in a computer room. On the first floor, reporters run in and out of the smoky restaurant, holding glasses of *shaay haleeb*—tea with milk.

We head to the Ministry of Information to get my press ID. This is no simple task. Qasim asks me to lie and say that I am a reporter for *The Week* in the United States, because an international press pass apparently grants greater freedom. I don't want to lie. I'm going to be living here for a year, and I will be found out sooner or later. But it's illegal for a foreigner to be running a Yemeni paper, Qasim reminds me. We compromise and put both the *Observer* and *The Week* on my tag, which is pink for "international reporter."

We hear rumors of election-related violence and killings in Ta'iz and other governorates, but most remain unconfirmed. It's funny how fast the news of these alleged incidents spreads. I even hear from several people that a man was arrested with explosives in Tahrir Square, just down the street from me. Misinformation seems to move much faster than fact.

My pink tag dangling from my neck, I climb into Qasim's car and we head to a nearby polling place. In the courtyard of the al-Quds School for Girls on Baghdad Street, a long black column of women stretches all the way down the hall leading to their voting rooms. Though it's now noon, many of them have been standing there since the polls opened.

Across the courtyard, men do not have to wait in line. They dart in and out, completing their votes in five minutes or less.

"The women take longer to vote because they are not educated," local election supervisor Ameen Amer explains. "Many are illiterate."

To assist the illiterate, the presidential ballot has color photos of each candidate, as well as his party's emblem, next to his name. A rearing horse symbolizes Saleh, while a rising sun is the sign of the Islah Party.

"Most of the women just registered this year and haven't done this before," says another election supervisor. "It's a matter of education, and now, democracy is proceeding, day by day, and getting better and better."

Others we speak to in the sunny courtyard suggest that men vote later in the day, after work, while most women vote in the morning. It's a frustrating wait in the hot sun for the women, who grow restless and shout out their complaints. "We have a crisis!" one woman cries. "Nobody is moving!" Yet they admirably do not give up, and most wait patiently for their turn in the voting booth.

As voters file into each room, they are given one presidential ballot, two ballots for governorate councils, and two for district councils. They then secrete themselves behind the gray curtains of a small booth, where they mark their chosen candidates. As each emerges, she stuffs her papers into the plastic ballot boxes, before dipping her thumb into the well of purple ink that brands her as a voter.

A row of seated representatives from each party observes the voting, often erupting into arguments but not becoming violent.

"Nobody is cheating," says observer Hanan al-Jahrani, who is representing the GPC (the ruling party to which President Saleh belongs). "We have had no problems."

For the most part, the process is going smoothly, concurs Amer. But at least fifteen people have come to the polls wearing T-shirts or hats emblazoned with their favored candidates, which is against election law.

A businessman tells us that the voting process has improved. "We have seen the competition getting stronger, and each party is more nervous this year, which means we are getting closer to democracy. If a voter senses this, he will be more likely to vote."

Outside each room stand two armed men in green camouflage and red berets. Despite the threat of violence, I don't see any reason to feel uneasy. Things seem to be moving more or less smoothly and thankfully the guns remain unused.

Back at the office, I write up my notes. Zuhra and Jabr bring me their stories from other polling centers, and I tuck them into my reporting. Farouq runs around between the SCER and polling centers all day, so I don't see him. Al-Asaadi is allegedly doing something similar.

Election results won't come in until the next morning, so I am able to leave work by eight thirty P.M. The next day will be long; I had better escape while I can.

The results trickle in all the next day, with Saleh unsurprisingly winning 77.2 percent of the vote. It's a disappointing anticlimax after the frenzy of the last few days. No serious election violence is reported, no riots, no major problems at the polls. And privately we had all hoped bin Shamlan would do a bit better.

On the upside, it's a bizarrely calm day. I sketch out the issue on my dry-erase board and get al-Asaadi's approval. He hasn't eaten breakfast so

I offer him some of my oat cookies. He takes four. "My food is your food," I say.

"My office is your office," he says, his mouth full of oats.

I am pleased that he's so cheerful, and even more pleased that he gets his pages to me on time. So does everyone else. It's not a perfect issue, but some of my ambitions for the paper will have to wait. When al-Asaadi leaves early to let me finish the issue on my own, I am downright astonished. Without his last-minute headline changes and layout shifting, we finish all the pages by midnight and I am out of the office by one A.M. Some nights, it feels good to be boss.

TEN

homemaking in the holy month

After a month in my little suite at Sabri's, I still haven't unpacked my suitcases.
My two rooms are certainly adequate, but they do not feel like home. I
have made no attempt to decorate the walls, put up photos, or stock my
kitchen. It seems a waste of effort when I know I am leaving. Living in a
dormitory with Sabri's young Arabic students has its perks, but I want a
place of my own. Once I have a house, I can get myself sorted. I can un-
pack, decorate, invite people over for tea. *Then* I can truly begin my
Yemeni life.

So far I have had no time to look. Faris found a house he thought I
might like, but it was far away from everything—far from the Old City,
shops, and my office. I want to be able to continue walking to work.
Karim gives me the number of a Yemeni man he knows, Sami, who can
find me a house in Old Sana'a. I tuck it in my purse and plan to call. Just
as soon as I have a free minute.

Work is beginning to follow something of a schedule when Ramadan
arrives abruptly. I am dining at Zorba's with Shaima, my worldly World
Bank friend, when she gets a text message from a friend telling her that
Ramadan will begin the next morning. She immediately texts others to
spread the news. I wonder how this was all done before cell phones.

No one is entirely sure when Ramadan will start until the evening before, as it depends on the first sighting of the crescent of the new moon. The Islamic calendar is lunar and shorter than our solar calendar. Islamic months thus rotate through the seasons, with Ramadan falling about eleven days earlier each year. Yemen turns upside down during this holy month. One of the Five Pillars of Islam is that Muslims must fast from sunup until sundown during Ramadan to burn away their sins. But in Yemen, after breaking their fast at sunset, everyone stays up until four A.M. binge eating and then sleeps half the day away. It seems a bit like cheating to me, to sleep until three P.M., when only three hours of fasting are left before sundown and *iftar,* the fast-breaking meal. But who am I to judge?

At the *Yemen Observer,* we don't go completely nocturnal, but our hours change dramatically. I have only just begun to inch our deadlines earlier when our Ramadan hours throw everything off kilter again. Our official hours during the Holy Month are ten A.M. to three P.M., and then nine P.M. until one A.M. (except on closing nights, when we're often there until five A.M.). But in reality, the men never straggle in before eleven and seem to find it a struggle to get back by nine, despite the six-hour break for *iftar.*

Unsurprisingly, everyone is much more productive in the evenings. During the day, they are cranky with hunger and thirst. My original impulse is to fast along with my staff. It seems like the right thing to do. I want to squeeze myself into as much of Yemeni life as possible. But at the moment, fasting is inconceivable. I am already losing weight and am constantly so tired I can barely stay upright. I often go days without eating meals—I have no time to cook or go out—but forgoing water just seems unhealthy. Fasting throughout Ramadan would indubitably weaken me too much to run this newspaper properly.

Al-Asaadi is quick to reassure me that no one will judge me. "We are open-minded," he says. "We understand you are being true to your own culture."

But I am careful not to eat or sip from my water bottle in front of my staff. Only when my office door is firmly shut do I delve into the secret stash of dried fruit, nuts, and oat biscuits I keep in my desk drawer for emergencies. Luke isn't fasting either and comes into my office to sneak food. Occasionally, a reporter will burst in and catch us with our mouths full and our hands dirty with crumbs. Like guilty children, we hide our hands under our desks and swallow hard. But our reporters never seem to mind; we are not Muslim and are thus held to different standards.

Luke and I have grown much closer as a result of an intimate hour we spent in my office while closing the election issue. This was when he finally confessed to me that he is gay, which I had suspected all along (the *Will and Grace* videos on his laptop, his love of *Project Runway,* etc.). I am curious about what it is like for him to live here, in a country where homosexuality is punishable by death.

Yet homosexual acts between men are hardly rare in Yemen, he tells me. A large percentage of the male population has sex with men. Luke, for one, is propositioned regularly. This doesn't surprise me; he is blond and blue eyed, attractive, and speaks charming Arabic.

"But how does it work?" I ask. "I mean, how do you know who it is safe to hit on?"

"Well, once in Aden a guy cruised me in an ice cream shop. When I left he chased me down, and I got his number and he came over later that night. Easy."

"Very interesting."

"Naturally, this does not leave this office."

"I wouldn't dream of saying anything."

In return, I confess my past romantic relationships with men and women alike. This is an enormous relief. I hadn't realized just how half-alive I was feeling, unable to be my full self with anyone here. Suddenly I can tell someone the truth about my sexuality and not risk punishment or judgment. I am so grateful for Luke I want to hug him. I feel lighter than I have in weeks.

☾*

ONE BENEFIT of our Ramadan schedule is that I actually have free time during the evenings. On the first day, I head home a couple hours after my staff have fled and make myself dinner for the first time since arriving in Yemen nearly a month before. I boil water and cook whole-wheat pasta. This feels like a major achievement. I take my bowl of pasta into my bedroom and eat it while watching a DVD on my computer. This is the first truly relaxing, nonproductive, leisurely thing I can remember doing in weeks.

But this would be more satisfying if I could do it in a real home. Maybe if I bought some spices and flour, I might start cooking for myself. I could fill a corner of my kitchen with water bottles so I wouldn't have to stop and buy water every day. I could make friends with my neighbors. I really have to ring Karim's friend Sami soon. I'm tired of living in between places; I want to be *here*.

Salem comes to take me back to work at eight thirty. My reporters arrive enormously cheerful after their massive *iftars*. Ramadan fasts are traditionally broken with dates, with which the Prophet Mohammed broke his fasts. These are followed by deep-fried samosa-type potato dumplings called *sambosas*, yogurt drinks, fruit juice, a pale wheat porridge, and then meat, rice, and bread. Before sunrise, everyone eats again to store up for the day. Ironically, many people complain that they actually gain weight during Ramadan.

Final election results are declared on the first day of Ramadan. We knew them already, but now it's official. The city goes wild with joy. Firecrackers explode the whole evening, and men on neighboring roofs empty rifles into the air. The country has been saved from a tricky transfer of power, saved from unpredictability.

I run out to go buy some gum and candy for the office, wanting to give the staff a treat after their day of fasting. Farouq stops me at the door. "Why don't you send someone to the store?" he says. "You are the boss; you don't have to go yourself."

"Because it's right there," I say, pointing down the street. "I can walk."

"But you don't *have* to walk."

"But I *want* to walk."

"Send someone! Someone can go for you!"

"Farouq! *I like to walk!*"

We both start laughing, and he finally moves aside and waves me down the steps. My days are filled with plenty of these small, happy moments with my staff, enough to keep me fond of them even when they are thwarting my deadlines or returning late from lunch.

☪

One of the most striking things about Ramadan is how clearly it illustrates the cohesiveness of the culture. I have never in my life lived anywhere where everyone belonged to the same religion (although Yemen is divided between Sunni and Shia Muslims, and within these groups are scores of subgroups). I have never lived in a country where everyone is doing exactly the same thing at exactly the same time. For example, at sunset during Ramadan, every single Yemeni is eating a date. This alone is remarkable. At this time, there is no one, *no one,* on the streets. Every single Yemeni man, woman, and child is home breaking his or her fast. No stores are open and no taxis are on the streets.

I don't find this out until the second day of Ramadan, when I go to the Sheraton in the afternoon, emerging from the hotel just before six P.M., in time to see a spectacular sunset over the city. The Sheraton is perched on a hill over the bowl of Sana'a, and the purples and pinks descending across the mountains above and valleys below take my breath away for a few moments as I stand on the totally abandoned street. But my awe is short-lived as I look up and down the hill. Not a car in sight. No taxis, no *dabaabs,* no trucks, nothing. How will I get home?

Fortunately, just as I am despairing of a ride, a Sheraton taxi driver who remembers me from June passes by and sees me standing in the empty road looking bewildered. He mimes eating gestures to explain where everyone is and drives me swiftly home. We make it from the Sheraton to Sabri's house in about three minutes—without stopping once—a miracle! Sana'a is a ghost town. We do not pass a single car or person. My driver speeds away as soon as he drops me, no doubt late for his own feast.

☪

ON SEPTEMBER 25, the kidnapped French tourists are finally released. Karim gets photographs of them as they disembark at Sana'a airport, and we run them on our front page. I'm relieved, although the Yemenis have all been predicting this outcome, so they didn't worry. While I am upstairs with Karim, Faris stops by. I tell him again how much I need more staff and that I can't hope to get the paper under control until I have an adequate number of reporters. I mention the hours I am working.

"Jennifer," he says, looking concerned, "I don't want 100 percent from you. Do this gradually. Aim for 40 percent improvement or 60 percent improvement. I am afraid you will burn out if you try to do too much."

Fine, I think. It's good to know his expectations are low. But how do I *do* that? I don't know *how* to give less than 100 percent.

Because I end up working until *iftar* most Ramadan days, I walk home for dinner. It's too hard to find a taxi. Besides, it's so lovely to walk home when the streets are near-deserted. As I pass the restaurants along Zubairi Street, I see men poised to break their fast. Some even have plates of food in front of them, which they poke at hungrily as they wait for the cannon to go off so they can eat. The expectation in the air accompanying the approaching *iftar* always feels festive. Watching them makes me wish for a kitchen of my own, an *iftar* dinner waiting for me. If only I had a wife!

One of these solitary nights, I finally ring Karim's friend Sami about apartments. A slender, handsome twenty-four-year-old who studies English and works as a fixer for foreigners living in the Old City, Sami does a small business in tourism, arranging drivers to take people around the countryside, finding homes for expats, running errands, and generally being the most helpful person I have ever met. He is enthusiastic about meeting me and finding me a home. It doesn't take long. In the last few days of September, at our third meeting (having looked at a house that was too vast and one that was too tiny), we find my gingerbread house in Old Sana'a.

☪

THE HOUSE SAMI FINDS for me is not just any house but my *dream* house. It's a three-story, boxy stone house of my own, tucked behind a pale blue fence overflowing with pink flowers. I know I want it after just having seen the kitchen. It is vast, with a long counter, a small table for eating, a stove, a refrigerator, and antique Yemeni bread-baking ovens (in case I get *really* ambitious). On the same floor are a bedroom and a small laundry room/bathroom. On the way up the uneven stone stairs to the second floor is another small room, about the right size for an office. The next floor holds a large bedroom, with Star of David *qamaria* (Jews built this house 350 years ago, the landlord, Mohammed, tells me) as well as a couple of circular alabaster *qamaria*. I immediately decide this is where I will sleep. On the same floor is a large, airy *mafraj* lined with red cushions and adorned with several half-moon *qamaria,* a guest room, and a Western-style bathroom—with a tub!

And there's more! The top floor includes a tiny jewel of a room that looks out over all Sana'a, a storage room, and a door to a wide roof.

A whole house! I have never had so much space in my adult life. Mohammed and his entire family follow me as I admire the house, and then we all take off our shoes and sit down in the *mafraj* of the neighboring house to sign the lease. The rent is $300 a month. Expensive for Sana'a, but worth every penny to me. Sami and Shaima translate each line of the lease. Ever since I moved here, Shaima has been my most loyal friend. We eat together once a week or so; she helps me run errands and introduces me to her family and friends.

Several westerners have warned me away from the Old City, the most conservative part of town. Here, people keep a very, very observant eye on their neighbors. I will be watched, and all my guests will be duly noted. But what is the danger in that? I don't have time to behave badly. Besides, there is nowhere else in Sana'a I can imagine living. I can think of no greater bliss than to inhabit these thick gingerbread walls in the cozy warren of cobblestone streets. In fact, I long for nosy neighbors. I am so incredibly lonely that the smallest kindness from strangers makes me teary. Sami lives right down the street and says he is willing to help me with anything, anytime.

I sign my name to the lease, in both Arabic and English. I have a home.

The morning I am to move into my new house, an exploded cyst in my ovaries sends me to the hospital. I've been bleeding, feverish, and in pain for days with no idea why. A female doctor assures me I'll survive and sends me away with antibiotics. I'm too weak to carry anything, so Sabri's guards kindly transport all my possessions to the Old City.

But I can't rest yet. I have no bed! I am so tired I can barely walk, but I head out shopping with Sami. The Old City streets are thronged with people; it is just before *iftar* and everyone is buying provisions. Around Baab al-Yemen, the main gate to the Old City, the ground is covered with cross-legged merchants selling heaps of dusty plastic sandals, pyramids of raisins, and bright red pistachios. Crippled children sit in cardboard boxes, their big dark eyes eloquent with despair; dwarves stretch out their palms for alms; and deformed children are pushed by their parents to beg for cash. The high rate of birth defects in Yemen is visible everywhere. I feel much less sorry for myself.

Sami weaves through the clusters of men as I hurry in his wake, breathing in a soup of male sweat, cumin, and exhaust. I am struggling to catch up when, a few blocks from the gate, a man grabs me hard, squeezing my left side and breast. My scream carries. Some 150 people turn around to look. Sami whips around and takes a step toward the man, intending to hit him.

But the man is clearly crazy. He is half-dressed, in what looks like a large white diaper, with no shirt. His arms and legs are bent and wiry; his shoulder-length hair is dirty and wild, sticking out from his head in all directions; and his grin is toothless. Madness glazes his eyes. When Sami realizes this, he lowers his arm.

"I would hit him," he says. "Only it wouldn't do any good because he is insane."

I concur, but the attack has shocked me into tears. Sami tries to find something comforting to say but is obviously unequipped to do this. Realizing how uncomfortable I am making him, I pull myself together. By the time we get to the mattress store, my eyes are dry. We pick out my bed things, and Sami negotiates the price. Finally, I have a place to lie down.

☪

SAMI HELPS ME furnish my house, fixes electrical and plumbing problems, and runs errands. Both he and Shaima are constantly trying to feed me. One night I enjoy a massive *iftar* at Sami's house, and the next day I am invited to Shaima's.

Shaima and her sister Nada live in Hadda, the fancy part of town, in a large, two-story home with vast carpeted rooms and a kitchen big enough for a sit-down dinner for twelve. A froth of flowers surrounds the house.

Shaima's father, currently away in Germany receiving treatment for lymphoma, was a diplomat. When he was posted to Algeria, he fell in love with an Algerian woman, taking her as a second wife, much to the distress of Shaima's mother, who stopped talking to him for a couple of years.

Shaima's stepmother (whom she despises) has children by Shaima's father, but she has not been told about his lymphoma.

Nada is married to an Italian man, Desi, who has also fallen in love with another woman. When he told Nada he wanted to make this woman his second wife, she was grief-stricken. This is why she is now living with Shaima. Desi comes to visit his daughters Ola and Mumina but doesn't want to give up the other woman. It all sounds horrible and painful. Shaima says that if he were her husband, she would have drawn and quartered him by now. Throughout the year, I hear many more stories like this one. These multiple wives cause immense pain. Yemeni men seem to be about as faithless as American men—only instead of keeping their mistresses secret, they marry them. Islam permits up to four wives, as long as the man commits to treating them all equally. But this is impossible. Even the most perfect of humans cannot love four women equally. And in reality, this is rarely how it seems to work out. The women always suffer.

Shaima herself was once briefly engaged to a man with a first wife in Aden. But she backed out of the deal after three days. "I am just too jealous to deal with another wife," she tells me.

When she was at university in Jordan, Shaima received several marriage proposals, which she turned down because she thought she wanted to marry a Yemeni. But when she returned to Yemen, she found Yemeni men not up to her standards. "They are not polite to women," she said. "They do not hold doors, they do not want to chew *qat* with their wives, they don't want to spend time together." Now she is hoping to marry a Muslim foreigner, like her sister. "Jennifer, I am an atom bomb for Yemen," says Shaima bitterly. "I am an educated woman. I won't stay home. I work with men."

I ask her if there is really no contact at all between men and women before marriage. "Oh, everyone here is in a relationship," she says. "They are just underground. Like people everywhere, they find a way."

"What kind of relationship?"

"Like by texting. People have relationships by texts or by e-mail. Or they Bluetooth each other."

This intrigues me. I wonder if Shaima has such a relationship, but she assures me she doesn't.

WE START THE *IFTAR* MEAL with dates, of course. Then comes *shafoot* with salad, and *sambosas* filled with vegetables and cheese. Shaima has made the whole meal vegetarian on my account, which touches me. No one seems to mind—there is such a vast amount of food. After *shafoot,* they go one by one to pray before eating the rest of the meal.

Shaima serves us bowls of Ramadan soup, which is made from coarsely ground wheat, milk, and onions. "High in fiber," Nada tells me.

I am already getting full. But there are still roasted vegetables with cheese, couscous and yogurt, and several breads. I keep protesting they are feeding me too much. Yet somehow, when Shaima brings out the crème caramel, I manage to squeeze it in.

Desi interrogates me in a friendly fashion. He's very interested to hear everything about my life and work. I'm curious about him, because of the other woman. He makes us Italian coffee after dinner, and he and Nada compete to see whose coffee I like better—Nada's Yemeni or his Italian. I pick Nada's in solidarity.

After dinner, he heads to work teaching English. The rest of us have just retired to the living room when all of the power goes off. This happens every day during Ramadan, often for hours at a time. Nada is on her feet in a shot. "Ola will cry," she says. "She hates this."

Sure enough, a second later we hear a wail from upstairs, where the girls are playing. I dig a flashlight out of my purse for Nada, who runs upstairs to fetch the girls. Once they join us, Mumina starts to dance. She is wearing a long, pink princess dress with spaghetti straps. Ola, who is wee at a mere one and a half, dances with her, making me want to kidnap them both for my own.

I HAVEN'T BEEN in my new house for a week when I slip on my uneven stone stairs and crack two ribs. I am carrying my computer in my arms, and when I fall my only thought is protecting it. My ribs catch the edge of the stone step so hard that I cannot move for nearly half an hour. I lie sprawled between my kitchen and the second floor, stunned with pain, thinking that it might be a good idea to have a roommate. Someone to call the ambulance. Were there any ambulances. At last, I roll onto all fours and crawl up the stairs to bed. There's nothing to be done about a rib anyway, even if it is broken. I take four ibuprofen and try to sleep on my left side.

This puts an end to my swimming for several months. Every time I try—which, given my obsession with exercise, I often do—there is such searing pain in my ribs that I end up in tears. How on earth will I cope if I cannot swim to release stress? I walk to work every morning, but it is not enough to ease the strangling amount of tension that builds up in me each day.

It doesn't help that I've been suffering from a flulike Yemeni virus for more than two weeks. Al-Asaadi and I have been sneezing so much we finally conclude we're allergic to each other. I've already had to make one trip to the hospital, and I am not keen to make another.

I keep thinking that I should go out on my days off, or call someone, or try to meet new people, but I am just too tired and sick to do anything. Hope begins to desert me. I worry I will never be healthy, never be without pain, never get the newspaper on a schedule, never teach my reporters anything. Work is an unending struggle. Reporters are constantly missing, our Internet connection goes down every few minutes, and photographers refuse to show up when I need them.

I want to believe that there has been some progress, that something good is coming of this. My standards for success have dropped dramatically. Give me just one grammatical headline. One issue closed before midnight. One day when my male reporters get to work on time. But I am still fighting simply to fill pages—forget trying to fill them with good reporting or decent writing. I still have no one to whom I can delegate any of my work and no one to cover for Luke over Christmas when he is gone for a month. Talha vanished from the office after I caught him plagiarizing an entire story from the IRIN news service and has not been seen since. Zuhra is out sick until after Eid al-Fitr, the festive holiday celebrating the end of Ramadan. Her doctor told her she has exhaustion and must rest. Whom can I turn to now to find stories at the last minute? Who will make me laugh when I am feeling cross? Who will walk me to the Jordanian sandwich shop? I miss my little shadow.

Giving up isn't an option. After all, I have no backup plan. But I feel so tapped out I just don't know where to turn. Everything overwhelms me. I remember that Faris gets back from a trip to Washington the next day, and I decide to talk to him. Maybe he will know where I can find good reporters. The number of applications I get from people with master's degrees in English who can barely write astonishes me. The résumés and cover letters are riddled with typos, malapropisms, and grammatical mistakes.

I've just reached the nadir of my despair, however, when I have my best closing night yet. Al-Asaadi is away, so I pull the entire issue together myself, and my skeleton staff pulls through for me. Thilo, a German freelancer I hired in desperation without ever having read his writing, turns in a wonderful piece about antiquities smuggling. Hassan writes several news stories. Ibrahim sends front-page stories from his home office, and I realize I will have enough stories to fill the paper after all.

I whip out my editorial in fifteen minutes and even enjoy the process. When no pressing issue is begging to be editorialized, I indulge my pet peeves. Tonight, it's honking.

Excessive, ear-ravaging honking of automobile horns is a pervasive problem in Sana'a, but perhaps never quite as terrible as it is during Ramadan. During the holy month of fasting, everyone in the city rushes home for iftar to break his or her fast at exactly the same time. The ensuing gridlock only aggravates the frustration of drivers, who turn to their horns to express their dissatisfaction with the situation.

But these are futile gestures. Blaring horns are powerless to move heavy chunks of automobile. Making screeching noises that harm the ears of passengers, pedestrians, and bystanders alike will not make the cars in front of you move any faster. Nor will it make other drivers behave any more kindly toward you. . . .

Scores of medical studies have found that exposure to elevated noise such as loud horns causes a range of physical and psychological problems, including: hearing loss, high blood pressure, stress, heart problems, increased levels of aggression, as well as vasoconstriction, which can lead to erectile dysfunction. Before leaning on that horn, perhaps a man should think about what it could do to his reproductive capabilities.

(This prompts an e-mail from my mother, who is concerned that perhaps attacking men's reproductive capabilities isn't a wise move on my part. "But, Mom," I protest, "that's a surefire way to get their attention.")

With much cajoling and limping up and down the stairs, I manage to squeeze all the photos I need out of the often-elusive Mas. He complains, but cheerfully. Noor surprises me by turning around a quick story on Eid al-Fitr, which she reports and writes in one day. It is a miraculous night all around. Perhaps I do better when I am not relying on al-Asaadi to do anything for me. We finish laying out the last page of the night at two forty-five A.M.—our earliest Ramadan close ever! I am jubilant. Luke looks at me with suspicion. "You're doing unusually well for three A.M.," he says. "What kind of cold medicine are you taking?"

I finish the last few captions and catch Farouq's eye. "What?" he says, alarmed. "What do you need from me?"

I smile and make a zero shape with my fingers. *"Nothing."*

Farouq raises his eyes and hands to the ceiling. *"Al-hamdulillah!"* he whispers thankfully. Praise belongs to Allah.

My neighborhood is silent as I unlock my gate and tiptoe through my courtyard, a slip of moon lighting my way. A cat darts across my feet and disappears under the water tank. I wonder if anyone is watching me, wondering at the hours I keep. I climb the stairs, shed my shoes, and turn the lights on in my kitchen. Boxes of tea and cereal line my counter, next to an enormous bowl of oranges, apples, and grapes. I flick the switch on my electric teakettle and pad upstairs (slowly!) to change into my pajamas. Ten minutes later I am curled in my bed, a cup of mint tea by my side and a history of Islam in my hands. I am home.

☪

AS SUDDENLY AS IT BEGAN, Ramadan is over. During the last few days, traffic comes to a complete standstill, as everyone in the city is out every night shopping to prepare for Eid. Old Sana'a is thronged with five times the average number of people, and the markets stay open until nearly dawn.

I have never been so happy to see a holiday. For the first time, I have more than one day off in a row! For the first time in nearly two months, a piece of unscheduled time! My first morning off I sleep and sleep. Eid has quite literally saved my life. It makes me feel so festive it's like Easter and Christmas all rolled into one. The little girls tear around the streets dirtying brand-new princess dresses, men fit themselves out with upgraded *jambiyas,* and women bake sweet cakes to feed visiting family and friends in preparation for these four days of celebration. Every single one of my journal entries during this time begins with "Eid is the best holiday *ever!*"

Now I finally have time to enjoy my new home. Solitude is a luxury after long days with my staff. I like the freedom to read over dinner. I like to take my clothes off and dance around my rooms to Fountains of Wayne and XTC. I like to write in my journal in bed. I like sprawling in my *mafraj* with a chunk of dark chocolate and a pile of books and magazines. I still long for more companionship, but I trust that it will come.

My Yemeni friends have trouble understanding why anyone would choose to live alone. For instance, when Shaima drives me to the supermarket one day, I tell her I need to find a little coffeemaker. I'm desperate for real coffee—I've been drinking the ubiquitous Nescafé since I moved here. But all I can find are giant, exorbitantly expensive family-size Mr. Coffee–type coffeemakers. Even I could not drink that much coffee. "No one lives alone here," Shaima explains. "They all live in big families. No one *needs* a little coffeepot." I hadn't thought about this. It's true; no one lives alone. Yemeni people live with their parents until they marry, and often married people stay in the same house as their parents. The concept of "alone time" does not exist. When I tell my Yemeni friends that I wish I had a bit more time to myself, they are baffled. *"Why?"* they say. "Why would you ever want to spend a minute *alone?*"

☪

ON THE FIRST MORNING of Eid, my elderly neighbor across the street, Mohammed, invites me over. He calls my home phone, waking me. I have no idea how he got my number, but he says he has seen me unlocking my gate, and won't I come for an Eid visit? I have a friendly neighbor! So I dress quickly and run across the street. Everyone in the Old City is so kind to me that it never even occurs to me to be afraid of strangers. Mohammed ushers me through halls hung with oil paintings of landscapes to a *mafraj* done all in blue, with white lace draped across the cushions. Across the carpet are scattered several little silver tables covered with dishes of pistachios, raisins, pastries, and chocolates. Mohammed pushes one of these little tables in front of me and tells me to eat. I nibble on raisins and almonds while he calls for his wife and daughter. "I've been to Arizona," he says. This is evidently a great source of pride.

His wife, a rounded, wide-hipped, hook-nosed woman with an enormous smile, comes in and sits beside me. Their daughter sets a glass of lime juice in front of me and settles on the other side of her mother. She's around twenty and rather plain. Both women, according to Mohammed, speak English but are too shy to speak it around me. Mohammed does most of the talking, telling me how much he loves America and Americans.

"Do you like Kenny Rogers?" says Mohammed. "I *love* Kenny Rogers." He gets up and puts on a cassette. Somehow I failed to imagine that an Eid celebration would involve suffering through "Coward of the County." Whenever his wife leaves the room, he turns it up. When she returns, she turns it back down. Eventually, when the first side of the cassette ends, she gets up and replaces it with a tape of Yemeni *oud* music.

"She *likes* this kind of music," says Mohammed disapprovingly.

"It's pretty," I say. "I like the *oud*."

They keep encouraging me to eat and ask me about my life. Mohammed hands me a large, illustrated book about Yemen and tells me all the places I have to visit.

"You must go to Soqotra," he says. "Or you have only half lived."

They ask if I have a husband and I lie. They ask if I have children and I tell the truth. "But maybe I would like some," I say.

This sends Mohammed's wife into fits of laughter. *"Maybe!"* she says. "Maybe!" I wonder if she simply thinks it is ridiculous for someone as old as I am—I've gotten so much more white hair since I got here—to consider children or if it is funny that I am not sure.

A similar scene repeats itself at Sami's house later that day. Sweets are served, tea is poured, I am again forced to explain my childlessness, and my teeth ache with all of the sugar. But I am grateful. For the first time, I feel a sense of community. I belong to my neighborhood.

☪

EID ALSO BRINGS ME the gift of Anne-Christine. A German woman about my age who has worked in Sana'a for several years in hospital management, Anne-Christine is living in a small flat under my house when I move in. But when its tenant returns from Denmark in October, she finds herself suddenly homeless. I discover her in tears one night on my stairs. Though I hardly know her, I invite her to live with me. I have so much space, and she is so distressed.

The arrangement works out marvelously for both of us. Anne-Christine is not only a vegetarian, and so shares my eating habits, but she is also a talented cook. She is happy to have someone to cook for, and I am ecstatic to eat something other than salad and bread, which is all I can ever muster the energy to throw together. For the entire two months she lives with me, Anne-Christine makes dinner every night. Even when she goes out to dinner with friends, she still cooks me an eggplant curry or stewed lentils and leaves the dish for me with a note. As if I couldn't possibly manage to fend for myself.

On nights that I fail to come home for dinner or am late because of work, Anne-Christine is distraught. "Oh, I just *wish* I knew when you would be home!" she says to me one night. Feeling a bit like a 1950s husband, I start to leave work earlier, so as not to upset her.

Al-Asaadi finds this greatly amusing. "You have a wife!"

"Yeah," I say, shutting down my computer. "She's the best thing ever. I can see why you guys would want four of them."

After she's been living with me a few weeks, I cannot imagine how I ever survived before Anne-Christine. It makes such a difference to come home to someone. I've also begun to recognize that it is a matter of survival to have a few non-Yemeni friends to whom I can confess the whole of myself. This keeps me sane and keeps me from overconfiding in people who do not have the cultural context to understand some of the decisions I have made. I am still feeling my way toward the boundaries of what I can tell and what I need to keep secret.

Anne-Christine is so integrated into the fabric of Yemen that she has a Yemeni lover, Yahya. I cannot hide my astonishment when she confesses that he is married. I wonder if she is risking her life with this relationship in a culture where adultery can be punishable by death. The night I meet Yahya for the first time, he's terribly shy and worried that I will think poorly of him, though Anne-Christine reassures him that in Germany and the United States, it is perfectly normal for a man to visit a woman in her home. When he rings to say that he is on his way, she becomes giddy as a schoolgirl, running around the house fixing her hair and changing her dress. I've never seen down-to-earth Anne-Christine like this. Her face has flushed crimson, and she looks pretty and all of sixteen.

Yahya is tall for a Yemeni, attractive, and very soft-spoken. He speaks English, though slowly. I speak too quickly for him, and Anne-Christine tells me to slow down. He seems kind and not at all the sort of man to take the risks he is taking. But people here, I am learning, are rarely what they seem.

☪

NOT ONLY DO I now have someone cooking for me and a few friends in whom I can confide, I also have what I consider the ultimate luxury: a cleaning woman. I've never had one before. No one but me has ever scrubbed my bathroom or washed my dishes. In New York, it was so expensive to hire someone to clean that I didn't even know anyone who had a cleaning woman. But Shaima has insisted that I have someone. "I don't know what we'd *do* without a housemaid," she says. She sends me Aisha, a Somali woman desperate for work.

Yemen is home to some 150,000 Somalis, most of whom have fled to Yemen to escape violence in their homeland. They are granted automatic refugee status in Yemen—as long as they can reach the country alive. Thousands of Somalis save their money to buy passage on tiny, over-crowded smugglers' boats across the Gulf of Aden. Many don't survive the journey. They are often victims of violence on the boat, and many of the smugglers transporting the Somalis dump them so far from Yemen's shores that they drown. But Aisha has survived. She doesn't speak a word of English, so I uncover her story gradually, as my Arabic improves. She lives in Sana'a with five children and a husband. A tall, heavy woman, Aisha wears a *hijab* but doesn't cover her face. When she smiles, she reveals a mouthful of enormous teeth. At first I ask Aisha to come just once a week—I don't make much of a mess given that I am rarely home. But she is so desperate for work that I relent and have her come twice a week. I pay her $10 per visit, which Shaima tells me is the going rate. This seems staggeringly little to me, but Aisha accepts it without complaint. She leaves my house gleaming, with the smell of bleach wafting up from my stone floors.

After the first couple of weeks, I start to give her things to take home, usually food. I give her whole cakes, boxes of cookies, chocolates, and even some jewelry and clothes, mostly gifts I have received for which I have no need. A few weeks later, I give her the keys to my house. I trust her.

☪

DESPITE THE REST and nutritious meals, my ribs refuse to heal. I still cannot laugh without agony, so finally our photographer Mas takes me to the hospital for X-rays. I don't know quite what the point is, because if they are cracked there is nothing I can do but rest. But it couldn't hurt to see a doctor.

We walk into an office in the emergency pavilion of the Yemeni-German Hospital, where three men sit idly shuffling papers. The one in the middle is apparently the doctor. I explain my problem, and he gives us a written order for an X-ray. We then find our way to Radiology, up and down stairs and through doorways. The technician ushers us right in and has me change into a hospital gown (even more modest than ours). I change in private, but during the actual X-ray, he allows Mas to stay in the room. Does the technician not know that he is exposing Mas to radiation? Or does he just not care? No one even asks me if I am pregnant. Do they know that pregnant women shouldn't be X-rayed? Maybe they just think I look too old to be pregnant?

We have to go to a different department to pay. It costs a whopping YR800, or about $4. We return to the doctor, who takes me to a room where a woman sits next to a tiny infant attached to an IV. It is screaming its lungs out.

The doctor sits me on another bed and draws a screen around us. My heart thuds nervously. I have not been to a male doctor in at least a decade. This man pokes and prods my rib cage, making me yelp with pain, and then moves his hand higher. I draw back in shock. "That is *not* my rib." I am too stunned to get up and walk out.

"I think you are having pain in your liver and gall bladder," he says. "You might have a liver disease."

I glare at him. "*I fell down my stairs and landed on a rib.* There is nothing wrong with my liver!" I struggle to pull down my shirt and stand.

He *insists* that I have a liver function test and asks me if I have been sick. Yes, for nearly three weeks, I say, desperate to escape him. He hems and haws and hands me over to the phlebotomist. I figure there is no harm in having the blood tests, so I let a gloveless woman take a couple of test tubes of my blood. She hands these to Mas and tells us to go to the lab. Clearly, there's no chain of custody for blood samples. I could stick any sort of substance in my test tubes, or even trade them for someone else's on the way to the lab. But I'm in a Third World country, I remind myself. I should know better than to have First World expectations of the medical care.

The lab is in a different building. We hand the unlabeled test tubes to a man behind a glass window, who struggles to write my name on them. He tells us they will be ready the next day and that the test will cost YR 4,300, nearly $25, a fortune here. I don't have that much left, so I will have to dig around the house for loose change. I don't get paid until next week.

A couple days later, Mas and I go back to the hospital, which is much more chaotic in the daylight. We want to pick up my X-ray as well as the test results, but the X-rays are nowhere to be found. The men in the emergency room walk about their office, looking under piles of paper. Then one of them finds a stack of dusty X-rays sitting unprotected on top of a metal filing cabinet.

"Here," he says, handing me the stack. "See if you can find one of ribs."

I stare at him in disbelief but thumb through the transparencies. There are legs and arms and collarbones. Finally, I find one rib cage and hold it up. The doctor looks at it. "It *could* be yours," he says. There is no name on the film.

We give up on the X-ray and go to fetch my blood test results, which of course show that I have the healthiest and happiest of livers. The entire experience has been nothing but a monumental waste of time.

☾

WHEN I RETURN to work after Eid, I am told that Hadi will be replacing our designer Samir, who is being moved to *Arabia Felix*. Despite my sadness at losing Samir, I quickly realize that Hadi is a big improvement. Samir is a lovely designer but slow. I like a pretty front page as much as the next editor, but newspapers are ephemeral things, and what's most important is that the news gets printed in a timely manner. With Hadi laying out our pages, we close earlier than ever. By eleven P.M., all of the pages are closed and we are in a van home, the men stunned to be heading out so early.

All of the hospitality I experienced around Ramadan and Eid leaves me feeling curious about something. Total strangers often invite me to their homes for meals or tea or *qat* chews, but my staff members never do. At first I take this personally. I figure that it isn't that they don't want to spend time with me. After all, al-Asaadi and Qasim have both invited me out several times. But I am never invited to their homes. Even odder is that Faris has never once invited me to his home.

I bring this up with Anne-Christine one night over dinner. She has lived in Yemen for much longer and is much more knowledgeable. "It just seems so un-Yemeni," I say, "given how hospitable everyone I meet outside the office has been."

"But they are afraid to bring you home," says Anne-Christine. "They are afraid of their wives. They cannot introduce them to you."

"Because I am a Western woman?"

"Because you are a beautiful woman. And women are very jealous. They would not allow their husbands to work—and until such late hours!— with a woman like you."

A woman like me. I'm not sure I even know what that means anymore.

ELEVEN

the trials of mohammed al-asaadi

The fanatics are calling for our heads. They've been calling for our heads since last February, when the *Yemen Observer* republished controversial Danish cartoons depicting the Prophet Mohammed, one of which shows the prophet with a bomb tucked in his turban. The paper reprinted three of the cartoons on the Op-Ed page, alongside an editorial condemning them. A large black X obscured the cartoons, yet this did nothing to temper their inflammatory impact. Islam considers even respectful depictions of the prophet to be blasphemy. The *Yemen Observer* and Mohammed al-Asaadi have been on trial for nearly ten months.

The twelve cartoons, originally printed in the newspaper *Jyllands-Posten* in September 2005 and reprinted by scores of Western publications, sparked outrage. Muslim protestors staged violent demonstrations throughout Asia, Africa, and the Middle East, during which at least fifty people were killed. The cartoonists received death threats, editors went into hiding, and Danish goods were boycotted.

Despite the *Yemen Observer*'s explicit condemnation of the cartoons, the Yemeni government insisted that the mere reprinting of them constituted an unforgivable offense against Islam. Fanatics called for the execution of al-Asaadi, and the courts shut down the paper for three months. Al-Asaadi spent twelve days in prison before he was released on bail. Yemeni prisons do not provide inmates with food and water, so reporters and family ensured al-Asaadi was fed during his internment.

Court date after court date passes without a final ruling. If we are convicted, the paper could be shut down. We could all lose our jobs. But the judges keep postponing the sentencing. The wait is taking a toll on al-Asaadi, who by November looks exhausted and drawn.

Al-Asaadi has worked for the *Yemen Observer* since 1999, when Faris plucked him out of an Internet shop in Ta'iz. "It was always my dream to be a journalist," al-Asaadi told me. "Since seventh grade. Either a journalist or a diplomat." But he was unable to study for either of those careers. Al-Asaadi grew up in the village of Ramadi in Ibb Governorate, the greenest, most fertile part of Yemen. He headed to nearby Ta'iz for university, where there were no courses in media studies or international relations. Media courses were offered in Sana'a, but al-Asaadi had no money to travel. So he studied English.

Just a couple months after graduation, al-Asaadi was working in an Internet café in Ta'iz when Faris walked in to check his e-mail. He was sitting there reading the *Yemen Times,* and Faris asked if he ever read the *Observer.* Al-Asaadi said he did. Faris then quizzed him about a recent issue, asking him what he thought of various stories, including one that he himself had written. Al-Asaadi gave his opinion, not suspecting he was speaking with the publisher of the paper. Faris said, "I am Hessam, the brother of Faris. If you want a job at the *Yemen Observer,* maybe I can talk with him."

"Yes!" cried al-Asaadi, feeling lucky indeed. The two men exchanged phone numbers and Faris went on his way.

Two days later, al-Asaadi rang Faris at the *Observer.* "I met your brother," he said. "And he said you might have a job."

Faris then confessed his true identity. "I just wanted to see how interested you really were," he said.

Al-Asaadi began working as an office assistant. Faris helped him to get training, and al-Asaadi received several grants to study journalism abroad. By the time I came to the paper, al-Asaadi had risen as far up the masthead as it is possible to go.

☪

I first accompany him to court in early November. "I just want a *verdict,*" he says. "But I know they are just going to postpone again." Faris claims that the delays are beneficial because they give the fanatics time to calm down and lose interest in the case. I repeat this to al-Asaadi, but it doesn't seem to quell his anxiety. Though al-Asaadi and I are increasingly at odds over how to run the paper, we put aside our differences when the trial date comes up. Neither of us wants to lose our job and I certainly do not want al-Asaadi sent back to prison—or worse, put to death.

One of the *Yemen Observer*'s early stories on the case (the paper continued to publish on the Web after it was shut down) reported that twenty-one lawyers for the prosecution called for the death penalty for al-Asaadi, as well as the permanent closure of the newspaper and the confiscation of all of its assets. The lawyers "recounted a story in which a lady was killed during the Prophet's lifetime after she insulted him, and that the Prophet then praised the killer. They said that they wanted the same punishment to be applied on 'those who abuse the Prophet' (PBUH)." This drives home to me the very real risk my reporters are taking by attempting to report what goes on in the world.

My reporters always follow the name of the prophet in their copy with PBUH, for "peace be upon Him." I am unsure how to deal with this. To me, newspapers are secular, reporting objectively on all issues, including religion. So for the paper to wish peace upon the prophet at first strikes me as editorializing. The articles about the cartoons naturally include scores of "PBUH"s in a concerted effort to prove how unlikely it is that the paper would insult the prophet.

The first few times I encounter "PBUH," I delete it, and no one complains. But eventually, this strikes me as overly pedantic. I am living in an entirely Muslim country. Does it hurt anyone to allow the "PBUH" to stay? Will this put the paper on the slippery slope to promoting a religion? My fears that the paper is biased toward religion feel slightly ridiculous in a uniformly religious society. I resolve to overcome my knee-jerk secularism. Besides, until our court case is over, I'm not taking unnecessary risks.

According to the *Observer,* lawyers for the prosecution also demanded "personal financial compensation for the psychological trauma they claimed they suffered by the actions of the newspaper, which they said has impaired their ability to do their jobs and follow their normal daily lives."

This is laughable. Reprinting the cartoons has psychologically dismantled the extremists? How mentally healthy can they have been to begin with if a mere cartoon can unhinge them? I despair of the Arab world ever achieving press freedom.

The defense team pointed out that the newspaper had condemned the cartoons, had defended Islam and the prophet, and had reported the different reactions from all across the Arab and Islamic world. But the prosecution said their case rested on the cartoons alone and that the accompanying articles were irrelevant.

The Ministry of Information first revoked the newspaper's license on February 8, 2006. At the same time, *al-Rai al-'Aam,* another weekly that reprinted the cartoons, was also shut down. And *al-Hurriyah* weekly not only lost its license, but its editor was jailed along with his assistant.

Prison had a profound effect on al-Asaadi. The following is an excerpt from a personal account he wrote of his incarceration, which we published on the anniversary of his arrest.

I held my breath as I was locked in a dark room in the basement of the same building, where I was interrogated. . . . Fifteen people were in that dark and dirty room. Some people, who were still asleep, though it was midday, were interrupted by noise. The inmates recognized that the new comer was a high-profile person as a result of the protest that could be seen from the only window in the room. "Who are you and why are you here?" I was asked by the inmates. I revealed my profession but concealed my name and the reason of my imprisonment. I dared not tell them that I republished the cartoons. Whatever was the context of my story, I would not be welcome. I was really afraid . . . that I might be attacked by the prisoners. That fear was justified the second day when two bedouins from Ma'rib were jailed. They asked about everybody. I was pretending that I was asleep. They asked about me and the inmates told them that I was the journalist who republished the Danish cartoons. They jumped and said, "This is the dog, then." They were calmed down by others who told them that I was defending the prophet. . . .

I was asked to pay YR 200 for the toilet water, like any new comers to the cell. Then my family sent me a mattress, blanket and pillow. My colleagues from my newspaper and other friends flooded me with food, fruit and all edibles. I offered my fellow inmates food and other stuff. They appreciated my offer and started asking seriously about my case. I put off telling them the story until after the prayers. I wanted to assure them that I pray like all good Muslims. It worked out and they trusted me. . . .

Mosque preachers and religious fanatics launched severe attacks against us. Many of our relatives and friends boycotted us, believing we really were offenders. Obviously, it was not only the government against me in this ordeal, but also influential Islamic hardliners. The latter, who proved to be the toughest, collected millions of rials to prosecute us. . . .

After 12 long days, painfully as long as 12 years, I was released on bail. Everybody was happy for my release except the inmates. . . . They told me that they would miss the food, lectures and the cleanliness of the room. I was released, but the trial continued and the newspaper continued to be suspended from printing, but continued to be updated online. The staff and top administration's determination to continue online was great. Their work during my stay in jail helped a lot to raise the profile of the case in the international community and contributed to my release.

When al-Asaadi parks his car near the courthouse for our November court date, at first I am unaware that we have arrived. The building, set in a dusty, rock-strewn courtyard, doesn't resemble any courthouse I have ever seen. It is devoid of grandeur and looks to me like an ordinary modern Yemeni house. A crowd of men bustles around the entrance, and we have to push our way through. All of the guards kiss al-Asaadi hello. Even the prosecutor on his case comes over to kiss him several times as we arrive at the gate. The prosecutor tells al-Asaadi that his sentencing has been postponed yet again, to December. This was just what al-Asaadi feared. To make absolutely sure that we cannot get a verdict, we push our way into the building. The prosecutor tells me that there are three similar cases going on, involving the other newsmen accused. "None of the judges wants to be the first to rule," he says. They are afraid of the response of the fanatics.

If al-Asaadi were not dragging me behind him into the building, I am not sure I would make it through the throngs. There are too many people. Too many men. Guards pat men down at the entrance to the building, but they have no female guards and so they don't search me, despite the fact that I am toting an enormous bag. I see no other women.

We pass through a grubby narrow hallway and start up a filthy set of stairs at the back. At the top, we pass from small square white room to small square white room, greeting people and moving on. I have trouble keeping up with al-Asaadi, who is tiny enough to slip easily through crowds. I am also very busy trying to keep from brushing against any of the men, which is no easy task. When we at last reach a small square white room with a judge, al-Asaadi is unable to persuade him to issue a verdict, and we are turned away. On our way out, al-Asaadi stops to kiss a few hundred more men.

"Do you want to see the prison cell where I was?" he asks me.

I do.

Al-Asaadi greets (and kisses) one of the guards and convinces him to unlock the prison underneath the courthouse. The low-ceilinged room is crowded with men. They have been sitting on their thin sleeping mats, but most spring to their feet when they see us. They stare at me.

"Salaam aleikum," says al-Asaadi.

"Aleikum salaam," they chorus back.

I gaze around. The dingy yellow walls are scrawled with graffiti. On my right, the entire corner is littered with empty water bottles. Just beyond them is the toilet. It doesn't smell all that horrible, though I have a cold again, so I'm not smelling much in general.

"That's where I used to sleep," al-Asaadi says, pointing to a corner toward the back.

The men continue to stare at us, silently, until we turn to go.

"They never let anyone in there," al-Asaadi tells me as we walk back out into the sunshine and the guard locks the door behind us. "But I formed a good relationship with the guards."

"I can see that." We climb back into his car and return to the office to work. And to wait.

When the next court date rolls around in December, everyone feels certain we will finally get a verdict. The day before, the Yemeni Journalists Syndicate, an advocacy group for journalists' rights, holds a rally to support al-Asaadi and the paper. I meet al-Asaadi and Farouq in the courtyard of the YJS first thing in the morning, and we mingle with the journalists trickling in.

The rally is held outside, under a blue-and-white-striped tent. Propress slogans demanding the unshackling of journalists have been printed on sheets of white paper and pasted on all the walls of the courtyard. The crowd of sixty or so journalists is almost entirely male, with two Yemeni women sitting quietly toward the back. Because the sexes are almost always segregated in Yemen, it is unusual for a woman to sit near men. But I take a seat in one of the front rows. I'm the editor of the paper, damn it. A series of journalists then make impassioned speeches in Arabic for about an hour (Ibrahim translates). It's all preaching to the choir—everyone present is on the same side. I wonder if the rally would be more effective if it were held, say, in front of the courthouse. This doesn't seem to have occurred to anyone.

Kamil al-Samawi, the lawyer representing us in court, makes a speech in defense of press freedom. He works with HOOD, a nonprofit, nongovernmental human rights organization. HOOD reports human rights violations and defends victims, offering free legal assistance. It is unpopular with the government, which doesn't like to be reminded of its shaky human rights record. A short, stocky man with glasses and a broad smile, Kamil is a passionate speaker, and the crowd murmurs its assent as he talks.

I am particularly fond of Kamil for helping Zuhra overcome many of her initial fears about becoming a journalist. She first met him at the courthouse when the *Observer*'s trial began, and they became friends. He was close to her oldest brother, Fahmi, so Zuhra felt comfortable with him. "I liked the way he speaks about human rights. He is very openminded," she said. "He feels it is important for victims to speak up. I have never seen a man that respects people like Kamil."

She had always thought she was "a coward journalist" because she avoided controversial stories. "This was before you came," she says. She worried that covering provocative topics would make her a target. "I remember Rahma Hugaira [a female Yemeni journalist]—her reputation was assassinated because she attacks the government." Rahma was called a whore and worse, just for having the courage to speak out. Zuhra was terrified of suffering a similar fate. But when Kamil took her to court to meet Anisa al-Shuaibi, Zuhra knew she had to write about her case.

In 2003, Anisa was accused of killing her former husband but was acquitted of the crime when no evidence was found against her—and her ex-husband was found to be living. At the time of her arrest, she was brutally dragged out of her home at night and locked in prison, where she was raped. When she was released, more than a month later, she accused the head of the Criminal Investigation Unit, Rizq al-Jawfi, and the head of the CIU's investigations department, Saleh al-Salhi, of illegally imprisoning her and of being responsible for her rape and torture in jail.

Zuhra interviewed her, as well as her two small children, and was shocked by the tale. "The Anisa case represents in all ways part of what we are suffering here as women," says Zuhra. The men who put her in prison knew that no one would support Anisa, she continued. "If you are being raped and speak out about it in Yemen, you are going to be scandaled and face social denial." It is unacceptable to talk about rape, and any woman who claims to have been raped is blamed for the crime and ostracized. Zuhra admires Anisa's bravery and hopes she will inspire other women to speak out. Since Anisa's protest, Zuhra adds, fewer women have been put in jail, because officials became afraid that they would be accused of abuse.

Zuhra's stories on Anisa have prompted threatening letters from readers. But while these frighten her, she has no intention of silencing her pen. "I was afraid to cover it, but it makes me feel good about myself," she says. She doggedly follows the story, never missing a court date and filing several front-page pieces on Anisa's plight. "I have started my war and I have decided not to stop."

☪

DECEMBER 6 IS D-DAY for al-Asaadi and the *Yemen Observer*. I am at the office by eight thirty A.M. to check in with my staff before heading to the courthouse. Najma and Noor are late with the Culture page, so I tell them they must stay and finish it. But I am forced to relent when Mohammed al-Matari says he has spoken to Faris, who wants everybody there. Al-Matari colors his graying hair black and dresses in suits that fit him the way a refrigerator fits a stick of butter. His lapels are often stained with something, spots of tea or dried beans. There's a kind of old-world gentle-manliness about him, a persistent chivalrousness.

Al-Matari's insistence that everyone attend the trial shames me—I should not have tried to make the women stay in the office on such an important day. Of course they should come with us. We should be filling the courthouse and squeezing out the fanatics who will be there in the hopes of seeing al-Asaadi laid low. I am surprised when Faris himself does not show. Since the fate of his paper hinges on this trial, one would think he might want to attend. When he doesn't appear by nine A.M., we all pile into the *Yemen Observer* van.

At the courthouse, Zuhra glues herself to me. We push through the mobs at the gate and building entrance and up the stairs to the courtroom.

"I haven't missed a single court date for this trial," says Zuhra. "Even al-Asaadi missed one date when he was sick, but I have never missed one!"

Zuhra makes Najma change places with her so she can sit next to me on the wooden bench lined with splitting, chocolate-colored cushions. The narrow courtroom fills up quickly, mostly with fellow journalists. My women are the only women in the room. I am the only westerner. I take several photographs of the crowd.

Faris never arrives.

☾⋆

AL-ASAADI IS LATE. He told me on the phone earlier that his lawyer had advised him to be a little late, to make a dramatic entrance I suppose. But he is so late that his lawyer finally calls him and says, "Where are you? Do you want to just go straight to jail?" (The lawyer is standing in front of us, and Zuhra translates.) He and Qasim and several other men in the front row laugh. There is much nervous laughter and chatter, but the anxiety in the room is palpable. We are all journalists; we all have a stake in this. If the *Yemen Observer* is shuttered, my staff and I will be jobless. I have no idea what I will do if this happens. I suppose stay and fight to get it reopened. I couldn't possibly go back to New York now. To return to New York would be admitting defeat. Besides, I have grown attached to my reporters. I cannot imagine abandoning them.

A cheer goes up in the courtroom. Al-Asaadi has arrived, making a grand entrance from the judge's end of the room. Men rush to the front of the pews and surround him, kissing him and squeezing his hand. He looks very sharp in a black suit and striped tie. I feel an impulse to hug him, but naturally this is impossible, so I settle for a wave and an affectionate nod.

By the time the judge arrives, the room is filled to overflowing. The back of the room is so packed that guards have to push people to keep them from surging forward. A dozen or so men dressed in army green and wearing red berets watch us intently, their hands fiddling with the triggers of machine guns and pistols. Their presence reminds me that violence is expected. If al-Asaadi and the paper are not convicted, the fanatics could go mad. Fortunately, there isn't much room in the courtroom for fanatics; we journalists take up almost all of the benches. I crane my neck to try to spot them. Zuhra says they are in the back, but I can't tell who they are.

Several more guards stream in with the judge, who takes a seat at the head of the bench.

I am so anxious I might throw up. My heart pounds so loudly I have trouble hearing Zuhra, and my hands tremble as I scribble notes.

Al-Asaadi stands at a small, low lectern on our right. His supporters close in, hovering protectively around him, clinging to each other's hands. I find it touching that Yemeni law allows someone about to be sentenced to stand surrounded by dozens of his closest friends.

His face solemn as death, the judge—gray hair, glasses, green sash—begins to read from a paper. Zuhra whispers a translation of his words while furiously taking notes. He begins by recapping the cases of both the prosecution and the defense. The only sound in the room other than his words is Zuhra's occasional "Oh my God!"

I hardly dare to breathe. Not knowing exactly when the sentence is coming, I watch the audience closely for clues. The men look stern and frightened. Al-Asaadi is slumped against his lectern, as though he can't quite hold himself up.

Finally, a murmur goes up from the crowd, and I hear the words "YR500,000." "Is that a fine?" I whisper to Zuhra. "Are we getting a fine?"

She nods and tells me that al-Asaadi has been convicted. I draw a sharp breath.

"Of insulting Islam?"

"Yes, by republishing the cartoons. The judge just confirmed that it was a crime."

But al-Asaadi will receive no jail term, she tells me. Even better, the paper will stay open!

There is a collective release of breath. Men begin to whisper to each other and shuffle their feet.

When the judge finishes reading, there is scattered applause. Along with relief for al-Asaadi, however, comes concern that this conviction makes him more vulnerable to being attacked by extremists. A conviction of insulting Islam is a serious thing, and the fanatics might just take it upon themselves to punish him, now that his crime has been confirmed.

Guards whisk al-Asaadi away to a holding cell until a guarantee can be deposited. We quickly follow, streaming down the stairs and out into the sunshine.

A Reuters television reporter has grabbed me in the courtroom and asked if he could interview me, so I follow him to an area away from the crowds. He asks my opinion of the verdict and the Yemeni courts, while al-Matari translates. A crowd gathers to watch.

"I am very pleased that the paper will remain open," I say, squinting in the bright sunlight. "That is a victory for freedom of the press. But I am very disappointed with the conviction. I am concerned that it puts our colleague Mohammed al-Asaadi at risk."

The men around me murmur to each other and ask al-Matari what I have said. Several of them seem to nod in agreement. When I am done, I turn and scan the crowds for Zuhra. She is busy interviewing people, darting from man to man. It's easy to spot her; she's the fastest-moving object in the courtyard.

Al-Asaadi has appeared in a window of the courthouse and is making the most of his audience, clinging to the bars of the window and posing for photographs. He calls out to me.

I climb up the embankment under his window.

"Mohammed! What are you doing in there?"

He looks awfully cheerful for a convicted man. "I'm in prison!" he chirps.

"How do I get you out?" This is a serious question. I wonder if I should pay the fine myself, so that we can take him back to the paper with us. But I don't have enough *riyals* on me. Where the hell is Faris?

"I will be out in a little while, after we make the guarantee. Go back to the paper and get the story online."

"Of course. Zuhra is on it. Do you need money?"

"No, not now."

"Well, I can get you some if you need it."

"Thank you."

I find Zuhra and try to take her to the van, but she keeps spotting new sources to tackle. We are about to make it out of the gate when she sees one of the men who want us dead.

"There's one of the fanatics!" she cries, recognizing a man she met in court before. "I have to get a quote!" I watch her flap away, bursting with pride.

Finally, we all pile into the van to go back to the paper. Zuhra and I decide that it will be fastest to write the story together. She has all of the quotes from the judge and other sources, and I have descriptions of the proceedings and quotes from al-Asaadi. We run to my office, and Zuhra pulls a chair up to my desk. We send someone out for tea.

"Have you had breakfast?" I said.

"No."

"Eat this. We can't have you falling over before deadline." I hand her an energy bar, a package of peanuts, and a parcel of toast from my secret food drawer.

We are a good team, working fast and efficiently, me typing, Zuhra reading and translating her notes for me. Our story is online within an hour—and we are the first to break the news, beating Reuters, Agence-France Presse, and the BBC.

I am very pleased and flushed with manic energy. Zuhra and I high-five each other and toast ourselves with sugary tea.

Ibrahim calls in the afternoon to congratulate me. "It was so brilliant, so professional, and you even got a quote from a fanatic!" he says.

"That's all Zuhra," I say. "She did all the real reporting."

"I called al-Asaadi to tell him what a wonderful job you did."

"You did?"

"I said, 'She even mentioned your tie!'"

"Well, it was a very nice tie!"

Al-Asaadi sends me a text later to thank me for my support and the story. I glow with happiness.

☪

OF COURSE, our busy morning means that we fall behind with the rest of the paper. So, feeling quite like Sisyphus, I put my shoulder to the stone and begin, slowly, to roll it back up the hill.

TWELVE

tug-of-war

Unfortunately, the solidarity al-Asaadi and I experience during our day in court is short-lived. Now that we have been reprieved, we resume our slowly escalating power struggle. I've tried my utmost to avoid conflict, but it's hard when al-Asaadi refuses to acknowledge deadlines. By now, I've realized that the first thing I need to achieve is a proper schedule. Not until I get the paper moving in an orderly way, with pages coming in at predictable times and issues closing on time, will I be able to turn my attention to the development of my staff's journalistic skills.

By December, the only thing standing between me and a regular schedule is al-Asaadi. The rest of my reporters now turn in their pieces on time, so we *could* close every issue by eight P.M. But al-Asaadi purposely withholds his stories until the last minute and drags out our closes for hours. To make a point, Luke and I finish absolutely every page, send everyone else home, and ring al-Asaadi to tell him we are just twiddling our thumbs waiting for his story, which is the last thing we need in order to close. This has little effect. Al-Asaadi still refuses to come to the office before eight P.M. on a closing day. He doesn't seem to care that he is holding us all hostage. Thursdays are particularly bad, because he spends all afternoon chewing *qat* with his friends and is reluctant to come to the office at all. When he gets there, he is so wired that he is perfectly happy to stay up all night—and keep us up with him—closing the paper.

Things come to a head during the Consultative Group for Yemen's donors' conference in London, held to encourage foreign aid to Yemen. Yemen is the poorest country in the Middle East, but it receives surprisingly low levels of development assistance. Now Western and Arab countries are meeting to discuss Yemen's development challenges and to pledge financial support. This is intended to help Yemen develop its economy, improve its infrastructure, and battle poverty and illiteracy. The money comes with strings attached, however. Donors insist that Yemen forge ahead with anticorruption reforms, bolster democratic institutions, create a more independent judiciary, and increase government transparency. Yemen has vowed its dedication to these reforms, but whether it will be able to fully realize them remains a great unknown.

Al-Asaadi has traveled to England with Faris to attend the conference and has promised us a front-page story. The biggest news, that a total of $4.7 billion has been pledged, breaks on a closing day. This is a major increase over amounts pledged at previous donors' conferences. Yemeni officials (and Faris) are euphoric.

But we hear nothing from al-Asaadi. All day, I edit the rest of the issue and wait for his news. We cannot run the issue without it; the donors' conference is the biggest story in the country. By seven P.M., we have edited everything else. I grow anxious. Just in case, I tell al-Matari to start putting a story together from the wires and calling local officials for comment.

We are still waiting when Luke begins vomiting. He thinks it's the pesticides on his *qat*. Pesticides illegal everywhere else in the world have a way of sneaking across Yemen's borders and ending up on *qat* plants. Luke chews Yemeni quantities of *qat* and by deadline can hardly speak, his cheek is so packed with greenery. "He's more Yemeni than most Yemenis," Zuhra says.

I send him home. Manel, a twenty-four-year-old Senegalese-American I recently hired to share the copyediting, stays to help me. Manel speaks fluent Arabic, French, and English and brims with infectious good humor. His copyediting is patchier than Luke's, but he has such a sunny attitude that his mere presence in the office inspires all of us. Handsome, with a lean wiry body and neatly cornrowed hair, Manel is particularly inspiring to the women in the office. But *everyone* loves Manel, who wouldn't even know how to go about getting stressed out. I'm hoping some of his Zen will wear off on me.

I have already written several e-mails to al-Asaadi, asking him how the conference is going and when I will receive his copy. No reply. When the rest of the issue is done, I write again to tell him that if I don't hear from him in the next half hour, I will have to run a wire story.

He rings me in response. "Zaid and I will have the story to you in a couple of hours," he says.

"A couple of hours? Al-Asaadi, the rest of the issue is completely done! Please get it to me in the next hour."

Our conversation is cut off just after that, and I get an e-mail from him that says, "I am the editor in chief, and if I tell you to hold the paper until I send you the story then you have to hold the paper. I don't have to answer to you."

Actually, I want to say, you *do* have to answer to me. It is in my *contract* that I am to have *complete editorial control* over this paper. Thus far, I have purposely avoided saying such a thing. I have never pulled rank on him, in an effort to preserve his dignity and our diplomatic relations.

Even Faris has warned me about al-Asaadi. "He doesn't like it when anyone else gets too good," he told me. The reason al-Asaadi has been sabotaging every issue, Faris believes, is that he can't stand to see me get the paper on a schedule. To see me succeed where he failed.

I do not respond to his e-mail. I sit and stew, while Manel holds my hand and tries to keep me from erupting into flames. As it becomes clear why we are stuck in the office so late, my staff also grow impatient. It's midnight by the time we get the story and photos from al-Asaadi. He fails to send me photo credits and doesn't respond when I ask for them by e-mail. I am forced to run the photos without credit and send everyone home. I've been at work for twenty hours.

I indulge in revenge fantasies all the way home. I imagine calling al-Asaadi and saying, "Why do you think they hired me? Because you were running the paper perfectly?" But I do no such thing. I go to bed with an aching stomach and dream that al-Asaadi is livid with me for not waiting in the office all night for him to send me photo credits.

(☾ ·

THINGS CONTINUE in the same vein after he returns from London. The very next issue, he e-mails me that he wants to write the editorial. So I save him that space. Luke and I finish every other page by seven thirty P.M. Al-Asaadi waltzes into the office at seven forty-five P.M. He hasn't even started his editorial. It's *textbook* sabotage.

I have been in a sunny mood all day, but now clouds are gathering. When he finally finishes his editorial, al-Asaadi decides to rearrange the entire front page and suggest additions to the Local page. I fight to keep my voice steady.

"I would have loved your feedback—*at four P.M. this afternoon*," I say. "When we had plenty of time to rework things before deadline."

"I can't come in at four P.M.," he says.

"Why not? Everyone else does. That's our work hours."

We are interrupted by his phone. Al-Asaadi has two mobile phones, both of which ring constantly. He chats for several minutes, his cheek bulging. While the entire rest of the staff has been hard at work, he has been at a *qat* chew with his friends.

Al-Asaadi seems to believe that holding the title of editor in chief entitles him to do less work than the rest of the staff. His time in prison has made him a bit of a celebrity. He's Yemen's poster boy for press freedom, and he milks this so much that Manel takes to calling him the "Boy Wonder" or the "Ghetto Superstar." He loves to go out to embassy parties, to meet and greet dignitaries, but isn't all that interested in the day-to-day sweat and toil of editing a paper. He spends no time training the staff to become better reporters, though they could use his help, and is impatient with their mistakes.

Luke and Manel and I confer about al-Asaadi's obstructiveness after we finally flee at eleven P.M. Compared to our first two months, this is still an early close, and I have worked a mere fourteen hours instead of twenty. Luke, who worked for the paper for several months before I arrived, says that before I came there was no order at all and they were often there all night. "We were here until five or six in the morning," he says. "You've done an amazing job."

Luke offers to come with me to talk to Faris, to support my complaints about al-Asaadi. "He has blatantly sabotaged you for the last three issues," he says. "All three issues would have closed at eight if not for him."

Faris, as is too often the case, is out of town. So we wait.

The weird thing is that I know al-Asaadi likes me in spite of himself. And I like him. He brought me a pretty souvenir candy dish from London, and on days we are not closing an issue, we often talk and laugh together. But throughout the fall, the tension has escalated. When he is in the office, he entertains a constant stream of visitors, who sit a few feet from my desk talking loudly and slurping tea. The incessant racket is deleterious to both my patience and my editing. If al-Asaadi isn't with a guest, he is shouting on the phone.

In Yemen, no one ever makes an appointment. People visit the editor of a paper when they feel like visiting, with no regard for the fact that she might be on deadline. Yet it is the height of rudeness to turn anyone away. I make this mistake one day, when a Yemeni reader drops in to talk with me about the paper just as I am editing several stories on a closing day. "Look, I'm really sorry, but I just don't have time right now," I tell him. "I am trying to close an issue. Could you please make an appointment next time?"

As soon as he leaves the office, al-Asaadi berates me. "You cannot *do* that," he says. "You must *always* offer them a seat and at least a glass of tea. That is how things are done here."

I feel terrible guilt for being so culturally insensitive. But I am also frustrated. If I am required to entertain endless visitors, as al-Asaadi does, how am I ever going to get my work done?

Yet sometimes, my visitors delight me. I am busy editing one afternoon when a tall, blue-eyed cowboy walks into my office. A real cowboy. From Arizona. This is Marvin. He steps hesitantly across my threshold, looking as though he's just been peeled off a Marlboro billboard. His gray hair is cropped short, and he sports a big mustache, jeans, and bowlegs.

I'd heard of Marvin. He is running a livestock program on Soqotra and splits his time between the island and Sana'a. Thinking that I could get an interesting story, I invite him to sit.

Goats run loose across the pristine island of Soqotra, he tells me, and they are slowly destroying its unique and delicate ecosystem. Marvin's plan, yet to be put into action, would help the local people learn how to keep their animals healthy, manage foraging, open a sanitary *halal* slaughterhouse, and sell meat to the mainland.

We commiserate about the difficulty of getting anything done here, the malingering of our workers, and the disorder of the country. Marvin tells me that one of his workers refused to come in one day because he'd skipped breakfast and his stomach hurt, while another didn't show up because his left pinkie finger had a paper cut.

"You know the Spanish word '*mañana*'?" says Marvin.

"Of course," I say. "Tomorrow."

"It doesn't really mean 'tomorrow,' " he says. "It means 'definitely not today.' "

I could see where this was going.

"And here, it's the same thing with '*insha'allah*.' "

"I know! It's the universal excuse for everything. If my reporters don't get a story done on time, well, it just wasn't *meant* to be done on time." This absence of personal responsibility bothers me. The general attitude of my male reporters seems to be "Why should I worry about it, when I can just leave it to God?" While my women will work themselves to exhaustion, refusing even to eat until a story is done, my men spend the bulk of their time justifying their minimal efforts. This is the result of privileging one half of society over another, I think. The men feel the world owes them a living and work only to get more money for *qat,* whereas the women work three times as hard in an effort to prove that they can do what everyone tells them they cannot.

Yet the men treat the women with condescension. One afternoon, al-Matari, who is Noor's cousin, comes into my office to tell me that Noor has gone home crying. "It is Farouq," says al-Matari. "He yelled at her."

This is not the first time this has happened. Zuhra recently ran into my office trembling. "Can I talk to you?" she said, closing the door and throwing back her veil. She was in floods of tears. Farouq had been taunting her, she said, accusing her of spending too much time talking with westerners, as if this were a betrayal of her people. By "westerners," he meant Western men, which meant Luke and Manel. Zuhra sees Luke as a brother and is nearly as comfortable talking with him as she is with me. Because Luke is Western, she knows he won't mistake her friendliness as a sign of loose morals. Over time, she has come to feel the same way about lovable Manel. It's agonizing to have these relationships misconstrued.

Today, it's been Noor's turn to play punching bag to Farouq. As she is already gone, I send her an e-mail saying that I am sorry Farouq has upset her and that she shouldn't hesitate to come talk to me if he bothers her at work.

The next afternoon, I pull Farouq into my office. He claims that Noor yelled at him first (which I doubt). "Farouq. You are an adult. No matter *what* Noor said to you, I need you to try to be kind to her in the office. If you have a problem with her, come talk to me about it, and I will deal with her. But this isn't the first time you've upset someone in the office, and I don't want my reporters leaving here in tears."

"I will have nothing to do with the women!" he says angrily. "I will never speak to them!"

"Well, you may *have* to, for work. So I need you to please try to be nice. And professional. Come to me with any problems. Okay?"

He gives me a curt nod and leaves my office.

I tell all of this to Marvin, who nods sympathetically. "Well, if you need to get away, come see us on Soqotra," he says. "There are plenty of stories for you to write there."

☪

I KEEP MARVIN'S INVITATION in mind as I redouble my efforts to work with al-Asaadi. The tension is not constant, and he can be quite charming. In late November, our relationship gets a boost from an out-of-town field trip. I haven't left Sana'a since I arrived (other than a long weekend in Istanbul) and am aching to see the countryside. Al-Asaadi says he wants to take me somewhere in honor of my birthday, which I think is the best gift possible. So one Friday in November, he and his two eldest daughters come to pick me up in the Old City to take me out to Wadi Dhar, a valley about a half hour from Sana'a.

Hulud and Asma, ages four and six, both tiny and shy with identically braided hair and long, curly eyelashes, stand in the backseat of the car for the entire ride, staring at me silently. I cannot get used to seeing parents fail to buckle their children safely into cars. There are no child safety seats, and older children never wear seat belts.

It is a bright, sunny morning as we head out of Sana'a, past the sprawling fruit and vegetable markets on the fringes of town and increasingly ramshackle homes, into the mountains. We are heading to Dar al-Hajar, the imam's palace built on top of a rock in Wadi Dhar.

On the way, al-Asaadi pulls over at a scenic overlook, where hundreds of tourists, both Western and Yemeni, mill around the edge of the cliff overlooking a deep, green valley. The four of us walk to the edge and stand looking down at the patches of *qat* and the squat homes beneath us. Mountains fill the horizon. Yemeni men sell trays of bright pink cotton candy, fruit, and nut brittles. A man with a falcon on a rope lets foreigners take pictures for a price. We take photos of each other and talk with a German family standing near us. Al-Asaadi is happy to see tourists in his country. "When bad things happen, like these terrorism things, it makes me worry about their future," he says, tapping his girls on their heads.

I want to say that one of the best things he can do for their future is to make them wear seat belts in the car, but I bite my tongue.

It is hot and dusty when we arrive at the palace. Just outside, men dance in a circle with unsheathed *jambiyas*. Even knee-high little boys wave their daggers around in the air as they try to follow the steps of the men. No one seems concerned about trusting preschoolers with lethal weapons. I am reminded of my sister's horrified reaction when, after my first trip to Yemen, I gave a tiny *jambiya* to my four-year-old nephew, Noah. "I can't let him have a *weapon!*" she scolded me.

We wander over to the entrance and make our way up the many flights of stairs, pushing through throngs of people. The five-story medieval Dar al-Hajar (Rock Palace) was expanded in the 1930s into a summer residence for Imam Yahya, who ruled Yemen from 1918 to 1948. It is a maze of gypsum-walled rooms, riddled with *qamaria* and nooks and crannies for children to crawl into. We lean out windows to gaze at the valley below. Hulud and Asma are interested in everything, touching the walls and looking around them with big eyes, but are almost entirely silent. They don't even jabber with each other.

When we're done exploring, al-Asaadi is in a hurry to get home in time for noon prayers. The dirt track winding back to the main road is lined with fruit sellers offering pyramids of plums and pears. I buy a kilo of tight-skinned purple plums and we eat them as we drive back, the sweet juice running down our arms and chins. When Al-Asaadi drops me home, he runs to the Qubat al-Mahdi mosque across the street, as he doesn't have time to get to his mosque. I ask if he is taking the girls, and he says no, they will wait in the car. The afternoon heat is sweltering and the car is overly warm. Trying to hide my horror, I ask, "Why don't they come stay with me until you're done?"

"Oh no," he says. "They're used to it." He opens a window and shuts them in the car.

I stand next to the car for a moment as al-Asaadi hurries across the street to pray. The girls sit quietly. It feels unconscionable to walk away and leave them there, but I don't have a choice. I turn to head toward home, hoping that al-Asaadi prays quickly.

☪

AT THE END OF NOVEMBER, two men from the South African embassy visit me. These men actually made an appointment, only I have completely forgotten. When they arrive, I am buried in work, but I set my editing aside to talk about the recent elections and press freedoms in Yemen. Ambassadors often drop by to quiz me about the Yemeni press. They want to know "where my red lines are"—what limits are put on free expression. I normally enjoy these ambassadorial briefings, but I am so overwhelmed by the work I have left to do that their visit sends me into a panic. Exacerbating matters, I return to my office to find a group of women students sitting there, waiting for al-Asaadi. Struggling to be polite, I chat with them briefly before he arrives.

Now I am even more behind, so I ask al-Asaadi to please take the students to a conference room, so I can catch up with my editing.

"No," he says with a note of defiance in his voice.

I look up from my computer, startled. "Why not? The conference rooms are both empty, and I have to be in the office to edit on my computer and e-mail questions to Hakim on his story."

"No. *You* go someplace else."

I am stunned, not just by his irrational obstinacy, but by the fact that he is arguing with me in front of a room full of women.

"Mohammed, I need to be in this office and you know that. Why do you need to be here to talk with these women? This is why we have conference rooms! For meetings like this!"

He refuses to leave. I attempt to work, but it is impossible with him talking at top volume to the students right next to me. Faris, for once, happens to be upstairs, so I run up to solicit his support. I interrupt his meeting with Jelena, the temperamental advertising coordinator for *Arabia Felix,* who has just had such a vicious fight with Karim that he threatened to quit.

"What is it?" says Faris, looking annoyed.

I explain the situation, and Faris immediately phones downstairs to tell al-Asaadi to take the girls to a conference room. I am well aware that tattling on al-Asaadi to Faris sounds the death knell of our relationship, but I don't know what else to do. I have five pages left to edit, and most of the day is gone.

I run back downstairs, but al-Asaadi, in defiance of Faris's orders, still refuses to leave. Faris sends down the big guns, in the shape of the formidable Doctor. I hide out in the newsroom with Luke while he goes to oust al-Asaadi and the girls from our office.

When at last they are gone, I go straight back to work. Al-Asaadi promptly returns to yell at me. I yell back.

"Why are you being so stubborn?" I say. "You know I have to be here for work. Why do you have to be here, when both conference rooms are free?"

"Because it's *my office!*"

"That is not rational! There is no reason you cannot talk to those women in the conference rooms!"

Al-Asaadi picks up things from his desk and throws them down again. "This isn't even an *office* anymore," he says. "It looks like a *grocery* store!" He waves angrily at the orange sitting on my desk.

"You know I keep most of my food in my desk drawers," I say, my voice starting to tremble. "And I *have* to keep food here, because I don't have a *wife* at home to cook me lunch." (Anne-Christine has moved to Syria, and I've gone back to a diet of cereal and salads.) "*This* is where I eat my lunch. I have too much work to finish to go home. What do you want me to do? Stop eating?"

Silence.

"Al-Asaadi, if you want me to move, I will try to move to a different office. Then you can do what you want. It is your office, after all."

"No," he says, relenting a little. "It is your office too. I am sorry. I want you to stay here."

"I am sorry too. I really didn't want to get into a huge argument about this, but you have to understand that I really need to get work done!"

I turn back to my computer, and al-Asaadi taps away at his keyboard, for once in total silence.

I finally get caught up on my editing, after skipping both the gym and lunch, enabling us to close by the not unreasonable hour of ten thirty P.M. I'm pretty pleased with the front page, although nervous about what Faris will think, as it is packed with what he is sure to see as negative stories. Headlines include QAT-CHEWING DOOMS YEMENI FOOTBALL TEAM, GUN-TOTING YEMENIS DISCOURAGE INVESTMENT, and ATTACKS ON JOURNALISTS CONTINUE.

I am even more nervous about my editorial, in which I attack President Saleh for not standing up for journalists. He has said nothing to condemn the imprisonment and harassment of journalists, and I think this is disgraceful, particularly given all his big talk about how Yemen is such a swell democracy.

Yet Faris doesn't notice. I start to suspect he doesn't even read the paper unless someone makes a complaint. I never hear a single word from him about anything we publish.

Qasim has begun giving me almost as much trouble as al-Asaadi. Noor comes to me one morning to say that she wants to cover a big concert for her Culture page. This sounds fine to me, so I agree to write her a letter confirming that she is a journalist. Faris is still refusing to give my staff press IDs, which means they are constantly getting thrown out of government buildings and hospitals for lack of credentials. He claims that my reporters must prove themselves trustworthy before they deserve IDs, although I point out that it is nearly impossible for them to do their jobs without identification.

Just after I give Noor permission to go to the concert, Qasim storms my office. "You cannot let Noor cover the concert!"

I am bewildered. "I want this story for the Culture page," I say. "Why shouldn't we cover it?"

"*Arabia Felix* is writing about it."

"*Arabia Felix* is a *magazine* and comes out twice a *year.* It's not exactly a conflict of interest for us both to write about it."

"Well, Noor can't get in. I only have two passes."

"I'll get her press passes then. Who is the press contact?"

"He only speaks Arabic."

"Fine. I'll find someone to call him."

Qasim is beside himself. "No! A professional journalist should cover this concert."

I stare at him. Noor is standing right in front of him.

"Noor *is* a professional journalist," I say coolly. "And I am sending her and Najma to cover the concert. I will buy their tickets with my own money if I have to."

I do have to. Qasim persists in refusing to help the women, so I give Noor and Najma enough cash to cover both their tickets and transportation, along with a letter stating that they work for me. They are delighted, thank me effusively, and write a colorful feature about the event. I wonder sometimes how much more we could get done if men were not constantly trying to stand in our way.

☾⋆

I HAVE BEEN at the paper for three months when the Ministry of Information telephones to ask about my specific role at the paper and for my visa number. Enass comes into my office to take my passport, sending me into a panic.

"Am I going to be thrown out of the country?"

She laughs and shakes her head.

Al-Asaadi says I must write a letter to the ministry saying that my title is merely honorary and that I make no editorial decisions at all. I agree to do this because it is illegal for a foreigner to run a Yemeni paper. But I am suspicious of the ministry's sudden interest. Why now, when I have been on the paper's masthead for three months? Have they just not been paying attention, or has someone tipped them off? I wonder briefly if my editorials criticizing the government are to blame, but they are unsigned.

The letter does the trick, and the ministry backs off. My title, however, has slipped down the masthead and been changed to consulting editor. Al-Asaadi must be thrilled. But it doesn't bother me. As far as I'm concerned, they can call me staff janitor as long as I can do my job.

☪

MY NEXT TACTIC in my campaign to get everyone, including al-Asaadi, meeting deadlines is a written schedule. In late December, I pass this out, along with a style guide I have been compiling since my arrival. We have already begun to close pages on a somewhat regular timeline, but too many of my reporters seem consistently surprised when their deadlines arrive. Now, with a written schedule in front of them, they cannot claim to be ignorant of when their pages are due. I have made a point of making al-Asaadi's pages due before lunch on closing day, given that he can't be trusted to get back to work after lunch. I'm hoping this will help keep things on track when I go off to Cairo for ten days' vacation over New Year's.

On Christmas Eve, I decide to leave work early because it's a holiday for me and I have an out-of-town guest. I edit manically to finish by eight P.M. I've already told al-Asaadi that I won't be coming in on Christmas, which falls on a closing day. For once, I am going to play the Christian card and claim a religious holiday of my own.

But when al-Asaadi shows up in the office close to eight P.M. on Christmas Eve, he tells me that he has decided to finish the paper that night, a day early.

"Why?" I am bewildered. "There's no reason."

"Tomorrow's Christmas!" says al-Asaadi.

I stare at him. "Mohammed. This is a Muslim country. There is no reason not to work on Christmas."

"We're all going to take a day off in solidarity with you."

"Why?" I ask again. "Do you feel like you won't be able to close tomorrow without me?"

He insists and says he will keep Manel with him in the office until the issue is done. This is incredibly unfair to Manel and the rest of my staff, but there is nothing I can do. I can't stay in the office myself when someone has traveled all this way to be with me. Just as I am about to pack up to go, al-Asaadi hands me several stories to edit.

"Al-Asaadi. It is Christmas Eve, and I would like to be able to go home and spend some time with my guest," I say.

"But I need you to edit these before you go."

"Why don't you just save them for tomorrow and have Manel do them?"

"We're closing the issue tonight!"

"Look, I *never* ask for time off. Just this *once,* I want to go home and spend time with someone who is in this country for only ten days and whom I will not see for months."

Al-Asaadi then informs me that not only has he decided to close this issue a day early, but he has decided that we should put out one more issue before Eid al-Adha, which falls just after Christmas this year. We have already decided, *together,* that we would not publish another issue before the holiday. Now everyone will have to work on Tuesday and Wednesday in order to put out that extra issue, when they have counted on having a holiday. What's even worse is that the reason we have to publish this extra issue is that Qasim has already sold advertising for it. Qasim had done the same thing during Eid al-Fitr, and I had made him promise me that he would never again sell advertising for an issue that would have to be put out over a holiday.

Fuming, I quickly edit the stories al-Asaadi has given me and am walking out the door when he says, "So, I'll see you here Tuesday!"

I whirl around. "Mohammed, I told you *a month ago* that I was taking time off this week. We also decided ages ago that this week was a holiday for all of us. So I am not coming in *at all,* except to collect my salary. It is nine P.M. on Christmas Eve, and this is the first that I have heard of this schedule change. If you want to do another issue before Eid, have fun. But I am not going to be here."

And with that, I leave. I cannot believe that al-Asaadi would behave so abominably on what—as far as he knows—is a holy day for me. He has done the barest minimum of work since I got to this country, and now he has the nerve to suggest that I am a slacker for taking time off? I fume all the way home and, despite a pleasant dinner, the Christmas spirit fails to materialize.

I throw a party on Boxing Day for those of my friends who didn't head westward for the holidays. Deputy U.S. Ambassador Nabeel Khoury, who has become a good friend, arrives first, with wine and flowers. Just as we've settled in the *mafraj*, Karim arrives, with several French friends, followed by the ever-charming Manel, a British journalist friend named Ginny, and several others. It's a low-key night, but to me the simple act of drinking wine and eating cheese in a room full of friends feels like an extraordinary luxury.

☪

WHEN I RETURN to Yemen after a brief holiday in Egypt, it doesn't take long for all of the familiar anxieties to catch up with me—as well as some new ones. I arrive home just after the second Eid holiday and Saddam Hussein's execution to find the entire country in mourning. More than half of Yemen's population is Sunni, and they *love* Saddam.

Yemen was one of the few Arab countries that refused to criticize Iraq's invasion of Kuwait in 1990. Every other Gulf state—Saudi Arabia, Bahrain, Qatar, the United Arab Emirates, and Oman—condemned the invasion. Yemen, the PLO, Jordan, and the Maghreb, areas with substantial Palestinian populations, abstained.

I've noticed a few correlations between Saddam and Saleh. Like Saddam, Saleh came from a military background and surrounds himself with a close circle of advisers who are military people. He places his trusted tribal associates in key positions of power, consolidating his control over the security apparatus of the state. In some ways, Saleh's Sanhanis are not unlike Saddam's Tikritis. But the comparison goes only so far. Saleh did not consolidate power by shooting family members who didn't agree with him, try to eradicate entire ethnic groups, or destroy the economy of Yemenis who didn't concur with his political or religious philosophy.

Saleh's support of Saddam during the invasion of Kuwait infuriated Yemen's neighbors. Every Arabian Gulf state expelled the majority of Yemeni expatriates working within their borders. Some two million wage earners were forced to return to Yemen jobless and unable to support their families, which had a hugely damaging effect on the Yemeni economy still felt to this day. It remains difficult for Yemenis to work in the Gulf. Kuwait has never really forgiven Saleh and has obstructed Yemen's attempts to join the Gulf Cooperation Council, the regional economic bloc.

In turn, Saddam expressed his appreciation for Yemen's solidarity by donating large sums of money to the country, both directly to Saleh and to the tribes. Members of Saddam's family have sought refuge in Yemen, which is home to an estimated one hundred thousand Iraqis. Not all of these were Saddam supporters; many came to Yemen to escape repression.

"Everyone in Yemen loves him [Saddam] because the official media told them to love him," a diplomat tells me. "And he was an important source of income to Yemen during a very difficult time."

Yemenis offer slightly different opinions. "He was good for Iraq because Iraqis need someone strong to keep them in line," a Yemeni Arabic teacher tells me. "Otherwise they are wild and difficult people." Posters of the dictator plaster storefronts and houses and the back windows of cars. Arabic newspapers sing his praises. Street vendors sell cigarette lighters that project an image of his face.

In the office, my men walk around with long, sorrowful faces.

"It's best if you don't bring it up," Manel warns me. "They're incredibly sensitive. Everyone here has been crying about him for days." He had made the indelicate suggestion that Saddam was a brutal tyrant responsible for the death of thousands, and was promptly abused. "They think he's a martyr." For once, I keep my mouth shut.

The video of Saddam's execution is disturbingly popular, and I keep catching the men watching it on the screens of their mobile telephones. I refuse to see it. Parents in Yemen apparently think it is appropriate to allow their children to watch such things, and in early January two young boys kill themselves in imitation of their hero. One hangs himself, and the other shoots himself. Their parents are quoted in the press as saying that their boys worshipped Saddam.

Angered, I spit out an editorial condemning the broadcast media for circulating the video and parents for letting children see it. We have just closed the issue when al-Asaadi demands to read my piece. With a sense of foreboding, I hand him the page. His face tightens as he reads. "You have to take out this part about Iraqis killing Saddam," he says. "Iraqis did not kill Saddam. Everyone knows Americans killed him."

He has a point. Americans have their fingerprints all over the execution, but it ultimately was Iraqis who hanged him, something no one in Yemen will admit. It doesn't even register in Yemen that the entire Iraqi population of Detroit danced in the streets at his death.

I am personally opposed to capital punishment, and I think that killing Saddam on the first day of Eid was a *terrible* public relations move. But it frustrates me that Yemenis refuse to acknowledge that Saddam did *anything* bad.

I keep all of this to myself. I tell al-Asaadi that I won't change anything that is factual.

"Your editorial isn't factual."

"It is."

"You need to say Americans killed Saddam."

"I am not going to perpetuate untruths."

"Then I will pull the editorial," he says imperiously, attempting to yank the paper out of my hands.

"You will *not* pull the editorial," I say, hanging on to the paper. "That is not your decision to make."

"Hadi, kill the editorial," he calls to our designer.

"Hadi, do *not* kill that editorial!"

Our reporters have all stopped working and turned around to watch us, their mouths hanging open. Their eyes are frightened, like those of children watching their parents fight. I'm glad the women aren't here to see this. They miss my battles with al-Asaadi because they're nearly always gone before he arrives.

We are both still tugging on the page. "Don't make me behave in a bad way," says al-Asaadi.

"You are responsible for your own behavior. If you behave in a bad way that's *your* decision, not mine," I say, refusing to loosen my grip.

He drops the page.

"You kill that editorial and I am going to Faris."

"Go ahead, call Faris."

I run to my office for my phone. My fingers are shaking as I dial. I have had it with al-Asaadi.

Faris, miraculously, answers his phone. I take the phone out to our courtyard and pour out my frustrations. I tell him about the editorial and about how al-Asaadi has been trying to sabotage every issue. I also remind him that my contract grants me total editorial control.

Faris tells me a story. "Jennifer, you know the tale of the robe?"

"No."

"A man went out shopping one evening, and his wife asked him, while he was out, to please pick up a robe for her. Well, when the man came back later, he had everything else but had forgotten the robe. And the wife was very angry and yelled at him, and they had a huge fight. But the fight was not about the robe; it was about everything else in their relationship. Do you understand me?"

I do.

Faris tells me to e-mail him the editorial. He reads it and rings me back immediately. "You can run this if you want," he says. "It would be best, however, if you run it as an opinion piece instead of an editorial. You see, I am trying to keep people from throwing bombs at the paper."

"This would get bombs thrown at us?" I have failed to consider this.

"It's possible."

"Which part?"

"You cannot say that there is any argument against capital punishment. It is part of Islam."

I am surprised. This is not the part of the editorial that I thought might get us killed.

"Oh," I say. "I hadn't realized."

"Other than that it's fine."

I think for a moment. "I think maybe I won't run it. Or I'll run it as an opinion piece in the next issue."

"It's up to you."

"I actually don't want to get the paper bombed."

Faris says he will sit down with us to talk this out on Saturday.

After I hang up, I tell al-Asaadi what Faris has said, adding, "You want a new editorial, you write it. I'm leaving. I've been here thirteen hours already and you've been here—what? Two?"

"Fine." He is sitting at his desk, waiting for me to leave. He often stays until I am gone so he can change things without me finding out until it's too late.

I pick up my things and go.

On my way out I stop in the newsroom, where only Hadi and Farouq are still working. I tell Hadi what we're doing with the page, thank him for his work, and say good-bye. When I thank Farouq, he says, "It will be okay. These things happen. Just be patient."

"Farouq," I say wearily, "I get tired of being patient."

He smiles at me. "Allah will help you."

"*Shukrahn*, Farouq, I hope so."

The worst thing about arguments with al-Asaadi is that by the end of them I feel as angry and disappointed with myself as I do with him. This is what I vowed I would avoid. The last thing I wanted to do was to come off like a patronizing, domineering, aggressive, culturally insensitive westerner steamrolling the locals. Yet somehow I too often end up in shouting matches with al-Asaadi, Qasim, or the Doctor. Given that *no one* ever shouts at the Doctor, there is great excitement in the office when this happens, and everyone gathers around to watch. I get the feeling that a few of them would cheer were that possible.

But I hate to shout. I've never been a shouter and I've certainly never yelled at anyone at work. I am uncomfortable with the discovery of this angry, frustrated, dictatorial part of me. After battles with al-Asaadi or the others, I am always in tears and full of self-loathing for losing control once again. Then I swear to myself that it won't happen again, that I will reason calmly with my staff and hope that I can cajole them around to my point of view instead.

Thankfully, I rarely have to yell at the women, mostly because they rarely argue with me. When I do raise my voice, I feel particularly awful because they would never do the same to me. This happened with Najma in the early months, and I called her into my office.

"I am sorry," she said as soon as she walked into my office. "I will do better."

"Najma, I am the one who should apologize to you. I should never yell at you; there is no excuse."

"No, you should. We deserve it." Her eyes are dark and earnest.

This breaks my heart. "You do *not* deserve it. No one deserves to be yelled at. I will try not to do it again."

"But you can——"

"I don't want to. I don't like to yell. I should be able to talk with you about work without getting upset. I make mistakes. I am sorry."

On Saturday, Faris finally appears at the office, and we talk about al-Asaadi. He does not seem surprised by his behavior and tells me that al-Asaadi has an ego problem. He wants to be a media superstar without doing any of the actual work. Al-Asaadi has the potential to become a really good reporter, I say, and a better manager. The problem is that he is unwilling to learn or to work within a schedule. Faris agrees that al-Asaadi is a poor manager and is better suited for a glad-handing job in public relations. He promises to have a word with him.

Then he introduces me to an attractive, charming young man named Ali who wants to join our staff. The product of a Yemeni father and American mother, Ali grew up in Oregon and speaks perfect English. I am thrilled to have him and put him straight to work. He immediately earns my undying gratitude by turning my reporters' stories into passable English.

The women are even more thrilled. They turn into adolescents around him, giggling and awkward and shy. When Zuhra comes to fetch her tea from Radia at reception, Radia tells her to go back into the newsroom. "I will bring you the tea," she whispers. "Just so I can come look at him again!"

Even Manel, a fine-looking man himself, is impressed. "He *is* the best-looking Yemeni I have ever seen," he says.

Ali is either unaware of the stir he creates or is simply accustomed to it. He types away at his desk, oblivious to the little black pillars of rayon swooning in his wake.

I'm feeling much more cheerful until Faris rings me again to tell me that al-Asaadi claims he cannot turn in his pages on deadline because he wants the news to be as fresh as possible. My dark mood instantly returns. "Look," I say to Faris, "if he cannot turn in his pages by one P.M., when precisely will he turn them in? The point is that I need him to pick a deadline that he can stick to *every single issue.*"

Faris suggests that I move into my own office. We could transform the conference room, he says. I remind Faris that al-Asaadi is due to leave the country in fourteen days, so it's absurd to move me now. I am thrilled that al-Asaadi has received a fellowship to spend four months studying in the United States, because this means that I might finally be able to do what I want with the paper.

ZAID HAS RETURNED to the paper on holiday from his studies in London. He is full of enthusiasm, and I am grateful to have him. Still, it surprises me to read his stories and to see that his English has not noticeably improved in the four months he spent in England. I hope that this will change in the second semester. In fact, I am counting on it. Now that it is clear that al-Asaadi is uninterested in learning anything new and has no intention of carrying on my reforms when I leave, I have become anxious about finding a successor. I'm determined to create changes that are sustainable.

I figure Zaid is my best bet. He is due to finish his program in London in June, which means I will have at least two months to train him before I leave. When he is back in December, I sit him down and explain that I would like him to succeed me—assuming we can get Faris's support.

It distresses me deeply that I have failed to win al-Asaadi over, even after months of attempting to bond. No one else at the paper is surprised, however. Luke tells me that no other editor has survived even this long trying to power-share with al-Asaadi.

Al-Asaadi has promised me, as a result of his conversation with Faris, that I will have his pages by six thirty P.M. Despite the fact that he himself picked that deadline, he fails to show up at the office until eight P.M. When I open my mouth to remind him of the deadline, he shrugs.

"You only have six more days, *khalas.*"

Six days, two issues, one hundred and forty-four hours. Not that I'm counting.

☾

AL-ASAADI COMES IN the next day around eleven A.M., dressed all in black and looking somber.

"*Kayf halak?*" (How are you?) I ask.

He shakes his head. "*Mish tammam.* Not good at all."

"Are you going to a funeral today?"

He looks surprised. "You knew?"

"You're dressed in mourning."

"Yes, a friend of mine died."

"I'm sorry to hear that."

A little while later I find out a second reason for his distress. "I didn't get my visa," he says. "So I cannot go to the States."

My heart falls straight through the floor.

"*What?*"

No sooner are the words out of his mouth than I am e-mailing my friend Nabeel, the deputy U.S. ambassador. I am desperate. All of my hopes and dreams for this newspaper are at stake. "Please," I beg him. "Is there anyway you can fast-track al-Asaadi's visa? If he doesn't go to the States I will never be able to do anything with this paper."

Nabeel's response is prompt and reassuring. He tells me that he is aware of the delay and says they are waiting for Washington to give al-Asaadi security clearance. "Tell him not to fret," says Nabeel. "We will take care of him (and you)."

A few days later, al-Asaadi is on a plane.

Now, I think, the work can really begin.

THIRTEEN

pillars of rayon

I am impressed that Najma is still with us in January. During my first few months, she often appears in my office panicky and on the verge of tears. She can't finish her story on time, she says. There is no driver to take her where she needs to go. Or she can't find the sources I want her to interview. She becomes so hysterical about these things that it is difficult for me to reassure her that we can find solutions. I keep expecting her to give up, to decide it is simply too much to handle.

But she doesn't. No matter how traumatized she is over a story, she always perseveres. If anything, Najma works too hard. She stays in the office straight through lunch and sometimes into the early evenings, struggling to finish her page.

She has only just finished university and has no journalism experience. She also lacks a sense of what information is critical to a story and what can be left out. Almost everything she turns in is three or four times the length it should be. To be fair, she is not the only one with this problem. My reporters seem to think that it is perfectly reasonable to fill an entire page with one twenty-five-hundred-word story.

"No one reads stories that long," I tell them. "No matter how interesting. You're lucky if people read past the first few paragraphs." I want three or four stories on the Health and Science page instead of one or two.

In my first month, Najma turns in a story on children's health that is thirty-six hundred words long. Two full pages.

"There is a lot of important information in it!" she protests.

"I am sure there is! But people don't need to know *everything*." My reporters themselves would never read a story that long. In fact, they don't read. Almost no one in Yemen reads. Even the most educated people I meet have few books on their shelves. The only book anyone ever seems to pick up is the Qur'an.

Granted, Arabs do have a strong oral tradition, so poetry and other literature have historically been transmitted that way, rather than through written texts. And half of Yemenis are illiterate. Yemenis' resistance to reading may also be due to their experiences in school, which often drain the joy out of books. They are beaten and mocked when they fail and so live in terror of making mistakes. Zuhra tells me how a teacher once used her, when she was just five years old, to punish another little girl. The girl had been unable to read an Arabic word on the board, and the teacher had asked Zuhra to read it, to show the girl how stupid she was. She then forced little Zuhra to write the insult "donkey" on the other girl's forehead. Zuhra was so horrified by this experience that she lived in fear of meeting a similar fate for the rest of her school years.

Yemeni culture overall doesn't encourage reading as a pastime. Leisure time is instead whiled away chewing *qat* and gossiping. The women don't have as much free time for this as the men, given that they are generally kept busy at home with children and cooking—or out herding or farming—while their husbands gad about with friends. Even my women reporters, who still live with their parents and thus have fewer responsibilities, do not read. Their leisure time seems to be chiefly occupied with helping cousins or sisters or friends prepare for weddings.

I remind them that reading is the best thing they can do to improve their language and journalistic skills. "It doesn't matter what you read. Novels, cereal boxes, comics. Find something you enjoy. But *read*."

This learned aversion to education and absence of a culture of reading puts my journalists and the entire Yemeni population at an immense disadvantage when it comes to understanding the world at large and the range of human experience. How can people understand other ways of life and the world beyond their borders without the aid of books and newspapers?

How does one develop compassion for someone with a completely different set of values without reading something from their point of view? Books are one of the few ways in which we can truly get into the heads of people we would never meet in our ordinary lives and travel to countries we would otherwise never visit.

I suppose that the harsh existence of most Yemenis leaves them little time to contemplate other ways of life. Perhaps it is only when our own lives are comfortable that we can afford to look out at the world beyond our personal borders.

☪

GIVEN ALL OF THIS, one would think Najma would understand why our readers would be unlikely to make it through a thirty-six-hundred-word story. I explain to her how to pare down quotes to a sentence or two, eliminate redundancies, and delete irrelevant information. This is a significant problem for all of my reporters, who include paragraph-long quotations in their articles rather than selecting one or two meaningful sentences. They also frequently include information that bewilders them. When I ask questions, they look at me with wide eyes and shrug. My reporters assume that their readers are much, much smarter than they are and will understand things they do not—perhaps because it saves them the effort of figuring things out themselves.

Despite their challenges, it doesn't take long for me to realize that my women are the paper's most reliable strength. While they have no more training than the men—indeed, often less—they have the requisite *will*. They are harder and more persistent workers than the men, and none of them chews *qat* or smokes. They arrive promptly and do not disappear for three or four hours during lunch. They either eat sandwiches in the back room or wait until they finish their work to go home and eat.

The discrepancy between male and female work ethics is not limited to the *Yemen Observer*. Friends who manage oil companies, NGOs, or embassies often rave to me about their female Yemeni employees and decry the sloth of the men. This is partly because the women don't have the same sense of entitlement that the men do; they feel fortunate to have the opportunity to work. It is still unusual for women to work outside of the home in Yemen, and it takes a tough, driven woman to convince her family to allow her to pursue education and seek employment. By the time women get to the workplace, they are already seasoned fighters, whereas men are often handed jobs simply because of family connections.

Najma is lucky; her mother has always encouraged her to do what she wants. "And your father?" I ask. She hasn't mentioned him. She waves a hand dismissively. "He's not like my mother."

But she still has to fight to prove to the men at the office that she is as capable as they are. In fact, she is quickly growing *more* capable, solely as a result of her determination. By late autumn, her Health and Science page is at last improving. One Saturday, she turns in a three-thousand-word breast cancer story. I had told her that the story must be at most a thousand words. "Most readers won't read past five hundred," I say. "Please make this a thousand words and then give it back to me. I want you to make the cuts yourself. And I need you to put the news up front. We are not producing a medical textbook; you can leave out these lengthy and technical medical explanations. What I want to know is, what is happening *in Yemen?* How many *Yemeni* women have breast cancer? And what treatments are available to them *in Yemen?* This is what our readers care about—not women worldwide."

Najma looks at me as though I have just shot her mother.

"Okay," she says bleakly.

"And I want it back before you leave today."

Her eyes widen over her *kheemaar.*

"You can do it," I say.

And she does. It takes her until nearly six P.M., working nonstop, but she does it. When she hands it back to me, it is twelve hundred words long (close enough) and she has reworked the structure and reporting exactly as I asked her to do. How far she has come! And Najma has found some real news, in that Yemen has just acquired its first clinic specializing in the treatment and prevention of breast cancer.

I am so proud of her! I thank her for staying late, and she tells me her mother is very upset with her. "Please tell her it's my fault," I say. "I promise to send you home early tomorrow."

When I arrive the next morning, I make a beeline for her.

"Najma, I was really happy with your rewrite of your story. You did exactly what I wanted you to do. So *shukrahn.*"

Her eyes crinkle with happiness over her veil. That look is enough to make me think, Well, maybe I'll try to survive another month.

☪

I GIVE NAJMA her biggest challenge yet on World AIDS Day, celebrated on December 1, which hands us a news peg for writing an update on the progress of the disease in Yemen. This is Najma's first attempt at tackling this subject, and I am curious to see how she will handle it.

This is how Najma begins her story:

A Muslim scholar has reached a result concluded by thought and study. AIDS is re-garded as one of God's strong soldiers. Any people contradict God's right way are pun-ished by a kind of torture. So AIDS is a torture firstly and violently infects some societies which have declared sexual revolution, allowed man to marry another man, and made the obscene acts as usual things.

It goes on like this for, uh, three thousand words or so and includes all kinds of misinformation, including the fact that Kofi Annan is the "secre-tary general of the United States." I am sure he would be interested to know that.

I don't know whether to laugh or cry. Particularly when I see passages like this:

The first cases infected with AIDS in the world comes as evidence to prove what is told in the *Hadith,* Mohammed's prophetic tradition. The prophet Mohammed has told us . . . the bad results caused by appearing and spreading practicing the adultery in one society. Declaring carelessly practicing such things bring God's torture. God may send the plague disease as a torture on those people or some other strange dis-eases which are not known by their ancestors. So AIDS . . . comes to prove the prophet's speech and as a torture fallen down on the humanity that keeps away from God's right way.

The disease, she also informs us, "is not limited to the sexual odd peo-ple" and will spread more rapidly with the advent of the Internet in Yemen, because education is very dangerous.

I cannot possibly run the story. It's a judgmental rant and contains almost no facts. I am sitting at my desk staring at the piece when Luke walks in.

"What *now?*" he says when he sees my face.

"Believe me, you don't want to know." What would Najma say, I wonder, if she knew that Luke is gay? The cognitive dissonance might just do her in. Everyone loves Luke.

"Let me see the story," he says when I tell him.

I do, and a few minutes later Luke is back in my office, equally appalled. "Okay, I can see why we're not running it."

"On a technical note," I say, "if AIDS is meant to punish homosexuals, why is it that lesbians have the lowest infection rate?"

"God likes lesbians better?"

"Funny, I always picture God as a straight man."

"Straight men *love* lesbians."

"Incidentally, what's the Arabic word for lesbians? For some reason my dictionary doesn't have it."

"There are no lesbians in the Arab world. There are women who have sex with each other, but no lesbians."

The next day, I call Najma into my office and ask her to sit down next to me. I am so nervous that my hands tremble and I hide them in my skirts. It is important to me that I do this right. I do not want to risk offending her religious beliefs or losing my temper. Keeping my voice as calm and steady as possible, I explain to her that the Health and Science page is no place for opinion or judgment. What you have written, I say, is more a sermon than a piece of journalism.

"I have great respect for your beliefs, and naturally you are free to think what you want, but you may not put your personal beliefs in this newspaper. The only place in the paper that should show any evidence of personal beliefs is the Op-Ed page."

She listens and nods, her dark eyes serious. She does not argue or resist what I am telling her.

I go through her entire story, line by line, explaining to her every error. I explain which contentions go against science and which are simply unprovable. Education, I say, is much more likely to *prevent* the spread of AIDS than to increase it. I show her places where she is judging people.

"It is not our role to judge," I say. "It is our job to lay out the facts for people and let them make their own opinions. Let's leave the judgment up to God."

She nods and seems almost ashamed. We talk about the definition of the word "fact." We discuss the importance of studies being conducted by reputable universities and medical research centers, published in reputable journals, and peer reviewed. This is all news to her.

And oh! I can't help myself! I have to know what she will say! I ask her why lesbians so rarely get AIDS if it is meant to punish homosexuals.

This is obviously not a point she has ever considered. "I don't know," she says.

"Maybe something to think about," I say.

While she seems to understand, I won't really know if I have gotten through to her until I see her next story.

Toward the end of our talk, she looks up at me pleadingly. "I worked so hard on this—"

I stop her. "I *know* how hard you work. And I really appreciate that. This isn't at all about how hard you work. This is just part of learning how to do this work better. It's a continual process. We are all constantly learning. But I am well aware of how hard you work."

And we are through. She thanks me and leaves. I feel limp with relief and happy that I have managed to get through the entire conversation without once raising my voice or getting angry. Progress for both of us!

The next time Najma turns in a story on AIDS, it addresses the bias against victims of the disease and the misperceptions about how it is spread. It is full of factual information and accurate statistics and contains no preaching whatsoever. I very nearly kiss her.

☪

A TINY BESPECTACLED WOMAN shows up in my office one morning, unannounced. She wears a *hijab,* but her face is uncovered. This is Adhara. "I want to be a translator," she says.

I sigh. She and half the country. Everyone who speaks even a few words of English thinks they can be a translator, and they all show up at the paper sooner or later.

I politely inform her that we are not hiring translators—though we desperately need them—as Faris won't give me the money to pay one.

"But I need practice," she says. "I will work as a volunteer. My translation is very bad."

Hardly an advertisement for her skills, but I'm impressed with her honesty. Most would-be translators consider themselves quite brilliant, despite the fact that they can't put together a job application that isn't riddled with errors. Still, I worry that shoddy translations will only create more work for me. I send her away.

She is back in my office the next day. "Please," she says. "Let me translate something! I must learn!" She stands stubbornly on my gray carpet, refusing to be dismissed.

I believe in rewarding persistence. I relent and let her translate part of the Q & A for Jabr. She's right; she's not a good translator. But at least I can figure out what she means, and as we are not paying her, I can't complain. I allow her to stay.

When I get to the office the next morning, Adhara is waiting. She comes again the next day and the day after that. Her translation slowly gets better. I assign her the Panorama page, which contains translated editorials from Arabic papers. This used to be al-Matari's responsibility, but he has constantly been out sick. Adhara, on the other hand, never misses a day.

One afternoon, she walks into my office holding a flash drive aloft.

"Zuhra asked me to write a back-page story. She said you needed one," she says. "And I did it!" There is triumph in her voice.

"Fantastic!" I take the disk. I am desperate for a back-page story.

It's a piece about the conflicting views of the Internet in Yemen. It is crudely written, contains no real news, and is mostly made up of huge blocks of quotations with no transitions. But my standards are not what they once were. I decide to run it anyway. Together, Adhara and I rework the structure and impose some segues. She is immensely pleased. She follows this first story with a piece on a new course that trains women to paint on glass and sell their art. It needs massive work, but I sit her down and explain what to do. Now that the paper is on a schedule, I have time for training. It's thrilling to be able to watch and aid Adhara's diligent and measurable progress.

She begins to tail Zuhra, who takes her on reporting expeditions to the Old City and shows her how to conduct interviews. My women welcome little Adhara into their fold, thrilled to see their ranks expand. I tease my men by telling them that soon we will have an all-female staff—this seems to motivate them more than anything else.

By the end of my year, I will have to officially hire Adhara. There is nothing else to do. She won't stop *showing up* and we cannot in good conscience let her keep working for free, I explain to Faris. He finds the money to pay her.

One day Zuhra runs into my office, Adhara on her heels.

"Tell her," says Zuhra.

Adhara shakes her head, turning red.

"*Leysh?* It's okay."

"Please," says Adhara. "*Please,* Zuhra."

"What is it?" I say.

Earlier, I had told Adhara to give her story to Ali to copyedit. It didn't even occur to me that this might be awkward. But the prospect of talking to the handsomest man in the office overwhelmed Adhara, who is painfully shy. It was as if I had asked her to please interview Brad Pitt. Petrified, she had gone to Zuhra for help.

"Ali is very nice," I reassure Adhara. "You don't need to worry."

"I told her!" says Zuhra, who no longer fears men, handsome or otherwise.

Eventually, Adhara and Zuhra together get the story to Ali. And over time, Adhara's fear ebbs. One day, I walk out of my office and look out the front door to see Adhara and Ali sitting on the steps side by side. Ali is smoking a cigarette, and Adhara is talking easily to him. Almost as if he is just another human being. I can't stop smiling at the sight.

☾⋆

LIKE NAJMA AND NOOR, Adhara is fortunate to have parents supportive of her ambitions. But this doesn't mean all three don't face barriers at work. The carefully cultivated modesty of women is at odds with the requirements of their profession. My women are often nervous about approaching men or about being perceived as too aggressive. Najma and Noor deal with this by working as a team. They accompany each other on reporting excursions, write stories for each other's pages, and edit each other's English. Rarely does one leave the office without the other. I'm impressed with their cooperation and the creativity they use to find their way around restrictions. The men could take a lesson.

Radia, whose official title is Faris's personal secretary, has also begun reporting and writing stories. Like Adhara, she doesn't ask me if she can become a reporter. She simply hands me a story one day. She writes in Arabic and gets one of the men or Zuhra to translate. Her reporting is good, though her writing and storytelling are weak. I spend hours with her, helping her find the news angles and fill in reporting gaps. One of her first pieces is a back-page story on the rising price of fabric. It sounds dull until she tells me that these rising prices are hurting brides in particular, many of whom have begun sewing their own dresses and settling for plainer fabrics. We refocus the story on the plight of brides, and it transforms into something eminently printable.

Soon, Radia isn't just writing back-page features. She is covering car accidents, human rights issues, and explosions, turning in several stories for each issue. One day she runs into my office to tell me that she has a good story about a "hot phone." I have no idea what she is talking about. When she can't make me understand, she fetches Enass, who laughs. "She means *hotline*," she says.

Yet she is not a reporter and continues to make the mere $100 a month Faris pays her to be his secretary. She asks Faris for more money, which he denies her, because she is "not a real reporter." Never mind that she writes more stories per issue than any of my men. She accepts this as something she is helpless to change. I've repeatedly tried to get higher pay for my women, but every time Faris just tells me he is paying the fair market wage. My hands are tied.

☪

ZUHRA IS ALSO FLOURISHING, largely because she asks more questions than anyone else and never leaves my side when I am editing her work. One day, Luke comes into my office after editing a raw story of Zuhra's. "I didn't realize how good her English has gotten!" he says. "It's been so long since I saw her raw copy. I'm amazed at how much better her stories are than they were in the fall."

Her stories are so intriguing that it is weeks before I realize how often she is quoting Kamil al-Samawi. It's clear why HOOD is such a crucial source of human rights stories, but Kamil can't be the organization's only lawyer.

"What's the deal with Kamil al-Samawi?" I ask her one day. "You've quoted him in your last three stories."

Zuhra smiles mysteriously. "He's the lawyer on all these cases. I have to quote him!"

"Well, try to figure out what cases the other lawyers are working on and write about them," I say. "You are banned from mentioning Kamil al-Samawi for a month."

☾

DESPITE HER NEAR-CONSTANT PRESENCE in my office, Zuhra is still careful about what she reveals to me about her life. She tells me all about her career ambitions, her mood swings, and her physical ills, but when she falls in love in the middle of my tenure, she holds this secret close to her chest. It will be months before she can confess it all to me. For a Yemeni woman to admit to love before marriage is to risk social ruin. Women are not supposed to have friendly contact with men who are not close relatives, let alone spend enough time with one to fall in love. Very few Yemeni women choose their husbands, and most matches are arranged.

Thus, Zuhra has plenty of reasons to keep quiet. To confess to even one person is to risk exposure and censure. She lives in a conservative neighborhood, where her neighbors gossip, and the women are particularly vicious about each other. "Sex is the most important thing in all of our society," Zuhra tells me with bitterness in her voice. "Even homosexuality isn't as bad as a woman committing sex outside of marriage. A woman isn't just representing herself as a person; she is representing the whole family, the whole tribe. If my sister's reputation is bad, my reputation is bad." When one of Zuhra's sisters broke off an engagement, the whole family suffered the condemnation of their community. Zuhra fears what her family would say if they knew of her secret love. Because her father is dead, Zuhra needs permission from her brothers and uncles in order to marry. Or to travel. Or to do so many things.

(☪

ON MY RECOMMENDATION, Zuhra has applied to the Columbia University Graduate School of Journalism, my alma mater. She is the one person on my staff with what my Columbia professors liked to call the "fire in the belly" necessary to become a brilliant journalist. So I think she would thrive there. I'd especially like her to be admitted because she plans to return to Yemen afterward and eventually launch her own newspaper. Then, in a way, she can carry on my work after I leave. As part of the application process, she is required to take a news-writing test, which I proctor on the last day before the deadline. It must be postmarked that day, but because it's the end of the month, no one has enough money to pay for postage with DHL, one of the only reliable mail services to the United States. I give Zuhra my last YR1,000, which isn't even close to enough. We have to take up an office collection. Manel, Hassan, Jabr, and Jelena all contribute their last *riyals*. We send Hassan off to fax a copy to New York, and Manel runs to DHL to mail it. It's inspiring to see that even the poorest among us empties her pockets.

To my great disappointment, Zuhra's improved English is not quite good enough to get her into Columbia. A professor on the admissions committee calls me personally to tell me that although the committee absolutely loves her application, they have reservations about her English. Zuhra takes the news like someone accustomed to disappointment and vows to try next year.

"We will find another way to get you to the U.S.," I say. "I promise." She needs to perfect her English abroad, as there is little chance of doing so in Yemen. Diligently, Zuhra begins applying for every fellowship abroad she can find. So many, in fact, that if a fellowship were offered for applying for the most fellowships, Zuhra would definitely win it.

It is Zuhra, and the rest of my women, I am most desperate to help. The men will be all right. They will always find work in Yemen; they will always have society's approval. My women I worry about. What will become of them when I am gone?

(☪

ONE DAY, I am editing a health story with Najma when she says, "Jennifer, I need to tell you something."

"Okay," I say, looking up from my computer screen. "What is it?"

"Are you really leaving in September?" She sits on the very edge of her chair, leaning toward me, her dark eyes serious.

"Well, that's my plan."

"Jennifer, this is a very big problem for us. A very big problem. Noor and I were talking. No one else will read our stories so closely; no one else will help us like you do."

"Najma," I say, tears pricking the back of my eyes, "my goal in coming here is not to help you for a year and then abandon you. My goal is to train you, and train a person to take my place, so that you won't need me as much."

I am suddenly panicked about my reporters' future. No matter how good Zaid is—and he has his flaws—he is not a woman, and Najma is right; he won't care as much about their work. This, unfortunately, will be truer than I could ever guess.

The men resent the attention I pay the women. "You like the women better," they say accusingly.

"I like all of you the same," I lie. "But the women happen to always show up for work on time. They don't take cigarette breaks. They don't chew qat. They turn their work in on time. If you want to be treated like the women, try following their example."

This makes them grumpy. They believe it is their God-given right to smoke cigarettes and chew qat! It is their God-given right to take a nap for several hours after lunch! They should be considered better reporters simply because they are men!

One day I am joking around with Bashir, who has written a story about a group that works for women's rights and to preserve culture. "Well, what if the culture they want to preserve doesn't grant women rights; then what?" I tease. "Then they have a conflict. They can either preserve the women's rights or the culture, but not both."

This is said in jest, and he laughs. But then I make a reference to women not being free in Yemen, and he looks shocked and retorts that women are *totally* free in Yemen.

"Women can do whatever they *want* here," he says. "Noor doesn't have to wear her *abaya* if she doesn't want to."

While it may be true that Yemeni women are legally freer than most women in the region—they can drive cars and the dress code is not enforced by law—they can hardly be said to be unfettered.

"Bashir," I say, "do you have any idea what it is like to be a woman here and walk around *without* an *abaya*? She would be harassed constantly. *I* get harassed constantly, even dressed as I am, and it is much worse for Yemeni women."

Zuhra once put it like this: "A woman in Yemen would get harassed even if she were wrapped in an *abaya,* shut in a cardboard box, and on the outside of the box was written 'THIS IS NOT A WOMAN.'"

My dark-skinned foreign friends who could pass for Yemeni get hassled even more on the streets because they appear to be fallen Muslims rather than heretical foreigners. My Dutch-Indonesian friend Jilles had acid thrown at her and was handed a slip of paper with an illustration of how women ought to dress.

When I tell Bashir what kind of harassment women would face on the street here if they went without an *abaya* or *hijab,* Noor turns around in her chair. "It's true," she says.

Thus begins a debate on the status of women in Yemen. Noor claims that Islam does not require the *hijab,* culture does. This is news to Bashir, who argues that the Qur'an orders the *hijab.* The conversation gets heated, with more reporters joining in, but I have so much editing to do that I retreat to my office. When I return to the newsroom a half hour later, they are still locked in combat. I have to break up the discussion three times before they settle down and focus on their stories. "I know this is my fault!" I tell them. "But could you please go back to work?"

They dutifully turn back to their computers. But the second I leave the room, I hear the battle resume.

☪

MY WOMEN ARE TEACHING ME at least as much as I teach them. Radia and Zuhra and occasionally the others take turns helping me with my Arabic, delighted to be able to correct *me* for a change. Every time I get something right, Zuhra claps her hands and says, "You're so smart!" I feel embarrassingly like I am five, learning how to talk all over again.

My Arabic lessons are a source of entertainment for the entire office. On the day I learned negatives—"I am not your mother, you are not a baker, he is not the president"—I rushed into the newsroom to practice on my staff. "I am not bread!" I announced proudly. It was the first word that came to mind. My reporters dissolved into giggles.

But it's not just Arabic they give me. They patiently explain to me bits of Yemeni history and culture, telling me about wedding rituals, Yemeni foods I haven't tried, and tribal honor. They bring in cakes for me to taste, such as *kubana,* a crumbly cornbread. They introduce me to their families at weddings and other celebrations. It's an enormous comfort to have such an enthusiastic pack of guides to help me navigate this multilayered world.

☪

IT TAKES A LONG TIME for me to get to know Najma and Noor more personally. They are both shy and seem to find me intimidating despite my best efforts. My relationship with Zuhra may also be a barrier. She has a sense of ownership of me, and the other women thus defer to her and stay respectfully at a distance. (Whenever someone else makes me tea or helps me with something, Zuhra asks why I didn't let her do it. "It's just, I think of you as *mine,*" she tells me. "You're *my* Jennifer.")

By mid-January, I still haven't seen Najma's or Noor's face, although Radia, Zuhra, and Enass all flip their veils back the second they cross my threshold. It takes another medical emergency for things to change.

It happens like this. One night we close the paper early. Manel and I are so pleased with ourselves that we head to his home in Hadda for a celebratory drink. Alex, Manel's roommate, has just returned from England with a bottle of duty-free green-apple vodka. It is sweet and synthetic and awful. But this is Yemen, and you drink what is available.

I hadn't thought I had had that much to drink, but I wake close to dawn feeling intensely nauseated. Thinking perhaps it hadn't been a good idea to skip dinner, I go downstairs and eat a yogurt. Then I remember that I have little green pills from an earlier Yemeni illness. They had worked wonders on nausea! I rummage through my drawers, find the green pills, and take two.

Half an hour later I wake again feeling worse. I take two more pills and crawl downstairs to make coffee. But I am too sick to drink it. When Aisha arrives to clean my house, she finds me sitting at my kitchen table, staring mournfully at my full cup. "Hospital?" she says, looking concerned. I shake my head. I'm just hungover, I think. I will get better. Going to the pool will probably help. I take two Advil and two more green pills and go for a swim.

My first flip-turn nearly makes me vomit, and I wonder if I will have to get out. But lap by lap I begin to feel better. After forty-five minutes, I climb out, shivering, and head to the sauna to warm up. But I can't seem to sweat; I just dry out and my fingers, oddly, stay cold.

The nausea worsens. I take two more green pills. After all, if I remember correctly, they can be taken every hour. I manage to keep from vomiting in the taxi and go home to collapse on my bed. I can't eat. I can't even get down water. I am exhausted but too ill to sleep. Zuhra calls me to find out why I'm not at work. She is worried.

"You should not be alone," she says. "You need a hospital."

"I'll be okay. I just need to rest."

I am still trying to sleep a half hour later when Noor rings me. "We are at your door," she says. "We have come to take you to the hospital."

Given my experiences with Yemeni hospitals, I'm not sure I want to go. But perhaps the doctors could give me some antinausea drugs, which might allow me to finally sleep.

I find Noor and Najma waiting at the bottom of my stairs. After removing their shoes, they stand to pull back their veils.

"This is the first time you have seen our faces," says Noor.

"Yes!" I stare from one to the other. Noor is much as I imagined her, very pretty, though with a rounder face and smaller chin than I had expected. Najma is also pretty, with a sparkly smile, despite crooked bottom teeth that bend inward.

"It is very sweet of you to come," I say. It is difficult for me to speak through the nausea.

They've been looking around my house curiously. "You don't live here *alone,* do you?" says Noor.

190

I nod. "Yes. It's just me."

They look at each other and then back at me.

"That is *terrible,*" says Najma. "You have no one?"

"We don't think you should be here alone," says Noor. "Not when you are sick."

"I'm okay."

They look deeply skeptical.

Outside, Salem is waiting in the van. I dread the ride, nauseated as I am, but Salem is as good a driver as there is in Sana'a. We head for the Yemeni-German Hospital, because it is the closest. This is the same hospital where I had the incompetent X-rays, but I don't know where else to go.

Najma and Noor tell the clerk at the front desk what kind of doctor I want, and he gives me a file. I pay him several thousand *riyals* and take the file to a main waiting room.

Several doors open off of the main waiting room, each for a different specialist. We wait for at least a half hour to see the internist, sitting mostly in silence, as I am too ill to talk. Men with their arms in casts come out of the orthopedist's office. Old women in *setarrhs,* traditional Sana'ani dresses of red and blue cloth, limp from the internist's office. Men sitting next to me cough and spit. I begin to wish I hadn't come, feeling that I am more likely to pick up an illness here than to cure one.

Finally, we see the doctor. He speaks English, so I tell Najma and Noor they can leave me. I explain to him the problem and say I hope he can give me something to ease the nausea. Then I show him the packet of little green pills I have been taking.

He pales. "Stop taking these immediately," he says. "These are for pain! Not for nausea."

I immediately realize my mistake. I have been taking the prescription painkillers I was given for my ribs, which are to be taken once every twenty-four hours, rather than the nausea pills, which are to be taken two every hour. Frantically, I try to remember how many I have taken. Six. Maybe eight. Will I be okay? Oh god, and I took two Advils!

The doctor assures me I will live, though I probably won't feel much better for twenty-four hours. I don't think I can survive feeling like this for that long and am grateful when he writes me a prescription for anti-nausea medication.

At the pharmacy, though, I am given an enormous bag of liquid, a needle, and a packet of powders. "To inject," he says. I stare at him in horror. He actually seems to expect me to mix up the powders with the liquid and inject the solution into myself. After what I have seen of the hygiene of Yemeni hospitals, I refuse to allow another needle into my arm.

We return to the doctor to argue about this. He says that I need the injection. I reiterate that I don't. Finally, clearly annoyed, he writes me a prescription for antinausea pills, which cost the rest of the *riyals* I have.

At home, I ring a friend in New York, who looks up the specific painkiller on the Internet to double-check whether I will die from the overdose. He also checks to make sure the antinausea medication they gave me is actually antinausea medication. It is, *al-hamdulillah*. But the list of warning signs he reads off to me about the painkiller makes me feel panicky.

"If you throw up something that looks like coffee grounds—"

"I don't have that."

"Or have pain and nausea in your stomach—"

"I have that!"

"Or you lose feeling in one side—"

"Nope."

"Headache—"

"Yes." My head is in searing pain.

He makes me promise that if I feel worse at all I will ring Nabeel and get someone at the embassy to help me.

In my journal, I make a list of lessons learned:

1. Never, ever, drink vodka selected by a twenty-four-year-old.
2. Never drink flavored alcohol, particularly green apple.
3. Never let a British person refill your glass while you aren't watching.
4. When you wake up nauseated three hours before your alarm, do not take little green pills for nausea without reading the packaging.
5. When you continue to feel nauseated, do not continue to take little green pills without reading the packaging.
6. When you purchase little green pills, try to make sure the packaging insert is in English.
7. Remember that lots of different kinds of drugs come in little green pills.

Seeing me weak and helpless has made me less imposing to Noor and Najma. They invite me to their relatives' weddings and talk to me about things outside of work. My illness has humanized me.

In February, Noor invites me to my first Yemeni wedding. She ducks into my office one day, aflutter with excitement, and shyly presents me with a beribboned card. I'm flattered to be asked and dying of curiosity about the ritual.

I have no idea what to wear. Everyone has told me that Yemeni women wear scandalously little to weddings, where there are no men to ogle them. All weddings are sex segregated. While the bride and groom do meet earlier in the day (or even earlier in the month) to sign the marriage contract, it astonishes me that the celebration of their union does not involve any actual union.

The men have big lunches followed by long *qat* chews, with music and maybe dancing, whereas women gather in wedding halls to sip tea, dance, and admire each other's outfits. Some more modern families allow the groom to pick the bride up at the end of the wedding, when almost all of the guests are gone, but this is not common.

While I've been told that it doesn't matter how much flesh I show at a wedding, I cannot bring myself to dress provocatively in this environment. I settle on a knee-length, blue silk dress with a fitted waist and spaghetti straps and wrap myself up in an *abaya*.

In the corridors of the wedding hall, swarms of women are shedding *abayas* to reveal spangled, candy-colored dresses and heavily made-up faces. The dresses resemble the most shameless of prom gowns or things a stripper might wear for the first thirty seconds of her act. There are women in see-through lace, women in black rubber miniskirts, women with trains ten feet long. It is impossible to overdress (or underdress) for a Yemeni wedding. Yards and yards of black hair, painstakingly straightened or curled, are sprayed into sticky towers or hang loose down girlish backs, a few strands tucked into a glittering butterfly barrette. In Yemen, my waist-length hair is merely average. The women's faces are painted with thick black eyeliner and colorful eye shadow, regardless of age. It looks as though they are all wearing masks by the same designer.

The married women wear small, round decorative caps and sit on cushions around the edge of the room, smoking *shisha* and chewing *qat*.

Feeling conspicuously modest and plain in my simple dress and bare face (save for lipstick), I wander down an aisle searching for familiar faces. Zuhra finds me first. She is encased in floor-length pink polyester with a sequined camisole top. Her thick black hair hangs in loose curls to her waist, and she wears tiny pink feathers as earrings. She looks *gorgeous*. She twirls in front of me, smiling, showing off a little. "Come," she says, taking my arm and leading me to a table near the front.

We sit and talk while Somali women circle the room with trays of milky sweet tea. Clad in a short, spangled dress, Noor hurries to greet me and introduce me to a dozen other cousins. Her mother comes over to introduce herself. "You are all Noor talks about," she says. "It's Jennifer *tammam,* Jennifer *tammam!*" ("Jennifer good!") I am enormously grateful. I had never been sure what Noor thinks of me.

Then the dancing begins. The whole outing is totally worth it just to see little Zuhra dance. One of the first to take the stage, she lifts her thin arms, gray from lack of sun, her hair swirling about her waist, lips curved into a sly smile, eyes downcast, hips a-shimmy. No Western woman in a disco could be more sultry a temptress than this candied mermaid, Zuhra, brushing back long strands of hair from her dark eyes and laughing.

Soon a flock of women converge upon the dance floor, a field of undulating butterflies. No two are wearing the same color. One fat woman has even squeezed herself into something that looks like a Hefty bag or an S and M outfit. Women form a circle on the stage, taking turns dancing in the middle to whoops of appreciation.

The dance is mostly in the hips. The upper body is still, arms carving slow arcs through the air. But what surprises me more than anything is the slackness and abundance of flesh. I had thought Yemeni women were all tiny, thin little things, but the fifteen hundred women on display are anything but. Their flesh is loose from lack of exercise, their backs utterly without tone, their arms jiggling when they wave. The physical consequences of their confinement. Their skin is mottled and pale, the result of being denied even a glimpse of sunlight through their *abayas*. When Zuhra returns, I look at my arm next to hers on the table and notice mine is browner.

When the bride finally arrives, she proceeds slowly down the raised stage running through the center of the room. Cameras flash and a black rayon wave ripples across the room as the women cover themselves with scarves to keep from getting caught on film. Only professionals take photographs; the rest of us had to leave our cameras at the door.

The bride is petite and dressed in a mass of Princess Diana–style white satin. I suspect her face is pretty, but it is obscured by thick layers of foundation, blush, eyeliner, and lipstick. I try to guess how she feels about her impending wedding night from her smile. It looks forced; she is posing for the cameras. But she doesn't look unhappy. She gazes down at the crowd with a sort of haughty triumph, as if lording her union over the poor, unfortunate spinsters around her.

"Tell me she is marrying someone nice," I whisper to Noor.

She nods. "She is," she assures me.

While I am pleased finally to experience a Yemeni wedding, the festivities ultimately make me restless. The music is so loud that we cannot talk, we can only dance or watch. After a while, women perch on the edge of the stage, dangling their feet and looking suffused with ennui.

So as soon as the bride is safely down the aisle and surrounded by women ululating and cheering her, I slip out with Zuhra. There is not much left of the ceremony, Zuhra tells me. The bride will hold court for a while and dance with the women. Eventually, she will either meet her groom at their new home later that night or return to her home and wait to meet him the next morning, when they are both fresh.

In the hallway, we pull on our long robes before heading out into the night. The streets are full of loitering men waiting for their painted women to emerge, once more swathed in anonymous black.

FOURTEEN

tropical depression

One day, the usually gentlemanly al-Matari marches into my office midmorn-
ing and announces, without preamble, "Then I will quit!"

"What?" I say, looking up from my computer.

"They have not given me my whole pay, so I will quit."

"Why didn't they give you your whole pay?"

"I don't know."

I march upstairs to the accountant's office with him. It turns out that
al-Matari has forgotten that he recently borrowed money from work to
buy a blender. Once he realizes where the money has gone, al-Matari tells
me everything is okay and goes back to work. I hope it's a good blender.

Then when the accountants dole out my own February salary, they give
me only $50. "That's all we have now," they say. *Right.* Still, this is plenty
for the moment, and it is more important that the rest of my staff gets
paid, which they haven't been this month. It's several days after payday,
and they lack the various safety nets I have in times of crisis, like credit
cards (which exist in Yemen but are not widely used).

My reporters don't just live month-to-month, they live in the future.
They spend every paycheck before it arrives, so delays are always harrow-
ing. A week before the end of the month, everyone starts coming to me to
borrow money for dinner or *qat* or their aunt's hospital bill, which quickly

drains my own pockets. By the second day of the month, every one of us—myself included—is flat broke.

I've been lending the little I have quite a bit. Now that my debts are paid off and my lifestyle costs very little, I have a few dollars to play with. I've loaned Zuhra $200 this week, though she has already paid me back. And I had to buy Samir dinner last night because he hadn't eaten. This is the first time in my life I have been able to do this, and it makes me happy. In New York, I could never buy anyone dinner.

I ask the Doctor to pay my whole staff, especially Manel, because he is leaving for Senegal, as well as my phone bill. I've made several international calls to report a story for *Arabia Felix,* and my phone bill is an unprecedented YR30,000 ($150). The Doctor refuses.

"But I only use this phone for work," I say. "I made those long-distance calls for *Arabia Felix,* which didn't pay me a single *riyal* for that feature story. If I have to fork out for the reporting that I did, you are essentially asking me to *pay* for the privilege of writing for *Arabia Felix.*"

The Doctor is unpersuadable. He tells me that the paper hasn't been making money (of course it hasn't—it hasn't turned a profit since it launched, according to Faris) and thus there is no money to pay my staff. Manel will have to wait for his salary. Which is a whopping $300.

"Manel is leaving the country *tomorrow,*" I say. "You will pay him *today!*"

The Doctor tells me that I should stay out of financial matters, because they are none of my business.

"When my staff threatens to quit because they have not been paid, it *is* my business," I say. "I do not expect anyone to work for free."

Desperate to get Manel paid before he gets on a plane, I finally ring Faris.

Within minutes, he e-mails me back with one word: "Done." Which is generally what he says when I ask him for something he thinks is reasonable. Sometimes this means he will immediately do what I want, and sometimes it doesn't. Sometimes it means he just wants me to shut up.

But ten minutes later, Mas comes in to tell me my phone bill has been settled. An hour later, Manel has been paid. I guess the Doctor found some money. Now all I have to worry about is editing a paper.

I AM WEARY. I'm still not sleeping enough, and I wish that getting even basic things done around the paper didn't require a full-scale battle. I'm also lonely. I'm without a roommate again and my nonstop schedule hasn't allowed many social excursions. So when the cowboy Marvin (who had first stopped by my office months ago and has since become a friend) and his wife, Pearl, invite me to join them for a week in Soqotra later in the month, I accept immediately. It will still be work; Marvin wants me to write about his livestock program, and I imagine Soqotra will have other stories to offer. But I will get a break from Sana'a.

"Just make sure you arrange for everything to run smoothly while you are gone," Faris says. Right. Like that has *ever* happened.

Jabr and Bashir try to hug me good-bye, but I won't let them. *"Why?"* they complain.

"Because you're Yemeni. And it's not the sort of thing Yemenis ought to do."

Really, it's that Yemeni men interpret casual physical contact much differently than Western men do. Western men don't think twice about being embraced by a woman, but a Yemeni man might immediately assume my morals were coming loose and that he could take advantage of this. I also refuse to hug my male reporters because I am scrupulous about leaving no room for misinterpretation of my relationship with them. Nothing is more important to me than maintaining this boundary and being taken seriously as a boss and a woman. I cannot bear the thought of them thinking of me sexually.

It already makes me uncomfortable that Jabr constantly proposes articles related to sex. He writes me reports on the increasing use of Viagra and other sexual stimulants, the rising popularity of pornography, the sexual side effects of Red Bull, and how young men and women are beginning to hook up via Bluetooth technology, which leads to all sorts of *haram* behavior. Though the tone of these articles is always condemning, a little too much glee goes into the writing of them.

When I hug Luke good-bye, the Yemeni men protest the inequity. "He's Californian!" I say. "It's an essential part of his culture."

☾

I HAVE A FIT of anxiety about leaving the paper and fuss at Luke and Zuhra, leaving them lists and making sure they know which pages are due when.

"Just go," says Luke. "We'll be fine."

"Okay. Just remember the Health page should be done the first day of the cycle. And try to keep on schedule." I pick up my suitcase. "Oh! I feel like a mother leaving her child with a babysitter for the first time."

"*Yalla,*" says Luke. "We'll try to keep the kid alive."

☪

MARVIN, PEARL, AND I catch the Yemenia flight to Soqotra, leaving in the middle of the night. None of us sleeps on the plane. Despite my exhaustion and anxiety over abandoning the office for a week, I am excited. I remember my neighbor Mohammed telling me that people who haven't seen Soqotra have only lived half a life. Yemenis speak rapturously about the tropical desert island, as one might speak of paradise. Even those who have never been there extol its charms. I prepare myself to enter a fairy-tale world.

We arrive at eight a.m. and emerge into oppressive heat—the kind difficult to imagine until it flattens you. The Soqotra "international airport" is one tiny building, thronged with people. Herds of foreigners from our plane mingle with crowds of Soqotri people hoping to get some work. The first thing I notice about Soqotris is their teeth. On the mainland, I am constantly confronted with rotting brown teeth. But Soqotris must not chew as much *qat* or smoke as much tobacco. Or perhaps they have been blessed with good genes. Their teeth are beautiful and white, dramatically so against their dark skin. A mix of Asian and African, Soqotris have very black skin and sculpted faces. I find them *gorgeous.*

Pearl and I go outside to find Rasheed, a Soqotri man who works with them and drives their company car, a monstrous white SUV. Rasheed is slim and handsome, with sparkling black eyes and a rascal's smile. With all the windows open, we cruise along a coast so spectacular I almost forget the heat. The ocean glitters in the morning sun to our left, and mountains rise precipitously to our right. The lower slopes are peppered with fat, fleshy trees topped with pink flowers—the Soqotri desert rose. The coastline scallops in and out, creating pretty little lagoons. It only takes about fifteen minutes to reach the wee village—excuse me, the hopping capital city—of Hadibo. At first I don't recognize it as even a town. It looks more like the ruins of something. Low stone walls, which apparently are buildings, crawl across the dust everywhere. At least, they're buildings according to the Soqotri definition of the word, which doesn't necessarily include a roof. This is the most populous area of the eighty-mile island. No exact census exists, but the population is estimated to be between forty thousand and a hundred thousand.

As we rumble down what passes for the main street, Pearl points out the Soqotra Women's Development Association, which sells local handicrafts and offers opportunities for female tourists to meet with local Soqotri women; the Soqotri honey store, run by a French man and Lebanese woman who have been training the Soqotris to manage hives; a tiny grocery store selling soft drinks, tinned beans, and candy; and plain, boxy hotels without signs.

On the other side of town (the foreigners' area, the Soqotri version of Hadda), we come to the house Pearl and Marvin rent from Rasheed. A metal door painted with red and blue diamonds opens into a pebbled courtyard. On our left is a raised, tiled area about the size of a large room, with only three walls. Just past that is an enclosed room. Across the courtyard is a kitchen containing only a sink, and opposite is a small, pink-tiled Yemeni bathroom with a squat toilet and a cold-water shower. (Cold being relative; the water in Soqotra is never less than warm.)

Pearl and Marvin insist I take the one closed room and string up their mosquito net on the tiles. I drag my things into my room and cover the tiny, thin mattress with my sheet. The small bed, adrift in a desert of linoleum, depresses me, making me feel acutely single. I lie down for a nap. It is stifling, nearly too hot to sleep, but I manage to slip into a tropical torpor for a bit before waking around noon. We all take quick showers to cool off and walk into town for lunch. It's so hot I have trouble making my legs move. The dusty main street is deserted. It feels like the American Wild West at high noon.

We find a restaurant at the other end of town. Lunch is cold slices of fish, rice, and tea. This is all there ever will be for lunch on Soqotra, unless you want meat, rice, and tea. There is almost no agriculture on the island, so fruits and vegetables don't appear in restaurants. But as it is my first meal, I enjoy it. We sit and talk and swelter. Marvin tells me more about the livestock project.

After lunch, we walk (slowly, as the sun is still burning down) to the small *souq,* where we peer into the shops. Goats are everywhere. They are not happy or healthy goats. Their fur is matted, their bellies bloated, and their tails coated with excrement. In the *souq,* several are tied under tables, ready for slaughter. In one of the small shops, I buy a light cotton dress for $3; everything I brought feels too warm. I wash it as soon as we get home and hang it on a line in the courtyard. A half hour later, it is dry.

Desperate for a swim, we all pile into the SUV and head to a beach on a protected little peninsula with two pointed rocks at the end called Di Hamri. A few camping shelters have been set up here, with an open-air shower.

The men wander off, to preserve our modesty, and Pearl and I drop our things on a sheltered stretch of rocky beach. After waiting for the men to disappear from view, I strip to my swimsuit and hurl myself into the water. It's crystal clear. I put my goggles on and am awestruck. Coral mushrooms up from the ocean floor, fanciful kinds of coral I could not have dreamed up—my previous encounters with coral being limited to jewelry shops. There is bloated round coral, branchlike coral, brain-shaped coral, and hundreds of kinds of fish. There are black-and-white-striped fish with yellow tails, black fish, long blue fish, and tiny little fish too small to eat. I have never been scuba diving or snorkeling and have never swum in water so clear. I am deliriously happy. I swim out and out, until men on the shore begin waving their kerchiefs at me to come back. But I can't stop, luxuriating in my newfound floatiness.

The sun begins to set around the corner on the cliffs, and I stay in the water until it dissolves. When I emerge, I feel near-human. On the beach, I shower in a little palm-frond-shaded booth on the rocks and talk to Pearl while I comb out my hair and pin it back up with chopsticks. It seems that last year, a couple of tourists swam out a bit too far and were caught in a riptide. Their bodies washed up the next morning.

"That is why those men were waving you in," she says.

The only thing missing from the afternoon is a stop at a roadside ice cream stand. In this climate, ice cream feels critical. But there is no ice cream on Soqotra. There is hardly any refrigeration, and what little exists is usually on only after dark, when the island's few generators are turned on.

We drive back past tiny villages of stone walls and palm-thatched roofs. Once we've changed, we eat dinner at the same restaurant where we had lunch. None of the restaurants have names; even the Soqotri can't tell you what they're called. They simply say "the restaurant of the Taj Hotel" or "the restaurant across the street from the Taj."

Dinner is *ful* and *fasooleah* with bread, and some sheep for the sheep eaters. Afterward, Pearl and I walk over to the Taj Hotel so she can show me where "all the cool people hang out." Most of the expats and tourists eat at this one restaurant, though all of the restaurants serve exactly the same thing: beans for breakfast, meat and rice for lunch, and beans for dinner. There are no menus.

The next morning, I head out for a walk before the heat becomes insufferable. In my new cotton shift, I trek up into the shrub-covered mountains. From a distance, the area looks bare and unpopulated. But every few minutes, I am surprised to stumble upon a house that blends so closely into the rocks around it that I haven't seen it. Every time I think I am alone, a child bursts from a bush and runs across my path.

I hurry back to shower because I'm going to a workshop conducted by U.S. veterinarians, here to teach Soqotri women how to care for their livestock. When we arrive at the training, held at the small, filthy local hospital, we are quizzed by Jennifer, a testy woman working for the U.S. embassy. She won't let men into the training, because it's full of Soqotri women, but says I may watch if I promise not to be disruptive.

In a small, airless room that reeks of feet, some thirty-five women, all in black *abayas, hijabs,* and *niqabs,* are gathered. A blond U.S. military veterinarian sits at her computer flipping through the slides of her PowerPoint presentation, while a male Soqotri veterinarian reads them out loud. They have been translated into Arabic. Occasionally there are English subtitles, such as "Disease History," "Prophylaxis," "Defecation," "Urination," "Gait," and "Voice."

"The goal is to teach women basic care, not to make them vets," Jennifer says.

I ask why only women are being trained, and Jennifer explains that women do most of the work on the island, particularly the herding. The women come from villages all over the island, handpicked by their local councils for their ability to speak and read Arabic. Soqotris have their own language, the origin of which is still debated. The women are dressed in their fanciest *abayas,* with spangled sleeves and embroidered trim, their feet shod in high heels. It is difficult to imagine an outfit less suited to examining livestock. Their fingers are stained with henna and *nagsh.*

I struggle to breathe in the stale air, and sweat runs down my spine, soaking my cotton dress. The heat and the stench are overwhelming. The women flip through handouts of the presentation, without taking notes, while the Soqotri vet explains how to examine animals for disease.

During breaks, the staff and I race outside for a breath of fresh air, but the Soqotri women do not leave the room. They are encouraged several times to go outside, but evidently neither the heat nor the funk bothers them.

By the end of the second lecture, I am drooping and in need of escape. I sneak out into the relentless midday glare, heading for the Tourist Information Office, as Pearl has suggested it might help me find things to do here.

At the office there are posters on the wall but nothing else, save a few DVDs locked in a display case. I ask the young man there—in Arabic, mime, and English—if he has any brochures. He shakes his head.

"We have no information."

"No information?" I am incredulous.

"Mafeesh." (Nothing.)

Well, if the Tourist Information Office is out of information, I doubt I will find it anywhere else, so I head home.

We lunch at the same little restaurant with the friendly French/ Lebanese beekeepers. We laugh at the décor, as the walls are plastered with photos of luxury travel destinations, mostly featuring pools of deep blue water and palm trees—places landscaped within an inch of their lives that could not possibly be mistaken for wild Soqotra. Rasheed helps me draw up a list of things to do and see. He's far more informative than the Tourist Information Office.

After lunch, he drives me in his pickup truck to Wadi Ayeft while Marvin and Pearl stay behind to work. The *wadi* (valley) is about a forty-minute ride away, and only the first quarter is on pavement. The rest is on rocky trails so bumpy that I get blisters on my back from bouncing against the seat. There is a handle on my side of the car (and no seat belt, natch), so I pull myself forward with that, clinging to the truck for dear life as we bounce our way up mountain trails.

Finally, we abandon the truck and continue on foot into the valley. Cliffs of red rock rise up on either side, and jagged peaks appear before us, including the tallest mountain on the island. We pick our way across rocky ground, Rasheed pointing out frankincense trees and all manner of other exotic and storybook-looking species. He shows me a plant whose pointy spines contain an antibacterial sap, and another with tiny yellow fruits that resemble cherries but taste woody, like mealy apple-apricots. He throws rocks at the tree until the fruits shower down, and we eat them. These are the first fruits I have seen here.

We pass some locals. The *wadi* dwellers herd goats up and down the cliffs, and many, including Rasheed's uncle, live in caves.

I notice that Rasheed greets other men by touching noses with them once or twice and making hand gestures. I ask about this. He tells me that the number of nose touches is important: If Soqotri men have not seen each other in more than a week, they must touch noses three times. "Otherwise, there is trouble." There are variations on the greeting for encounters with people one's own age and with older people.

We continue along a dried-up riverbed for nearly half an hour before it opens into a pristine pool of freshwater, next to a small cascade that stretches across its far end. Tiny red crabs cling to the sides. Rasheed walks a few yards from me, keeping passing men away while I change and slip into the water. It is delicious to paddle around in its silky coolness. When I climb out, Rasheed joins me, and we sit on the rocks at the edge and talk.

There, a rare feeling of relaxation spreads through me. I am cool, I still have energy, and there is nowhere else I need to be. It is a whole, perfect moment and the first glimmer of pure happiness I've felt in weeks.

Rasheed tells me endless stories, first about his deep friendship with the French ambassador. On the ambassador's first trip to Soqotra, Rasheed had welcomed him to Hadibo by joking, "Welcome to Paris."

"Have you ever been to Paris?" the ambassador asked.

"No. Just the Paris of Soqotra."

"Would you like to go?"

"You must be joking."

But the ambassador wasn't. A few weeks later, Rasheed had a visa, plane tickets, and hotel reservations in Paris. He was instructed to leave his Soqotri *mahwaz* behind and dress as Parisians do.

So Rasheed went to Paris. The girl who was to meet him there rang to ask what airport he was coming into. This was his first shock. "There is more than one?" As the girl tried to explain to him how enormous and overwhelming French airports are, Rasheed assured her that he had been to an international airport, as Soqotra had one. We both laugh when he says this.

In Paris, he was immediately confronted with confounding things, such as an escalator, which he had never seen. He told me he had been afraid to step onto it and had called back to the only other Yemeni on the plane to ask him if it was safe to get on.

Then the girl who met him at the airport had kissed him on both cheeks! He was mortified. "This made me very shy," he said. "And she said to me, 'You are in Paris now, you must leave your Soqotri self in Soqotra.'" She made him take her arm (another shock) as they left the airport. He had yet another jolt when they got on an elevator, which he had never seen. "What was that?" he said in alarm when it began to move.

The French girl instructed him how to use silverware. "And then after three days of practicing with silverware, she took me to a Chinese restaurant!"

"And you had to use chopsticks!"

"Yes!"

We collapse in giggles.

Rasheed's stories get more personal as the sun slides down the sky. He is the sole male supporter of fourteen women. His wife and two children are currently in Sana'a. He doesn't sound too fond of his wife. "There are problems," he says. "But my family likes her."

Rasheed has only ever truly loved one woman. They were childhood sweethearts, always competing with each other in school for first place in their class—so fiercely that she once stole his books right before an exam to try to keep him from studying. Before unification with the more conservative North, boys and girls went to school together, and girls didn't cover their faces. When Rasheed was later sent to the mainland to study, he mourned this girl. Something was missing from his life, he tells me. He missed her so much he called his mother and said he was coming home. But his mother chastised him, reminding him of the money spent on his education. So he called another relative and came home.

He told the girl that he loved her and wanted to marry her. Neither family was happy. Soqotris are not supposed to choose whom they marry. But the girl said she would wait for him while he studied abroad for three years. He set off once more.

While abroad, he heard that her mother had married her off to a wealthy man from the United Arab Emirates. The girl had refused to marry the man, but her family had forced her. She is now living in the Emirates and has children, but it is obvious that Rasheed still loves her.

"I will not make trouble for her life," he says. "But I hate people from Emirates now."

I murmur sympathetic things and try to distract him from his evident sadness by asking him to describe local weddings. Soqotri mountain and coastal dwellers have very different ways of celebrating weddings. People on the coast, he says, have music and drums and dancing, because they are more African. But people in the mountains instead have fierce poetry contests, usually among five groups of people, each group reciting a poem. "It's a very *hard* competition," says Rasheed. "Until around four in the morning. They argue by poetry, one guy saying something like 'You don't have enough *qat,*' or 'You are not serving enough meat at your wedding.'"

Mountain weddings also apparently involve jumping contests, during which men leap up and down while the crowd makes "jumping noises" to accompany them.

The sun turns the cliffs above us red and darkens the palm trees around the pool of water into silhouettes. We continue to sit by the pool until the rocks become too sharp against our bottoms, and we have just a half hour of daylight left to get back.

Something about the air of camping and summer vacations and days at the beach here makes me feel nostalgic and melancholy. I find myself dwelling on happy summers of my past, appreciating them anew. In the car on the way home, Rasheed and I both fall silent as we watch the sky darken.

"I like this time of night," I say.

"It is the time when each person is alone with his thoughts, thinking about things," he answers. Exactly so. Our silence is companionable after our long afternoon of talking. I drift off into memories of other vacations in wild lands—happy times bicycling through the mountains, climbing peaks, rock climbing, running through rain, eating meals of fresh corn and blackberry pie, drinking by campfires, and basking in warm companionship.

I don't think I took these things for granted then, but they are even more precious to me now. Here on Soqotra, away from the distractions of work, my solitude feels acute. I feel a sudden longing for a lover, someone with whom I could share this. It occurs to me that this is the longest time I have been alone since I was a teenager; I have always been romantically involved with someone. I want to climb a mountain again with someone I adore, pick blueberries, tell each other stories as we clamber our way through rocks and trees before sunset. Though I have long avoided lifetime commitment, I now think that maybe it would be nice to stay with someone for a while. A long while.

Chances are I won't find this person in Yemen. Not with my work schedule and the dearth of romantic prospects. I resign myself to months more of solitary nights and wonder if it would help if I made some more friends.

I'm jolted out of my reverie as Rasheed pulls the truck up by our house. He smiles at me. "I'll come find you tomorrow."

☾

FOR THE REST OF MY WEEK on Soqotra, I rise at five A.M., when the rooster goes off. This is the only time the heat is bearable. Still, when I climb the hills near town, there is no cover, no shade, no relief from the sun. When I return from a two-hour walk my second or third morning, I am dizzy and on the verge of vomiting. Pearl is anxious that I have sunstroke. I strip and get into the shower. I soak my hair in the hopes that it will keep me cool.

Pearl disappears and comes back with a straw hat for me. "Are you going to make it?" she asks. "There's a plane out on Monday."

I am appalled that my discomfort is so apparent.

"I'll be okay," I reassure Pearl. I'm determined to stick this out.

In the late afternoon, Rasheed comes to fetch me for another adventure. Our second trip is to Diksam, a cooler, mountainous region in the center of the island. The mountains are barer than I had expected, save for the fantastical dragon's blood trees, which look like giant stalks of broccoli standing on end. Rasheed shows me the red resin in the trunk that Soqotri women use for makeup.

On our way up into the mountains, we pick up several men, including one of his uncles. There are always men on the road needing a ride, and Rasheed always picks them up. They stand in the back of the truck or crouch low. Occasionally, one shouts at Rasheed to slow down. Because Soqotra has had a road for only a few years, every driver on the island is a novice.

When we reach the top of one mountain, we pull over next to two tiny stone huts, to have tea at Rasheed's uncle's home. The inside of the house is cool and welcoming. We sit on the floor, which is covered with thin woven mats and uncluttered by any furnishings. A woman brings us sweet tea made with goat milk and fresh flatbread that we dip into our mugs. Children, dirty and half-dressed, with enormous brown eyes, gather around me to stare.

The women question me, wanting to know (of course) if I am married and have children. In my lonely, travel-weary state, it makes me sadder to have to lie about having a husband and to tell the truth about the absence of a child. A young woman, in her early twenties and newly married, is the most interested in me and aggressive in her questioning. She wants me to stay the night. But we peel ourselves away close to sunset and drive home mostly in silence, picking up men along the way.

☪

I LOOK FORWARD MOST to my afternoons with Rasheed. It is fun to travel with him, to listen to his stories and not have to talk. The next afternoon, he drives me to a protected lagoon near Qalansiyah. It takes an hour or so to get there. As we approach the rocky cliffs above the sea, he slows down and tells me to close my eyes. The truck lurches forward.

"Now open."

Framed between two walls of rock is a vast expanse of pristine white sand and a lagoon of clear, aquamarine water, sparkling in the sun.

"*Jamil*," I say. *Beautiful*.

Our last and best adventure is the Hoq cave. I've been dying to see it, but Rasheed initially resists, saying that it is too late to set out. "It's an hour-and-a-half hike," he says. "To tell you the truth, I am feeling lazy about hiking."

Well, I am not feeling lazy about hiking, so I put my foot down. We drive along the northeastern shore until we come to the fishing village closest to the cave. Soqotri law holds that cave visitors must take a guide, so that locals benefit from the tourism. We pick up a man who says he is afraid to go into the cave himself, but he can show us the way. He doesn't have a flashlight but assures us that a group has gone up before us and that they will have one.

The three of us set off up the mountain. It is a steep, difficult climb, and our guide sets a breakneck pace, which is all the more impressive given that he does it in purple plastic flip-flops. Still, I manage to keep up. I am happy to be getting some real exercise. I even have to prod Rasheed along at one point. "I'm stepping on your heels," I tease him. "Pick up the pace."

We make our way past dozens of the pulpy fat-trunked desert rose trees. They are so adorable that every time we pass a good one, I cry aloud, "Fat tree!" and throw my arms around it. Rasheed finds this so entertaining he begins pointing them out. "There's one over there," he says. "Hug that one too!"

Our guide becomes noticeably nervous as we near the top and falls behind. You can't see the black maw of the cave until you are right upon it. Then it opens before you, a wide dark gash in the mountain's side. I pause, panting, and turn to look down at the sea below. The mountainside falls away dramatically, and the sky is just turning pink over the water. Rasheed catches up with me and we stand gazing down.

"I'll wait outside," the guide says in Soqotri. "There are *jinn*."

Jinn are mentioned in the Qur'an. As my friend and Arabic teacher Hamoudi explains: "Before the God made humans, he had only angels and *jinn*. Iblees was the king of the *jinn*, who were all made of fire. God made the *jinn* of fire and the angels of light. The God then said, 'I will make a human, Adam, from mud, and everyone should pray to him, just once.'

"Iblees, the king *jinni*, was the first person to say no to the God. He said, 'No, I will not worship humans, because they are mud and we are fire. We are better!'

"God said, 'Go away.'

"The *jinn* said to God, 'Then we will make humans do bad things.' . . . God said, 'Go, and try to make humans do bad things. But if they do, you and they will both be in hell.'"

Muslims believe the *jinn* can enter a person's blood and force him to commit terrible crimes. A human can either follow the *jinn* to hell or choose a higher path. A human possessed by a *jinni* often requires an exorcism, which involves an imam reading the Qur'an over the afflicted.

Not all *jinn* are evil, however. There are Muslim *jinn*, who have been convinced of the righteous way. But these are apparently not what our guide is worried about encountering in the cave.

There is no sign of any other tourists, and we have no flashlight. I fish around in my purse and find a lighter with a tiny bulb at the end. Rasheed and I step into the cave.

"Here, *jinni jinni!*" he calls, to torment the guide.

We pick our way across the uneven rock floor, skirting pools of water. "Look up," says Rasheed.

Stalagmites of astonishing length hang everywhere, like Stone Age chandeliers. A thousand dripping daggers of stone hang over my head. I've never seen anything like them. Around us crowd accidental statues and gargoyles in a Gothic sculpture garden. Pools of water form in bizarrely symmetrical basins. Cathedral ceilings stretch away into blackness. It is the Notre Dame of caves. It catches up all of my breath. Silently, Rasheed and I pick our way as deep into the cave as is possible with our tiny light.

When I stop again to gaze up at the magnificent stalagmites, Rasheed whispers, "Turn out the light."

We stand in the total darkness, listening to the drip of the water and the silence in between and our breathing and the rustle of—bats?

I want to go all the way to the back of the cave, but we do not have enough light or time. It is nearly dusk, and we still have a long climb down the mountain. "I promise, the next time you come, we will go to every cave on Soqotra," says Rasheed. "We will do the all-cave tour."

Our guide is pacing anxiously outside. We join him and hustle down the path. I take the lead, full of renewed vigor. We race the sun down the mountain and emerge from the scrub at the bottom just as the sky turns deep blue and the first few stars wink on.

After dropping our guide at his village, we stop to visit a friend of Rasheed's mother's. The sky is heavily salted with stars when we arrive at the little stone hut by the sea. A woman comes out to greet us and ushers us into a small courtyard. As we settle ourselves on mats laid on the ground, the family gathers around us, friendly and inquisitive. A pot of a reddish fish stew is set before us, and we dig in. It is delicious, the fish falling apart in our fingers. It must have been caught just hours before. We follow this with fresh flatbread and the usual milky sweet tea. Afterward, I am offered a bowl of sour milk. I expect it to resemble yogurt, but it tastes like rotten milk. I gag and pass it to Rasheed. I politely decline the dates fermented in goat skin.

As we sit there, eating and talking with the family, a wave of tranquility washes over me. For a moment, I feel a second flash of pure happiness, to be outside on a cool, starry night, with warmhearted friends, and eating simple food. I could sit there for hours.

Travel is always like this, I remind myself. Uneven, with stretches of loneliness and anxiety followed by unparalleled moments of bliss and discovery. In the droughts, I have to learn to trust that the joy will come.

FIFTEEN

the artificial man

Six months into my tenure, the paper is on a regular schedule, I'm sleeping more, and I've started to do some of my own reporting. Most significant is a whirlwind trip to the Kharaz refugee camp, home to some ten thousand refugees, mostly Somali. I go with officials from the United Nations High Commission for Refugees. We fly to Riyan in the South and drive west along the coast to Shabwa and the Maifa'a Reception Center, where the Somalis who wash up on Yemen's shores are processed—if they survive the journey. My cleaning woman Aisha probably landed here.

It's much hotter than in Sana'a, and our driver blasts the air-conditioning. Red cliffs that remind me of the Grand Canyon rise on our right. To our left, the sea is dotted with colorful fishing boats. I'm squished in the backseat next to a Yemeni UNHCR official and Amal, a tiny woman reporter for the *Yemen Times*.

No matter where they come ashore, Somalis either find their way to the Maifa'a Reception Center, or villagers who see the refugees on the beach alert UNHCR, which sends transport, says Aouad Baobaid, a field specialist who travels with us.

"When we can't get to people—we can't find everyone—the villagers take care of them," he says. "They feed them and put them up for the night, women with women, and men with men. They even bury the dead."

There are plenty of dead. In 2006, UNHCR reported that some twenty-seven thousand people made the perilous voyage, with three hundred and thirty dying on the way and another three hundred still missing.

Maifa'a, a cluster of whitewashed cinder-block shelters baking in the southern sun, was established in 1996 to register the refugees. They are asked when they left Somalia, how their journey was, why they fled, and where they arrived. We wander around, asking questions, examining food stores, and interviewing workers. Afterward, we visit several other spots along the coast where refugees often wash ashore.

In the morning, we fly to Aden and drive two and a half hours inland to the camp. Kharaz sprawls on an isolated expanse of steaming-hot desert, many miles from towns, roads, water, and work. It was the only land on offer, say the UNHCR officials leading us around. There are no walls around the vast complex of look-alike cinder-block shelters mingled with a cluster of tents for new arrivals, and refugees come and go as they wish.

Only about 5 percent of refugees stay at the camp. The rest head for urban areas, where they hope to find jobs washing cars, cleaning houses, or doing other sorts of menial labor. The lives of camp refugees consist primarily of waiting—waiting for Somalia to calm down enough so that they can return, waiting for job opportunities, waiting for better food, better shelter, better health care, waiting for something miraculous to lift them out of their misery.

For this reason, any visitor to the camp is instantly surrounded by scores of anxious Somalis who hope that this person is the miracle they have awaited, that help has arrived at last. Many carry handwritten or mimeographed letters that they press into the hands of visitors. Most are addressed to the UNHCR and request all manner of aid.

A woman named Asli Abdullahi Hasson hands me a letter describing the bombing of her home in 1991, the death of her relatives, and her flight from Somalia. On her way to Yemen, men "tried to rape [her] in front of [her] husband," she writes. "He defended me unfortunately he was fired bullets. He was not dead but had a bad wound." She ends her tale with a simple plea. "Please," she writes. "Assist me to look for a better future." There are countless stories like hers, and as many letters.

In February, the air already feels stifling, and my clothing is quickly drenched in sweat. By summer, the heat grows deadly, and many refugees fall ill, says Dr. Fawzia Abdul Naji, the gynecologist/obstetrician in residence at the camp. She is one of three doctors working full-time at Kharaz.

We visit refugees in the cinder-block homes and the cluster of tents. In one of the homemade tents lives Khadija Mohammed Farah, who shares three tiny rooms with six people. Inside, the air reeks of excrement, and flies coat every surface. A woman lies motionless on a thin mattress. "She is very ill," says Khadija. In another room is a rudimentary kitchen with a camp stove and kerosene lamp. Khadija has been at the camp for two years and is still awaiting a more permanent shelter. Her four children cling to her while she complains about the conditions. Twenty-five or so Somalis crowd around us to add their own laments.

"Many journalists come here, and nothing ever changes," cries one.

Khadija says that she wants to return to Somalia, when it is safe. But until then, she feels trapped.

"Look," she says, pulling down the front of her colorful dress. "I was burned horribly."

Her entire chest is a mass of scar tissue, caused when a lamp accidentally ignited a fire in the camp.

A man pushes to the front of a crowd. "Won't you help me!" he cries, pulling down the front of his own shirt to reveal a crater-shaped scar. "Help me, I am all alone with four kids."

The psychological scars many bear from witnessing unthinkable brutality are even worse. Issa Sultan, fifty, originally of Mogadishu, tells me he was forced to flee to Yemen with his wife and three children in 1995 because of the terror of the wars between Somali clans.

I interview scores of Somalis, scribbling furiously in my notebook. Working keeps me from becoming overwhelmed by the sheer misery of the place. I cannot get my mind around desolation on such a mass scale. I will never complain about my life again.

By the end of the day we are exhausted, overheated, emotionally drained. Yet we are lucky. We have the luxury of climbing back into our refrigerated Land Cruiser and driving away. So much of what I see in Yemen is a constant reminder of my good fortune. Every day I witness scenes of poverty and deprivation, yet my American passport allows me to walk away at any time. After living here, I can never again take any of my privileges for granted.

☪

I AM WORKING on the Somali story at my desk in Sana'a the next day when I get a phone call from customs.

"You have a package," the man says.

"Great." I am expecting a box with a replacement battery for my computer, a power cord, chewing gum, and medicine from a friend in New York. It's been taking ages to arrive. But I can't imagine why this man is calling me; usually packages are delivered without preamble. "Well, bring it on over then."

There is a silence on the line. Then, "Ah . . . Well, you see, there's a problem. It contains something offensive to the Muslim faith."

"*What?*" I stop looking at my computer screen and turn my attention to the call. "What is it?"

"Ah . . ." The man clears his throat. "It's . . . It's some sort of . . ." The customs officer stumbles over his words. "It's—an *artificial man!*"

Suddenly I know what it is. A friend in Manhattan has joked about sending me a vibrator to keep me company in this lonely place. Oh dear.

"I'm not sure I know what you are talking about," I say carefully. "Could you describe it to me?"

"It's—!" The man is deeply uncomfortable. "It's—! It's *purple!*"

I suppress a wave of hysterical laughter. "I see." I twist the phone cord around my finger and wonder how much trouble I am in. "A purple artificial man."

"Yes!"

I don't know what I am supposed to say. "Well, I don't think I know what you are talking about," I tell him. "But if it's offensive to you, why don't you just throw it out and bring me the rest of the package?"

"It will be destroyed."

"Great, destroy it! That's fine. But you can bring me the rest of the things, right? All the rest of it is legal? Because I am expecting some very important computer parts and medicine." I am desperate for the rest of that package. My battery has been recalled, and Luke and I have been sharing a power cord for weeks.

"I don't know," says the customs man.

"Look, there is no reason why you can't bring me things it is legal for me to receive. I want the rest of that package, okay?"

The man mumbles something and I hang up. I have a story to write after all, and I am on deadline. I push aside the unsettling conversation and go back to work.

Haleema Mohammed, 45, of Galkayo realized that staying in Somalia was no longer an option one unforgettable night in 1991, when she was forced to watch as her brothers were slaughtered in front of her eyes.

"Forty people were killed that night in Galkayo," she said. "Five were my brothers."

Mohammed, sitting in a tent at the al-Kharaz refugee camp in Yemen's Lahej Governorate, speaks with calm stoicism, her gaze defiant and unwavering. Her eyes, which she says were black in Somalia, are now blue. They were bleached by Yemen's merciless desert sun, she says. . . .

I am deeply engrossed in my writing when Radia comes into my office and hands me a DHL slip. "Where is the package?" I say.

"No package."

"No package?"

"No. At customs."

Now I'm worried. Why would they drop off a package slip but no package? What are the customs agents planning to do with my things? What am I supposed to do?

"Radia," I say, "I have to find that package." I explain to her that something that was in the package offended the customs agents and that I told them to throw out that item and bring me the rest of it. I cannot see why this would be a problem.

"I will send a driver," says Radia. "Salem can get it for you."

But a few minutes later she is back in my office. "The Doctor won't let us have a driver," she says. "He says you should go."

"I can't go! I'm on deadline!" Not only do I have to finish writing my refugee story, I still have to edit the rest of the paper. Work on my story has already slowed me down.

Radia shrugs. "He says you have to go."

The Doctor has been sulky and resentful ever since I forced him to pay my employees, which I must say I don't think was an unreasonable request. "It's a closing day! Tell him that if I have to go to the airport myself, the paper will close four hours later." The Doctor hates it when we close late.

She disappears again.

When she leaves another reporter comes in to tell me that my phone bill is overdue. Sabafon has changed the amount of my bill four times in the past month, by wildly varying amounts. I have no idea how to tell which total is accurate.

I'm stewing over this when a series of reporters come into my office asking for my camera, which we use for almost every story now because the photographers rarely can be bothered to work. But I can't give it to them, because I have two hundred photos of refugees in my camera. I can't download them because my computer has no memory or battery left. "Go tell one of the photographers to do his job," I say crossly.

Zuhra comes into my office, anxious to help, but I am so distraught I am almost inconsolable. "You need someone to do things for you," she says. "Faris should hire someone just for you, so you don't have to cope with all of these things."

I manage a weak smile. "That is unlikely," I say. "I can't even get him to pay for business cards for my staff; forget an extra employee."

Still, I run upstairs to ask Faris for help. I explain to him why I need a driver to go to the airport and fetch this package, which contains computer parts we need for work. The entire paper runs on my computer, after all. I don't mention the vibrator. Faris promptly sends Salem off to the airport.

An hour later, Zuhra comes into my office looking anxious. "Salem is calling from customs. They need to know, the power cord that is in your package, is it a . . . a *sexual* power cord?"

I stare at her. "No," I say. "It is the power cord that goes to this computer." I tap my Apple.

"Oh. Okay." She hurries out of the room.

A few minutes later, she is back. "Um, they have to know, is the battery in the package, is it a *sexual* battery?"

"Zuhra. It's *square*."

She looks at me quizzically.

"I mean, I just can't imagine how it could be used sexually. Look, the battery has a serial number and an Apple logo. They can look it up online if they want. It's a standard Apple battery."

She nods and heads off again but is back a few minutes later.

"Sorry! But they want to know if the chewing gum is *sexual* chewing gum."

I despair. "Zuhra! How on earth could chewing gum be sexual? Are these men completely out of their minds?"

"I don't know!" Zuhra twists her hands together.

She looks extremely distressed to have to ask me these awkward questions. I feel sorry for having put her in this position.

"No," I finally say. "The chewing gum is absolutely not sexual."

I feel compelled to explain to her why the police are asking such interesting questions. Mortified, I say that my friend has included this one verboten item but that the rest of the package was completely innocent.

She listens calmly and goes back to the telephone. Moments later, she returns to tell me that customs has determined that everything in the package is sexual. They will not give it to Salem.

I nearly lose it. "Are these men *stupid*?" I say. "The battery is obviously a computer battery!" I am trembling, despite my dim awareness of the humor of the situation. I cannot believe that the customs officers are about to get away with stealing hundreds of dollars of things from me. No matter how offended they are by the vibrator, there is no reason they cannot deliver my medicine and computer parts.

I start to cry from sheer frustration but quickly dry my eyes when Faris comes in and hesitates in front of my desk. "Jennifer, if you want to receive things like this, you should tell me. I could have had it routed through the embassy. Salem almost got arrested at the airport. I just had to talk to the police to get them to release him."

I want to dissolve into my carpet. I cannot remember ever feeling so completely humiliated.

"I didn't know what he was sending," I say. "All I want is the computer battery and the cord and the medicines that are in that package. I had no idea they would try to arrest Salem. I'm really sorry."

He says he will try to get those things for me but chastises me for not talking to him earlier, so things could be done "a different way."

Now everyone in the entire office knows what was in my package. I am ashamed to face them, but I have no choice but to brazen it out. I go about my work as normally as possible, and no one says a word. I don't even catch anyone smirking. Zuhra comes in my office later that afternoon to tell me that her family supports me. "My sister says it's unfair, that it's personal and what they have done is wrong."

I am embarrassed that she has told her sister but grateful for her compassion. I never would have expected such a response from a conservative Muslim, but my Yemeni reporters are always surprising me.

When I have calmed down a bit, I finish my refugee story. My staff is still being kind, particularly Hadi, who invites me outside to eat with him. He shares his pan of *ful* and his bread. I am not hungry but I eat anyway, thankful for his gesture of friendship.

☾

A WEEK LATER, I go to Faris to ask if he has made any progress in obtaining my package. He avoids looking me in the eyes, fiddling with a pen on his desk.

"You see," he says, "the problem is that customs doesn't have your package anymore."

"It doesn't?"

"No. Ah, security has it."

"Security?"

"Well, apparently your package is now considered a national security threat. And, ah, they are testing the chewing gum."

"They are *testing the chewing gum?* For what?"

"For, you know, Viagra or something. Like a sexual stimulant."

What on earth would I do with a sexual stimulant in this country? I want to say. I am completely alone.

"Faris, it's *Trident*. It's a famous brand. They can look it up on the Web!"

"These are not educated men, Jennifer."

"Apparently not."

"They don't know how to look anything up. They might not be able to read."

I sit in silence for a moment. "I bet they took it all home," I say. "I bet they just want it for themselves."

Faris nods slowly. "They probably do."

We sit in silence. "I guess I wouldn't want it back now anyway then." I look up at him.

He nods gravely. "You probably wouldn't."

SIXTEEN

the power of peanut butter cups

There are moments, even whole days, when everything falls into place. Reporters give me coherent stories, photographs come in on time, and the men actually return from lunch at a decent hour. Progress is irrefutable. But just when I am feeling most hopeful, I run up against obstacles that it is not in my power to remove. I can edit poorly written stories. I can assist shoddy reporting. I can enforce deadlines. But some things, only Faris can remedy.

Staffing is one of these. Every time I feel I have enough reporters, somebody quits. They all leave for the same reasons: They are not paid enough, they receive no health insurance or other benefits, and the administration treats them shabbily.

My reporters are attractive to international employers, who constantly poach them, because they are educated and speak English. When the Red Cross offers Hassan a job with decent pay and benefits, he has no choice but to accept, though he loves being a reporter. He and his Yemeni wife have just had a baby, he's having expensive medical problems, and he's just taken a Canadian second wife. But he also leaves because of the Doctor. For months, the Doctor has been harassing Hassan, withholding his salary until I march into his office to remonstrate. This happens with monotonous regularity. The Doctor claims that Hassan isn't working. I tell the

Doctor that Hassan certainly *is* working, and that if he weren't, I would be the first to know. Hassan has no idea why he is singled out for abuse, and the Doctor gives me no reason other than Hassan's alleged laziness—which is laughable. He is one of my most reliable men.

I am heartbroken to lose Hassan. He is a passionate journalist, dedicated to improvement, and without a disagreeable bone in his body. Unlike the other men, he relishes criticism of his work so he can learn. But Faris refuses to invest in his staff. Every time I tell him how important this is, that without decent reporters the entire enterprise is worthless, he tells me he pays them a livable wage. While it may be true that $200 a month is relative riches in Sana'a, it is obviously not enough to support a family or to keep reporters from looking for other jobs.

"It takes me *months* to train a reporter," I tell him. "When they quit I have to start all over again with someone new. The paper is constantly losing its most valuable people."

Faris shrugs. "So you can feel you are doing some good in the world," he says. "You train them so well they get other jobs and succeed."

I didn't come here to train journalists so that they could leave the profession, I say. "I came here to make this a better paper and to help the staff to become more professional. I cannot do this when everyone keeps quitting."

☪

NOT LONG AFTER HASSAN GOES, Bashir gives notice. For once, his chubby face isn't smiling. His wife is pregnant, and he has been offered a well-paid job with a telecommunications company. I've spent six months training him. Now all of my careful cultivation has been rendered meaningless. Again, Sisyphus springs to mind. I can't help tearing up when he tells me. Bashir is sad too. "I don't want to go," he says. "But I have no choice. I don't make enough here to support a family."

Whenever I tell Faris that low wages and lack of benefits are losing us valuable employees, he reminds me that the paper isn't making money. He seems to think that if only we wrote better stories, we'd all be rich. I remind him that it is not the mission of the editorial staff to make money; it is our mission to create a brilliant product. It is the job of marketing and advertising to *sell* that product. Faris has no idea what marketing means. I try to explain a few of the things that the marketing department of *The Week* did while I was there. It hosted lunches with famous speakers; it held film nights with celebrities; it gave copies of the magazine to colleges and schools. It did demographic surveys and sent direct mail to the likeliest readers. Not all of these are possible in Yemen, but they could be adapted.

Faris is reluctant to take the publisher's responsibility for marketing and advertising problems. After all, he is working full-time for the president. So he wants me to find someone who can market. He's already paying five men to do marketing, he says, but they have no impact. I have no idea where to start. I want to help him, because I want people to read the product I work so hard to edit. But I only stretch so thin. I cannot be both editor and marketer, even if that were ethical.

It's clear that Faris's loyalties are to the regime, not to reporting. And he mistakes public relations for journalism. In that case, why does he even have a paper? He has given me his reasons: to encourage tourism and development by writing about Yemen's attractions. By writing about Yemen in English, he believes he can communicate Yemen's charms to a broad international audience.

But this still fails to explain Faris's lack of interest in quality. Even if he wants the *Yemen Observer* to be no more than a cheerleader for the country, I would expect him to care about how well it is written and reported. I would expect staff retention to *matter*.

Zuhra offers an explanation. "In Yemen there is no such thing as bad paper and good paper. The quality of journalism overall is bad." Because all newspapers in Yemen—both Arabic and English—contain legions of mistakes, expectations are low. Quality doesn't matter. Publishing a paper in English is prestigious enough, she says. Who's going to complain about quality, other than me and a few ambassadors? And why should Faris invest in quality when he can expect such low returns for it?

Owning a paper also gives Faris power, she says. He can protect himself through media, using it to further his own goals. Publishing in English also allows him access to the international community. If the paper lands in trouble with the government, the case gets international attention.

Zuhra respects Faris, who has been generous and kind to her. But she thinks him too pragmatic to produce brilliant journalism. He cares more about selling ads than he does about printing stories that could change the country.

☪

COME APRIL, Faris is chronically absent. Even if he does manage to slip upstairs to his desk while I am in the building, he avoids me. Never once does he poke his head in to see how things are going. Never once does he tell me I am doing a good job. Or a bad job, for that matter. Sometimes I wonder if he remembers I am here.

This is not the relationship I've dreamed of having with my employer. After his effusive warmth during my first trip, I had hoped to be invited to dinner at his home, introduced to important Yemenis, confided in about national affairs. I had imagined us meeting over coffee or lunch to brainstorm new ideas for the paper and to discuss our progress. I had thought he would be someone I could turn to for guidance, or at the very least information about Yemen's inner workings. It would have made all the difference.

These dreams have vaporized. Not only is Faris physically not present most of the time I am in the office, but when we do meet, our conversations average forty-five seconds. I can always sense his impatience to finish with me and get back to his Really Serious Work for the President. Talking with him makes me so anxious that I nearly always decide that several of the urgent matters I needed to discuss with him are not so urgent after all. Maybe Hassan can wait another week to get paid. Maybe I don't need that plane ticket back to New York. Maybe I can do without a copy editor. I begin to come to him with a list. Otherwise, his snapping fingers and persistent "Next?" drive all of my carefully considered concerns from my head.

I'm busy editing one evening in April when Faris is spotted in the office and someone races to tell me. Back when Manel was around, he'd run to my office and say, "Porsche parked outside. World's handsomest Yemeni spotted upstairs. Hurry."

But tonight when I run upstairs to ask him for five minutes—just five minutes!—he tells me he must speak with Jelena of *Arabia Felix* first. He, Jelena, and al-Matari then have a screaming fight in his conference room for an hour. It seems unwise to interrupt. I've finished my work, but I loiter downstairs, waiting for my five minutes.

Because I'm in my office, I don't see Faris slip out the front door. Only when I emerge to ask Enass if he's free yet do I find out he has escaped once again.

In the hope that Yemenis understand Faris better than I do, I consult my reporters. They have no suggestions. To them, Faris is a godlike, mythic presence. Zuhra aside, most would never dare question anything he does. Even al-Asaadi is cowed by him. Ibrahim takes me out to dinner one night, and I spill my woes over fried fish, hummus, and chewy flatbread. He is mystified. "You've done *wonderful* things for the paper," he says as I glumly tear off strips of the bread and stuff them into my mouth. "He should be grateful to you."

"I'm not sure Faris ever *looks* at the paper," I say. "And I definitely haven't sensed any gratitude."

On April 13 (oh, notable day!), for the first time in months, I spy Faris's silver Porsche in the street. I toss my purse and books in my office and take the stairs two at a time. The door to Faris's office is open, and when I peek in I can see him sitting in the yellow light of a lamp, staring meditatively at his computer screen.

"May I come in?"

He nods, without enthusiasm and without looking at me.

"Faris," I say, perching on the edge of a chair opposite his desk, "I have been trying to get in touch with you for weeks. I am very concerned that you are not answering my phone calls or my e-mails. Did you read my e-mail?"

He glances at his screen. "Frankly? No." He touches his mouse nervously, glances again at the computer screen, and shrugs. "It was too long."

I look at him in disbelief. My e-mail was a paragraph long. A short paragraph.

"Just tell me what you want."

This is hardly encouraging. "Well, first of all, I want a better relationship with you. It feels terrible when you ignore my calls and e-mails. I don't like being avoided. I mean, I *am* running your newspaper. There are many things I would really like to discuss with you."

"To tell you the truth, I have been avoiding you because it makes me feel bad to see you," he says. "I cringe inside myself when I see you."

His words are a dozen *jambiyas* hurled through the air and pinning me to my chair. Everything I've struggled for, and he hates me. "Why?" I look at him with helpless bewilderment. "What have I done?"

He pauses, fiddling with his pen. "You are doing an excellent job with the paper," he says. This is the first positive feedback I have gotten since I arrived back. "But you don't seem to want to work with the advertising and marketing guys. If they ask you to do something, I want you to help them. Not tell them, 'Stay away from my reporters.'"

"But, Faris, I—"

"I want you to help them. The paper doesn't make any money."

That argument again. "Faris, may I explain something?"

"Yes."

"You brought me here to make the paper more professional, right? And to increase its credibility."

He nods.

"The key to doing that is keeping a firm wall between advertising and editorial. If our readers see that we are writing about our advertisers, if they see that we write about people who give us money, they will think that every story we print we only write because someone paid us to run it. It destroys our credibility."

Faris nods as if he might understand.

"I don't want them using my reporters for that reason—it teaches them the wrong ideas about journalism. Also, I am short-staffed as it is. I can't spare news reporters to do advertising."

"I know you need people."

"So we should hire advertising their own people. Qasim obviously needs a staff."

I have become so fed up with Qasim stealing my reporters that I ran a help-wanted classified seeking an advertising intern. But when a man showed up who was eager to help, Qasim sent him away.

Faris has no suggestions. He just reiterates how much he needs me to help the advertising people. But he isn't done with me yet.

"Regarding al-Huthi," he says. "Tone it down. Do you hear me?"

"Tone it *down*? It's the biggest story in the country!" The Huthis are conservative Shiites in the North who have been periodically battling the government since 2004. Their specific demands are unclear, but they seek the restoration of Zaydi Shia dominance in Yemen and denounce Saleh's close relationship with the West.

In January, fighting between Huthis and the government resumed, and hundreds are rumored to have died. We are not allowed to send a reporter to Sa'dah, the northern province where the fighting is centered, because the roads are blocked and there is a complete media blackout. So Ibrahim has been reporting the story based on phone calls to the governor of the region and other sources.

"I am telling you: Do not run it on the front page of every issue. Do you hear me? *Tone. It. Down.*"

"I hear you, but—"

"There were errors in the last story."

"If the government doesn't want us to make mistakes, then it should let us into Sa'dah so we can see what's going on for ourselves."

"You want to go to Sa'dah?"

"*Yes,* I want to go to Sa'dah!" How thrilling it would be to be able to do some real reporting on this story. I am certain that the information we get from the government is far from accurate.

"Fine. I will see if I can get you in. I would love it if I could send you to Sa'dah."

"Why? Anxious to get rid of me, Faris?" Small smile.

"No—we'd have an exclusive."

"And possibly some real information."

Ignoring this, Faris comes to what seems to be an even bigger problem: I've fired our photographer Mas. I explain again why I dismissed him: He did no work. He sat around listening to music on his laptop and complaining about being bored, but the minute I needed him to photograph something, he was nowhere to be found. After months passed without Mas producing a photo, I fired him.

Yet some people in the office seem to think I should have kept him, largely because he is the Doctor's son and a favorite of Faris's.

They may be right. It has hurt my standing with my staff and it has upset Faris deeply.

"When Mas was young and had leukemia, I paid for his treatment,"

Faris says. "Mas is like a son to me. I like to see him around the office." His eyes glisten with tears. I am consumed with self-loathing. How could I be such a beast? I knew about Mas's cancer. He had told me after doing a photo essay on a little boy in a Sana'ani cancer ward. "If you don't want to work with him, couldn't you still have kept him around the office?" says Faris.

I'd love to work with him, if he would actually *work,* I think. Instead I say, "Faris, I am sorry."

I feel terrible that I have failed to understand the intricacies of Faris's relationship with Mas, and also the difficulties of firing someone in an office controlled by nepotism. I might have avoided this pitfall had Faris spent a little more time with me, helping me to understand how things work here. Now I find out these things too late.

I apologize abjectly, saying that I will do anything to make things right. Faris says he hasn't told me this before because he didn't want to cry in front of me. And on cue, he sheds two tears. I feel sick.

Before I leave the office, we go quickly through the other things on my list. For example, I need the plane fare to the United States for my two-week break, as my salary is not enough to cover it.

Without a word, Faris pulls a wad of $100 bills the size of a grapefruit out of his pocket. I stare wide-eyed, never having seen that much cash in my life. He peels off thirteen bills and hands them to me. Feeling that I am being paid to go away, I crumple the bills in my fist and slink out of the office.

☪

A FEW DAYS LATER, I am scrambling to finish an issue early enough to attend a Dutch friend's farewell *qat* chew before meeting a Jordanian friend for dinner when Faris rings.

"This is really important. There's this British guy here, head of Middle East security or something. We need an interview with him. Set something up immediately and get back to me."

"Great," I say. "We can interview him Saturday." It's a Thursday, and I am looking forward to having a night off and a free day Friday to pack for my trip home.

"Saturday is too late, he'll be gone. Arrange it for before then."

So much for my evening plans. But I need to get back into Faris's good favor. "I'll talk with him tonight," I say. "What did you say his name was? And his title?"

"I don't know," says Faris. "Something to do with the Middle East. Find out."

I ring the British Embassy, but because it is the weekend for the rest of the Yemeni world, it is closed. There's an emergency number on the recording. I hesitate. This isn't exactly an emergency. But I really need to make Faris like me. I think about his disappointment if I fail to get this interview, and my fingers start to dial the emergency number all by themselves.

The woman on duty says she'll pass on my message, and five minutes later, Ambassador Mike Gifford calls me back.

"Look," he says, "I am having a dinner at my house tonight for Peter Gooderham," (my target, the director for the Middle East and North Africa in the British Foreign and Commonwealth Office) "Why don't you join us? We have plenty of room. And you can interview him there."

"If you're sure it won't be a problem. I hate to intrude on his dinner."

"No problem at all. We would be delighted to have you."

So relieved I'm bordering on happy, I ring Faris and give him the good news.

Mike Gifford's wife, Patricia, welcomes me warmly and introduces me to a few others, including a chatty man named Khalid who works for Islamic Relief and has been to Sa'dah. I question him furiously about the situation there. I also talk with a reporter from *26 September,* also there to interview Peter; a British man working with the Yemeni Coast Guard; and a member of the British House of Commons. I drink a gin and tonic and enjoy myself immensely. There are worse jobs.

Peter Gooderham is seated near me and is quite charming, quizzing me about my work. He finishes eating before I do, so I regretfully abandon my third helping of fish and brussels sprouts to interview him in the living room. He talks for nearly an hour, and I fill my notebook. I hardly have to ask any questions. He just rattles on until the other journalist gets impatient.

I stay until close to eleven P.M., heading out with the last stragglers. At home, I kick off my boots and write the entire interview by twelve thirty A.M. The photo is e-mailed to Faris by one A.M. I fall asleep feeling very pleased with myself indeed.

☾

I RETURN from a brief holiday in New York in early May with renewed determination to work on my relationship with Faris. There are urgent reasons for this. Al-Asaadi and Zaid are both due back in Yemen in June, and I need to figure out whom I am training to be my successor. It seems obvious to me that it won't be al-Asaadi, because he hasn't shown any interest in learning from me or in perpetuating my reforms at the paper. Zaid, on the other hand, has been eager to learn and seems ripe for training. One of my main reasons for doing this job is to create reforms that outlast me.

My first discussion with Faris on this topic is not inspiring.

"Al-Asaadi will be editor in chief and Zaid will be managing editor," he says when I ask him what will happen in June.

My heart sinks. This will never work. Al-Asaadi and Zaid cannot stand each other. When they both come back, I expect nothing short of total catastrophe.

"Faris," I say, "you know those two do not get along."

"I need everyone to work as a team," he says.

"Of course. But I need al-Asaadi not to disrupt what I have done. We have a terrific schedule now, but when he was here before, he constantly tried to sabotage me. We do get along as people, you know. We've even been e-mailing each other since he's been gone. But I do not want all of my work undone." Faris seems to have the wild idea that he can just throw us all together, establish no clear hierarchy, and let us fight it out. I don't know what to do. My reporters need a clear hierarchy. I need a clear hierarchy. Zaid and al-Asaadi will definitely need a clear hierarchy. I dread June.

☾

I ALSO RETURN from New York with a secret Faris-softening weapon. His two older sons have advised me to use, in times of crisis, Reese's Peanut Butter Cups as a way to get their father to pay attention to me.

"He'll give you anything you want if you bring peanut butter cups," they tell me.

You cannot find peanut butter cups in Yemen, so it isn't until April that I can get my hands on a good supply. I've brought back five bags.

So when Faris comes into my office one day to ask me to cover a story, I tell him I would really like to sit down and have a leisurely talk about my successor and the future of the paper.

"Sure, yeah, okay, but not now, I have a meeting," he mutters while backing toward my door. It is clear that he has no intention of having a talk with me, leisurely or otherwise.

"Faris," I say, "I have peanut butter cups."

He stops in his tracks, turns to look at me, and walks back toward my desk. His eyes dart around my office. "Where?"

"I'll tell you," I say, "when you sit down and talk with me. Not before."

"Ah," he says, looking crestfallen. "I'll get back to you." And with one last wistful look at my desk drawers, he turns and walks slowly out my door.

A few days later, he waylays me at a party at Nabeel Khoury's. I'm standing in the courtyard, halfway through a gin and tonic, being bored rigid by a series of earnest young men from the American Embassy, when Faris grabs my arm. "You wanted to talk?" he says, pulling me up the stairs to the house.

Yes, I think, though this wasn't exactly the venue I had in mind. Still, Faris wanting to talk with me is so novel that not for anything would I miss this opportunity. I let him lead me into the empty living room, where we settle on the sofa.

"Now we can have that leisurely chat you've been wanting," he says as he reclines.

Grateful for the gin in my hand, I explain how I would like to see things unfold. I would like Zaid to work under me, shadowing me until I leave, and then to take over the paper. "Al-Asaadi has *had* his chance to be the editor, and he is not a good manager," I say. "He could be a great reporter, or maybe do something else—you mentioned the magazine—but I really feel that it is time to let Zaid have a chance to run things." I need someone with Zaid's passion, someone open to my ideas.

Faris nods and listens attentively, not interrupting or rushing me. I am beside myself with delight. He says that he will talk to al-Asaadi (I am not to attempt this myself) and work things around the way that I want them. "Just keep in mind," he says, "Zaid is not a marathon runner, he's a sprinter. He'll go all out and then give up suddenly."

"I'll keep a close watch on Zaid," I promise. "I will keep him in line."

We then discuss several story ideas Faris has from his sources at the top. He tells me about the panic going around that cell phones are mysteriously killing people. I've heard this rumor from my staff, who have all become frightened of their phones. "There are some people who are afraid to take my calls," Faris says. "They say they can't answer something that says 'private number,' because it might kill them."

He gives me several other ideas. I am thrilled. This is the most productive talk I have ever had with Faris. I tell him so. After forty-five minutes, I actually feel satisfied, and we stand to rejoin the party outside. A rain shower has released a cool, starry night.

"So," says Faris, looking at me expectantly as we walk toward the door, "do I get my peanut butter cups now?"

☾⋆

IN EARLY JUNE, I screw up again. The first Thursday of the month, I am having a bad closing day. Hadi has taken off just before deadline to attend a wedding, leaving me with no designer. Samir is enlisted to help us finish the issue, but he is slower than Hadi, and I get impatient and storm around the office.

Things are going much better overall, so why do I still have fits of temper? I think about my former editors. I remember Jim McGarvey at the Morris County *Daily Record,* who would scream that I was the most disastrous reporter on the planet one minute and then shower me with praise the next. Yet he was a brilliant editor. I think about all of the other editors I have known. Few of them were particularly stable, with the possible exception of my editor at *The Week,* but the pressures there were not the pressures of a daily. Maybe these fits of impatience on deadline simply come with the job.

Feeling better, I write the final captions and pack up my bags. At seven thirty, just as I am grabbing a bottle of French wine from my house and heading for dinner with a new neighbor, my phone rings. It's a private number. Faris.

"*Salaam aleikum*," I say.

"I need you to go back to the office," he says. "Did you put something on the front page about the Huthis being behind the explosions at the armory?"

It takes me a minute to remember. My brain erases each issue from its data banks as soon as it's put to bed. The Huthi rebels in the north of Yemen were rumored to have caused explosions in a cave near Sana'a.

"Yes," I say. "But we quoted someone from the Ministry of the Interior."

"The minister is denying it," says Faris. "Get back to the office and change the front page or the paper will be closed down and we will be taken to court. And I want you to fire whoever wrote that story."

"Farouq and Radia wrote it," I say. I presume Farouq did the interview, because he is the one with the contacts.

"People have to double-check their facts," says Faris. "Radia should have—"

"Don't blame Radia for this!" I'm incensed. Why is Faris jumping to the conclusion that Radia is at fault? Didn't I just say Farouq *and* Radia wrote it? "Farouq worked with her, and he was the one who gave me the story." He also has several more years of experience as a reporter, I want to point out. He is the one responsible for overseeing Radia's work.

Yemeni men immediately blame the women for anything that goes wrong. If the accountant makes a mistake, he blames Radia. If an administrator makes a mistake, he blames Enass. God forbid the men ever take responsibility for their own mistakes.

A male Yemeni friend explains the phenomenon to me this way: "They cannot admit a mistake because they are afraid of the punishment. We're used to being punished every time we make a mistake."

I am immediately abashed that this had not occurred to me; it makes sense in a culture in which children are beaten for not having the right answers. Plus, Yemen is a country in which the government crackdown on any misstep can be severe. No *wonder* they don't want to admit mistakes.

But Faris is hell-bent on punishing someone. "Well, when I find out who wrote it . . . !" he says.

"Faris, I just *told* you who wrote it." He doesn't want to have to fire Farouq, I think. Farouq is a man and therefore less dispensable. "Anyway, have you told the designers to hold the paper?"

"I have."

"How did the ministry know about the story?"

"Apparently Enass posted it online and someone saw it and called the ministry."

Well, that was fast! We finished the story five minutes before I left the office.

"Is Luke still in the office? I was on my way to meet people . . . ," I say lamely, knowing there is no way I can get out of going back to work. Yet a dinner date is such a rarity that I hate to miss it.

"Jennifer, this is the news business and in the news business—"

"You don't need to tell *me* about the news business. I've been in it for twelve years." Which, I want to point out, is longer than the *Yemen Observer* has been in print. I am also tempted to point out that no *real* newspaper would let the people in power tell us what we can write. "Anyway, I am on my way."

I race back to the office. By the time I arrive, I have calmed down. Luke is still there, chewing *qat* with the guys. Faris had phoned and made Luke read him the story. It wasn't even anonymously sourced—we used the name of the director of the interior minister's office. Enass actually heard Radia interview the man, so there is a witness to the conversation. Of course, women aren't taken seriously as witnesses. Luke and I figure that the director must have spoken out of turn, and then, when the story was posted, he got in trouble and was forced to deny his statement.

Luke has already found some additional photos for the front page, and together we reconfigure it. It all goes smoothly. We are just finishing when Faris calls to check in.

"What story did you put on the front page?" he says.

"A cheerful little story about Yemeni expatriates getting surveyed so that they can be provided with new services," I say. "Do you want to know what is on the rest of the front page?"

"No," he says. "I trust you."

He trusts me?

I tell Faris our theory that someone at the ministry had spoken out of turn, got in trouble, and then retracted.

"But he's denying it," says Faris.

"Yes, I *know*. But I am quite certain that Radia would never lie." On this point, I will not budge.

Faris has calmed down and seems almost willing to accept that Radia hasn't committed a crime. He asks me to promise that I will call him if we run anything else on the Huthis. Saleh is very touchy about any story about these rebels. God forbid we actually find out what the government is doing up there in the North.

Later that night, after a glass of wine with my neighbor, it all seems funny. We laugh about it until after midnight, when I reluctantly head home to bed.

☪

THE STORY ABRUPTLY CEASES to be humorous the following Wednesday, when Faris summons me to his office.

"I need to speak with you," he says. Faris never needs to speak with me if things are going well. Heart racing, I leap up the stairs to his office.

"We're in trouble," he says. "The minister of the interior is suing us. What do you think we should do?"

"But we never printed the story!"

"About twenty Arabic papers managed to pick it up from the Web before we took it down."

"Christ."

"He denies that he said anything. He is denying that he even spoke to a reporter. That anyone in his office spoke to a reporter."

"But Radia did speak to someone in his office."

"He's saying she didn't."

"I really don't think Radia would lie."

"Well, either he is lying or she is lying."

"He has a motive to lie; she doesn't."

"Look. . . ." Faris clicks through a few Web pages. "He put it on the Web. That he is denying everything."

"Hmmm."

"So what should we do?"

"Well . . ." I think for a minute. I am glad that Faris is asking my advice and has not just called me to his office to chastise me. "In the States what we would do is write another article, with the minister's reaction to the previous story. Set the record straight." I still think the minister is lying, but we have no way to prove that anyone spoke with Radia because we have no way to record phone calls. And Faris is basically asking me how to cover our asses and not get the paper closed.

"That won't work."

"But then it would be on record that we wrote the 'correct' version."

"That would just make everything worse. Things aren't done like that here."

"Okay, so what are our other options?"

"I don't know." He fidgets with his mouse, clicking on and off websites and twirling in his chair. "Jennifer, the minister of the interior refused to shake my hand yesterday at the Italian embassy. I have never been snubbed like that. Do you know what that is like?"

"No . . ."

"I have a lot of enemies here. There are a lot of people who are after me, and I want to keep them from getting at me through the *Yemen Observer*. You understand? So the next time we have a story like this, just print the official government press release and that is *all,* okay?"

I nod. So much for holding power accountable.

We sit quietly for a few minutes.

"I mean, who is going to take responsibility for this?" he says. "They could put someone in jail."

"I will." I am not going to let Radia—or any of my reporters—go to jail. But they will never send me to jail. It would be political suicide. Besides, it would be far too embarrassing for Faris; he simply would not let it happen.

By the time I'm dismissed, I have the feeling that Faris didn't really want my advice after all. What upset him most was that the minister had refused to shake his hand. People in power were irked with him. And he wanted to make it clear to me that this was my fault and unacceptable. I could do anything I wanted to with the paper—so long as I didn't lose him any friends in power. One more false step, I think, and even peanut butter cups won't be able to save me.

Slowly, it dawns on me that this is not going to change. There will always be limits to what we can write. Faris will never allow me to hire the staff we need. Salaries are not going to rise. My reporters won't all stick around, and those who do are not going to become paragons of the profession in one year. This is what I have to work with. These are the parameters within which I will have to find new ways to define success.

SEVENTEEN

a world beyond work

Now that my reporters are submitting almost all of their stories promptly on deadline, I'm spending more time with them than ever before. It's immensely gratifying to have the luxury of explaining all of my edits to them and chatting with them about their lives. I've even changed my routine; I go to the gym before work, so I can lunch with my staff.

My favorite lunches are at the fish *souq,* where al-Matari or one of the other men picks out a large fish or two and we take it to a restaurant to be roasted and served with squishy, buttery bread called *ratib.* I am always the only woman there, and men stare at me the entire time. But surrounded and protected by my male staff, I don't mind. Some afternoons we go for *saltah,* a Yemeni meat stew with a bubbling broth of fenugreek, in Baab al-Sabah, the market street near my house. The men spread strips of cardboard on the stones for me to sit on and run off in different directions to buy *saltah* and bread and tangy raisin juice. They even order me my own little pot of vegetarian *saltah,* which tastes like a spicy potato stew. We squat in a circle while passing men stare at the oddity of a woman eating in public. It makes all the difference that I now have time to do this; my relationships with my reporters become easier as we spend more non-work time together.

The mere act of getting the paper on schedule has transformed my life.

Not only can I spend more time with staff, but for the first time in six months, I have time to go out with friends after work. Of course, I first need to find friends. I have some, but I've spent so much time in my newsroom that I've hardly met anyone outside of work other than Shaima, Marvin, and Pearl. My solitary times on Soqotra musing on distant loved ones reminded me of how critical my friendships are. The e-mails I get from faraway friends are a comfort, but I need people *here*.

Anne is the first to step into the void. I'd met her a couple of months earlier at my first diplomatic party, but now I finally have time to see her. An intern at the Dutch Embassy, Anne is twenty-two, but age has ceased to mean anything to me. In New York, most of my friends were close to my age or older. But in Yemen, I collect friends from ages twenty-two to sixty-seven. There are so few expats in Yemen that just living here gives us a strong common bond. Besides, Anne is precocious. She grew up in Saudi Arabia and has traveled extensively. A voracious reader, she often whips through a book a day, speaks perfect English and decent Arabic, makes friends easily, and is consistently sunny and cheerful. I am a little bit in awe of Anne. Our mutual love of books initially brings us together; there are few books in English available in Yemen, so we trade our stocks. In the evenings, she is often the person who drags me from the office after a long day. We make dinners together at my house or go out to eat, and she introduces me to her legions of friends.

In early spring, she invites me on a trip to Kamaran Island with a group of mostly Dutch friends. I've gotten bolder about taking time off, and so without even telling Faris, I leave the paper in Luke's hands on a closing day and head for the Red Sea. I don't want to miss a chance to meet people away from work.

The occasion is Floor's birthday. Floor is Ali's new girlfriend; they began dating while he was working for me (much to the dismay of my women). When we go to Kamaran, Ali is temporarily away in the United States. Floor is slender and blond, easygoing, and drives her own car, a massive army-green jeep. With her is her best friend, Serena, an Australian doctoral student in political science, and Matt and Nina, a couple from New York.

Xander, a tall, dark-haired Dutch development worker, drives the second car, with Anne and her new Dutch boyfriend Florens. I am squeezed into the last car with Yahya, a Yemeni; Lama, a tiny, wild, married Yemeni woman; and Zana, a vastly fat Albanian with short-clipped blond hair and watermelon breasts.

Zana is from Kosovo and works for the National Democratic Institute with Floor and Lama. We pass the time asking Lama how to say various things in Arabic, focusing on phrases to make men leave us alone. Zana asks how to say "It is nothing that would interest you."

"There is no Arabic translation for that," says Lama, "because here, everyone is interested in everything."

We drive up over the jagged peaks of the Haraz Mountains, majestic and misty. It is cool in the mountains, and I am astonished at their greenness. The color comes from the crops planted in diminishing terraces rising up the slopes all around us. On one peak, our three cars meet up at a bootleg alcohol shop. I am amused to find the tiny, unmarked shed plastered with enormous photographs of Saddam Hussein and stocked with bottles of Glen's gin, Bell's whiskey, and Heineken. When I ask what other contraband is available, Serena says, "Anything you want." Several of the Dutch buy hashish, and we all chip in for cases of beer.

As we descend from the mountains toward Hodeida, the air grows softer and warmer, and the valley alongside the road greens with banana trees. Soon, it is so hot that we have to roll our windows all the way down.

We arrive at the boat launch in Selim just after dark. The air is thick, warm, and sticky. The police at the docks make a big fuss over our papers, delaying us while they hold conferences among themselves. The man who seems to be in charge is very confused about how many of us there are. Serena tells him there are fourteen of us, but he doesn't understand. "Five and five and four," she says, pointing out our three groups. He cannot add, and she shows him on her fingers. He frowns and scribbles and counts us again.

Finally, we are allowed to board three rickety fishing boats, our bags of contraband clanking as we heave them over the sides. Even then, the boat drivers are in no hurry to set off. They busily compare cell phone features while we grow impatient. We have already been traveling for seven hours.

After sitting for ages breathing exhaust fumes from the boat, little Lama finally loses patience. *"Mumkin,"* ("Can we . . . ?") she says, tapping the driver. And we all join in with the *"YALLA!"* (Let's go!)

With a sudden push, we are speeding across the water. I look up. The stars are bright and the moon fuzzy with humidity. There are no lights anywhere. Our boats themselves lack headlights and the water is dark around us. The enchantment hits us all in a rush. Our boats fly, faster than our cars had on land, through the dark. Our wake and the waves around us glow white in the moonlight.

"Wow," we say in one awestruck voice. I trail my fingers in the water.

"This is my first time on the Red Sea," says Nina.

I'm suddenly excited. "Me too!"

Our driver asks Nina for her flashlight, and she hands it over. It strikes me as odd that he doesn't have his own. He flashes the light skyward and then toward the other boats. They flash back, directing us.

It takes us twenty minutes to cross the water. As our boats push up against the rocks of Kamaran, which is still invisible in the dark, a voice booms from above.

"Welcome to Kamaran!" It is a Yemeni voice speaking warmly in English. As I clamber across the other boats and up the rocks, a strong hand grips mine and hauls me to the top. Mohammed al-Zubairy's round brown face appears in the dark, glistening. He introduces himself and turns to the next guest. "Zana! You made it!" He remembers the name of everyone who has been there before, particularly the women.

From the top of the cliff, I see the modest buildings of the Two Moon Tourist Resort silhouetted in the moonlight. Those on land are already scurrying to pick out their round, pointy-roofed, thatched Tihama huts. These are scattered across the sandy plain around a circular, stone main building that houses the dining room, kitchen, and bathrooms.

I follow the group slowly, wondering who might let me share their hut. All the seventh-grade anxieties about not fitting in with the popular crowd surge up from my unconsciousness. Everyone else already knows each other. Anne is the only person I really know, and she is sharing a hut with Florens.

"Jennifer!" calls Floor. "Do you want to be in our hut?"

Rescued from social rejection! Floor is the ringleader of this group, and I am grateful for her warmth. I hurry to join her and Serena.

By the time we've dropped our things and run into the main building, everyone is lounging in wood and rope chairs, sipping their first cold beers. Floor announces that she is going for a swim, followed by Anne. I waver long enough that they head out without me. (Alcohol or swimming? It's a tough call.) But I finally decide I want nothing more than to be underwater, and Mohammed leads me across the sand in the dark.

He remembers having seen me before, somewhere in Sana'a.

"I was attracted to your face," he says. "And here you are, on my island!" I am flattered.

We walk across a dune, passing the dripping Floor and Anne on their return trip, to a small square building. Not until we get there can I make out the outline of the shore. I start for my swimsuit, but Mohammed tells me I don't need it here. "Just swim! Be free!" he says. "It is night. There is no one to care."

These are magic words to a girl who has been swaddled from head to toe for months. Euphorically, I strip off my long skirts and walk naked across the sand. Mohammed has gone discreetly ahead and is already out in the water, wearing his boxers, far from me.

The water is deliciously cool. We swim out, Mohammed (staying a respectful distance ahead) guiding me away from underwater hazards. I flip onto my back to see how the moon looks from the Red Sea. It looks fuzzy. My worries about the paper dissolve and float out to sea. I follow Mohammed's instructions and feel free. I am tempted to float out here all night, but I remind myself that I didn't come here to be alone.

I join the others for a beer before dinner. We've all shucked our Yemeni drapery—even Yemeni Lama has stripped down to a tiny pair of shorts. It feels like the first day of summer vacation. Mohammed and his staff have whipped up a vast feast of seafood and salads, which we boisterously inhale before heading outside to relax under the stars and fuzzy moon. Nina passes me a joint, and I take a couple of hits. I never smoke hashish, and the drug immediately blows me sideways. I fall asleep in my chair, and when I open my eyes Anne is watching me. "You look tired," she laughs. I stumble over to our hut, curl up on my rope cot, and am instantly asleep.

We wake early to find crepes and mango juice already waiting for us. After breakfast, everyone heads in different directions—some to swim, some to take a boat to a nearby island, some to read in the shade. I linger in the main lodge with Mohammed, curious to know more about his resort. "I wanted to create a place where people could be free," he says. "This is why I came here." He opened the resort in 1997, after President Saleh gave him the land to open the island to tourism investment.

"I like the sea," he says. "I grew up close to the sea. I wanted to protect the environment in some way, in my way."

Using only natural, local materials, he followed the traditional building methods of the Tihama region, the western coastal area, to build the huts. The resort is isolated from the rest of the island, where some thirty-five hundred Yemenis make their living from the sea.

There are two reasons the island is called Kamaran, says Mohammed. First, if you sit at the very tip of this spit of land, just as the full moon rises in the sky, you can see its reflection on either side of you. *Qamaran* is a transliteration of the Arabic word for "two moons." Second, for two weeks a month it is possible to see the moon shining in one side of the sky while the sun is shining in the other.

The forty-two-square-mile desert island is fringed with white sand beaches and surrounded by coral reefs. I'm eager to see these reefs but have never snorkeled, so Mohammed teaches me. I have seen coral before only off Soqotra. In flippers and masks, we drift over what looks like heads of cabbage. Tiny silver fish dart in and out of them. Beside these are the labyrinthine shapes of coral folded in upon itself to resemble the cerebellum of a sea monster. Spiky sea urchins abound. Branch coral reaches purple-tipped fingers toward the sky. A rainbow-colored fish swims by, flapping tiny wings, and an enormous mussel (which Mohammed calls a "murder shell") opens and closes its rippled blue lips. A shoal of long, cylindrical fish—the kind served for dinner the night before—dashes quickly away as if suspecting the fate of their missing brethren.

As we swim, Mohammed silently points to things and I gurgle my awe. After an hour of exploring, I head to shore and trek across the dunes, thick with crushed white shells, to join the others on a distant beach.

It is early evening when we all return. I take some photos of the sunset and join the others for a riotous cocktail hour. Florens and Xander amuse us by covering their sunburned bodies with yogurt. We trade our Yemeni adventure stories and laugh and then eat another fish and vegetable feast.

Afterward, we move outside to celebrate Floor's birthday with more drinks, dancing, and even a fireworks display. We crank up the stereo. I lift my arms to the starry desert sky, relishing the tickle of my loose hair across my spine, and feel happier than I have felt in months. Festivity, food, and, finally, some nonwork *friends.*

Close to midnight, boats arrive to take us to the mangroves. We climb into two fishing boats, clutching bottles of whiskey and beer, and zoom off into the dark sea, the moon our only light. Drenched by the sea spray, we toss beers from boat to boat, teasing each other. At a spit of sand near the entrance to the mangroves, we all strip down for a moonlight swim.

When we grow chilly, we climb into the boats and race each other back, drinking and egging each other on. By the time we get to sleep, there are no moons left on Kamaran Island.

The trip to Kamaran throws open doors to the outside world. I return with a host of new friends, who will introduce me to still more new friends, and at long last, a social whirl begins. I still have to work six days a week. I am still the first to leave parties on Wednesday nights, because my staff and I are among the few people in Sana'a who work Thursdays. I still have moments of impatience and exhaustion. But now, I have learned to walk out the door in time for dinner. I have learned to leave things un-done on my desk. After all, as I am always telling my reporters, the great thing about the news business is that there is always a next issue.

EIGHTEEN

dragging designers from the qat shed and other drug problems

Whenever I leave the newsroom for too long in the afternoon, my men dis-
appear. Initially, I have no idea where they go and send other reporters to
find them. But it doesn't take long for me to discover their hideout: the
qat shed. This is a grimy little room tucked just inside the *Observer*'s gates.
Dirty *mafraj* cushions are squeezed against the walls, and boxes of newspapers are stacked in the corners. Here, the men smoke cigarettes, stuff
their cheeks with leaves, and try to hide from me. I stand in the doorway
of the *qat* shed calling, *"Amal!"* (Work!) until they reluctantly hoist themselves from the cushions and follow me inside. Of course, this doesn't
happen right away. They first try to convince me to join them. "Chew, Jennifer!" they urge. "It's nice!" Farouq holds up an alluring branch of green
leaves and waves it at me. "It will relax you." On occasion, I give in and
chew a little with them, though I can't say it makes me any calmer.

My male reporters chew every day, often late into the night. Most
Yemeni men chew, though not all make a daily habit of it. The nationwide
dependence on *qat* is perhaps Yemen's greatest development hurdle. The
thirsty plant drinks the country's aquifers dry, sucks nutrients from the
soil, steals hours of productivity from workers, and causes a wide range of
health and social problems.

I don't need scientific reports to know the adverse effects of *qat;* I see them every day. My men constantly complain of insomnia and lack of appetite. Many of them are painfully thin, the result of skipping supper in favor of a cheekful of greenery. Their teeth are brown with decay. Several have complained to me about the depression that follows a good chew, which I've experienced myself. "But that's when you just chew some more!" say my reporters.

Qat also keeps journalists from meeting deadlines, which causes *me* health and social problems. When the typical Yemeni workday ends, at two P.M. (not ours, alas!), many men rush from work to stuff themselves with stews and breads to line their stomach in preparation for a five-hour *qat*-chewing session. Because my reporters work evenings, they chew in the office (or the shed). On closing days, the drivers bring us rice and chicken for lunch so we don't need to leave the newsroom—but the men still manage to sneak out to buy *qat*. Often, we will be ten minutes from finishing an issue, and all of my male reporters will simultaneously vanish. They cannot fathom getting through an afternoon without their fix.

Qat has been cultivated in Yemen for centuries—some evidence suggests it grew here as early as the thirteenth century. Ethiopia and Yemen are the two biggest producers, although it also grows in Kenya, Uganda, Tanzania, Rwanda, Zimbabwe, Turkmenistan, and Afghanistan. There is some disagreement as to whether the plant originated in Ethiopia and spread to Yemen or vice versa. An Ethiopian legend holds that a goatherd was the first person to chew *qat*. One night he noticed that his goats were particularly wakeful and frolicsome. So the next day, he followed them and found them munching green *qat* leaves. The herder tried some for himself, and a habit was born.

Until the 1960s, *qat* chewing in Yemen was mostly an occasional leisure activity for the rich. But in the 1970s and '80s, rising household incomes and increased profitability for farmers contributed to the spread of the practice. Now, about three-quarters of men and a third of women chew *qat,* according to a 2007 World Bank report. Other studies have found chewing even more prevalent. Most *qat* chewers are habitual users; more than half of those who chew do so daily.

☾*

MUCH OF WORK LIFE in Yemen revolves around *qat* chews. Friends working as consultants for government ministries report that decision making often happens in the *qat* chews that precede official meetings, rather than in the meetings themselves. "Which means that Yemeni policies are often made by men who are high as a kite," says one consultant.

It's easy to see how *qat* became so prevalent. For farmers, *qat* is lucrative—ten to twenty times more profitable than other crops. Its contribution to the economy is equivalent to two-thirds of the contribution that oil makes (oil revenues make up 75 percent of Yemen's budget), according to the Ministry of Planning. Thus, farmers are understandably in no hurry to switch to alternatives—even when rising global food prices threaten to starve the country and increasing cultivation has led to a serious water crisis.

Qat production and distribution also employ about one in seven Yemenis. But while it may supply jobs, the drug bleeds money from Yemeni families. A tenth of the typical Yemeni household income is spent on *qat*, and some poor households spend more than a quarter of their income on it. Money spent on *qat* is money that isn't spent on food, medicine, or other necessities—hitting children hardest.

My male reporters, who are always out of grocery money weeks before payday, somehow still manage to buy *qat*. So it doesn't surprise me to learn that 94 percent of nonchewers and 77 percent of chewers admit that *qat* has a deleterious effect on the family budget. Just under a fifth of Yemenis are forced into debt to finance their drug habit. It's not unusual for a reporter to stand in front of my desk with a cheek full of *qat* asking to borrow money for dinner.

Qat eats up hours as fast as it eats money—hours that might be spent on more productive pursuits. More than a third of *qat* chewers indulge their habit for four to six hours a day and nearly a quarter chew for more than six hours a day. When men joke that *qat* is Yemeni whiskey, I say, "Yes, but we don't tend to drink whiskey for six hours a day, seven days a week."

One of the most entertaining bits of information I found in the World Bank report was that men dramatically underestimate how much *qat* their wives are tearing through. Fourteen percent of husbands said that their wives chew, but 33 percent of their wives reported chewing. This may be because there is more of a stigma attached to *qat* for women than for men. Or it could be that men are just out of touch with what their wives are doing, given that they spend little time together.

Because men and women chew separately, the practice contributes to sex segregation as well. Primarily, it keeps men away from their families. My reporters, for example, would rather spend all night chewing with their male friends than go home to their wives and children.

Before coming to Yemen, I was very curious about *qat,* and I have chewed my fair share in my efforts to assimilate. It's nearly impossible to avoid *qat* chews, as almost all social life revolves around them. Even the expat community has adopted the tradition. Whenever someone leaves the country—and there is always someone whose contract has just ended or whose diplomatic term is up—there is a farewell *qat* chew. There are also housewarming *qat* chews, birthday *qat* chews, and just-because-it's-Friday *qat* chews. The main difference between Yemeni chews and expat chews is that at a certain hour, the expat *qat* chews turn into cocktail parties when everyone spits out their leaves and picks up a glass of wine.

Overall, I probably wouldn't mind the whole *qat* phenomenon were it not for its interference with work. I don't try to ban the practice; it would trigger mutiny (though the *Yemen Times,* I find out later, bans chewing at work). But I do try to keep the men from running out to buy it while we are closing an issue. It's a losing battle but one, for some reason, I don't seem able to abandon.

"This has got to be the only country in the world where reporters are allowed to run out and buy drugs when on deadline," I say to Luke.

"It's not *drugs,*" says Farouq. This is a regular argument. Yemenis do not consider *qat* to be a drug.

"It's a mood-altering stimulant. What else could it be?"

"It's just *qat,*" says Farouq.

Hadi sides with him. Hadi, Farouq, and al-Matari are my most devout chewers, though Jabr often chews with them. He has trouble talking with his mouth full and sometimes spits bits of leaf at me when trying to explain a story. I try to imagine the reaction of my editor at *The Week* if I did this to him.

At least Luke admits it's a drug. One day he comes to my office to report a conversation with Hadi.

"Hadi just came in and said, 'The *qat*, it is killing me, I can't sleep at night. I am spending all of my money on it. It is making my wife mad at me. It takes away my appetite!'"

"That's because *it's a drug*," he told Hadi. "When the negative consequences outweigh the benefits, and you still continue to do it, then that means *it's a drug*."

Hadi just shook his head sadly and stuck another leaf in his mouth.

Another reason I don't try to ban *qat* is that I am not sure that my men could do their jobs without it. They might fall asleep on their keyboards. Or go home for a nap. Journalists on *qat*, I figure, are better than journalists suffering from *qat* withdrawal.

In contrast, my women are almost universally opposed to *qat*. Najma constantly writes health stories about its deleterious effects as a passive swipe at the men. Here is an excerpt from one of her masterpieces: "The *qat* chewer is prone to a lot of bad effects after taking *qat*. He becomes unable to sleep and he feels lazy and worried. He is also prone to be weak in sexual performance, focusing on things or information and to lose control on sperm. His appetite is badly affected by chewing *qat* and he tends to sit alone. He also suffers from some difficulties in urinating."

But there's some evidence that my men are coming to grips with what *qat* really is. One day in May, Farouq pops into my office as I am finishing editing a front page.

"Do you need me?" he says.

"Why?" I ask warily. "Where do you need to go?"

"I need to take your permission to go buy some drugs," he says, grinning broadly.

I laugh. "Well, since you put it that way, you have my permission to go buy drugs."

"Shukrahn!" And he's off like a shot.

I don't complain. Farouq has been inordinately kind and respectful lately and receptive to my thoughts and criticisms. We've just finished going over a story he wrote about a graduation project that two Sana'a University students did on religious conflict. Islam is vastly misunderstood, both by "bad" Muslims (who use Islam to justify terrorism) and non-Muslims, the students say. To address this, they wrote a booklet and held a workshop to increase the understanding of Islam in a post–September 11 world. A few parts of the story made me cross, particularly the sections that referred to the Western media as a homogenous entity, as if every newspaper and magazine in the Western world were conspiring together and speaking with one voice, when, in my experience, the Western media is a multiheaded beast encompassing an infinite number of voices. Doesn't it include both *Mother Jones* and the *New Republic*? *Playboy* and the *Wall Street Journal*? While it's true that some voices are louder than others, I've personally found the "Western media" to be pretty free and various.

When I try to explain this to Farouq, he responds, "But don't the Jews control all the media?"

"Farouq," I say, "tell me what percentage of Americans you think are Jews."

"I don't know."

"Just guess. I am curious what you think."

He considers for a moment. "Twenty percent?"

I hold up two fingers. "*Ithnayn.* Two percent. Tops."

He is shocked. He had assumed that the entire United States was ruled by a Zionist cabal.

I sigh. "Farouq. I have been in the media for twelve years and I don't recall ever having been controlled by Jews." In fact, I reflect, my last three bosses were Catholic. "And while there are certainly plenty of biases evident in newspapers and magazines, I've read quite a few pro-Muslim stories. Even in the *New York Times.* Which is, in fact, owned by a Jew. The U.S. media is not one big anti-Muslim block."

The United States was founded on the idea of religious freedom, I add. "It's illegal to persecute anyone for his or her religion."

It's strange to hear myself sounding so patriotic. I've spent a great deal of time agitating *against* the U.S. government—going to anti-Bush demonstrations, signing petitions, marching for peace, and supporting gay rights. Yet in Yemen, I find myself defending the government I have done nothing but complain about for years. And it's true that in comparison with the corrupt and inefficient Yemeni government, mine is beginning to rise—just a bit—in my esteem.

Farouq is surprised that it is illegal to persecute Muslims in the United States and surprised that any paper has written anything pro-Muslim.

Even more, he seems surprised that the United States encompasses diverse viewpoints.

In his story about the students' Islam project, a source claims that the reason the United States is so afraid of Islam is that it is worried that its entire population will convert.

"I don't think that's *quite* it," I tell Farouq. "The reason some people in the U.S. worry about Islam is that terrorists have used it as an excuse to attack our country." But I leave the quotation in anyway.

Farouq doesn't argue with me. He listens. This alone is progress. He has begun to ask me more questions and seems to be trying harder to impress me. Last week he redesigned the front page. He does this fairly often now, coming into my office to show me the two pages side by side in the hopes I will choose his. Sometimes he is right; I am the first to admit I have little design sense. But in this issue I have been quite firm about where I wanted which stories, and when I express this to Farouq, he just shrugs. "You're the boss," he says. "It's your call."

His deference makes me feel so warm and fuzzy that when he tells me he needs to leave just before deadline to go buy drugs, I don't try to stop him.

NINETEEN

bright days before the deluge

*I have stopped fantasizing about going back to New York. I have stopped think-*ing of anywhere as home other than my own lovely gingerbread house in Sana'a. I sleep through the night more often than not. I eat meals. When I return to the Old City at sunset and see the gold and rose evening light setting the houses aglow against a darkening sky, I feel like the luckiest person on earth. The paper has never run more smoothly; we're on such a predictable schedule now that I can make plans with friends even on closing days.

This is how it happens. My canny reporters figure out that meeting deadlines means getting out of work earlier. Getting out of work earlier means spending more time napping, chewing *qat,* or, in rare cases, with their families. In other words, all it takes is for them to realize that they are not just making me happy—there is something in it for *them.*

It sounds so simple. I suppose every manager realizes this at some point: that you must convince your staff that they themselves will benefit from doing what you want them to do. There's a big difference, however, between reading this seemingly simple philosophy in a management self-help book and trying to implement it at a newspaper in a foreign culture. Not that I've ever read a management book. Or—until now—been a manager in a foreign culture. I just fumbled in the dark until one day, light dawned, the paper closed at three P.M., and we all sat around marveling at ourselves and wondering how it happened.

Almost everything I learn in Yemen happens through improvisation, through feeling my way over each hurdle, each newsroom battle, and—after 1,001 mistakes—actually hitting upon a successful strategy. For example, one closing day in June, I discover that it isn't just Faris who can be manipulated with peanut butter cups.

I arrive at work that morning feeling cheerful and excited about social plans I have later. "I don't feel like dawdling around here today," I announce to the newsroom. "How about we have the earliest close ever?"

My reporters look up from their computers. *"Insha'allah,"* they say, looking dubious.

I have three front-page stories edited before eleven thirty A.M., which gives me plenty of time to hustle my staff. It is then I am struck with genius.

"The first person to get me his or her front-page story gets five peanut butter cups," I say. "The second person gets four, the third person gets three, et cetera. Now, go!"

I cannot believe how well this works. Noor gets her story in first, followed by Jabr and Radia. Soon, the men all have chocolate-swollen cheeks, and the women's hands keep disappearing under their *niqabs.*

As I am in the middle of designing a page with Samir, who is filling in for a tardy Hadi; ringing Sharabi to demand that he come in and give us photos; and ordering my reporters about, Luke swings away from his computer to look at me.

"When you leave here, you really ought to think about joining the circus," he says. "You have all the skills to be a ringmaster."

My stomach tightens. *When I leave here?* The phrase fills me with panic.

It is a frenetic day, but we do indeed close early. Farouq turns in a decent story about two brand-new X-ray machines that were intended to screen containers entering Yemen's ports but that failed embarrassingly in a public demonstration. When the officials put a machine gun through one of the machines, it failed to detect it.

Ibrahim files a story about three officials in Dhamar who were fired on corruption allegations. Zuhra writes another story about Anisa al-Shuaibi, whose rape case goes to trial this week. Luke and I joke that Zuhra is on the sodomy beat after she turns in a series of stories on abused prisoners, raped women, and sodomized men. Every story she reports seems to involve some kind of bodily violation. My little human rights crusader.

Najma gives us a story about how an overabundance of fluoride in the water of some villages is turning children's teeth brown, and Noor writes a piece about a march through Sana'a to demand funding for children's programs.

All of our pages are done by two P.M., though I stick around a bit to prod my staff along, proof pages, and make sure all of the captions are written and grammatical. "Do you need me?" I ask Hadi before making my escape.

"No," he says without hesitation. "Go home."

"Yes," says Luke, turning to me. "*Please* go home."

☪

EVEN WHEN DAYS don't go this smoothly, I now find my reporters' mistakes more entertaining than exasperating. Take Bashir's translation of Farouq's story about the Huthis: "The minister of endowment and giddiness Hamoud al-Hitar said, 'We will try to convince the rebels to surrender and lay down arms and stop the war against the camps of the State.' He adds, 'Last Saturday, the scholarship committee arrived to Sa'ada to transfer massage from the scholarship to the rebels about the war there.'"

I am sure that a massage by the minister of endowment and giddiness could play a productive part in conflict resolution. But it seems unlikely to happen.

Jabr turns in another of my favorite leads, for a story about a fundraiser for a charity that helps children with cleft palates. "One thousand and seven hundreds dollars for work of Yemeni smile that provide operations for children who have genital problems and who can not smile, said Nerys Loveridge, the Principle of the school. The money delivered to the ambassador of British during the open day that held in Sana'a British School on Wednesday."

It's common for Arabic speakers to mix up the P and B sounds. There is no P in Arabic. Thus I often get sentences like this: "There are some teams of masked soldiers called IRF (Instant Response Force). 'They enter the cell and beat the crab out of the prisoners,' he said."

Zuhra pulls her weight in the malapropism department too. When she is assigned to write a story on the celebration of Passover by fifty Yemeni Jews who live in the North and are under government protection in Sana'a after threats were made against them, she describes their food restrictions as such: "Jews are not allowed to eat inflated bread during this time." In a story about a group of people protesting shoddy medical treatment, she refers to them as "people who have had kidney plantations."

But perhaps my favorite is this paragraph from a health story she wrote on fertility treatments, which—alarmingly, given the country's already astronomical birth rate—are increasing. "Women must take medicines that stimulates the ovaries to produce eggs, and the men must stimulate their male liquid. Then, the mother will be in stupefaction in order to take out the eggs. Laser peels the chosen egg from the surrounding cells to guarantee that it will be fertilized appropriately."

I relish having time to discuss these errors with my reporters. The macro structure of our paper has fallen into place, allowing me to focus on the micro structure of my staff's stories. Now, instead of hurriedly rewriting everything alone in my drab office, I have reporters come sit with me while I edit their stories. This allows me to explain every change I make.

It's good that I now have time for these editorial tête-à-têtes, because in the spring I acquire Zaki, who replaces Hassan as the Business page editor. Charming to the point of obsequiousness, pudgy, bespectacled Zaki has a mere passing acquaintance with the English language. I spend hours coaching him and trying to break his habit of using meaningless business jargon sure to befuddle our readers. His stories are full of sentences like this: "Professor, Mohammed Muammar al-Shamiri, Supervisor of Group Insurance, said awareness on the importance of securing is very important either individuals or institutions on the all economic fields in Yemen." Decipher if you dare.

Zaki is eager to learn and gets me his page before deadline, so I don't complain. Besides, by now my standards for staff run something along the lines of "Must type with at least two fingers and sometimes show up."

Zaki is also a source of intriguing cultural information. One afternoon, he bursts into my office, wildly excited.

"Jennifer," he says, settling into the chair next to my desk and leaning toward me. "I met with the *jinni* yesterday!"

"Oh, great!" I say, thinking he has met my journalist friend Ginny. "I had dinner with her just last night!"

Zaki looks at me in horror. "You *did*?"

"Yeah," I say. "At the Indian restaurant."

"At the *Indian restaurant*?" Zaki looks very confused. I suddenly realize that Zaki means *jinni* as in *jinn*—the oft-evil spirits made of fire and capable of possessing people. It turns out that Zaki was recently called in to help with the exorcism of a possessed woman. And this may not surprise anyone, but it turns out that the bad *jinni,* in this case, spoke English, with an American accent. This is why the sheikh who was reading the Qur'an over the possessed woman needed Zaki to translate.

"Her face changed shape!" he says. "And she turned colors!"

"You saw this?" I say, eyebrow arched.

"Yes!"

"And you really believe in the *jinn*?"

He looks offended. "Every Muslim believes in the *jinn*!"

"Ah," I say. This was all before I actually read about the *jinn* in the Qur'an some months later. Not only do all Muslims believe in the *jinn,* they find it inconceivable that there are countries without *jinn.* I tell my Yemeni friends that the closest thing I can think of are ghosts, but they are the leftover energy or spirits of dead people, whereas the *jinn* were never human. I suppose the evil spirits or demons that possess evangelicals in the South and make them speak in tongues are the best Western version of the *jinn,* but with a different backstory.

Zaki describes how the woman writhed and moaned in American English before he returns to the newsroom. I've told him that he can write about the *jinn,* but I would like to see if scientists and doctors have any possible alternative explanations for the physical changes in the woman. Perhaps this is too secular a demand, but I am curious to hear what they might say.

I sit mulling this all over and then walk to the newsroom. Something is bothering me.

"Zaki," I say. "Did this woman know English?"

"No!" he says. "She is completely illiterate!"

"Hmmm."

"I know a woman like that too," says Bashir (who often stops in to help, despite having quit months ago). "She was completely illiterate, but when the *jinni* possessed her, she spoke perfect English with an American accent."

It turns out that pretty much everyone in Yemen knows a woman like this. At a loss for words, I turn back toward my office.

"You had better watch out," says Najma. "Since the *jinni* is American!"

"If the *jinni* is American," I say, smiling, "then I don't think I have to worry."

☾*

I AM GROWING CLOSER to all of my reporters. It's easy to spend time with my men outside of the office, because they can go where they want whenever they want. But my women all have curfews. They can't be out after dark, and I can't take them to dinner at a restaurant. Most women don't go to restaurants. (It's nearly impossible to eat while wearing a *niqab*.) Also, when I invite my women to lunch, they often decline because they are fasting. My women are frequently fasting, sometimes just because they want a little spiritual extra credit. Still, many afternoons I eat with Zuhra at al-Mankal, the nearby Jordanian restaurant where I now have lunch most days and where the manager brings us a wooden screen to hide her from view. Other days, I buy falafel sandwiches for me and Radia, who never goes home for lunch, and we sit eating them at her desk. None of the men are around then, so she flips up her veil while she eats and helps me with my Arabic homework.

My women are, however, more likely than the men to invite me home. It's easier for them; they don't have to worry about jealous wives. The first time I have lunch at Zuhra's house, I am struck by how joyful a place it is. She and her three sisters drag me to their bedroom after we eat, and we lie on the bed looking at scores of photos and a series of home movies. One stars Zuhra and Shetha (her sister now married and living in Dubai) playing old village women wrapped in the traditional Sana'ani *setarrh* (a red and blue cloth now worn only by the elderly). Ghazal, Zuhra's youngest sister, dances toward them in a skimpy dress. She doesn't cover her face or glittering eyes and exudes self-confidence. "Put something on!" Zuhra says in the film. Aping the old gossips who sit around judging the younger generation, they ask Ghazal if maybe she is *American*. Are you *praying* in America? Who is your father? (Two questions Zuhra says are often asked of young girls.) We all roll around on the bed laughing and poking each other.

"This is what we are like all the time," Zuhra says. I have a pang of envy. When I was a child I fantasized about having a big, noisy family. Zuhra and her sisters and mother are as close as I can imagine any family being. "We're like *Little Women*!" Zuhra says. I am surprised she knows the book. And I think they might have a bit more fun than those March sisters.

☾*

IBRAHIM IS ONE OF THE FEW MEN who dares to invite me home. I go to his house, some forty minutes outside of Sana'a, for lunch one Friday afternoon. Ibrahim and his wife, Sabah, live with a passel of relatives and children. Upstairs, I take off my shoes and settle in a large carpeted room, where the curious eyes of little people soon surround me. A plastic sheet is spread on the ground, and platters of fish, salads, breads, rice, chicken, radishes, and *zahawek* (the spicy Yemeni salsa I love) are piled in front of me. Because I am the only non–family member present, men and women eat together. If I were a man, I could eat only with the men. Sabah is very pretty and asks me the usual questions. Am I married? Yes, of course. Do I have children. I hesitate. No, I say, waiting for the usual cry of dismay. But to my surprise, she brightens. "Like me!" she says. "You are like me." I hadn't realized that Ibrahim had no children. He and his wife are both in their thirties and have been married since they were around twelve. Such early marriages are common in Yemen, though there is a growing movement to increase the minimum matrimonial age. I constantly hear reports, from both Yemenis and westerners, of young girls forced into marriage before their bodies and psyches are prepared. These appall me, and I find it horrifying that it is acceptable for grown men to find twelve-year-olds sexually appealing.

But Ibrahim and Sabah share a genuine affection that isn't often obvious between husbands and wives here. It is unusual for a Yemeni man to stay with a woman who hasn't given him children. Yet Ibrahim and Sabah occupy themselves with caring for their herd of nieces and nephews and appear happy.

☪

ALL THIS PROGRESS with the rest of my staff leaves me with just two people to worry about: al-Asaadi and Zaid. Faris has promised to keep al-Asaadi out of my hair by making him the editor of a new magazine he's launching and has approved my choice of Zaid as my successor. While I am dismayed that I only have a couple of months to get Zaid up to speed when he returns from London, I have high hopes that his journalism studies abroad have molded him into something resembling an editor. All I will have to do, I hope, is polish his edges. Yet I am plagued by anxieties. I have no idea what Zaid will be like as a manager. I have no idea how al-Asaadi will take to his new job.

My relationship with al-Asaadi has improved with distance. He calls and writes me enthusiastic e-mails from upstate New York, where he is studying and working as an intern at a newspaper, congratulating me on what I have done with the *Observer* (which he reads online). "Only now can I appreciate what you did for us," he says. "I am so grateful for all I have learned from you." I am astonished. Who is this man, and what has he done with my belligerent little fellow editor? Yet this doesn't quell my fears that our old battles will resume once we are face-to-face again.

Al-Asaadi arrives in Yemen a week before Zaid. He demonstrates his Americanization by kissing me once on each cheek, a first. We have lunch together soon after his return, at al-Mankal, my favorite haunt. We chatter easily about his time in the United States and about work. Jamal Hindi, the Jordanian owner of al-Mankal, comes over to tell us that he is going organic. He spent eight years living in Hong Kong and the Philippines, where he learned about macrobiotics and became interested in organic food. Once he began eating organic, he says, he lost seventy-five pounds. Now, Mr. Hindi is still a very large man, so it's a bit alarming to imagine what he looked like before.

The first organic restaurant in Sana'a! I pull out a notebook and interview him. I also interview the manager and several people eating nearby. In between, al-Asaadi tells me his plans for the new magazine, called *Yemen Today*. I look at his list of proposed sections and story lineup and am very impressed. *Newsweek,* look out! We discuss stories and timelines, and I'm amazed at how well al-Asaadi and I get along when we aren't battling for supremacy. A huge burden has been lifted from my shoulders; now all I have to worry about is Zaid.

☾

ZAID ARRIVES FROM LONDON about a week later, and I take him to the same restaurant. Like al-Asaadi, he greets me with a kiss on each cheek. Yemeni men who have been abroad are particularly fond of this Western custom. Frankly, I prefer not to be kissed. I've become incredibly protective of my physical space here; every touch begins to feel like a violation after a while in a country where most men and women never even speak to each other.

We have a fantastic lunch. He tells me about his studies in London, although he spends more time talking about all of the women he got to hug and all the whiskey he drank. He also tells me about the scandal he created when he arrived at Sana'a airport. "When I was in London, people asked me what was the first thing that I wanted to do when I got back to Yemen," he says, "and I said that the first thing I wanted to do was to kiss my wife. I missed this woman like you would not *believe.*"

So when his wife met him at the airport, he lifted her veil and he kissed her. "She was angry at me for about twenty seconds," he says. "Then she kissed me back."

Her relatives are less forgiving. His wife's father and brothers are still furious with him. Heaven forbid a man demonstrate his love for his wife in public.

I update Zaid on life at the paper, give him an outline of our schedule, and talk with him about how I would like our relationship to work. Until I leave, I am in charge. To present a unified front, I want him to run anything he says to the reporters by me first. Zaid concurs.

He then announces that he has given up *qat* entirely. I find this hard to believe, as I have rarely seen Zaid in the newsroom without a massively swollen cheek.

"You should ban it from the newsroom," he says.

"There would be mutiny!"

"No, the men would thank you for it in the end."

Oh really?

This lunch leaves me feeling even more relaxed. At last, I have someone willing to help me! At last, I can begin to shift a bit of my burden and
begin to think about the future.

☾

AT HOME, I've started building a family. My new Scottish housemate, Carolyn, whom I met at the Soqotra airport and who had originally planned
to stay for just a month, moves in for the rest of my time in Yemen. This
delights me, as I'm not eager to evict someone who does my laundry, occasionally cooks, and entertains me endlessly with her adventures following in the footsteps of Ibn Battuta and leading tour groups through Iran,
Saudi Arabia, and Tashkent.

Just when I've settled into domestic life with Carolyn, my Dutch
friend Koosje rings one morning while I am making coffee.

"Remember how you said that maybe I could live with you if I had to
move out of my house?" she says.

"Yeees . . ."

"Well, I do actually have to move out. So, would it still be possible?"

"When?" I stir my coffee.

"Twenty minutes? I'm already packed."

What can I do? I can't leave a pretty blond Dutch girl to the streets. So
half an hour later, I have a second housemate. They bookend me agewise;
Carolyn is forty-nine and Koosje twenty-two. Koosje is an intern at
UNHCR.

It surprises me to find that I love living with other people. For years I
have thought I could only live alone. After all, I have lived alone quite happily for the better part of twelve years. Now I find I am a communal crea-
ture after all. I love coming home and sprawling in my *mafraj* with Carolyn
or Koosje. I love the flurry of their comings and goings. I love that there
are always other people around to help, say, fix the washing machine.
Funny how you can get to thirty-eight and still find out so many new
things about yourself.

We all get on famously, spending our free evenings lounging in our *mafraj,* talking over drinks. My friends are more diverse than ever before: Dutch students, German development workers, Ethiopian housecleaners, Kenyan consultants, and Yemeni economists. It occurs to me how insular my world was in the cosmopolitan city of New York. I could not have anticipated, for example, that it would be a Republican oil company executive from Texas, a man named Don, who would become one of my most loyal friends in Yemen.

(*

OF COURSE, my life is never quite trouble free. Just when my reputation is beginning to recover from my little run-in with customs, it suffers a new insult. One Thursday afternoon, Floor rings. She has the alcohol left over from Kamaran; may she drop it off for the party we are throwing at my house that night? No problem, I say. Swing by the office. There are three bottles of whiskey and two of vodka, which clank suspiciously as I trot from Floor's jeep back to my desk. I stuff them into my gym bag, which is sitting on a chair by the door, and go back to editing a front-page story.

A few minutes later, I hear a sharp clang, followed by the shattering of glass. My gym bag has thrown itself from its chair, as if offended at being asked to carry the contraband. I look up, horrified to see the spreading pool on my carpet. Immediately, my office smells like an Irish bar at closing time. I panic. I've wasted alcohol, in a dry country! I should be taken out back and shot. Worse, my door is open and any minute a reporter is going to walk in and step into a puddle of vodka. Just one bottle has broken, thank god. I vault over my desk and begin to frantically pick up the pieces of glass. I am grateful it wasn't the whiskey.

I am still on the floor, my knees soaked in booze, when Qasim walks in.

"Dageega!" (One minute!), I say. *"Law samaht, ureedo dageega."* (Please, I need one minute.) I wave my hand at him, trying to send him away, but he just walks all the way in and looks over my shoulder at the three bottles of whiskey I have just rescued from certain ruin.

"Oh!" he says.

I curse my ineptitude. Qasim leaves my office, probably to go tell Faris

I'm a mad dipsomaniac bent on destroying the remaining morals of my staff. First vibrating artificial men, now this!

I open all my windows and stash the other bottles under my desk, but my office still reeks like a tavern.

Luke strolls in, stares at my carpet, and sniffs the air. "Well," he says. "There goes the rest of your reputation."

"Hey," I say with false cheer. "At least vodka doesn't stain. My carpet has never been so sterile."

Our stalwart receptionist, Enass, without saying a word, walks in and hands me a bottle of carpet cleaner.

I have another special delivery that day. Abdurahman, Ali's dad, calls to say he's bringing me a bag of organic avocados, which cannot be found in Sana'a. I am so ecstatic I briefly forget the vodka. That evening, in my taxi home, I stroke them, just to feel their firm roundness under my palms. I can't remember the last time I was so excited to put something in my mouth. Anne and Florens come over to help me mash the avocados into a dip for the party. Which turns out to be a roaring success, in that few people can remember the details of it the next day. I've never had such a crowded house. My *mafraj* overflows with people, several of whom I've never met. Everyone from Kamaran is there, plus Marvin, Pearl, and Ginny. I wear a short, sleeveless dress and savor the feel of it sliding up my thighs as I raise my arms to dance. It's springtime, and it feels like it.

After we've all been dancing for a while, Marvin requests cowboy music. I put on a country song and he and Pearl actually two-step around the room, knocking over several drinks as they swish around. It feels like a real party. (Yemenis of course have parties too, but they are always sex segregated and usually revolve around *qat* and sugary tea.) The only thing missing tonight, I think, is romance.

☪

IT ISN'T LONG, HOWEVER, before this last void in my life is delightfully filled by a twenty-six-year-old German water researcher for the Dutch Embassy. Tobias is intelligent and attractive, tall, with oversized feet and hands, like a puppy that hasn't quite grown into his extremities. His square Germanic face is softened by floppy dark hair, large blue eyes, and an infectious grin. I meet him through Kamaran Island friends, and when he moves into a house nearby he begins inviting me over to parties and *qat* chews. Our mutual attraction is increasingly obvious, but weeks pass before we admit it to each other.

It happens on a weeknight. I'm exhausted from work but when Tobias asks if he may come over, I perk up. It's the first time we've been alone together. We make drinks and curl up in the *mafraj*. After a while, he suggests watching a movie. I put on *Half Nelson,* and we press close together in front of my twelve-inch computer screen. Tobias moves his arm around me and I slide into his embrace. I have no idea how *Half Nelson* ends. I'm not even sure if we turned it off or just left it running as we made love, first in the *mafraj* and again, moments later, in my bed.

He wakes me at dawn. After we say good morning properly, he sneaks home and I get ready for work, feeling more cheerful than I have since I got to this country.

I skip the gym and walk to work. The spring is back in my step, the kind of spring that makes men on the street pay twice as much attention to me as usual. I dare not meet anyone's eyes, I feel so incandescent with sensuality. When Luke walks into my office, he says, "Okay, what happened to you? Why the Cheshire cat smile?"

I say nothing at all.

☾

TOBIAS SPENDS ALMOST EVERY NIGHT with me that week, and on Friday, we don't leave my house. We spend about twenty-one of twenty-four hours naked and entwined, until hunger drives us finally out of bed, and Tobias cooks us pasta, which we wash down with a bottle of wine in my *mafraj*. The *muezzins* keep calling out Friday prayers, the wail of the preachers prompting Tobias to cry out, "You people don't know what you are missing!" But we are praying, in our own way, to our own decadent gods.

As the sun slides down over the rooftops around us, filling my *mafraj* with gold, Tobias falls asleep in my lap, looking angelic and terribly young. I stroke his hair and run my fingers over the decorative curl in his earlobes, his dark eyelashes, his flushed cheeks, his pale, flat stomach. I like him. The age gap between us and his return to Germany in a few months makes a future unlikely, but for the first time all year, a simple glow of well-being makes worry feel impossible.

I dream that night that I have a good fairy who has been watching out for me. She looks like a middle-aged housewife, plump, with short dark hair, and she seems slightly annoyed.

"Well, it looks like things are now going exceptionally well for you," she says, a touch resentfully. "So I am going to go find someone else to help, someone with *real* problems."

☪

THERE ARE PEOPLE in this world who can go for years without being touched. I am not one of them. I can't survive more than a month of physical loneliness without wanting to crawl out of my skin. Which means that I've been wanting to crawl out of my skin almost since I got to Yemen. I am deeply physically needy, and I refuse to be ashamed of this. So when one of my closest Yemeni friends, a virgin, confesses to me that she also thinks constantly about sex, I try to reassure her that she is not an immoral freak. Don't you think Allah gave us these desires for a reason? I say. That he gave us these bodies for a reason? This does not shock my Yemeni friend. In fact, she seems quite heartened. "This is true," she says happily. "Why *would* we be given bodies like this?"

Shaima, on the other hand, simply buries her desires. One night as she drives me home from dinner, we chat about men and relationships.

"I have never kissed a man, Jennifer," she confesses.

"Never?" Shaima is over thirty years old. I kissed my first boy in fifth grade. No, wait—first grade! I still remember his name. Bobby Woodward. Audacious tyke.

"Never."

"So how do you . . ." I want to say, how do you survive never being touched? How can you bear the loneliness? But I swallow the words.

"Jennifer, I just ignore my body," she says in answer to my unasked question. "I try to forget it is there."

☪

MY RESEARCH for our next health page gives me a little more insight into Yemeni sexuality. While searching for interesting new studies, I stumble across a piece in *New Scientist* on how oral sex causes cancer. Apparently anyone who has had five or more partners is about a trillion times more likely to develop throat cancer. While I am spiraling into despair about this, Jabr comes into my office. He is my only reporter not working on something.

"Jabr," I begin cautiously, "do you think we could get away with a story on oral sex?"

He looks at me blankly. "What is oral sex?" he says. From the awkward way he forms the words, it is clear that he has never heard the phrase.

I am shocked. Most of my male reporters (according to Luke) are surfing porn sites every time I turn my back, so I thought they had a pretty graphic image of what oral sex is.

I start to explain, but for the first time in my life, I find myself too embarrassed to describe a sex act.

"Don't be shy," says Jabr encouragingly.

My stomach twists. "I'm not! It's just . . ." It's just that I don't want to accidentally excite you, I think to myself.

Instead, I pick up the dictionary from my desk and read him the definition. Neither of us cracks a smile.

"Um, so, what I am wondering is, are we going to get in trouble for writing about this? Is it okay according to Islam? Between married people, of course!"

"Let me check," says Jabr gravely. "I will read the study."

A half hour later, I stop in the newsroom to find Jabr reading through everything Google has turned up on oral sex. He has consulted with Noor and Najma, neither of whom has heard of oral sex. All three reporters are single, so perhaps this is not surprising.

Noor turns to me and says, "We don't have such a thing in Yemen as oral sex."

"You don't?" This cannot be true.

"No," Jabr agrees.

"We are a conservative country," says Noor. "We don't do this."

"Not even married people?"

All three shake their heads.

"But it's . . ." A thousand inappropriate explanations of why it's healthy and necessary threaten to burst out of my mouth. I bite my tongue. "Let's drop it then. We'll run the iPod story instead."

This is absurd, given that the iPod story is about the effect of iPods on pacemakers, and hardly any Yemenis own either gizmo. But at least it won't scandalize anyone.

Curious to find out the truth, I report the conversation to Luke. "They claim there is no such thing as oral sex in Yemen."

"Oh yes there *is!*" he says, laughing.

"I figured you would know."

I guess the gay men have all the luck. Once you're engaged in one illegal activity, you might as well go all out.

Later, married Yemeni women tell me that oral sex *does* exist but that many people consider it shameful. "Women are not honest with each other," says one Yemeni woman. If a woman admits that her husband "kisses her vagina," others disparage the act as disgusting. Some think that a man who performs oral sex is being too servile to his wife and unmanly. "It's just how we are trained, to think our bodies are disgusting," says my friend. "Some women don't feel husbands should witness birth because they will be disgusted. Women think organs are a disgusting place. Women internalize these sexist ideas. In Islam, you should take a shower after sex."

☪

IT MAKES ALL THE DIFFERENCE to have Tobias waiting for me after work. Someone to whom I can pour out the frustrations of my day, someone to hand me a drink and sit with me looking out over the boxy brown houses of Old Sana'a glowing in the dark, holding my hand. Someone with interesting stories of his own. My reporters sense a new lightness in me. The women tell me I look pretty twice as much as usual, looking slightly suspicious. How do they get through their lives? I wonder. How can they bear sleeping alone every night? They must have passions of their own, but what do they do with them? Offer them to God? Perhaps that is it. Perhaps if I had God, I could be happier alone. I could be happier without fingers brushing against my skin, without a warm body curled around me. But I do not have God. All I have is a persistent and not necessarily wise openness to love, and a relentless desire to be loved in return.

Despite how well things are going, I've been looking forward to a break from my six-day week, from my twelve-hour days. But the thought of returning to a job in New York, the thought of once again climbing onto the endless treadmill of work and rent paying and rushing from place to place in anonymous crowds, fills me with dread.

I have no idea what I will do at the end of this year. I've scarcely had time to look up from my desk. But now that I have become human again and made room for joy and leisure in between manic workdays, my brain finds itself with time to look up at the horizon. There is nothing there.

TWENTY

the deluge

Just when I am at my happiest personally and most optimistic about my paper's future, harbingers of doom appear. It takes less than a week for me to realize that Zaid's English has failed to improve one iota during his ten months in London. How he managed this is beyond me, but I struggle to edit his stories and it becomes clear that he is not remotely capable of editing anyone else's work. After fighting so hard to sell Faris on Zaid, now I am going to have to do some rethinking.

Zaid already seems to have lost his resolve to give up *qat*. The day after our lunch, I walk into the office to find him stuffing a leaf into his mouth. I raise an eyebrow.

"It was a gift!" he says. "I couldn't refuse it! It would be rude!"

I have also begun to have trouble with Hadi, who has always been the most reliable and devoted of designers. He has been coming in later every day, sometimes not appearing until noon. This mystifies me. One morning, desperate to lay out a page, I collar Luke.

"Hadi hardly ever gets here on time anymore! What is going on?"

"Did you know he got a car?"

"He got a car?"

"So that's why he's been coming in late."

I don't get it. Shouldn't a car get him here even earlier?

"He's been working as a taxi driver in the mornings."

Ah. This is not unusual. Many Yemenis string together several jobs to make ends meet. If Faris raised staff salaries, it might keep them from taking side jobs that distract them from their work. Even al-Asaadi worked for UNICEF while editor in chief of the paper. This not only took him away from the office too often but was entirely unethical, as the newspaper regularly covers UNICEF's activities.

Some reporters make it difficult for me to agitate for higher pay. When the men want a raise, they begin doing less and less work, if they bother to show up at all. I try to explain to Hadi—who just asked for a raise—that if he wants to be paid more, he should prove that he is worth it. He should be showing up *early* and getting an exceptional amount of work done. That is what would make me want to help you get more money, I say. This baffles him.

The Missing Link does the same thing. A day after asking for a raise, Jabr doesn't show up at work or even call in with an excuse. When I finally get him on the phone, he says he is napping.

"Jabr, if you're hoping for a raise, it's not terribly wise to start skipping work. You should be demonstrating how much you deserve it, not what a shirker you are."

My frustration with Hadi builds until one morning in late June. Hadi, who was the happiest with our new schedule, has begun to drag our closes.

"You cannot keep coming in this late!" I say, accosting him as he walks in the door one closing day at noon.

"Do you have any pages?" he says belligerently.

"Yes, I have pages! But that isn't the point. You are supposed to be here in the morning. You have a *job!*"

Things escalate until we are shouting at each other in the hallway. I ask Zaid for help, saying I have to get Hadi to the office earlier. He goes outside to talk with Hadi, and I retreat to my office.

A few minutes later, Zaid appears in my door.

"Hadi has a big problem," he says.

"I know, he can't get to work on time," I say crossly.

"No, he has a big problem at home. He said he wants to sleep in the office and never go home. It has to be serious for him to say that. He was crying just now."

I feel guilty for yelling at him. "If he has a reason he can't get here on time, he should tell me."

"I think you should talk with him."

I go outside and find Hadi on the front steps, leaning against the building. I touch his arm.

"Hadi, I am sorry I yelled at you. I don't like yelling at you. I love working with you, and I want things to be good between us," I begin.

His anger is gone. He smiles at me, his long black lashes still damp with tears.

"If you have a problem, some reason you can't come in, you can tell me," I say. "You can talk to me."

"Thank you," he says, reaching out to pat my arm, an unusual gesture. "Thank you." He's short of money for things he needs at home, he says. He's also been having bitter arguments with his wife. It's unclear if the two problems are related. I promise to try to get him a little more money from Faris and he promises to try to get to work earlier.

☾

ON JUNE 26, I must somehow sense what the day has in store, because I wake too depressed to eat and cry all the way to the gym. It all builds up, my worry about Zaid, my fear about leaving the paper, my anxiety over the future, and the floodgates open. Thank god I'm wearing dark glasses. I run five miles on the treadmill and bike half an hour, as if I can somehow get away from myself. I head out afterward to find that none of the hotel taxi drivers will give me a ride, because they are all curled up in the trunks of their cars, green leaves sticking out of their mouths.

Irritated, I stride out to the main road and hail a cab. The driver argues about the price, but I get weary of fighting and climb in. I just want to get to work.

I am staring out the window for the first half of the ride, watching the storefronts and child salesmen and pyramids of tomatoes and watermelons spin by, so I don't notice my driver's activities. Then a frenzied movement in my peripheral vision arrests my attention. I look over to see that my driver has his grubby hand around his penis and is vigorously and quite openly jerking off.

At first I refuse to believe it. But then I look again. I am *not* imagining it.

In horror, I pull some *riyals* out of my purse and throw them at him, leaping from the car in the middle of a major intersection. "You *disgust* me!" I yell. Dodging cars, I run panting and nauseated across the street, my bags banging against my back. I cannot get over his complete lack of shame. Did he think he could get away with that, just because I was a foreigner? I wish I hadn't paid him. I wish I had remembered the Arabic word for "shame." I wish I had hit him. I stop and look around. I have no idea where I am. I am probably only halfway to work. But I have been on this route so many times, I figure if I just keep walking I will see something I recognize. It's hot, and the sun and dust press down on me. Once again I am grateful for my dark sunglasses as I stumble crying down the street, trying to stifle my sobs as I pass groups of construction workers. I walk and weep all the way to the office. My women are gathered at the gate, as if expecting me. It is lunchtime, and the men are gone.

"Do you have a cold?" says Zuhra, looking anxious.

"No, I just . . ." I start crying again, and Zuhra and Radia follow me to my office. I tell them the whole story, but they don't look impressed.

"This happens to all of us," Zuhra says. "It is normal."

Radia concurs. They are harassed constantly, both by taxi drivers and men on the streets. Even fully covered, fully disguised.

"One time a man even offered me money to go to a hotel with him," says Radia. "But what can we do? This is what men are like."

This is what men are like.

"You should not be subjected to this!" I cry. "It is *not* normal. I can't bear the fact that you think of this as normal! You should not have to suffer these horrible men."

They concur. "But what can we do?"

☾⋆

AT THE END of the month, the rains come with a vengeance. While the mornings are still sunny and clear, by the afternoons dark clouds have filled the sky. It's unwise to start walking anywhere between lunch and dinner; that's when the deep purple bellies of the clouds tear open, flooding the city.

It's nearly rain time one closing day when al-Asaadi rings to tell me he has a front-page story. A group of Belgian tourists was barred by the Tourism Police from traveling to the picturesque village of Kawkaban and are outraged. They complained that they had read in our paper that Yemen was inviting and safe, and now the minister of tourism is holding them captive in Sana'a. Al-Asaadi wants the headline to be GOVERNMENT KIDNAPPED US, SAYS TOURISTS.

I politely suggest that the word "kidnapped" may be slightly loaded, and al-Asaadi concurs. We change it to TOURISTS BLOCKED FROM TRAVEL. I'm trying to explain how I want things laid out to Hadi, but both al-Asaadi and Zaid are hovering, blocking my way.

"Three editors in one place is two too many," I say in frustration. "Could I please have some space to finish telling Hadi about this paragraph?" No one moves, and I throw the pages I'm editing to the floor. It's a bit melodramatic, but experience has taught me that my reporters don't respond to subtlety.

This jolts the men into action. Al-Asaadi slips back upstairs to his new office, and Zaid storms off in an adolescent funk.

"Do whatever you want with the paper. I'm leaving," he flings at me before toddling huffily off down the road, despite the fact that I have invited him to chew qat at my house after work.

This is the first of several dozen times that Zaid will "quit." He'll tell me he's done with the paper, storm off in a sulk, and then the next morning at the office he'll be back in front of his customary computer. "Funny," I'll say, "I could have sworn you quit yesterday." It gets so the day doesn't feel quite complete if I haven't driven Zaid to quit.

With Zaid gone, I quickly finish my edits and find Ali, who has come back from the United States to work for me again. Luke has been moved upstairs to edit Arabia Felix, so Ali temporarily fills his shoes. Rain spatters my hair as we walk to his antique powder-blue car. By the time we are on the road, the rain is coming down in blinding sheets. It's the hardest rain I have ever seen here. Knowing the Sayilah—the moat-like road around the Old City—will be flooded, we turn off Zubairi Street to wind our way through the back alleys. But the windows have fogged so badly we cannot see out the back or side. I pull Kleenexes out of my purse and daub at the windshield, but it refogs as fast as I wipe. The streets are flooding with fast water, and I am genuinely afraid that we will be swept along into the Sayilah and go under the rushing muddy river. At last, unable to see and unable to find a passable street, Ali stops the car on a hill. We sit, waiting out the storm.

"Too bad we don't have a flask," I say, fiddling with the broken radio.

"I was just thinking that."

While we are waiting, I get a text from Zaid.

"I thought u'll show me more respect, but girls and Ibrahim are your favorite and me at the end of your list. U made me feel empty and nothing. Thanks and sorry can't understand u anymore."

What am I going to do with him? I myself am no model of comportment, but I can at least say with a clear conscience that I have never once threatened to walk out on my job. At least the girls never fling themselves out of the office in a funk or threaten to quit.

"Ali, help me," I say. "Couldn't *you* take over the paper?" He is half-Yemeni, after all. His English is flawless. He's ideal.

"No *way*," he says without pausing for reflection. "I just don't care about it enough—not like you do."

Maybe I care about it too much. I want to control what happens to it after I leave; I want to shape Zaid into a model editor; I want my reforms to be immortal. I want better conditions for my reporters and a better reputation for the paper. I want the *Observer* to be *effective,* to influence public thought. But I'm starting to realize that no matter how hard I work, no matter what kind of plans I make, these things are beyond me. I cannot single-handedly save this paper. I'm still pondering this when Carolyn rings. "Now don't panic," she says. "But I thought I should warn you. . . ."

As if it had absorbed the full weight of my hopes and dreams for the *Observer,* a large chunk of the roof of my 350-year-old gingerbread house has collapsed. A massive pile of ceiling, dirt, and rubble has tumbled to the hallway of our top floor, just outside the room where a houseguest was sleeping. And the rain is pouring in.

I panic, picturing a massive river of water cascading down my stairs, sweeping away our shoes from the landings. "I should get home," I tell Ali.

The rain has eased a bit, so Ali and I park and pick our way through ankle-deep water to my ruined home. Outside, crowds line the flooded Sayilah and its series of bridges. A carnival atmosphere prevails, adults as excited as the children to see the sudden river circling the city. I've never seen the water so high; it must be more than ten feet deep. Children slither down the stone embankments and splash into the muddy brew. A taxi floats by. A large truck is semisubmerged under the bridge. Forgetting my roof for a moment, I pull out my camera and begin snapping photos. Men walk by with their white *thobes* pulled up, revealing their undershorts. When they do this, they wrap their robes around their *jambiyas,* so it looks like they are all walking around with enormous erections. Sometimes men even hold on to each other's *jambiyas* as they walk, with no apparent thought for the overt eroticism of the gesture.

Fifty photos later, we tear ourselves away from the spectacle and splash down the street to my house. When I unlock the gate, Ali and I race to the top floor. An avalanche of mud, straw, plaster and rock litters the last staircase. I stop short of the landing, because there is nowhere left to stand. A waist-high pile of roof fills the hallway. A few drops of water hit my hair and I look up. Sure enough, above us is only a jagged chunk of Arabian sky.

My home, the paper, this city—always falling apart, always needing to be rebuilt. This is the ride I am on.

TWENTY-ONE

bombs, breakups, and bastille day

On the first Monday in July, an unlikely event restores my faith in my staff— a bombing. That afternoon, I put the paper to bed early and go home to try to nap. Sleep refuses the invitation, and I get up to check my e-mail, to find messages from Fox News, CBS, and Global Radio Network asking if I am still in Yemen and if I have any more information about the terrorist bombing in Ma'rib, a city a hundred miles east of Sana'a that is popular with tourists for its spectacular dam and ancient ruins. Why hasn't anyone on my staff called me?

I'm dialing the office before I even finish reading the e-mails. Al-Asaadi is still there, *al-hamdulillah,* working on *Yemen Today.*

"Don't let them send the paper to the printer!" I say. "We have to add the Ma'rib story." Al-Asaadi has only just heard the news himself. This is, I think, as close to a "Stop the presses!" moment as I am ever likely to have. In a flurry of excitement, I ring Farouq and Ibrahim and ask them to report the story pronto and file it directly to me. I can edit it from home and send it to Zaid at the office for layout.

While waiting for them, I ring the spokesmen at the Ministry of the Interior and the Ministry of Information. I don't get anywhere. They just keep giving me each other's phone number and don't seem to know anything. If I were in the United States, I think, I would just get in a car and go to the scene of the bombing. But this kind of on-the-ground reporting is nearly impossible here. Getting to Ma'rib would mean not only finding a car, but crossing some thirty military checkpoints. For non-Yemenis, getting through those requires a sheaf of travel permissions: sheets of paper containing the name of the traveler's organization, vehicle number, and dates of travel, authorized by the Tourism Police. Who has time for that on deadline?

If you are one of the rare foreigners who track Yemeni news, you notice after a while that there are almost never witnesses to newsworthy events. You never get the story from the guy who lives near the site of the car bomb, who heard it go off and watched the car go up in flames while bystanders raced for shelter. This is partly because journalists are rarely allowed anywhere near a crime scene and partly because witnesses would never speak to a journalist. They're too afraid of getting into trouble. Of course, it also doesn't often occur to Yemeni reporters to interview anyone but official sources. When I ask my reporters to find out what regular people on the street think of a proposed law, for example, their typical response is, "Who cares about regular people?"

The dearth of eyewitnesses and other nonofficial sources makes for dull and often misleading stories. I don't trust the Ministry of the Interior to feed me anything but fraudulent pap, the aim of which is to make the government look good and anyone in conflict with them look bad.

I hound Ibrahim and Farouq until they e-mail me their stories, and I weave them together. Nine people are believed dead, seven Spanish tourists and two Yemeni drivers. They were ambushed by a suicide bomber who drove a truck full of explosives through their convoy at the site of the Ba'ran Temple, also called Arsh Bilqis (the Queen of Sheba's Throne) in Ma'rib.

I e-mail the finished story to Zaid, tell him which photo to use, and send a copy to al-Asaadi to put on the Web. It's a little exciting. Despite the tragedy, and the sorrow and fear it evokes, I can't help but feel that familiar guilty journalistic thrill at a major news story breaking.

The story requires weeks of follow-up. This has never been the paper's strong suit, but my reporters amaze me. They interview a surviving Yemeni driver who still has shrapnel in his right eye and left ear. They write about the financial hardship facing the families of the two dead and two injured Yemenis, who have no way to support themselves now that their sons and cars are gone. They write about the decline in tourism.

The bombing, we report, has all the hallmarks of an al-Qaeda attack. Yet some sources suggest that it is the work of a new al-Qaeda cell, not of the veterans who trained in Afghanistan. Zaid writes a piece exploring the differences between the old and new al-Qaeda and why young men might be drawn to careers in terrorism.

Yemen is a fertile breeding ground for terrorists for many reasons. It is one of the poorest countries in the world, with a corrupt government. This corruption results in major inequities between rich and poor, fostering a strong sense of injustice. Despite significant oil revenues over the past thirty years, the government has failed to provide effective education and health services, sustainable water supplies, and reliable power to its people. The regime gives land and commercial contracts to its supporters while neglecting areas controlled by its opponents. Rumors abound that the president's cronies profit from smuggling of arms, oil, and drugs; after all, little effort has been made to stop such smuggling. Exacerbating matters, a corrupt and incompetent judiciary makes it difficult to address grievances. No wonder people feel angry and impotent.

A weak government, poor intelligence services, and lax immigration procedures also mean that terrorists can operate more freely in Yemen than they can in stronger neighboring countries, such as Saudi Arabia. The Saudi government has attacked terrorism with will, determination, and resources not found in Yemen and made it very difficult for terrorists to operate there—so many have moved to Yemen.

My staff reports all of this. I am bursting with pride in my reporters for continuing to generate story after story in the wake of the attack. It's a huge reminder of how far we have all come.

☪

NOW THAT ALI has taken over as copy editor, we fly through pages. Closing is faster than it was with Luke, who was rather Yemeni in his approach to closing times. Ali doesn't loiter in the *qat* shed shooting the breeze with the guys, doesn't vanish for four hours at lunchtime, and doesn't chew at work. He even helps my other reporters with their writing, and they help him to conduct interviews in Arabic (which Ali speaks, but not confidently enough to interview government officials).

With the notable exception of Zaid, progress is all around. Sure, I still see atrocious stories. Editing itself doesn't get that much easier. But there's no denying the changes in every single one of my journalists. And that *matters*.

My grand delusion that I can spread democracy in the Arab world by loosening the stays of the Yemeni press has dwindled, as have my illusions that any story we write could have the smallest impact on government policy. But in the place of these lofty dreams are smaller, more stably built achievements. My reporters almost always use more than one source per story. They can integrate statistics into trend pieces. They've got a rudimentary grasp of ethics and journalistic integrity. Some of them even occasionally write a good lead. These modest achievements will outlive me. That is something.

Sometimes, when I look at my work at the newspaper and squint in just the right way, I can even see it as a microcosm of democracy itself. After all, every staff member participates in the creation of each issue. I solicit their ideas. I value the contributions of women and minorities. Of course, I wasn't democratically elected, but what newspaper chief ever was?

☾

ONLY AFTER THE ADRENALINE of writing about the bombing has worn off do I turn my thoughts to my own safety. Throughout all of my months in Yemen, all of my late-night walks through the Old City, never once have I felt in danger. Yes, men harass me constantly and everyone stares, but I haven't felt threatened with violence. The Ma'rib bombing suggests that perhaps I've become too complacent. Just a couple weeks before, Koosje and Tobias had traveled to Ma'rib, to the same temple where the Spanish tourists and Yemeni drivers were killed. It could have been them. For a few weeks, my friends and others in the expat community seem a bit edgier than usual, but eventually we all go back to worrying about our work and love lives. It is impossible to live on full alert all the time. I wonder why the bombing doesn't make me feel like fleeing the country, but then I think, September 11 didn't make me feel like fleeing New York, did it? There's danger everywhere, and attempts to predict the terrorists' actions in an effort to dodge it are a fool's game.

☪

NOW THAT I'M BACK to worrying about more personal things, my thoughts turn to Tobias. He will leave soon, before I do. We've only been together a couple of months, but we're about to be forced into some decisions. Either we go our separate ways and call this a summer fling, or we try to keep going. Staying together would involve either a long-distance relationship (which I don't want) or one of us moving. Tobias is heading back to graduate school, to work on a doctorate. And I am—well, I don't know yet. I guess I'm flexible. The truth is, neither of us is sure what we want. I genuinely adore Tobias. He's smart, he's sexy, and he makes me laugh. But I have no idea if we'd be a good match in the longer term. We're at different places in our lives; my student days are long past and his are not yet over.

During Tobias's last few weeks, we don't have time to see much of each other, which makes our parting less dramatic. Still, resigned though I am to the logical end of our romance, I'm sad to see him go. Maybe he isn't the perfect life partner for me, but a small part of me wishes we'd at least had time to let things run their natural course, whatever that might be. I never have an easy time saying good-bye. We set all of our concerns aside to spend one last night lying under my stained glass windows, in each other's arms. Then he is gone. A group of us walk him to the taxi, and I am the last to hug him. In full view of my neighbors, the driver, and our friends, I stand on my toes and kiss him. "You'll get in trouble," he whispers. "I don't care," I say. And I turn away, before anyone can see my tears.

In the morning, I listen to the new Wilco album, *Sky Blue Sky.* The first song reminds me of an empty summer day in a small New England town. The kind of day on which I had a lemonade stand to raise money to buy a water pistol, but no one passed by, and the air was still and quiet except for the occasional drone of a plane overhead or a passing fly. That feeling . . . like a pause in the middle of life, after which anything could happen.

☪

I ESCAPE LONELINESS by burying myself in work, spending even more time with my staff as our time together shortens. Zaid can't seem to make up his mind how he feels about me. One moment he's telling me that I taught him everything he knows and that he reveres me, and the next he's quitting again because I haven't been respectful. But I'm still trying with him, still hoping that somehow he will manage when I am gone.

One mid-July closing day, he's already quit once, so I'm surprised when he approaches me as Ali and I are finishing photo captions. "Are you going to the Bastille Day reception at the French ambassador's house Saturday night?" he asks. I want to go, but I don't have an invitation. Because I cannot legally be listed as the editor in chief on the masthead, all invitations now go to Zaid. Before he arrived, when they were still addressed to al-Asaadi, Enass passed everything to me.

"I have an invitation," Zaid says. "Wanna be my date?"

"Okay, I'll be your date." It's my peace offering. It is also a decision that will change the course of my entire life.

ON BASTILLE DAY, the day of the French ambassador's party, I have an unusually productive day. I edit all three health stories, including Adhara's piece on the danger of listening to headphones in a lightning storm. She mistakes thunder for lightning, however, and keeps referring to "thunder strikes." I also edit Jabr's surprisingly adequate report on the harassment of women by taxi drivers. Near and dear to my heart.

My male reporters are terribly excited about the French party (the women of course are not allowed to go) and arrive at the office decked out in smart Western suits, their hair neatly combed or slicked back. I feel slightly less spectacular in plain black pants and a long royal-blue embroidered Turkish tunic. Nothing to be done. Useless to worry about fashion in Yemen. I put on exceptionally bright red lipstick and hope that will spruce me up.

Zaid, Jabr, Bashir (who still drops by to help us on closing days), and I all pile into photographer Mohammed al-Sharabi's battered car, and away we go. Zaid makes me sit in the front, and the three men squish together in the backseat. Zaid rings someone on his cell. *"Feyn ant?"* he says. Where are you? Yemeni men begin every phone conversation like this. They cannot possibly talk to someone if they don't know exactly where that person is.

"Do you know what that means?" asks Bashir.

"Of course," I say, mildly insulted. "That's baby Arabic!"

"No one speak Arabic!" says Bashir. "She can understand us now!"

We arrive early at French Ambassador Gilles Gauthier's house and loiter outside the gates with a few other overeager invitees. At last, we are all admitted to the front garden, where we are subjected to a very thorough security check. My laptop, gym bag, and purse are taken away, and I am marched through a metal detector. In the wake of the Ma'rib bombing, everyone has tightened security.

A path of fairy lights leads us past a gauntlet of solemn French officials, who shake our hands and murmur, *"Bonsoir."* Beyond them, rows of bushes open into a large backyard sheltered by tents. At least a dozen banquet-sized tables are covered with food, and the bar stretches about a city block long. Waiters circulate with platters of juices, wine, and shrimp. I take a glass of wine and look around. No wonder security is so tight; the place is teeming with ambassadors. Just then, the new Deputy British Ambassador Chris Shute, who arrived recently and has become a friend, catches my elbow. "Come," he says. "I'll introduce you to the new British ambassador." I'm eager to meet him, since former Ambassador Gifford had been so helpful to me.

Chris leads me through the growing crowds to a tall, dark-haired man in a pinstriped suit, with the sparkliest blue eyes I have ever seen. I offer him my hand. "I'm Jennifer Steil, editor of the *Yemen Observer.*"

"Tim Torlot," he says, twinkling at me.

My heart trips over itself. *This is the man I want to marry.* The thought flashes through my mind only seconds after our hands meet. It's completely irrational. He's a stranger. Marriage is not on my agenda. But suddenly I'm more wide awake than I have been since I got to this country. I'm awash in joy and sorrow all at once. Steady now, Steil. Ambassadors are all married. I want to check his left hand, but I can't look away from his eyes. I wonder how old he is. There's no white in his hair, and his body is straight and slender.

Pulling myself together, I ask him how long he's been here and what he's seen of Yemen. He's only been here three days.

"Where were you posted before Yemen?"

"Iraq, most recently. Shorter stints in Afghanistan, Chad, and the Central African Republic . . ."

"So really this is the safest country you've been to in years."

"Yes. I'm beginning to wonder if the Foreign Office hasn't been trying to tell me something," he says, smiling. His eyelashes are curly and tipped with gold. Focus, Steil!

He asks how long I've been in Yemen.

"About a year. I'm leaving in a month and a half," I say. "My contract is up at the end of August."

He looks disappointed. Or am I projecting? I don't want to leave Yemen, I realize. I desperately do not want to leave Yemen.

"Everyone I meet seems to be about to leave."

"Yes," I say. "High turnover rate, I'm afraid."

We make small talk. What about the press in Yemen? he asks. Is it free? Which subjects are taboo? I talk about the *Observer* while he listens attentively. It must be something they teach diplomats: Never look away from the face of the person you are addressing.

Neither of us looks away, until I begin to worry I am monopolizing him. The line of dignitaries waiting to meet him has grown to unwieldy proportions.

"I'd love to talk longer," he whispers. "But I am supposed to be meeting all these people."

"Right. Sorry! I'll leave you to it then. I've got a few people to meet myself."

"I'm ever so pleased to meet you. Here—I've even got my cards already." He hands me one.

"How efficient. It took me three months to get mine. And now I'm out. But it's terrific to meet you." He takes my hand one last time, and I reluctantly release him to the queue.

Feeling slightly dizzy, I head to the bar. It takes forever to get there. Every person I have ever met in Yemen is at this party. There are close to a thousand guests. I feel like I end up talking to most of them.

But there is only one conversation I record in my journal.

TWENTY-TWO

pomegranate season

Zuhra comes flapping into my office one late spring day at twice her normal speed. "I got it!" she says, her smile so big I can see it through her *niqab*. "They gave it to me!"

"What?" I say. "Who gave what to you?"

"The embassy! The fellowship!"

"Which one?" Ever since Zuhra was rejected by Columbia, she has been madly applying for every fellowship that might take her out of the country.

"*Your* embassy!" Zuhra says. "They are sending me to America!"

"They are?" I hug her. She's too excited to stand still and is bouncing on her toes as if her grubby sneakers have grown springs. "Zuhra, that's fantastic news! Tell me about the program."

The Near East and South Asia Undergraduate Exchange Program is offering Zuhra full tuition and living expenses at an American university for one semester. Zuhra already has an undergraduate degree, but this does not disqualify her. Besides, given what I know of the Yemeni education system, a bonus semester couldn't hurt. The embassy won't tell her the exact dates of travel or where she will be placed until later.

I'm thrilled, and relieved that I will not be leaving her behind when I go. How could I walk out of the *Yemen Observer* while she was still there?

How could I leave her in the hands of Zaid, whose inability to fill my editorial shoes grows more apparent every day? We cross our fingers and hope she gets sent to New York, where I think I will be in autumn and where her oldest brother, Fahmi, lives. A friend of a friend has offered me a free apartment in Manhattan for two and a half months, which at least gives me somewhere to land and sort out my future. Zuhra and I talk about what she will need to take with her. "I need some long skirts and shirts!" she said. "Modest things."

I laugh, because the things Zuhra ends up buying to go to the United States are the same things that I bought to come here. Because Yemeni women wear *abayas* over their outfits every day, many hardly own any modest clothing. Underneath those polyester sacks are usually tight T-shirts and jeans, nothing they would want men to see.

Packing up to go is easier now that I know Zuhra will also be leaving. Not that I've done much packing—I'm still working the same schedule and haven't had time. Nothing about these last couple of months feels final. There is no gradual decline of workload, no slowing of pace. I work flat out until the day I walk out the door. Is there any other way to do it with a newspaper? Issues still have to be closed, on the same deadlines. There is little time for reflection and no easing of pressure. I feel a desperate need to experience as much as possible before I go.

Thus, when my friend Phil Boyle calls from the British Embassy to offer me an interview with Shahid Malik, parliamentary undersecretary of state for international development and Britain's first Muslim minister, I jump at the chance. Malik is in town for just a couple of days, and Phil is offering interviews to only the *Yemen Observer* and an Arabic paper. "I'll do it myself," I say. I suppose by now I should trust my staff to interview ministers, but I want this one. Editors shouldn't get too far away from reporting, I rationalize. I don't want to forget how to do it.

So a little before six P.M. one Wednesday afternoon in early August, I appear at the gates of the stately British ambassador's residence. I'm riding a wave of euphoria, happy with work, happy to see the guards who swing open the vast metal doors to admit me, and, I can't deny, excited to see the man whom all of this is arranged to protect.

Only a minute after I'm inside, standing between the vast lawn and the house, the gates swing open again and a forest-green Land Cruiser whips around the corner and into the driveway beside us. Several men with machine guns leap out and begin searching nearby rooftops with their eyes. Just behind them is Ambassador Tim Torlot, who springs from the backseat with the enthusiasm of a seven-year-old released from school.

"It's terrific to see you!" he says, having landed practically at my feet. "But I presume you're here for work and not pleasure?" He's all a-twinkle.

"Well, I don't believe I've been invited for *pleasure* yet." I can't believe I just said that out loud. Am I *flirting* with the ambassador?

But he laughs and flushes. "I'm afraid we haven't had time to organize a single event for pleasure yet."

We stand there talking for so long that he nearly makes me late for my appointment with the minister. At last, he ushers me into the house and parks me in his study while he goes to track down the minister. I examine the bookcases lined up against the wall. Books in English! Hundreds of them! It's been so long since I saw this many books in one place. I run my fingers along their spines with undisguised lust. Isabel Allende, Shakespeare, A. S. Byatt, Iain Banks, Tim Mackintosh-Smith, Freya Stark, Oscar Wilde, Philip Larkin, W. Somerset Maugham, a host of *reference* books! Every book on the shelf is something that I have either already read or am longing to read. I wonder whose books these are, Tim's or his wife's. (He is, of course, married.) Who is the reader? I want to ask Tim, but he has vanished.

A man from the embassy comes to fetch me. I have only fifteen minutes, so I get right to my questions. What does the minister see as the most pressing issue facing Yemen? (Population growth.) What are the most important aspects of the ten-year development plan the UK is signing with Yemen? (Population, education, water, the usual.) How does the UK plan to help Yemen integrate economically into the Gulf Cooperation Council? This one throws him. He stammers and gives me something vague. Phil commends me for that one as he ushers me out of the room. As usual, I've used up more than my allotted time. I'd been trying, unsuccessfully, to get him to say something that fizzed a bit, something not quite on script. When I walk out of the house, Tim comes bounding from the porch to meet me. I ask what he has done so far with Malik, and he tells me about various development projects they have visited. I'm facing the long rectangle of lawn, gazing at it longingly. "Do you have a croquet set?" I ask.

"Not here."

"You've got a good lawn for it."

"But I don't. It's all this weird spongy stuff. Here—come see." He touches my arm and we walk onto the grass. Our feet sink into the springy loam with every step.

"I see what you mean."

"We'll have to do something about it."

We stand there idly talking as the sun slips down over the mountains and the air cools. "I should go," I say. "I have my roommate's farewell dinner."

"And I had better be getting back inside."

But neither of us moves. I suddenly have an overwhelming desire to kiss him. He's almost close enough and sparking away at me like a firefly in the dusk. The thought flusters me, and I tear myself away.

The guards let me out the gate, and I walk down the street in a daze, practically vibrating with joie de vivre. I could gallop the entire way home. But I would be late for Koosje's last night. I turn the corner and keep going, heading to the main street to find a cab. At home, I run all the way up my seven or so staircases and fling myself into the kitchen, where Carolyn is waiting.

"I'm in *love* with the new British ambassador," I say, throwing myself into one of our plastic chairs.

Carolyn looks at me with calm skepticism. "There's a new ambassador?"

"Yes, oh yes. And he's the loveliest man on the planet."

"Isn't he married?"

I sag. "Yes," I say. "I'm not going to run off with him or anything. I just *love* him."

Fortunately for Carolyn, I get too distracted by preparations for Koosje's last supper to keep obsessing about Tim. We're always saying good-bye to someone. Our usual crowd meets at the Arabia Felix hotel, where we have the usual curry and *shisha* blowout bash. Afterward, the whole gang of us escorts Koosje to a taxi and runs waving after her. "*Ma'a salaama!* Safe journeys to the First World!"

Koosje's departure is the beginning of the end of our home. She and Carolyn have become my family, and I miss Koosje like a sister. I'm terribly glad Carolyn has decided to stay.

Later that month, Carolyn and I go to a quiz night at the British Club. Our team does quite well, and I can't help beaming often and inappropriately at Tim, who is also here, standing across the room at the bar. His wife and their visiting daughter, a vivacious seventeen-year-old, are here too, but in another part of the room. It takes me a while to figure out who they are. I don't speak to Tim, but we smile at each other an awful lot.

"Incorrigible flirt," Carolyn says accusingly before heading over to Tim to introduce herself. "He's *my* ambassador, after all," she says. They talk for ages, and when she returns to our table, she looks at me significantly and says, "I see what you mean."

(*

LOCUST SEASON, WEDDING SEASON, and pomegranate season arrive simultaneously; in August, Sana'a is taken over by bugs, brides, and wheelbarrows spilling over with round yellow-green fruit. On my way to work, I see small boys chase fist-sized locusts, catching them with dusty palms and stuffing them into plastic bottles. They carry these bottles home, where the bugs are roasted and eaten.

The locust infestation inspires my hands-down favorite editorial. One Thursday, we finish the paper by four P.M., and I am closing down my computer when Ali pops his head back into my office, looking alarmed.

"Editorial?"

I look up at him. "Oh *no*. I totally forgot!"

"So did I."

I switch my computer back on and open the folder of front-page stories for this issue. Nothing inspires me. Then Jabr's piece catches my eye. He's done a marvelous locust story, including the fact that people in the streets are rejoicing in the bounty and eating them. It sports one of my all-time favorite headlines: LOCUSTS INVADE SANA'A, BECOME SNACKFOOD.

"Ali," I say, "can you get on the Internet and find me locust recipes?"

"Yeah," he says, laughing. "Let's do that."

A few minutes later, he sends me a list of recipes from the UN Food and Agriculture Organization's website, and I write a brief editorial on why we should eat the critters.

HOW TO MAKE THE MOST OF YOUR LOCAL LOCUSTS

Swarms of hopping, soaring locusts have begun encroaching on our territory. These pests are a plague to farmers whose crops they threaten. But in the cities, many of us are rejoicing at the ubiquity of one of our favorite snacks. And why not treat yourself to a handful of locusts? They're cheap, tasty, and readily available. Besides, you'll be doing your bit to help protect crops from their deadly munching. So, with a little bit of help from the Food and Agriculture Organization of the United Nations, here are a few recipes to help you make your locusts even tastier. After all, given that these critters are so intent on eating our food supply, it's only right that we bite back.

Try these at home:

Tinjiya (Tswana recipe)

Remove the wings and hind legs of the locusts, and boil in a little water until soft. Add salt, if desired, and a little fat and fry until brown. Serve with cooked, dried mealies (corn).

Sikonyane (Swazi recipe)

Prepare embers and roast the whole locust on the embers. Remove head, wings, and legs . . . and the rest set on the coals to roast. The roasted locusts are ground on a grinding stone to a fine powder. This powder can be kept for long periods of time and can be taken along on a journey. Dried locusts are also prepared for the winter months. The legs, when dried, are especially relished for their pleasant taste.

Cambodia

Take several dozen locust adults, preferably females, slit the abdomen lengthwise, and stuff a peanut inside. Then lightly grill the locusts in a wok or hot frying pan, adding a little oil and salt to taste. Be careful not to overcook or burn them.

Barbecue (grilled)

Prepare the embers or charcoal. Place about one dozen locusts on a skewer, stabbing each through the centre of the abdomen. If you only want to eat the abdomen, then you may want to take off the legs or wings either before or after cooking. Several skewers of locusts may be required for each person. Place the skewers above the hot embers and grill while turning continuously to avoid burning the locusts until they become golden brown.

Locust Bisque, serves 6

1 gallon locust shells
2 onions, roughly chopped
1 clove garlic, chopped
1 celery stalk
2 carrots
1/2 tsp. powdered mace
1 cup whipping cream
salt and pepper to taste

Put all ingredients except whipping cream into a large stew pot, and fill with water. Bring to the boil, reduce heat, and simmer for three hours. Process in blender or food processor in batches, and strain before returning to clean pot. Add whipping cream, being sure not to allow it to boil. Serve with animal crackers.

My dad writes from Vermont immediately, asking for a recipe for beetles, too. "They're ruining Mom's garden. She wants to bite back."

☾

WHILE I HAVE MINIMAL CURIOSITY about the taste of locust, I've become obsessed with pomegranates (*romaan* in Arabic). I eat at least three a day. Unlike the small, red pomegranates for sale in New York, Yemeni pomegranates are yellowish green and the size of grapefruits. But their seeds are crimson and swollen with sweet, addictive nectar. An inconvenient fruit, they require such intense effort to peel and open that it is impossible to do anything else while dismembering one. I've learned how to run a knife along the rind, weakening it just enough so that I can pry it apart with my fingers, sending ruby-red seeds spraying across my desk. Rarely do I bother anymore to pick the seeds out one by one. Rather, I break the fruit apart and gnaw on the berries inside, red juice dripping down my chin and often onto my shirt. Pomegranates are directly responsible for the slow start to my days my last few months, and for the dire condition of my blouses.

The proliferation of brides also takes a toll on work. Most of my reporters are either preparing for weddings or attending them. Everyone is rushing to get hitched before Ramadan. From nearly every house emanate the yodels of Yemeni women celebrating a bride-to-be. Several parties precede the actual wedding, parties during which brides are painted with whirly designs, decked in traditional gowns, and feted with sweet tea and biscuits.

Wedding sites in the Old City are marked by strands of bright white bulbs strung along streets and across alleyways. Under the bright glare of these lights, men dance outside to deafening music blared through staticky loudspeakers and climb into a nearby tent to chew *qat*. I grow to dread seeing these lights near my house, as weddings often go on until the following morning, meaning no one nearby can sleep.

Women gather indoors to celebrate, away from the male eyes. It never ceases to feel odd that the bride and groom rarely meet. It's a stark example of the gender segregation that is so integral to Yemeni life. What's the fun of a wedding if you cannot dance with your loved one? What is the fun of a wedding devoid of flirting and champagne? Yet for Yemeni women, it is enough to look pretty for each other, to move their hips on the dance floor with a freedom they don't have in front of men, to drink tea and gossip.

In mid-August, Noor invites me to a pre-wedding party for her sister Rasha. It's a *naqsh* party, at which a local artist paints the assembled women with intricate botanical-looking designs in an inky black dye. These designs, a traditional wedding adornment, stain the skin for weeks. Radia, Jelena of *Arabia Felix,* and I travel together from work to Noor's home, a large modern house in a wealthy part of town. We are seated in the front *mafraj,* where women are unwrapping themselves, drinking tea, and passing plates of date and sesame cookies. Several girls and women dash in and out of other rooms, changing clothing, fixing their hair and makeup, and helping the hidden bride. I hardly recognize Najma when she emerges from another room, after shedding her *abaya* and *hijab*. She is wearing a form-fitting leopard-print top, revealing more than a hint of cleavage, with tight jeans. Her thick hair is tied in a ponytail. I've seen her face many times before, but never her hair. She laughs to see me stare at her and takes my hand to lead me outside, to show me a tent filled with fancy candelabras for the wedding.

Noor rushes around attending to her sister and other family members, also in jeans and a top, her hair pulled back.

A long-haired woman sitting near me asks me what other Yemeni weddings I've attended, and I tell her that I went to the wedding of one of Noor's cousins.

"That was my wedding!" I look closely at her. I would not have recognized her. Like all Yemeni brides, she had been buried in layers of cosmetics, her hair tightly curled and sprayed into rigid obedience. Now she wears a bit of eyeliner but little else on her face, and her hair hangs straight down to her hips.

"Wow!" I say. Then, to cover my surprise, "That was a beautiful wedding."

"Thanks!"

"So how is it going, married life?"

"*Al-hamdulillah.*" She laughs.

What I really want to ask is, How's the sex? But I'm fearful of offending. "I thought you were going to China."

"We *were* going to China, but I have two more years of school so we decided to stay here." I am pleased to hear that she has a husband willing to make concessions for his wife's career. It is the rare Yemeni woman who is granted all the rights we take for granted in the West: the right to work, to choose a career, to decide whether to bear children, to get on a plane by herself, to direct her own life.

Someone hands me a cup of tea, and I am introduced to a dozen more women, who all kiss my cheek several times before moving to kiss the rest of the room.

At last, the *nagsh* is ready, and Jelena and I, as the guests of honor, are shepherded into an adjoining *mafraj* to be painted. Jelena goes first. She wants to get her whole body decorated with the black ink (which I much prefer to the reddish henna that some Yemenis use instead) but settles for both arms and her chest. I sit next to her and watch as an elderly woman still wrapped in her *abaya* paints on the ink with a small brush in short, rapid strokes. She's remarkably fast, and yet each shape looks perfectly formed.

Then it's my turn. "I just want a little," I say, indicating my wrists. The woman protests. Too small a canvas! Why don't I want my whole arms done? But it's my first time, and I am not sure I like the way it looks all the way up the arm. Fading *nagsh* or henna can resemble a skin disease.

Najma and Radia perch on cushions near me, watching closely, as the woman paints bracelets of flowers and leaves around each of my wrists, the designs extending down the tops of my hands to my knuckles. I won't let her do my fingers. "I wash my hands so much!" I say.

"So don't wash them for a few days!" says Najma.

"Impossible!" Some Western habits are just too hard to break.

The ink is cool on my skin, and as it dries, the tattoos tighten around my wrists like ethereal handcuffs.

But the process isn't over when the ink is dry, we discover. We still must be basted with Vaseline and patted with flour before getting wrapped in plastic, to preserve the design. I watch Noor work on Jelena, smearing Vaseline over her *nagsh*. When Jelena is completely greased up, Noor takes out a large blue cloth and drapes it across her lap and the floor. From a pan next to her, she scoops out handfuls of white powder, which she pats onto the Vaseline, sending clouds of it into the air. A woman brings a roll of plastic wrap decorated with green flowers from the back room, and each of Jelena's arms is encased in plastic, another sheet wrapped across her chest. I am very glad that I have just asked to have my wrists done.

Noor works on me next, greasing and powdering each of my wrists and hands before sticking my hands into plastic bags and tying the ends tightly around my wrists.

"How long do I have to keep these on?" Losing the use of my hands and fingers makes me mildly panicky.

"At least an hour."

"An hour!"

"But you really should leave them on all night."

"All night!" I am invited to a dinner party later, and I don't think I'll want to attend with plastic mittens dangling from my arms.

When at last we're finished, we wait for Rasha, the bride, to emerge from one of the back rooms, where she has been suffering body waxing in preparation for her wedding. Yemeni women take everything off—leg hair, arm hair, pubic hair, *everything*.

It's been hours since we got here, and we're growing restless. The girls and women around me began to whoop and clap, prompting Rasha finally to begin her slow progress down the hall to a chair that has been set up for her. She wears a dress of gold lace and a gold tulle veil over a black ski-mask kind of hat. Once again I regret not being able to take a photo. Her eyes are very serious.

I stand around with the other women a while, clapping and attempting the distinctive Yemeni ululation, before pulling on my shirt over my plastic-bag-wrapped arms. I can only ululate for so long before tedium overwhelms me. Najma and I share a taxi. I ask about her family's upcoming trip to Saudi Arabia, and she says that they hope to do *umrah* to Mecca. "I love this place," she says passionately. "I cannot tell you how much I love it." I ask about what she will be doing there, if it will be mostly praying. She said yes, mostly praying. "I pray to my God for things," she says.

"Like?"

"I pray to him for a good husband," she says, laughing.

TWENTY-THREE
she's leaving home

Zuhra hasn't even left yet, and already I miss her. She is suddenly very busy, with all kinds of visa interviews, doctors' checkups, and shopping for her trip to America. We still don't know when she will leave, and I am in a panic at the thought of going even a couple of weeks without her. Whenever I am short of stories on a closing day, Zuhra says, "I will find you one." And she does. Luke said that on the rare occasions I am gone from the office, she takes over control of the copy flow, running around with a chart of stories and bossing people.

Now Zuhra is preoccupied with her own problems. Once the thrill of receiving the fellowship has dimmed, she starts to worry about her family. She will not be able to travel to the United States unless she gets permission from her male relatives. It never occurred to me that she might not be able to go. I feel sick at the thought of anyone keeping her from this opportunity.

Strategically, she first tells Fahmi, her eldest brother who lives in New York. Fahmi is the most westernized and open-minded of her siblings and is utterly devoted to his little sister. He is thrilled and promises to speak on her behalf to her other brother. Aziz, who still lives with Zuhra in Yemen, is initially resistant.

"I am afraid that if they say no I will lose a chance," Zuhra frets, rocking back and forth on her sneakers. "If I don't go, I might not be given a fellowship again."

Zuhra had thought she'd be sent to Washington, DC, because the administration of the fellowship program is there. Her family fretted about the safety of the city, but Fahmi worked hard to reassure them. "It's safer than Yemen," he told them. Then she found she was being sent to Mississippi, and no one knew quite what to think about that.

At last, Aziz relents. "He was only afraid that I would be alone in the U.S.," Zuhra says. "But Fahmi convinced him after long discussion that I would be okay and that he would take responsibility for me."

Amazingly, Zuhra, who has never been on an airplane or spent a night away from home, has no trepidation about the journey. "Not for one single moment," she says. "I am only happy. It is an opportunity, it's great, and it's not fair to feel nervous."

Privately, she is sad to be traveling away from Kamil al-Samawi, the human rights lawyer. While it will be some time before I find out, Zuhra has been falling in love all year. She first realized she was in love with Kamil last autumn, after fainting while covering a story in a Sana'ani hospital. The chemical smell of the place had made her ill. When she regained consciousness, Kamil was the first person she rang. He had been so supportive of her, such a close friend, that he was the one she trusted to come and get her. It was Ramadan, but Kamil gave her juice and food to revive her and took her safely home. That was before they were in love, she said. "After this incident I realized I was in huge love with him. I see him and thought oh my god I want to spend my life with this person. It was deep down. Lots of changes that happened to me were because of Kamil. He made me feel confident, he made me love myself, he made me feel I am beautiful. We knew we were in love after this incident. But it took time. It's not acceptable to be in love here."

Which is why she stayed silent.

Kamil supports her trip to the United States. They have been discussing marriage, and she wants to start a life with him, but he promises to wait. I'll just be gone a little while, she tells herself. I'll be back soon.

☪

In mid-August, I start to panic about my own future. Two weeks left, and I have made no preparations for my departure, other than to try to sort out visas, which as usual has gone wrong. The immigration authorities didn't renew my residency, which will be two months expired by the time I leave. And the exit visa they gave me runs out before I even get to the airport!

I ambush Faris the next day to ask him for help. I also tell him that Jamal Hindi, the owner of al-Mankal restaurant, has offered to host my farewell dinner with my staff. What day would be good for him? He doesn't know. He'll get back to me. He doesn't seem particularly broken up about my imminent departure. Everyone in the office has asked me to extend my contract—everyone, that is, except Faris. I remember sadly the huge banquet he threw for me at the end of my first trip to Yemen and wonder what went wrong. Then he had given speeches lauding me and handed me a pile of Yemeni gifts. Now he can't seem to get me out the door fast enough. He can't bring himself to look at me but fiddles with his pen and stares at his computer.

"Faris? Is everything okay?"

"You've made me a lot of enemies," he says. "Everyone in the government hates the paper. The minister of the interior will not speak to me to this day."

I look at him levelly. "It is not the job of a newspaper to *befriend* the *government*," I say. "We should be the *watchdog* of the government and make sure that it is fulfilling its promises. And frankly, I am not at all convinced that it generally is."

He nods, but not in agreement.

"And everyone I have spoken to, every diplomat, every expat, and even Yemeni officials, has told me how far the paper has come in the past year." I am desperate for just one tiny shred of recognition.

"Yemeni officials? I doubt it."

"Even your friend Jalal." Jalal is now deputy minister of finance.

"Oh, really? What article did Jalal like?"

"Faris, I can't remember a specific article. Look, are you saying you are unhappy with my work?"

"No. I am just telling you the whole picture. Didn't I tell you lately how

I heard everyone is begging you to come back and offering you their houses?"

I stare at Faris. He looks away, at the wall, the desk, anywhere but at me. I linger, hoping vainly for a few kind words about the changes I have wrought in his paper, but Faris is obviously done with me. I get up to leave. If I were to wait around for Faris to pat me on the back, I'd be waiting an awfully long time.

☾

MY STAFF HELP make up for Faris's apathy. Hadi gets more despairing every day. "I will suffer when you leave," he says, likely remembering the pre-Jennifer closes that went on until dawn.

Even my new business reporter Zaki is inconsolable. One day, I am working on the business page with him for one of my last issues, chastising him for forgetting to use quotation marks and to attribute important contentions. He also uses too much incomprehensible business jargon.

"You have to understand that politicians and government officials speak in *bullshit*," I tell him. "It is your job to translate that bullshit into something anyone can understand."

Zaki laughs but says that his story is meant for businesspeople, who are sure to understand this technical jargon. It's his customary argument.

"Any story in a newspaper is a story for all people," I say. "Business can be fascinating even to people not interested in business if you write it engagingly. The more complicated the story, the more important it is that you make it clear to your readers."

Zaki looks at me, his eyes solemn behind his glasses.

"It will be bad when you go," he says. "I learn so much working with you. No one else will help me like this. You have improved me so much."

These conversations always make me feel like a traitor.

"But why do you have to leave?" my reporters ask me. "What are you going to do now?"

I have no answer for them. Perhaps I will find another country that needs a journalist trainer. I've noticed that an NGO in Sierra Leone is hiring, and I've sent in my résumé. How scary could Sierra Leone be after

Yemen? The idea of being a journalist trainer to the world at large, moving from one chaotic country to the next, is rather exciting, too.

My only other prospect is the book proposal I've been putting together about my time here, which I am hoping to show a friend with a brilliant agent in New York. But I can't pin my future to a pipe dream like a book contract.

Faris has finally agreed to give my reporters press IDs, which I've been requesting for eleven months, but this leads to new problems, because now everyone wants one. Hadi walks into my office one day and demands one.

"Why? You aren't a reporter. They are for reporters, so they can get into government events." Hadi's duties don't take him out of the office.

"I *want* one," he says like a child demanding candy.

"But why do you *need* one?" I cannot imagine what use it could be to a designer.

"I just *want one,*" he says, pouting.

"Hadi, I am prepared to give you one if you can tell me why you need it."

"I want one!" he says, stomping out of my office. *"I want one!"*

I sigh. Two more weeks, I think. Just two more weeks.

☾

I INVITE TIM TORLOT to my first farewell party. It's almost all staff, but several of my friends are coming, and I suppose I am looking for an excuse to see him again. He responds immediately. He's terribly sorry, but he has a dinner engagement that night he cannot escape. But he adds how sorry he is that I am leaving and promises to call me before I depart.

I sit at my computer rereading this and finally respond that there's a second farewell for me later that week, at my friend Phil's house. Could he come to that one? He writes immediately that he could! He also says that he will see me even sooner, at his deputy's house the following night, as we're both invited to yet another (nonfarewell) party there.

The next evening, I am nervous as I dress in the black-and-gray sundress I've been wearing to parties for about seven years now. It's a bit shabby around the edges, but I trust the lights will be dim.

At the party, I talk with a friend for a while on the porch, where Tim eventually joins us. My friend fades away and then there is just Tim, standing close to me, his pupils dilating into saucers. I have no idea what we talk about. The newspaper, probably. The vacation to Jordan, Beirut, and Ethiopia I am planning before returning to New York. Things he hopes to do in Yemen. But really, I have no idea. Everything that happens between us has nothing to do with words. I know his wife is somewhere in the room, but I am never introduced to her. I wonder why. Not that it matters. Tim and I are only talking, and what could possibly ever really happen between us? My love for him has no expectations; it just *is*. But why, why must there be a wife?

It's been a funny week. People keep coming into my office just to sit with me. Even Qasim came in the other day as I was closing an issue and just sat watching me.

"What can I do for you?" I inquired, figuring he had come in to try to pressure me into writing about an advertiser.

"Nothing," he said mournfully. "It's just that you are *leaving*." And he continued to sit there, gazing at me.

Luke visits several times, coming downstairs from his new job at *Arabia Felix*. It reminds me how much I miss him. He makes me laugh. As does Ali, who also comes in between editing stories. In my final days, I manage to talk Ali into staying at the *Observer* beyond my departure. He had planned to quit when I did. "I couldn't survive this place without you," he says. But I beg and plead. I tell him I can't bear to see the paper descend immediately into chaos. I tell him that the women need him and that Zaid can't edit. At last, in exchange for a hefty raise, he agrees to step into my shoes. Both Yemeni and a native English speaker, he is the ideal person to be editing the paper. I know he won't last long, but at least I feel better about the paper's next few months. "Write me," I say. "Let me know if you need help with anything."

Ali laughs. "You'll get more e-mails than you could possibly want."

☪

AFTER LUNCH ONE AFTERNOON, Zaid, Ali, and I are chatting in the newsroom about why tattoos will keep you out of heaven, as well as the Arabic words for bellybutton *(seera)* and monkey *(kird)*, when Zaid reaches into his black briefcase.

"I have something for you," he says. He presses play on a small tape recorder, and I hear a familiar voice.

"I have seen quite a lot of progress over the few weeks I have been here . . . but I have a few recommendations as you go forward."

It is the speech I gave to my class a year ago, at the end of my first trip to Yemen. It's the voice of someone with answers, someone who knows a few simple steps to turn the paper around. Someone almost unrecognizable.

". . . and I recommend that you create the position of assigning editor, or editor in chief . . ." It is the voice of someone sentencing herself to a very interesting life.

The day of my first farewell dinner, I look around my office. The windows are tilted open, letting in cats and wind and fluttering curtains. I run my fingers across the dusty gray desk that used to be al-Asaadi's. There is nothing particularly attractive or memorable in this room. Yet I will remember all of it. My wheeled blue chair. The dry-erase board across from my desk. The battered filing cabinet where I lock my wireless keyboard each night. I will remember the sound of men arguing in the hallway. The distant sound of prayer. The not-so distant sound of prayer. Radia and Enass's voices, high-pitched with excitement. Their serious brown eyes peering over their *niqabs.* The Doctor screaming in the hallway.

I sit with myself. I can't do this for long without crying, so I close my computer and pick up my gym bag, and lock my door behind me.

☪

DESPITE MY NERVES, the farewell dinner is lovely. Some fifty people come to bid me good-bye, including Bashir and Hassan, who arrive in suits; Ibrahim; and most of my women. Only Najma and Zuhra are forbidden by their families to come, even though I have arranged for the women to be seated in a separate room. Carolyn comes, as do my friend and fixer Sami, an American filmmaker, Shaima, Phil Boyle, and others. It's a full table.

Most of my reporters come bearing gifts, wrapped in silver paper covered with hearts or red roses. Shaima and her friend Huda give me jewelry. Jabr and Zaki each bring me a spray of flowers tucked into crepe paper. Zaid gives me a pretty bracelet with a handwritten note.

I'll always remember you, no matter what. I wrote this small poem for you last night. It was 3 o'clock in the morning and I hope you'll like it. I wish you all the best and don't worry about the paper.

I will try to hide my tears
I will try to give it a laugh
You might leave Yemen,
But you'll never move a bit
Out of our hearts and minds.

Zaid al-Alaya-a
your successor
Tue 3 A.M.

Al-Asaadi fulfills a promise he made ten months ago and brings me the Yemeni raisins he claims are the best in the country. This perhaps touches me the most.

Faris is late. When he does finally come, he sits in the middle of the table, ignoring me. Despite the odds, I've been hoping that finally Faris will offer me a tidbit of recognition, throw me some crumb of acknowledgment that will somehow validate my year here.

I wait in vain, as I circle the table trying to talk with everyone individually and run in and out of the room where my women are dining without their *niqabs*. Everyone waits. My staff also expects Faris to say something. At least a few parting words. At least good-bye and good luck. That would give me an opening to say a few words of thanks to my staff.

But he does nothing. He sits there, complaining that the main course is too slow to arrive, and then leaves before the end of the night with a hasty "Thanks for the invitation" before practically running for the door.

I stand there in the emptying restaurant, feeling stunned. Just a few of us are left, as some of my male reporters have gone back to work, the women have curfews, and the expats have scampered to have drinks at someone's house. They've invited me, but I've never felt less like a drink.

Shaima and her friend Huda come around the table to comfort me. "He can't even manage a *thank you*?" I say. I am so hurt that I can hardly speak properly. Shaima tries to console me, telling me that everyone else appreciates me, and isn't it my reporters who matter? She is right, of course. My reporters are why I came, and they are why I stayed.

"It isn't Faris's nature to be thankful," says one of the women. "You can't take it personally."

I look at them, so kind and concerned. I try to inhale their patience. They smell of frankincense. They smell of Yemen.

"Thank you," I say, squeezing their hands. "I'm sorry to be so emotional."

They go, and I head home for almost the last time, alone.

☪

THE SECOND FAREWELL PARTY is for people who drink. Phil Boyle from the British Embassy has generously consented to host and does a spectacular job of it. He places little bowls of nuts and chips on the tables and lines up bottles of wine in front of his liquor cabinet. "My farewell gift to you," he says. He's also filled an entire refrigerator with beer and sodas.

I wear a clingy fairy dress in sparkly green, in complete contrast to the modesty I'd demonstrated the night before. My hair is down, and I'm wearing lipstick the color of a stop sign. I'm heading back to the Western world, after all, so I must start to adjust!

Carolyn is the first to arrive, followed shortly by Tim, who comes without his wife. I perch on the arm of the sofa next to him, and we talk about my imminent trip to Jordan, as I have just gotten off the phone with a Jordanian friend who is helping me with arrangements. Tim asks me about my staff, but the second I start to talk about leaving, I am in tears.

"Sorry—we'll change the subject," he says kindly.

My oil worker friends arrive next, followed by a passel of other friends and neighbors, bearing food and drink. Just as the bulk of people begins arriving, Tim tells me he must leave early. He's heading to Aden the next day. I'm sad to see him go. "But I'll be back," I tell him as I walk him to the door, where he kisses me chastely on each cheek. "I know I'll be back."

What happens next depends on whom you believe. I swear that Tim kisses me full on the lips before turning to go, but he is equally convinced that I am the one to kiss him.

"I was stunned all the way back to the house," he says later. "I hadn't thought you liked me like that. Like I liked you."

I find it hard to focus on anything after that. Around eleven thirty, Phil taps on his glass to get everyone's attention and gives a little speech, saying all the things I wished Faris had said, albeit with a wry British spin. He talks about how I have revolutionized the newspaper, turning it from a paper that was "a total rag" into one that is "just a little bit of a rag." But perhaps the nicest thing he says is that I probably have "more Yemeni friends than anyone else here." It's so easy for expats to operate in their own social bubble, but I have striven to integrate myself with Yemenis. They *are* the reason I am here. Phil's speech makes me feel, for a warm minute, that I've gotten something right.

☾*

THE NEXT DAY, Thursday, August 30, is my last day of work. Tears stay close to the surface all day; I can barely hold myself together. Noor rings me in the morning to ensure that I am coming in and can edit her interview. I had stayed late at work the night before to edit Najma's last piece before the party. She had sent me an emotional e-mail. "Please Jennifer, edit this yourself and make it a beautiful shape for me, don't give it to anyone else to edit." I honor their last wishes.

As a parting gift, I write recommendations for every single one of my staff members. I rather enjoy doing this, not just to help them, but to remind myself of just how far each one of them has come this year. Farouq now writes in English. Najma, who was unable to keep personal emotions out of her health stories and who had no idea how to incorporate studies into a real story, now is a capable health and science writer. Radia, who was a receptionist when I came, is now a novice reporter.

Noor and Najma come into my office together at the end of the day to say good-bye and to present me with a Yemeni purse woven from goat hair. None of us can speak for the tears. They just hug me, look at me with damp eyes, and hurry away. Even Jabr has to blink back tears as he shakes my hand good-bye. I am glad Zuhra has already left. I could not have handled all of the good-byes at once.

☾

ZUHRA CAME INTO MY OFFICE the day before and stood uncommonly still in front of my desk. "I am going to say good-bye now."

I stopped slicing the skin of the pomegranate on my desk and put down the knife on an old copy of the paper. Pomegranates were taking over my life. I couldn't go a day without them. I thought about Persephone and how eating six pomegranate seeds in Hades consigned her to spending six months of each year in hell. One month per seed. If I were to spend a month in Yemen for every seed that I have eaten, I could never leave.

I was not ready to say good-bye to Zuhra. Someone is *there* every day of your life for a year, and then she isn't. There is no transition. Wait, I wanted to say. I need time.

She came around the side of my desk and I hugged her tightly, my little bundle of rayon, like holding a Christmas present with all of its wrapping still on it.

I couldn't say anything. There were no significant last words, no best wishes, no declarations of love. I could not talk. She didn't say anything either. We just looked at each other.

Then she was gone.

Feeling numb and slightly queasy, I sat back down at my desk. I picked up the pomegranate.

When I emerged from my office to throw away the peels, Zuhra was still standing by Enass's desk, gathering a cluster of plastic bags full of her possessions.

"If you stay any longer I am putting you back to work," I said.

Zuhra smiled. Or I imagined she did, from the way her eyes glinted for a moment. "How many times have I said good-bye?" she asked Enass. And she walked by me to the door. "I'll see you in New York."

I nod.

She hurried across the courtyard, and I turned to follow her. I couldn't help it. She didn't see me. I walked out of the office to stand at the top of our three marble steps. She walked quickly, a bustle of black skirts and plastic bags, with her fringed, brown leather purse banging against her side. I watched her until she stepped out of the gate and was gone. She did not look back.

☪

I WAS AT MY COMPUTER half an hour later when my phone beeped. It was a text from Zuhra, her last before getting on the plane: "I LOVE U."

TWENTY-FOUR

reasons to return

During my worst months in Yemen, when I fantasized only about sleep, broccoli, two-day weekends, and having access to cheese, a friend asked me how my love life was going. "You must be joking," I said. "Even if I had time, everyone in Yemen is married, Muslim, or twenty-three. But knowing my luck, I'll fall in love with someone my very last day and get stuck here."

This, it turns out, is exactly what happens.

During my three-week trip in September to see friends in Jordan, Lebanon, and Ethiopia—my victory lap of the region to celebrate surviving the past year—I find myself horribly homesick, for Yemen. I miss my gingerbread house. I miss the Old City at dusk. I miss my reporters. I miss Carolyn and Koosje. I find myself eager to get back to Sana'a, although I will have only three days there before flying to New York.

I'm obviously not ready to leave. But there's no question of changing my ticket. I now have a meeting with an agent in New York; I have a free apartment and a large orange cat waiting for me to take care of them; and my family would kill me if I didn't return. But I've started to think of the upcoming months in New York as a visit rather than a permanent move.

Going back to *The Week* does not even cross my mind. To return to that office would be to resume being someone I no longer am. What new

challenges would there be for me there? The things I want to learn can't
be learned doing a comfy job in a comfy First World country. I need new
cultures, new people, new languages. I couldn't go back to a predictable
work life. Having survived the hardest year of my life, I am suffused with
a new sense of confidence. Got a difficult job in a chaotic country? *Bring
it on.*

The Sierra Leone job looks good, if they decide to offer it to me. I
haven't spent much time in Africa, but I *know* I could handle the work. In
fact, despite the myriad challenges of the *Observer,* the idea of training a
whole new staff at a whole new newspaper is thrilling. It's particularly alluring because I wouldn't also have to be editor in chief. I could focus *just*
on training. It sounds positively *cushy.*

I decide to give up my Manhattan apartment, which I've been sublet-
ting. While I have no idea where I'll end up living, I know I am not done
traveling. If I sell my book proposal, I'll have to come back to Yemen anyway, at least for a few months to do research. How much fun it would be
to live in Yemen while not running a newspaper! I'd get to travel more
around the country, spend time with friends, and focus on Arabic. Most
important, I'd have time to *write.*

Of course, I don't have to decide just yet. These three weeks I spend
traveling are supposed to be pure pleasure, pure respite, before plunging
back into New York life and the decisions that await me there. But it's
tough to keep my brain from dwelling on these thoughts. It keeps trying
to figure out how I could stay in Yemen a bit longer and how I could earn
enough money to support myself while writing a book.

And then there's Tim.

☪

DURING MY TRIP, I strike up an unexpected correspondence with Tim. I
first write to him from a dingy little Internet café in Amman, to thank him
for attending my party and to tell him a bit about my visit to the spectacular ruins of Petra, where I spent three happy days climbing around ancient temples with *bedouins.* He writes back immediately and at length.
Thus begins near-daily communication that continues the entire time I
am gone.

Every night before I go to sleep in another strange bed, I write him about my day, and just about every night, I dream about him. Vivid, passionate dreams. I don't understand it. I've never dreamed so much and so intensely about someone I hardly know. I dream that I go to his house. I have a piece of paper with notes on it, which I show him. We talk about these notes with great excitement. He is happy to see me. Then his wife comes in. At first she is kind and then sees right through me and realizes that I am in love with her husband. She looks at the notes I have written and she knows. Her face darkens. She begins to yell at me and at Tim, saying cruel things.

I expect Tim to rush to reassure her, but he does not. She leaves, and he turns to me. "I don't love her," he says. "It's terrible to say. But I don't. This won't last much longer, and I adore you. And we can be together. We could marry."

When I wake, my head whirls. It has never occurred to me he could actually leave his wife. I reassess how much I am enamored. Do I really want him on a permanent, long-term basis? I *must* love him that much if he is to sacrifice his marriage for me. To my surprise, I feel simply joyful, without a shred of doubt, at the prospect of a life with him. Of course, in *real* life, this is not exactly on offer.

By the time I arrive in Addis Ababa for Ethiopian New Year, I can hardly think of anything but Tim. What is happening to me? All this from a flurry of e-mails from a married man?

☪

I RETURN TO SANA'A on September 16, 2007, the day before Tim's birthday. As my plane descends into Arabia, the sight of the cookie-colored cubes below brings tears to my eyes. I'm practically soggy with love for this city, this country, these familiar streets. If I didn't have a lunch scheduled with a literary agent in New York, I don't think I would leave at all. As the plane taxies down the runway and the Yemenis begin leaping out of their seats, I switch on my phone. Tim has texted to welcome me home. Sami is waiting for me at the airport and takes me to my beloved house, where I want to hug everything. Carolyn has left for China, but there is too much to do to wallow in lonesomeness. I have to pack up a year of my life in less than three days. The first two I spend stuffing all I can into two suitcases, giving away the rest, and seeing friends.

The third and last day I have saved for Tim, who has asked if I have time to see him before I go.

That morning, I am awakened by a telephone call from one of his bodyguards. They'd like to come check out the house, if that would be convenient. Still groggy, I agree. Tim texts me, apologizing for the invasion. An hour later, a very polite Yemeni in a crisp white shirt comes to my gate and asks if this is where the ambassador will be coming later. I say it is indeed and promise to keep him safe from all harm.

By the time Tim rings to say the ambassadorial procession is under way from the embassy, I am completely organized. My two overloaded suitcases sit waiting for their trip to the airport; my house is spotless; Sami has taken the last of my DVDs and books; and my refrigerator is empty except for a bottle of champagne, a Marlborough white wine, and a yogurt. Two pomegranates sit in my kitchen waiting for breakfast tomorrow. In my *mafraj,* I light the candles and sit reading until Tim rings me from the gate.

He slips in, smiling like a schoolboy playing hooky, and kisses me on the lips, right in front of the two Yemeni bodyguards who follow him into my courtyard. But the kiss is chaste enough simply to be a friendly greeting; I shouldn't read anything into it. Flustered, I start to lock the gate, but Tim reminds me that with two armed men parked at my door, this is hardly necessary. I lead him upstairs, heart hammering, all the way to the roof, shedding my *abaya* on the way. I want to show him my city. Most of the dirt from the roof has been carried away, and the ceiling has finally been repaired, albeit not with the traditional materials UNESCO guidelines require. Tim has to duck through the low doorway to the roof, and then we are standing under the Sana'ani stars. Leaning our elbows on the dusty parapet around my roof, we admire the glowing *qamaria* and watch children playing under clotheslines before turning to look at each other. A crescent moon plays in his eyes, and I can't stop smiling. In a striped shirt and jeans, Tim looks all of seventeen and profoundly unambassadorial. This is one of the perfect moments of my life. We stand there until a little girl on a nearby roof spots us and begins waving and calling. Having promised to protect him, I hurry Tim back down to the *mafraj* and fetch the bottle of champagne.

Never has my *mafraj* witnessed such an enchanted evening. We talk for so long—about his work in Iraq, Chad, and the Central African Republic, about my uncertain future—that I almost worry that I have misread him. But when we finish the champagne and he opens the wine, I know. We've barely tasted it when he slides a hand under my hair to cup my neck, says, "We probably shouldn't do this," and kisses me.

Something wild takes hold of me, something that immediately eclipses every passion I've ever felt. It is a vertiginous, irresistible fall. How could I have believed I loved anyone before this? How could I ever have been with anyone else when there is a Tim in this world? I can feel, vividly *feel*, my heart leave my body. I'd think this mere romantic fantasy if not for everything that follows.

As we tilt back into the cushions, he stops for a minute and takes my head between his hands.

"Promise me," he says. "Promise me it won't be the last time."

"Promise *me*."

"I promise you. I promise."

"Then I promise," I whisper.

Even after we've made love, he doesn't loosen his grip but wraps me closer in his arms. We stay like that until long past a reasonable hour.

"Why are you leaving?" he says in a pained voice, his arms bruising my rib cage. "Don't go."

"It's a good thing I'm leaving." I'm trying to talk myself into it. "If I stayed, I would be in terrible danger of falling in love with you."

"It's too late," he says, his fingers digging into my shoulders. "Don't you know it's too late?"

☾⋆

I DO LEAVE YEMEN, but not Tim. During my three months in New York, we write every day, unfolding our entire lives. Everything that happened between us in Sana'a happened so fast that I had hardly any time to think about the repercussions. But now, I worry. I worry about feeling so strongly about a man who isn't mine. I worry that he is toying with me and will never leave his wife. I worry about the pain it will cause his family if he does leave his wife.

I share these worries with him. I also tell him about every past lover, every mistake I have ever made. If anything is going to scare him away, I want to know now. But Tim doesn't scare easily. Every revelation only brings a new declaration of love from him. Every time I hit send, I worry I will never hear from him again, but every time I check my in-box, he is there.

Tim tells me about his large, close-knit family; his years living in New Zealand, Chile, Austria, and France; that his daughter has been his greatest joy. He tells me about the women he has loved. And finally, he tells me about his wife. There have been problems for years. They don't share the same values or enjoy doing the same things. He would not have embarked on this relationship had he been happy in his marriage.

Someone once told me that women leave a bad marriage because it is a bad marriage, but that men never leave until they find someone else. Perhaps that's true. I think Tim felt that he couldn't leave unless he had a really good reason—his unhappiness alone wasn't enough to justify hurting someone else.

When I am out with friends in New York, I find myself rushing home as if Tim were actually there waiting for me and writing to him for hours. It scares me how completely I love him. I have made it clear that I cannot continue this, I cannot keep falling in love with him, if there is no chance of a future together. This is what makes him different from other men I've loved—I actually *want* a future with him. I ask to have him all to myself.

"I need to see you," he says. "We need to see each other, to be sure." We worry aloud that maybe we're creating a fantasy relationship and that reality will disillusion us. Tim warns me that he snores. I warn him that I grind my teeth at night. We agree to meet in London.

By then, I have accepted the job training journalists in Sierra Leone. I agonize over the decision, calling my parents, my new agent (the lunch went well!), my friends, and Tim. My parents are not enthusiastic about me heading off somewhere possibly more dangerous than Yemen, but they know better than to try to change my mind. My agent encourages me, reminding me that we haven't yet sold the book I'm writing. It might be

good to have a backup plan. Tim withholds his opinion, telling me to follow my heart. He will wait for me, he says. While I have dreams of staying
in Yemen to be close to him, I am not making any decisions in my life contingent on a married man.

I take the job. After meeting Tim in December, I will fly to Yemen with
him and stay with friends for two months. The Sierra Leone job starts in
February. I figure that even if I do sell my book, I'll have two months to
get cracking on it before I head to Africa.

☪

DECEMBER 7 IS THE BEST DAY of my whole life. It begins before dawn in
New York, when a friend drives me to JFK. I've spent the week meeting
editors but still don't know the fate of my book. The flight to London is
empty. I lie down across empty seats but am unable to sleep. My heartbeat
is too loud. Customs detains me at Heathrow, so I am the last person to
emerge. And there he is, waiting for me. His face is utterly familiar, as if
I've been meeting him at airports all of my life. *"Jenny,"* he says.

He whisks me to a hotel, where I find the room filled with all of my favorite foods. He's memorized them from my e-mails. There are peppered
cashews and blueberry muffins and grilled shrimp. A bottle of champagne
waits on ice. I get teary at the sight of it all. But before I get comfortable,
I have to call my agent. "You have a publisher!" she says without preamble.
I promptly begin to faint and have to lie down on the bed to continue the
conversation. Tim is as ecstatic as I am and uncorks the champagne.

We drink champagne at every meal that week. We go to the theater, the
ballet, and the movies. We ice-skate in front of Somerset House. We wander through art galleries. We walk absolutely everywhere. On our penultimate night, we are eating dinner at a dimly lighted French café when
Tim says he wants to talk about us. "I have met the person I want to spend
the rest of my life with," he says. "And it's you. And I need to know how
you feel before I go about disrupting a lot of lives."

Oddly, I don't need time to think about it. In thirty-eight years, I've
never felt this way about anyone. It's funny that I will remember exactly
what he said but not my own words. I am crying with wonder and relief
and love. But somehow, I get my answer across.

Tim had planned to wait until after the holidays to leave his wife, but it doesn't work out that way. By Christmas Eve, he's told her everything, and by January, she is gone. It's messy, complicated, and horrifically painful for his wife and daughter. It's excruciating for me to know I am hurting people I have no desire to harm. But not once has either of us had a nanosecond of doubt that we are doing the right thing. The most inexplicable thing is that we have been so sure, right from the start.

For a few weeks, I hardly see him. I stay with friends while he sorts out his separation and is busy working. The wait is agonizing. I can't bear to be apart from him and keep worrying that he will change his mind. Fortunately, now that I have sold my book, I have plenty of work. I keep distracted with a strict writing schedule and with frequent visits from Zuhra, who returns to Yemen from Mississippi the same time I return from New York.

I've been wrestling with what to do about Sierra Leone. Tim has told me he will wait for me and that he wants me to move in with him as soon as I finish the eight-month assignment. But it has become clear that I will struggle to balance writing my first book with training Sierra Leonean journalists. And every time I think about leaving Yemen, I burst into tears. While I've all but concluded I should turn down the job, I am afraid to tell Tim. I don't want him to feel I am rushing things or putting any pressure on him by staying in Yemen.

Zuhra is dead set against me leaving, worried that she will be replaced in my affections.

"You'll find a new Zuhra there!" she says. "An African Zuhra!"

I tell her about Tim, whom she thinks I would be crazy to desert for eight months. "You would be in huge torture apart from him," she says. "You don't need to go. You deserve to stay with the person you love."

(☾ ⋆

IT IS A SUNNY WINTER DAY when Tim and I take our first Yemen outing together. Thus far, we've only spent time together in private, at his home when the domestic staff is gone for the day. But now that he has announced his separation from his wife and his relationship with me to the embassy, I am no longer a secret. The armored cars drop us off at Bait

Bous, an ancient village on a cliff overlooking Sana'a, and we set off on a long walk. A few of his bodyguards scramble up the mountains ahead of us, and several others follow at a discreet distance.

At the top of a ridge, we stop to catch our breath. We've been talking the whole way up but fall silent as we turn to look down at the city of Sana'a sprawled beneath us. It looks like something I might have made out of sand as a child, with its fanciful minarets and gingerbread houses. No clouds mar the clear blue of the sky. Across from us, distant mountain peaks sharpen in the midday light. Tim takes my hand.

Nervously, I draw a breath. "I've been thinking about Sierra Leone. . . ."

When I finish explaining to him the reasons I shouldn't go, he smiles. "You're absolutely right. Frankly, you'd be mad to try to write a book while working the kind of schedule you were working here. And you really need to be *here* to write this book, don't you?"

"I just didn't want you to feel that me staying means we have to move things any faster. . . . I am sure you need time, and I don't want to interfere with your work—"

"Jenny," he says, cutting me off. "Can I tell you something? I am *so* glad you aren't going to Sierra Leone."

"Are you?"

"I don't think I could actually stand being apart from you that long."

"I can stay with friends for a bit. . . ."

"But I want you to live with me, as soon as it's possible. Will you, Jenny? Will you come and live with me?"

I don't need time to think, but for a minute I can't speak. I look down at the city I love before turning back to the man I love even more. It seems too good to be true that I could have both of them.

"I don't think I could be happy living anywhere else."

 EPILOGUE

*Since we both left the **Yemen Observer,** Zuhra and I have become closer than* ever. She visits me in New York, while on vacation from her fellowship program at Jackson State University in Mississippi, a state that she describes as "just like the Third World! Not so different from Yemen."

It doesn't take her long to adapt to American culture. She revels in her freedom, living on her own in a dormitory, mingling openly with peers, and peeling away her *kheemaar.* She is shocked, she writes, to discover that she is beautiful!

"A handsome man told me that i am so pretty. i was happy. many pple here told me so. and the best thing that i make lots of freinds here. pple here are so freindly, most of them are balcks. They have a good heart. i befreinded with an old police officers. i befreinded the women in the dorms. Aaah, i met the avengilicans, the invited me to the church to teach me English!!!!!i will go to do this."

I get a flurry of excited e-mails during her first month in America. "I bought a jeans and short shirt," she writes. "i look pretty. Jennifer, you won't belive how many men praised me, and there is a handsome and old man said that if i am in 40s, he won't hesitaite to marry me. I don't realise that i am so attractive to this level. Really i mean it, i thought that i am not beatiful and have not attractive personality that people will be hit on."

But for Zuhra there is also a dark side to being found beautiful. When men begin to flatter her, ask her out, and make declarations of love, she feels that she must have done something wrong to attract such attention. *Am I still a good girl?* she asks me in a million ways. Yes, I tell her. The best girl ever.

The first thing I notice when I finally meet her at her brother's home in Brooklyn is that she is wearing purple. "You're in color!" I say. I pick her up in my arms and spin her around. I'm wearing a sleeveless, knee-length dress. I had asked if I should dress modestly, but Zuhra reminded me that we were in *my* country and I should dress however I want. We can't stop talking, sharing one chair in the living room, until her brother Fahmi jokes that he is starting to worry about our relationship.

For Zuhra, returning to Yemen is a much harder adjustment than leaving it. She begins to fret even before she leaves the United States. How can she go back to a life of restriction with the taste of freedom lingering on her tongue? Zuhra knows what awaits her in Yemen, and—Kamil aside—she dreads it.

I arrive back in Yemen a few days before her, and we cling to each other in a time of major upheaval. I am staying with a series of friends and struggling to write while Tim is sorting out his separation. Zuhra is debating a return to the *Yemen Observer* and readjusting to a sheltered life. Ultimately, she decides to take a job with Kamil's human rights organization HOOD, writing and reporting for their website. "I can't go back to the *Observer* without you," she says. "They wouldn't let me report the truth."

It saddens me that so many of my reforms die after I leave. My women, without exception, loathe Zaid, who they say runs the newsroom like a tyrant and is too much a pawn of Faris. Ali, who was keeping things relatively on track, quits in protest when Faris tries to force him to report something he knows is untrue. Noor leaves to work on a newsletter for the German development agency GTZ. "I'm still a journalist!" she reassures me. Radia stops writing entirely, refusing to work for Zaid, and goes back to being a secretary. A few months later, after Qasim quits to start his own business, she is promoted to his position. She's brilliant at the job, says Zuhra, and has received a huge raise.

Farouq, Jabr, Hadi, Ibrahim, al-Matari, and Najma continue to work at the *Yemen Observer,* where they are now among the most senior staff members. Najma's Health and Science page is the best page of the paper. So there's that.

I visit the paper as often as I can and spend time with my reporters, the women in particular. Adhara finishes university in May 2008, and I attend her graduation with Radia, Enass, and Najma. I tell them about Tim, and they are thrilled. No one is more excited than Zuhra, who is the first person Tim and I invite for tea at the residence. The two of them get on so well I don't get a word in edgewise the entire evening. And when I climb into a taxi to escort Zuhra home afterward, she turns to me and says, "I love him at first sight."

"Yes," I said. "I know the feeling."

Adhara stays at the paper for another year, before her frustrations with Zaid drive her to take a job at an organization working on food security. When her new employer asks her to serve as interpreter at their meetings, she shows up on my doorstep in a panic, terrified at the prospect of talking in front of people. I am pleased that she has come to me and help her deal with her anxieties. When I call a week later, she says her job has gotten easier, and she is much happier.

Not long after we are both back in Yemen, Zuhra finally confesses her own secret love. I am pleased that he turns out to be someone I know and respect. "Now I know why you quoted him so much last year!" I tease.

The only drawback is that Kamil already has a wife. I would not have chosen the life of a second wife for Zuhra, and we spend entire afternoons discussing the implications of this decision. Are you sure you want to share your love with another woman? I say. Is it fair that you are giving him all of you, and he is giving you only half of him? Have you thought about how his first wife must feel?

"You are in the same situation!"

"But Tim isn't *keeping* his first wife," I remind her. "And I can't bear to spend one night apart from him."

But Zuhra is a stubborn little thing and will not be dissuaded. No one else will do, she says. You cannot control love. Again, she has to fight for her family's permission and defend her decision to become a second wife. The experience gives her empathy for all minorities, she says. "People say,

'Why you pick a married man?' and I feel like I am a gay person, because people don't understand me." While it's not uncommon in Yemen for a man to take several wives, many families don't desire such a fate for their daughters. But ultimately, Zuhra's family supports her decision and rejoices in her happiness.

I give her my blessing as well, and attend her wedding in August 2008. She is at least choosing her own husband, which is a daring break with tradition. She is also choosing a man who will allow her the freedom to continue her career and to travel whenever she wishes. This is no small benefit. Nothing is as important to Zuhra as her career, and she reassures me she will not give it up. By June, she has sold major stories to both *Stern* magazine in Germany and the Sunday magazine of *El País* in Madrid. She has begun to surpass her teacher.

I'm curious to hear about her married life. "How do you divide Kamil?" I say. "Is there a schedule?" There is. Zuhra gets Kamil every other night. "Do you make him shower when he comes over?" I ask, but she just laughs. Kamil's children visit her often and call her Aunt Zuhra. She loves them but is not ready for her own children. Like me, she worries it will stifle her work. "I have enough to do getting used to a husband," she says.

Zuhra hasn't given up her dream of running a paper of her own someday. She does some freelancing for the *Yemen Times* and hopes that once she has HOOD's website in shape, she will again work as a journalist.

As I write this, Zaid is still the editor of the *Observer.* He calls me every few weeks to ask why I don't visit more often and to tell me he misses me. I'm impressed that he has stuck it out, but I can't bring myself to say how devastated I am by what he's done with the paper. My few remaining staff members are preparing to leave, mostly because they take issue with his management style. Before Adhara quits, she writes me a desperate e-mail telling me how much she and the others are suffering. Faris and Zaid don't respect women, she says. The *Yemen Times* has offered her a job, but she is afraid to take it. "I am afraid Mr. Faris would do something to hurt me," she says. I hope this fear is unfounded.

I hate seeing my women treated poorly. I feel guilty and responsible.

I invite Adhara as well as Zuhra, Radia, Enass, Najma, and Noor to lunch. I now live with Tim in the residence of the British ambassador, surrounded by ten bodyguards and a household staff of five, It's a major adjustment. This morning I get up from my desk in my airy office overlooking our garden and stop short on my way downstairs to the kitchen to discuss the menu with our cook; I cannot believe this is my *life*.

Over shrimp soup, we discuss the paper's dramatic decline and wonder why Faris isn't interested in doing anything about it. "Why does he keep Zaid, when he treats the staff so poorly and publishes such crap?" I ask. In perhaps not those exact words.

"No one else will do it," says Radia.

"No one else is willing to run the paper?" I say.

They all shake their heads.

"But why? It's so easy!"

My women look shocked for a moment and then start to laugh.

"I guess maybe I have to come back."

"If you go back, I will go back too," says Zuhra.

"Really?" I say. I think about it. There are at least two more years left in Tim's posting. And then I remember that Faris will not have changed. He'll still want my staff writing advertorials. He'll still want us to avoid news that reflects poorly on Yemen. He may still want Zaid at the head of the masthead. In practice, he would almost certainly not be willing to re-hire me, a fact that doesn't seem to occur to my reporters. But I also think about my staff and what I could do with them with world enough and time. I've got two more years to kill, after all.

I can't believe I am even thinking about it.

ABOUT THE AUTHOR

JENNIFER F. STEIL spent a year as editor of the *Yemen Observer*, a twice-weekly English-language newspaper published in Sana'a, Yemen. Before moving to Yemen in 2006, Steil was a senior editor at *The Week*, which she helped to launch in 2001. She has also worked as an editor at *Playgirl* and *Folio* and as a reporter at several newspapers. Her work has appeared in *Time*, *Life*, *Good Housekeeping*, and *Woman's Day*. Steil has an MS in journalism from the Columbia University Graduate School of Journalism and an MFA in creative writing from Sarah Lawrence College. She lives in Sana'a, Yemen, with her fiancé, Tim Torlot, the British amabassador to Yemen, and their daughter, Theadora Celeste.

HOLY WARS

HOLY
WARS

3,000 YEARS OF BATTLES
IN THE HOLY LAND

BY GARY L. RASHBA

CASEMATE
Philadelphia & Newbury

Published in the United States of America and Great Britain in 2011 by
CASEMATE PUBLISHERS
908 Darby Road, Havertown, PA 19083
and
17 Cheap Street, Newbury RG14 5DD

ISBN 978-1-61200-008-4
Digital Edition: ISBN 978-1-61200-0190

Cataloging-in-publication data is available from the Library of Congress
and the British Library.

10 9 8 7 6 5 4 3 2 1

Printed and bound in the United States of America.

For a complete list of Casemate titles please contact:

CASEMATE PUBLISHERS (US)
Telephone (610) 853-9131, Fax (610) 853-9146
E-mail: casemate@casematepublishing.com

CASEMATE PUBLISHERS (UK)
Telephone (01635) 231091, Fax (01635) 41619
E-mail: casemate-uk@casematepublishing.co.uk

CONTENTS

CONTENTS *(continued)*

MAPS

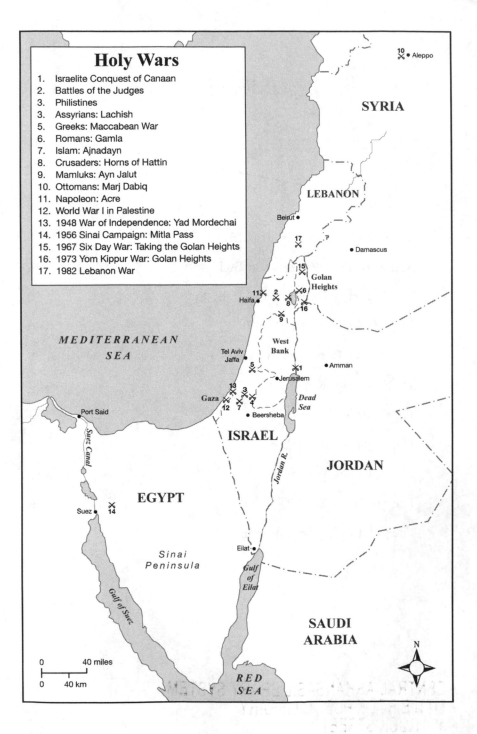

Holy Wars

1. Israelite Conquest of Canaan
2. Battles of the Judges
3. Philistines
3. Assyrians: Lachish
5. Greeks: Maccabean War
6. Romans: Gamla
7. Islam: Ajnadayn
8. Crusaders: Horns of Hattin
9. Mamluks: Ayn Jalut
10. Ottomans: Marj Dabiq
11. Napoleon: Acre
12. World War I in Palestine
13. 1948 War of Independence: Yad Mordechai
14. 1956 Sinai Campaign: Mitla Pass
15. 1967 Six Day War: Taking the Golan Heights
16. 1973 Yom Kippur War: Golan Heights
17. 1982 Lebanon War

SYRIA

LEBANON

Aleppo

Beirut

Damascus

Golan
Heights

Haifa

MEDITERRANEAN
SEA

West
Bank

Tel Aviv
Jaffa

Amman

Jerusalem

Gaza

Dead
Sea

Port Said

Beersheba

ISRAEL

JORDAN

Suez Canal

EGYPT

Suez

Jordan R.

Sinai
Peninsula

Eilat

Gulf
of
Eilat

Gulf of Suez

SAUDI
ARABIA

N

0   40 miles

0   40 km

RED
SEA

PREFACE

Holy Wars is intended to give an overview of the Holy Land's profound military history—a history which teaches many lessons, including the importance of timing, speed, stealth, good intelligence, and the danger of complacency or letting down one's guard—issues as relevant today as they have been throughout the history of warfare. Examples of experiences and lessons from history transcending time abound. Napoleon, who was well-versed in both the Bible and Josephus' writings, opted to avoid the difficult terrain of the Judean hills, where he knew many armies had met their demise. During World War I, there was British Major Vivian Gilbert, serving in the British Commonwealth army fighting the Ottomans in Palestine. Recalling the Biblical story of King Saul's son Jonathan who, accompanied only by his shield bearer, attacked and routed a Philistine garrison at Michmas by flanking the position and attacking from an unexpected direction (see chapter 3), the British officer devised a plan replicating Jonathan's attack route to overtake an enemy position in that very spot.

I do not wish to bog the reader down with overly detailed accounts of which unit moved on a specific flank, as I find that such micro-analyses of battles tend to either lose the reader's interest or can be difficult to follow. On the other hand, overly general accounts tend to gloss over fascinating military history.

Though I aim for accuracy, I am more a storyteller than historian, striving to bring both ancient and recent events to life in an interesting and readable way. That isn't to say that writing this book did not involve extensive research: *Holy Wars* is the culmination of some twelve years of work, compiling sources and materials to piece together a coherent account of events. Working at times with ancient or archaic sources that are prone to exaggerations, such as numbers of forces that simply could not have been sustained, or Goliath's height, I have tried to qualify such points with credible modern interpretations or clarifications. Historical accounts often exaggerated the strength of one's enemy (and reduced the actual number of the victor's force) to make a victory seem all the more impressive. When possible, I consulted with experts in the field. However, this is by no means a definitive history. Both archaeology and other historical research are ongoing pursuits within which new discoveries can revise contemporary accounts of historical events.

The land stretching between the Mediterranean Sea and the Jordan River that I am calling the Holy Land has been known by different names over the millennia, its name changing with the ebb and flow of peoples, empires and civilizations. Within chapters the contemporary names for the region are used.

My stimulus for researching the topic was that I simply wanted to know more about the Holy Land's military history, yet could never find the version I wanted—one that gives a sense of the fight and the context in which it was fought. My quest ultimately resulted in my writing the account. Rather than presenting an exhaustive rendition of every battle fought during the periods covered, the focus is usually on one of the significant battles—not necessarily the best known, but one that captures the essence of the war or campaign. I wrote a chapter. Then another. And another, and it began shaping up into a book. While *Holy Wars* runs chronologically, chapters are self-contained, meaning readers can choose a specific chapter for a snapshot of a particular period of interest without having to read the previous or subsequent chapters.

I hope that you, the reader, finds the subject as fascinating as I do!

ACKNOWLEDGMENTS

The author would like to thank Professor Mordechai Gichon, professor emeritus of Military History and Archaeology at Tel Aviv University; Dr. Yehuda Dagan of the Israel Antiquities Authority for his assistance with chapters 3 and 4; Dr. Danny Syon of the Israel Antiquities Authority for his invaluable comments on chapter 7; Professor Reuven Amitai, Dean of the Hebrew University of Jerusalem Faculty of Humanities, for his comments on an early draft of chapter 9; Professor Michael Winter of the Tel Aviv University Department of the History of the Middle East and Africa, and Professor Carl Petry of Northwestern University's Department of History, for assisting me with chapter 10; the late Munio Brandvein for recounting his wartime experiences to me for chapter 13, Dr. Arieh Gilai for his assistance with chapter 14; Kibbutz Yad Mordechai Archive; and the Israel Air Force History Department. Additionally, I'd like to thank Alan Merbaum, Yossi Sorogon, Curt Fischer, Dick Osseman, Marshall Editions and Kregel Publications for the photographs and images they were kind enough to permit me to use.

I would also like to thank my wonderful wife Sigal for all her love and support; my editor Ruth Sheppard whose extensive knowledge and keen eye helped shape this work; Steve Smith, Libby Braden, Tara Lichterman and the team at Casemate; and my friends at *Military History* Magazine.

INTRODUCTION

*They shall beat their swords into ploughshares, and their
spears into pruning-hooks; nation shall not lift up sword
against nation, neither shall they learn war any more.*
Isaiah 2: 4

In the Holy Land, this ancient hope and prayer remains as elusive
today as it was when written. Today's Arab-Israeli conflict, ever
present in the news, is merely the latest iteration in an unending
history of violence. While each side in the modern dispute blames the
other for its origins, the truth is that the Holy Land has been contested for millennia.

Beginning with the Israelites' capture of Jericho and ending with
the 1982 war in Lebanon (the last time Israel fought a nation-state),
Holy Wars describes 3,000 years of war in the Holy Land, uniquely
focusing on pivotal battles or campaigns to tell the story of a historical period. An epilogue covers the low-intensity, or asymmetric,
conflicts Israel fought in the first decade of the 21st century.

Sitting at a strategic crossroads between continents, the Holy
Land has been the scene of conflict for many of the world's great civilizations. The Israelites took Jericho and secured a foothold in what
was to them the Promised Land. The native Canaanites resisted the
newcomers, just as the Israelites would later fend off desert dwellers
attracted to the land's bounty, and would counter invading powers.

13

Many of the world's great empires would leave their footprints in the Holy Land. Rome demonstrated its might after the Seleucids, successors to Alexander the Great—fielding one of the most modern armies of the day—met defeat at the hands of insurgents dead-set on defending their faith, a theme that resonates in wars being fought in modern times. Both the Mongols and Napoleon suffered their first defeats in this contested land.

Great stories of history took place in the Holy Land: the walls of ancient Jericho crashing down; the battle of Lachish described in detailed reliefs decorating the Assyrian palace at Nineveh; the armies of the new faith of Islam bursting out of the Arabian desert to wrest control of the Levant from Byzantium; crusaders from Europe liberating Christianity's holy sites from what they considered infidel Moslem hands; and modern Israel's legendary military victories. The fact that the land is holy to the three monotheistic faiths, with some invoking claims of divine right to the land, has helped fuel dispute. The conflicting commitments made by the British during World War I to both Jews and Arabs promising them the same territory only exacerbated the situation and almost guaranteed continued strife. Today both Palestinians and Jews consider the Holy Land their rightful home, with both sides claiming Jerusalem as their capital.

Further conflict may be predicted in the New Testament's Book of Revelation, which indicates that the war of wars will take place at Armageddon (a corruption of the Hebrew *Har Megiddo*, located not far away from the northern fringe of the Palestinian Authority's territory), where the forces of good will battle those of evil. It truly takes a great deal of optimism to believe the Holy Land may one day enjoy the blessing of peace, rather than enduring conflict.

CHAPTER 1

LATCH OF THE LAND OF ISRAEL

Israelite Conquest of
the Promised Land, 1400 BCE

Circling Jericho's massive walls, the Israelite men had their doubts. Armed with only knives, swords, spears, lances, and bows and arrows, the Israelites had nothing with which to knock down such walls. They also lacked equipment to scale, tunnel, or breach the ramparts. Yet their plan for the conquest of Canaan hinged on first taking Jericho. Looking up at the fortified city's defenses, some of the men became demoralized and questioned how they could possibly succeed. It was 1400 BCE, and the Israelites were following Joshua to take possession of their Promised Land after spending forty years in the desert.

Bountiful with food and water in an arid, inhospitable land, Jericho was a way-station for caravans and travelers moving between and along the two banks of the Jordan River. A lush green oasis whose palm trees contrasted with the surrounding desolate brown terrain, Jericho was accustomed to attacks by marauding nomadic tribes. The city had gone to great lengths to protect and defend itself:

> Jericho was surrounded by a great earthen rampart, or embankment, with a stone retaining wall at its base. The retain-

ing wall was some four to five metres (12–15 feet) high. On top of that was a mud brick wall two metres (six feet) thick and about six to eight metres (20–26 feet) high. At the crest of the embankment was a similar mud brick wall whose base was roughly 14 metres (46 feet) above the ground level outside the retaining wall.[1]

There was no question that Jericho could hold out against the Israelites. Secure behind its walls, the people of Jericho were confident they could withstand any siege. They had proven it time and again. Not only did the city have strong defenses, it was also well-provisioned. The Israelites approached the city just after the spring harvest, so the stores were full of wheat, dates and other foodstuffs; and the perennial Spring of Elisha, or Ain es-Sultan, provided ample water. Despite the obvious mismatch, morale in Jericho was low and its people scared. It wasn't only that recent earthquakes could have damaged the protective walls. There was something different about this enemy. It is very likely that stories about these people who had defied the pharaoh's power and left Egypt (the power that dominated Canaan), of their crossing the Red Sea and later military victories across the river were known by Jericho's citizenry, putting them on edge.[2]

Before the Israelites had crossed the Jordan River into Canaan, Joshua looked across the valley at the lay of the land before him, with Jericho and its defenses visible in the distance. After succeeding Moses, Joshua began formulating a plan for the Israelite advance, bringing to fruition his people's aspiration to return to the Promised Land, a longing maintained throughout the generations by oral tradition. No newcomer to the battlefield, Joshua had already made a name for himself as a military leader, but planning an invasion was something else. He knew the Israelites lacked the capability to attack the Canaanites' secure stone-walled cities. His force was also at a disadvantage in open-country warfare against chariot-equipped and heavily armed Canaanites regulars. The Israelites also had to consider the Egyptian reaction, as Egypt claimed suzerainty over Canaan. But with internal problems and troubles on its borders, Egypt could no longer safeguard all of Canaan; its influence was hardly felt on the frontier. The Israelites' best chance for successfully establishing themselves in Canaan lay in the sparsely populated hills in the center of the country. Later called the "latch of the Land of Israel" in ancient Jewish writings, Jericho controlled the route into the mountainous heartland of Canaan. If they could take Jericho, the Israelites would have a bridgehead west of the Jordan River, a foothold they could expand into a much larger area for permanent settlement.

Requiring intelligence on Jericho's defenses, Joshua dispatched a two-man reconnaissance team to scout out approaches and the city's defenses. Jericho's well-developed defensive network noticed the spies' arrival. Jericho's king received a report that Israelite men had come to search out the land.[3] The pair of Israelites would gain the confidence of, and lodge with, a woman named Rahab, who provided assistance. When townspeople hunted the two strangers, Rahab hid them and helped them escape. For her actions, Rahab and her family were later spared during the Israelite killing spree.

The reconnaissance report Joshua received indicated disunity in the city, and a fear of the Israelites, whose reputation had preceded them. Armed with this knowledge, Joshua conceived his plan.

United in their purpose of conquering the Promised Land, the Israelite host—ripe for action—set off from their encampment across the Jordan River. Years in the desert, often under attack by other nomadic tribes, had forged them into a hardy fighting force. Encouraged by recent military successes over the Ammonites and King Og, and motivated by their commander, the Israelite soldiers were raring to fight.

They crossed the Jordan River at an easily passable ford. The Book of Joshua states that the river was in flood, but that when the priests carried the Ark of the Covenant to the edge of the river, it stopped flowing until all the Israelites had crossed. Some scholars argue that an earthquake occurred at the time of the crossing and may have caused the steep banks to collapse, damming up the Jordan River for several hours.[4] The Israelites crossed over on dry land, until the build-up of water forced through the obstruction. Already instilled with the zeal of God, this was seen as divine intervention, reinforcing their faith.

The appearance and disappearance of the two Israelite spies had

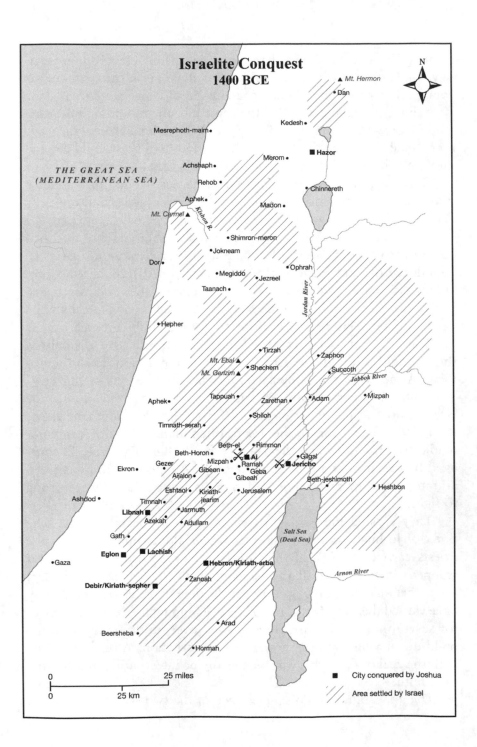

Israelite Conquest
1400 BCE

N

▲ Mt. Hermon

• Dan

Kedesh •

Mesrephoth-maim •

Merom •

■ Hazor

Achshaph •

Rehob •

• Chinnereth

Aphek •

Madon •

Mt. Carmel ▲

Kishon R.

• Shimron-meron

• Jokneam

Dor •

• Megiddo

• Ophrah

• Jezreel

Taanach •

THE GREAT SEA
(MEDITERRANEAN SEA)

Jordan River

• Hepher

• Tirzah

• Zaphon

Mt. Ebal ▲

• Shechem

• Succoth

Mt. Gerizim ▲

Jabbok River

Aphek •

Tappuah •

Zarethan •

• Adam

• Mizpah

• Shiloh

Timnath-serah •

Beth-el •

• Rimmon

Beth-Horon •

✕ ■ Ai

• Gilgal

Mizpah •

• Ramah

Ekron •

Gezer •

Aijalon •

Gibeon •

• Geba

✕ ■ Jericho

• Gibeah

• Beth-jeshimoth

Eshtaol •

Kiriath-jearim •

• Jerusalem

• Heshbon

Ashdod •

Timnah •

Libnah ■

• Jarmuth

Azekah •

• Adullam

Gath •

Salt Sea
(Dead Sea)

Eglon ■

■ Lachish

■ Hebron/Kiriath-arba

• Gaza

Debir/Kiriath-sepher ■

• Zanoah

Arnon River

• Arad

Beersheba •

• Hormah

0 ————— 25 miles

0 ————— 25 km

■ City conquered by Joshua

╱╱ Area settled by Israel

alerted Jericho that trouble was literally on the horizon. Walls damaged by recent tremors were hastily repaired. People living outside the city sought refuge within Jericho's protective walls, and the city gates were closed. From the vantage of their ramparts, Jericho's defenders now followed the Israelites' approach. Rumors and talk about the Israelites exacerbated the already tense situation. Morale plummeted as fear took hold in the city, and there was little will to fight. The Jordan River ceasing to flow, allowing the Israelites to cross with ease, was taken by the local people as a very bad omen.

Lacking the means with which to attack the city, Joshua put a different weapon to work: psychological warfare. Led by the Ark of the Covenant, containing the stone tablets inscribed with the Ten Commandments that Moses had received on Mount Sinai, and seven priests blowing rams' horn trumpets, the 40,000-strong Israelite host set off from their encampment and approached the city walls.

Jericho's defenses sprang into action, reinforcing defensive ram parts and towers. But the Israelites did not attack. They circled Jericho's walls, parading around the city in a huge procession. After completely circling the city once, the Israelites retired to their nearby camp.

For the next five days, the Israelites repeated this drill, marching around the walls once before returning to camp. Jericho's defenders were wary and suspicious, amused and frightened by these strange desert nomads' unusual procession around their city. There were no demands from the Israelites; the siege was anything but conventional. Blasts of the Israelite priests' rams' horns sowed fear among the besieged city's inhabitants, who were discomfited by the sight of an army laying siege to their city. Unsure how to respond, Jericho's defenders made no sallies against the Israelites.

On the seventh day of the siege, as the Israelites were completing their circuit, blasts from ram's horns signaled a change: the Israelites were to continue circling the city. The Israelites circled a second time. Then a third. And a fourth. . . . Jericho's nervous apprehension turned to fear as what had become habit veered to the unknown. With each additional lap around their city, the feeling of impending doom among the defenders grew. The noose was slowly tightening. Many prayed to Reshef, the Canaanite god of war.

After circling the city seven times, the Israelite priests blew the rams' horns, making a great noise, and the men began to shout. The ground began to shake, and a rumbling sound could be heard, growing louder and louder. The noise grew in intensity as stones and bricks began to dislodge from the wall's upper portions. Cracks appeared and grew larger, growing into large fissures until the great stones at the base broke free and rolled down the slope, kicking up a thick cloud of brown dust. In several places, the mud brick city wall collapsed down onto the retaining wall, forming a ramp. During her 1950s excavations, the late British archaeologist Kathleen Kenyon found "fallen red bricks piling nearly to the top of the revetment. These probably came from the wall on the summit of the bank."[5]

The Israelite troops rushed up the earthen embankment, over the collapsed walls and into the city. Shocked by the tumultuous collapse of the walls and their sudden vulnerability, the townspeople were overcome with terror and became paralyzed by fear.

From pessimistic doubts to what they now saw as divine intervention, the Israelites were imbued with religious fervor, faith in their mission restored. So inspired, they rushed through Jericho's streets freely killing everyone in sight. Townspeople fled among the streets and alleyways; others tried to hide. The invaders ran through the town with gusto, euphorically killing man and beast alike. Jericho's fighting men hardly resisted, and many people merely submitted themselves to slaughter by the rampaging invaders:

> They were afrighted at the surprising overthrow of the walls, and their courage was become useless, and they were not able to defend themselves; so they were slain, and their throats cut, some in the ways, and others as caught in their houses,— nothing afforded them assistance, but they all perished, even to the women and the children; and the city was filled with dead bodies, and not one person escaped.[6]

Joshua had ordered his men to completely exterminate Jericho's population, and this order was carried out without exception. Save for the pledge made to Rahab, the Israelites "utterly destroyed all that was within the city by the edge of the sword." The city was not plundered; it was destroyed and set on fire.

"The destruction was complete," wrote archaeologist Kathleen Kenyon. "Walls and floors were blackened or reddened by fire, and every room was filled with fallen bricks, timbers, and household utensils. . . ."[7] While the level of destruction and killing may seem excessive, the Israelites knew their arrival posed a true threat to all Canaanites, who might very well have taken the opportunity to wipe out this new force in their midst. And with plans to advance into, and establish themselves in, the Canaanite hinterland, their actions at Jericho were preemptive—killing off enemies who could threaten their rear while also establishing a reputation for ferocity. Jericho was left unoccupied and cursed, and the Israelites moved on.

While archaeological evidence over the last century corroborates the Bible's version of a fortified city destroyed after a short siege, its walls collapsed and the city wrecked by fire, the debate continues over when this occurred. Kenyon and others date Jericho's destruction to 1550 BCE—too early for the aggressors to have been Joshua and the Israelites. Challenging Kenyon's methodology, contemporary archaeologist Bryant Wood dates Jericho's destruction to 1400 BCE, which aligns with the timing of the Biblical account. Further debate surrounds the arrival of the Israelites to Canaan, with many scholars believing the Israelites arrived some 200 years later—in 1200 BCE—long after Jericho was destroyed.

Ai

. . . take all the people of war with thee, and arise, go up to Ai; see, I have given unto thy hand the king of Ai, and his people, and his city, and his land.
Joshua 8: 1

Their bridgehead west of the Jordan secured, the Israelites next set about penetrating the Judean mountains. Whether the Israelite conquest was as rapid as portrayed in the Bible is questionable. It seems they linked up with local tribes related to them—those who had not gone to Egypt and others who joined them. Thus, rather than a pure *blitzkrieg* of Canaan, it was more likely both conquest and a gradual process of encroachment and infiltration through which the

Israelites established themselves in Canaan.[8]

The mountainous areas were only lightly settled, meaning little was in the way to impede them. In planning his strategy for the initial conquest of Canaan, Joshua was careful to avoid the heavily populated, well-defended plains and valleys. The Israelites also had to steer clear of the major Egypt to Syria trade route—later known as the Via Maris, or Sea Route—to mitigate risk of Egyptian interference.

Their target along their route to Canaan's central highlands was the city of Ai. Rather than attacking the fortified city of Beth-el, Joshua set his sights on Ai, which shielded Beth-el, or may have been a fortified city in its own right. Eliminating Ai would give the Israelites access to the country beyond, central to their plan for securing the heartland of Canaan.

Buoyed by their success at Jericho, the Israelites were overconfident. When reconnaissance suggested Ai was lightly defended and could be easily taken, Joshua dispatched a force of only 3,000 men to capture the town, allowing the bulk of his men to rest. The Israelites climbed the steep trails from the Jordan Valley and attacked. The intelligence proved faulty; the Israelites met strong resistance and were forced to retreat. Ai's defenders pursued the Israelites to the descent from the heights, killing 36 Israelite men. Not only did this blow hurt the Israelites' morale, but it also tarnished their reputation of invincibility—dangerous as it could embolden their enemies. Understanding the serious consequences of this defeat, Joshua was livid. "For when the Canaanites and all the inhabitants of the land hear of it," he angrily exclaimed to his lieutenants, "they will compass us round, and cut off our name from the earth . . ."[9]

Resigned to attack again without delay, Joshua ordered a 30,000-strong ambush force to infiltrate the area and lie in wait behind Ai. Under cover of darkness, Joshua led a second force to a staging area on some heights to the city's north before moving down into the valley before Ai. Five thousand men were dispatched to serve as a blocking force concealed between Ai and nearby Beth-el to thwart any relief efforts.

When Joshua's force was spotted in the morning, the alarm was raised in Ai. Joshua led the attacking force in a feeble frontal assault, repeating their earlier folly. For a second time, the Israelites found themselves attacking Ai's well-entrenched defenders with insufficient force to oust them. Now experiencing for himself the city's fervent defense, Joshua ordered a retreat. Seeing an opportunity to annihilate these nomads who had now twice attacked his city, Ai's king rallied his forces for a counterattack. This chance for a *coup de grace* against the feared Israelites and opportunity to make a great name for himself was enticing; the king ordered his entire force to leave their posts and to pursue the retreating Israelites.

Once they were a distance away from the city, Joshua used his spear to signal the main ambush force lying in wait to move on the now undefended city. "And the ambush arose quickly out of their place, and they ran as soon as he had stretched out his hand, and entered into the city, and took it; and they hastened and set the city on fire."[10] The retreat had been part of a carefully planned ruse, and Ai's king had taken the bait.

After capturing and setting fire to the city, the Israelite ambush force attacked the Ai force's exposed rear flank. Joshua's "retreating" force stopped in its tracks and made an about face.

Believing they were chasing frightened Israelite troops fleeing from battle, the men of Ai were now confused to see their city in flames, and to find themselves being assaulted from both front and rear. Dumbfounded by the sudden change, Ai's men were decimated in a scene of great carnage. The Israelite men then set about carrying out orders that had been handed down: "do to Ai and her king as thou didst unto Jericho and her king . . ."[11] All 12,000 citizens of Ai were put to the sword, their king captured and hanged, and the city destroyed.

With each engagement, the Israelites became better fighters. Word of their skill and ferocity spread, sending shock waves through Canaan. Rulers of the Amorite cities Jerusalem, Hebron, Jarmuth, Lachish and Eglon united in a defensive coalition against the vigorous newcomers. Another bloc, a federation of four cities led by Gibeon, in the mountains north of Jerusalem, made a peace pact with the Israelites to ensure their safety.

Rather than focusing its attention on resisting the Israelites—the more pressing threat, the Amorite alliance, very angry with the Gibeon-led collaboration with the enemy invaders, moved against the

federation cities to punish them. "Therefore the five kings of the
Amorites . . . gathered themselves together, and went up, they and all
their hosts, and encamped against Gibeon, and made war against
it."[12] This split illustrated a lack of unity that would prove the
Canaanites' downfall.

The besieged cities appealed to Joshua for assistance, invoking
their treaty of friendship. Joshua responded to their call, which also
served his purpose of weakening potential adversaries in his conquest
of Canaan. Leading his force on a strenuous 15-mile (25-km) night-
time march, the Israelites covertly approached besieged Gibeon.
When the Israelites made a simultaneous three-pronged assault, the
Amorites were caught completely unawares. Panicked, the Amorites
fled towards the Beth-Horon pass, on the route down through the
Ayalon Valley to the coastal plain. The Israelites pursued them, aided
by a chance hailstorm that slowed the Amorites' flight and killed
more fleeing soldiers than the Israelites killed. Deep in unfriendly
territory and far from their base, the Israelites had to finish off the
Amorites before nightfall to prevent their opponents from extricating
themselves in the darkness and potentially regrouping.

Joshua beseeched the sun and moon to stand still, lengthening the
day to allow the battle to continue. "'Sun, stand thou still upon
Gibeon; And thou, Moon, in the valley of Aijalon.' And the sun stood
still, and the moon stayed, Until the nation had avenged themselves of
their enemies."[13] The Amorites were soundly defeated in what was
described as "a great slaughter." The Amorite kings were captured,
put to death and their corpses hung from trees. It was a complete victory, which reinforced the Israelite reputation.

A string of victories followed, allowing the Israelites to further
secure their position in Canaan. Their successes precipitated a showdown with a powerful combined Canaanite force led by the city of
Hazor in the north. In what was considered one of Joshua's greatest
victories, the Israelites defeated a chariot-equipped force by the waters
of Merom. The fighting continued, with more Israelite victories. "So
Joshua took all that land, the hill-country, and all the South, and all
the land of Goshen, and the Low-land, and the Arabah, and the hill-
country of Israel, and the Lowland of the same; . . . even unto . . . the
valley of Lebanon under mount Hermon; and all their kings he took,

and smote them, and put them to death."[14] "So Joshua took the whole land, according to all that the Lord spoke unto Moses; and Joshua gave it for an inheritance unto Israel according to their divisions by their tribes. And the land had rest from war."[15]

Notes

1. Bryant Wood. "The Walls of Jericho." *Creation* (21:2, March 1999), pp.36–40.
2. Joshua 2: 8–11. *The Jewish Bible: Tanakh: The Holy Scriptures* (Philadelphia: The Jewish Publication Society of America, 1985).
3. Joshua 2: 2.
4. Situated astride the Syrian–African rift fault line where two of the massive plates making up the earth's surface meet, the Jordan Valley is prone to earthquakes caused by friction as the plates move.
5. Wood, "The walls of Jericho."
6. Josephus (translator William Whiston), *Antiquities of the Jews*, Book V, Ch. I:
7. *The Complete Works of Josephus* (Grand Rapids, MI: Kregel Publications, 1981),
7. Bryant Wood. "Is the Bible accurate concerning the destruction of the walls of Jericho?"
8. Hanoch Reviv, "The Canaanite and Israelite Periods (3200–332 BC)" in Michael Avi-Yonah (ed.) *A History of the Holy Land* (Jerusalem: Steimatzky's Agency Ltd. 1969), p.49.
9.Joshua 7: 9.
10.Joshua 8: 19.
11.Joshua 8: 2.
12.Joshua 10: 5.
13.Joshua 10: 12.
14.Joshua 11: 16–17.
15.Joshua 11: 23.

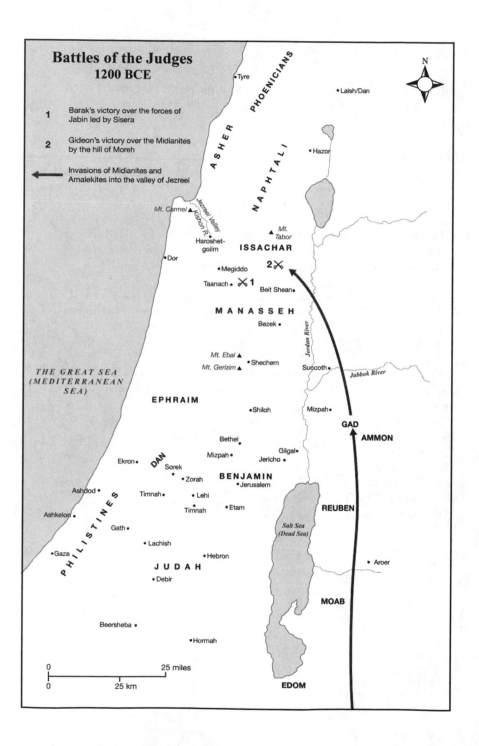

Battles of the Judges
1200 BCE

1 Barak's victory over the forces of
Jabin led by Sisera

2 Gideon's victory over the Midianites
by the hill of Moreh

← Invasions of Midianites and
Amalekites into the valley of Jezreel

N

• Tyre

PHOENICIANS

A
S
H
E
R

• Laish/Dan

N
A
P
H
T
A
L
I

• Hazor

Jezreel Valley

Mt. Carmel ▲

Kishon R.

▲ Mt.
Tabor

Haroshet-
goiim

ISSACHAR

• Dor

• Megiddo

2 ✗

Taanach • ✗ 1

Beit Shean •

M A N A S S E H

Bezek •

Jordan River

Mt. Ebal ▲

Mt. Gerizim ▲ • Shechem

Succoth •

Jabbok River

THE GREAT SEA
(MEDITERRANEAN
SEA)

E P H R A I M

• Shiloh

Mizpah •

GAD

AMMON

Bethel •

Mizpah •

Gilgal •

Jericho •

Ekron •

D
A
N

Sorek

• Zorah

B E N J A M I N

• Jerusalem

Ashdod •

Timnah •

• Lehi

Timnah

• Etam

REUBEN

Ashkelon •

P
H
I
L
I
S
T
I
N
E
S

Gath •

Salt Sea
(Dead Sea)

• Lachish

• Hebron

• Gaza

J U D A H

• Debir

• Aroer

MOAB

Beersheba •

• Hormah

0   25 miles

0   25 km

EDOM

CHAPTER 2

TIMES OF TROUBLE

BATTLES OF THE JUDGES, 1200 BCE[1]

Do unto them as unto the Midianites;
as to Sisera, as to Jabin, at the brook of Kishon
Psalms 83: 9

Stung by a Bee: Deborah & Barak vs. Sisera

At first it was only harassment. Canaanite chariots constantly tormented the Israelites on the main roads of the Jezreel Valley, becoming such a menace that Israelites were forced to travel by secondary routes. Over time the situation deteriorated, with Canaanites entering Israelite villages to stir up trouble before returning to their secure walled cities. Fragmented following Joshua's death, the Israelites had no means with which to counter the Canaanites or retaliate.

When Joshua died, Canaan was still far from being in Israelite control. The coastal plain was in Philistine hands, and strong Canaanite enclaves remained. It would be another two centuries before the Israelites were securely established in Canaan. Leaving their nomadic ways behind them, the Israelite tribes divided up Canaan into areas for permanent habitation and settled down. The people busied themselves with mundane matters like working the land. With no clear successor to Joshua, the Israelites lost their cohesion, and they became a fragmented tribal society. There was no political unity;

the tribes acted completely independently, and at times even fought.

While the Israelites were weak and unorganized, Canaanite cities were thriving, following the weakening of the Egyptian hold on Canaan. The Canaanites were able to act at will against the Israelites. The harassment intensified into persecution and outright oppression. The Israelites were forced to pay such a heavy tribute that they were working mostly to pay off obligations to the Canaanites. This degrading situation went on for twenty years, so the downtrodden Israelites were almost resigned to such treatment at the hands of their much stronger neighbors.

Hazor's king Jabin particularly resented the Israelites, who had laid waste to his city under Joshua. Overcoming their traditional divisiveness, several Canaanite cities in the Jezreel Valley, including Hazor, Taanach, Megiddo and Yochneam, allied themselves under Jabin to form a league of northern Canaanite cities. Dubbing himself "king of Canaan," Jabin set out to exert his power. With his general Sisera commanding a force of 10,000 infantrymen supported by an arsenal of 900 iron chariots positioned by Haroshet-goiim, a strategic outlet from the Jezreel Valley to the coast, the Canaanites now threatened to drive a wedge between the Israelite tribes of Galilee and those in the center of the country.

Despite their independence, the Israelites' shared religion and experiences kept them united in a loose confederacy. Only the re-emergence of old enemies and the appearance of new ones led to inter-tribal cooperation. "In the absence of any central authority the Israelites had to invent some original solution to the problem of evolving a leadership and a defensive system which would ward off the threats of their enemies and the risk of foreign domination."[2] Judges were the answer. In difficult times, these divinely guided ad-hoc leaders united the people to some common cause.

Though she lived in an area removed from the Canaanite league in the north, the prophetess Deborah, whose name means "bee" in Hebrew, formulated a plan to stand up to the Canaanites, and mobilized the people to action. Deborah was already a judge, with the clout to call on Barak ben Avinoam, a leader from the tribe of Naphtali in northern Israel, and instruct him to raise a force from Naphtali and the neighboring tribe of Zebulun. "The God of Israel commanded," Deborah told him. "Go and draw toward Mount Tabor, and take with thee ten thousand men of the children of Naphtali and of the children of Zebulun. And I will draw unto thee to the brook Kishon Sisera, the captain of Jabin's army, with his chariots and his multitude; and I will deliver him into thy hand."[3] Lacking confidence in his own abilities or in the situation they faced, Barak balked and insisted Deborah go with him. She agreed, but told Barak it would cost him the glory of victory.

Barak issued a call to arms that was met with an enthusiastic response, especially by those closest to the Canaanite threat. Detachments from the tribes of Naphtali, Zebulun and Issachar in the north and from as far south as Manasseh, Ephraim and Benjamin joined in. Deborah and Barak went to Kedesh, where Barak mustered the ten thousand men before moving the force to Mount Tabor, whose steep slopes afforded protection against Canaanite chariots and a clear view of the surrounding terrain. Mount Tabor was a safe place to wait for the heavy winter rains they knew would soon come—rains with the ability to quickly turn surrounding areas into a mire that could potentially bog down the enemy force.

A Kenite man named Heber tipped off Sisera about the Israelite troop concentration. The Kenites lived in peace with both the Israelites and the Caananites. Heber had severed himself from his people and was living near Kedesh with his wife Yael. After observing the force being assembled by Barak at Kedesh, Heber reported their movements to Sisera. His motives are unclear. Maybe he was trying to ingratiate himself with the Caananites, or perhaps the pursuit of money or other benefit motivated him. There was clearly some type of arrangement, for we are told "there was peace between Jabin the king of Hazor and the house of Heber the Kenite."[4]

The Israelite deployment on the strategic vantage point challenged Canaanite hegemony. Sisera's initial response was concern, as Mount Tabor stands between the military position at Haroshet-goiim and his patron's city of Hazor. The Israelite force—a fraction the size of Hazor's army—posed no true threat to the city that Josephus tells us "had in pay three hundred thousand footmen, and ten thousand horsemen, with no fewer than three thousand chariots."[5] But with the Via Maris travel and trade route cutting through the Jezreel Valley on its way from Egypt to Syria and Mesopotamia, the Israelites might strike at their economic lifeline by disrupting this profitable trade route. The Israelite massing of forces and deployment on Mount Tabor was more an affront than anything, but it did provide Sisera with an enticing opportunity to deal the Israelites a painful blow. Pulling out of his position at Haroshet-goiim, Sisera advanced with his chariots and infantry across the open plain towards the mountain, kicking up great clouds of dust like a sandstorm as they went. The Israelites' confidence was shaken when they saw and heard the mass of chariots and infantry approach and pitch camp near the mountain.

Sisera knew the Israelites were secure in their mountaintop deployment and that he would need to draw them onto the plain. As long as the Israelites remained on Mount Tabor, his chariots were useless. Deborah and Barak also understood this well, which was precisely the reason they had opted for this defensive posture. Sisera was confident he had the Israelite force contained on the mountain, where he could keep his eye on them. They could not remain there forever, he reasoned, and would have to come down at some point. With a large infantry force and armada of chariots under his command, Sisera had every reason to be confident. On level ground, his chariots were an excellent shock weapon against poorly organized forces like the Israelites' makeshift militia. With the chariots' speed and maneuverability, the Israelite infantry force had no possibility of escape.

Surrounded by Sisera's forces, the Israelites—civilians pressed into military service—must have been terrified when they looked at the forces massed on the plain below them. Armed with little more than bows and arrows, swords, and spears, the Israelite men felt powerless. Their apprehension grew, and many wanted to disband and slip back to their villages. With the mountain surrounded, this would not be easy, even with their familiarity with the local terrain. The two armies were in a standoff. Deborah retained the men and commanded them to remain and fight.

Deborah had devised a plan to draw Sisera's forces away from the mountain and back towards the Kishon River, which she knew the imminent rains would turn into impassable swamp. As she had earlier told Barak that she would lure Sisera's force to the Kishon River, it seems likely that Deborah had initially intended to lead a decoy force—possibly striking at Sisera's rear—but Barak's hesitation forced her to delegate its command. The decoy force skirmished with Canaanite forces in Taanach by the waters of Megiddo.[6] When word reached Sisera, his confidence was shaken. He wondered whether it was a trap, with a larger force maneuvering against him. Information on this second force was sketchy whereas the force on Mount Tabor was a known element. It certainly explained why the Israelites had deployed on such a visible position where all he had to do was wait for them to come down. Sisera quickly dispatched forces to find and engage the second Israelite force, creating some confusion and disorder in his camp as men, animals, and equipment were regrouped and moved out.

The wind was picking up, and threatening gray storm clouds overhead were a good omen for the Israelites. With the Canaanites taking the bait of the decoy force, Deborah gave the fighting men a very inspiring pep talk assuring them of divine assistance that would lead them to victory. Then she issued orders to attack. Barak and his men charged down the mountain. As if on cue, it began to rain in one of the sudden downpours common to the region. The rain intensified into a torrential downpour interspersed with hailstones, which pounded the combatants. Strong winds blew down the mountain, directing the brunt of the storm on the Canaanites, who were unable to use their arrows and slings, "nor would the coldness of the air permit the soldiers to make use of their swords."[7]

Viewing the storm as the intervention Deborah had spoken of, the Israelites drew inspiration and charged wholeheartedly into battle, slaying a great number of Canaanites. Agitated by the storm, panicky horses were soon out of control, trampling men beneath their hooves or running them over with chariots.

Withdrawing from Mount Tabor, Sisera's force ran into trouble by the Kishon River. The torrential downpour caused the normally gentle Kishon River to swell and overflow its banks. Its waters swept away men and horses, and tracts of land turned into a huge mud bath, bogging down chariots and heavily armed infantry in the suddenly muddy terrain. The Israelites came down on them with a vengeance. Horses harnessed to chariots stuck in the mud cried loudly, adding to the grunts of men fighting hand-to-hand for their lives. Canaanite charioteers abandoned their vehicles and joined infantrymen fleeing on foot, most heading west towards the safety of Horoshet-goiim or other friendly city. With flooding in this area slowing their retreat, Barak's forces harried the fleeing Canaanite soldiers all the way back to Horoshet-goiim, routing Sisera's army.

Rather than rallying his troops in the confusion of the storm and Israelite attack, Sisera panicked and fled the battlefield by foot. Heading east, away from the flooding—probably on the way to Hazor, Sisera found refuge in the tent of Yael, wife of Heber, the informant who had earlier assisted him. Yael welcomed Sisera into her tent and comforted him. Physically and mentally exhausted from the sudden turn of events and his flight, Sisera desperately needed rest. Drenched from both rain and sweat, the shivering general found the dry, warm tent very inviting. As he began to catch his breath, he asked for some water to quench his thirst before continuing on. Yael brought him some milk, which he quickly drank. Exhaustion overcame him; Sisera realized he could not yet go on and accepted Yael's hospitable offer to lie down and rest. Sisera had already been assisted by Heber, and had possibly met Yael, so he had enough faith to trust her guard and let his own down while he rested. Yael covered him with a coarse blanket and he quickly fell fast asleep.

When his deep rhythmic breathing confirmed his slumber, Yael "took a tent-pin, and took a hammer in her hand, and went softly unto him, and smote the pin into his temples, and it pierced through into the ground; . . . he swooned and died."[8] One can only speculate what motivated Yael to interfere in a conflict that was not hers and kill the Canaanite general. Perhaps Sisera had mistreated her husband or not delivered, or maybe Yael acted out of some affinity with the Israelites.

Barak, in hot pursuit of the Canaanite general, came across Yael's tent. Hearing someone approaching, Yael went outside and was relieved to see it was not a Canaanite. When Barak asked if she had seen any fleeing Canaanite soldiers, Yael replied, "Come, and I will show thee the man whom thou seekest." Barak entered the tent and, as his eyes adjusted to the smoky darkness, was shocked to find Sisera lying on the tent floor in a pool of blood. And so the glory of the *coup de grace* was stolen from him, just as Deborah had foretold when Barak had hesitated to accept her appointment. Barak went on to fight Jabin at Hazor, where he killed the so-called "king of the Canaanites" and punished the city.

The defeat of Jabin's alliance did not finish off the Canaanites, but did severely weaken them. The Israelites were freed from subjugation by the Canaanites, who no longer posed a significant threat. Barak's military force demobilized, and there were forty years of calm. With no strong, centralized Israelite leadership to step in following the collapse of Canaanite power, a power vacuum resulted, leaving the region susceptible to desert raiders.

The Sword of Gideon: Gideon vs. the Midianites

The Israelites worked the soil of the Jezreel Valley, where its wheat fields earnt it the title of the Israelites' "breadbasket." Fertile and abundant with water, the Jezreel Valley proved particularly tempting to marauding tribes from across the Jordan River, primarily the Midianites, joined by Amalakites and Arabians.

Come harvest time, these fierce desert raiders would sweep in on their camels, stealing crops, and hustling livestock and beasts of burden. With no organized defenses, the Israelites had to withdraw at the hint of danger, taking with them whatever food they could carry to their cave hideouts. Unable to harvest their crops, the Israelites began facing food shortages. It was humiliating that the little wheat they managed to spirit away had to be threshed in secret lest the Midianites steal it. Threshing yielded the flour used to bake bread, a staple of the local and neighboring Israelite tribes.

The forty years of quiet that the Israelites had enjoyed under Deborah and Barak were over, and now they found themselves in distress. Israelite submissiveness encouraged and emboldened the Midianites. This persecution went on for seven years, resulting in serious famine. Still the Israelites would sow the fields, only to have their produce taken from them in violent raids. Many people chose to forsake their livelihood and left the fertile Jezreel Valley for the safety of the mountainous hill-country.

When a huge Midianite-led force crossed the Jordan River and pitched camp in the Jezreel Valley by Gibeath-moreh (hill of Moreh), a young man named Gideon, whose brothers had been killed during a Midianite raid, took the lead in opposition. Gideon put out a call to arms to his own tribe of Manasseh and the neighboring tribes of Asher, Zebulun and Naphtali, all of whom were suffering food shortages. The Midianite threat unified the normally fragmented tribes, and the call to arms received an enthusiastic response. Thirty-two thousand men rallied to the cause and assembled by Ein Harod, the Spring of Harod, a move that did not go unnoticed by the Midianites.

Even with the large turnout, Gideon knew his force of amateurs was no match for the Midianites, who had the upper hand in terms of numbers, superior weapons and mobility. Gideon knew his only chance lay in neutralizing the Midianites' advantages. It seemed a surprise nighttime attack, when the enemy would be dismounted from their camels, would best prevent them from exploiting their edge. Such an operation would require detailed coordination, planning and execution, so the force would have to be small. Far too many men had answered his call to arms, so 22,000 men whose initial enthusiasm was greater than their actual will to fight were released, leaving Gideon with a force of 10,000 men. This was still far too many, as Gideon conceived a lightning assault by a small force rather than an attack en masse.

During the heat of day, Gideon brought the men to a spring to drink. Observing them carefully, Gideon paid close attention to those who took water with one hand as they held their spears with the other—alert to the possibility of ambush or attack by Midianite forces, exhibiting a soldierly trait. The vast majority of volunteers kneeled down on their knees to drink, without concern for the danger of their position. These latter men were dismissed.

By this method, Gideon pared his force down to 300 men. While his plan would rely on a small force initially, Gideon knew he would need all the help he could muster should his attack succeed. Careful to keep noise levels down to prevent being discovered, Gideon moved his force to high ground above the Midianite camp.

Under cover of darkness, Gideon personally reconnoitered the massive Midianite encampment, the sheer size of which awed him. They were "like locusts for multitude; and their camels were without number, as the sand which is upon the sea-shore . . ."[9] The light of fires dotted the landscape before him, illuminating tents, groups of men, camels and supplies. But Gideon was not deterred. Closing to within earshot to listen in on conversations, Gideon approached a tent where he overheard some Midianites speaking of "this Gideon and the army that was with him . . ."[10] Fear of the large Israelite force they knew had assembled seemed to be affecting their morale and was something Gideon could exploit to his advantage. Since word that he had dismissed the bulk of his volunteers had yet to reach the Midianites, Gideon knew he must attack without delay.

En route back to his camp, Gideon put together the final touches to his plan. Speaking to his men, Gideon described what he had seen and heard, and laid out his plan. He divided his 300 fighters into three companies, equipped each man with a sword, ram's horn, and a torch whose flame was hidden in a pitcher. The force stealthily approached the Midianite encampment from three directions and laid in wait by the camp perimeter for the middle of the night change in guard shift, when tired guards from the early watch had returned to their tents, where they would quickly fall asleep. New guards, still groggy from being woken up in the middle of the night, would be fighting off the nighttime chill.

Immediately after the change of guard shifts, Gideon blew his ram's horn—the sign for each of his men to do the same and to attack. Gideon's men exposed their torches and converged on the camp. The sudden commotion of 300 men attacking and blowing horns and the light of their torches startled man and beast alike. Encouraged by the sound of the rams' horns, the men howled excitedly as they set upon the Midianite camp. Coming from three directions, the Israelite attack had the appearance of an assault by an overwhelming force.

Gideon's men slew desert raiders and began setting fire to the camp, lighting up the night with flames. Confusion and panic took hold in the camp. Frightened men and animals cried out, and camels struggled to free themselves.

"A disorder and a fright seized upon the other men while they were half asleep, for it was night-time . . . so that a few of them were slain by their enemies, but the greatest part by their own soldiers. . . ."[11] The camp layout, divided by different nations, many speaking different languages and dialects, made it difficult to differentiate friend from foe. The result was utter chaos: "Once put into disorder, they killed all that they met with, as thinking them to be enemies also."[12]

The Midianites began fleeing, mostly heading eastward, toward their homes. Gideon's unscathed force chased the Midianites, but it was not large enough to finish off the fleeing army. As his men pursued the retreating Midianites, Gideon dispatched urgent messages to tribes in the vicinity to harass the retreating enemy, and to the tribe of Ephraim to block the Jordan River crossings to prevent the Midianites from escaping.

Exhausted from the attack, the killing and pursuit, Gideon and his men stopped at the settlement of Succoth for food and water, but were refused. They continued on to Penuel, where they were again turned away. Both towns refused assistance out of fear of Midianite reprisals. Though 120,000 Midianites were reported killed in the nighttime attack and subsequent pursuit, some 15,000 Midianite men—including the two Midianite kings Zebah and Zalmunna—escaped. Succoth and Penuel's hesitance illustrated the need to completely eliminate the Midianite threat, though Gideon would later return to these settlements to deal with them harshly.

The Midianites made it across the Jordan River. Believing they had finally reached safety, they stopped to rest. In relentless pursuit, Gideon's force spotted the Midianite camp and attacked. Caught unawares, Gideon's force destroyed the Midianites and captured the kings. After interrogating the kings for knowledge about his brothers, Gideon personally killed them. With revenge very much on his mind, Gideon had no problem taking spoils from his defeated enemy and allowing his men to do the same. Gideon claimed the Midianite king's royal pendants, garments and crescent symbols from their camels, and a percentage of each of his men's take.

The victory made Gideon a hero among the Israelite tribes. The people asked him to lead them, but he refused. Having avenged those responsible for his brothers' deaths and freed his people from the yoke of Midianite persecution, his work was done. There would be 40 years of rest for Israel, and for Gideon a timeless legacy. Rule by judges would continue until the system was deemed inadequate to address the threat posed by the Philistines around 1000 BCE.

Notes

1.The Bible's Book of Judges, the source for the events covered in this chapter, seems to have been written shortly after the "judges" period ended, probably around the time of the new monarchy. Josephus' *Antiquities of the Jews* is based on the Bible.

2. Reviv. "The Canaanite and Israelite Periods (3200–332 BC)," p.58.

3. Judges 4: 6–7.

4. Judges 4: 17.

5. Josephus (trans. Whiston). *Antiquities of the Jews*, Book V, Ch. V: 1.

6. Judges 5, The Song of Deborah.

7. Josephus. *Antiquities of the Jews*, Book V, Ch. V: 4.

8. Judges 4: 21.

9. Judges 7: 12.

10.Josephus. *Antiquities of the Jews*, Book V, Ch. VI: 4.

11.Josephus. *Antiquities of the Jews*, Book V, Ch. VI: 5.

12.Josephus. *Antiquities of the Jews*, Book V, Ch. VI: 5.

CHAPTER 3

TWO PEOPLES, ONE LAND

PHILISTINES AND ISRAELITES, 1000 BCE

Choose you a man for you, and let him come down to me.
If he be able to fight with me, and kill me, then will we be your
servants; but if I prevail against him, and kill him, then
shall ye be our servants, and serve us. . . . Give me
a man, that we may fight together.
I Samuel 17: 8–10

Goliath, the Philistine champion, challenged the Israelites with
these words each day for forty days, inviting a man from the
Israelite army to come out and fight. Goliath—a giant standing six to
nine feet (2–3m) tall,[1] was decked out in a coat of mail armor and leg
protectors, topped off by a brass helmet, and was armed with a spear,
javelin and sword. Terrified by his massive size, impressive armor and
formidable weapons, not a man among the Israelites was willing to
accept the challenge.

The Philistine and Israelite armies were arrayed for battle in the
Elah Valley in the Shephelah foothills, the border region between
Philistia, as the Philistine areas were known, and Judah. The year was
around 1000 BCE, and the Israelite army was blocking a Philistine
push inland towards the hill country, the heartland of Judah. Were
the Philistines to successfully cross the Elah Valley, one of the few
easily passable routes inland from the coast, the Israelites' firm grip

39

on the interior highlands would be at risk.

Conflict between the Philistines and Israelites had begun not long after the Philistines reached Canaan, roughly a century or two after the Israelites. The Philistines came from a group known as the Sea Peoples, proto-Greek seafaring invaders from the Aegean and central Mediterranean (possibly the island of Crete) uprooted by regional upheavals, which wrecked havoc in the area. The Sea People met defeat when they invaded Egypt in 1188 BCE, and the Philistines settled along the southern coastal plain in neighboring Canaan, where they established the cities of Ashkelon, Ashdod, Ekron,[2] Gath,[3] and Gaza.

With two peoples vying for the same land, it was only a matter of time before they would clash. The militarily powerful Philistines set out to enlarge the territory under their control. The Israelite tribes lacked the centralized power to deal with Philistine encroachment on their territory. There was ongoing conflict, including long periods of Philistine occupation when the Israelites were held in degrading servitude. The Philistines' well-organized military, equipped with iron weaponry and chariots, posed a very real threat to the Israelites' survival.[4]

Chariots gave the Philistines a huge advantage when operating in lowlands and on plains. But advancing inland towards the Elah Valley, the chariots lost their effectiveness as the topography changed. With the Israelites ensconced on the high ground, the Philistines feared venturing into the valley with their chariots. In these cases, the Philistines left their chariots behind and adopted a policy of establishing outposts. After conquering an area, the gains were secured and control imposed with military garrisons. Forces manning these positions also enforced the Philistine ban on ironsmithing—technology they strived to keep for themselves. The Philistines were skilled ironsmiths, providing them the best and most advanced weapons of the day, so they zealously enforced their ironsmithing monopoly to keep such weapons out of Israelite hands.

The Philistine camp was deployed on several hills on the southern side of the Elah Valley, centered around a hill known as Socoh while the Israelites were opposite, to the north, at Azekah. Both armies were arrayed defensively. Each day, the Israelite army would form up for combat but would not join battle with the Philistines. Goliath the

Philistine would then appear before the Israelite army and challenge one man to fight him. With the Israelites failing to accept Goliath's challenge, a precarious stalemate resulted. This situation was already affecting the Israelites, who could not remain mobilized indefinitely, for supplies were being depleted.

Goliath's threats, which added an element of psychological warfare designed to cause fear in the Israelite camp, only contributed to the stalemate. An adolescent named David was sent to the Israelite camp with food for his three brothers serving in the army and their officer to supplement their dwindling provisions. When David observed Goliath's daily challenge, he was embarrassed by the fear Goliath caused among his people's army and ashamed by the Israelites' failure to respond. David volunteered to fight the giant. It was not an act of reckless abandon in declaring his readiness to fight the Philistine, for the Prophet Samuel had told David that God had chosen him to become their king and "that he should overthrow the Philistines; and that against what nations soever he should make war, he should be the conqueror, and survive the fight; and that while he lived he should enjoy a glorious name, and leave such a name to his posterity also."[5] With such God-ordained invincibility, David was confident he could not lose.

When Saul heard of David's resolve, the king sent for the boy. "Thy servant will go and fight with this Philistine," David volunteered. Seeing the young boy before him, Saul dismissed the idea outright, saying, "Thou art not able to go against this Philistine to fight with him; for thou art but a youth, and he a man of war from his youth."[6] Saul had offered rewards for the man who would accept Goliath's challenge, but there had been no takers. That the Israelites did not simply decline the Philistine challenge and fight suggests there was more to the challenge than meets the eye. It may have been as it appears: an attempt to spare the death and destruction that would come from the two armies fighting. According to Goliath's challenge, the loser's side would surrender its weapons and submit themselves to be slaves. Such a challenge was a departure from the norms of warfare known to the Israelites, who had been fighting the Philistines for some time already. While foreign to the Israelites, such arrangements were an accepted tradition in the Philistine army.[7]

The challenge may also have been for a representative battle of which people's god would prevail. If this were the case, failing to send a warrior for this test of the gods would show a lack of faith in the Israelite god.[8]

In pleading his case to Saul, David cited examples of divine providence. David added: "the Lord . . . will deliver me out of the hand of this Philistine." Now that someone had come forward—albeit a boy—Saul had to accept lest he question his god's omnipotence. Acquiescing, Saul said, "Go, and the Lord shall be with thee."[9]

David had observed Goliath, noticing how cumbersome his armor was, and that the Philistine was equipped and armed solely for close-range or hand-to-hand battle; Goliath had no bow and arrows nor any other long-range weapon. But arrows were not effective against an individual mobile target wearing the armor the Philistine expected his opponent to have. It was clear to David that Goliath intended to lure his opponent in close where his advantage in size and strength could be brought to bear. Goliath would thrust his heavy spear at David when there was no time to escape the danger. The weight of the spear and iron spearhead, matched with Goliath's strength, made it likely that armor could be pierced at close range. If his opponent were wounded or if he missed his mark, Goliath had his other weapons to rely on.

Against the heavily armed and armored Philistine, David opted to go into battle without armor, armed only with a slingshot, the weapon he knew best. King Saul had offered David his armor, helmet and sword, but after trying these unfamiliar items, David declined. The sling was definitely not the weapon of choice against a single, mobile, well-armored opponent. In armies, slings were used against large targets, such as massed forces. For single combat, the user would have to be extremely skilled in its use. A shepherd, David had had ample time to practice in the fields while tending his family's flocks. Knowing that accuracy was not the sling's best feature, David collected five stones for the battle. Exposed but nimble, David set off to engage Goliath. Surprised his opponent was not fielding the same weapons and armor, and dismissing the young boy approaching him as an unworthy opponent, Goliath became angry and abusive. David's retort that he would "cut off thy head, and cast the other parts of thy body to the dogs. . . ."[10] was more than Goliath could bear.

Goliath went for the young upstart in haste but was slowed by the weight of his armor. David ran towards Goliath but stopped a safe distance away. With his target in effective range, David placed a stone in the pouch of his sling, raised it above his head and began swinging it around, harder and harder. David released the stone, which flew with great force towards the Philistine. It smashed into Goliath's face—left exposed by his helmet to provide a wide field of view—and "sank into his brain."

Mortally wounded by the blow, Goliath fell to the ground. With the heavy armor—estimated at around 125 pounds (57kg) weighing him down, Goliath was dazed, helpless and suddenly vulnerable. David rushed to him, drew the Philistine's sword from its sheath, and cut off his head. To those watching from the surrounding hilltops, the sight of David holding the Philistine champion's head aloft eliminated any doubts about the battle's outcome.

Panicked by this unexpected loss, the Philistines began fleeing en masse. If the battle had truly been an alternative to combat, then the Philistines were violating the agreement inherent in Goliath's challenge. If meant to showcase whose god would prevail, then the results were a clear harbinger of things to come. The Israelite army pursued the Philistines to the borders of their cities, killing some 30,000 and wounding double that number. Goliath's armor, weapons and kit were taken and put on display, perhaps as a tangible example of the Israelite god's power, just as the Philistines had done earlier in the conflict after capturing the Israelites' holy Ark at Eben Ezer.

The battle between David and Goliath was neither the beginning nor the end but rather the best-known event of a much larger military struggle between the Israelites and Philistines. The conflict had been going on for decades and would continue after this particular Philistine defeat.

The Israelites' first major engagement with the Philistines was the disastrous battle at Eben Ezer, near the modern town of Petah Tikva. After 4,000 Israelites were killed early in the fighting, the Ark of the Covenant was brought to the front to rally the troops. Containing the tablets inscribed with the Ten Commandments, the Ark was the most important symbol of the Israelites' faith and served as the only physical manifestation of the Israelite god. Its arrival inspired the Israelites and scared the Philistines.

As the battle continued, it went very much awry for the Israelites. In a humiliating defeat, 30,000 Israelite men were reportedly killed and, in a devastating national loss, the Ark was captured by the Philistines. This bounty would be only shortly in Philistine hands, for sickness and pestilence struck whichever Philistine city hosted the captured prize, so it was returned.

The Philistine gains from their victory at Eben Ezer were later erased, seemingly by divine intervention. When the Philistine army was poised to attack the Israelite force massed at Mitzpe, a natural disaster struck, with the ground shaking and thunder and lightning causing the Philistines to drop their weapons and flee. The Israelites pursued and killed them, and Israel recovered the cities and territory the Philistines had occupied.

In response to deprivation suffered under Philistine occupation and the on-going confrontation with the Philistines and other threats, including conflict among the tribes, pressure grew from the tribes to establish a monarchy. The Israelites were still confronting the Canaanites, but the Philistines were the more formidable enemy. At times, the Philistines occupied large swaths of Israel. The only resistance to speak of was the judge Samson's one-man war against the Philistines during a 40-year-long period of Philistine domination, yet Samson's motivation was revenge over being jilted rather than his people's freedom.

"It was necessary they should have with them one to fight their battles, and to avenge them of their enemies."[11] Responding to the will of the people, the prophet Samuel appointed a king, choosing Saul. "Be thou a king, by the ordination of God, against the Philistines, and for avenging the Hebrews for what they have suffered."[12]

Despite his mission, Saul's baptism of fire was actually against the Ammonites, east of the Jordan River. Tribes from the east were taking advantage of Israel's precarious position and the Ammonites, a neighboring tribe which had been persecuting the Israelites of Jabesh-Gilead, were laying siege to the town. With the inhabitants ready to surrender and submit to every male having his right eye put out, a call went out for help.[13] Hearing of the situation, Saul acted immediately, mobilizing a rescue force of more than 300,000 men. The speed of Saul's response allowed his force to take the Ammonites by surprise and defeat them. With the siege lifted, Saul earned a reputation for valor. This debt was later repaid following Saul's death when the men of Jabesh-Gilead risked their lives to rescue the corpses of the decapitated king and his sons, displayed ignominiously by the Philistines on the Beit Shean city wall.

Since the force he had mustered and led to the rescue of Jabesh-Gilead had been mobilized by Saul's threats, Saul saw the need for a standing army. Saul therefore established a royal army, with 2,000 men under his command and another 1,000 under his son Jonathan. There were chariots, drivers, horsemen, guards and runners. Officers commanded units of 100 and 1000, with an arms industry of skilled craftsmen making armor, chariots and other implements.

It was not long before the Philistines moved in and seized Israelite territory again, putting Saul's new force to the test. Philistine garrisons began imposing their repressive yoke over the Israelites. Jonathan's force attacked and wiped out a Philistine position at Geba, one of the hated symbols of Philistine occupation. Angered by the attack, the Philistines brought in reinforcements, amassing 300,000 infantry, 30,000 chariots and 6,000 horses, establishing a camp at Michmas. Philistine raiding parties began ravaging the countryside in reprisal. Vastly outnumbered, the Israelites were paralyzed by fear; many soldiers deserted. In an act exhibiting great courage, daring and élan (and a good measure of luck), Jonathan broke the deadlock when, accompanied only by his shield-bearer, he slipped into a Philistine position under cover of darkness and killed about 20 enemy soldiers. Alerted that something was going on, the rest of the camp reacted. Assuming they were under attack by a large force, different groups of Philistines unknowingly began fighting one another. In the ensuing melée, many Philistines were killed and a large number fled. The situation turned into a rout when an earthquake struck, causing a mass panic among the Philistine forces. Saul's force, camped nearby, took advantage of the confusion to attack, and killed some 60,000 retreating Philistines. The Philistines' hold on the center of the country had been pried open and they were chased back to the coastal plain.

Next came the Philistine thrust through the Elah Valley, which ended with the ignominious retreat following the defeat of their champion Goliath. Changing approach, the Philistines began advancing up the coast in friendly territory in an attempt to drive a wedge between the Israelite tribes in the north and center. After massing at Aphek, by a pass on the Via Maris, the Philistines cut inland to the Jezreel Valley. Monitoring their progress, Saul led his force through the highlands to reach the valley, where he deployed his men on the lower slopes of Mount Gilboa. When Saul asked God what would be, he received no answer—striking fear in the king's heart. Saul betrayed his serious concerns when he sought the services of a soothsayer before the battle. When he was told: "The Lord will deliver Israel also with thee into the hand of the Philistines; and tomorrow shalt thou and thy sons be with me; the Lord will deliver the host of Israel into the hand of the Philistines," his confidence was shattered. In what would become a self-fulfilling prophecy, the battle was doomed from the start.

The attack began the following morning at dawn. From their assembly point at the hill of Moreh, the Philistines advanced towards the Israelite camp. When they joined battle, the combat was described as a "sharp engagement" in which "the Philistines slew a great number of their enemies." The flat valley allowed the Philistines to fully employ their chariots. Saul and his sons fought "courageously and with the utmost alacrity," killing many Philistines.[14] Even when the Philistines had them surrounded, the Israelite leadership continued to fight tenaciously. In the fighting, Saul's sons Jonathan, Adinadab, and Malchishua were killed. Israelite soldiers began fleeing for their lives, hiding in the groves of the highlands. Disorder and confusion prevailed, and the Philistines slaughtered many of the fleeing Israelites.

Saul fought on, retreating up Mount Gilboa with a strong body of soldiers. The Philistines pursued them relentlessly and their archers wiped out all but a few of the Israelite force. Despite suffering from multiple wounds, Saul fought until he was too weak to continue. Rather than face capture by the Philistines, Saul committed suicide by falling on his sword. Saul had dedicated much of his energy countering the external threats to his kingdom, and died doing so. The place of his death (on Mount Gilboa) was cursed with barrenness, ironically by the young hero David, on whom Saul had expended so much effort out of spiteful jealousy: "Ye mountains of Gilboa, let there be no dew nor rain upon you, neither fields of choice fruits; for there the shield of the mighty was vilely cast away, the shield of Saul, not anointed with oil."[15]

Following his victory over Goliath, David had become a hero of Israel, receiving great acclaim—sometimes more than the king himself. David became an officer in Saul's army, where he brought more praise upon himself in further defeats over Philistines. David was held in high esteem by all the people, except for Saul, who was horribly jealous and came to hate David. Saul went as far as trying to kill David on grounds that he was a threat to the king's grip on power. Fleeing Saul's jealous wrath, David was forced into life underground. Joined by his family and others who feared the king, David became leader of a band of outlaws. With his cadre of followers, David supported himself by protecting local villages for a tribute.

Though he had opportunities to kill Saul, David refrained from doing so. But the king's relentless pursuit ironically led David to seek refuge with the Philistines. In fact, his fighting force accompanied the Philistine host on the northern offensive that culminated with the combat at Mount Gilboa until other Philistines voiced their concern and David and his force departed the area.

Following Saul's death in around 1005 BCE, David was moved by Israel's predicament. Israel's army had been decimated, civilians had fled large areas of the north and the Philistines occupied the abandoned cities. David became king, first of Judah and then of all Israel. He earned a great name for himself by unifying the Israelites into a united monarchy, through successful military campaigns and the establishment of Jerusalem as capital and religious center, where he installed the revered Ark of the Covenant. His reign was considered a golden age, and it was said that he was respected by all the peoples from the Euphrates to the Nile.

As king, David led the Israelites to defeat the Philistines, driving them back and containing them along the coastal plain. The Philistines lost their pre-eminent position in the region, although they would endure until the time of the Babylonians in the 5th century BCE. Ultimately, "in the ebb and flow of warring nations over this land it is more than probable that they were gradually absorbed and lost their identity."[16]

However, in an enduring legacy, the region continued to be called Philistia, and by this name—in the form of the word Palestine—the whole country became known. While the Philistine people may have disappeared, their name lives on with the Palestinians, the people who contend with modern-day Israel in a conflict reminiscent of the Israelite–Philistine wars, with two peoples struggling for this ancient land.

Notes

1.Moshe Garsiel's "Elements of History and Reality in the Description of the Ela Valley Warfare and the Combat Between David and Goliath (1 Samuel 17)" *Beit Mikra* (Vol. 41, 1997) has an excellent discussion of Goliath's height. Garsiel's bottom line is that "One needs to relate to the height not as an exact height, but rather as a typological number." It seems that Goliath's unusual height was further exaggerated by scribes over time who believed they were adding to the glory of Israel. Since Goliath was the Philistine champion, it stands to reason he was indeed a large, impressive figure, rejecting theories that his extreme height was the result of a growth disorder.

2. Identified as Tell Mikne, near Kibbutz Rivadim.

3. Identified as Tell Tzafit, near Kfar Menachem.

4. New archaeological evidence suggests the Philistines did not have chariots (personal interview with Yehuda Dagan, Israel Antiquities Authority, Shephelah region expert). However, chariots are mentioned in both the Bible and in Josephus' *Antiquities*, so remain in this account.

5. Josephus, *Antiquities of the Jews*, Book VI, Ch. VIII: 1.

6. I Samuel 17: 32–33

7. Garsiel, p.299.

8. Garsiel, p.301.

9.I Samuel 17: 37.

10.Josephus, *Antiquities of the Jews*, Book VI, Ch. IX: 4.

11.Josephus, *Antiquities of the Jews*, Book VI, Ch. III: 6.

12.Josephus, *Antiquities of the Jews*, Book VI, Ch. IV: 2.

13.Putting out a man's right eye was an ancient form of "demilitarization" as it prevented the man from fighting as a soldier. Since soldiers carried shields on their left side, visibility from the left eye was obstructed, meaning the right eye was necessary to see what was happening while protected by the shield.

14.Josephus, *Antiquities of the Jews*, Book VI, Ch. XIV: 7.

15.Samuel II 1: 21.

16.Driscoll, J. F. "Philistines." *The Catholic Encyclopedia* (New York: Robert Appleton Company, 1911) http://www.newadvent.org/cathen/12021c.htm (accessed March 14, 2011).

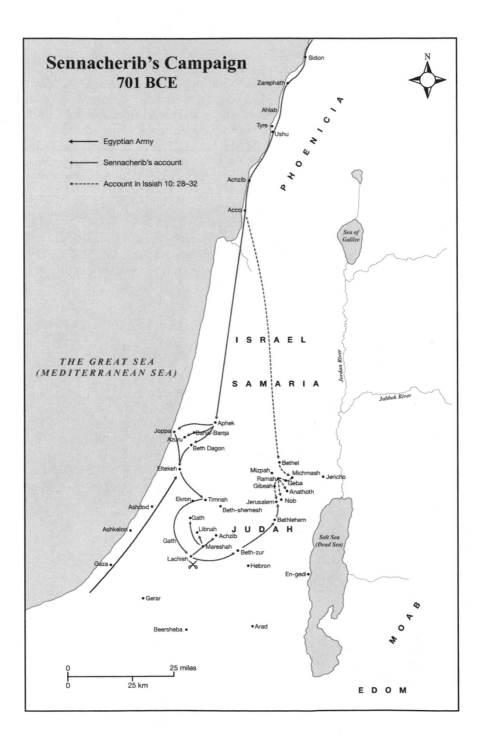

Sennacherib's Campaign
701 BCE

— Egyptian Army

— Sennacherib's account

•----- Account in Issiah 10: 28–32

N

Sidon

Zarephath

Ahlab

Tyre
Ushu

Achzib

Acco

PHOENICIA

Sea of
Galilee

ISRAEL

THE GREAT SEA
(MEDITERRANEAN SEA)

SAMARIA

Jordan River

Jabbok River

Aphek
Joppa
Bana-Barqa
Azuru
Beth Dagon
Eltekeh
Bethel
Mizpah
Michmash
Jericho
Ramah
Geba
Gibeah
Anathoth
Ekron
Timnah
Jerusalem
Nob
Ashdod
Beth-shemesh
Gath
Bethlehem
Libnah
Ashkelon
Achzib
JUDAH
Gath
Mareshah
Salt Sea
(Dead Sea)
Lachish
Beth-zur

Gaza
Hebron
En-gedi

Gerar

MOAB

Beersheba
Arad

0   25 miles
0   25 km

EDOM

CHAPTER 4

SENNACHERIB'S CROWNING ACHIEVEMENT

Assyrians at Lachish, 701 BCE

The Assyrians had never before seen anything like it. Of the 46 fortified towns and villages they would destroy on their 701 BCE campaign against rebellious Judah, nowhere else would they encounter such elaborate defenses as at Lachish, Judah's most important city after Jerusalem. Guardian of the southwestern approach from the lowlands (Shephelah) into the Judean mountains, Lachish was Assyrian monarch Sennacherib's first major objective during the punitive expedition.

Assyria was the Near East's strongest regime, with its empire stretching from modern-day Iraq to the Mediterranean Sea, down to the Egyptian border. The southern kingdom of Judah had been submissive to the Assyrian superpower while the northern kingdom of Israel had earlier risen up in revolt.[1] A punitive force sent by the Assyrian king laid siege to Samaria, the Northern Kingdom's capital, and the city fell in 722 BCE. The people were banished, thus beginning the saga of the ten lost tribes. At that time, Judean king Hezekiah had steered clear of anti-Assyrian activity.

But with Judah enjoying a time of prosperity that begat confidence, King Hezekiah felt the time was ripe to free Judah from the yoke of foreign subjugation and began preparing for revolt. The most illustrative example of the great lengths undertaken during these preparations is the 500m-long (1,640 foot-long) tunnel hewn from solid rock to bring the Gihon Spring's waters into Jerusalem, securing the water source for the city while denying it to invading armies. Knowing that unity and centralized leadership would be necessary if Judah were to withstand an Assyrian onslaught, Hezekiah instituted reforms designed to consolidate Jerusalem's power. Assuming the outlying areas would bear the brunt of an invasion, foodstuffs and supplies were distributed and stockpiled, and it seems the people were behind Hezekiah.

When a revolt against Assyrian rule broke out upon the death of King Sargon II in 705 BCE, Hezekiah took an active role. Babylon rebelled against Assyria, joined by Philistine Ascalon and Judah with Egyptian support, revolting against Assyrian dominance and taxation. Furious over such insubordination, Assyrian monarch Sennacherib organized and led an expedition to punish the recalcitrant lands and force payment of taxes.

The Assyrians first crushed the revolt in Babylon before setting their sights on the rebellious provinces to the west. Sennacherib's army invaded and subdued the coastal territory of the Philistines. Sennacherib recorded in his annals the capture of towns from the rebellious kingdom of Ascalon: "In the course of my campaign I besieged Beth Dagon, Joppa, Banai-Barqa, Azuru. . . . I conquered [them] and carried their spoils away."[2] When an Egyptian force rushed north to challenge the Assyrians, they were soundly defeated at the battle of Eltekeh, as Sennacherib described: "In the plain of Eltekeh, their battle lines were drawn up against me and they sharpened their weapons. Upon a trust [-inspiring] oracle [given] by Ashur, my lord, I fought with them and inflicted a defeat upon them. In the . . . battle, I personally captured alive the Egyptian charioteers with the[ir] princes and [also] the charioteers of the king of Ethiopia."[3]

Then he turned east to conquer the rebellious mountain kingdom of Judah. The Bible tells us that "In the fourteenth year of King Hezekiah, Sennacherib, king of Assyria, went on an expedition against all the fortified cities of Judah and captured them."[4] "I laid siege to 46 of his strong cities, walled forts and to the countless small villages in their vicinity," Sennacherib wrote, "and conquered [them] by means of well-stamped [earth-] ramps and battering-rams brought [thus] near [to the walls] [combined with] the attack by foot soldiers, [using] mines, breeches as well as sapper work."[5] As the largest citadel guarding the western border of the Kingdom of Judah, Lachish was Sennacherib's first major objective in Judah. More heavily fortified than all the other Assyrian objectives in Judah, it was clear to the Assyrian invaders that Lachish's formidable defenses would pose a serious challenge—even with their siege works, equipment, and experienced troops.

Sitting on high ground dominating the surrounding countryside, Lachish was a formidable citadel. Surveying their objective in hopes of finding its weak link, the Assyrian combat engineers were awed by the town's defenses. Cities and towns, generally sited along roads or trade routes, were built with thought to ensure ample water supplies and defensive considerations. To defend against the threat of invasion, cities tended to be built on high ground. A *tel* is an artificial mound created when cities were built upon the ruins of a previous city. Debris of destroyed towns was never completely cleared but merely leveled off, a base upon which the survivors or newcomers would build anew. Thus, a town originally settled on high ground continued to grow with each subsequent resettlement, resulting in easily defendable steep slopes. This was precisely the situation at Lachish, which was at such a great height that it was afforded a view of the surrounding territory for miles. Its height, and its double set of city walls, made it one well-protected city. We first learn of Lachish as a fortified Canaanite city conquered by Joshua around 1400 BCE.[6] The city was later fortified as part of a defense system based on a string of forts blocking enemy penetration into Judah.

The city was surrounded by two walls: the main defensive wall made of bricks on stone foundations standing around six meters (18 feet) high with towers protruding at regular intervals, and a stone (and in some places topped with brick) revetment wall along the middle of the slope. Though intended as a retaining wall supporting the upper wall and glacis, the revetment wall added to Lachish's defenses. The two walls joined together at a gate structure, the largest and most impressive of its kind—with massive wooden doors and flanking towers, all serving to deter assault. From their camp on the neighboring hilltop, the Assyrians could appreciate the massive scale of Lachish's palace-fort in the center of the city, which rose high above the surrounding buildings.

Fortified towns posed no real obstacle to the Assyrian military machine, with its seasoned troops and arsenal of battering rams. Its army had specialized units, including cavalry, sappers, combat engineers, snipers, and foot soldiers. The combat engineers were well versed at building siege ramps against walled cities, laying the groundwork for assault units to move battering rams into place to bash down the walls, which they did throughout Judah. But with its defensive arrangement of walls, gatehouse complex, well, and inner fort, Lachish was no ordinary adversary.

The Assyrians knew what would be in store were they to assault through the main gate complex. Cities generally had several gates through which an attacker would need to penetrate. Defenders with bows and arrows, slingshots and other weapons would be stationed on the towers, bombarding attackers to keep them at bay. From its appearance alone, the Assyrians could be certain that Lachish's gate structure would incorporate additional defenses designed to complicate an enemy attack.

The alternative was breaking through its walls. The outer wall was designed to slow an enemy's advance on the city once they were within effective range of the defenders' bows and slings, while also protecting the base of the walls from undermining and breaching. Just approaching the walls meant climbing a glacis, a protective lime-plastered ramp, while exposed to defensive fire, ruling out an assault in force to scale the barrier.

Rather than accepting the heavy casualties a direct assault on the gate structure would entail, the Assyrians opted to build a siege ramp. The southwest corner of the town was decided upon as the main attack point, for here Tel Lachish joins another hill, forming a topographical saddle. Though the city's fortifications would clearly be stronger in this area, its low height relative to other potential routes convinced the engineers that this was the best option. And so they began constructing a siege ramp, carrying boulders from the surrounding countryside to build it up. Rocks were heaped against the slope; the ramp grew larger and larger, slowly climbing over the revetment wall and up towards the main city wall. Not only was the construction physically demanding, but construction teams were constantly under fire from defensive positions on the city walls. The city's defenders constructed a counter-ramp inside the city to raise the city wall's height. This forced the Assyrians to raise the height of their ramp, as they knew their battering rams would be most successful against the upper portion of walls, as the stones at the thicker, stronger base of a wall were harder to dislodge. With the Assyrian ramp nearly complete, stones at the top were cemented together with lime-plaster, and logs laid to prepare the ground for the battering rams. Construction work became even more dangerous as building details put on the final touches, with defenders firing at near point-blank range.

Anxiety and apprehension in Lachish mounted as the Assyrian ramp grew closer to the city's main wall. Lachish was rife with a sense of helplessness and of inevitable defeat at the hands of their powerful adversary, an adversary unlikely to be merciful after suffering heavy losses during the long and difficult siege.

With the ramp complete and all preparations in order, the long-awaited attack on Lachish began. Under a hail of arrows and missiles from the defenders, armor-clad and helmeted Assyrian infantrymen—archers, sling-throwers, and shielded spearmen—advanced up the ramp. The counterfire intensified as they closed range and began rolling the feared battering rams up the ramp and into place at several locations. The defenders threw flaming torches down upon them but the Assyrians were ready with buckets of water to douse the flames. Chariots—useless in a besieged city—were set ablaze and thrown down on the battering rams, which had begun pounding the walls.

Assyrian archers took aim at the men on the parapets and in the towers. Despite the heavy suppressing fire, Lachish's defenders perched on its ramparts shot arrows and hurled stones and firebrands down on the attackers without pause. In the fierce battle, there were many casualties on both sides. Under intense fire, many of Lachish's defenders fell—the lucky ones falling back into the battlements where they could get medical treatment; others tumbling over the walls, where some were impaled and displayed by the Assyrians. Dead

Assyrian soldiers were strewn about the ground, some where they had fallen, others moved from the ramp to make room for more assault forces.

Battering rams continued pounding the walls, dislodging stones until the walls began collapsing under weight of the powerful blows, taking parts of the battlements down as the walls crumbled. With the wall breached, defenders in the towers maintained fire at the Assyrians who were now charging into the city over debris of the fallen wall. For a time, the defenders held the Assyrians at bay, but force of numbers and the Assyrians' determination after the long and difficult siege made them unstoppable. The Assyrian forces fanned out past the mud-brick shops and houses lining the main street into the town. The Assyrian calls for surrender long ago rejected, Lachish's men knew they would face the sword, and so they made for the fortified palace for a final stand. But with Assyrian soldiers now pouring through the breach, the situation was hopeless. There was no stopping the determined Assyrian war machine, and the palace was taken as well.

After securing the city, the Assyrians were amazed by the elaborate gate structure. They had been right to build a ramp as troops assaulting the gate would have been exposed to fire on their vulnerable right side (shields were typically carried with the left arm) from archers on the walls. At the top, after breaking through the outer gate, they would have found themselves channeled into a small courtyard where they would have needed to break through an inner gate while exposed to deadly crossfire from above.

Troops rounded up Lachish's frightened residents from the densely populated residential quarters. Allowed to take a few belongings, the people were forced from the city. Captives and deportees were then paraded before Sennacherib before being taken away as slaves. The city was ransacked and looted. Ceremonial symbols and other booty were carried off and displayed before the king. Corpses of some 1,500 casualties were dumped into a deep pit. The Assyrians then set fire to the town, burning Lachish to the ground.

Jerusalem

While at Lachish, Sennacherib sent a task force 30 miles (50 km) northeast to Jerusalem, perhaps to defend against the dispatch of relief forces. Jerusalem was besieged, and King Hezekiah was unable to direct the defense of his kingdom. Sennacherib gloated in this fact, writing in his official annals: "As to Hezekiah, the Jew. . . . I made a prisoner in Jerusalem, his royal residence, like a bird in a cage. I surrounded him with earthwork in order to molest those who were his city's gate."[7]

The Assyrian force pressed Hezekiah to surrender, claiming that the God of Israel had abandoned the Jews. Caged in as he was, Hezekiah apparently had time to consider all that was going on. The revolt was not going nearly as hoped. Neither the Egyptian force nor the Philistines had succeeded in standing up to Assyrian assault. And with reports reaching the king of events at Lachish and destruction throughout Judah, King Hezekiah became wary of a fate like that of the defeated northern kingdom of Israel, meaning he could be Judah's last king, a reputation history would not treat kindly.

And so Hezekiah decided to appease Sennacherib with a declaration of submission. Hezekiah sent word to Sennacherib at Lachish, saying, "I have offended; return from me; that which thou puttest on me will I bear."[8] Sennacherib demanded a large tribute, as recorded in his annals: "Hezekiah himself . . . did send me, later, to Nineveh, my lordly city, together with 30 talents of gold, 800 talents of silver, precious stones, antimony, large cuts of red stone, couches [inlaid] with ivory, nimedu-chairs [inlaid] with ivory, elephant-hides, ebony-wood, boxwood [and] all kinds of valuable treasures, his [own] daughters, concubines, male and female musicians. In order to deliver the tribute to do obeisance as a slave he sent his [personal] messenger."[9]

The tribute was evidently not enough to appease Sennacherib's anger, as the king was determined to thoroughly punish Judah for its role in the revolt. A massive Assyrian force was encamped around Jerusalem, and its citizens were subjected to demoralizing psychological warfare when Assyrian commanders speaking Hebrew denigrated the God of the Jews and King Hezekiah before his people. "Let not Hezekiah beguile you, for he will not be able to deliver you," the Assyrians called out. "Neither let Hezekiah make you trust in the Lord, saying 'The Lord will surely deliver us; this city shall not be given into the hand of the king of Assyria.'"[10] They continued their harassment, suggesting that the Lord had abandoned the Jews. With Jerusalem under siege and humiliated by the Assyrians' daily harangues, King Hezekiah prayed to God for help. The king's prayers were answered: "The angel of the Lord went forth, and smote in the camp of the Assyrians a hundred fourscore and five thousand [185,000]; and when men arose early in the morning, behold, they were all dead corpses."[11] Perhaps this was an outbreak of plague, as disease could be rampant in areas where people lived in close quarters for an extended period. Greek historian Herodotus, writing in the 5th century BCE, attributed the outbreak to field mice. Whatever its cause, the disease spread like wildfire through the Assyrian ranks, resulting in mass death.

After this horrible setback, Sennacherib, who had moved on from Lachish to besiege another objective in Judah, called off the campaign. The Assyrians broke camp and left Judah without completely subduing it, though they may have later returned to take care of unfinished business. While the Bible tells us Sennacherib returned home shamefaced, the real loser was Hezekiah. Though he survived the ordeal and retained his reign, the revolt had been a disaster. Forty-six cities, forts and villages had been destroyed, their populations taken away as slaves, and captured parts of Hezekiah's kingdom distributed to kings who had remained loyal to Assyria. Sennacherib recorded the aftermath: "I drove out [of them] 200,150 people, young and old, male and female, horses, mules, donkeys, camels, big and small cattle beyond counting, and considered [them] booty."[12] On top of these spoils, Assyria demanded an even higher annual tribute than before, meaning that Judah would now be even more subservient to Assyria.

Having failed to take Jerusalem, Sennacherib had to settle for second best: Lachish. Sennacherib considered his conquest of Lachish the crowning achievement of the campaign, as evidenced by the prominent placement of reliefs depicting events at Lachish in his palace in Nineveh, in modern-day Iraq. These reliefs, now exhibited in the British Museum in London, along with the Bible and Sennacherib's own royal annals, give us a detailed account of what transpired at Lachish. Archaeological excavations conducted under the direction of David Ussishkin of Tel Aviv University's Institute of Archaeology corroborate these accounts.

In 681 BCE, Sennacherib was murdered by his sons as he worshipped in the temple of his god Nisroch. His death ushered in a period of upheaval. Assyria's power ultimately waned and they disappeared into the history books. As for Lachish, the city was later rebuilt and fortified, only to be destroyed again in 586 BCE by the Babylonians when Judah stood up to Babylon's rising influence and authority. In a campaign of reprisal, Babylonian King Nebuchadnezzar presided over the destruction of Jerusalem and the Jews' Temple—which had been built in 957 BCE by King Solomon—followed by the forced exile to Babylon (present-day Iraq) made famous by Psalm 137: "By the rivers of Babylon, we laid down and wept, for thee, Zion." The exile was short-lived due to Babylon's defeat by Persian King Cyrus, who allowed the Jews to return home and rebuild their Temple. Work began in 538 BCE on a new Temple, whose desecration at the hands of Greek influence would usher in a new period of turmoil.

Notes

1. The monarchy established by King David and carried forward by his son Solomon unraveled when Solomon's son Rehoboam became the third king of this dynasty (reign 928–11 BCE). The northern tribes, seeking relief from excessive taxation, were rebuffed by the new king, leading to secession and establishment of the Kingdom of Israel. Relations between the two kingdoms varied from one of friendly allies to conflict.
2. Prism of Sennacherib. Retrieved at http://staff.feldberg.brandeis.edu
3. Prism of Sennacherib. Retrieved at http://staff.feldberg.brandeis.edu
4. 2 Kings 18: 13.
5. Prism of Sennacherib. Retrieved at http://staff.feldberg.brandeis.edu
6. Joshua 10: 1–32.
7. Prism of Sennacherib. Retrieved at http://staff.feldberg.brandeis.edu
8. 2 Kings 18: 14.
9. Prism of Sennacherib. Retrieved at http://staff.feldberg.brandeis.edu
10. Isaiah 36: 14–15.
11. 2 Kings 19: 35.
12. Prism of Sennacherib. Retrieved at http://staff.feldberg.brandeis.edu

The Maccabean War
175 BCE

- —·—·— Boundaries of the Jewish state
- — — — Border with the Ptolemaic Kingdom
- - - - - Other borders
- ■ Greek cities

■ Sidon
Sidon

Paneas
● Paneas

■Tyre
Tyre

Ladder of Tyre

Kedesh/
Kudisos

Asor/ ●
Hazor

Ptolemais/Acre ■

Arbela ●
*Sea of
Galilee*
Galilee

Philoteria ■

*THE GREAT SEA
(MEDITERRANEAN
SEA)*

Dora ■

Great Plain

Arbatta

Scythopolis/
Beit Shean

Samaritis

■ Samaria

● Sichem
▲ *Mt. Gerizim*

Parathon ●

Tephon ●

Acrabatha ●

Apollonia ■

Jordan River

Paralia

Joppa ■

Ramathaim/Arimathea ■
● Thamnatha

Adida ●
Lydda ●
Modin ●
Gazara ●
✕

Port of the Jamnites ■

Jamnia ■
Accaron ●
Cedron ●
Emmaus ●

Judea

see inset

Azotus/
Ashdod ■

*Lake
Asphaltitis
(Dead Sea)*

Ashkelon ■ ● Ascalon

Adullam ●

Marisa ●

Adora ●
● Hebron

Gaza ■ ■ Anthedon

Engaddi ●

Idumea

■ Raphia

● Alusa

**NABATAEAN
ARABS**

N

Inset

● Beerzeth

Lower
Beth-Horon
✕ ● ●✕
Elasa Berea/
Beeroth

Bethel

● Aphaerema

● Maspha/●
✕✕ Mizpeh
Caphar Adasa
Salama

● Michmas

● Dok ●
Jericho

Jerusalem ●

● Bethbassi
✕● Beth Zecharia

● Bethzeth ● Tekoa

Beth-Zur ● ● Asphar

*Desert of Judah/
Wilderness of Tekoa*

*Lake
Asphaltitis
(Dead Sea)*

0 —— 25 miles
0 —— 25 km

0 —— 10 miles
0 —— 10 km

CHAPTER 5

PUSHED TOO FAR

THE MACCABEAN WAR, 175 BCE

"Avenge the wrong done to your people."
I Maccabees 2:67

With these deathbed words, Mattathias, patriarch of the priestly Hasmonean clan, bequeathed his sons responsibility to continue their struggle against the Seleucids, one of the most advanced and powerful militaries of its day.

During his conquests, Alexander the Great reached the walls of Jerusalem in 332 BCE, where he was said to have been so gratified that the Jews, led by the high priest, opened the city gates and came out in festive dress to greet him that he would not permit the city to be plundered. Following his death in 323 BCE, Alexander's generals divided the lands he had conquered, creating three main empires: the Ptolemies in Egypt, the Antigonids in Macedonia and the Seleucids in Syria, Asia Minor and the Middle East. In a process known as Hellenization, imported Greek ways and culture joined and slowly replaced the indigenous cultures of the conquered peoples. The division it would cause among the Jews, and the subsequent infighting and then war are spelled out in the Books of the Maccabees and in Josephus' *Antiquities of the Jews*.

Judea[1] lay between the Ptolemaic and Seleucid empires. It was ruled by the Ptolemies of Egypt until it was captured by the Seleucid king Antiochus III (the Great) in 200 BCE. There was tolerance towards Jewish religious practices, but many Jews, especially the urban elite, were attracted to Greek ways and willingly took to them. Hellenism, they believed, was the future, representing the modern world. Viewing Judaism as archaic, these apostate Jews embraced Hellenism with a passion, abandoning all connections to Jewish customs. Some went as far as undergoing a surgical procedure that hid their circumcision so that when they were seen naked during athletics, they would appear Greek.

The ascension to power of a new Seleucid ruler in 175 BCE brought an end to the benevolent autonomy Jews had been enjoying. The new ruler, Antiochus IV, dubbed himself "Epiphanes," or God Manifest, for he considered himself divine. His detractors called him "Epimanes," or mad-man, due to his vagaries and excesses, which he lost no time in demonstrating.

Hellenized Jews took advantage of the change in rule to advance their agenda. Approached by the apostate Jews with ideas on how to expedite the process of Hellenization in Judea, the new king was pleased to hear them out. The assimilated Jews' scheme built on the appointment of a Hellenized Jew named Jason as high priest—the spiritual leader of Jewry. With their proposal sweetened with a hefty tribute, the king consented.

Having one of their own in power gave the Hellenizers undue influence in Judea, and accelerated the pace of Hellenization. Yet when Jason's tenure failed to meet the king's expectations, the king removed him and replaced him with extreme Hellenist Menelaus, whose bribes and radical outlook pleased the king. Scorning the responsibilities of the priesthood, Menelaus opened the Jews' Temple to the worship of Greek gods and went as far as allowing the altar to be defiled by the sacrifice of pigs—an unforgivable sacrilege.[2] Menelaus' behavior was a serious affront to traditional Jewish ways and resulted in the alienation of a large proportion of the Jewish population, most of whom were simple farmers and artisans. Backlash over the Seleucid king's interference in the appointment of the high priest exacerbated the divide between the Hellenized Jews and those who continued to observe Jewish religious and cultural traditions.

The new king made two expeditions against his rivals in Egypt, the first, successful one in 170 BCE and a second a year later that was curtailed due to Roman diplomatic pressure. The Seleucids were seething from this embarrassing capitulation to Roman power and while crossing Judea en route home in 169 BCE, they found a way to reassert authority by entering Jerusalem and plundering the Temple of its holy vessels and going on an unprovoked killing spree before retiring to Antioch, their capital on the Mediterranean in northwest Syria.

Despairing of the rich and mighty Hellenizers and their powerful Seleucid backers against them, Judea's traditional Jews turned to their religion and became more observant, widening the divide. When Jason—now supported by the majority—sought to regain the high priesthood by force, a cry from the apostate Jews went out to Antioch for help. Triggered by unrest and instigation by the radical Hellenized Jews, in 167 BCE the Seleucids returned with a vengeance.

The Seleucids stole everything of value remaining in the Temple, set fire to parts of Jerusalem, leveled the city walls and wrought destruction. This time, the Seleucids established a permanent occupation presence when they built an imposing fortress overlooking the Temple. Known as the Acra, the fortress was garrisoned with troops both to intimidate and repress the local population, and to safeguard their allies among the Hellenized Jews, whose extreme views and support for the king had put them at risk. Jewish collaborators took refuge within the Acra.

From its new permanent base, the Seleucids terrorized the Jewish population, many of whom fled the city. The situation deteriorated with prohibitions on Jewish religious practice, part of a drive to unify the entire Seleucid kingdom under Greek customs. It was likely external threats to the Seleucid Empire that led the new king to accelerate the imposition of Greek religion and culture on the peoples over whom he ruled to create a loyal, uniform Hellenized population. This policy of crash Hellenization was not targeted only at the Jews; Hellenism was imposed on all Seleucid subjects. Seeing no alternative, the conquered peoples acquiesced. But the Jews of Judea mostly objected, angering the king. Considering himself a Greek god, the king expected complete submission to his commands. The Jews' obstinate rejection of Greek ways infuriated the king, bringing on more repression.

The prohibitions forbade Jewish religious practice. No longer could Jews observe the Sabbath, circumcise their children or follow their traditional way of life. Not only were Jewish rites and customs forbidden, but edicts were issued ordering the Sabbath and festivals be violated—all so that the Jews would forget their ways. Inspectors were appointed to ensure compliance with the new rules; failure to obey was punishable by death. Many Jews complied—some willingly and others out of fear of the consequences, but most refused to forsake their ways, which put their lives at risk. Thousands were martyred. Jews throughout Judea fled to the wilderness.

The Hellenizers were pleased that a mechanism was now in place to eliminate what they considered their people's antiquated customs. Knowing it was unusual for the Greeks to repress a particular religious group, the traditional Jews correctly inferred the moves came from the extremist apostate Jews, and blamed them for inviting the harsh Seleucid measures.

The Spark

Spreading throughout Judea's towns and villages, the Seleucids enforced the new edicts, epitomized by the compulsory sacrifice of pigs. When a Seleucid contingent arrived in the outlying village of Modiin, northwest of Jerusalem, they called on Mattathias, a well-respected community elder from the priestly Hasmonean family, to publicly sacrifice a pig. When the old man refused, an apostate Jew came forward and carried out the order. Mattathias' defiant refusal in itself meant a condemnation to death. Infuriated by the Jewish collaborator and with nothing to lose, Mattathias struck out, killing the Jew and the Seleucid official supervising. Mattathias' five sons led the villagers against the accompanying troops, killing them. A revolt had begun. Knowing word would soon reach the authorities and would bring on reprisals, Mattathias and his sons fled to the rugged hills of Gophna, between Jerusalem and Samaria, for refuge.

Joined by other Jews who had already fled their homes, Mattathias and his sons organized themselves and others in the hills and began training in guerilla tactics. The small group, none with military training, recruited members to its ranks. Arming themselves with farm implements and weapons they fashioned themselves, these men on the run became a people's militia. They established contacts with villages throughout the countryside, developing these relations into an effective intelligence-gathering organization. The rebels began by attacking towns where Hellenizers were strong, killing traitors and collaborators and destroying Greek idol altars—symbol of the hated Greek oppression. Next came more brazen guerilla attacks against Seleucid military patrols. Ambushing and killing the troops, the Jewish rebels supplemented their arsenal with captured weapons before melting back into the countryside.

Learning as they went along, the rebels used tactics improvised to suit each situation. Attacks on collaborators and Seleucid patrols showed that surprise and stealth worked best—they could achieve their aims and return home unscathed. Using their intimate knowledge of the countryside, the Jewish fighters struck at their enemies with near impunity, becoming known as Maccabees for the hammer-like blows they dealt their enemies. The Maccabees became the law of the land, in effect nullifying the Seleucid edicts against Jewish practice.

After a year of difficult living in the hills, Mattathias passed away, although not before delegating command to his son Judah and instructing his sons to avenge the wrongs the Seleucids were doing to the Jewish people.

The Seleucids, after encountering mainly sycophant Hellenized Jews, were amazed by the Jews' commitment to their faith, and their willingness to fight and die for their beliefs. Seleucid forces were occupying Jerusalem, a puppet government had been installed, and the Temple had been desecrated, yet the Jews would not submit. What the Seleucids did not understand was that the Maccabees were committed to a cause: fighting for religious freedom in their homeland, defending their way of life. Empowered by their passion for a cause charged with religious zeal, the Maccabees gained control of the countryside. Jerusalem and its Seleucid garrison were in danger of being isolated.

Apollonius

With rebels gaining the upper hand, word reached Antioch that authority was deteriorating throughout Judea. In 166 BCE Seleucid regional governor Apollonius set off from his base in Samaria with troops to locate and destroy the rebels.

Presumptuous and overconfident, Apollonius marched his troops along the Samaria–Jerusalem route, right into the Maccabees' stronghold, perhaps expecting that the rebels would be terrified into submission by a show of force by heavily armed Seleucid regulars. Apollonius miscalculated. Accustomed to being stationed among docile peoples, his troops were not prepared to face determined rebels.

When word reached Judah that Apollonius was on the move towards the Gophna area, he employed his knowledge of the territory to plan an attack that would not allow his powerful enemy to bring its superior numbers to bear. On the Seleucids' route of advance the logical place to attack was a long defile that Judah sensed would be perfect for an ambush.

As the Seleucids approached unawares, the rebels could not help but feel nervous in the face of the largest Greek force they had ever encountered. With Judah reassuring them, the Maccabee fighters maintained discipline as lead elements of the Seleucid force proceeded through the winding ascent, close to where the rebels lay hidden in the brush. When its vanguard rounded a bend and could not be seen by the main body, Judah signaled his troops to attack. Apollonius never even saw the attack coming. The Maccabees showered the Greeks with a deluge of arrows and rocks. Before the shocked troops could react, the Maccabees rushed them, slaying soldiers with their motley assortment of captured swords and improvised weapons. The Seleucids' heavy weapons proved useless in the restricted space of the passage. The terrain also restricted them from forming up into defensible array, leaving each man to defend himself. When Apollonius was killed in the fray, true panic broke out, with soldiers trampling one another in their haste to escape. Many of the Seleucid troops were killed, but far more were wounded and managed to flee, abandoning in the process a large quantity of weapons and gear to the Maccabees. Judah claimed Apollonius' sword as his own personal spoil, with which he would fight all subsequent battles.

Seron

With Apollonius' defeat, King Antiochus realized the situation in

Judea was far more serious than he had imagined. Embarrassed by the defeat and continued challenge to his authority, he was determined to teach this band of rebels a lesson. The king dispatched another general, Seron, who gladly accepted the mission thinking it would bring him glory. Dismissing Apollonius' expedition as a bungled mission, Seron set out in 165 BCE at the head of a strong army certain that the Jewish rebels would be no match for his professional soldiers.

Confident in the strength of his force yet careful not to repeat Apollonius' mistakes in the unfamiliar territory, Seron led his force southward along the coastal road, steering clear of the Maccabee stronghold. After turning inland on the route to Jerusalem, they were joined by Jewish collaborators familiar with the lay of the land. Seron's force pitched camp at Beth-Horon. To advance towards Jerusalem they needed to march through the adjacent pass. While navigating the narrow pass, the Seleucid force would be open to attack. Judah took men out towards the advancing Seleucid force. He could not believe a second Seleucid general was making this same critical error, which he knew would mean victory for the Maccabees. Despite their commander's confidence, the rebels were naturally intimidated by the heavily armed Seleucid force, and felt uneasy.

Summing up his plan in a talk with his men, Judah explained: "It is easy for many to be hemmed in by few"—recalling the tactic already proven successful in their victory over Apollonius. Judah reminded his men that they were fighting for their homes, families, and religious beliefs. "They come against us in great insolence and lawlessness to destroy us and our wives and our children, and to despoil us," he said. "But we fight for our lives and our laws. The Lord himself will crush them before us; as for you, do not be afraid of them."[3]

Judah deployed his men along the Beth-Horon pass, concealed along the steep slopes commanding the narrow pass. As the Seleucid force made its way up the ascent, Judah noticed large gaps between units, which he reckoned was a defensive measure allowing troops to come to the aid of any part coming under attack. The distance between the units grew as the soldiers trudged up the long, windy route, encumbered by their heavy weapons and equipment.

Maccabee slingers and archers deployed along the sides of the defile opened up with a barrage into the Seleucid ranks before Judah led his men in with swords and knives, sending the Selecuids reeling. Despite being a true combat unit, trained in Greek combat doctrine to fight in set-piece battle formations, the Seleucids were completely neutralized by the terrain, which allowed no room to maneuver. The Seleucid host was decimated, with 800 men left dead, including its commanding general. Word of Seron's death spread quickly, causing panic to break out among the Seleucid forces. Abandoning their weapons and gear, the Seleucid soldiers fled in disarray down the treacherous pass, with the Maccabees in hot pursuit.

After the rout, the Maccabees helped themselves to the weapons and equipment abandoned in the pass, putting them to use in arming the scores of new volunteers who joined their cause and in training for what they knew would be another showdown.

This second victory proved that the first was not a mere fluke. As stories of his legendary acts began to circulate, reaching as far as the palace in Antioch, Judah's reputation became well-known. Hellenized Jews and collaborators in Judea were terrified of him, and he was viewed as a true threat to the integrity of the Seleucid Empire.

The rebels in Judea were an embarrassment, but they were not the only trouble facing the Seleucid Empire. Parts of the empire were refusing to pay taxes, and the royal coffers were running low. King Antiochus was preparing for a campaign to Persia to forcibly collect taxes, but saw that more attention needed to be given to stamping out the rebellion in Judea. Before setting off on his expedition, the king appointed royal family member Lysias to act as regent for his son and to be in charge of affairs. The king allocated half his forces and elephants to Lysias with which to "wipe out and destroy the strength of Israel and the remnants of Jerusalem; . . . banish the memory of them from the place, settle aliens in all their territory, and distribute their land by lot."[4]

Taking no chances, Lysias resorted to overkill, assembling a massive force of 40,000 infantry and 7,000 cavalry under the command of three generals: Ptolemy, Nicanor and Gorgias. The force set out along the coast in 165 BCE, taking a cautious approach steering clear of the mountains, and established camp at Emmaus (near Latrun), close to where the modern road to Jerusalem begins its climb through the hills. The camp was situated on open terrain well-suited to the

Seleucid army's strengths. Various camp-followers, including slave dealers and other profiteers, descended on the Seleucid camp, waiting for action.

The Seleucid army's power centered on the phalanx. A large square-shaped tactical formation, the phalanx was a formidable array designed to smash an enemy force. The smallest building block for the formation was the 256-man syntagma, arranged in eight or 16 rows. In battle mode, a phalanx's first five ranks held their spears (sarissa) horizontally, creating an impenetrable barrier. The remaining rows rested their spears on the shoulder of the soldier in front of him, ensuring cohesion. A phalanx not only delivered a powerful punch, but was also an intimidating spectacle that had psychological impact.

Judah knew his force had no chance in a set-piece battle against a Seleucid phalanx. But he also knew the phalanx had its faults. The formation was not very mobile, it could not change its front in face of an enemy, and if penetrated it was ill-suited for hand-to-hand combat. For protection, its vulnerable flanks and rear were guarded by cavalry and light forces. In a confined area or on broken ground, a phalanx could not form up or maintain cohesion—the precise circumstances that had allowed Judah his first two victories over the Seleucids.

Given the Seleucids' cautious deployment, Judah was almost forced to allow them to take the initiative while he remained ready to immediately react to their moves. His only hope for victory lay in responding unconventionally, where advantage could be drawn from the fact that the two forces were so disparate.

With no intention of being lured into the Judean mountains where the rebels held sway and could hit them with a surprise attack, the Seleucids deliberately situated their camp on open terrain. With their overwhelming force, supplemented by reinforcements from Judea's southern neighbor Idumea and auxiliaries, the Seleucids were totally convinced of victory.

From guerilla band, the Maccabees had developed a more formal military structure, with officers commanding units of 1,000 men, companies of 100, platoons of 50 and sub-units of 10. Despite their progress and past successes, the Maccabees were still merely a militia, and thus were understandably wary of confronting such a massive fighting force, many times larger than anything they had faced before.

After initially assembling at Mitzpe, northwest of Jerusalem, Judah moved his force closer to the enemy, allowing them to observe the Seleucid camp from the hills. From the somewhat fatalistic talk to his men, it seems Judah's confidence was also shaken. Calling on his men to "be courageous," Judah told them: "It is better for us to die in battle than to see the misfortunes of our nation and of the Temple. But as the Lord's will in heaven may be, so shall He do."[5]

Knowing the Maccabees fought unconventionally, Seleucid General Gorgias tried to follow suit. Abandoning standard doctrine and tactics, he led a crack force of 5,000 infantry and 1,000 cavalry under cover of darkness against the insurgents, hoping to catch the Maccabees in their camp unawares. When Maccabee scouts reported on the preparations and departure of this force, Judah saw the opportunity to lure them away by ordering bonfires lit in the Maccabee camp to give the impression that his forces were concentrated there. Leaving behind a small decoy force, Judah evacuated the camp and led his men on an overnight march along a circuitous route down to the coastal plain.

When Gorgias' force reached the Maccabee camp, they found it empty, yet spotted what they believed was the tail end of the Maccabee army withdrawing. Gorgias immediately set off in pursuit, leading his men deeper into the hills, away from their base camp.

Reacting to the Seleucid initiative, Judah may not have had the necessary time to coordinate an ambush; it was enough to neutralize Gorgias with an aimless pursuit in the hills. With the Seleucids' best troops thus occupied, Judah led his men towards the main Seleucid encampment at Emmaus, which he hoped would have relaxed its guard in the knowledge that Gorgias' force was in the process of attacking and destroying the Maccabee camp. The Maccabee force approached the Seleucid camp at daybreak. Seeing the rebel force drawing near, the alarm was raised. Men scrambled out of their bedrolls, with the rush of adrenaline overcoming the early morning chill. Some Seleucid forces formed up into a phalanx on the plain while others scrambled to defend the camp. Exposed on the plain and with Gorgias' force in the hills, there was no option for retreat. Judah ordered an attack.

The Maccabees maneuvered and hit the Seleucid phalanx on its vulnerable flank. With the unexpected rebel attack, the Seleucids may not have fielded their full complement of light cavalry to protect the phalanx. The Maccabees penetrated, breaking up the formation's integrity.

Finding their long spears unwieldy, the Greek soldiers were hard pressed to fight off the Maccabees, who were adept in hand-to-hand combat. The Maccabees reached the Seleucid camp, and in an instant, the Seleucids' confidence deteriorated into fear, and utter confusion broke out. Horses and other animals—excited by the noise of battle—trampled soldiers in their own panic. In a chain reaction, individuals and then masses of men began fleeing, leaving 3,000 casualties in their wake. The Maccabees pursued, but Judah called off the chase as there was still the unfinished business of Gorgias' force. The massive Seleucid camp, largely destroyed by the fighting and panicked flight of so many men, was set on fire.

Gorgias' men, descending from their frustrating overnight search through the hills, saw their comrades in flight and parts of their camp on fire, and understood that something had gone very wrong. The sense that they might next fall victim set off a panicked retreat towards the coast, without even attempting to engage the Jewish rebels. Judah and his men looted what remained of the Seleucid camp, where they acquired more arms and equipment plus other booty and spoils with which to feed the needs of their growing army.

Lysias

Lysias was livid. Determined to see the Maccabees crushed, Lysias himself organized and led a force estimated at 20,000 infantry and 4,000 cavalry[6] and set out from Antioch in 164 BCE. Traveling by the safe corridor of the coastal plain, the force headed further south (towards Ashkelon) before wheeling inland, all within friendly territory. From the route they traveled, it was clear the Seleucid host was headed for Jerusalem, most likely to relieve the Acra garrison before moving against the rebels.

Judah moved to counter the Seleucids with a force some 10,000 strong. Fed with intelligence on their whereabouts by his scouts, Judah tracked the Seleucid advance, looking for an opportunity to attack. The Seleucids were slowed at Beth-Zur, a fortress on Judea's southern border with Idumea that the Maccabees had occupied, buying time for defensive preparations.

With the Seleucids poised to drive on, Judah searched for a spot from which to launch an ambush—resorting to the Maccabees' tried and true tactic of attacking where the enemy would be hard-pressed to defend itself. The Maccabees' new organization seems to have paid off, with their large force well-coordinated to strike a blow that inflicted heavy casualties on the Greek forces. While details of the confrontation are scarce, it was said that Lysias observed how bold the Maccabees were, and how ready to die nobly, such that he began to truly appreciate what the Seleucids were up against.

What happened next came as a complete surprise to the Maccabees. The massive Seleucid army broke camp and began pulling back. The Maccabees could not believe their eyes. Judah ordered scouts to track the Seleucid host to ascertain what they were up to until word reached him of King Antiochus' death, the probable reason for the withdrawal. Indeed, when word of the king's death reached Lysias, he decided to quit Judea and return to Antioch, where he would reign as regent for Antiochus' son. Given the Seleucid army's withdrawal from Judea and the mad king's death, Judah believed the Maccabees had won a reprieve for some time, and hoped there might also be a change in Seleucid policy. The time was ripe for a move on Jerusalem to reclaim the Temple.

Return to the Temple

Religious freedom was finally at hand. When the city's Hellenized Jews heard the Maccabees were making for Jerusalem, many fled. With great joy, the Maccabees cleansed the Temple and rededicated it, resuming religious sacrifices. Tradition has it that the sole cruse of ritually pure olive oil found in the Temple—a one-day's supply—miraculously burned for eight days.[7] The festivities marking the rededication have been celebrated by Jews ever since as the holiday Chanukah.

The story does not end here. The menacing Acra citadel was not only a reminder of Seleucid authority, but its garrison actively opposed the Jews. Additionally, in a move to frustrate upstart Judea and ingratiate themselves with Antioch, Judea's neighbors began a campaign of persecution against Jews living in their lands. Judah responded with punitive expeditions against the perpetrators in neighboring territories and lands. Confident from his successive victories, Judah was ready to move against the Acra fortress.

When the Jerusalem garrison pleaded for assistance, Antioch responded with an invasion on a scale that far surpassed that of all previous campaigns. Taking heed of the lessons from his earlier campaign, Lysias knew more troops were required. Leading a Greek and mercenary force of 50,000 infantry, 5,000 cavalry and a complement of war elephants, Lysias marched on Judea accompanied by his charge, the young King Antiochus V Eupator.

After marching along the same approach corridor as before, the Seleucids were again forced to invest the fortress at Beth-Zur, which the Maccabees had fortified, before continuing towards Jerusalem. Moving rapidly yet cautiously, the Seleucids advanced steadily and in good order, with their flanks protected by forces spread out in the hills. They were an impressive sight, with rank after rank of soldiers carrying golden and brass shields that flashed in the afternoon sun like flaming torches. They intentionally made a great deal of noise as they marched, with their shouts echoing through the hills causing fright among Judah's men.

Judah had mustered a fairly large force with which he tried to block the Seleucids at Beth Zecharia. The Maccabees were awed by the size of the enemy force—the most impressive the Seleucids had yet fielded in Judea—but more so by the elephants. Around "each elephant they stationed a thousand men armed with coats of mail, and with brass helmets on their heads, and five hundred picked horsemen were assigned to each beast."[8]

Seleucid forces advanced through the hilly area, carefully sending forces to secure the high ground, yet the Maccabees managed to launch an attack that hit the Seleucids hard, leaving 600 casualties. The Seleucids quickly recoiled and began rallying forces. The elephants' shock effect had its intended impression; many of the Jewish fighters were paralyzed by fear. Judah's brother Eleazar, attempting to inspire the rebels, went after an elephant he believed carried the Seleucid general. After fighting his way through the guard, Eleazar stabbed the elephant in its belly with his sword. The elephant collapsed on him, crushing him to death.

The Seleucid force far outclassed the Maccabees, who broke and retreated. Judah fell back to Jerusalem to organize its defenses before retiring to his base in the mountains of Gophna. From this safe haven, the Maccabees could return to guerilla warfare against the occupation force Lysias would undoubtedly leave. The Seleucids regained control of Jerusalem until, for a second time, the day was saved when external events forced Lysias to withdraw, this time to prevent his rival Philip from usurping power in Antioch. For the Maccabees, aided by a strong dose of luck, victory had been snatched from defeat.

Seeking quiet in Judea to free him to address domestic matters, Lysias lifted decrees forbidding religious observance, eliminating the Jews' primary grievance. The majority of the rebels were content to lay down their arms and return to their lives now that the revolt had achieved its aim of religious freedom, albeit under continued Seleucid rule. To Judah, the Seleucid concessions were not enough. Convinced that religious freedom could not be preserved under Seleucid rule, Judah wanted full political independence.

In an unexpected turn of events, the young Seleucid king Antiochus V was ousted by his cousin Demetrius, who had the deposed king and his guardian Lysias put to death. Quick to seize the opportunity presented by the new leader in Antioch, apostate Jews convinced Demetrius to intervene in Judea. To shore up the situation, Demetrius appointed a new high priest, Alcimus, who arrived in Jerusalem accompanied by a military escort under Bacchides, sent to establish and bolster the new priest's authority. The Seleucid contingent entered Jerusalem unopposed.

The new high priest and the general were quick to alienate the people through killings and other vindictive measures, proving correct Judah's skepticism. In response, the Maccabees mobilized and fought back, leading to calls for Antioch to assist. This renewed instability in Judea coincided with revolts in the Seleucid Empire's eastern satrapies, presenting a very real threat to the empire's unity.

Demetrius responded by despatching Nicanor at the head of a large force to deal with the revival of the Maccabean revolt. When the force he led was ambushed and routed at Capharsalama (Kfar Shalem), Nicanor withdrew to Jerusalem to await additional manpower. When his reinforced army resumed operations in the countryside, Judah ambushed them at Adasa, north of Jerusalem, and succeeded in killing the Seleucid general. Word of Nicanor's death in battle caused the Greek troops to panic and flee.

To counter the renewed Seleucid aggression, the Maccabees made an approach to Rome, then a regional power. Seeing an opportunity to check the Seleucids, Rome was receptive, and a treaty recognizing Judea's independence was concluded.

Angered both by the military defeats in Judea and the political maneuvering with Rome, Demetrius sent Bacchides back to Judea with a 20,000-strong infantry force backed by 2,000 cavalry. Knowing that the Maccabees lacked the strong support they had previously enjoyed, Antioch pressed its campaign to wipe out the Jewish rebels.

Death of Judah

Sources report Judah succeeded in mustering only 3,000 men with which to counter Bacchides. Seeing the Seleucid army arrayed against them on the battlefield at Elasa, the force began hemorrhaging deserters, leaving Judah with only 800 men. Given accounts of the battle, which we are told lasted from morning to night and described as severe, Judah's force was likely much greater.[9] In a brilliant maneuver, Bacchides' forces caught the Maccabees in a pincer, sandwiching them between the two flanks of his army. There were many casualties on both sides, the legendary Judah the Maccabee among them.

After recovering Judah's body from the battlefield, the Maccabees fled, taking their commander's body back to his family village of Modiin for burial. The Seleucids were back in control. Bacchides put Hellenizers in charge of the country, and they began pursuing Maccabee supporters. Judah's brothers would carry on the torch; Jonathan took on the task of breathing life back into the resistance. Bacchides returned to Antioch to help address the deteriorating situation in the east. The Maccabees' strength grew once again to the point where they were the *de facto* rulers of most of Judea. Bacchides was sent back to Judea to crush the rebellion but was himself defeated. This time, he agreed to peace terms and departed Judea for good. Demetrius was killed in battle fighting a rival for the throne. Jonathan, free to govern Judea, went on to become high priest, and purged the nation of Jewish Hellenizers. In coming to an understanding with the Seleucids, Jonathan was able to consolidate his power and expand Judea's territory until he was murdered by the treachery of Seleucid general Trypho, who feared his rising power.

Simon, the last surviving son of Mattathias,[10] stepped in to fill the void, and would go on to distinguish himself in his own right. Simon presided over the surrender of the menacing Acra, symbol of Seleucid oppression. Simon secured concessions from Antioch, chief among them freedom from taxation, which in effect was a recognition of independence. In 141 BCE, Judea was granted formal independence from Seleucid rule—the fruits of more than 30 years of resistance from the time Seleucid hostilities began. Thus began the Hasmonean Dynasty, which would rule for a century.

This is the true accomplishment, or miracle, if you will, of the Maccabees: Judea was an independent Jewish state, while the mighty Seleucid Empire slowly declined into irrelevance, all brought about by the knee-jerk reaction of a proud old man who refused to forsake his faith.

Rome, eclipsing the Seleucids as the great power in the region, granted the Hasmoneans limited authority under the Roman governor of Damascus. The Jews became hostile to the new regime, and the following years witnessed frequent insurrections. The Hasmonean dynasty's reign came to an end when Herod the Great became king of the Jews, ushering in the next chapter of foreign-domination-inspired revolt by the Jews.

Notes

1. Note the Greco-Roman spelling (formerly Judah).
2. II Maccabees 4: 24, *The Apocrypha, or Deuterocanonical Books* (New Revised Standard Version) (Cambridge UK: Cambridge University Press, 1989).
3. I Maccabees 3: 20–22.
4. I Maccabees 3: 35–36.
5. I Maccabees 3: 58–60.
6. Far less than the highly exaggerated figure of 60,000 troops reported in I Maccabees.
7. Judah ordered the Temple cleansed, a new altar built in place of the one desecrated by the sacrifice of pigs, and new holy vessels made. When the fire had been kindled anew upon the altar and the lamps of the candelabra lit, the dedication of the altar was celebrated for eight days amid sacrifices and songs in a similar fashion to the holiday Sukkot, the Feast of Tabernacles, which also lasts for eight days. (II Maccabees 10: 6)
8. I Maccabees 6: 35.
9. Bezalel Bar-Kochva. *The Seleucid Army. Organization and Tactics in the great Campaign* (Cambridge, UK: Cambridge University Press, 1979: reprinted with corrections), p.185.
10.In the period following Judah's death, younger brother Yochanan was killed by tribesmen east of the Dead Sea.

The Zealot Rebellion
67 CE

Phoenice

Gaulanitis

Ptolemais

Jotapata

Gamla

Sepphoris

THE GREAT SEA
(MEDITERRANEAN SEA)

Galilee

Galatis

Jordan River

Caesarea

Dekapolis

Samaria

Peraea

Beth-Horon

Jerusalem

Bethlehem

Herodium

Salt Sea
(Dead Sea)

Judaea

Idumea

Masada

0   25 miles

0   25 km

N

CHAPTER 6

IVDAEA CAPTA

THE RAGE OF ROME, 67 CE

Roman hegemony over Judaea had begun with Jerusalem's capture in 63 BCE by Pompey, which brought Jewish independence to an end. The province the Romans called Iudaea (Judaea) became a vassal state, and the Romans appointed Herod as King of the Jews. Initially, Rome respected some local sensibilities and granted the Jews a measure of autonomy in internal affairs. Rome generally tolerated conquered people's beliefs and ways; Roman customs were infused into conquered lands while some aspects of the conquered people's cultures might be adopted.

After enjoying a century of independence under the Hasmonean Dynasty, the Jews had a hard time accepting subjugation, which they considered a blow to national pride. While most Jews found a way to compromise between Jewish law and their new circumstances, radical Jewish nationalists, known as Zealots, virulently opposed foreign occupation. Since Rome expected complete loyalty from its subjects, the Jews did not ingratiate themselves with their new rulers. The Romans never came to understand the Jews. When Pompey captured Jerusalem, he had upset the Jews by entering the Holy of Holies—their

Temple's sacred inner sanctum entered only by the High Priest once a year—to see for himself that the Jews had no manifestation of the god they worshipped, as it was inconceivable to him, and many Romans, that the Jews worshipped an invisible god. Rome's view of the Jews deteriorated and grew into a deep-seated hatred, with Jews receiving perhaps the harshest treatment of all Rome's subjects. A hint of Rome's attitude toward the Jews can be found in Roman historian Tacitus' *Histories*, where he calls Jews "this race detested by the gods" and "the vilest of nations."[1]

Rome later moved to direct rule of Judaea by procurators: administrative officials with the power of a provincial governor. The procurators selected for Judaea were largely inept, excessively greedy, and exhibited a disregard for the Jewish people they governed. Abusing their authority to plunder for personal gain, the procurators callously bled Judaea of its wealth. Excessive taxes forced Jews from their lands and a great many into poverty, thereby alienating their subjects and increasing support for the Zealots.

Gessius Florus, who took office as procurator of the province in 64 CE, soon surpassed his predecessors with his abuses and excesses, pushing the mainstream Jews to the side of the Zealots. Josephus noted that "Gessius Florus, as though he had been sent on purpose to show his crimes to every body, made a pompous ostentation of them to our nation, as never omitting any sort of violence, nor any unjust sort of punishment."[2] Roman soldiers and locals took their cue from the procurator, who propagated incitement and violence. Intentional provocations against the Jewish community in the Roman provincial capital of Caesarea erupted into a riot that ended with the Jews' expulsion from the city, an event considered a trigger to the war. Florus' greed was so great that he raided the Temple treasury, crossing a line that inflamed the Jews' passions. When some Jews sarcastically collected alms for the procurator—a brazen insult—Florus responded with violence, unleashing his soldiers on murderous rampages that left thousands of Jews dead. His provocations and incitement worked: urged by the Zealots, the bulk of the Jews became convinced that Roman occupation was untenable; conflict was the only alternative. Florus couldn't have been happier, for war would obviate him from being called to account for his actions before Caesar. As Tacitus put it, "the Jews had patience till Gessius Florus was made procurator. Under him it was that the war began."[3]

In 66 CE, Florus left Jerusalem for Caesarea. In short order, Masada, once King Herod's desert mountain-top fortress, was seized by a band of extremist Zealots known as the Sicarii (for the daggers they carried and freely used against their enemies), who killed the Roman force stationed there and seized its arsenal. In another overt act of mutiny, the Temple priests stopped the requisite daily sacrifices for the Roman emperor, a profound move that signaled a break with Roman rule. Finally, the populace of Jerusalem rose in revolt. The local Roman garrison was massacred by revolutionaries.

Internecine fighting now broke out among the Jews, many of whom disagreed with the provocations against Rome. Aristocrats and others seeking maintenance of the status quo (with optimistic hopes that the next procurator would be better) fought the revolutionaries, who they felt were encouraging Rome to make war against them. Ill-effects of the uprising were immediate, with local populations in Judaea, Egypt and Syria attacking Jews with impunity.

Following events in Judaea with grave concern, Roman governor of Syria, Cestius Gallus—who held responsibility for Judaean affairs—marched from Antioch in November 66 CE at the head of Legion XII, supported by cohorts of infantry, troops of cavalry and auxiliaries, including many archers, to quell the Jews' uprising. Plundering and setting fire to Jewish villages en route, the Roman force reached Jerusalem and besieged the Jewish insurgents in the Temple. After undermining the Temple wall and making preparations to burn its gate, Cestius Gallus inexplicably ordered his forces to withdraw. The Jews harassed the retreating Romans and repeatedly attacked them by the Beth-Horon pass, the narrow defile where the Maccabees had defeated a Seleucid army in their fight for independence. Nearly 6,000 Roman soldiers were killed, and only by a stratagem did the governor manage to escape with some of his forces.

Though exhilarated by this victory and inspired by its symbolic location, the Jews had no illusions that Rome would tolerate such insubordination. Not only was it an embarrassment for Rome, but the Jews' insurrection threatened the important link between Alexandria in Egypt and Antioch in Syria, the Empire's greatest cities after Rome.

With its massive empire held together in a delicate balance, Rome had to send a strong message that all its ruled subjects would understand quite well—that Rome would destroy those who upset the *Pax Romana*, while also dissuading Rome's rivals, the Parthians, from intervening.

Rome's response came in the form of three legions. Burning, stealing, pillaging and murdering their way across Galilee, the Roman forces quickly subdued many Jewish towns and villages. Sepphoris (Zippori), Galilee's largest city, saved itself by pledging allegiance to Rome, siding against their own countrymen, which did not say much for the Jews' unity.

Military governors had been appointed by the aristocrats in Jerusalem organizing the war effort to prepare the country's defenses. Joseph ben Mattathias had been named to the critical post of commander of the Galilee region. It was believed the Romans would first focus their efforts in Judaea's north to conquer Galilee before moving on Jerusalem or other parts of the province. A strong stance against the invading Romans would embolden the country and might encourage intervention by the Parthians. If the Romans were to be stopped, it needed to be in Galilee.

Joseph prepared Galilee's cities and towns for defense, and assembled a force that by his account numbered 60,000 infantry, 250 horsemen, 4,500 mercenaries and 600 guards, all armed with old weapons he had collected and prepared. The force was organized according to the Roman model, with captains of tens, hundreds and thousands. Joseph trained them to "give the signals one to another, and to call and recall the soldiers by the trumpets, how to expand the wings of an army, and make them wheel about; and when one wing hath had success, to turn again and assist those that were hard set, and to join in the defense of what had most suffered."[4] He exercised them for war while impressing upon them the importance of soldiers maintaining good conscience.

Their adversary was the Roman general Titus Flavius Vespasianus (Vespasian), an experienced and well-regarded veteran of successful campaigns in Germany and Britain. Vespasian arrived at Ptolemais (Acre/Akko) with Legion XV *Apollinaris* and was joined in theater by his son Titus with Legions V *Macedonica* and X *Fretensis*. Vespasian's legions were supplemented by cohorts, troops of cavalry and thousands of auxiliaries, including cavalry, archers and infantry provided by local Roman vassal kings. In all, Vespasian commanded a force of 60,000 men with which to crush the Jews. With so many elements under his command, the Roman general needed time to organize his force before moving out in April 67 CE.

The military force Joseph had organized was quick to desert in the face of Roman legions, finding refuge in Galilee's walled cities. The training they had undergone was for naught; there would be no set battles with the Romans, only resistance in the walled cities. In effect, this acknowledged eventual defeat, for the cities and towns could not hold out against the Romans, who were masters at siegecraft. Ideas of thwarting the Romans and petitioning for a settlement would not be realized, nor would other subjected peoples join the revolt now that the Jewish War, as the revolt came to be known, was seen as a lost cause.

Joseph fled to the walled city of Jotapata (Yodfat). Roman intelligence reported the bulk of the Jewish rebels were also in the city, which was considered the strongest of the cities. Vespasian determined to demolish Jotapata and capture Joseph, thinking that the capture of the Jewish general would be a major blow to the Jews' morale and will to fight, and might frighten other cities into surrendering.

Jotapata put up a tenacious resistance throughout May 67 CE. Repeated Roman assaults were repulsed, and Roman losses were heavy, with even General Vespasian wounded in action. Only when a deserter treacherously tipped off the Romans about when the city's sentries would be sleeping were the Romans able to finally overcome the city's defenses after 47 days of siege.[5]

After convincing so many of his countrymen to give their lives for their cause, Joseph put saving himself above his ideals and turned himself over to the Romans, with whom he would collaborate. He took the Roman name Flavius Josephus and chronicled the Jewish War; his accounts are the primary source on the war. His countrymen would brand him a coward and deserter.

Gamla

After Jotapata, the Romans moved down the coastal plain to secure

Jaffa and its environs before returning north to take Tiberias and then
Taricheae (Migdal) in a land and naval battle. Intimidated by Roman
successes, most towns and villages surrendered. With Galilee almost
completely in Roman hands, the Romans turned their attention to the
city of Gamla east of the Sea of Galilee, in the Gaulanitis region, part
of what is today known as the Golan Heights.

Considered a strong and safe refuge, Gamla's population swelled
with refugees fleeing the Roman army's rampage in Galilee, and villagers from surrounding areas seeking shelter. The influx of refugees
had turned Gamla into a Zealot stronghold.

Naturally secure atop a steep hill resembling a camel's hump
(from which the city drew its name—*gamal* is Hebrew for camel),
Gamla is protected on all sides by nearly impassable ravines. The city
is approached from the east by a dip in the terrain, called a saddle,
connecting the hill to the plateau above. This was the only side protected by a defensive wall. Before going over to the Romans, Galilee
commander Joseph had helped the city to shore up its defenses. The
wall facing the approach to the city was fortified by evacuating houses
abutting the wall and filling them in with stones, entrances and gaps
between houses and other structures along the wall were filled-in or
sealed, and the wall was thickened. Trenches and underground mines
were dug across the city's approach to impede access. And for morale,
coins were minted honoring Jerusalem, perhaps as a way of reminding
citizens that their preparations were part of a greater national and
religious effort.

Confidence in the city's strength had been reinforced when Jewish
vassal King Agrippa II, a grandson of Herod the Great, who ruled a
region north of Galilee, had unsuccessfully besieged the city for seven
months earlier in the year.

Marching through difficult volcanic rock terrain cut by deep river
canyons, the Roman column comprising General Vespasian and his
guard, three legions and auxiliary forces, cavalry, siege equipment and
baggage—some 30,000 men—arrived at Gamla in September 67 CE.
The Romans established camp on a plateau overlooking the city.
Normally the Romans intentionally sited their camps to be visible
from their objective for its psychological impact on the enemy, but the
terrain around Gamla did not allow for this.[6] The ground in their

encampment was leveled and prepared, walls built and buildings erected. Sentries were posted around the city in an effort to prevent escape and block reinforcements or supplies from reaching the city.

Surveying the city wall, the Romans identified weak points where they would position battering rams. Knowing where to focus their attacks may have been made easier with the help of collaborator Josephus, who was familiar with Gamla's defenses from when he had surveyed them and advised on their improvement.

Roman engineering units quickly went to work filling in the city's defensive trench, raising a bank against the wall and preparing the ground for the siege engines. Work details set out to supply the engineers with the necessary timber, earth and rocks to build platforms for the siege engines, siege works, ramparts and lines of wooden hurdles and screens. In addition to their disciplined military drill regimen, Roman soldiers were also trained in construction.

The speed and efficiency with which the Romans went about their work shook the confidence of the defenders of Gamla. The Jews fired at the workers relentlessly, hurling rocks and projectiles, to no avail. Working behind protective screens while archers and slingers provided steady cover fire, the engineers built ramps that crept steadily towards Gamla's walls.

King Agrippa, who joined the Roman siege force at Gamla, approached the city wall calling for surrender. Gamla's response came in the form of a slinger's well-aimed rock, which sent the king reeling. Roman soldiers became apprehensive given the Jews' response to Agrippa; if the Jews would respond to one of their own this way, the Romans reasoned, they could expect a savage reception. At Jotapata, the Romans had seen how ferociously the Jews could fight, including pouring boiling oil on attacking Roman troops, proving they would resort to any means to defend themselves.

Defenders on Gamla's wall did their best to beat back the teams bringing the engines forward until cover fire became so intense that no one could oppose them from the parapet, freeing the Romans to bring up the battering rams.

Following Roman assault doctrine, the attack on Gamla began with an intense barrage. Stone balls launched from ballistae crashed down with great force. Projectiles shattered the great synagogue's roof, killing those sheltered inside. Catapults fired missiles and darts with such intensity that some reached as far as the city's western quarters, nearly 1,000 feet (300m) from the city wall. Archaeologists discovered some 2,000 basalt ballista balls and 1,600 iron arrowheads in and around the city—more than any other site in the Roman Empire, giving testimony to the intensity of the barrage.[7] Archers composed largely of auxiliary units from ethnic groups skilled with the bow, and slingers added to the fray, forcing Gamla's defenders to seek cover. The Roman artillery made a terrifying noise, both the machines' groaning and their projectiles screaming through the air.

The battering rams went to work, Gamla's wall reverberating with each blow. At Jotapata, the siege engines had been set alight several times by desperate sallies, so the Romans may have outfitted the rams with hurdles and skins to protect both their soldiers and equipment. At Gamla, they went about their work unmolested. Shaken by these huge wooden beams capped by a heavy iron tip in the shape of a ram's head, it wasn't long before the wall began giving way. Assault troops amassed behind protective screens, waiting for a breach. Soldiers equipped with ladders and hooks prepared to scale the wall in a bid to overwhelm defenses in force.

When repeated blows dislodged stones, the wall began to crumble. Led by Vespasian, the Roman assault team secured their helmets and armor, drew swords, raised protective shields and rushed forward towards the V-shaped breach in the two meter-thick section of wall just below the synagogue, shouting as they charged. Backed by archers and slingers, they climbed through the breach in the wall and penetrated the city, their assault heralded by trumpet blasts.

Gamla commanders Chares and Joseph deployed forces to the breach points, where the Jews resisted the first wave streaming in. As more and more Romans poured over and through gaps bashed through the wall, Gamla's defenders could no longer stop them. The Jews retreated, pulling back towards the upper parts of the city. In what Vespasian later described as a hasty rush to victory, the Romans pursued the retreating Jews with gusto. Following the Jews into the confusing maze of passageways and streets, the Romans were not prepared when the Jews turned around and counterattacked. With their intimate knowledge of the city, Gamla's men trapped and began repulsing the invaders while Roman soldiers continued to pour into the city.

"Jammed inextricably in the narrow alleys," Josephus described, "the Romans suffered fearful casualties."[8] The topography dictated a cramped city, with houses built nearly on top of one another. Fleeing both the Jews' counterattack and crush of their comrades' advance, Roman soldiers climbed onto rooftops for safety. Unaccustomed to such weight, the reed and packed-earth roofs and houses alike collapsed. Built so close together, the collapse of one house brought others crashing down, kicking up a huge cloud of brown dust that made it nearly impossible to see. Josephus recounted: "A great many [Roman soldiers] were ground to powder by these ruins, and a great many of those that got from under them lost some of their limbs, but still a greater number were suffocated by the dust that arose from those ruins."[9] Jews threw darts and rubble at the Romans, who struggled to extricate themselves. Those able to find their way out of the melée withdrew through the breaches in the wall; others lost in the confusion were killed by Gamla's defenders or stabbed themselves in desperation. Roman corpses littered the city; the Jews collected a bounty of metal weapons from dead and wounded Romans.

After initial euphoria over routing the Roman assault, confidence and morale plummeted as they realized their vulnerability. Gamla's defenses had been breached with ease, and now they had no hopes of any terms of accommodation. Escape or fighting to the end seemed the only options. The one bright spot was that the difficult terrain surrounding Gamla prevented the Romans from entirely encircling the city with earthworks, an omission that had allowed small groups of Jews to escape from Gamla throughout the brief siege. Those who could fled; townspeople remaining suffered from shortages of water and provisions exacerbated by the influx of refugees.

Vespasian consoled his dejected troops, reminding them that "it can never be that we must conquer without bloodshed on our own side."[10] The general assured his men that the setback was not a poor reflection of them nor related to valor among the Jews, but rather Gamla's very difficult layout. Roman over-zealousness is what had resulted in their failure to take the city, with Vespasian to blame, for he had led the way and fought himself deeply into Gamla's upper sections and only narrowly escaped. One might consider it a forgivable misstep; being in the heat of action, leading his troops into battle and withdrawing last were qualities that inspired his men.

Regrouping after the failed breach, the Romans sent sappers against Gamla's round tower, which they had determined lacked strong foundations. The sappers excavated the soft chalk on which the tower was built and managed to dislodge heavy stones, undermining the tower's integrity. Late at night, the tower, which sat prominently on the city wall, came crashing down, causing panic in the city. Gamla's defenders braced for the expected Roman assault, but the Romans waited for daylight before venturing into the city.

Having learned from the first assault, the Romans limited the number of troops penetrating. Early morning on October 20, 67 CE, Vespasian's son Titus led 200 chosen horsemen and infantry into Gamla. Sentries raised the alarm, mobilizing defenders to meet the Romans at the hastily repaired breaches. While the men resisted the attack, Gamla's non-combatants took refuge in the upper part of the city.

Jews fired arrows, threw rocks and "recycled" ballista balls, and fought hand-to-hand with the Romans who were pouring through breaches in the wall, but this time the Roman war machine plowed through the resistance. Gamla's two commanders were dead, one having been killed by a Roman dart, the other having succumbed to illness. The Jews were pushed back; panicked masses fleeing the Roman onslaught crowded the way to the upper city.

With the breach secured, Vespasian led a second Roman wave with a larger assault force. The Romans killed without respite; Josephus described the scene as a slaughter, with blood flowing down the streets from the upper part of the city. Gamla's people fled to the summit of Gamla's northern slope beyond range of Roman arrows. On the exposed bluff, powerful gusts of wind blew in the Romans' favor. Clouds of dust blown by the wind blinded the Jews, adding to their desperation. The Romans began killing the cornered Jews, including those trying to surrender. Their only remaining hope was to escape down the steep slopes away from the city. In the rush, some of the panicked people fell to their deaths, tumbling down the steep slope, while others were inadvertently trampled. As Jews reached the summit and began their descent, disappearing from sight, it appeared to some of the Romans that the trapped Jews were leaping to their deaths from the steep cliffs. Gamla was once called "the Masada of the North," with the belief that 5,000 of its citizens had thrown themselves to their deaths in a mass suicide, but modern researchers refute this. The Romans showed no mercy, sparing "not so much as the infants, of whom many were flung down by them from the citadel."[11] In all, some 9,000 Jews were killed at Gamla.

With the city finally secured, the Romans stripped Gamla of valuables, collected their dead for cremation and destroyed their camp to prevent it from being of any use to their enemies. Mules and beasts of burden were loaded with baggage, the troops formed up into marching order and left the area, leaving Gamla's survivors to trickle back to rummage through their destroyed city and bury their dead. Gamla was abandoned, left as it was after its defeat, and lost to history for 1,900 years until its rediscovery and identification.

Word of Josephus' capitulation at Jotapata had inflamed the volatile situation in Jerusalem, exploding into civil war among the Jews. The in-fighting served the Romans well; having suppressed the rebellion in nearly all of Judaea, the Romans stood down and besieged Jerusalem as they waited out the tumult in Rome following Emperor Nero's suicide. In a span of a year, Rome had three emperors in rapid succession before Vespasian returned to Rome and was proclaimed emperor in late 69 CE, as Josephus had conjectured in his life-saving pitch to the Roman general following his capture. "Thou O Vespasian," Josephus had said, "art Caesar and emperor, thou, and thy son."[12] Titus remained to continue the siege of Jerusalem, a task he carried out with relish. When the city finally fell in 70 CE after bitter fighting, the Romans perpetrated a bloodbath, destroying the Temple and carrying its sacred vessels off to Rome, never to be seen again. Jerusalem was left in ruins.

Masada

With all of Judaea—save for the desert fortress of Masada—now subdued, the Jewish extremists who had taken refuge on Masada were the last vestige of the Jews' revolt. Under Flavius Silva, then procurator of Judaea, Legion X *Fretensis* moved in to destroy them. In a demonstration of Roman resolve, the Romans completely surrounded Masada and constructed a massive assault ramp up the side of the mountain in order to deploy siege engines against the rebel compound. Hopelessly surrounded and facing certain defeat, the 967 Jewish rebels holed up on the mountain committed suicide in 73 CE, dying as free men. Masada has become part of modern Israel's national ethos, a symbol of heroism, a place where few stood against many and opted for an honorable death rather than defeat and slavery.

The results of the Jewish War were disastrous: hundreds of thousands of Jews were killed, thousands more sold into slavery and exiled, and the Temple destroyed. Josephus, who returned with the victorious Titus to Rome, may have exaggerated his account of Jewish resistance and casualties as a way of accentuating the Roman victory, thus ingratiating himself with his Roman sponsors. But the minting of Roman coins publicizing the victory with the inscription "*Ivdaea Capta*" (Judaea Captured) suggests that this was considered a very real war. The victory was celebrated in Rome with a triumphant procession, a scene captured for posterity in a frieze on the Arch of Titus, a triumphal arch erected in the forum at Rome. The Arch of Titus remains to this day, showing Roman soldiers parading the Temple's sacred vessels. At some point, a visitor etched telling graffiti in Hebrew just opposite the frieze: "*Am Yisrael Chai L'Olam va'Ed* (The Jewish People Will Live Forever)."

Several hundred years later, the Roman Empire would split into western and eastern empires. The Western Roman Empire ended in the 5th century CE, while the Eastern Empire later became known as the Byzantine Empire, lasting until the 15th century. The Holy Land remained under Roman/Byzantine rule until the armies of Islam swept through the region in the 7th century.

Notes

1.Tacitus (translators Alfred Church and William Brodribb). *Histories* (London, UK: Macmillan, 1864–77), Book 5: 1, 5: 8.

2.Josephus, (translator William Whiston). *The Complete Works of Josephus* (Grand Rapids, MI: Kregel Publications, 1981). *Antiquities*, Book 20, Ch.XI: 1.

3.Tacitus: *Histories*, 5: 10.

4.Josephus, *Wars of the Jews*, Book II, Ch. XX: 7.

5.Josephus, *Wars of the Jews*, Book III, Ch. VII: 33.

6.Josephus, *Wars of the Jews*, Book III, Ch. VII: 4.

7.Syon, Danny. "Gamla—City of Refuge." In A. M. Berlin and J. A. Overman (eds.). *The First Jewish Revolt. Archaeology, History and Ideology* (London and New York: Routledge, 2002), pp.141–2.

8.Josephus, *Wars of the Jews*, Book IV, Ch. I: 4.

9.Josephus, *Wars of the Jews*, Book IV, Ch. I: 4.

10.Josephus, *Wars of the Jews*, Book IV, Ch. I: 6.

11.Josephus, *Wars of the Jews*, Book IV, Ch. I: 10. This is understood to mean "the summit" as no archaeological evidence supports the existence of a citadel fortress, nor does the battle account refer to Gamla's defenders taking refuge in and attempting a last stand from such a fortress.

12.Josephus, *Wars of the Jews*, Book III, Ch. VIII: 9.

Visitors standing above the excavation site of ancient Jericho, the world's oldest city. The Israelites' plan for the conquest of Canaan hinged on taking this heavily fortified desert oasis. (Yaacov Sa'ar, Israel Government Press Office)

Jericho, 3,000 years later. (Courtesy of Alan Merbaum)

Above: Jews working wheat fields in the fertile Jezreel Valley in 1938. Some 3,000 years earlier, Israelites sowed these very fields, only to have their produce taken from them in violent raids by Midianites and other marauding tribes until a young man named Gideon swore to put an end to such persecution. (Kluger Zoltan, Israel Government Press Office)

Left: The Kishon River overflowing its banks following a winter rainstorm. Mount Tabor was a safe place for the Israelites to wait for the heavy winter rains which they knew could quickly turn the Jezreel Valley into a mire. (Yossi Sorogon, Kishon River Authority)

Left: Aerial View of Mount Tabor showing its prominent position over the valley below. Responding to Canaanite persecution, a call to arms went out, and 10,000 Israelites volunteered. The force deployed to Mount Tabor, whose steep slopes afforded protection against Canaanite chariots and offered a clear view of the surrounding terrain. (Moshe Milner. Israel Government Press Office)

The Philistine and Israelite armies faced off in the Elah Valley, one of the few easily passable routes inland from the coastal areas, where the Philistines were dominant. The Philistine camp was deployed on several hills on the southern side of the valley while the Israelites were opposite, to the north. (Dr. Yehuda Dagan, Israel Antiquities Authority)

Copy of Verrochio's 15th-century bronze sculpture of David with the head of Goliath at his feet. (Author's collection)

Ruins of Roman-era Beit Shean are seen before the *tel*, or archaeological mound, an area of older settlement. Following the death of Israelite King Saul in battle against the Philistines on Mount Gilboa, the men of Jabesh-Gilead risked their lives to rescue the corpses of the decapitated king and his sons, displayed ignominiously by the Philistines on the Beit Shean city wall. (Curt Fischer)

Artist rendition of Sennacherib's siege of Lachish. Under a hail of arrows and missiles from the defenders, armor-clad and helmeted Assyrian infantrymen, archers, sling-throwers and shielded spearmen advanced on the embattled city and began moving up the ramp. The counter-fire intensified as they closed range and began rolling the feared battering rams up the ramp and into place at several locations. (Courtesy of Marshall Editions)

Tel Lachish on fire, as the city may have appeared following the Assyrian capture of the city. After ransacking and looting the city, the Assyrians set fire to the town, burning Lachish to the ground.
(Dr. Yehuda Dagan, Israel Antiquities Authority)

Aerial view of Tel Lachish.
The Assyrian assault ramp
is to the right, between the
tel and the modern
moshav, believed to be the
site of the Assyrian camp.
The Assyrian assault came
from their camp. The
photo clearly shows the
tel's dominant position
over the surrounding
terrain. (Dr. Yehuda Dagan,
Israel Antiquities Authority)

Hezekiah's Tunnel.
Preparing for an Assyrian
reaction to Judah's revolt,
King Hezekiah wanted to
secure the Gihon Spring's
waters while denying them
to enemy invaders. A 500-
meter long tunnel was
hewn from solid rock to
bring the waters into
Jerusalem. (Moshe Milner,
Israel Government Press Office)

Reconstruction of the battle of Beth-Horon. Boxed in by the narrow defile, the Seleucids had no room to maneuver, leaving them vulnerable to attack. Maccabee slingers and archers deployed along the sides of the defile opened up with a barrage into the Seleucid ranks before Judah led his men in with swords and knives, sending the Selecuids reeling. (Courtesy of Marshall Editions)

Judah's brother Eleazar, attempting to inspire rebels paralyzed by fear of the Greek war elephants, went after an elephant he believed carried the Seleucid general. Eleazar stabbed the elephant in its belly; the elephant collapsed on him, crushing him to death. (Image of "Eleazar's attempt to kill Antiochus" taken from *The Complete Works of Josephus*, copyright 1981, translated by Wm. Whiston. Published by Kregel Publications, Grand Rapids, MI. Used by permission of the publisher. All rights reserved.)

Naturally secure atop a steep hill, Gamla is protected on all sides by nearly impassable ravines, with the city accessed from the east in a dip in the terrain. Note the reconstructed round tower in the photo's center. (Author's collection)

Depiction of the battle at Gamla. Boulders launched from ballistae crashed down with great force while catapults fired missiles and darts with such intensity that some reached as far as the city's western quarters. Archers swept the parapets clean, allowing the battering rams to approach and smash the city's walls. Assault troops amassed behind protective screens, waiting for a breach. (Gamla Excavation Project)

Masada, the isolated mountaintop fortress where 967 Jewish rebels held out against Roman Proconsul Lucius Flavius Silva's Legion X *Fretensis* between 72 and 73 CE, was the last vestige of the Jews' revolt against Rome. In a demonstration of their resolve, the Romans completely surrounded Masada and constructed a massive assault ramp up the side of the mountain to reach the rebel compound. Hopelessly surrounded and facing certain defeat, the Jewish rebels holed up on the mountain committed suicide, not out of desperation but rather in a conscious decision to die with dignity as free men. (Author's collection)

Wreckage from the Roman rampage. Building blocks thought by archaeologists to be from the Jews' Temple complex, toppled by the Romans following their suppression of the Jews' revolt against Roman authority. (Author's collection)

View of the lower reaches of the Yarmuk River gorge, in whose upper areas the Byzantines suffered their crushing defeat in 636 CE that left Syria in Muslim control. The area's deep gorges restricted Byzantine defensive movements, allowing the smaller Muslim force to drive a wedge between the Byzantine force, breaking their integrity and leading to total defeat in a bloody battle with heavy losses on both sides. (Moshe Milner, Israel Government Press Office)

As the Holy Land's new rulers, Muslims built the Dome of the Rock on the Temple Mount in Jerusalem as a shrine for pilgrims, but also to rival Christendom's impressive churches. The building's original dome was replaced by the current gold one in a 20th-century restoration. (Author's collection)

View towards the Sea of Galilee from the Horns of Hattin. Tightening their chokehold on the Christians, Saladin's forces set fire to the dry grass and thistle. Hot, thirsty, stressed from the incessant fire from Saladin's archers and now with smoke and heat from the brush fires adding to their misery, some Christian soldiers wandered off in a desperate search for water, only to be killed or captured. (Author's collection)

The Horns of Hattin, a barren plain in the hills above the Sea of Galilee, behind Tiberias, where the Crusaders and Muslims had their showdown. (Author's collection)

Aerial view of the Horns of Hattin (background). The shores of the Sea of Galilee can be seen along the bottom of the photograph, showing how close the thirsty Crusaders were to this fresh water lake. (Moshe Milner, Israel Government Press Office)

View overlooking Mount Gilboa to the valley below. Egypt's Mamluks dealt the Mongols their first defeat on the open ground at Ayn Jalut (Goliath's Spring) at the foot of Mount Gilboa, on September 3, 1260. The valley was an ideal battleground for the two cavalry-based forces. Two millenia prior, Israelite King Saul committed suicide on Mount Gilboa by falling on his sword, rather than face capture by the Philistines. (Moshe Milner, Israel Government Press Office)

Ruins of the Crusader castle at Atlit. Consolidating their hold on power after their victory at Ayn Jalut, the Mamluks systematically destroyed Crusader positions until all that remained was the Templar fortress at Atlit, known as Chastel Pelèrin. It was abandoned in 1291. (Teddy Brauner, Israel Government Press Office)

Ruins of Montfort Castle. After their victory at Ayn Jalut, the Mamluks viewed the remaining Crusaders not only as foreign implants and infidels, but as impediments to full Mamluk hegemony. In their systematic campaign to destroy the Crusaders, the Mamluks besieged the Teutonic Knight's fortress Montfort until it surrendered. (Author's collection)

The Temple Mount in Jerusalem during the Ottoman era. Beyond the city walls is the Dome of the Rock and behind it, to the left, the al Aqsa Mosque. The Dome of the Rock and Al-Aqsa were built following the Muslims' capture of the Holy Land. The Temple Mount is Islam's third holiest site, celebrated as the spot from which the Prophet Mohammed embarked on his night-time visit to heaven. After their victory over the Mamluks, the Ottomans rebuilt Jerusalem's walls and gates, which had been in ruins. (Photographed by The American Colony, Israel Government Press Office)

Aleppo Citadel, Aleppo, Syria. Following their defeat at the Ottoman-Mamluk clash at Marj Dabiq, most of the Mamluk recruits were allowed to flee towards Aleppo. Upon arriving there, the Mamluks found themselves locked out by local inhabitants. When Ottoman sultan Selim arrived at Aleppo, he was hailed as liberator. Selim had earlier boasted that his weakest man would take Aleppo's citadel. Keeping this vow, he sent in an aged clerk to view treasures abandoned there by the Mamluks. (Dick Osseman)

Jerusalem's Tower of David. The minaret of the mosque at the citadel was built by the Ottomans, complementing the mosque built by the Mamluks. Today the entire citadel complex is a museum of the history of Jerusalem. (Author's collection)

French General Kleber at the assault on Acre. Each time Bonaparte sent his forces to breach the walls, Acre's defenders held their ground. In one attack, the French succeeded in penetrating into the city. Acre's defenders withdrew; when the French troops advanced they found themselves in a carefully prepared ambush, where many were cut down in a hail of fire. (The Weider History Group Archive)

Situated on a peninsula jutting out into the Mediterranean Sea, Acre is protected on three sides by the sea. Napoleon's army set about taking the city, but Acre's defenses and defenders proved tenacious, and ultimately the French gave up. Its walls and dry moat can be seen in the photo slightly left and below of center. (Moshe Milner, Israel Government Press Office)

CHAPTER 7

THE KORAN, THE TRIBUTE,
OR THE SWORD!

ISLAM'S CONQUEST OF THE MIDDLE EAST, 634 CE

When a lone Muslim Arab warrior reconnoitered Byzantine lines and killed 19 of the 30 men dispatched to challenge him, the Byzantine Army—successors of the great Roman Legions—saw it best to attempt buying its way out of battle. With conquest their aim, the Muslim Arab army would not be deterred. Their response was succinct:

"The Koran, the tribute, or the sword!"

It was July 30, 634 CE, and the two armies were deployed at Ajnadayn along the road between Beit Guvrin and Jerusalem. With the Byzantine offer rejected, battle was now unavoidable. As the two armies formed up for combat, champions from both sides met in duels where the Muslims proved superior by killing several Byzantine officers and champions. Byzantine archers opened the attack with a massive barrage against the Muslims. The Muslims failed to respond, giving the impression they were unprepared for battle against such a modern army. Dressed in a motley assortment of robes and armor and equipped with a range of weapons and gear, the Muslim army lacked the appearance of a serious foe. But their restraint was due not to a lack of conviction or capability but rather to Muslim General Khaled ibn al-Walid's orders not to attack. Known as "the Sword of Allah," Khaled counseled discipline and patience to his men. The Arabian tribesmen were raring to fight, yet Khaled held them back while they absorbed the Byzantine barrage. The men implicitly trusted Khaled, an experienced and highly respected commander. When he determined the timing was right, Khaled finally gave the order to attack. In only two days of battle, the Muslims would break the Byzantine juggernaut.

The prophet Mohammed himself had initiated this *jihad*, or campaign of expansion from the Arabian Peninsula via conquest, but early defeats, the prophet's unexpected death from illness in 632 and then rebellion had proved setbacks. It had all begun in 610, with Mohammed's revelation of faith in, and total submission to, a single God, Allah, who punished evildoers and rewarded the righteous. Empowered to spread God's message, Mohammed converted Arabia's tribes to Islam, and the faith spread rapidly. Following Mohammed's death and the contentious appointment of Abu Bakr as caliph, or successor, to Mohammed, a number of Arabian tribes broke with the *ummah*, or community of followers. The response was heavy-handed; the *riddah* (apostasy) against Islamic authority was crushed, resulting in a powerful, consolidated caliphate. With the rebellion suppressed, the new caliph renewed military campaigning in the name of their faith.

Caliph Abu Bakr told the men that "fighting for religion is an act of obedience to God,"[1] but it was not initially a campaign of religious warriors as the tribes were not necessarily religious at this stage. Motivation may have come from the mundane lure of plunder, as much as in the name of Islam.[2] Even legendary General Khaled seems to have been indifferent towards Islam; he reportedly had his way with captive women on the battlefield following victory, and was said to have bathed in wine—hardly examples of righteousness.[3]

After consolidating power in Arabia by force of arms, the Muslims began moving beyond the Arabian Desert in a campaign of conquest and expansion. Abu Bakr began with the Persian Sassanid Empire's province of Iraq. Under Khaled, who had made a name for himself suppressing the tribal rebellion, the Muslims won a string of victories over the Persians in 633. Confident from his army's successes, the caliph set his sights on Syria.

Palestine[4] was part of Syria, which had become "Byzantine" when the Roman Empire's center of gravity shifted eastward and became the Eastern Roman, or Byzantine, Empire. It was Emperor Constantine's personal embrace of Christianity and his instituting it as the empire's official religion during his reign of 306–337 that ushered in the Byzantine period, named for his capital Byzantium in Asia Minor, which he renamed Constantinople after himself. The Roman adoption of Christianity brought Palestine new status as the Holy Land. Palestine prospered. Great edifices, such as the Church of the Holy Sepulcher and Church of the Ascension in Jerusalem, and Church of the Nativity in Bethlehem, were built. Churches and monasteries, many with exquisite mosaics—at which the Byzantines excelled—dotted the landscape, and pilgrims from throughout the empire visited sites associated with the life of Jesus.

Focused on the Persian Sassanids, the Byzantines did not fully perceive the threat emanating from Arabia. The nomadic Arabian tribesmen were known for stealing and pillaging from settled areas before disappearing back into the desert—a reputation that no doubt contributed to Byzantine emperor Heraclius' initial dismissal of the threat they posed. The Romans had fought the Persian empires for over seven centuries, so the Byzantines maintained a wary eye on this traditional enemy and the bulk of Byzantine defenses in the region were concentrated in northern Syria. Only a few years had passed since Palestine and adjoining areas were recovered after 15 years of Persian occupation, and the Byzantines were still securing and reasserting authority in these relinquished territories. The incessant fighting had taken a toll: both empires were exhausted from years of warfare. Ironically, while the Byzantines were rolling back the Persians, Mohammed was forging the power that would burst out of remote Arabia and eventually defeat both empires.

Declaring intentions to "send the true believers into Syria to take it out of the hands of the infidels,"[5] Abu Bakr dispatched four separate forces to Palestine and Syria,[6] each with its own commander and mission. A force entered Palestine north of modern Eilat and moved up the Arava Valley before cutting inland while the other three forces advanced northward up the caravan route on the east side of the Jordan River, one towards Damascus, one intending to take Jordan, and the third advancing on Emesa (now known as Hims or Homs, in Syria). Caravans from Arabia plied the ancient trade route through Syria to Mediterranean ports, so the Arabians were well aware of Syria's fertility. The Byzantines had checked Muslim Arab encroachment in the 629 battle of Mu'ta (in today's Jordan), where a Muslim force in which Khaled commanded was defeated. The battle of Mu'ta was a harbinger of Muslim intentions. As a precaution, Heraclius ordered the fortification of towns and cities in the region, some with permanent garrisons, and appointed military commanders over cities and the surrounding regions—expenses he authorized despite his efforts to reduce defense expenditures. These steps may also have been taken to discourage cities from surrendering to the Muslims, which would bring both a loss of prestige and valuable tax revenue needed by the empire's already strained coffers.

Due to competition for troops on its empire's other exposed borders, the Byzantines faced a manpower shortage on its eastern fringe. Friendly Arab tribes—best known among them the Ghassanids—helped fill the void by guarding the desert frontiers. The Byzantines lacked the resources to maintain permanent frontier garrisons, a limitation that dictated a reactive defense. This meant an enemy would be allowed to penetrate its territory before being met by mobile forces that would expel them. Ironically, as part of Byzantine cost-saving efforts, payments to their Ghassanid allies were cut off, removing one of the first lines of defense. In around 633, the Muslim forces had easily penetrated Byzantine territory and soon had multiple forces operating deep inside. When Muslim Arabs defeated a Byzantine force in early 634 at Dathin near Gaza, Heraclius responded by mobilizing forces from throughout Syria, yet evidently not enough. Some historians say Heraclius allocated an inadequate force of 10,000 men, with heavy reliance on local troops.[7]

In contrast to his personal involvement in leading the campaign that ousted the Persians, Heraclius did not fight in this campaign, perhaps a sign of failing health. Heraclius entrusted command to his brother Theodore, who was experienced from operations against the

Persians. Command may have been shared with another experienced officer named Wardan, commander of Syria's major military base at Emesa. It took two months for the Byzantine force—cavalry and infantrymen trailed by their baggage train and followers—to assemble at Emesa and make its way south, via Palestine's main military base of Caesarea Maritima, to Palestine's hinterland.

Converging on Ajnadayn

The Byzantine army converging on Palestine threatened both the Muslim force operating in Palestine and the three other Muslim forces in Syria. Following developments from Medina, the caliph responded by calling on Khaled to quit his campaigning in Iraq and to assume command of Muslim forces in Syria. Khaled united his dispersed forces by ordering them to Ajnadayn.[8]

"Know that thy brethren the Moslems design to march to Aiznadin, where there is an army of seventy thousand Greeks, who purpose to come against us. . . . As soon therefore as this letter of mine shall be delivered to thy hands, come with those that are with thee to Aiznadin, where thou shalt find us if it please the most high God."[9] Khaled hurried his force across the desert towards Palestine, taking the Byzantine city of Busra en route in mid-July 634. Khaled also made an attempt on Damascus, but withdrew after a short siege.

Camels and horses lent the Muslim forces mobility that, along with their short logistics tail and legendary hardiness and endurance (they were said to be able to survive for weeks on only dates and water), allowed them to quickly deploy and concentrate power. The agile Arabians assembled their force at Ajnadayn by July 24, 634. Armed with lances, javelins, spears, swords, daggers and bows, the Muslims deployed with a center and two wings.

Concentrating at Ajnadayn was a departure from traditional Arab fighting tactics that centered around the desert where the Arabs found refuge. These were no desert raiders; taking on the Persians and Byzantines meant the Muslims must have been a coherent force. Its make-up of tribal units from all over the Arabian peninsula gave the Muslim army inherent structure. They were also well-led, as Khaled's skillful combination of tactics and strategy would prove. But their true strength came from Islam, the force that was forging them into a nation instilled with purpose.[10]

According to doctrine, the Byzantines should have drawn up for battle in two lines, the second a reserve to exploit successes, or alternately to provide support in the event of an enemy breakthrough.[11] Heavily armed cavalry, and infantry with lances or bows, supplemented by local allies, were about to fight the first major battle between the Byzantine Empire and the Muslims in a clash in which the ultimate outcome would change the face of the Middle East and beyond.

Looking across at the Muslim Arab army, whose appearance was anything but uniform, the Byzantines were not impressed. Limited interactions between the disparate peoples had propagated stereotypes of Arabians being primitive and backwards; the Byzantines looked down on them. Though spies had brought back information on the Muslims, and the Byzantines were aware of Muslim victories against large armies in Iraq and over their own compatriots, the Muslims remained an obscurity. Not even a contemporary Byzantine military manual known as the *Strategikon* offered advice on fighting Arabs.[12]

The Byzantines arrayed at Ajnadayn got an early taste of Arabian bravery and resolve when a young Muslim warrior named Dhiraar ibn al Azwar made an aggressive reconnaissance of the Christian camp. While many of his comrades-in-arms wore hardened leather or mail armor and head protection, Dhiraar wore none. Wearing only his loose-fitting trousers and armed with his personal weapons, Dhiraar mounted his horse and approached Byzantine lines. When thirty men were sent after him, Dhiraar hastened back towards his army's lines, with the enemy in hot pursuit. Once they chased him a distance from their camp, Dhiraar spun his horse around and went on the offensive. Fighting with lance and sword, Dhiraar killed 19 of his pursuers; the others broke off pursuit and returned to camp to tell of the fearless and invincible Arab champion who came to be known as the Naked Warrior.[13]

The Byzantines knew how to fight formally organized armies like the Persians, whereas the Muslim Arab army was less conventional. Emperor Heraclius had thus warned his brother Theodore to beware of the Arabs, and avoid engaging in open battle with them. The two sides faced off for a week—time that the Byzantines probably used attempting to divide the enemy coalition, and hoping that the Muslims might possibly tire of campaigning and return home, as they were known to do after past raids. Contemporary Byzantine military strategy counseled such caution over decisive action. When the Muslim Arab army proved unwavering, the Byzantines opted to invoke a common practice of negotiating to avoid battle.

An old bishop approached the Muslim army asking to meet their commander. The bishop pitched to Khaled the Byzantine offer to give each Muslim "a dinar, a robe and a turban; and for you there will be a hundred dinars and a hundred robes and a hundred turbans" if the Arabs would withdraw from Syria.[14] "Ye Christian dogs, you know your option," Khaled immediately responded. "The Koran, the tribute, or the sword!"[15] meaning convert to Islam, pay the submissive *jizya*[16] tribute, or war. "As for the dinars and fine clothes," Khaled reportedly added, "the Muslims would soon possess them anyway, by right of conquest!"[17]

While accounts of the battle are sketchy, the engagement was thought to be unremarkable, with none of the clever maneuvering or stratagem for which the Muslim armies would become known. The Byzantines espoused a massive opening assault with arrows raining down on the enemy to distract their foes until mounted lancers plowed through enemy lines. Apparently the Byzantines' shock assault was either thwarted or somehow failed to deliver its desired effect. After the Muslim Arabs absorbed the opening Byzantine barrage, the two sides fought a conventional battle in which casualties would have been high on both sides. Questionable Muslim sources tell us the Byzantines suffered massive casualties in the tens of thousands while the Muslims were relatively unscathed. With neither side managing to get the better of the other, the Byzantine commander attempted to break the deadlock by means of a ruse to lure Khaled into an ambush. Wardan asked under false pretenses to meet the Muslim commander to discuss peace terms—a classic Byzantine strategy of using cunning and duplicity to win battles. A Christian Arab betrayed the plan to Khaled, and it backfired; instead Wardan was said to be killed when he went to the designated meeting place. With the Byzantines reeling from the death of a senior commander, Khaled ordered his army to attack. Again, it was a physical and exhaustive exchange. When the

Muslims penetrated a gap in Byzantine defenses, Byzantine front-line troops fell back, banking on protection by their rear lines. But the Christians could not coordinate their defense, despite their training in mutual support—perhaps the reliance on local troops had come at the expense of cohesion. Fresh Muslim reserves helped penetrate Christian lines, causing a breakdown of Byzantine resistance. Troops began fleeing the battlefield towards Jerusalem, Gaza and Jaffa in disorganized flight while Muslim horsemen ran them down. Given the battle's outcome, Byzantine accounts are sparse while Muslim sources cite a serious defeat with extremely heavy Byzantine casualties. Muslim historian al-Waqidi put the Byzantine casualties at a highly exaggerated 50,000 versus 450 Muslims.

As Khaled had confidently declared before the battle, the booty—consisting of multiple banners and large crosses of gold and silver, precious stones, silver and gold chains, and suits of the richest armor and apparel—was indeed his by conquest. Adding insult to injury the Muslims offered to sell the booty back to the Byzantines. Also captured were countless weapons that the Muslims would put to use against the Byzantines in subsequent battles. The Muslim victory foreshadowed what would come two years later in the better-known Battle of Yarmuk, the outcome of which resulted in the loss of Syria to *Dar al-Islam*, the House of Islam.

Aftermath

Like so many of his troops, Theodore fled to Jerusalem before making his way north to report the defeat to Heraclius, who ordered his brother imprisoned. The defeat created a vacuum in Byzantine authority in Palestine that gave the victorious Muslims nearly free reign. With Palestine in disarray, the Byzantines assumed a defensive posture. People sought safety in walled cities and towns, which were isolated from each other, resulting in fear and a sense of insecurity.

Receiving reports of the Muslim victory, the caliph encouraged a continuation of the campaign. Khaled's army headed north, taking Tiberias and Scythopolis (Beit Shean/Beisan) before besieging and capturing Damascus. The victorious Muslims imposed only a poll tax on Damascus—these were very generous terms that likely contributed to more surrenders. While many Christians abandoned their homes and fled for safer parts of the Byzantine Empire, the Muslims' unexpected victory was embraced by the many people discontent with Byzantine rule. Syria's Christians—the majority of the population—were alienated from the official Byzantine Church over theological differences, local Arabs shared a cultural connection to the victorious Muslims, and even Jews welcomed the change, despite having brought on the Muslims' wrath when they rejected Mohammed's claim to be a prophet. The Muslims would bestow the special second-class *dhimmi* status on Jews and Christians, tolerating their religions in recognition of their shared heritage.

Seething over the defeat at Ajnadayn, Heraclius was determined to push the Muslims out of Syria. Reallocating forces, the emperor managed to assemble an army claimed to have numbered 100,000 men.[18] Units formed up into brigades and divisions and deployed to Syria intent on overwhelming and destroying the Muslims. Consolidating his forces, Khaled withdrew from Damascus and other areas and concentrated 25,000 men on the left bank of the Yarmuk River gorge where the two armies faced off. In typical Byzantine military fashion, the army did not make any decisive moves nor press its advantages but rather trod cautiously while possibly looking for ways to avoid combat. For nearly two months the two armies sparred until the Muslim Arabs took decisive action on August 20, 636. On a hot summer's day when clouds of dust limited visibility, the two armies came to blows. Muslim maneuvering seems to have split the Byzantine force, whose movements were restricted by the area's deep gorges. It was a bloody battle with heavy losses on both sides, but the smaller Muslim force succeeded in crushing the Byzantines. Only a small number of Byzantine forces survived to report the defeat to Emperor Heraclius.

The Muslims returned to all their earlier conquests vacated before the showdown at Yarmuk. As word quickly spread of the major Byzantine defeat, the Muslim Arabs took Byzantine towns in succession, leaving Syria in Muslim control, save for Caesarea and Jerusalem which both held out for some time. Jerusalem fell in 638, with the city's surrender personally received by new caliph Omar, who had assumed leadership following the death of Abu Bakr.

Heraclius had spent six difficult years the previous decade fighting the Persians to liberate the Holy Land, which he had now lost for Christianity. His desperation could be felt in his parting words: "Farewell, O Syria! What a wonderful country you are for the enemy."[19] Heraclius worked his way back to his capital of Constantinople, where he died in 641, by which time the armies of Islam had taken the Fertile Crescent, Iraq, Syria, Palestine, and Egypt. At its height, the Muslim Empire would stretch from Spain in the west, across North Africa, the Middle East and into Asia. In taking the Middle East, the Muslims destroyed the Sassanid Persian Empire and captured vast territories from the Byzantines. Byzantium regained its balance and was able to halt the Muslim advance on its territory, and its empire survived until 1453.

Over time the Muslims began changing the face of Palestine. Masterpieces such as the Dome of the Rock and Al-Aqsa mosque were built, the provincial capital city of Ramla was established and coastal areas prospered. Ultimately trade routes shifted eastward, away from Palestine, causing decline. When European Christians began to view as sacrilege that the birthplace of Jesus was under Muslim control, Europe would be galvanized to embark on a crusade to free the *terra sancta* from Muslim rule.

Notes

1.Edward Gibbon. *The History of the Decline and Fall of the Roman Empire.*
2.A. A. Vasiliev. *History of the Byzantine Empire, Volume 1, 324–1453* (Madison: University of Wisconsin Press, 1958), p.208.
3.Arthur Goldschmidt Jr. *A Concise History of the Middle East* (Boulder: Westview Press, 1979), p.51.
4.Following a Jewish anti-Roman revolt between 132–135 CE, Roman Emperor Hadrian changed the name of Judaea to Syria Palaestina, or simply Palestine.
5.Gibbon, *The History of the Decline and Fall.*
6.Historians disagree on the actual number of Muslim fighters involved as sources vary from about 1,000 men per army to 7,500.
7.There is no precise account of the size of either the Byzantine or Muslim armies, nor of the battle fought at Ajnadayn. Accounts of the battle come mostly from Arab sources recorded long after the events occurred, and tend to be biased. Arab historian al-Waqidi's descriptions of the early Islamic campaigns were written more than a hundred years later, and his works have been considered literary rather than history. For example, al-Waqidi put the Byzantine forces at 90,000. Sources provide figures that vary wildly: 10,000–45,000 Muslim combatants

versus 10,000–90,000 Byzantines. Arab sources tend to exaggerate in order to glorify the Muslim victory. See A. I. Akram. *The Sword of Allah—Khaled bin Al-Waleed*. October 1969.

8.According to Israel Antiquities Authority Shephelah region expert Yehuda Dagan, the battle site has not been precisely located. Expert assessments put the site somewhere between Beit Guvrin and Ramle.

9.Gibbon, *The History of the Decline and Fall*.

10.Fred Donner. *The Early Islamic Conquests* (Princeton: Princeton University Press, 1981).

11.*The Strategikon*, Byzantine military manual.

12.Walter E. Kaegi. *Heraclius. Emperor of Byzantium* (Cambridge, UK: Cambridge University Press, 2003).

13.Khaled was angry at Dhiraar for losing sight of his reconnaissance mission, to which Dhiraar responded that concern over upsetting his commander prevented him from taking on the 11 Byzantines who escaped.

14.Akram. *The Sword of Allah*.

15.Gibbon, *The History of the Decline and Fall*.

16.A tax levied on non-Muslims.

17.Akram. *The Sword of Allah*.

18.Bernhard Bischoff and Michael Lapidge. *Biblical Commentaries from the Canterbury School of Theodore and Hadrian* (Cambridge, UK: Cambridge University Press, 1994), p.39.

19.Moshe Sharon, "The History of Palestine from the Arab Conquest Until the Crusades (633–1099)" in Michael Avi-Yonah (ed.). *A History of the Holy Land* (Jerusalem: Steimatzky's Agency Ltd. 1969). p.196.

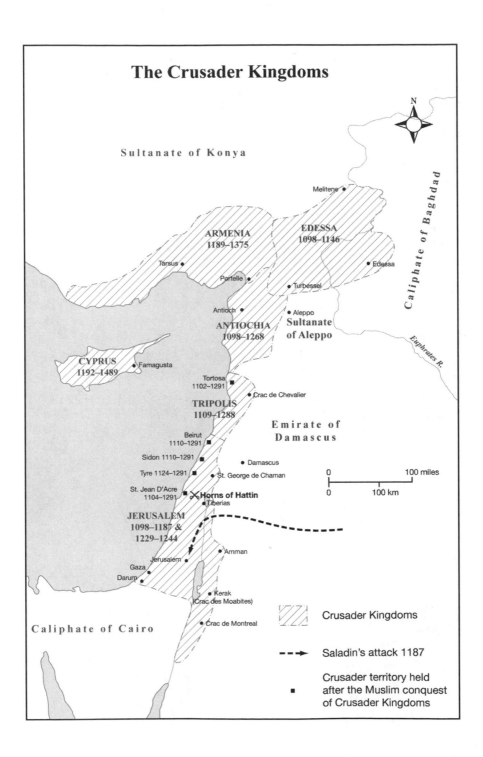

The Crusader Kingdoms

N

Sultanate of Konya

Caliphate of Baghdad

Melitene

ARMENIA
1189–1375

EDESSA
1098–1146

Tarsus

Portelle

Edessa

Turbessel

Antioch

Aleppo

ANTIOCHIA
1098–1268

Sultanate
of Aleppo

CYPRUS
1192–1489

Famagusta

Euphrates R.

Tortosa
1102–1291

Crac de Chevalier

TRIPOLIS
1109–1288

Emirate of
Damascus

Beirut
1110–1291

Sidon 1110–1291

Damascus

Tyre 1124–1291

St. George de Chaman

St. Jean D'Acre
1104–1291

Horns of Hattin

0   100 miles

Tiberias

0   100 km

JERUSALEM
1098–1187 &
1229–1244

Jerusalem

Amman

Gaza

Darum

Kerak
(Crac des Moabites)

Caliphate of Cairo

Crac de Montreal

///// Crusader Kingdoms

- - -► Saladin's attack 1187

■ Crusader territory held
after the Muslim conquest
of Crusader Kingdoms

CHAPTER 8

IMPALED AT THE HORNS OF HATTIN

TWILIGHT FOR THE CRUSADER KINGDOM OF JERUSALEM, 1187

When the Crusader host stopped for the night far from both the springs where they had last watered on a scorching hot summer's day, and from their destination of Tiberias, Lord of Galilee Raymond knew it did not bode well. Galloping back from the army's vanguard, Raymond exclaimed:

"Alas, Lord God, the battle is over! We are dead men. The kingdom is finished!"

More than 450 years passed after the fall of the Holy Land to the Muslims before Christian Europe took decisive action to wrest back control of the Christian holy places. Europe's masses were riled up with fabricated accounts of persecution of Christian citizens and religious pilgrims by Muslims. Joining the holy expedition, known as a crusade, would fulfill religious duties and absolve the participant from sins, along with bringing the mundane benefit of spoils. For those who fell, a glorious death with heavenly rewards was promised.

After the first wave, known as the People's Crusade, was easily defeated at the hands of the Turks in 1096, the professional knights and soldiers that followed successfully reached the walls of holy Jerusalem in 1099, three years after setting off from Europe. On July 15, 1099, after a five-week siege, Jerusalem—the city in which Jesus had died—fell to the Crusaders.

The victory was celebrated with a murderous rampage. Hell-bent on destruction, the Crusaders attacked Jerusalem's residents with a vengeance. "Thousands of non-combatant Jews, Muslims, and even native Christians were beheaded, shot with arrows, thrown from towers, tortured, or burned at the stake. Human blood flowed knee-deep in the streets of Jerusalem."[1]

The Crusaders set about transforming Jerusalem from a Muslim into a Christian city. They restored the Church of the Holy Sepulcher, believed to be the site of Jesus' crucifixion and burial, and built or rebuilt churches, hospitals and hospices. The Temple Mount—Islam's third holiest site, celebrated by Muslims as the spot from which the Prophet Mohammed embarked on his night-time visit to heaven—was declared Christian, and a great golden cross erected above the Dome of the Rock.

Word of such indignities reached Arab capitals, leading to outrage. An Egyptian force challenged the Crusaders the following month but was firmly defeated near Ascalon (Ashkelon), securing the Crusaders' place as the new masters of Jerusalem.

Groups of Crusader knights seized control of interior regions, expanding and reinforcing their rule. With more towns and cities captured, the Franks, as the Crusaders were known to the Muslims, consolidated their power and secured their borders, establishing the feudal Kingdom of Jerusalem, with the holy city as its capital. While many of the knights returned home, a stream of immigrants arrived in the new Christian kingdom. City walls and defenses were beefed up, and massive stone fortresses were built to safeguard highways, frontiers and interior regions. Despite a Muslim call for *jihad* against the foreign invaders in *Dar al-Islam*, divisions and rivalries among Muslim leaders prevented them from destroying the fledgling Crusader kingdom, whose borders would ultimately encompass modern Israel, Lebanon, Sinai, Jordan, and Syria.

The Crusaders suffered some reverses, most notably the fall of the Crusader principality of Edessa to Zengi, a Turkish emir, in 1144. But the Crusaders would find their nemesis in an ambitious Kurd who rose to power in Egypt. Salah al-Din Yusuf bin Ayub, better known as Saladin, would establish the power base necessary to challenge the Crusaders. Considered Islam's greatest military leader, Saladin understood that Muslims would first need to be unified before they could defeat the Christians. From Egypt, where he had become vizier, Saladin embarked on a unification campaign that extended his rule to Syria and Iraq by 1183, uniting the provinces into one state with the resources to take on the Crusader Kingdom.

In 1185, a time when the Crusaders were plagued by internecine feuding over succession following the death of the leper King Baldwin IV and threatened by famine, Lord of Galilee Raymond III of Tripoli suggested a four-year truce with Saladin, until new arrivals from Europe would invigorate the kingdom. Raymond's pragmatic approach, approved by the barons, was hindered by the notorious Reynaud de Châtillon, Lord of Oultrejordain, the Crusader territories east of the Jordan River. From the vantage of Kerak fortress in modern-day Jordan, presiding over a trade route between Egypt and Syria, Reynaud raided and pillaged caravans and attacked Muslim religious pilgrims on their way to Mecca. Reynaud's audacity was such that he had led a campaign along the Red Sea that threatened Mecca, the holiest of Muslim cities. Saladin was so outraged by these actions that he vowed never to forgive them. Saladin twice besieged Reynaud's fortress at Kerak but was forced to withdraw both times in face of Crusader relief forces.

Paying no heed to the truce, Reynaud hijacked a massive caravan passing by Kerak in 1186, killing its military escorts, taking the merchants prisoner and confiscating the cargo. Saladin sought to resolve this matter diplomatically but Crusader King Guy, who owed his throne in part to support from Reynaud, had little influence over the unwieldy baron. Reynaud's provocations could not go unanswered, and now Saladin wielded the necessary muscle.

Responding to Saladin's call to arms, troops began pouring in from territories he controlled, growing into the largest army he had ever commanded, numbering 30,000 soldiers, including 12,000 cavalry. Saladin boasted that the "dust it raised on the move would darken the eye of the sun."[2]

Wanting no part of the troubles brought on by his rivals, Raymond of Galilee made an independent treaty with Saladin. This was an affront to King Guy, who had outmaneuvered Raymond for the Kingdom of Jerusalem's throne. The Crusader king threatened to move militarily against Raymond's city Tiberias, which would have amounted to civil war, adding to the already tense situation.

Under his treaty with Saladin, Raymond allowed a Muslim force passage into his lordship of Galilee. At the same time, a delegation including the grand masters of both the Orders of the Hospital and of the Temple (known commonly as the Knights Hospitaller and Knights Templar) were en route to Raymond to arrange a reconciliation between him and the king. Hospitallers, as their name suggests, had originally cared for sick pilgrims before taking on the military role of providing armed escort. Templars, whose name came from their headquarters in the expropriated Al-Aqsa Mosque on Jerusalem's Temple Mount, ensured the safety of Christian pilgrims. These military orders, which combined military and religious life, were a key element in Crusader power.

Having ignored the instructions that they had received from Raymond telling them to wait for the Muslim force to leave Galilee before traveling in the area, the Templars and Hospitallers encountered the large Muslim force at Cresson springs near Nazareth and recklessly attacked, resulting in a complete Crusader rout. One historian described it as a massacre rather than a battle.[3] Holding himself responsible for the deaths of his compatriots, Raymond abrogated his treaty with Saladin and paid homage to the king, which he had previously vowed never to do. The Crusader kingdom was now unified.

Crusader unity was in itself an accomplishment given that Reynaud did not consider himself subject to the king's authority, and the military orders were exempt from all authority save that of the pope. All responded to the royal decree for a general mobilization. Eager for vengeance for the massacre at Cresson, the Hospitallers and Templars contributed all their available knights, leaving only small garrisons to defend their castles. In this critical time, the Christians were feeling the pinch of a manpower shortage brought on by a drop in immigration to the kingdom, so literally all able-bodied men were called to arms. "Not a man fit for war remained in the cities, towns or castles without being urged to leave by the King's order."[4]

Saladin sent reconnaissance units to collect information on the Crusader mobilization and, according to Christian sources, the scouts "laid waste and set fire to vast areas from Tiberias to Bethany . . . up to Nazareth and around Mount Tabor."[5] Saladin's full force crossed the Jordan River south of the Sea of Galilee and established camp. Though he could not sustain a prolonged military mobilization lest his disparate army dissolve, Saladin knew better than to risk attacking the Crusaders where they held the advantage; he would need to draw them out where he could press his advantages. Knowing that a Christian army would undoubtedly come to the city's rescue, Saladin moved against Tiberias, capital of Galilee, on Thursday July 2, 1187. Tiberias held out for only one hour before its garrison, led by the Countess Eschiva, Raymond's wife, yielded the ramparts and city and withdrew to its citadel. Messengers were sent to Raymond and to the king entreating them to "send help at once or we shall be taken and made captive."[6] Leaving a small force to maintain the siege, Saladin moved the bulk of his army to Kfar Sabt in the hills above Tiberias.

In response to Saladin's move on Tiberias, Crusader King Guy held a war counsel, where Christian unity proved short-lived. Given the Muslims' unprecedented cohesiveness and power, and—no less important—the intense summer heat, Raymond called for restraint, suggesting Saladin's army be allowed the prize of Tiberias as a way of buying time. Christian reinforcements were promised from Antioch and he also figured that the Muslim army would soon tire of campaigning, disperse and return home.

"Tiberias is my city and my wife is there," Raymond began. "None of you is so fiercely attached, save to Christianity, as I am to the city. None of you is so desirous as I am to succor or aid Tiberias. We and the King, however, should not move away from water, food, and other necessities to lead such a multitude of men to death from solitude, hunger, thirst and scorching heat . . . "[7] King Guy was convinced by this sincere, sound advice.

Reynaud de Châtillon and the influential military orders wanted to fight. Led by Grand Master of the Knights Templar, Gerard de

Ridefort, this camp rejected a non-militant approach as shameful and suggested that King Guy and Raymond were cowards. Guy had been criticized four years earlier in 1183 when, despite the encouragement of Reynaud and the military orders, he opted not to attack a numerically superior Muslim army at the Pools of Goliath (Ein Harod/Ayn Jalut). His restraint had earned him a reputation for weakness and caused him to be deposed as Crusader King Baldwin's regent. Not to face off against Saladin at this time would go counter to the momentum for war. The entire kingdom had been mobilized, and mercenaries hired and paid with a special treasury deposited by King Henry II of England. There was no backing down. Seeing an opportunity to restore his image, the fickle king decided to commit the Crusader army.

Hattin

The Crusader force of 1,200 knights and 20,000 infantrymen and light cavalry assembled at Sepphoris (Zippori), where they had the advantage of springs and pasture for their horses. It was the finest army of Christendom's kingdom in the Holy Land, with the cross emblazoned on each fighting man's tunic, shirt or shield. The Bishop of Acre carried the kingdom's holiest relic: a fragment of the True Cross on which Jesus had been crucified, brought to provide inspiration and providence.

The next morning the Crusaders set out in the repressive heat via the northern route towards besieged Tiberias, some 18 miles (30 km) away, down in the Sea of Galilee basin. Despite his opposition to confronting Saladin, Raymond led the army's way as the enemy was being engaged in his lordship and the custom was for the baron of the lordship to lead the first division. The deployment for the march called for the royal battalion (commanded by the king) and the battalion of the Holy Cross to come next, with Reynaud and the military orders forming the army's rear guard. With each knight requiring several horses to carry himself and his equipment, and assistants who prepared him for battle and helped him mount his sturdy horse, the Crusader army and its accompanying train was huge.

Closely following Crusader movements, Saladin moved his force towards the hills of Hattin, where the road begins its descent towards the lake, and dispatched mounted archers to harass the Crusaders. In swift attacks, Muslim archers descended on the Christians, unleashing volleys of arrows before quickly retreating, vanishing as rapidly as they had appeared. Each attack brought death to more men and horses, sowing fear in the Crusading army, slowing their advance and harming morale. With the heat, their thirst, and continual harassment wearing down the Crusaders, progress was slow.

By afternoon, the Christians were close to the Horns of Hattin, where two peaks (the Horns) rise above a barren plain in the hills above the Sea of Galilee, behind Tiberias. Harried by Muslim archers throughout the day, the Templars could go no further; King Guy gave orders to stop and establish camp where they were, halfway to Tiberias.

Raymond knew their precarious location would not bode well. He galloped back from the front crying: "Alas, Lord God, the battle is over! We are dead men. The kingdom is finished!"[8]

Saladin's forces took the springs where the Crusaders had last watered en route, cutting off the possibility of returning to them. The Muslim army closed in and surrounded the Christians during the night, blocking their option of retreat. Parched with thirst after a day of marching in the intense summer heat, Crusader morale was not good. Hearing the Muslims all around them made it worse. Saladin remained awake all night seeing to logistical matters; he was leaving nothing to chance. Saladin had fought battles and led campaigns against the Crusaders over the previous decade, yet victory had eluded him. This time victory was within reach. Not only did Saladin have the Crusader army surrounded, but they were on hilly terrain that limited the effectiveness of their heavy cavalry. Furthermore, while the Crusaders were parched with thirst, Saladin's forces had access to ample fresh water.

Saladin's presence inspired his men, who were strengthened by the sight of him. The Muslim leader personally commanded his army's center, with his nephew Taqi al-Din commanding the right wing and Muzaffar al-Din commanding the left. Tightening their chokehold on the Christians, Saladin's forces set fire to the dry grass and thistle. The cordon around the Franks was said to be so complete that not even a cat could get through. Hot, thirsty, stressed from the incessant fire from Saladin's archers, and now with smoke and heat from the brush fires adding to their misery, some Christian soldiers wandered off in a desperate search for water, only to be killed or captured.

After their miserable night, the sun rose over the heights across the Sea of Galilee, its sweltering heat beating down on the battlefield, prolonging the hell the Crusaders had been enduring since leaving Sepphoris the previous day. Saladin's archers unleashed an intense barrage of arrows into the Crusader camp. The Muslims were armed with 400 loads of arrows, plus a further 70 camel-loads. One calculation put the total at more than one and a quarter million arrows in the Muslim arsenal.[9] The Christian foot soldiers, with only light armor, suffered the brunt of the Muslim attacks. The knights were well-protected in their long-sleeved chain-mail coats, mail hoods topped with iron helmets, mail gloves and leggings, and shields, but their mounts were not. Muslim chronicler Ibn al-Athir described: "The Muslim archers sent up clouds of arrows, like thick swarms of locusts, killing many of the Frankish horses."[10] Killing these specially bred horses in battle effectively neutralized the knight, who could not easily remount a replacement while weighed down by his 70–90lb (30–40kg) suit of armor. While providing much-needed protection, the complement of armor and protective under- and outer-garments was unbearable in the summer heat.

The king's brother Amalric, the Constable, began marshaling the forces. Lingering flames from the still-burning brush and scrub bore down on the demoralized Crusaders, their heat accentuating the soldiers' thirst. Saladin's secretary chronicling the battle described the Crusaders as panting dogs.[11]

Daylight revealed how precarious the Crusaders' situation had become. Surrounded, under constant barrage, hot, thirsty, afraid, with their eyes burning from smoke and sweat, a breakdown in discipline was almost inevitable. At some point, the bulk of the infantry, desperate for water, broke ranks and fled in an ill-fated attempt to break through Muslim lines and reach the lake below them. The Muslims contained them, corralling them up a hill. The knights and infantry had a symbiotic relationship, reliant on one another. The king and the bishops pleaded with them to return, to no avail. Without the knights' protection, the Muslim cavalry was free to ride the infantry down, killing and capturing large numbers of men. A Christian source recounts: "Thousands and thousands of Syrians were charging at the Christians, shooting arrows and killing them."[12] Crusader foot soldiers dropped their weapons and willingly surrendered themselves.

So pitiful was the Christian predicament that five of Raymond's knights purportedly went to Muslim lines begging them to attack, preferring death in battle to the torture of dying from thirst. They may have had ulterior motives given what would transpire.

Though the Muslims were a more agile force, with mobility that limited the effectiveness of the Crusader knights' charge, the king ordered Raymond and the vanguard to attack. A knights' charge was a potent weapon. Just the sight of him mounted on his horse with his armor, shield, sword, and lance was fearsome and intimidating. The weight of his armor and the momentum of his heavy steed made blows from his lance, broadsword, mace or battle axe all the more lethal. A close-formation charge would smash through enemy formations. Crusader infantry would follow on the knights' heels, finishing off those knocked from their horses, trampled or pushed aside in the knights' wake.

When the king gave the order to attack, Raymond and the knights charged. With the Christian knights rapidly approaching their lines at a gallop, the Muslims responded by simply opening their ranks, allowing the Franks to pass through, and then closed their lines behind them.

Some Christian sources claim Raymond's charge was a tactical break-out from encirclement, others describe it as an escape from impending defeat. Whatever the motive, Raymond and his knights were cut off from their compatriots, and in grave danger. Besieged Tiberias was too dangerous a destination, so they fled north to safety in Tyre, Raymond abandoning his wife and Tiberias to their fates. However, Raymond had previously established a trust with Saladin; he and the sultan had exchanged gifts, so his escape may have been pre-arranged. Raymond's wife, the Countess, was later given free passage by Saladin to join her husband, who would take ill and die a few months later.

Cut off as they were from their ground troops, the mounted

Christian knights were denied the benefit of the infantry's protective screen against enemy cavalry, and foot archers, who kept Muslim archers at enough of a distance that they couldn't attack the cavalry. "Enemies sprang up on every side," one of the sources describes, "shooting arrows and killing them."[13]

Capitalizing on the flight of the Crusader infantry, Saladin became more aggressive, sending his cavalry on repeated charges against the Christian knights, wearing them down. The Christians pulled back to the Horns of Hattin, where some ruins offered protective cover. The king's red tent was pitched towards the summit, and more tents set up as obstacles to thwart Muslim attacks. Saladin moved in for the kill, unleashing his cavalry in an uphill attack towards the Crusaders' royal tent.

The remaining knights closed ranks around the tent to defend King Guy and the relic of the True Cross. Despite their difficult circumstances, the Crusader knights mustered a cavalry charge whose power was augmented by the momentum of attacking downhill. Focusing on the inviting target posed by the concentration around Saladin's tent, the Crusader charge threatened the Muslim center where Saladin commanded the action, nearly overrunning them. Nervously tugging at his beard, Saladin encouraged his troops to rally for an uphill counterattack that forced the Crusaders back. The Crusaders charged again. Saladin rallied his men; the Muslims again fought their way uphill.

The dwindling numbers of knights fought on foot in a steadily shrinking ring until they were simply overwhelmed. The king's tent and standard collapsed, and the relic captured, perhaps more of a blow to the fighting men than the capture of their king. Christians surrendered by the thousands; dead and wounded lay on the battlefield. Arab chronicler Ibn al-Athir wrote: "When one saw how many were dead, one could not believe there were any prisoners, and when one saw the prisoners, one could not believe there were any dead."[14]

As Saladin's men began rounding up survivors, they found many of them too exhausted to surrender. Grasping the extent of his victory, Saladin raised his eyes to heaven and thanked Allah.

A tent was set up for Saladin, who sat drinking water cooled by ice brought from Mount Hermon while the surviving Christian leaders were rounded up and brought before him. Weary from battle, parched from thirst, and fearful of what would become of them, King

Guy, Reynaud de Châtillon, Gerard de Ridefort and other lesser barons stood before Saladin. The Muslim leader greeted them graciously, offering King Guy a drink from his goblet, a gesture that according to Muslim hospitality meant that his life would be spared.

After quenching his thirst, the king handed the goblet to Reynaud—Saladin's sworn enemy, who stood beside him. Saladin knocked the cup to the ground. Some accounts purport that Reynaud, in a final act of bravado, defiantly slandered the Prophet Mohammed. Saladin drew his sword and beheaded the arrogant knight on the spot, and then rubbed some of Reynaud's blood on his own face as a sign of vengeance done. Saladin then reassured the startled Crusader king and his other captives and gave orders for them to be treated well. Saladin's mercy toward defeated enemies was intimidating as it demonstrated that he had nothing to fear from them.[15] Those who could afford to pay were ransomed, leaving the surviving common soldiers to be force-marched to the Damascus slave markets and sold off. King Guy was later released under oath.

Saladin's mercy did not apply to the 230 captured knights of the military orders, whose belligerency and reputation among the Muslims for being untrustworthy warranted that each Templar and Hospitaller be executed. All were summarily beheaded, save for Templar Grand Master Gerard de Ridefort, who later gained his freedom by collaborating with Saladin to secure the surrender of the Templar fortress at Gaza.

Soldiers wishing death rather than a life of slavery in the service of infidels claimed they were Templars. Denied by Christian sources, a handful of surviving Christians apparently were spared by accepting an offer to convert to Islam. Their supposed descendants survive to this day as the Salibiyya (Crusader) tribe in north Arabia.[16]

Aftermath

Saladin moved his army away from Hattin, leaving the battlefield full of rotting corpses. A Christian chronicler wrote: "throughout the three following nights, while the bodies of the holy martyrs still lay unburied, rays of divine light shone clearly above them."[17] Despite the holy spin put on the battle, the reality was that the greatest army the Crusaders had ever fielded had been decimated, its leaders killed or captured, and the relic of the True Cross lost. Arab chronicler Ibn al-Athir wrote: "Never since their invasion of Palestine had the Franks suffered such a defeat."[18] Saladin ordered a Dome of Victory erected at the battle site to commemorate the event.

Tiberias' garrison surrendered to Saladin, the first of a series of Crusader cities and towns to surrender or fall over the next few weeks. Having thrown all their forces into the showdown, the Christians had no reserves to call upon; nearly the entire Crusader kingdom fell to Saladin in short order, culminating in the capture of Jerusalem on October 1, 1187. Only Tyre and a handful of Crusader fortresses held out.

Saladin's army entered the holy city and immediately began restoring Jerusalem's Muslim face, epitomized perhaps by the dismantling of the gold cross from the Dome of the Rock.

The defeat of the Kingdom of Jerusalem came as a shock to Europe. Pope Urban III was said to have died of grief upon hearing the news. Guilt over allowing the kingdom to fall provided the impetus for a new crusade, led by three of Europe's kings. In the spring of 1191, Richard I, King of England, known as Richard the Lionheart, arrived in the Holy Land at the head of the Third Crusade.

Richard's forces would defeat Saladin in battles at Arsuf and Jaffa in 1191 and 1192, recovering coastal territories previously in Crusader hands. However, he understood that without an accommodation with Saladin, there would be no quiet, and he might have to remain in the Holy Land indefinitely. Richard never even attempted to take Jerusalem; he sought a treaty. In 1192 the Peace of Ramla was concluded, acceding Palestine's coast to the Crusaders while Jerusalem remained Muslim, although Christian access to its holy places was guaranteed. Having previously sworn to see Jerusalem only as its conqueror, Richard refused to visit the holy city. Five subsequent crusades followed, but none was remarkable, as the Crusader period by and large had come to an end with Richard's treaty with Saladin, although the Christian kingdom managed to maintain its holdings along the Mediterranean coast for another hundred years.

Saladin died in 1193 having achieved the goal of liberating Jerusalem. The dynasty he founded, known as the Ayyubids, named after his father Ayyub, ruled for nearly 60 years, with lands stretching from North Africa to the mountains of Armenia. It is a tribute to his character that he is held in high regard in both western and oriental sources.

The final end for the Crusaders came with the fall of Acre in 1291 to the Mamluks, former slave warriors who ruled Egypt at the time, whereupon the remaining Crusader holdouts abandoned their positions in favor of Cyprus, bringing an end to the Latin Kingdom's two-century reign in the Holy Land.

Notes

1. Arthur Goldschmidt Jr. *A Concise History of the Middle East* (Boulder: Westview Press, 1979), p.87.
2. "The Horns of Hattin," www.website.co.uk/knights_templar/templar4_7.html
3. Runciman, p.453.
4. Joseph Stevenson (ed.). *De Expugatione Terrae Sanctae per Saladinum*, [*The Capture of the Holy Land by Saladin*], Rolls Series, (London: Longmans, 1875), translated by James Brundage, *The Crusades: A Documentary History*, (Milwaukee, WI: Marquette University Press, 1962), pp.153–159, at www.fordham.edu/halsall/source/1187hattin.html (accessed March 14, 2011).
5. Stevenson. *De Expugatione.*
6. Stevenson. *De Expugatione.*
7. Stevenson. *De Expugatione.*
8. Stevenson. *De Expugatione.* French accounts and Ernoul the Frank blame Raymond for advising the king to halt the advance and to establish camp where they were.
9. Smith, John Masson, Jr. "Ayn Jalut: Mamluk Success or Mongol Failure?" *Harvard Journal of Asiatic Studies* (Vol. 44:2, December 1984), p.322.
10. Silvia Rozenberg (ed.). *Knights of the Holy Land. The Crusader Kingdom of Jerusalem* (Jerusalem: The Israel Museum, 1999), p.153.
11. Elizabeth Hallam (ed.). *Chronicles of the Crusades* (London: Weidenfeld & Nicolson, 1989), p.158.
12. Stevenson. *De Expugatione*
13. Stevenson. *De Expugatione*
14. Kenneth Czech, "City Taken and Retaken." *Military History* (February 1984).
15. William Hamblin. "Saladin and Muslim Military Theory" in B. Z. Kedar (ed.). *The Horns of Hattin: Proceedings of the Second Conference of the Society of the Crusades and the Latin East* (London, UK: Variorum, 1992), pp.228–38: p.237.
16. John J. Robinson. *Born in Blood: The Lost Secrets of Freemasonry, Vol. I.* (M. Evans, 1989).
17. Hallam, *Chronicles.*
18. Czech, "City Taken and Retaken."

CHAPTER 9

WA ISLAMAH! WA ISLAMAH!

MAMLUKS STOP THE MONGOL HORDE, 1260

As the Egyptian Mamluk army arrived and deployed at Ayn Jalut in northern Palestine on September 3, 1260, the Mongols were undaunted. The Mongols had already met and defeated many a formidable army, from Asian warriors to heavily armored European knights. To throw the Mamluks off balance before they could take any initiative, the Mongols, who were already deployed at Ayn Jalut, immediately went on the offensive. Seeing the command flag signaling the attack, mounted archers charged the Mamluk forces and unleashed an initial barrage from their deadly recurved composite bone and wood bows, said to be superior to all other contemporary bows in accuracy, force and range. Unit after unit galloped at the Mamluks, firing arrows from short range. As each wave galloped away to prepare another charge, a subsequent wave immediately came forward and unleashed a salvo in a blitz that threw the Mamluks off-balance. This was precisely the Mongol plan, with the mounted archers softening up enemy formations with their opening onslaught until their armored comrades in tough boiled leather armor charged in on their mounts for the kill.

Recoiling from the ferocity of this initial onslaught, the Mamluk lines wavered. Confusion broke out in the Mamluk ranks as the Mongols pounded them with this well-orchestrated lightning attack. The Mamluks were getting their first taste of the Mongols' characteristic organization, speed and ferocity, justifying the anxieties many Mamluks had going into this.

The Mongols had never been defeated, and they were heading towards Egypt, leaving destruction in their wake. With the Mongols' hatred for Islam, the future did not bode well for the Mamluks. Looking to Baghdad, the Mamluks could see their likely fate if they submitted to the Mongol advance. Much of Baghdad lay in ruins following its defeat. The city had suffered heavily in its resistance against the Mongol siege and assault, then after its fall in February 1258, Baghdad was sacked and pillaged. This cultural and intellectual center's schools, libraries, mosques and palaces were destroyed. The Mongols moved in and occupied Baghdad, where they committed horrible atrocities. Nearly the entire Muslim population—numbering in the hundreds of thousands—was killed. The ruling caliph and the entire Abbasid family were executed, bringing an end to the once-glorious Abbasid Empire. Such was the Mongol treatment of those who refused to submit.

Nomads from the Eurasian steppe, the Mongols had emerged as a new force on the horizon in the thirteenth century. It was Genghis Khan (1167–1227) who united the scattered Mongols into a strong tribal confederation that he called the "Great Mongol Empire." And great it was, as it became the largest empire ever in history, stretching across China, Russia, Central Asia and into Europe. Though referred to as "barbarians" or a "horde," Mongol conquests could not have been achieved without brilliant organization and military skill.

With hardy horses and basic yet superb quality weapons of bows, arrows, and axes that each warrior fashioned with his own hands, the Mongols perfected tactics of harassment, attack, evasion against counterattack, pursuit, and encirclement. Successful execution required a high degree of organization and cooperation, aspects in which the disciplined, orderly, and efficient Mongols excelled.

However, their reputation was scarred by their brutality in laying waste to areas they conquered. Tens of millions of deaths are attributed to them, even though the intention may have been to frighten future targets of their aggression into easy submission. Travelers in Mongol-captured territory reported destroyed towns and mounds of human bones as a common sight.

The Mongol invasion into what is today known as the Middle East was led by Hulegu, a grandson of Genghis Khan. Departing Mongolia in 1253, Hulegu's forces took Persia (Iran) in 1256 and Iraq in 1258 before moving against Syria. In January 1260, Aleppo was captured and sacked after a siege; its rulers and commanders either fled to Egypt or joined the Mongols. The Syrian cities of Homs, Hama and Damascus all subsequently fell to the Mongols.

With Syria secured, the Mongols set their sights on Egypt, and it seemed they would easily steamroll over Palestine and into Egypt. Mongol forward elements moved into Palestine—some reaching as far south as Gaza, and Hulegu sent envoys carrying a threatening letter to the Mamluk sultan of Egypt demanding submission. "You should think of what happened to other countries and submit to us," he wrote. "You have heard how we have conquered a vast empire and have purified the earth of the disorders that tainted it. We have conquered vast areas, massacring all the people. You cannot escape from the terror of our armies. . . ."[1]

The Mamluks saw the Mongol advance not only as an existential military threat to Egypt, but an assault on Islam. It was cause for consternation in a country still in disarray following the Mamluk overthrow of their masters, the Ayyubids, whose dynasty had been established by legendary Muslim leader Saladin.

Since the 9th century, young boys chosen for their physical excellence had been brought from Central Asia by the Ayyubid sultans of Egypt and Syria, to be trained, educated, converted to and steeped in Islam, becoming life-long elite Mamluk (meaning "owned") slave-soldiers in service to sultans and senior officers. When Ayyubid Sultan al-Salih died in 1249, the Mamluks, who had become extremely powerful, murdered his son and successor al-Muazzam Turan-Shah and seized power. Internal conflicts marred the new Mamluk sultanate, and there followed a turbulent decade of civil strife and intrigue in Egypt, ending with the murder of the new Mamluk ruler, Aybek. After more unrest, the murdered sultan's most senior Mamluk,

Sayf al-Din Qutuz, emerged as sultan in 1259.

With all this instability, the Mongols had little reason to believe Egypt could withstand invasion. However, despite the disarray, the Mamluks understood the gravity of the situation and were defiant. When the Mongol envoys delivered their threat to the Mamluks, Sultan Qutuz had them killed and their heads hung in the capital—a morale booster for his people. Knowing his actions would likely unleash the fury of the Mongols, the sultan set about uniting the people. Using the banner of holy war as a rallying call, Qutuz was able to enlist the support of influential Islamic scholars. Qutuz raised funds and prepared for a military campaign, all the while consolidating his own hold on power.

Though professional soldiers, many Mamluk *amirs*, or officers, were wary of Sultan Qutuz's combativeness. Unexpected support for the aggressive approach towards the Mongols came from Baybars al-Bunduqdari, previously one of Qutuz's rivals. Due to their combined efforts, the military elite was convinced and the die cast for confrontation with the Mongols. The Mamluk army, its ranks supplemented with Syrian troops who had fled the Mongol onslaught, and auxiliaries, was equipped with the latest weapons and gear including helmets, body armor, an arsenal of bows and arrows, lances, javelins, swords, axes, maces and daggers. Though well-armed and trained, the Mamluks had heard of the Mongols' seeming invincibility, and even as they prepared to embark on this expedition, they were scared.[2]

Mongol plans to invade Egypt in force were derailed when Mongol leader Hulegu received word of the death of his brother, the supreme khan. Hulegu was obligated by Genghis Khan's laws of succession to return to Mongolia to the *Khuriltai*, the congress of nobles, to elect the new *khakan*, or great khan. Hulegu withdrew eastward, taking with him the bulk of his forces, leaving his lieutenant Kitbuqa Noyon in charge with only a small part of the original Mongol expeditionary force. The timing for the departure worked out well, for with the hot summer just around the corner, grass and water would not have been plentiful enough to sustain the large Mongol force, whose horses—several per warrior—relied on grazing for sustenance. But the small force that remained was not adequate to take on the Mamluks in Egypt. Augmented by Georgian, Armenian, and locally recruited auxiliaries, possibly including some Franks, Kitbuqa's force could consolidate Mongol control of Syria and hold the line. Whether Hulegu was truly comfortable with the situation due to the continued disarray in Egypt; was unaware of Mamluk military prowess; trusted Kitbuqa's force could hold its own; or simply had no choice, he withdrew.

News of Hulegu's departure certainly helped impel the Mamluks to action against the vastly reduced Mongol force rather than waiting and possibly facing the full strength of the Mongol war machine. Even so, there were many among the Mamluks who still feared what they were getting themselves into. Sensing this undercurrent of fear, Qutuz had to lecture his reluctant army repeatedly on how crucial their mission was to the survival of Egypt and Islam, not to mention all they risked losing if Egypt were to submit.

Perhaps to reward him for his support (or alternatively, to put him in the line of danger—he was a rival after all), Sultan Qutuz gave Baybars command of the Mamluk vanguard. This force engaged forward elements of the Mongol army that had reached as far south as Gaza during the summer of 1260, and the Mongols pulled back. The main Mamluk force, commanded by Qutuz, caught up with the vanguard and moved northward up Palestine's coast. With Crusaders still entrenched in cities stretching up the Mediterranean coast as well as some inland fortresses which could pose a threat to the Mamluk army, especially if they were to ally themselves with the Mongols, Qutuz made it clear to them that they would regret their actions should they make hostile moves. Still smarting from past defeats at the hands of the Muslims, the Crusaders were wise enough to watch from the sidelines, and even allowed the Mamluk army to camp by Crusader Acre (Akko) for several days. Upon learning the location of the Mamluk encampment by Acre and anticipating its route inland through the Jezreel Valley, Mongol commander Kitbuqa moved his forces southward from their positions in what is today Lebanon's Bekaa Valley. Though the Mongols traveled light, carrying little equipment and making do with few provisions, they moved slowly. Their trademark rapid movement in combat required a large number of horses. Stalwart like their masters, the horses survived by the process of grazing in the wild, which made for slow progress.

The Battle

The two armies met in the Jezreel Valley at Ayn Jalut (Goliath's Spring, or Ein Harod)[3] during the early morning hours of Friday, September 3, 1260. The open ground at Ayn Jalut at the foot of Mount Gilboa, where there was room to maneuver and a plentiful water supply, was an ideal battleground for both the cavalry-based forces. Accounts of the size of the opposing forces and details on the course of battle differ considerably. It is believed the Mamluks had a slight numerical superiority over the Mongols, who were thought to field a 10,000-man unit known as a *tuman*.[4]

Differing, sometimes contradictory accounts make a precise econstruction of the battle impossible. The following account is pieced together working with sources and common Mamluk and Mongol tactics.[5]

Though skilled mounted archers themselves, the Mamluks were hard-hit by the opening attack of the "devil's horsemen," as the Mongols were known. When the Mamluks stabilized the situation and counterattacked, the highly mobile Mongols retreated to the safety of their rear ranks, where men on fresh horses were ready to attack again. Though riding larger mounts and better equipped, the Mamluks quickly tired out their horses in their attempt to close ranks with the Mongols in order to bring their heavy weaponry to bear. Lacking pastureland, Egypt's geography dictated that the Mamluks could not support a large cavalry, and each man had only a single warhorse.[6] This meant that the Mamluks could not hope to catch their attackers, with their abundance of spare mounts. Without the luxury of spare horses, Sultan Qutuz saw they would be doomed if they allowed the Mongols to dictate the terms of battle. They would need to conserve their horses' energy and rely on their expertise in archery. Qutuz ordered his Mamluks to hold steady and calmly fire at the successive waves of Mongol attackers, taking advantage of their training and archery skills rather than futile counter charging.

Reading the Mamluks' failure to pursue them as a sign of weakness, the Mongols again went on the attack. Charging forward in another lightning assault, a rapid succession of Mongol horsemen unleashed their arrows. The Mongol army's right flank began overpowering the Mamluks' left flank. When his forces on this flank began retreating,

Qutuz is said to have climbed on a large boulder and begun shouting "*Wa Islamah! Wa Islamah!* [Oh, Islam! Oh, Islam!]" Seeing their commander so courageously invoking their faith evidently inspired his forces to hold steady and keep fighting. Rallying his troops, Qutuz repeated his orders. The Mamluks held their ground and began firing steadily at the attacking Mongols. Unlike the nomadic Mongols, Mamluks had time for regular individual and large-unit training. Shooting faster and straighter, unleashing deadly long-range fire from atop their stationary horses, Mamluk prowess with the bow began taking a heavy toll on the Mongols, neutralizing their short-range hit-and-run horse archery.[7] When the Mongols halted, the Mamluks went on the offensive with their larger, stronger horses. Qutuz led the charge into the enemy ranks, where he is credited with killing a number of Mongols. In the course of the battle, Qutuz's horse was hit, but the sultan was unscathed.

As the Mamluks were gaining the upper hand, the Mongol force was hit by the desertion of Homs ruler al-Ashraf Musa, a Syrian Ayyub who had gone over to the Mongols (whose practice was to incorporate into their ranks those that had submitted to them). Al-Ashraf Musa's intention to desert with his troops during the battle had been conveyed in advance to the Mamluks. In the heat of battle, when these front-line forces abandoned the Mongols' left flank, the Mamluk right flank plowed through the void and moved on the Mongols' center.

Some modern historians claim the bulk of the Mamluk army laid in wait while Qutuz, leading a small detachment, engaged the Mongols before feigning retreat—drawing them into an ambush.[8] However, the false retreat routine was a known Mongol tactic, casting doubt on claims that the Mongols would fall for their own trick. It was also Mongol practice to send large scouting parties in advance, so they were very likely to have known the true size of the Mamluk force they were facing.

However, whichever version of events is accurate, the results are not in dispute. By day's end, the Mongol army was devastated, with 1500 dead, plus casualties and prisoners. Dead and dying men and horses were strewn about the broad Ayn Jalut valley. Despite the deteriorating battlefield situation, Mongol commander Kitbuqa remained in the thick of battle and was killed.[9] Leaderless, the remnants of the Mongol army fled the battlefield, only to be pursued by vengeful Mamluks led by Baybars. Riding hard on their heels, the Mamluks chased the fleeing Mongols, killing any they could find. A group of Mongols attempted a stand on a nearby hill, but they were no match for the force pursuing them. Others tried hiding in some nearby fields of reeds. When the Mamluks spotted them, they set fire to the fields.[10] Some Mongols did succeed in escaping northward, though Baybars' force pursued them into Syria.

Ayn Jalut was the Mongols' first true defeat. This time, the Mongols were not carrying out their custom of cutting off an ear from each enemy corpse to aid them in counting their victims. Instead, those that lived to tell about it only did so because they had fled for their lives. The Mamluks had routed the army that had brought terror to so many, and about which Hulegu had bragged: "Our horses are swift, our arrows sharp, our swords like thunderbolts, our hearts as hard as the mountains, our soldiers as numerous as the sand."[11]

When news of the Mongol defeat reached Damascus, the local Muslim population rose up against its Mongol occupiers. In disarray following the power transition in their capital, the Mongols were unable to stabilize the collapsing situation in Syria, and power struggles would prevent them from avenging their defeat. The Mongols pulled back, creating a power vacuum that left the Mamluks masters of Palestine and Syria. Though defeated, the Mongols continued to pose a very real threat. The Mamluks' chief opponent over the next half century would be the Il Khanate dynasty established by Hulegu in Persia in 1260. This dynasty would grow from its beginnings in Persia to encompass vast areas from Turkey to Pakistan.

Ironically, Hulegu's state—who had laid waste to Baghdad before the elements under Kitbuqa Noyon were defeated at Ayn Jalut by an army rallied to action on religious grounds to fight the infidel—embraced Islam and adopted it as their state religion in 1300 under Hulegu's great-grandson Ghazan. But not even their conversion to Islam could erase their legacy of ruthlessness in the Muslim lands.

During the march back to Egypt in October 1260, Baybars added another chapter to Mamluk Egypt's decade of turbulence by stabbing Sultan Qutuz to death. His motive may have been disappointment at not receiving Aleppo as a reward for his support and exemplary service in the conflict, or pure calculated ambition. Upon returning to Cairo, Baybars declared himself sultan, assuming the title *al-Malik az-Zakir*, The Triumphant King. Though not its first sultan, Baybars is considered the true founder of the Mamluk sultanate by virtue of his extremely capable leadership and ability to govern. An excellent soldier, administrator and politician, Baybars is credited with reversing Egypt's decline.

Baybars invested in his army's strength, building it up to resist and deter further Mongol attempts. In fact, the Il Khanate would attack Syria a further six times, never successfully. In addition to battling the Mongols, Baybars would direct his attention to another enemy: the infidel Crusaders.

Viewed by Muslims as foreign invaders, the Crusaders were an impediment to full Mamluk hegemony, and could serve as a bridgehead should Europe get ideas of renewed crusade. Beginning in 1263, Baybars turned his forces on the Crusaders in a concerted but gradual effort to drive them from Mamluk territory. One by one, the beleaguered Crusader positions fell.

After Baybars' death in 1277 (purportedly from drinking poison he had intended for a rival), the Mamluks continued their campaign against the Crusaders. With the 1291 fall of Acre, the last major Crusader city in Palestine, the remaining Crusader holdouts abandoned their positions for the safety of Cyprus, bringing an end to the Latin Kingdom in the Holy Land.

Left without any true enemies, the Mamluks prospered. Directing their energies to the arts and culture, they set about building civic works and improving infrastructure. In Palestine, the Dome of the Rock was renovated, and the area around the Temple Mount was built up with madrassas, hostels and charitable institutions to aid pilgrims. Palestine also benefited from Mamluk projects linking Egypt with all parts of the sultanate. Roads and way-stations were built, improving movement, communications and security; it took only four days for post to travel between Cairo and Damascus. Jindas bridge in Lod, the "White Mosque" tower in Ramla and parts of Nimrod's fortress in the Golan Heights all give testament to the Mamluks' building spree. Beyond changing the face of Palestine, these former slaves from the European steppe built their state into the center of Muslim power, wealth and learning that dominated the landscape for 250 years.

Notes

1. David W. Tschanz "History's Hinge Ain Jalut" *Saudi Aramco World* (Vol. 58:4), www.saudiaramcoworld.com.
2. "In the light of the relative combat power of both armies . . . the Egyptians feared an unavoidable clash with an equally strong and seemingly invincible Mongol army." Thorau, Peter. "The Battle of 'Ayn Jalut: a Re-examination." *Crusade and Settlement*—Papers read at the First Conference of the Society for the Study of the Crusades and the Latin East and presented to R. C. Smail. (University College Cardiff Press, 1985), pp.236–241: p.237. Smith writes: "The soldiers in Egypt knew the Mongols' record and feared meeting them; many surely evaded doing so." John Masson Smith Jr. "Ayn Jalut: Mamluk Success or Mongol Failure?" *Harvard Journal of Asiatic Studies* (Vol. 44:2, December 1984), p.313.
3. Northwest of Beit Shean and east of Afula, near the modern village of Gidona.
4. Thorau, "The Battle of 'Ayn-Jalut," p. 237, writes: "we may certainly take it for granted that in the time of the confusion and upheavals of the decade 1250–1260 the Egyptian regular army would have numbered no more than 10–12,000. It would thus seem probable that the army, including all the auxiliary units, at Qutuz's disposal in 1260 for his war with the Mongols could not have been stronger than 15–20,000 men." As for the Mongols, Professor Reuven Amitai notes "the figures of 10,000–12,000 give it the most credence, although these numbers are not a certainty." Amitai-Preiss, Reuven. "Ayn Jalut Revisited." *Tarih—Papers in Near Eastern Studies* (Vol. 2, 1992), p.124.
5. Amitai writes: "It is difficult to establish an acceptable and realistic account of the battle because none of the sources gives the complete picture and they often contradict each other; at the same time some events are unclear or completely unreported." "Ayn Jalut Revisited," p.129.
6. Smith "Ayn Jalut: Mamluk Success or Mongol Failure?" p.321.
7. Smith, "Ayn Jalut: Mamluk Success or Mongol Failure?" pp.324–5. With a different view, Professor Amitai wrote: "You overrate the Mamluks. They had just gone through 10 years of political confusion—certainly not conditions for building a regular army." (Personal correspondence)
8. Thorau. "The Battle of 'Ayn Jalut: a Re-examination," p.237.
9. One source (Rashid al-Din) claims he was captured and executed.
10. Amitai-Preiss. "Ayn Jalut Revisited," p.142.
11. Goldschmidt. *A Concise History of the Middle East*, p.91.

CHAPTER 10

OUTGUNNED

Mamluk Cavalry Scorn
Ottoman Firearms, 1516

In a traditional ceremony affirming allegiance, soldiers passed through an arch made of two swords, and Egypt's Mamluk sultan Kansuh al-Ghawri swore his officers to loyalty on the Koran. Not far away, the mighty Ottoman army was deployed with its modern weapons ready for battle. The Mamluks, maintaining their contempt for firearms to the very end, still believed their traditional ways of battle would lead them to victory.

Late in the thirteenth century, groups of Turkish-speaking Muslims in Anatolia were united into a confederation by a minor chieftain named Osman. The Ottomans, as his descendants are known, were militant and expansionist. Legend has it that Osman's sword was passed down to each successive Ottoman sultan with the understanding that they keep up the way of the sword, and most lived up to expectations. Spreading rapidly east and west, over time the Ottoman Empire came to fill the power vacuum created by the decline of the Byzantine Empire. From humble origins, the Ottoman Empire became the predominant power in Asia Minor.

Ottoman strength centered around the elite Janissaries. These imported slave soldiers, carefully selected on the basis of physique and intelligence, were educated, trained and imbued with the tenets of Islam. Well-equipped with modern firearms, the highly disciplined Janissaries were a formidable fighting force. Confined to barracks except during campaigns, the Janissaries' sole purpose and focus was military, ever loyal to the sultan and the state.

The Safavids

The emergence of a new state in Persia under Shah Ismail as-Safawi at the beginning of the sixteenth century challenged Ottoman power. Though both states were Muslim, the Safavids adhered to the Shiite sect whereas the Ottomans were Sunni.[1]

Ottoman eastern Anatolia was populated by a large number of Shiites—an inviting audience to the Safavids. Shah Ismail, an ethnic Turcoman, like much of the population of these Ottoman provinces, reached out to the Shiites with a message of revolt. Difficult to rule on the best of days, the nomadic Turcoman tribes idolized Shah Ismail, undermining Ottoman authority over entire areas of Anatolia. Encouraged by Shah Ismail, insubordination grew into an uprising in 1511.

Ottoman sultan Bayezid was not particularly aggressive in countering this threat. With his sons quarreling over succession to the throne, and with civil war a very real possibility, Bayezid had not been free to focus on the rebellious Shiites. Claiming that stronger leadership was needed to deal with the Safavid threat, Bayezid's son Selim, whose warlike nature was admired by the Janissaries, forced his father's abdication in 1512. By killing his four brothers, their sons, and four of his own five sons, Selim eliminated threats to his power and secured his position. Selim quickly adopted a far more bellicose nature towards the Safavids.

In 1513, the new Ottoman sultan launched a vicious campaign against Safavid supporters in eastern Anatolia, killing thousands of tribesmen. His determination and ferocity were notorious. Mere mention of Selim's name invoked terror, and the sultan became known as "Yavuz"—the Grim. The Safavids could not sit by idly as their supporters were massacred, and ultimately the conflict escalated to war, with the Ottoman and Safavid armies meeting at Chaldiran in

Azerbaijan on August 23, 1514. No match for the artillery and firearm-equipped Ottoman forces, the Safavids were soundly defeated and retreated into the Persian interior.

In the lead-up to Chaldiran, Egyptian Mamluk client Ala al-Dawla of Albistan had refused Sultan Selim's request for assistance as the Ottomans crossed his territory. The Mamluks quietly applauded him for this, fearing Ottoman moves and hoping for an Ottoman defeat to bolster their own position in the Taurus frontier region between the two empires. Consequently, Ala al-Dawla was killed by Selim and his land annexed to the Ottoman Empire in 1515, in clear violation of Cairo's rights. Adding insult to injury, Selim sent al-Dawla's head to Mamluk Sultan Kansuh al-Ghawri along with an announcement of the conquest. With the Ottomans also extending their control over Kurdistan, the balance of power in the region between the Ottomans and Mamluks was shifting in favor of the Ottomans. Kansuh saw that he must react to the Ottoman provocation.

For two and a half centuries, the Mamluks had ruled the Middle East, but by the start of the 16th century their grip had weakened. A deterioration of Mamluk government and other factors had led to internal dissent, exacerbated by external threats, posing serious challenges for the Mamluk sultanate.

Domestically, the Mamluk sultanate had been in a process of steady economic decline since the beginning of the fifteenth century. Egypt had been hit by plague, drought, famine, and war, all of which had taken their toll on the economy. Falling revenues for the government meant less money to distribute, and this led to insubordination among the Mamluk recruits, who had become quite greedy. By imposing high taxes, debasing the currency and carrying out mass confiscations, Sultan al-Ghawri was able to supplement the state's coffers enough to appease his soldiers, for the sultan knew his survival depended on keeping the men in arms happy. But his actions depressed the economy and angered and alienated the populace.

Once the bulwark of stability in the central Muslim world, the Mamluk sultanate now found itself threatened by both Portuguese maritime encroachment and aggressive Ottoman expansion. After rounding the Cape of Good Hope in 1497, the Portuguese established themselves in the Red Sea. The discovery of an all-water route around southern Africa replaced the taxable land route that passed through Egypt—a serious blow to the Mamluk economy that aggravated their financial troubles. Mamluk excesses have been blamed for the Portuguese search for a way of bypassing Egypt.

In the face of the Portuguese threat, the Mamluks strengthened coastal fortifications and built a naval fleet, which the Portuguese sank in 1509. The Mamluk sultan turned to the Ottomans for assistance. Angered by Portuguese support for their Safavid enemy, the Ottomans sent munitions, naval supplies and advisors to the Mamluks—support that would serve the Ottomans well. Not only did it give the Ottoman advisors their first taste of Portuguese naval power (which they would later face), it also gave them a glimpse of the poor state of the Mamluk army.

A tradition-bound military society, the Mamluks stubbornly resisted the introduction of the modern firearms such as artillery and arquebuses into their ranks. These new weapons threatened their traditional ways, which centered on horsemanship. Cavalrymen through and through, the Mamluks remained loyal to outdated equestrian battle methods employing sword, lance, and bow, from which they derived their pride and feeling of superiority. "Since the arquebus could not be operated from horseback, its adoption would end a very long and deep-rooted tradition and cause a profound transformation of the structure of the army, and hence of the ruling elite."[2]

Shortly after he became sultan, al-Ghawri revived traditional cavalry training exercises and military displays. These exercises strengthened Mamluk reliance on horsemanship as the foundation of their military might. Visually impressive performances meant to showcase Mamluk military power, these exercises and displays proved an intelligence bonanza for the Ottoman envoy in Cairo, who could clearly see that the Mamluks remained loyal to outdated weapons and tactics rather than adopting firearms, which were already used so effectively by the Ottomans.

Renewal of these exercises intensified Mamluk contempt for both artillery and guns. Mamluks regarded equipping a unit with firearms insulting and dishonorable. That the Ottomans had adopted and mastered such weapons only added to the enmity Mamluks already held towards the Ottomans. Mamluks looked down on the Ottomans, denigrating them for having no knowledge of what they considered honorable traditional warfare. The Mamluks thought that their ways could prevail over forces equipped with firearms—a belief which would cost them heavily.

It wasn't that the Mamluks had no guns. Egypt was casting cannon, destined mostly for coastal defenses. Others went to the citadel in Cairo, yet none was directed to any of the provinces bordering the Ottomans. This had nothing to do with Egypt's poor financial situation—it was solely due to the Mamluks' reluctance to adopt firearms. In 1511, al-Ghawri even created a rifle corps known as the "Fifth Corps." To circumvent opposition, members of the Fifth Corps were recruited from outside the mainstream. The arquebusier, or rifleman, was socially inferior to traditional fighting men. Men of the Fifth Corps were paid less than a standard soldier's salary, and their pay came on a special fifth pay session—separate from all other units, from which came their name.[3] Extra expenses incurred in creating, equipping and maintaining this corps were blamed for the chronic shortages in the treasury. Despite the difficult economic situation, al-Ghawri realized their importance and always found funds to pay his new unit. So upset were the Mamluks by the mere existence of the Fifth Corps that relations with the sultan became strained, and rumors of revolt were ripe. The Fifth Corps was deployed on two occasions: guarding Suez against the Portuguese in 1513, and on a voyage to India in 1515.[4] Since those involvements were outside the traditional realm of the Mamluk cavalrymen, use of the firearms-equipped Fifth Corps was condoned.

That the Ottomans had assisted the Mamluks against the Portuguese a few years earlier had been long since forgotten. The Mamluks were seething from Ottoman aggression along their common frontier, and so Egypt began preparations for war during the early months of 1516. Resolved to confronting the Ottomans, "al-Ghawri now assumed the demeanor of a commander in chief who would personally lead his troops to battle against this aggressor."[5] Aleppo's governor, fearful of an Ottoman move against his city, sent a message urging al-Ghawri to hasten his departure from Cairo. Al-Ghawri busied himself with preparations for the campaign, mustering troops and reviewing weapon inventories.

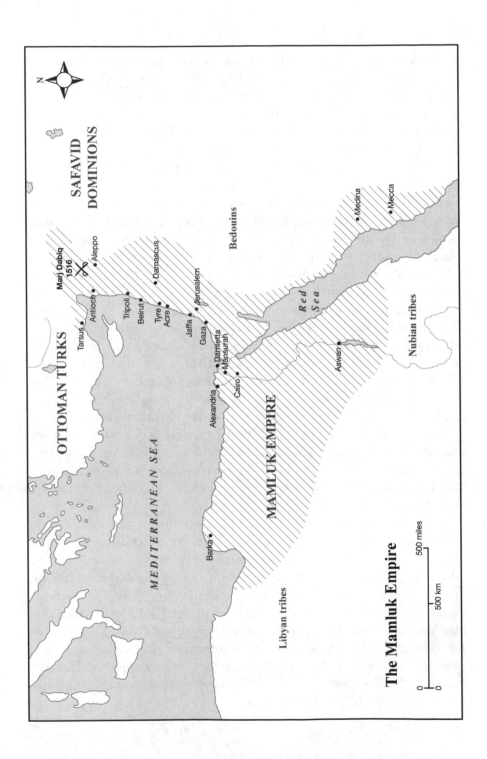

The Mamluk Empire

On April 21, 1516, al-Ghawri issued official orders for the campaign. Less than three weeks later, detachments were on the move. The sultan's battalion set out from Cairo on May 13 to the nearby camp at Ridaniyya on Cairo's outskirts. Al-Ghawri himself set out from Cairo a few days later, joining the forces at Ridaniyya. There he stayed for eight days arranging riding orders and attending to matters in preparation for his absence. The sultan ordered the caliph al-Mutawakkil III, the four chief *qadis* (judges) and other religious figures to join the army on its march to offer prayers for victory. Physicians, clerks and artisans were also ordered to join the campaign. Distinctly absent from the Mamluk host was the Fifth Corps with its guns. Given the poor state of relations between the sultan and the Mamluks because of the Fifth Corps, this decision is understandable.[6] If the expedition resulted in battle, the sultan would have to rely on his Mamluks, and he could not risk divisiveness.

Al-Ghawri appointed his nephew Tumanbay to rule as his deputy. Trusting no-one with his wealth—not even his nephew, al-Ghawri emptied Cairo's citadel of all the gold and silver treasures he had accumulated during his rule beginning in 1501 (all the while claiming financial hardship) and took with him all the funds from the national treasury.[7]

The Mamluk vanguard set out for Syria. Along the way, they were joined by Bedouins conscripted by local sheikhs. On May 24, as al-Ghawri was finalizing his preparations, a courier arrived at Ridaniyya camp with a message from Ottoman sultan Selim calling for peace and offering an explanation about the al-Dawla affair.

After quickly recovering from the blow dealt them by the Ottomans at Chaldiran, the Safavids had raised a new army and had even defeated an Ottoman force. Though Selim had provoked the Mamluks, his main enemy remained the Safavids, whom he passionately hated. Dismissing Selim's overture as a manipulative ruse designed to free the Ottomans to deal with the resurgent Safavids without Mamluk interference, al-Ghawri continued as planned, setting off for Syria with the main Mamluk force the very next day to follow events from that vantage.

Chronicler Ibn Iyas observed that the Mamluk army was smaller and less impressive than it had been in the past. "There were only 944 royal Mamluks and the whole army numbered approximately 5,000 soldiers, or according to another estimate, some 7,000 men."[8] Ibn Iyas described the army's opulent outfittings, but none was modern. And so it was an outdated, ill-equipped army that set off in the spring of 1516 to face the battle-hardened troops of the modern Ottoman army.

The Mamluks' route took them through Gaza, Damascus and Aleppo. Throughout the journey, al-Ghawri had to contend with conflicting information. False reports were being provided by Khayrbak min Yilbay, governor of Aleppo province, about an incursion of Shah Ismail's forces into Mamluk territories and their occupation of other areas.[9] Damascus' Governor Sibay reported no enemy in sight, but warned that economic conditions in his area were not conducive to sustaining a large army. In Damascus, al-Ghawri successfully pressured Sibay to join the campaign.

Al-Ghawri believed that a confrontation between the Ottomans and Safavids was imminent. Adding credence to his belief were assurances brought to him in Aleppo on July 11 by two Ottoman emissaries that the Ottoman dispute was with the Safavids, not with the Mamluks. The Ottoman message requested the Mamluks not to interfere. Still angry at Selim's patronizing attitude towards him in diplomatic correspondence, and certain the Ottomans would next turn on him, al-Ghawri detained the Ottoman emissaries and treated them poorly.

The Ottoman host set off from Istanbul on June 5, its supply train stretching as far as the eye could see, with animal-drawn wheeled carts, carriages, wagons and camels carrying copper cannon, gunpowder, lead, iron and other war materiel. Selim moved his forces to the plain of Malatia, from which he could easily travel eastward towards the Safavids or south towards Syria, according to circumstances.

Along the way, Ottoman spies brought news of the Mamluk army advancing towards Aleppo. Regarding the Safavids as the more dangerous foe, Selim planned to resume the offensive against them. But the Safavids had pulled back, and memories of their successful scorched-earth tactics during their previous confrontation were still fresh in Selim's mind. In mid-July 1516, it was still not clear which enemy would be the Ottomans' priority, but he could not ignore the Mamluk force now poised in Syria. Al-Ghawri's plans of facing an Ottoman army weary and weakened from battle with the Safavids were starting to backfire.

Perhaps sensing the change in Ottoman intent, al-Ghawri now scurried to avoid the prospect of war by releasing Selim's emissaries and dispatching an emissary of his own to the Ottoman sultan carrying a message of neutrality. At this point, Ottoman sources claim that they intercepted a message from al-Ghawri to the Safavids pledging mutual support.[10] It is likely that the Ottomans fabricated the story of the Mamluk message of mutual support to the Safavids as a way of justifying combat against fellow Muslims. It made no sense for al-Ghawri to have entangled himself when he had no interest in fighting at that time.

Outraged by al-Ghawri's alleged duplicity, short-tempered Selim decided on war with the Mamluks. When the Mamluk emissary arrived at Selim's camp carrying al-Ghawri's neutrality offer, his entourage was killed, and the emissary sent back to al-Ghawri with the message: "Meet me at Marj Dabiq!"[11]

The Ottoman army marched towards Aleppo, Syria, and stopped at Marj Dabiq, the plain north of the city. Leaving its treasury and baggage at Aleppo, the Mamluk army marched from the city. Chronicler Ibn Iyas' writings illustrate the glorious manner in which the Mamluks described themselves: "The Sultan called on the army to march out of Aleppo, and the whole army went forth, and they were like shining stars with their arms and prancing? [sic] horses: and every horseman was a match to a thousand infantrymen of the army of the Ottoman Sultan."[12] They went towards Marj Dabiq and set up camp at the adjacent town of Haylan. Al-Ghawri personally inspected the area's layout and deployed his units in preparation for battle.

Marj Dabiq

The Ottoman–Mamluk clash took place at Marj Dabiq on August 24, 1516. Mamluk Sultan al-Ghawri deployed at the head of his army, with the caliph, the four *qadis* and all the religious functionaries at his side, and the Mamluks. On the right flank was the Damascus regiment commanded by its governor Sibay; on the left was Aleppo's Governor Khayrbak and his men. Auxiliary infantry composed of Bedouin, Turcomen, and Kurds supplemented the force. Ottoman sources estimated the Mamluk force at 20,000 to 30,000 men.[13] Against them, Selim fielded a well-trained, well-organized, and experienced body of infantry and cavalry, supported by long-range muskets and artillery. Though awed by the size of the Ottoman army, said to number anywhere from 60,000 to an exaggerated 100,000, the Mamluks were not deterred.[14] They remained confident in the superiority of their traditional ways of war.

At the forefront of al-Ghawri's own contingent were the seasoned veterans—Mamluks purchased and trained by previous sultans. Al-Ghawri's own Mamluk recruits were not battle-tested, so it was not certain how well they would stand firm in combat. With these doubts, the sultan ordered the veterans into battle first. The veterans were clearly more experienced, but he was accused of favoritism, sparing his own Mamluks at the veterans' expense. There is probably some truth to these charges—with intrigue and conspiracy commonplace in the Mamluk political process, it was common for Mamluk sultans, out of paranoia, to purge their predecessors' Mamluks to avoid the prospect of revolt while favoring their own and thus maintaining their support through favoritism and largesse.[15]

The backbone of Mamluk tactics was the cavalry charge followed by rapid withdrawal. Mamluk veterans, followed by the horsemen from Aleppo and Damascus, made the first charge while unleashing a deadly hail of arrows. In this ferocious opening assault, they proved their superior horsemanship by ably maneuvering around the Ottoman artillery, breaking through the Ottoman ranks and driving back the Kurds and Turcomans on the Ottoman flanks. The Mamluks even succeeded in capturing seven Ottoman standards and cutting down some of the arquebusiers. In this close combat, Ottoman firearms could not be brought to bear, and as chronicler Ibn Tulun wrote, "Early in the day the Mamluk army had the upper hand. By noon they were busily engaged in pillage and plunder."[16]

The tide turned when the Ottoman cannon and arquebuses opened fire. The sound of guns firing was deafening, causing panic among the Mamluk men and horses. Artillery projectiles and musket rounds slammed into the Mamluk ranks, causing great numbers of casualties. Experienced after having fought firearm-equipped enemies in Europe, the Ottomans had become quite adept with both artillery and muskets. The Janissaries, formerly the infantry archers of the Ottoman army, had easily taken to firearms in place of traditional weapons. And artillery, though still more of a siege weapon, was proving to be an effective weapon on the battlefield.

"In Marj Dabiq 'every cannon killed some fifty or sixty or a hundred people until that steppe resembled a slaughter-house from the blood,'" wrote Mamluk historian Ibn Zunbul.[17] He noted that most of the dead Mamluks were killed by cannon and arquebus.[18]

Stunned by the heavy losses they had taken in this unfamiliar form of warfare, the Mamluks seemed to realize their predicament. Ibn Zunbul wrote fatalistically, "We cannot resist the Ottoman army and its great numbers and its firearms."[19] "At this critical moment when a resolute advance might yet have won success, Kansuh al-Ghawri and his own Mamluks remained inactive."[20] When he called on his recruits to fall back, the veterans who were bearing the brunt of the fighting felt they were being sacrificed and lost their will. Dissension in the ranks resulted in a loss of cohesion. In the ensuing confusion, Governor Sibay was killed, leaving his Damascus contingent leaderless.

With the situation unraveling, Governor Khayrbak added to the confusion by spreading the rumor that al-Ghawri had fallen in battle. Khayrbak had long been in traitorous contact with the Ottomans, arranging to defect in exchange for a prominent position with them. Keeping his agreement with the Ottomans, Khayrbak broke ranks and withdrew his forces in the midst of battle and fled the field. Khayrbak's treachery was not limited to desertion—he had also been passing valuable intelligence to the Ottomans and misinformation to his own side. In fact, he is said to have played a large role in convincing Selim to move against the Mamluks. Khayrbak's treachery would be well rewarded with his appointment as the first Ottoman governor of Egypt.

With the battlefield situation rapidly deteriorating and groups of his army fleeing, al-Ghawri fell from his horse and died minutes later, apparently from a stroke. His body was whisked away and never found. When the Ottomans learned of al-Ghawri's death, they pressed their attack. After a brief resistance, the Mamluks broke and fled. All the Mamluk standards fell into Ottoman hands, along with baggage belonging to al-Ghawri and the senior Mamluk officers. The plain was littered with mutilated remnants of this confrontation:

> Corpses lay in heaps, many without heads. Faces of the fallen were smeared with blood and grime, disfiguring their features. Slain horses lay scattered about, their saddles thrown from their backs. Gold-embossed swords, steel-mail tunics, tatters of uniforms were strewn all over. . . .[21]

While casualties among officers were high, most of the Mamluk recruits survived and were allowed to flee towards Aleppo. Upon arriving they found themselves locked out. Angry about the treatment they had received from the Mamluk army when it was billeted there, local inhabitants fell on them in revenge. Abandoning their war material and huge treasury in Aleppo, the survivors fled for their lives south toward Damascus.

Among those captured by the Ottomans were the caliph and three of the four *qadis*, one having fled with the retreating forces. Selim received the caliph and treated him well, though he was later deported to the Ottoman capital as a tangible signal that Egypt was no longer the seat of the caliphate—the legitimate religious authority, but merely a province administered from a distant land. Four days after the battle, Selim arrived at Aleppo, where he was hailed as liberator, freeing the populace from the Mamluk yoke. The fleeing Mamluks had left Aleppo's citadel unguarded. Selim had earlier boasted that his weakest man would take Aleppo's citadel, where al-Ghawri had deposited his huge treasury before setting off for Marj Dabiq. Keeping this vow, he sent in an aged clerk to view the treasures. When the clerk reported riches beyond calculation, Selim had to see for himself and was similarly overwhelmed. This windfall for the Ottoman treasury no doubt contributed to continued Ottoman conquests, beginning with the campaign against Mamluk Egypt.

In a matter of weeks, the Ottomans occupied all of Syria and Palestine. Hoping to avoid the grueling march across the Sinai Desert to take Cairo, Selim proposed to al-Ghawri's nephew Tumanbay, who had assumed power in Cairo, that he submit to the Ottomans and govern Egypt as the Ottoman viceroy. Rather than conceding to this common Ottoman practice, Tumanbay was defiant. Left with no alternative, Sultan Selim ordered the Ottoman army across the Sinai, arriving in the Cairo area in late January 1517.

Tumanbay prepared to make a stand at Ridaniyya military camp at the approaches to Cairo. Finally comprehending the necessity of firearms, the Mamluks had hastily assembled what weaponry they could muster to fortify Ridaniyya. All Egypt had however, was siege artillery—unsuited for the type of war it was about to face. When the Battle of Ridaniyya was fought on January 23, 1517, the 20,000-strong Egyptian army was defeated within twenty minutes after the Ottomans swept around the heavy artillery and attacked from the rear. Since the Egyptians could not turn their heavy siege artillery, most of the Egyptian guns did not fire a shot.

Sultan Tumanbay managed to escape and organize some resistance, but it was quickly broken, and he was captured and hanged. The Mamluk sultanate had come to an end; Egypt became a satellite of the Ottoman Empire.

After taking Egypt, the Ottomans continued on to Arabia. Selim doubled the size of his empire, adding all the lands of the Islamic caliphate, save for Persia (Iran), and Mesopotamia. With sovereignty over all the holy places of Islam and possessing vast wealth and power, Selim became the most prestigious ruler in the Muslim world. His reign is considered the prelude to the Ottoman Empire's golden age.

As a way-station on the pilgrim's route to Mecca, Selim wanted to ensure that Palestine had law and order and good services and facilities. When he died in 1520, Selim was succeeded by his son Suleiman. Jerusalem flourished under the new sultan, who became known as Suleiman the Magnificent. Suleiman rebuilt Jerusalem's walls and gates, which had lain in ruins since their destruction in 1219. When Suleiman learned that the architects literally cut corners when they left Mount Zion outside the walls, he had the two men executed, and legend has it they are buried just inside Jaffa Gate. Suleiman's improvements for the city included repairing the city's ancient aqueduct and installing public drinking fountains, building new markets and restoring old ones, refurbishing mosques, and other projects, most notably the Temple Mount's Dome of the Rock, where exterior mosaics were replaced with colored tiles.

After Suleiman's death, Jerusalem lost its prominence in Ottoman eyes. Over time, the Ottoman Empire suffered from a general disintegration of law and order, and Palestine was not immune. Corruption, rebellious governors and simple neglect took their effects, and the Holy Land became a backwater. American writer Mark Twain reported Palestine's poor state in his 1860's travelogue *The Innocents Abroad*, calling Palestine "desolate and unlovely" and saying that it "sits in sackcloth and ashes." Of Jerusalem he wrote: "Renowned Jerusalem itself, the stateliest name in history, has lost all its ancient grandeur and is become a pauper village. . ."[22] Palestine would remain that way until World War I would reshuffle borders, bringing an end to 400 years of Ottoman rule over the Middle East.

Notes

1. When the Prophet Mohammed died in 632, his father-in-law Abu Bakr took over as the first caliph, or successor, leading the *ummah* (community of followers). Abu Bakr was succeeded by Omar, Uthman and then Ali, who was Mohammed's cousin and brother-in-law. The Sunni branch of Islam accepts the legitimacy of the first four caliphs whereas Shiite Muslims believe that Ali, as a relative of Mohammed, was the only rightful successor, and that only his descendants are rightful successors to Mohammed. While both Sunni and Shiite Muslims share the same beliefs, there are differences in religious practices of Sunnis and Shiites, and the split between these two streams remains divisive until today.
2. Michael Winter. "The Ottoman Occupation," in Carl Petry (ed.). *The Cambridge History of Egypt. Volume I: Islamic Egypt, 640–1517* (Cambridge, UK: Cambridge University Press, 1998), p.499.
3. Carl Petry, "The military institution and innovation in the late Mamluk period" in Carl Petry (ed.). *The Cambridge History of Egypt. Volume I: Islamic Egypt, 640–1517* (Cambridge: Cambridge University Press, 1998), p.480.
4. Petry. "The military institution and innovation in the late Mamluk period," p.482.
5. Carl Petry. *Twilight of Majesty. The Reign of the Mamluk Sultans Al-Ashraf Qaytbay and Qansuh Al-Ghawri in Egypt* (Seattle: University of Washington Press, 1993), p.214.

6. "The regulars suspected that al-Ghawri routinely located funds to pay his new corps, while claiming insolvency in the face of their own bonus requests." Petry. "The military institution and innovation in the late Mamluk period," p.482.

7. Petry writes in "The military institution and innovation in the late Mamluk period," p.473, that "Al-Ghawri moved beyond exigency to opportunism as he made mass-scale confiscation a reliable instrument to raise revenue."

8. Winter. "The Ottoman Occupation," p.496.

9. Khayrbak had already concluded a deal with Selim to betray his sultan. Winter. "The Ottoman Occupation," p.496.

10. Winter. "The Ottoman Occupation," p.495.

11. Petry. *Twilight*, p.224.

12. David Ayalon. *Gunpowder and Firearms in the Mamluk Kingdom: A Challenge to Mediaeval Society* (London: 1956), p.77.

13. Winter. "The Ottoman Occupation," p.498.

14. Winter. "The Ottoman Occupation," p.498

15. Petry "The military institution and innovation in the late Mamluk period," p.469.

16. Ayalon. *Gunpowder and Firearms*, p.127.

17. Ayalon, *Gunpowder and Firearms*, p.89.

18. Ayalon, *Gunpowder and Firearms*, p.89.

19. Ayalon, *Gunpowder and Firearms*, p.88.

20. M. A. Cook (ed.). *A History of the Ottoman Empire to 1730* (Cambridge: Cambridge University Press, 1976), p.74.

21. Petry, *Twilight*, p.227.

22. Mark Twain. *The Innocents Abroad* (1869), p.442.

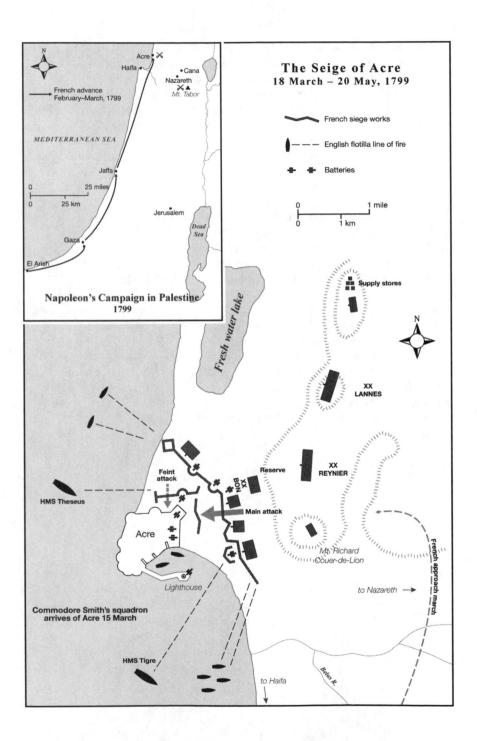

The Seige of Acre
18 March – 20 May, 1799

⌇⌇⌇ French siege works

◖ — — — English flotilla line of fire

✛ ✚ Batteries

0 _____ 1 mile
0 _____ 1 km

Napoleon's Campaign in Palestine
1799

N

← French advance
February–March, 1799

Acre ✕
Haifa •
• Cana
Nazareth •
✕ ▲
Mt. Tabor

MEDITERRANEAN SEA

0 _____ 25 miles
0 _____ 25 km

Jaffa •

Jerusalem •

*Dead
Sea*

Gaza •

El Arish •

Fresh water lake

Supply stores

**XX
LANNES**

**XX
REYNIER**

Feint
attack

Reserve

**XX
BON**

Main attack

HMS Theseus

Acre

*Mt. Richard
Couer-de-Lion*

to Nazareth →

French approach march

Lighthouse

**Commodore Smith's squadron
arrives of Acre 15 March**

HMS Tigre

to Haifa
↓

Belus R.

CHAPTER 11

PLAGUED BY DELAYS, AND DELAYED BY PLAGUE

NAPOLEON'S HOLY LAND CAMPAIGN, 1799

When it comes to Napoleon Bonaparte's defeats, the first ones that come to mind are usually the Russian campaign or Waterloo. Yet he was stung by his first defeat years earlier during his Holy Land Campaign, at Acre (Akko). After taking El Arish, Gaza and Jaffa, an overconfident General Bonaparte (as Napoleon was then known) declared: "The army of the Republic is master of the whole of Palestine."[1] This ambitious statement was a bit premature as his army's momentum ran out just two weeks later at the walls of Acre.

Bonaparte's campaign into Palestine was an outgrowth of his conquest of Egypt. When Bonaparte dreamt up the idea of a campaign into Egypt, his intention may have been to threaten rival England's interests in India, although this is unclear. There may also have been more than strategy at play. In proposing such a campaign, Bonaparte, who enjoyed reading military history and perhaps saw himself among the likes of Alexander the Great, may have been acting out his delusions of grandeur.[2] Whatever the reason, in 1798 the French set sail for Egypt in the first European military expedition against the Middle East since the Crusaders.

In July 1798, the 30,000 strong French Armée d'Orient landed and marched on Cairo. Local resistance was no match for the French army; three weeks after the French arrival, Egypt's Mamluks were defeated in a battle within sight of the pyramids. Egypt was theirs. But Bonaparte's jubilation was short-lived as only a few days later, an English fleet under Rear Admiral Horatio Nelson located the French fleet anchored at Aboukir Bay by Alexandria and destroyed it in the misnamed Battle of the Nile. Not only were the French cut off from reinforcement, but the battle left the British masters of the seas.

As Egypt was a suzerain territory of the Ottoman Empire, the French invasion was, in effect, an unprovoked attack on Ottoman hegemony. In response, the Turkish sultan allied with Britain and planned a two-fold assault to oust the French: a ground force sent from Damascus via Palestine, and once the weather improved, a second force being transported by sea from the island of Rhodes.

Rather than waiting for these forces to advance against him, Bonaparte seized the initiative with a preemptive march into Palestine. More than military maneuvering, the move into Palestine may have also been designed to forestall mutiny by his disgruntled army. With its fleet destroyed, the Armée d'Orient was stranded in Egypt. Knowing the dangers of an idle army, yet with desert to the west and south, east towards Palestine was the only option for keeping his forces occupied. Bonaparte planned to advance with his army into Palestine, seize the fortress of Acre (the region's de facto capital), defeat the Damascus army, and then hurry back to Egypt before good weather would allow the Ottoman Army of Rhodes to make its voyage and land in Egypt. Meeting these goals dictated that speed would be the critical element; Bonaparte announced the entire campaign would last one month.

The French army set out from Egypt on what was known as the Holy Land, or Syrian, campaign, with Bonaparte's carriage leading the way for some 13,000 infantry, cavalry, artillerymen and auxiliary, backed by 52 light cannon. On horseback, camel and foot, the Armée d'Orient began crossing the Sinai Desert towards Palestine.

Lead elements advanced from a forward base on February 6, 1799, with the rest of the army following. When they reached El Arish, they were surprised to find their route blocked by a fort defended by 1,500 Ottoman soldiers. This first encounter at El Arish would prove a precursor of the difficulties to come.

After the French took the village of El Arish, the entire Ottoman force sought refuge inside the fort. Having expected a clear route into Palestine, Bonaparte had lightened his army's load for the difficult desert journey by sending its heavy siege artillery by sea. Lacking the artillery necessary to topple the fortress walls, the French had no option but to lay siege—a time-consuming prospect.

While the French were making their preparations to besiege the fort, a 2,000-man force of Ottoman cavalry and infantry sent by Ahmed Jazzar, Syria and Palestine's local ruler, arrived to relieve the Ottoman force. Taking up a position to the rear, this force cut off the French army's option to retreat. But before they managed to move against the French, they were surprised by a French night attack with a deep flanking maneuver that circled behind and attacked their camp. The Turks were completely routed, although most of the men succeeded in escaping.

After the relief force was defeated, additional French forces arrived with field artillery. Once the guns were ready, the battery fired for a whole day until the fort's walls were breached, leading its commandant to surrender. Bonaparte was surprisingly lenient in his surrender terms: paroling the defenders on condition they not take arms against the French for one year. He would not have been so lenient had he known how this unexpected delay, from February 8 to 19, 1799, would impact the outcome of the entire campaign.

Setting off from El Arish, the French force continued its desert journey. By Gaza, their advance was challenged by 3,000–4,000 Ottoman cavalrymen. French cavalry and infantry charged the Turks, who gave way. The French performance was impressive as they had not had a decent meal nor drunk sufficiently for several days after getting lost in the desert.[3] When Gaza was taken, the French supplemented their arsenal with captured cannon and ammunition and replenished themselves with rations and water.

Proceeding up Palestine's coast, on March 3, 1799, the French arrived at the port city of Jaffa, which Bonaparte considered vital for his sea lines of communication with Egypt. Bonaparte deployed his forces around the city, with a blocking force stationed to the north along the Nahr al-Auja (Yarkon River). A French offer of surrender was refused. With its garrison of several thousand men backed by more than fifty cannon, Jaffa's defenders were confident they could withstand the French siege. The French set about preparing their siege works, making up for time lost at El Arish by positioning their artillery under cover of dense groves surrounding the town without wasting time digging trenches. Slowed by effective sallies from the garrison, French preparations took several days.

Before attacking on March 7, 1799, Bonaparte sent an envoy with a final offer for surrender. When the headless corpse of this envoy was thrown from Jaffa's walls, the French were riled up and raring to fight. They opened fire with their artillery and mortars in a bombardment that lasted several hours. The garrison put up a fight, with "lively and sustained fire," as Bonaparte described, but they were no match for the French.[4] By afternoon, Jaffa's southern wall was breached and deemed passable. Grenadiers—the army's assault forces—began storming through but were repulsed several times with heavy losses. Later, forces penetrated through breaches in the wall and through a large undefended passage they discovered next to their breach in the south of the city. Fanning out in the town's narrow lanes, the French overran Jaffa in a quick, violent battle. By nightfall, the French controlled the city.

Although it was common to sack a town that had refused surrender, at Jaffa the French soldiers went on a rampage. They plundered, looted, and killed as they went, leaving Jaffa ravaged. When order was restored, the French were angry to discover among the captured defenders Turkish troops paroled not three weeks earlier at El Arish—in violation of their parole terms. Lacking the resources to guard and feed them, and without ships to carry them back to Egypt, Bonaparte reasoned that he had no choice but to execute the prisoners, and some 2,000 to 3,000 Ottoman prisoners were killed.[5] With so many corpses, bubonic plague broke out in the city, which, with a hint of poetic justice, also affected the French, haunting them throughout the campaign.

Acre

Their advance sustained by the booty of supplies, cannon and ammunition, the French continued north towards Acre. Given his successes until that time, Bonaparte grew complacent and assumed Acre would similarly fall with relative ease. First seeing the city's protective walls and defensive towers from the Carmel Mountains above Haifa, Bonaparte sent a letter to Ahmed Jazzar recommending surrender, tempting Jazzar with promises of commerce and mutually beneficial relations.

Word of the atrocities committed at Jaffa had already made their way to Acre. While Bonaparte hoped this might intimidate the people of Acre into surrendering, Jazzar had no intention of capitulating. With no guarantee that surrendering would prevent a similar massacre, the French actions in Jaffa instead strengthened Acre's resolve.

The French reached the walls of Acre on March 18, 1799 and began their siege. Bonaparte soon discovered that Acre was in a different league to Jaffa. Not only was Acre situated on a peninsula jutting out into the Mediterranean Sea, offering protection on three sides by the British-controlled sea, but its walls, at 25–30 feet (8–9m) high, and an average of 5 feet (1.5m) thick, were of far better material and construction than those at Jaffa. The base of the walls—the primary target for breaching artillery—was even wider, and further protected by a dry moat. Toppling these walls would not be easy. Compounding the challenge, the French would have to make do without heavy guns. In a disastrous setback, the French heavy breaching, or siege, artillery, which Bonaparte had put aboard transport ships sailing to meet the French army at Acre, had been captured at sea by the British and turned over to Acre for use against the French. Left with only field artillery, Bonaparte would need to take the city by direct assault.

Given the circumstances, victory over Acre was far from guaranteed. Not only were the French without the cannon needed to knock down the walls, but Acre had become a proxy battlefield with France's chief rival, Britain. The delays experienced at El Arish and Jaffa had allowed time for the arrival of a British fleet under command of an old adversary of Bonaparte: British Commodore Sir Sidney Smith. Smith had been burned by Bonaparte six years earlier, when the French general, then an artillery officer, had used his guns to drive Smith's ships away from the besieged French port city of Toulon. Arriving at Acre just days before the French, Smith and his

friend Colonel Louis Phelippeaux, a French royalist during the revolution who had been a rival of Bonaparte since their days together in
the French War Academy, assisted Ahmed Jazzar and Acre's 5,000
defenders in hastily preparing defenses.

Were it not for the delays along the way, Bonaparte might have
marched into Acre; but when he arrived on March 18, Acre was being
brought into a condition to resist him. By the time the French were
fully deployed and ready to launch their first attack, Phelippeaux, an
expert in artillery and defenses, had had nearly two weeks to shore up
fortifications. Walls were reinforced, and some 250 artillery pieces—
including the heavy guns the English fleet had taken from the French
ships—had been positioned on the town's fortifications. As a further
defensive measure, underground passageways in the ancient Crusader
city were restored to be used as a means of escape inland in the event
the French penetrated the city walls.

When the first attack came on March 28, the town was in good
order to withstand assault, with nearly every point of approach
covered by at least two directions of fire. Crossing the dry moat under
enemy fire, the French assault forces found their siege ladders too
short to mount the walls and were forced to withdraw with heavy
losses. With this attack, Bonaparte finally understood that taking
Acre was going to take time.

While handicapped by the lack of siege artillery, the French did
have field artillery, supplemented by captured Turkish artillery. This
was one of the campaign's ironies: heavy cannon seized from the
French were defending Acre's walls while the French were firing
Turkish artillery at its former owners. The French light artillery, unable
to knock down Acre's walls, could be used for counter-battery and
harassing fire. To bring both their artillery and soldiers closer to more
efficient ranges, rows of trenches were dug parallel to Acre's walls.
Digging and manning these trenches was dangerous business. Constant
artillery fire from the walls and from the British ships at sea not only
demoralized the French, but also took its toll. The Turks, who excelled
in artillery marksmanship, had ironically been taught artillery techniques by French advisors.

Unable to topple Acre's walls with artillery, the French tried undermining them. Tunnels were dug in an attempt to cave the walls in,

to blow up their foundations or to gain entrance to the town underneath the walls. When the French were tunneling beneath the city's walls, Jazzar's forces dug counter-tunnels to disturb the French efforts. Acre's defenders made courageous sallies against the French trenches and tunnel works. Extra motivation was provided by a bounty Jazzar paid on each French head brought in. When these were displayed on the city's walls, it did little for the rapidly plummeting French morale.

While unable to break the deadlock at Acre, the French won a string of victories in Palestine's Galilee region—the most spectacular at Mount Tabor. The Turkish Army of Damascus, the ground forces dispatched by the Turkish sultan to drive the French away and retake Egypt, was crossing the Jordan River into Galilee. The French engaged the Turks throughout Galilee. At times, so many French troops were in the field that the siege of Acre was left in the hands of relatively few. The bulk of this Ottoman force—a motley mixture of Turks, Arabs (Bedouin), Albanians, Bosnians, Mamluks, Moroccans and Sudanese numbering some 25,000 cavalry and 10,000 infantry—had reached the Plain of Esdraelon (Megiddo, or Jezreel Valley) on April 13 and, joined by 7,000 locals, apparently planned to attack the French forces operating in Galilee and then those besieging Acre.

General Jean-Baptise Kleber—who Bonaparte would soon after entrust with ruling all of Egypt—was sent to Galilee to reinforce a small French force already operating there. When Kleber's combined force of 2,000 men came upon the massive Turkish force, he had no real option but to go on the offensive and attack despite being so vastly outnumbered—better on his terms than waiting for the Turks to decide the battlefield. In prior council with Bonaparte, it was agreed that the best approach would be a surprise night attack on the enemy camp by means of a deep flanking maneuver, like the one successfully executed at El Arish. This was not as preposterous as it sounds, for the professional French soldiers had already proven their mettle successfully fighting off elements of the Army of Damascus many times their number.

At Mount Tabor, poor timing in the night attack found the French forces revealed at daybreak of April 16 while still on the move maneuvering in order to attack the Ottoman camp. Kleber and his force came under attack by nearly the entire enemy host. Hastily preparing a defensive position, the French fought a desperate battle. Throughout the morning, the hopelessly outnumbered French, with only muskets and a few cannon firing grapeshot, withstood wave after wave of enemy cavalry charges and assaults. The disciplined French troops were managing to hold their ground, but surrounded and with ammunition running low, they knew there was no chance for victory against such odds. When all seemed lost, a cannon shot caught everyone's attention. Coming to the rescue in the nick of time—like the proverbial cavalry arriving to save the day—was a French relief force led by General Bonaparte himself. Perhaps after reconsidering the likelihood of Kleber's force single-handedly taking on nearly the entire Army of Damascus, and knowing that this Ottoman force had to be destroyed, Bonaparte opted to take them on in the open field rather than with his back to the sea at Acre.

Having approached undetected, the appearance of this fresh force at their rear—seemingly from nowhere—startled the Turks, who panicked and dispersed. "Terror seized the enemy ranks," Bonaparte wrote. "In an instant, this host of horsemen melted into disorder and headed for the Jordan. The infantry headed for the heights and the night saved them."[6] Lacking the necessary reinforcements to press their advantage, the French pursued the enemy as best they could. The battlefield was strewn with thousands of Turkish dead, and several villages were burned to punish the locals for joining the Turkish ranks. What had been a desperate situation was turned into a great victory.

Despite successes in the field, victory continued to elude the French at Acre. Each time Bonaparte sent his forces to breach the walls, Acre's defenders held their ground. Not one attempt created a true bridgehead into Acre. In one attack, the French succeeded in penetrating into the city. In the face of the French breakthrough, Jazzar's forces seemingly withdrew and the French thought they were finally gaining their foothold. But they had entered a carefully prepared ambush and were cut down with a hail of fire. As in all the attacks, there was heavy loss of life on both sides. Among the casualties were the French expatriate Phelippeaux on one side, and a number of Bonaparte's generals.

Bonaparte remained optimistic of victory, writing: "I shall rain down a great number of bombs and these, in such a confined space, should cause no small amount of damage. And when I have reduced Acre to rubble I shall go back across the desert and be ready to receive any European or Turkish army which . . . wishes to disembark in Egypt."[7]

Despite Bonaparte's sanguine outlook, Acre held the advantage of reinforcement and supply by sea. Late in the siege, the arrival of some 24-pounder heavy siege cannon brought overland allowed the French to renew attempts to knock through Acre's walls. Their arrival, however, was too late. A Turkish fleet with a relief force for the besieged city was due any day. Lacking reserves, and with ammunition for his heavy guns in short supply, Bonaparte understood he would not be able to overcome this additional challenge should the Turkish forces land. Preempting their arrival, Bonaparte ordered an eighth and final attack on Acre in hopes of taking the city on the eve of its relief. In this attack, the newly arrived artillery successfully breached the outer wall. When the grenadier assault forces penetrated, they were surprised to find themselves blocked by an internal wall secretly built under Phelippeaux's direction, and this attempt—like all the others—failed.

With this latest failure to take Acre, Bonaparte took stock of the situation at hand. His army was in a wretched state, with one-third of his men dead, wounded or sick. Morale was at a low ebb, as were supplies. His army simply lacked the wherewithal to take Acre. Adding to his troubles, there was unrest back in Egypt, and Turkish ships were preparing to transport the Army of Rhodes now that the weather was good enough for their voyage and landing. In short, he had run out of time, or—as Bonaparte later explained the defeat—luck. Though victory had many times seemed within his grasp, on May 10, 1799, Bonaparte lifted the siege of Acre.

Despite the military successes against the Turkish field forces, this was Bonaparte's first true failure. Even Bonaparte's tone in one of his dispatches suggests defeat. "I have been perfectly content with the army in circumstances and a type of war very new to Europeans" he wrote. "They have shown how real courage and military talent fears nothing and bears every sort of hardship. The result will be, we hope, an advantageous peace and greater glory and prosperity for the Republic."[8] On May 20, 1799—after 63 days outside Acre—the French forces began withdrawing.

There was jubilation in Acre. Ahmed Jazzar's steadfast determination had prevailed, saving Acre. Leaving nothing to chance, Jazzar took the precautionary measure of building up the city's defenses even though the French had withdrawn.

The vanquished Bonaparte last viewed the city that had proved his nemesis from atop the mountains above Haifa. Then, in an act of vengeance, the French set fire to everything in their wake, burning villages and crops—using a scorched-earth tactic that the Russians would use against them 13 years later.

To facilitate evacuation of the sick and wounded, all able-bodied men traveled on foot as far as Jaffa. Even Bonaparte gave up his own mount to a wounded man. Still not enough mounts were available for all the casualties, so the sick and wounded dragged themselves behind the retreating French columns. Bonaparte's secretary De Bourrienne described the scene: "The entire countryside was on fire. . . . We were surrounded by nothing but dying men. . . . To our right was the sea; to our left and behind us, the desert we were creating . . ."[9] Their pace slowed by both heavy cannon and the many invalids, at Tantoura (south of Haifa) it was decided to throw the artillery into the sea, freeing up more horses and mules to carry the injured and sick.

When the sick and straggling army arrived at Jaffa, Bonaparte saw what a burden the sick were imposing on his battered army. Even though he had earlier risked his well-being by visiting soldiers inflicted with plague in hospital, Bonaparte now ordered the poisoning of plague-infected soldiers and prisoners. When his chief medical officer refused, the general was forced to find someone less scrupulous to carry out this macabre task.

While claiming in his dispatches that only 500 of his men had been killed and twice that number wounded (versus 15,000 enemy casualties), his army was down some 4,000 to 5,000 men when it returned from its tortuous journey back to Egypt in mid-June. To mask the defeat, the return was given an air of victory and triumph; losses were downplayed by spacing out the arrival in Cairo of wounded generals and senior officers, and wounded soldiers carried captured Turkish flags. Three full days of celebration and festivities marked their return.

Bonaparte's army, though having taken a beating, joined with the forces left in Egypt and proved it was still in fighting form when it took on the Turkish Army of Rhodes. Arriving at Aboukir on July 12, the 15,000-man Army of Rhodes landed and quickly established a beachhead. Mustering all available men to fight, Bonaparte's force of 10,000 infantrymen and 1,000 cavalry met the Army of Rhodes and defeated it on July 25, 1799 at the Battle of Aboukir.

That threat defeated, Bonaparte returned to Cairo. His position in Egypt now more secure, Bonaparte turned his attention back to Europe. With forces arraying themselves for another major assault on France, Bonaparte saw it would be best if he were to return to France. Late that summer, he secretly departed, leaving General Kleber in charge. Not long after, Kleber was assassinated while Napoleon's stellar rise is well known.

The French Armée d'Orient was ultimately surrendered after a subsequent joint Ottoman/British attack. As part of the treaty arrangements, the French troops were transported back home on British vessels in March 1801—a humiliating end to Napoleon's grand dreams of conquest in the East.

Notes

1. Bonaparte's Despatches from Egypt, part IV.
2. David Chandler, *Campaigns of Napoleon* (Weidenfeld & Nicolson, 1966), pp.209–211.
3. Bonaparte's Despatches from Egypt, part IV.
4. Bonaparte's Despatches from Egypt, part IV.
5. Bonaparte reports 4,000 prisoners killed in his Despatches (Part IV). Gichon suggests 2,000, but cites other references to numbers ranging from 800–900 to 4,000. "Jaffa 1799," p.30.
6. Bonaparte's Despatches from Egypt, part V.
7. Bonaparte's Despatches from Egypt, part V.
8. Bonaparte's Despatches from Egypt, part V.
9. Shelly Wachsmann and Kurt Raveh. *An Encounter at Tantura with Napoleon*.

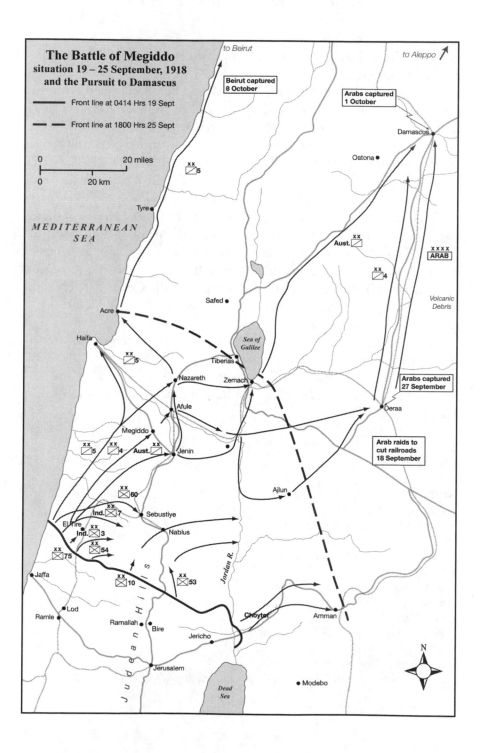

The Battle of Megiddo
situation 19 – 25 September, 1918
and the Pursuit to Damascus

——— Front line at 0414 Hrs 19 Sept

- - - - Front line at 1800 Hrs 25 Sept

0   20 miles

0   20 km

to Beirut

Beirut captured
8 October

to Aleppo

Arabs captured
1 October

Damascus

Oatona

XX
5

Tyre

Aust. XX

XXXX
ARAB

XX
4

*MEDITERRANEAN
SEA*

*Volcanic
Debris*

Safed

Acre

Sea of
Galilee

Arabs captured
27 September

Haifa

Tiberias

XX
5

Nazareth

Zemach

Deraa

Afule

Megiddo

Arab raids to
cut railroads
18 September

XX
5

XX
4

Aust. XX

Jenin

Ajlun

XX
60

Ind. XX
7

Sebustiye

El Tire

Ind. XX
3

Nablus

Jordan R.

XX
75

XX
54

Jaffa

XX
10

XX
53

Lod

Ramle

Ramallah

Bire

Choytat

Amman

Jericho

Judean Hills

Jerusalem

N

*Dead
Sea*

Modebo

CHAPTER 12

BY WAY OF DECEPTION

WORLD WAR I IN PALESTINE, 1917–18

British Commonwealth troops were finally in control of the heights commanding Gaza's approaches, and the city's defenses were on the verge of collapse. Some mounted forces had even penetrated into Gaza and were watering their horses. The battle seemed won; Gaza—gateway to Palestine—was almost theirs. Then orders came down to withdraw. Reactions ranged from shock to disbelief. One commander exclaimed: "But we have Gaza!" Tala Bey, Turkish commander of Gaza, was said to have laughed at the spectacle of seeing the victors pulling back.[1]

Unlike their colleagues bogged down in static trench warfare on the Western Front in Europe, the British Commonwealth forces in the oft-overlooked Palestine theater fought a mobile campaign involving some of the best strategizing of the war.

With the Allies' failure at Gallipoli in 1915–16, it became clear that the only way of forcing Turkey out of the war was through breaking its control of Palestine and Syria. As the Turks had been entrenched in these areas for some 400 years, prying open the Ottoman's hold on this territory would be no simple task.

When World War I began in August 1914, Turkey joined Germany and Austria-Hungary against the British Empire and other members of the Western alliance, which was known as the Triple Entente. Germany had taken an interest in the Ottoman Empire at the very end of the previous century and Kaiser Wilhelm II had established economic and military ties with the Turks. The relationship had grown to the point where the Germans effectively controlled the Turkish army. It was said Turks provided its army's brawn while the brains were supplied by Germany, which provided core services such as communications, transport, and air support.

Encouraged by its victory at Gallipoli, the Turks entertained notions of taking Egypt, especially the strategically important Suez Canal. Lifeline of the British Empire, the Suez Canal allowed British Commonwealth countries to supply Britain with men and resources for the war without exposing them to the dangers of attack by German warships and submarines in the Atlantic Ocean. The Germans supported the Turkish moves, as an assault on the canal would tie down a large number of British troops, siphoning off men and supplies from the main war effort in Europe.

Though vital to the defense of its Egyptian base of operations, the British considered the canal as an obstacle that protected Egypt. After the Turks moved across the Sinai Desert and made their first attempt to attack the canal in February 1915, the British view changed. After repulsing Turkish attacks, it was seen that rather than being a defensive barrier, the Suez Canal was an asset that needed to be protected. This was accomplished by moving the British Commonwealth Egyptian Expeditionary Force, or EEF, into the Sinai Peninsula. Their mission ultimately grew to include the capture of Palestine and beyond.

A success against the Turks would be a much-needed morale-booster for the British, whose forces were stalemated on the Western Front. But there would be no quick victory on the Palestine front, as the EEF's advance across the barren desert was contingent upon a supply of clean water.

Supplying an army in the desert—especially an army with horses—requires a well-developed supply network. Camels heavily laden with supplies followed on the heels of the fighting men, but this was not adequate to meet supply needs. Water was often in short supply, and only drinkable after boiling. The British set about building a railway and water pipeline as they proceeded eastward across the desert, with the construction setting the pace of the army's advance. As the front advanced, the pipeline of water was extended. After steadily advancing across the Sinai Desert, pushing the Turkish army back, the EEF reached Palestine's borders at the end of 1916.

"But we have Gaza!"

While some serious clashes had taken place between the two sides while the EEF advanced across the Sinai, particularly in a battle at Romani, the relative ease with which Sinai was taken from the Turks led General Sir Archibald Murray, commander of British forces in the Middle East, to believe his forces would also take Palestine with little difficulty. There was no clear dividing line between the opposing armies along the Gaza–Beersheba line; vast desert stretches—into which each army probed—separated them. Over-confident after recent successes, EEF commanders believed that if pressured, the Turks might pull out of Gaza, opening what was called the "gateway to Palestine." But the Turks had other ideas. Deployed in strength in the coastal fortress of Gaza, Turkish forces under German General Friedrich Kress von Kressenstein had no intention of relinquishing their positions.

General Murray determined to surprise Gaza and capture its garrison, estimated at 4,000–5,000-strong. Ringed with Turkish positions commanding the approaches, chief among them the formidable defenses at Ali Muntar Hill, and further protected by loose sand dunes and huge cactus hedges, Gaza would be no easy take.

Logistics limitations, allowing the forces to operate only one day ahead of its supplies, dictated that Gaza be taken in one day. Lieutenant General Sir Charles Dobell's Eastern Force, the name for the EEF forces operating east of the Canal, would have to quickly take Gaza in order to water its horses in the town's wells. The attack plan called for infantry to take Ali Muntar Hill early in the day as a springboard to a push from the south and southwest. Mounted forces were to circumvent Gaza to block a Turkish withdrawal or efforts to reinforce the position.

Through a series of night marches, with two infantry divisions numbering some 20,000 troops concealed from enemy air patrols by sand dunes and palm trees, the EEF avoided detection while advancing eastward. Major General A. G. Dallas commanded the infantry assaulting the positions at Ali Muntar. In the early hours of March 26, 1917 Dallas' force set out from their staging area southwest of Gaza. Their first challenge was crossing Wadi Ghuzzee, a dry watercourse, which cut across the terrain, with steep banks that could only be crossed at certain places. It was a black night, so traversing the wadi was no easy task. A dense fog rolled in from the sea in the pre-dawn hours, making navigation extremely difficult. While the fog protected the EEF's advance from detection by Turkish observers, it also caused disastrous delays in the attack plan.

When the fog lifted after six in the morning, there were further inexplicable delays in the infantry's progress. Mounted forces successfully penetrated deep into Turkish territory undetected, sealing off Gaza. Yet despite the time constraints so crucial to the operation's success, there was no sign of the infantry division tasked with taking prominent Ali Muntar Hill. It turned out they were still deploying south of Gaza preparing for the attack, and its commander could not be reached for some time. Poor communications and slow execution of orders down the chain of command plagued the operation, and would continue to do so throughout the day. When Lieutenant General Sir Philip W. Chetwode, commander of Eastern Force's advance troops, finally established communications with Dallas, he exhorted Dallas to get moving.

The attack on the Ali Muntar Hill area only got underway at noon under heavy Turkish artillery and machine-gun fire. The Turks had been alerted to the advance when one of their patrols encountered the attackers, resulting in a brief skirmish. Hearing shots, two German aircraft stationed nearby took off, spotted and strafed the host before flying back to raise the alarm. When the attack finally came, the well-concealed Turks manning positions on the high ground had an easy time cutting down the infantry advancing over the open country towards them. The EEF lacked adequate artillery support due to a shortage of ammunition, and what little they did have was missing its mark. Considered of secondary importance compared to the

Western Front, the Palestine front was receiving low priority in resource allocations.

Efforts to adjust the fire support to more relevant targets were slow, again due to communications. Despite these difficulties, the EEF infantry fought courageously and managed to make their way through the maze of cactus fields. By evening they had secured Ali Muntar Hill and driven the Turks from the high ground overlooking Gaza. The EEF's right flank was protected by a thin line of mounted troops.

With the delay in the infantry attack, it was decided shortly after noon to put the mounted forces to work exerting pressure on the Turks in an effort to accelerate Gaza's collapse. Originally slotted a secondary flank security role, the mounted forces were ordered to assault Gaza from the east. Again, orders took an excessive amount of time working through the chain of command, and it was not until day's end when all was ready for the attack to begin. The mounted forces fought their way through the Turks' rear lines and reached Gaza's streets by nightfall. "Every indication pointed to a rout and general surrender at any moment."[2] The battle seemed won; Gaza was almost theirs.

Then orders came down from General Dobell: Withdraw. There was shock and astonishment. One commander demanded to see the order in writing. Lieutenant General Harry Chauvel, commander of the Australia and New Zealand Mounted Division, epitomized the reaction with his exultation: "But we *have* Gaza!"

The troops in action did not have the benefit of reconnaissance reports from British airmen and cavalry patrols reporting Turkish reinforcements en route. While in retrospect the order for general withdrawal appears folly, at the time EEF command was seriously concerned about the Turkish relief force, unconvinced that they would be able to protect all their exposed flanks. Moreover, mounted forces deep behind Turkish lines desperately needed to water their horses. "Many horses had been 36 hours without water. It was, therefore, necessary to bring in the mounted divisions; and, it was then considered unsafe to leave the infantry on the captured ground with their flank exposed. . . . Thus we gave up the commanding position gained."[3]

With the cumbersome communications, EEF commanders were evidently not fully aware of actual developments in the field, with their infantry securely on Ali Muntar Hill and some of the mounted forces already watering their horses. Given the information available to them, the mounted divisions were ordered to withdraw and the infantry to quit Ali Muntar Hill—the position for which they had fought so hard, and for which they had paid the price of some 400 dead and 2,900 wounded—and establish defensive positions in the adjacent high ground for the night. It was with great consternation that they pulled back after what, for all intents and purposes, was a victory. The defeated Turks were amazed to see the EEF force withdraw.

Turkish reinforcements entered Gaza during the night. When EEF infantry tried to retake Ali Muntar the following day, they met stiff resistance and abandoned the effort, withdrawing during the early hours of March 28, 1917 and ending what would become known as the First Battle of Gaza.

"A Second Gallipoli"

Based on overly positive accounts of the attack in inaccurate dispatches to the War Office in London, such as General Murray's report of "a most successful operation. . ."[4] and exaggerated assessments of the relative ease with which Gaza could be taken in a second attempt, another attack on Gaza was authorized.

The mission again went to General Dobell. The attack plan he came up with built largely on "First Gaza": a frontal attack by infantry against the full strength of the Turkish position, with the mounted forces assaulting the flank. Learning from his first attempt, the general added a third infantry division to assist in dislodging the Turks from their positions. It was said that all soldiers involved, from commanders down to the troops, were convinced the plan would fail.

Beginning early in the morning of April 17, the EEF unleashed a punishing artillery bombardment on Turkish positions by field guns and naval vessels anchored offshore. Following the barrage, the infantry attacked Turkish lines, supported by six "landships," as the new battlefield innovation that came to be known as tanks were then known. But the Turks were ready. From German aircraft observations, the Turks were well aware of EEF preparations. They had reinforced their 20,000-strong garrison with ample machine guns and artillery, which were ranged to cover every immediate approach to their lines. Additional trenches had been dug and protected by barbed-wire obstacles.

When the attack came, the EEF was dealt a punishing blow. Nearly every attempt by infantry and mounted troops to reach Turkish lines failed. Tanks, used as portable machine-gun nests scattered along the front in advance of the infantry, proved magnets for Turkish fire, which knocked them out of action. The Turks held their ground and then counterattacked against the EEF's exposed flanks. German aircraft ruled the skies, strafing and bombing the attackers. There were some EEF successes, but none significant enough to affect the course of battle. When headquarters took stock of the failures after three days of fighting with no significant gains while suffering upwards of 6,000 casualties, the offensive was called off. British military command in London began referring to Gaza as "a second Gallipoli."

After twice resisting assaults on Gaza, the Turks began to doubt British military capabilities. Colonel T. E. Lawrence, better known as "Lawrence of Arabia," wrote: "The Turks . . . had been puffed up by successive victories to imagine that all British generals were incompetent to keep what their troops had won for them by dint of sheer hard fighting."[5]

The Turks reinforced their lines, ushering in a frustrating six months of static warfare. While the Turks dug in, changes were taking place on the British side. In a command shake-up, General Murray was removed from his post and replaced by General Sir Edmund Allenby, who arrived in theater in June 1917. His assumption of overall command of the Egyptian Expeditionary Force would teach the Turks that they had been wrong about British generals. Full of energy and purpose, Allenby drove and inspired his forces. "The Bull," as Allenby was known, reorganized the troops into a new force structure, inspected the entire front, personally reconnoitered the no-man's land separating the two armies and regularly visited his men along the front. In both a symbolic and practical move, he moved headquarters from Cairo to Sinai. His forces trained hard and drilled, regaining their morale. A few months after his arrival, Allenby was ready to attack along the entire front.

Allenby's arrival coincided with a greater commitment by the British War Office to the Palestine theater of operations, epitomized by Prime Minister Lloyd George's instructions to Allenby to take Jerusalem as a Christmas present for the British people. With the war in Europe bogged down in static trench warfare, Lloyd George knew the people needed a morale-booster. To accomplish this task, Allenby's arrival was accompanied by additional troops, munitions, heavy guns, equipment and supplies, including Bristol fighters, which would clear the skies of German aircraft.

While the EEF was busy training, the Turks continued to dig in. Gaza had become a fortified camp protected by lines of trenches reminiscent of the European front. Secure behind their defenses, the Turks were confident.

Even though Gaza was the Turks' strongest point, the EEF had twice attacked it head-on. Unable to break the Turkish grip on Gaza via conventional means, a clever plan relying on deception, surprise and speed was devised. A feint would be made at Gaza, quickly followed by a powerful thrust against the Turkish left flank deep in the desert at Beersheba—some 35 miles (60km) to the southeast— which the Turks thought unapproachable by a powerful force due to the distances involved and the lack of available water. Once Beersheba and its precious water supplies were secured, the EEF would then roll up the Turkish line towards Gaza. Though its lines were less developed around Beersheba, Turkish defenses had every advantage of observation. Situated in a shallow depression, Beersheba is surrounded by high ground that commands its approaches, especially Tel Sheva on Beersheba's eastern side—site of an ancient Canaanite city, which the Turks had fortified and entrenched with machine gunners. Strong Turkish defenses lay to the west and southwest of the town.

The plan posed a number of challenges. In order to be within striking distance of Beersheba, situated in the heart of the desert, great distances would have to be crossed over open country. This was overcome with a series of night marches, bringing forward overwhelming numbers of men and guns, backed by transport, all undetected by German aircraft. By night, the barren dry plains came alive with columns of men and horses. Water continued to pose the most serious hindrance. Allenby's plan hinged on one crucial point: capturing Beersheba's wells intact. The assault would need to be quick—lasting no more than one day—completed before the attackers' water supplies were exhausted.

An elaborate ruse was devised to convince the Turks that the main attack was on Gaza and the attack on Beersheba a mere feint. False army papers indicating "wrong positions for Allenby's main formation, a wrong direction of the coming attack, and a date some days too late" were allowed to fall into enemy hands."[6] The ruse was said to have been read by General Kressenstein himself, who believed it unquestioningly. That the Turks took the bait was evident from their work on Gaza's defenses to the detriment of preparations along the Beersheba line.

EEF infantry divisions were concentrated opposite Gaza's defenses. All began with a massive bombardment of Gaza on October 27, days before the actual assault. Joined by French and British naval vessels anchored offshore, EEF land- and ship-based artillery—aided by balloon observers—pounded Turkish trenches and artillery batteries. After serving earlier in the war on the Western front, Allenby "was full of Western ideas of gun powder and weight."[7] The attention on Gaza reaffirmed the belief that this is where the EEF would again strike.

After the last of their series of night marches towards Beersheba on the night of October 30, 1917, over 40,000 EEF troops were in position for the attack on Beersheba, which would begin the next morning. The plan called for the infantry to smash the town's defenses to the south and west while the mounted forces were to envelop the town and attack from the east, adding further pressure to the Turkish defenses as well as preventing Turkish reinforcement or escape, and being prepared to quickly secure the town upon capture.

In the early hours of October 31, Turkish trenches to the west and southwest of Beersheba were hit by a cruel artillery bombardment by more than one hundred guns. The first phase of the assault on Beersheba came after the artillery barrage, with two infantry divisions attacking Beersheba's western fortifications. As the EEF infantry advanced, Turkish machine guns raked the plain with heavy, accurate fire while German aircraft bombed and strafed the attackers. Infantry made their way forward and charged through the Turkish defenses, fighting with bayonets in savage hand-to-hand fighting until the Turks were driven from their positions at around 13:00.

After crossing difficult ground en route, the Desert Mounted Corps, recently created as part of Allenby's force reorganization, attacked strongly fortified Tel Sheva. Concealed Turkish machine guns and German aircraft dropping bombs and diving with machine guns blazing slowed the advance. The heavier than expected fighting delayed the plan for a combined infantry and mounted assault. Tel Sheva's defenses broke and fell by 15:00—far later than intended, threatening the entire operation, which hinged on capturing Beersheba's wells. Only one and a half hours of daylight remained, yet the wells—the pivotal element of the attack— remained in Turkish hands. More Turkish positions stood between the precious water and EEF forces. The mounted forces had ridden through the night and needed watering. It had been anywhere from 26–48 hours since their horses had last drunk water. When word got back to Allenby's headquarters that the force had been held up and was considering alternate watering options in the event that Beersheba's wells were not taken, Allenby reportedly said "water your horses in Beersheba tonight—no more than that, no less . . ."[8] With the next nearest available water twelve hours away, there really was no alternative. The horses' speed was the only hope of overcoming the last Turkish positions between the EEF and the wells. English Yeomanry cavalry had been detached for a covering role and were not readily available; the only option was the Australian Light Horse. A mounted force whose mobility and speed allowed them to cover great range, the Light Horse were infantry who rode horses for transportation but dismounted to attack; they were not cavalrymen. This did not stop Brigadier General William Grant of the 4th Light Horse Brigade from offering to take on the assignment of a mounted cavalry charge.

Despite the urgency, it was some time before the units were formed up for attack, for the men and horses had been dispersed as a protective measure against German air attacks. At 16:30, Grant led two mounted regiments against Beersheba's eastern defenses, advancing in the face of Turkish machine-gun fire. Brandishing their bayonets like cavalry swords, the Australian Light Horsemen—in what has been called one of the last great cavalry charges in history—charged the Turkish lines at full gallop. As the Turks discerned the horsemen through the clouds of reddish dust, they became very uneasy in the face of this surprise mounted advance, for they feared the cavalry. Turkish fire was largely ineffective. "Habitually, rifles and machine guns fire high at rapidly incoming targets and the less steady the soldiers the more is forgotten in sight correction."[9]

The light horsemen reached the Turkish lines, some leaping over the trenches on their way into town to secure the wells while others dismounted to engage the Turks in savage hand-to-hand combat. "You can't imagine Light Horsemen with bayonets . . . charging across the trenches and that sort of business to clean out the fort . . . it was just a matter of winding the whole show up then. We did finish up by watering in Beersheba that night."[10] The wells, so vital to the EEF, were captured intact, despite having being prepared for demolition.

The fall of Beersheba—which the Turks had considered an impenetrable position—made them uneasy about their ability to hold the entire sector. Germany's official observer, Gaston Bodart, noted in his report that "the position at Gaza, in consequence of this victory, now became untenable."[11] When a 70-strong EEF camel-borne raiding force sent to harass Turkish troops retreating from Beersheba cut the road south of Hebron, the Turks mistakenly thought Allenby's force was moving on Jerusalem via Hebron. They countered this perceived threat by pulling troops away from Gaza. With the EEF controlling Beersheba, they now threatened to outflank Gaza and choke its supply routes. However, water shortages north of Beersheba slowed the EEF's next moves. Attacks on Turkish positions continued against Gaza's left flank; the pressure on Gaza was mounting.

On the morning of November 2, 1917 EEF infantry captured Gaza's first line defenses. While they paused to consolidate their lines around Gaza, pressure was maintained by other units chipping away at the Turks' defenses until the Turks caved in and withdrew their forces, which pulled back and redeployed around Jerusalem.

With Gaza's left flank broken, the attack on the city was renewed at midnight on November 6, 1917. The EEF attack met little opposition, and the mostly abandoned city was taken the next day. This time, Gaza was unquestionably theirs.

By Way of Deception—Part II

It had taken three attempts—the last one involving an elaborate ruse—to finally break the Turks' hold on the Gaza–Beersheba line, unlocking the so-called gateway to Palestine. Now the Turks were on the run. After months suffering from heat and boredom while slowly pushing the Turks out of the Sinai desert in 1917, the British-led EEF troops were now in motion. With both Beersheba and Gaza captured and the Turks in disarray, it looked to General Sir Edmund Allenby as if he was on his way to quickly accomplishing his mission to "conquer the city of Jerusalem and bring about the downfall of the Ottoman in Palestine."[12]

The early days of November 1917 were characterized by days and nights of ceaseless activity as the EEF advanced rapidly, constantly fighting. The Gaza–Beersheba defensive barrier had been shattered; thousands of Turkish prisoners, heavy guns and supplies had been taken. But water shortages slowed the force, which was being pressed relentlessly by Allenby in an effort to achieve a massive Turkish surrender. Even the legendary Australian Light Horsemen, known at times to forgo their own needs in favor of watering their thirsty horses, had their limits. Despite their best efforts, the lack of water proved as much an enemy to the EEF as the Turks themselves. Turkish forces retreated, saved at times only by brave rear-guard holding actions by German machine gunners and Austrian artillerymen, who slowed Allenby's forces long enough to allow the Turks to retreat and redeploy.

Allenby's forces advanced up Palestine's coast, conquering the coastal plain as far north as Jaffa on November 16, and the following month reached the Nahr al-Auja (Yarkon River) and beyond, but water shortages foiled the British general's hopes of destroying the Turkish army in a *coup de grace*. Delivering British Prime Minister Lloyd George's request to capture Jerusalem as a morale-boosting "Christmas present for the British nation" would now require a slow campaign through Judea's hills.

The rapid advances on the open plains ended with the change in terrain. After withdrawing from Gaza, the Turks had managed to redeploy in the narrow passes and exposed ridges around Jerusalem. Flushing out the well-entrenched defenders would be a slow and tedious process. Geography dictated the assault would essentially be an infantry campaign, with machine guns, rifles and bayonets doing the brunt of the work. The infantry's task was complicated by a supply bottleneck, with only the main highway from Jaffa fit for wheeled transport, supplies and heavy guns.

Just as so much had depended upon it in the desert, water again had an impact on campaigning, this time in the form of rain. When the rains hit on November 19, Palestine, where seasons can change almost overnight, saw a complete shift in weather conditions. Bitter cold weather, for which the EEF was completely unprepared, set in. The combination of exposure and lack of sleep from constant fighting took its toll on the fighting men, and many became sick. Supplying the men on the front lines became even more difficult, with transportation grinding to a halt as all turned to mud.

Between the weather and the defensible mountainous terrain, the EEF's advance slowed to a crawl. When better weather returned, allowing transport to resume, the Turks' luck ran out. Trucks and thousands of camels and donkeys pressed into service moved supplies along the difficult Jaffa–Jerusalem road. With its supply network back in place, the EEF steadily flushed the Turks out of their defensive positions ridge by ridge, suffering heavy losses.

Another EEF force was moving up the southern approach to Jerusalem, from Beersheba towards Hebron. Out of respect for the holy places, EEF forces halted south of Hebron until learning it had been evacuated by the Turks, and then proceeded to the outskirts of Bethlehem, which was taken after it, too, had been abandoned. Jerusalem's southern approaches were now cut.

The final thrust against Jerusalem began on December 8 with a heavy artillery bombardment of Turkish positions west of the city. Allenby recounted: "The troops . . . pressed steadily forward. The mere physical difficulty of climbing the steep and rocky hillsides and crossing the deep valleys would have sufficed to render progress slow, and the opposition encountered was considerable."[13] When the EEF reached the Jerusalem–Nablus road, on which the city was now dependent for supplies, Jerusalem was in danger of being completely cut off. On the night of December 8, 1917, Turkish soldiers fled from the city towards Jericho and Nablus. The following morning, on December 9, Jerusalem's mayor delivered a formal letter of surrender. Jerusalem was surrendered to the EEF without a shot being fired within the city limits. The EEF moved in and established a perimeter around the city, although Turkish resistance sought to confine the EEF victory to just the city itself.

Jerusalem's capture became official with General Allenby's entrance to the city on December 11, 1917, which became famous for its simplicity. Riding a tall white horse, Allenby approached Jaffa Gate of the walled Old City along a route lined by representatives of the Allied forces. Forgoing the ostentatious entrance into the city that was becoming for a conqueror, the large, impressive figure of Allenby, with white hair and mustache, ruddy cheeks and protruding chin, dismounted out of respect, choosing not to ride over the stones on which Jesus had walked, and entered Jerusalem on foot, followed by his staff and guests. The ceremony itself, devoid of bands, flag-raising ceremony or other fanfare, was also a simple affair. Allenby stood on the steps of the historic citadel, or Tower of David, adjacent to Jaffa Gate, and pledged to maintain and protect the status quo in the holy places "according to the existing customs and beliefs of those to whose faiths they are sacred."[14]

Allenby's thoughts were likely on the mission that lay ahead, for Turks remained well entrenched throughout central and northern Palestine. Jerusalem had been taken as ordered, but the battle for Palestine was far from over. The British war cabinet ordered further operations, with the ultimate aim of capturing Damascus and Beirut.

With the ground too wet for movement beyond limited operations to secure his lines, Allenby saw there was no choice but for a break from major offensive operations. Across the Jordan, Colonel T. E. Lawrence was busy harassing the Turks with a band of Arab rebels and fomenting Arab rebellion against Turkish rule in support of the British war effort. Among the few indigenous groups who had not remained loyal to Turkey, Arabs in the Hijaz region (encompassing today's Saudi Arabia and Jordan) commanded by Emir Feisal, son of the Sharif of Mecca, attacked sections of the 800-mile (1,300-km) Turkish-built Damascus to Medina Hijaz railway line—lifeline of the 20,000 Turkish troops stationed south of Amman. Attacks on the railway had contributed to Jerusalem's capture by squeezing the Turks around Jerusalem as the EEF threat to the city had intensified.

More than just carrying out acts of sabotage, the Arab uprising attained some very real gains. Following their capture of Aqaba in July 1917, the Arab rebels began acting as Allenby's right flank. To mark their elevated importance in British eyes, Emir Feisal's army was put under Allenby's command, with the general responsible for their operations and equipment. Lawrence served both as Feisal's advisor and liaison officer to Allenby. The Arab uprising was estimated to have tied down or affected 40,000 Turkish troops and a good amount of their artillery, imposing a very real strain on Turkish fighting strength. "Their active revolt had been of immense advantage to the British in western Palestine. Without their cooperation, spasmodic and uncertain as it was, the force opposed to Allenby would have been substantially stronger, his right flank would have been always exposed to heavy pressure, the local Arabs might have been openly hostile, and the whole course of the campaign must have been seriously affected."[15] Not everyone held the same view. Colonel Richard Meinertzhagen, the intelligence officer who masterminded the ruse used to break the Gaza–Beersheba line, wrote in his war diary that Lawrence's Arabs were "a looting rabble" and "had little more than a nuisance value."[16]

Allenby planned a move on Jericho as a preliminary step towards a thrust across the Jordan River. By mid-February 1918, better weather and an improved supply situation opened the way to a renewed offensive. With EEF lines stretching across western Palestine from the coast to Jerusalem, Allenby could strike anywhere. Faced with such uncertainty, the Turks were forced to spread their forces thinly. As in many places, the force defending the Jericho route was not particularly strong. After a break of more than two months, the EEF renewed its offensive on the morning of February 19, 1918. EEF infantry backed by artillery advanced down the Jerusalem–Jericho road, with the right flank guarded by a force moving over mountain passes from Bethlehem towards the Dead Sea. Turkish defenses were concentrated on the main road, with additional forces deployed in the barren, rocky hills on its flank. The fighting moved quickly down to Jericho and the Dead Sea, the lowest point on earth. The situation on the flank was more difficult, where geography made for tough going over the precipitous hills. The Turks, well entrenched in the ridges, swept the EEF advance with machine-gun and artillery fire. But when the main EEF advance threatened to cut off their lines of communication, the Turks withdrew, evacuating even beyond Jericho, across the Jordan River or northward. Jericho, which the Turks had stripped of supplies and any booty of benefit, was taken on February 21, 1918, only two days after the offensive began, in a spiritual victory emulating that of Joshua and the Israelites. Though its capture offered little in material terms, it did open the door for operations across the Jordan River.

Allenby's focus shifted eastward. The Arab Northern Army, as Lawrence's Arab forces were known, was striking northwards, drawing Turkish forces away from Amman. Allenby sought to move against Amman, relieving pressure from the Arabs and allowing them to strike even further north, perhaps as far as a vital railway junction at Deraa (in modern-day Syria) that could affect the entire Turkish logistics system in the area. But the EEF's forays across the Jordan in the spring months failed. EEF troops crossing the Jordan River took a beating from the Turks, suffering heavy casualties. The plans to take Amman were abandoned—a setback for the EEF and a morale-booster for the Turks, who hadn't had much to be happy about since the early days at Gaza. A second foray across the Jordan similarly ended in withdrawal, with the Turks sending the EEF reeling. In a further setback for Allenby, large numbers of seasoned troops were pulled out of his theater of operations and hastily transferred to the Western Front. While failures, the two thrusts across the Jordan diverted Turkish troop strength eastward, a result that would greatly serve EEF efforts in the upcoming operation to dislodge the Turks from the rest of Palestine.

After the unsuccessful attempts on Amman, the EEF hunkered down in the Jordan Valley. Reinvigorated by their recent successes, the Turks became more aggressive—keeping EEF forward positions under regular artillery fire. The Desert Mounted Corps—champions of the earlier campaign in the desert and the capture of Beersheba and Gaza—was stationed in the Jordan Valley. Hot, dusty, and infested with flies by day and malaria-carrying mosquitoes by night, the Jordan Valley was a miserable posting for the mostly Australian and New Zealander mounted corps. Allenby knew the Turks were terrified of the horsemen and that they thought wherever they were, the EEF would next strike. This played into a larger plan Allenby was formulating to defeat the Turks in a *coup de grace* that would bring total enemy defeat in his theater of operations—the victory that had eluded him right after taking Beersheba and Gaza.

Building on the Turks' fear of the mounted forces, Allenby embarked on an ambitious plan to convince the Turks that his attack was to be to the east by means of a fictitious reinforcement of the mounted corps' Jordan Valley positions. In a masterful feat of deception, rumors were spread about plans for a renewed assault across the Jordan River. Troops marched down into the Jordan Valley by day and were trucked out at night. Dust was deliberately generated both to create the appearance of heavy activity and to make life difficult for Turkish observers. They went as far as to construct dummy horses of wooden frames covered with blankets. In actuality, the mounted divisions left the Jordan Valley, though leaving their camp intact to add to the deception. With all the "evidence" of reinforcement, Turkish observers could not discern the camp was empty. Aggressive air activity kept the EEF lines and rear largely free of enemy aerial observation. Air service overflights and Turkish deserters added to the intelligence information on Turkish dispositions, all of which confirmed the Turks had taken the bait. Convinced that the threat lay across the Jordan River, Turkish heavy artillery, dumps, stores and camps were all positioned and reinforced accordingly. Meanwhile, during the first weeks of September 1918, Allenby was massing artillery, infantry and mounted troops on Palestine's central Sharon plains, all without Turkish knowledge.

A confident Allenby visited his men, camouflaged among the Sharon region's orange and olive groves, his presence inspiring them. By midnight of September 18, 1918, with all the necessary elements in place, Allenby gave the green light. The operation began at 01:00 on September 19 with a bombing run by the single Handley-Page bomber in the theater. Targeting the Afula railway and communications junction, the aerodrome at Jenin and Turkish army commands at Nablus and Tulkarm, the attack wreaked havoc on Turkish communications just as the battle was to begin.

Before dawn, some 300 artillery pieces in the Sharon sector (running from coastal Arsuf inland) opened up on the Turkish lines. After the intense barrage softened up Turkish defenses, EEF infantrymen in their dome-shaped steel helmets, with fixed bayonets, crossed the open ground towards the Turkish trenches. The Turks resisted but the EEF infantry quickly punched through the Turkish lines, creating a breach they immediately set about expanding. A massive mounted force of 9,000 horsemen then charged through the gap the infantry had forced in the coastal sector and raced northward across the Sharon plain heading towards Galilee, with the objective of seizing Afula and Turkish headquarters in Nazareth before heading southeast down the Plain of Esdraelon (Megiddo, or Jezreel Valley) to Beisan (Beit Shean) on the Jordan River, some 80 miles (130km) from where they had begun their advance. This would be accomplished in a mere 34 hours. Turkish forces astride the breach were to be of no concern to the horsemen; the infantry would take care of them. The horsemen were instructed to remain focused on their mission of reaching Galilee to encircle the Turks.

Allenby's plan, which built on the superiority in both quality and quantity of his mounted forces, was for the infantry to drive the Turkish forces back and into the horsemen's hands, who would be waiting to collect them in their dragnet. The Turks had actually been correct in their belief that the mounted forces they feared so much would spearhead Allenby's next move, only they believed these forces were still deployed in the Jordan Valley.

The mounted forces raced northward towards their objectives. Time was of the essence as two critical mountain passes through the Carmel Mountain range to the Plain of Esdraelon in Lower Galilee had to be traversed by the horsemen before the Turks could organize resistance which could cause delays that might endanger Allenby's entire plan.

When a Turkish force was spotted en route from Afula to block the pass leading to that town, the horsemen pressed their advance, travelling the long, narrow, winding pass in the dark. In the morning, they attacked the unsuspecting Turkish unit as they were deploying, eliminating that threat. The way to Afula was cleared, and they went on to capture the town.

General Otto Liman von Sanders, who had taken over command of all Turkish and German forces in Palestine in February 1918 following the loss of Jerusalem and other defeats, followed the attack from his headquarters in Nazareth. Sanders was keeping track of the EEF breakthrough on the Sharon plain but, not realizing that Galilee was teeming with EEF mounted forces, he did not fear immediate attack. When EEF cavalry rode into Nazareth at dawn on September 20, they occupied most of the town without event. When some resistance was organized, the horsemen pulled back, allowing Sanders the opportunity to escape in his pajamas.

With such a rapidly moving advance, EEF generals criss-crossed the country in their cars, staying forward to keep abreast of rapidly changing events. Air service flights and new radio communications technology helped in coordinating the multiple forces involved and following events on the ground in this highly mobile environment.

On the Turkish side, the situation was not clear at all. EEF infantry was attacking across the width of the country, up the Sharon plain and in the hills astride Nablus. Without the benefit of telephone and telegraph connections, Turkish commanders had little access to situational reports other than the often-incoherent reports from soldiers fleeing the EEF onslaught.

British observer W. T. Massey wrote: "Our progress during September was rapid, and the extent of our advance, on a very wide front, is so great that it may be the impression at home that we were weakly opposed. That would be wholly wrong."[17] It wasn't that the Turks did not resist; they were simply outclassed. Allenby's plan had so completely fooled the Turks that the attack had come as a complete surprise. When Turkish troops realized their rear lines were swarming with EEF mounted forces, they correctly feared they were being cut off. Panicking, they began fleeing while they still could, which fit nicely into Allenby's plans.

Within only two days, the Turkish retreat deteriorated into a rout, assisted by EEF air service and cavalry attacks on retreating enemy columns. The battered Turks were more than happy to surrender when they fell into Allenby's cavalry cordon. Allenby was said to have been so certain of success that situation updates he received in the midst of the battle of various victories were almost old news to him.

Allenby's report of September 20, 1918 noted: "On the north our cavalry, traversing the Field of Armageddon, had occupied Nazareth, Afule, and Beisan, and were collecting the disorganized masses of enemy troops and transport as they arrived from the south. All avenues of escape open to the enemy, except the fords across the Jordan between Beisan and Jisr-ed-Dameer were thus closed."[18]

The Turks evacuated the coastal cities of Haifa and Acre (Akko), and Allenby's forces moved in and took both without a fight. The Galilee town of Safed, already clear of Turks, was also taken. The next step was to capture Tiberias and Zemach on the Sea of Galilee, opening the way for an advance on Damascus. With these last objectives secured, the so-called Battle of Megiddo came to an overwhelmingly successful end. A line across the width of Palestine, from Haifa–Nazareth–Tiberias had been secured; all Turkish railway and road lines of communication were now in EEF hands; some 70,000 prisoners had been taken; countless guns, transport and other equipment were destroyed. The Turkish 7th and 8th Armies had by and large been destroyed, and few Turkish troops remained between Allenby's new lines and Damascus. "Allenby concluded proudly and with truth: 'Such a complete victory has seldom been known in all the history of war.'"[19] Even Gaston Bodart's official German report concurred, calling the victory "beyond doubt the most complete victory of the Entente in the war . . ."[20]

But the job was not yet complete. Allenby ordered the advance to reach Damascus. Forces were sent across the Jordan River to capture Amman and up the Golan Heights to Kuneitra as a prelude to a move against Damascus. On September 30, 1918, Damascus was taken, although not before the Turks and Germans fled. French forces, recently contributed to the theater so their country could have a say in the post-war settlement, occupied Beirut on October 6, 1918.

The advance pressed a further 200 miles to Aleppo, which was taken on October 26, 1918. The Turks finally sued for an armistice, which was agreed to on October 30, bringing the war in the theater to an end. On November 11, 1918, an armistice was signed with Germany, ending what became known as the war to end all wars.

In post-war arrangements, Palestine became a British protectorate under League of Nations Mandate, while Syria came under French control. The British, initially welcomed as liberators in Palestine, soon found themselves at odds with the Jewish population. A slew of contradictory and conflicting British wartime promises to both Jews and Arabs also came to light, planting the seeds for today's Arab–Israeli conflict.

Notes

1. Steven Allan. "Gaza: The Unsurrendered City." *ERETZ Magazine* (Issue 49, November–December 1996), pp.36–41, 63: p.40.
2. H. S. Gullet. *The Australian Imperial Force in Sinai and Palestine—1914–1918.* (Queensland: University of Queensland Press, 1923), p.282.
3. Sir M. G. E. Bowman-Manifold. *An outline of the Egyptian and Palestine campaigns, 1914 to 1918* (Chatham: W. Y. J. Mackay & Co., 1922), p.31.
4. Gullet. *The Australian Imperial Force in Sinai and Palestine*, p.296.
5. T. E. Lawrence. *Seven Pillars of Wisdom* (Penguin Books, 1926), p.392
6. Lawrence. *Seven Pillars of Wisdom*, pp.393–4.
7. Lawrence. *Seven Pillars of Wisdom*, p.330.
8. http://www.jcu.edu.au/aff/history/net_resources/ellwood/ellwood10.htm
9. David L. Bullock. *Allenby's War: The Palestine-Arabian Campaigns 1916–18* (Blandford Press, 1988), p.75.
10. http://www.jcu.edu.au/aff/history/net_resources/ellwood/ellwood10.htm
11. Bodart, Gaston. "Report on the Fall of Jerusalem, 9 December 1917," in Charles F. Horne (ed.). *Source Records of the Great War, Vol. V* (National Alumni, 1923), www.firstworldwar.com/source/jerusalem_bodart.htm (accessed March 14, 2011).
12. Allan. "Gaza: The Unsurrendered City," p.37.
13. Allenby, Sir Edmund. "The Fall of Jerusalem," in Charles F. Horne (ed.). *Source Records of the Great War, Vol. V* (National Alumni, 1923), www.firstworldwar.com/source/jerusalem_allenby1.htm (accessed March 14, 2011).
14. Allenby, Sir Edmund. "The Fall of Jerusalem," in Charles F. Horne (ed.). *Source Records of the Great War, Vol. V* (National Alumni, 1923), www.firstworldwar.com/source/jerusalem_allenby1.htm (accessed March 14, 2011).
15. H. S. Gullet. *The Australian Imperial Force in Sinai and Palestine—1914–1918.* (Queensland: University of Queensland Press, 1923), p.659.
16. Colonel R. Meinertzhagen. *Middle East Diary* (London: The Cresset Press, 1959), p.41.

17.Massey, W. T. "Allenby's Progress," in Charles F. Horne (ed.). *Source Records of the Great War, Vol. VI* (National Alumni, 1923), www.firstworldwar.com/source/allenby_massey.htm (accessed March 14, 2011).
18.Allenby, Sir Edmund. "The Battle of Megiddo," in Charles F. Horne (ed.). *Source Records of the Great War, Vol. V* (National Alumni, 1923), www.firstworldwar.com/source/megiddo_allenby.htm (accessed March 14, 2011).
19.Chauvel, p.173.
20.Bodart, Gaston. "The Fall of Turkey," in Charles F. Horne (ed.). *Source Records of the Great War, Vol. V* (National Alumni, 1923), www.firstworldwar.com/source/turkey_bodart.htm (accessed March 14, 2011).

British General Edmund Allenby, Commander of British forces in Palestine during World War I, rides a horse alongside the walls of the Old City of Jerusalem in December 1917. Jerusalem was surrendered to the British-led Egyptian Expeditionary Force on December 9, 1917 without a shot being fired in the city limits. Allenby had been asked by British Prime Minister Lloyd George to capture the holy city as a Christmas present for war-weary England. (Eric Matson, Israel Government Press Office)

Mounted Australian soldiers leading Turkish prisoners. The legendary Australian Light Horsemen had more than proven their mettle in breaking the Ottoman hold on the Gaza-Beersheba front, and would continue to carry out crucial roles in operations against Ottoman forces. (Eric Matson, Israel Government Press Office)

Yad Mordechai before the onslaught. Named after Mordechai Analevicz, the 22-year-old leader of the 1943 Warsaw Ghetto uprising against the Nazis, the kibbutz stood in the way of the Egyptian thrust toward Tel Aviv in May 1948. A number of the collective farm's members were Holocaust survivors who had made their way to Palestine as illegal immigrants and now stood ready to defend their new home. (Courtesy of Kibbutz Yad Mordechai Archive)

Guardhouse with barbed wire. Kibbutz Yad Mordechai was certainly not prepared to withstand a thrust by the Royal Egyptian Army with infantry brigades, heavy artillery, tanks, and armored units, supported by an air force. Courtesy of Kibbutz Yad Mordechai Archive

Egyptian howitzers in action against Yad Mordechai, footage from Egyptian film. (Courtesy of Kibbutz Yad Mordechai Archive)

Egyptian infantry advance on Yad Mordechai, footage from Egyptian film. (Courtesy of Kibbutz Yad Mordechai Archive)

Yad Mordechai defenses. Bren Gun. Yad Mordechai's fortifications consisted mostly of trenches and sandbag-reinforced bunkers. With a small arsenal of light weapons and hand grenades, just over 100 defenders held off a brigade-size Egyptian force. (Courtesy of Kibbutz Yad Mordechai Archive)

Yad Mordechai, completely destroyed. (Courtesy of Kibbutz Yad Mordechai Archive)

Yad Mordechai's damaged water tower, seen after the kibbutz was retaken. Egyptian artillery used the kibbutz's water tower to range their guns. The tower was hit repeatedly, and precious water streamed from holes. The collapsed tower remains to this day, riddled with holes from the 1948 shelling.
(Courtesy of Kibbutz Yad Mordechai Archive)

Yad Mordechai following recapture by Israeli forces.
(Courtesy of Kibbutz Yad Mordechai Archive)

The shore Battery at Ras Nasrani prevented Israeli or Israel-bound shipping from entering the Gulf of Eilat. Notice barrel has been spiked after capture. (Israel Government Press Office)

After being dropped deep into Egyptian territory on October 29, 1956, Israeli paratroopers prepare trenches and clean their weapons at their deployment just outside Mitla Pass. (Avraham Vered, Israel Government Press Office)

Light aircraft helped maintain communications with IDF troops engaged deep in the Sinai. (Israel Air Force History Dept)

Southern Command Chief of Staff Lieutenant Colonel Rehavam "Gandhi" Zeevi flew out in a Piper Cub the morning of October 31, 1956 to meet Paratroops commander Ariel Sharon for an on-site assessment. Zeevi stressed the need to avoid unnecessary operations in order to minimize casualties, but authorized Sharon to dispatch a patrol to reconnoiter Mitla Pass. (Israel Air Force History Dept)

IDF paratroopers on a practice jump from an Israel Air Force C-47 Dakota. (Israel Air Force History Dept)

The Golan Heights are a formidable natural barrier. The Syrians had established a network of heavily fortified positions along the border, with all possible routes of attack mined and covered by pre-ranged firing positions. Dug into the rough volcanic basalt was a Soviet-designed defensive network that was nearly impervious to air and artillery attack. (Moshe Milner, Israel Government Press Office)

The assault on Tel Faher. Making their way up the twisting route to Tel Faher, the Israeli infantrymen had to cross dense layers of barbed wire and a minefield before reaching Tel Faher's trenches and bunkers. (Israel Defense Forces Archive)

The Golani attack on Tel Faher. With the Israeli attack plan in shambles, communications confused, its tanks knocked out of action, and the few remaining halftracks drawing heavy fire, the Israelis decided to dismount and continue their assault on foot. (Israel Defense Forces Archive)

Tel Faher's reinforced bunkers and pillboxes, some cut into the rock, were interconnected via rows of concrete-lined communications trenches. Manning the positions and dugouts was a company from the Syrian 187th Infantry Battalion armed with anti-tank guns, recoilless rifles, heavy machine guns and mortars. (Israel Defense Forces Archive)

Israeli M-3 Halftrack knocked out of action during the advance on the Golan. With the Syrians' advantageous firing positions, antitank fire targeted Israeli armor with great effectiveness. None of the Israeli tanks made it up to Tel Faher, and more than half the halftracks were damaged or stuck on the attack route. (Israel Defense Forces Archive)

Specially improvised bulldozers cleared the way for the armored columns to advance. Combat engineers were at the forefront, removing mines and carving a path for the tanks while under heavy fire. (Israel Defense Forces Archive)

IDF forces in action by Tuwafik. In the southern Golan Heights, Israeli tanks and mounted infantry fought their way up the treacherous, winding mountain road, breaking through the Syrian defenses at Tuwafik. Paratroopers helicoptered ahead behind Syrian lines, but for the most part found only isolated pockets of Syrian resistance. (Israel Defense Forces Archive)

Damaged IDF tank under repair. Technical teams rapidly returned damaged tanks to service. (Israel Defense Forces Archive)

Israeli AMX-13 light tanks during a short stop on the Syrian frontier before going into action on the Golan Heights. (Ram Lahover, Israel Government Press Office)

Memorial to the Golani Brigade soldiers who fell at Tel Faher, which was renamed "Golani Lookout." (Israel Defense Forces Archive)

IDF Centurion tanks moving into positions for a counter-attack on the Golan Heights. The fresh Israeli reserve units halted the near–and, in some cases, actual–retreat of what remained of their front-line forces and set about checking the Syrian advance. By midnight on day two of the war, the reserves had managed to stabilize what had been a disintegrating front. (David Rubinger. Israel Government Press Office)

IDF convoy moving northwards past a destroyed Syrian tank on the Golan Heights. Hundreds of wrecked and burnt Syrian tanks and armored vehicles and other vehicles littered the landscape. (Zeev Spector, Israel Government Press Office)

Syrian T-62 tanks and bridging equipment knocked out by the Israeli anti-tank ditch. Syrian mine-clearing tanks and bridge-layers led the way to overcome the Israeli obstacles, like the 20 mile (30km)-long anti-tank ditch along the border from Mount Hermon to Rafid, an obstacle Syrian armor had to cross under fire from Israeli tanks positioned behind ramparts. (Eitan Haris, Israel Government Press Office)

Syrian T55 and T54 tanks knocked out of action on the Golan Heights. (Menashe Azouri, Israel Government Press Office)

IAF F-15 "Baz" from the Knights of the Twin Tail Squadron credited with downing 4 Syrian aircraft. Between June 7–11, 1982 IAF F-15s downed 34 Syrian aircraft while the F-16s surpassed them with 46, decimating the Syrian Air Force. (Israel Air Force History Dept)

Destroyed Syrian air defense ZSU-23-4 "Shilka" antiaircraft quadruple-barrel 23mm gun vehicle. With its integrated radar, this highly capable weapon system could detect and hit low-flying aircraft in a two-mile range with a wall of fire, making it ideal for protecting Syria's SAM sites.
(Israel Air Force History Dept)

IAF C-2 Kfir of the 1st Fighter Squadron taking off from Hazor Air Force Base for a mission over Lebanon. The Kfir is armed with AIM-9D Sidewinder air-to-air missiles, 500-lb Mk.-82 bombs, and jettisonable fuel tanks. (Israel Air Force History Dept)

E-2C Hawkeye airborne early warning (AEW) command and control aircraft gave the Israelis an advantageous aerial battlefield picture. Packed with powerful computers, situational displays and secure communications, the Hawkeye is capable of detecting and assessing threats from approaching enemy aircraft over ranges of about 300 miles—more than enough to peer into Syria. Operators tracked Syrian aircraft as they took off from their airbases and vectored F-15 and F-16 fighters to intercept them. (Moshe Milner, Israel Government Press Office)

CHAPTER 13

ISRAEL'S "MAGINOT LINE"

1948 WAR OF INDEPENDENCE

"Go and rest," Colonel Nahum Sarig, the *Palmach*'s commander of the southern Negev region, told them. "You all deserve it."[1] After six days holding up an Egyptian brigade-size force, the fighters of Kibbutz Yad Mordechai certainly did deserve a break.

In May 1948, Egyptian media trumpeted news from Kibbutz Yad Mordechai as the capture of "one of the fiercest and most powerful strongholds of the Zionist settlements, built according to the most modern defense plans."[2] Dubbed a "Maginot Line," it was described as having two-story-high heavy-gun posts and "surrounded by a trench three feet deep—after ten steps there was another trench five feet deep and still further on one six feet in depth. The final defense line was electrified barbed wire."[3]

The description was far-fetched. Yad Mordechai's fortifications were far more humble, consisting mostly of trenches and sandbag-reinforced bunkers. With those simple defenses and a small arsenal of light weapons and hand grenades, just over 100 defenders held off a brigade-size military force from May 18 to 23, 1948, buying vital time that the fledgling state of Israel needed in the desperate first days of Israel's War of Independence (also known as the 1948 Arab–Israeli War). For that, the battle has been called one of the most decisive of the war.

The conflict officially began with Israel's declaration of statehood on May 14, 1948. Half a year before, on November 29, 1947, the United Nations passed a resolution calling for the partition of the British Mandate of Palestine into separate Jewish and Arab states. The so-called Partition Plan was accepted by the Jews and rejected by the Arabs. Determined to prevent the establishment of a Jewish state in Palestine, the armies of Egypt, Syria, Transjordan, Iraq and Lebanon attacked the day after Israel declared independence.

Kibbutz Yad Mordechai, a collective farm situated just over a kilometer from the Gaza Strip on the main road leading north, stood in the way of the Egyptian thrust toward Tel Aviv. The settlements—especially those on the frontiers—were being counted on by the *Haganah*— the pre-state underground army that, upon statehood, became the Israel Defense Forces (IDF)—to be centers of resistance, holding out against the expected onslaught. All able-bodied Jewish men and women in Palestine belonged to the *Haganah*. Originally a loose structure of local defense groups, the *Haganah* had grown into a large organization charged with the defense of Palestine's Jewish settlements. With its limited forces and equipment, the *Haganah* relied on every Jew to stand and fight.

Kibbutz Yad Mordechai

Kibbutz Yad Mordechai was named after Mordechai Analevicz, the 22-year-old leader of the 1943 Warsaw Ghetto uprising against the Nazis. A number of its members were Holocaust survivors who had made their way to Palestine as illegal immigrants after World War II, and now stood ready to defend their new home. Defensive preparations for the kibbutz were organized by Grisha Zilberstein, who was in charge of headquarters and disposition of manpower and arms, and Munio Brandvein commanded the defensive positions. A command post was built with communication links to 10 sandbag-reinforced outposts on the kibbutz 1.8 mile-long (3km) perimeter, each to be manned by a force of three. The kibbutz strongpoint was a pillbox built to the south, some 1,000 feet (300m) outside the perimeter fence.

Yad Mordechai's defensive force consisted of fewer than one hundred men: a mix of kibbutz members and newly arrived refugees from Europe being housed at the kibbutz. Its arsenal included antipersonnel "Shoe Mines" planted in front of the defensive posts, one PIAT antitank weapon with three rounds, a pair of 2-inch mortars with 50 shells, one Browning .30-caliber machine gun, one German-made light machine gun, four submachine guns, 37 rifles and about 400 hand grenades, supplemented by Molotov cocktails. With that, the defenders were expected to hold off several months of sporadic attacks by lightly armed Arab irregulars. That was nothing new, as the kibbutz had already faced such assaults. Yad Mordechai had been isolated and, at times, cut off completely during the spring 1948 "battle of the roads," when local Arabs blocked the routes connecting Jewish settlements, effectively putting them under siege.

Yad Mordechai was certainly not prepared to withstand a thrust by the Royal Egyptian Army with infantry brigades, heavy artillery, tanks, and armored units, supported by an air force. The new Israeli state's defensive strategy was built on the premise that Egypt would largely sit out the war. Initially intending not to intervene in the conflict, Egypt was almost forced to enter it due to competing interests and rivalries. Fearing that Transjordan's British-trained and -led Arab Legion—the best force in the region—would seize the lion's share of liberated Palestine and gain prestige, Egyptian King Farouk committed some 10,000 men against Israel in a two-pronged attack. One column moved towards Beersheba, planning to continue on to Jerusalem, while the second headed north up the coastal route, expecting to reach Tel Aviv within days. With friendly Arab villages along the way, the road to Tel Aviv would be virtually clear once the border settlements were passed.

The Israeli Palmach (an abbreviation for *"Plugot Machatz"* or Strike Companies of the *Haganah*) left a force of 16 men at Yad Mordechai, supplementing the kibbutz's strength and arsenal with its rifles and two British Bren .303-inch light machine guns. Field commander Brandvein spoke of the kibbutz's important strategic location: "Here we sit on the main road between Cairo and Tel Aviv. We are a barrier. You see how we have been able to cut off Arab traffic. If this place is captured, the Egyptian army can go straight north to the center of the country."[4] Palmach commander Nahum Sarig echoed those sentiments, writing that "the fighters knew that the battle wasn't only for Yad Mordechai but also for Tel Aviv and the entire country."[5]

Planning on penetrating deep into Israel, the Egyptian forces required secure lines of communication, to which Yad Mordechai, sitting alongside the main road, posed a potential threat. After unsuccessfully attacking two Jewish settlements further south, the Egyptians saw that it would be a mistake to attack every one along the way. Yad Mordechai's location, however, dictated that it could neither be bypassed nor merely contained—the Egyptian command ordered it to be taken. Soldiers of the Egyptian army's Seventh Brigade moved in, and the 1st Battalion was charged with taking the kibbutz.

While the kibbutz was implementing its defense plan on the evening of May 18, 1948, a pair of Royal Egyptian Air Force (REAF) Supermarine Spitfires strafed and bombed it. Faced with the reality of imminent attack, the Palmach evacuated 70 children and 42 others from the kibbutz, including children's caretakers, pregnant women, mothers with babies, and the sick. One hundred and thirty people remained: the kibbutz members (including 30 women) and the small Palmach contingent. The women prepared refreshments for the men in the positions and helped care for the wounded. Three women also served as runners after communications were knocked out by Egyptian artillery, and one held a command position in the trenches.

The Egyptians' first serious assault began on the morning of May 19. Egyptian aircraft dropped incendiary bombs, setting off fires throughout the kibbutz. Then their artillery, situated a few kilometers back, opened fire, using the kibbutz's water tower to range their guns. The tower was hit, and precious water streamed from holes caused by shell fragments (The collapsed tower remains to this day, riddled with holes from the 1948 shelling). Directed by a spotter plane, Egyptian 25-pounder field guns, 6-pounders and mortars bombarded the entire kibbutz in a methodical pattern for four hours. The only lull came after the Egyptians dropped leaflets announcing an hour-long truce for the kibbutz to surrender. When the hour passed, the bombardment resumed.

The Egyptians directed particularly heavy fire at the pillbox, making their intentions quite clear. Blocking their advance from the south, the pillbox would need to be taken if the Egyptians were to make an infantry assault on the kibbutz. The seven men manning the pillbox followed the Egyptians' progress through binoculars. With armored cars providing cover fire, Egyptian soldiers began traversing a deep ravine known as a wadi, and then advanced toward the pillbox. After patiently waiting for them to come within effective range, the men in the pillbox opened fire. Riflemen picked off the Egyptian officers while a Bren gun fired into the ranks. The attack dissolved into confusion and the Egyptians retreated, seeking cover. After regrouping, the Egyptians came at the pillbox a second and third time. Both times, they broke and fled in the face of carefully directed fire from their objective.

With three infantry thrusts defeated, the Egyptians renewed their artillery barrage on the pillbox, as if to exact revenge. Fires broke out in the fields between the pillbox and the kibbutz, leaving the men inside feeling their isolation. When Egyptian infantry came at them a fourth time, the defenders prepared grenades and allowed the attackers to approach, nervously waiting as the Egyptians came closer and closer. When the order came, each man threw his grenade and opened fire. Some soldiers took cover behind fallen comrades, while others fled. A few Egyptians, however, managed to probe around the pillbox and approached from behind, cutting through its wire defenses. The situation in the pillbox had become grave. Surrounded, with only a few grenades remaining, their Thompson submachine gun out of ammunition and the Bren firing only single shots, the pillbox commander ordered a retreat to the kibbutz, which was successfully accomplished after the Egyptians inexplicably pulled back.

With the pillbox neutralized, the Egyptians could now reach the kibbutz. Protecting its southern approach were posts 1 and 2, which would bear the brunt of the Egyptian attack. Built on top of small hills, those positions had clear views of the approach and good fields of fire. Emerging from behind White Hill, a low mound about 300 feet (100m) in front of the posts, some 60 Egyptian soldiers came at the kibbutz under heavy covering fire. Brandvein had ordered the defenders to "shoot only when the Egyptians get to the fence."[6] With great discipline, the Israelis held their fire. As they approached, the

Egyptians tripped antipersonnel mines, resulting in casualties. More fell when the defenders fired mortars, threw grenades and opened small-arms fire. In another wave, the Egyptians made it to the barbed wire entanglements just 30 feet (10m) below the positions, and many were killed while cutting the wire. Seeing their comrades fall, a number of Egyptians turned and fled. Brandvein told how he helped stop one thrust when he "hit them with enfilading fire with the machine gun and saw them drop."[7]

In all, three or four Egyptian assaults were repulsed. This did not come without cost to the kibbutz—six men had been killed and about 20 wounded. Egyptian casualties were much heavier, estimated at between 100 and 200.

With ammunition already running low and some weapons out of action, the Israelis scavenged a dozen British rifles, ammunition, a PIAT antitank rocket launcher with 12 rounds and two Bren guns from dead and wounded Egyptians on the battlefield during the night. They also laid additional antipersonnel mines and burrowed protective cavities into the trench walls.

With morning, the Egyptians renewed their attack. This time the mortar and artillery barrage was more precise, seeking out the trenches while machine-gun fire continually raked the kibbutz. Then smoke shells were fired, which the defenders knew was meant to mask an infantry advance. When the wind shifted, the smoke cleared, revealing Egyptian troops working at the entanglements with wire-cutters. The attack was stopped with rifle fire and hand grenades. Armored cars led the second Egyptian assault with machine guns blazing, but mortar fire from the kibbutz kept them at bay. That and the third attack were also repulsed, each with heavy losses to the Egyptians. With its own casualties mounting, the kibbutz pleaded with Israeli command for reinforcements, but Israel was under attack on all fronts. In addition to the Egyptian thrusts, Transjordan's Arab Legion was threatening Jerusalem while Syrian, Lebanese, Iraqi and irregular guerilla forces kept the pressure on Israel's north. Resources had to be dedicated to defensible positions and not to isolated settlements.

Israeli Command was able to dispatch one platoon of 30 Palmach men, with their standard equipment plus some additional weapons and ammunition, as replacements for Yad Mordechai's dead and wounded. When they succeeded in reaching the kibbutz at 02:00, the Palmach men helped repair trenches damaged by Egyptian artillery and relieved some of the posts. Their arrival brought welcome additional manpower, as well as the morale-building knowledge that Yad Mordechai was not completely cut off.

Yad Mordechai was not alone in calling for reinforcements that night. The new Palmach arrivals told of an Egyptian radio communication reporting 300 to 400 Egyptian casualties, with 1st Battalion no longer in fighting form. The 2nd Battalion was ordered in to finish the job.

During World War II, the British had recognized that their Egyptian allies "had neither the will nor the capability to undertake a serious military role."[8] The 1948 campaign proved that little had changed, in spite of the infusion of weapons and equipment the Egyptians had inherited from the British. Faced with unexpected resistance and heavy losses at Yad Mordechai, the Egyptian offensive lost momentum. The shelling continued day and night for two days. An Egyptian convoy bypassed the kibbutz while soldiers deployed in the surrounding hills, tightening the stranglehold on Yad Mordechai. Wishful thinkers among the defenders hoped that the Egyptians had decided to leave the kibbutz alone, but they were using the lull to organize newly arriving reinforcements and additional assets.

On May 23, Egyptian artillery opened a ferocious barrage. Believing this to be another diversionary bombardment while the Egyptians bypassed the kibbutz, Yad Mordechai's defenders crouched in their trenches. When they lifted their heads, they were surprised to see tanks—being deployed against the kibbutz for the first time—and Bren carriers (light, tracked armored vehicles mounting machine guns) advancing, trailed by infantry. While tanks fired into the kibbutz's defensive posts, the Bren carriers pressed forward.

An Egyptian tank and some troops managed to penetrate the kibbutz and stopped behind Post 1, which the Israelis abandoned. A runner confirmed the position's loss: "Position 1 retreated. Armored vehicles broke through the fence."[9] Converging on the area where the tank stood, the kibbutz defenders threw hand grenades and fired PIAT rounds, all to no effect. The tank remained stationary, firing its machine gun. It was not clear whether it had been damaged. Perhaps the crew was disoriented—all alone, lost in a built-up area of the kibbutz and not really sure what to do next. The Israelis fired more PIAT rounds, again without success. Improvised fortified grenades— two grenades combined with a quantity of TNT—also failed to penetrate the tank's armor or dislodge its treads. After some time, the tank began to move again. Finally, one of Yad Mordechai's fighters charged the tank and threw a pair of fortified grenades that exploded next to the machine-gun slit. As he rushed the tank, he was cut down with machine-gun fire, but the tank had finally been disabled and had to be towed out by a second Egyptian tank during the fighting. Men were pulled from other posts to help fend off the Egyptians. Post 1 was reoccupied, and the Egyptians were driven from the kibbutz. More Egyptian soldiers tried to enter the kibbutz through the torn fence but were stopped by machine-gun fire while mortar fire held off their armor. As dusk settled, the Egyptians broke off their attack and pulled back.

The price of the day's fighting had been high. When they took stock of their losses the Israelis found that seven men had been killed, bringing total casualties up to 23 dead and 35 wounded. The kibbutz had also suffered equipment losses. In the course of fighting, the mortar and Browning machine gun had been destroyed. Many guns were out of commission, and those that remained were low on ammunition. The kibbutz fences had been destroyed, defensive positions were in poor shape from the constant artillery barrage, and some positions were without hand grenades. Worst of all, the defenders were exhausted.

"By this time our position was completely finished," Commander Zilberstein recalled. "We had run completely out of ammunition and we had nothing with which to fight. After this I returned to the central command and there we began to discuss what we should do. We immediately decided that unless we got help to relieve all the fighters at their posts, who had reached the end of their strength, we could not stay here any longer."[10]

Responding to the kibbutz's status report, the Israelis tried to send relief forces. A Palmach unit set out with 10 armored trucks from nearby Kibbutz Gvar Am late that night. Attacked by Egyptian forces along the way, only three of the convoy's trucks managed to get through, reaching a point 1,000 feet (300m) from Yad Mordechai. The trucks carrying weapons and most of the reinforcements did not get through. Two Palmach company commanders slipped into the kibbutz to assess the situation. Appalled by the level of destruction and nearly overcome by the dizzying stench of corpses and the suffocating heat of the crowded shelters, one of the officers noted, "We felt the people had reached the end of their strength."[11]

"We can hold out," one of Yad Mordechai's commanders persisted, "but we must rebuild our fortifications, and that can only be done at night. But the people here simply don't have the strength for this type of work, and without fortifications we can't hold out."[12] The kibbutz pleaded for more weapons and reinforcements, with which they vowed to continue holding off the Egyptians. With its convoy blocked, all the Palmach could offer was to evacuate the wounded and leave a small force to supplement the kibbutz's defenders. Fourteen of Yad Mordechai's wounded were evacuated in the armored trucks, along with a number of the women.

Knowing there would be no additional relief, Zilberstein noted, "We decided that we would retreat from here that same night." After checking that nobody was left behind, the men and women gathered at a staging area, took a final look at their destroyed home, and headed off into the darkness through Egyptian lines towards Kibbutz Gvar Am.

Palmach forces attacked the Egyptian position that had blocked the convoy's route, providing a diversion that helped the trucks carrying the wounded to get through. Off in the distance, the Israeli troops could see the people of Yad Mordechai making their way to safety. When the Egyptians discovered the evacuees' movement, they opened fire. In the confusion of the nighttime evacuation under Egyptian fire, two stretcher-bearers and the wounded man they carried became separated from the group and were captured. Nothing was ever heard of the three again and they were added to the list of dead, increasing the number of deaths in the stand at Yad Mordechai to 26 (18 from the kibbutz and eight Palmach men). Such heavy losses were representative of the War of Independence, in which 6,000 citizens—one percent of the entire Jewish population of Israel—lost their lives, and 15,000 were wounded.

"We really managed to get out under their noses and by dawn we managed to reach Gvar Am," Zilberstein recalled. In the morning, the Egyptians resumed their bombardment of Yad Mordechai. Only after several hours of shelling did they realize that the kibbutz had been abandoned. In the afternoon, 2nd Battalion finally entered the kibbutz.

The Egyptian newspaper *Al-Musara* reported, "After conquering Yad Mordechai, the route to Tel Aviv is open before the Egyptian forces."[13] But that was not the case. After occupying the kibbutz, an Egyptian column of some 500 vehicles began its delayed drive north up the coastal road towards Tel Aviv. But the combat at Yad Morde-chai had sapped the offensive of strength and broken its momen-tum—it took the Egyptian column four days to reach what is today the port city of Ashdod, just 15 miles (24km) north of Yad Morde-chai, where it was halted by a bombed-out bridge, now known as *Gesher Ad Halom* or "Up to Here Bridge." Palmach southern commander Nahum Sarig called each day gained at Yad Mordechai "more precious than gold in that it gave sufficient time . . . to concen-trate a blocking force, to organize a line of defense, which was what stopped the enemy advance at Ashdod."[14]

Truce and Counteroffensives

Now an officially recognized state, Israel was busy purchasing artil-lery, military matériel and aircraft. The country had been in the gravest danger during those early days when all it had was the meager supply of arms illegally imported or otherwise acquired during the Mandate period. Among the weapons to arrive that month were Israel's first fighter aircraft, Avia S-199s (re-engined Czechoslovakian-made Messerschmitt Me-109Gs). The first four hastily assembled aircraft were pressed into service on May 29, when the Israel Air Force 1st Fighter Squadron set off on its debut mission against the Egyptian column halted at Ashdod. Each aircraft swooped down, dropping bombs and strafing the column. Their untested 20mm cannons and machine guns quickly jammed, and overall the air attack resulted in little actual damage, but the Egyptians scattered in face of the unexpected air attack, and lost the initiative. Bogged down some

23 miles (37km) from Tel Aviv, the Egyptian threat to Israel's center was over.

A truce came into effect on June 11, allowing each side to retain its territorial gains. Yad Mordechai was in the area controlled by Egypt. When the Egyptians refused to honor a truce provision allowing for the resupply of surrounded Jewish settlements, fighting erupted again. The newly reinforced Israeli army launched Operation *Yoav*, which drove the Egyptians from most of the territory they had seized.

Israeli forces would go on to take the entire Negev Desert, as far south as Um Rashrash, known today as Eilat. In the north, Syrian and Lebanese gains were reversed, and Arab volunteer forces known as the Arab Liberation Army were pushed out of Israeli territory. Only Transjordan's Arab Legion held its ground, remaining entrenched in the salient at Latrun commanding the main road to Jerusalem, and maintained its hold on Jerusalem's walled Old City.

On November 5, 1948, the Israelis retook Kibbutz Yad Mordechai. Zilberstein described the Egyptian retreat as "made with such haste that Yad Mordechai fell into our hands like fallen fruit. On that very day we returned and since then we started to rebuild the place with energy."[15]

Having fought so hard for their home, the people of Yad Mordechai gladly returned to their border location rather than opt for a safer place in the center of the country. Haganah Commander in Chief Israel Galili told the residents upon their return: "Your battle gave the whole south six precious days for fortification, for organization, for the securing of additional arms. The Egyptians learned here the valor and the obstinacy of the Jewish fighter. They recognized how much they would have to pay in lives and material if they were to go forward. The nation owes much to Yad Mordechai."[16]

Notes

1. Margaret Larkin. *The Six Days of Yad Mordechai* (Yad Mordechai Museum, Israel, 1965), p.238.
2. Larkin. *The Six Days of Yad Mordechai*, p.246
3. Larkin. *The Six Days of Yad Mordechai*, p.246.
4. Larkin. *The Six Days of Yad Mordechai*, p.79.

5.Brandvein, Munio (editor and compiler). *B'Mabat M'haHutz* [*A Look from the Outside. Listings of the Yad Mordechai Battles from May 19–23, 1948*] (Yad Mordechai: 1984). Nahum Sarig in *Sefer haPalmach*, p.6.

6.Brandvein, Munio. Interview with author.

7.Brandvein, Munio. Interview with author.

8.Steve Rothwell. "Military Ally or Liability, The Egyptian Army 1936–1942" *Army Quarterly & Defence Journal* (Vol. 128: 2, April 1998).

9.Brandvein. *B'Mabat M'haHutz*. Pinchas Shaish in *"B'ikvot haLochemim":
Sufot baNegev,* p.10.

10.Zilberstein, Grisha. Transcript of undated interview.

11.Brandvein. *B'Mabat M'haHutz*. Simcha Shiloni in *Sefer haPalmach*, p.12.

12.Shiloni. *Sefer haPalmach*.

13.Brandvein. *B'Mabat M'haHutz*. Egyptian materials reprinted in *"B'ikvot haLochemim": Sufot baNegev,* p.16.

14.Brandvein. *B'Mabat M'haHutz*. Nahum Sarig in *Sefer haPalmach*, p.6.

15.Zilberstein, Grisha. Transcript of undated interview.

16.Larkin. *The Six Days of Yad Mordechai*, p.252.

CHAPTER 14

ATTACKED, CAPTURED
AND ABANDONED

1956 Sinai Campaign

The aggressive brigade commander got what he wanted: authorization to send a patrol to reconnoiter Mitla Pass. Colonel Ariel Sharon's 202nd Paratroop Brigade was 125 miles (200km) behind Egyptian lines, deployed just east of this crucial mountain pass connecting central Sinai with the Suez Canal and the city of Suez in Egypt proper. His brigade's 890th Battalion, under Major Rafael "Raful" Eitan, had parachuted in the previous day. The Israel Air Force's entire fleet of 16 Douglas C-47 Dakota transports, under the protective cover of ten IAF Gloster Meteor jet fighters, dropped the 395 paratroopers deep into Egyptian territory at 16:59 on October 29, 1956. After landing several miles off mark, Eitan (a future Chief of Staff of the IDF) organized his men and marched two hours to their deployment by a crossroads known as the "Fork," near the Parker Memorial landmark east of Mitla Pass. The Israeli paratroopers dug in and awaited the eight jeeps, four 106mm recoilless antitank guns, two 120mm mortars, ammunition, equipment and supplies that were dropped to them later that evening.

What became known in Israel as Operation *Kadesh*, or the Sinai

Campaign, was underway. The paratroop drop at Mitla was actually a pretext for a larger Israeli-French-British tripartite action against Egypt. Israel would focus on Sinai, the triangular-shaped desert peninsula to its southwest, while France and Britain would launch their own offensive, Operation *Musketeer*, aimed at taking control of the Suez Canal, nationalized by Egypt just three months earlier. France was at odds with Egypt over its military support for anti-French forces in its colony Algeria, and Britain—with economic and commercial interests at stake—had much to lose from Egypt's nationalization of the canal. A joint Franco-British attack plan was born even before Israel was approached to join in September 1956. At the time, Israel was deeply concerned about a massive influx of modern weapons to Egypt from Czechoslovakia that would give Egypt the means with which to carry out its threats to destroy Israel. Egypt had already flexed its muscles three years earlier when it closed the Straits of Tiran to Israeli or Israel-bound shipping, effectively blockading Israel's southern port of Eilat. Egypt was also actively supporting terror attacks against Israel by Arab infiltrators known as *fedayin*. The frequent fedayin attacks against Israel and the Israeli reprisals were resulting in heavy casualties. Israel was ready to strike at Egypt's growing military might, re-open the Gulf of Aqaba and destroy the fedayin terrorist infrastructure.

In an agreement concluded at Sèvres, France, just five days before the Paratroop drop, a plan was created whereby Israel would initiate hostilities against Egypt, creating an alleged threat to the Suez Canal. France and Britain would then issue an appeal-cum-ultimatum they knew Egypt would reject, thereby justifying Franco-British military intervention. The Israeli *casus belli* was an airborne incursion deep behind enemy lines. The Paratroops were selected for the mission because the Israeli military leadership knew, based on previous performance, that they could hold their own. "Naturally," said IDF Paratroop Brigade reconnaissance company commander Lieutenant Micha Ben-Ari (Kapusta), "the IDF put the whole fight on the paratroopers' shoulders."[1]

Taking into account the possibility that the French and British could fail to keep their commitment to launch airstrikes against Egypt twelve hours after the ultimatum was issued, Israel's opening move was limited in scope so the troops could be withdrawn, conveying that the Israeli airdrop at Mitla was no more than a retaliatory raid for Egyptian-sponsored terror activity. Initially Israeli Chief of Staff Lieutenant General Moshe Dayan envisaged the war plan as an infantry campaign, with the armored forces relegated to a support role. Israeli Prime Minister and Minister of Defense David Ben-Gurion was concerned Egypt would react to anything more than an infantry incursion by sending its Ilyushin IL-28 bombers against Israeli cities. To defend against this eventuality—and to reassure Israel—the French agreed to provide Israel with air cover. French Air Force, or *Armée de l'Air*, Dassault Mystere IVA fighters and Republic F-84F Thunderstreak fighter-bombers were based at Israeli airfields to defend Israel's skies.

While Eitan's paratroopers were digging in at Mitla in the early evening of October 29, 1956, a convoy of airborne troops led by Paratroop Brigade commander Ariel Sharon was making its way across 180 miles (300km) from the Jordanian border, across Israel and through the Sinai desert to link up with them. Prior to the campaign, Sharon and the rest of his 202nd Brigade had been positioned on the Jordanian border to give the impression that the Israel Defense Forces were poised to strike eastward. Tensions with Jordan were running high given that country's support for terrorists acting against Israel, and Israeli reprisals seemed likely. It certainly explained Israel's military mobilization. A large reprisal attack against Jordan earlier that month at Kalkilia by Sharon's paratroopers had caused Jordanian King Hussein to invoke its defense treaty with the United Kingdom, ironically at the same time that the UK was discussing military co-operation *with* Israel. Carrying on the tradition of Sharon's legendary Unit 101 commando force, which was merged into the Paratroops, the 202nd Brigade executed Israel's policy of aggressive retaliation against its neighbors that supported terror. There was talk of Iraqi forces intervening to bolster Jordan, which Ben-Gurion had made clear would trigger an Israeli military response. Jordan reinforced defenses along its border with Israel.[2]

Sharon's column included two mechanized battalions in M-3 halftrack armored vehicles, field artillery and mortars, and thirteen French-built AMX-13 light tanks. The convoy—hundreds of vehicles in all—cut across southern Israel and crossed into Egypt. The difficult desert terrain took its toll on the vehicles, but Sharon pressed his column forward. The paratroops fought and took the Egyptian position at Kuntilla northwest of Eilat. At dawn they defeated Themed after a short battle and by late afternoon captured Nakhle. Many Egyptian soldiers were killed in the battles, and allegations emerged that the Israeli troops killed Egyptian soldiers and non-combatants surrendering to them rather than taking them prisoner. At 22:30 on October 30—after some 30 hours on the move since crossing into Sinai, Sharon's convoy linked up with Eitan's force dug in east of Mitla. A line of communication had been established; Eitan's battalion was no longer isolated.

Sharon found the deployment at Mitla vulnerable and in need of improvement. They were now a full brigade—some 1,200 men—exposed on low, open ground, providing an inviting target to both air and ground attack. Before Sharon's force had arrived, a number of Eitan's men had been wounded in a strafing run by a formation of Egyptian Air Force Mikoyan-Gurevich MiG-15 fighters. The Israelis had also been hit by mortar fire from the pass. Sharon was up in arms that the elite paratroops were under orders to remain at the rendezvous—vulnerable and idle in the midst of a war, even though the fact that they were the IDF's most experienced troops was precisely the reason they were in that position.

Mitla Pass

The restless 28-year-old Sharon began pressing his superiors for a thrust through Mitla Pass. A force was organized and ready to move into Mitla Pass by 04:00. A winding 15-mile (25-km) long pass, Mitla is enclosed by high ground to the north and south. At both the western and eastern extremes, the pass narrows to easily defended chokepoints, the eastern-most being known as Heitan defile. Control over these two narrow straits controls Mitla Pass, blocking access either to the Suez Canal or into central Sinai. From the intelligence in hand, it was believed there were no significant Egyptian forces deployed in the pass. The original war plan called for the Paratroops to jump west of the pass—some 20 miles (30km) east of the Suez Canal, but aerial reconnaissance photos revealed what was believed to be Egyptian military activity, so the jump destination had been moved to the eastern terminus.

Sharon's request to enter Mitla was denied by General Officer Commanding (GOC) Southern Command, Major General Assaf Simhoni. By this time, the Franco-British appeal had been issued calling on Egypt and Israel to accept a cease-fire, withdraw their forces to a distance of ten miles from the Suez Canal and accept temporary occupation of key positions along the canal to ensure free passage through the waterway, or else the British and French would force compliance. The combatants were given twelve hours to respond. Israel accepted the terms of this precoordinated ultimatum on condition that Egypt also accepted. The Israeli leadership knew their French and British allies were to begin airstrikes on Egypt the following morning. Israeli Chief of Staff Moshe Dayan's orders were clear: 202nd Brigade was "to reorganize in its present location and not to advance westwards to capture the Mitla Pass."[3]

Sharon held the view that staff officers could not fully appreciate the situation on the ground, and therefore "the upper echelon should intervene only if they are actually on the battlefield, if they know everything intimately, if they are forward where they can see and understand all the elements that affect the conduct of the battle."[4] Sharon undoubtedly expressed his opinion accordingly, reasoning that Israel Air Force over-flights reported no enemy between the Suez Canal and Mitla, while they *did* indicate an Egyptian armored brigade about 40 miles (65km) to the north at Bir Gafgafa, moving towards Mitla. Entering Mitla Pass would provide adequate positions for his brigade to defend itself. In the morning, when the French and British were supposed to launch airstrikes on Egyptian airfields, they instead extended their ultimatum by another twelve hours, casting doubts on whether they would come through as promised. Sharon and others—apparently including GOC Southern Command Simhoni—were already weary of this reliance on outsiders, especially the British, who until recently had been so hostile to Israel. When informed the night before that the French and British would not launch their air attacks in the morning, David Ben-Gurion—whose recollection of the paratrooper blocking force cut off in enemy territory during the recent Kalkilia operation was still fresh in his mind—considered recalling the paratroopers from Mitla.

Southern Command Chief of Staff Lieutenant Colonel Rehavam "Gandhi" Zeevi flew out in a Piper Cub the morning of October 31 to meet Sharon for an on-site assessment. Evidently Sharon was convincing, at least partially; he received permission to send in a patrol to reconnoiter the pass. Zeevi stressed the need to avoid unnecessary operations in order to minimize casualties, stating, "We must not pay a price in Jewish blood."[5]

Sharon took the liberty of sending in a much larger contingent than authorized: he organized a battalion-sized force comprised of two infantry companies mounted on halftracks, three AMX-13 tanks, the brigade reconnaissance company and 120mm mortar batteries, followed by an ambulance and trucks carrying fuel, supplies and ammunition. While the IDF battled Egyptian forces across Sinai, the Paratroops' commanders felt all they had done was drive across the desert, so they were itching to fight and be the first to reach the Suez Canal. Perhaps they were too eager, as there was a cavalier attitude; advancing to Mitla was approached like an excursion rather than a wartime mission. Sightings of men moving about the hills flanking the pass were dismissed as likely being fellow paratroopers, or perhaps Egyptian stragglers, with no need for concern, and no force was sent to secure the flanks in the heights above.

"I gave specific instructions not to enter into battle with the enemy," Sharon would later say. "The patrol, we hoped, would reach the other end of the Pass, 25 kilometers away, unheeded. It was a daring action, and therefore the force had to be well protected."[6]

Just before the paratroopers made their jump to Mitla, specially equipped IAF North American Aviation propeller-driven P-51 Mustangs had severed Egyptian communication lines in Sinai. While causing disruptions, this effort did not prevent word of the Israeli airborne and ground attack from reaching Egyptian command. Though Egyptian Chief of Staff General Abd el Hakim Amer was out of the country attending a conference of chiefs of staff of Egypt, Syria and Jordan in Amman, Egypt's defenses sprang into action. Even Moshe Dayan was complimentary of the Egyptian response, noting that "it must be said that they lost no time in reacting to [Israeli moves]."[7] All Egyptian forces were put on alert, and the Egyptian 2nd

Infantry Brigade dispatched its 5th Battalion, reinforced by a company from the 6th, to Mitla on October 30 to counter the Israelis. Deploying to prepared defensive positions on both sides of the Heitan defile with an arsenal that included 40 recoilless guns, 14 medium machine guns and twelve antitank guns, the Egyptians established themselves in caves, natural obstacles and other well-concealed defensive positions. Though the mountain pass was honeycombed with Egyptian positions, they were not visible from the air. The Israel Air Force attacked convoys of vehicles and artillery moving from the Canal Zone towards Mitla, including a convoy in the defile that turned out to be the empty vehicles belonging to the Egyptian troops entrenched in the heights. The latest IDF intelligence assessment was that the pass was free of Egyptians.

The paratrooper "patrol" set off for Mitla Pass at 12:30 on October 31, with force commander Major Mordechai "Motta" Gur, commander of the 88th Battalion (and a future IDF chief of staff) riding in a halftrack with his battalion's reconnaissance company in the vanguard. Sharon's deputy brigade commander, Lieutenant Colonel Yitzhak "Hake" Hoffe, followed with the tanks. Eitan's men complained that they made the jump to Mitla yet the other guys were getting the action.

The convoy had barely entered Mitla when it was greeted by Egyptian fire from the ridges commanding the pass. Assuming the fire was from a small defensive force, the paratroopers pressed ahead. When the lead halftrack entered the Egyptian killing zone, the Egyptians unleashed a barrage from bazookas, recoilless guns and machine guns. The halftrack was hit and disabled; both its driver and commander killed and men in the exposed back of the vehicle were hit. The vehicles following raced ahead through the Egyptian barrage, bypassing the damaged lead vehicle. With destroyed Egyptian vehicles cluttering the way, turning around or reversing out of the pass under heavy fire did not seem viable; they had no choice but to press ahead. The halftrack in which Motta Gur rode made it only another 500 feet (150m) past the lead halftrack before it was hit and stopped, with Egyptian fire pinning its soldiers down in the middle of the pass. Smoke from smoldering vehicles and the intense Egyptian fire obscured visibility as vehicles rushed through. Deputy brigade commander Hoffe, with a number of halftracks and two of the tanks, made it through to safety about two kilometers past the firestorm, believing Motta Gur was ahead of him. More halftracks and an ambulance were knocked out of action further back by the lead halftrack, with dead and wounded. The mortars and the brigade reconnaissance unit were instructed not to enter the pass. The convoy was now divided into four groups, spread out and intermingled. To further complicate matters, not all the groups had communications with one another.

Preoccupied with the potential threat posed by the Egyptian tank force to the north, brigade commander Sharon delegated to *Daled* (akin to Delta) battalion commander Lieutenant Colonel Aharon Davidi the mission of destroying the Egyptian resistance. Motta Gur would later accuse Sharon of cowardice for remaining behind while a battle raged to save the trapped force. The armored force about which Sharon was so concerned pulled back that night, eliminating the threat.

Motta Gur, in contact with Davidi, called for the reconnaissance unit to be sent into the heights flanking the pass to relieve pressure on the forces trapped within. The paratroops' supporting heavy-mortar batteries were deployed to open counterfire on the northern ridges while the brigade reconnaissance unit under Lieutenant Micha Ben-Ari was sent up the steep northern slopes to outflank the Egyptians and descend on them from higher ground. Ben-Ari described seeing the Egyptians firing down onto his fellow paratroopers. "Groups of them were sitting, filling magazines and running them to the soldiers sitting and firing down towards Motta's force trapped in the pass."[8] Once the reconnaissance unit was spotted, the Egyptians opened fire on them from all directions. The paratroopers charged and killed a number of Egyptians, but under intense fire, they had no choice but to pull back. They would attack two more times in an attempt to relieve pressure on their comrades trapped in the pass below, suffering heavy casualties as they went. Ben-Ari recalled charging the Egyptians under a hail of murderous fire. "Segev, the radioman who was on my right was hit by a bullet and died right there. Yaakobi, my good friend, charging a meter to my left, was killed by a burst of gunfire."[9] Moments later, Ben-Ari took a bullet in his chest—

his fifth combat injury—but made his way to safety.

Attempts at attacking the entrenched Egyptians were hampered by Egyptian fire from the opposing ridge and by the difficulty of discerning their precise firing positions.

Davidi thought of sending a jeep into the pass to draw Egyptian fire, thus revealing their source. Davidi's driver, 21-year-old Yehuda Kahn-Dror, volunteered for what amounted to a suicide mission. His face pale, Kahn-Dror drove off to near-certain death. He was badly wounded in the effort, yet managed to crawl out of the pass. Later succumbing to his wounds, Kahn-Dror was posthumously awarded the *Itur haGvura*, or Medal of Valor. This was but one example of selfless bravery demonstrated in this battle. With sketchy communications due to heavy screening in the confined pass, Motta Gur's radioman, Dan Shalit, repeatedly risked himself by climbing to exposed ground to maintain communications, for which he received a commendation, and in the ensuing battle to weed out the Egyptians, Lieutenant Oved Ladijinsky, commander of one of the companies battling the entrenched Egyptians, threw a grenade at an Egyptian bunker, only to have the grenade roll back towards him. To save the life of a soldier beside him, Oved shielded the soldier with his body and was killed, for which he was posthumously awarded the *Ot haOz*, or Medal of Courage. Ten soldiers were decorated for their exemplary bravery, gallantry, and for risking their lives in the battle at Mitla.

A halftrack was now sent into the pass to draw fire—again to identify the hidden Egyptian firing positions, and to attempt to evacuate some of the wounded. Despite heavy Egyptian fire, the halftrack succeeded in reaching the trapped force, evacuating six wounded men and reporting back on the sources of Egyptian fire. Its commander, Second Lieutenant Dan Ziv, was awarded the *Itur haGvura*. Around this time, a formation of four Egyptian Air Force Meteors bombed the paratroops' deployment outside the pass, knocking its mortar battery out of action and setting off their ammunition truck in a massive explosion.

The Israelis gained the upper hand when they used darkness to their advantage. Not only would the Egyptians' weapons be less effective, but the paratroopers were highly experienced in night training and operations, when darkness offered cover and protection. Venturing into Mitla in the light of day was not an ordinary operation for them.

Armed with a better sense of the Egyptian deployment, Davidi formulated a plan for a nighttime two-pronged attack. The men with deputy brigade commander Hoffe at the western side of the confined defile took to the hills and attacked the Egyptians from the west. Once they had secured their objectives, a large force went into action from the eastern side. Fighting the Egyptians at close range—at times hand to hand—the paratroopers overcame the Egyptians' hidden firing positions. Paratrooper Avshalom Adam stayed close to the cliffs to remain hidden in the shadows. He came so close to enemy positions that he could not respond to fellow soldiers calling to him lest the Egyptians hear. With one unit providing cover fire, he closed in on Egyptian machine-gun positions, waiting to hear ammunition belts run out, when he "would jump up and throw a grenade inside."[10]

After taking out a fortified Egyptian bunker with a grenade and then finishing off survivors with his Uzi submachine gun, paratrooper Muni Maroz came across a makeshift Egyptian position of rocks and boulders shielding soldiers firing away. Preparing a grenade as he moved in, protected by the darkness, Maroz took out the position with his grenade but spotted one enemy soldier getting away in time and lying down nearby. "With my weapon cocked," he recounted, "I moved towards the Egyptian soldier lying on his stomach pretending to be dead. When I pulled the trigger, I heard the blood-curdling click of a bolt finding an empty magazine. When I bent over to take the Egyptian's rifle with fixed bayonet, he came to his senses, got up on his knees and grabbed a hold of my leg, trying to pull me down to the ground." Maroz called out for help from another paratrooper he knew was in the area, who arrived "like a guardian angel." The second paratrooper—apparently also out of ammunition—smashed the Egyptian soldier in the head with the stock of his Uzi. The Egyptian's rifle bayonet was used to complete the job.[11]

The Israeli paratroopers neutralized the Egyptian positions in the pass one by one, first on the southern heights, which eased the situation for the paratroopers embroiled in fighting on the northern heights. By midnight it was over, the Egyptians having been flushed out of every bunker, burrow and cave. The Israeli casualties, who had been trapped in the pass all day, were finally evacuated; the rest of the paratroopers regrouped at the positions east of the pass. Summing up the action at Mitla, Chief of Staff Dayan wrote: "The Pass was therefore attacked, captured and abandoned."[12]

French and British forces entered the fray on the night of October 31 with an air attack by Royal Air Force (RAF) English Electric Canberra and Vickers Valiant bombers. "During the first twenty-four hours of their involvement, British and French aircraft flew over five hundred sorties . . . and destroyed more than one hundred Egyptian aircraft."[13] The Egyptian Air Force reacted by dispersing their aircraft or sending them out of the country for safety, relieving pressure on the Israeli forces on the ground in Sinai. Ongoing French and British airstrikes would destroy a further 100 Egyptian aircraft on the ground.

Once the French and British began their attacks, Egyptian President Gamal Abdel Nasser began pulling his Sinai forces back towards the canal, supporting the contention that if Sharon and the paratroopers had held their ground, the costly battle at Mitla would have been avoided. Chief of Staff Moshe Dayan was furious about Sharon's disregard for orders. In his *Diary of the Sinai Campaign*, Dayan wrote: ". . . my complaint, a grave complaint, against the paratroop command is not over the battle itself so much as over their resort to terming their operation a 'patrol' in order to 'satisfy' the General Staff."[14] In the ensuing fallout, actions of the senior commanders at Mitla were scrutinized, and Sharon was ultimately replaced as brigade commander. Years later Sharon would serve as a minister of defense and prime minister of Israel. About the paratroopers' performance the chief of staff was unequivocally positive, noting: "I doubt whether there is another unit in our army which could have managed in these conditions to get the better of the enemy. . . . The valor, daring and fighting spirit of the paratroop commanders are qualities which should be applauded and encouraged, but the battle was not essential."[15] The paratroopers were able to turn the tide at Mitla because of their collective experience gained from dozens of reprisal actions and cross-border missions over the previous three years. It was during this period of reprisals that the Paratroops' *esprit de corps* and fighting spirit of which Dayan wrote had been born.

Dayan bemoaned both that the action at Mitla was taken against his orders and its "murderous consequences": 120 paratroopers were wounded and 38 killed. Egyptian losses were significantly higher, with some 260 dead counted; the rest had slipped away.[16]

After a two-day rest, the paratroopers were called upon for the assault on Sharm el-Sheikh at the Sinai Peninsula's southern tip. The primary political objective of the campaign, capturing Sharm el-Sheikh, would re-open passage through the narrow Straits of Tiran in the Gulf of Aqaba, which, we recall, Egypt had closed to Israeli shipping. With the infantry brigade tasked with capturing Sharm el-Sheikh advancing slowly down Sinai's difficult eastern coast, Eitan's battalion was ordered down the Sinai Peninsula's western route while a reinforced company of paratroopers that had motored across Sinai was now given the opportunity for a combat jump to take the Egyptian airfield at A-Tur. The two groups of paratroopers linked up, and with the infantry brigade captured Sharm el-Sheikh. A pair of the threatening Egyptian coastal guns that had enforced Egypt's blockade is now housed at an IDF museum in Tel Aviv.

The IDF Armored Corps Proves Its Mettle

By the time Sharm el-Sheikh was taken, Israeli armored, mechanized and infantry units, formed into divisional task forces, had already met their objectives of breaking through the line of fortified Egyptian defenses at Abu Agheila, Rafah, and El Arish, the so-called triangle built to block any Israeli attempt on Sinai. Surrounded by minefields and barbed wire and backed by dug-in tanks, artillery, mortars, and antitank guns, these positions blocked the three main routes traversing Sinai: the flat Mediterranean coastal route in the north passing through the Gaza Strip and El Arish through Romani to Kantara, the central axis through Abu Agheila and Bir Gafgafa to Ismailia, and the route through Mitla Pass to Suez, reached by lateral crossroads. Most of the 30,000 Egyptian troops in Sinai and Gaza were concentrated in this sector.

Impatient with the infantry's progress at Kusseima—an important crossroad near the border and one of the IDF's early objectives—on October 30, GOC Southern Command Simhoni ordered the 7th Armored Brigade into action. Chief of Staff Dayan was furious, as the use of armor at that stage contravened his orders and risked an escalated Egyptian response. When his anger subsided, Dayan realized the benefit of their position and ordered the 7th Armored Brigade to capture the central axis. A probe revealed an undefended defile called Daikla Pass that would put the Israelis behind the Egyptian positions by Abu Agheila compound, yet only tracked vehicles could maneuver the pass. In an audacious move, 7th Armored Brigade's tanks left their wheeled fuel, ammunition, and supply vehicles behind and pressed on, putting them in position to attack Abu Agheila from the rear.

Despite stubborn Egyptian resistance, the Israelis broke through the Egyptian line of static defenses. Soon Israeli armored columns were racing across Sinai towards the Suez Canal on both the Mediterranean coast and central axes. The IDF Armored Corps proved its mettle in this war, earning their prominent place in future Israeli war planning. Gaza with its fedayin terror bases and training camps was the last objective secured in this sector.

In little more than 100 hours of fighting, Israel seized the entire Sinai Peninsula at a cost of 181 killed, 800 wounded and 4 captured. Egyptian losses were about 1,000 killed, 4,000 wounded, and 6,000 captured. Israel's victory brought with it a windfall of captured war bounty, including some 100 tanks, 200 artillery pieces, 1,000 vehicles and an Egyptian Navy destroyer, the *Ibrahim el Awal*. While shelling Haifa, the Egyptian vessel was intercepted by French and Israeli navy boats and rocketed by the Israel Air Force, leading to its surrender. Coupled with its heavy loss of aircraft, Egypt had suffered a serious blow. Despite the losses, Egyptian President Nasser, who had taken power in Egypt in 1954, came out a winner. His defiance and heroic stand against colonial powers of France and Britain earned him acclaim in the Arab world, leading to his becoming considered a leader of the Arabs.

British and French forces launched an airborne and amphibious operation on November 5, seizing both Port Said and Port Fuad in the northern extremity of the Suez Canal. The 90,000 men, 130 warships—including aircraft carriers—and more than 500 aircraft committed to the operation by France and Britain, would be reined in after less than two days, the result of intense international diplomatic pressure, including ultimatums from the United States and Soviet Union. In a miscalculation, it was thought the United States would be distracted by its presidential election and the Soviets by revolt in Hungary, but both countries took a firm stance against the invasion. For France and Britain, the war was a political disaster, seen as two fading powers' last attempts at exerting influence. For Israel, their role was critical. Without the French and British, Moshe Dayan wrote, "it is doubtful whether Israel would have launched her campaign."[17] The cooperation only added to the affinity France felt towards Israel and cemented the relationship; France would supply Israel with its armament needs for the next decade.

Israel also consented to the diplomatic pressure being exerted to withdraw its forces from Sinai, but it won the concession of a UN peacekeeping force known as the United Nations Emergency Force (UNEF) positioned at Sharm el-Sheikh and the Gaza Strip. By March 1957 the last Israeli forces pulled out of Sinai.

Only eight years after its precarious establishment, Israel had exhibited military prowess, proving it could fight and win on the battlefield. Beyond achieving its objectives for the campaign, Israel had demonstrated deterrence in a way her neighbors could not ignore, and was no longer diplomatically isolated. Perhaps for the first time Israel could enjoy a sense of security.

Notes

1. Avi Zur. Interview with Micha Ben-Ari.
2. Dayan described: "It is apparent that our deception plan was successful. Up to the last minute, that is, up to our paratroop drop at Mitla, the General Staffs of all the Arab armies believed that it was our intention to march on Jordan. Jordan accordingly reinforced her defense system along her border with Israel . . ." Dayan, *Diary of the Sinai Campaign* (New York: Schocken Books, 1965), p.89.
3. Dayan. *Diary of the Sinai Campaign*, p.95.
4. Ariel Sharon and David Chanoff. *Warrior: The Autobiography of Ariel Sharon* (New York: Simon & Schuster, 1989), pp.137–8. Sharon wrote this about Operation *Shomron*, the paratroopers' raid on Kalkilia earlier that month, when he had held differences of opinion with his superiors. He clearly states: "there should be as little interference as possible with the commander in the field."
5. Oren, Amir. "38 soldiers killed. Who approved the action?" www.haaretz.com. October 29, 2006.
6. Matti Shavitt. *On the Wings of Eagles: The Story of Arik Sharon, Commander of the Israel paratroopers* (Tel Aviv: Olive Books of Israel, 1970), p.137.
7. Dayan. *Diary of the Sinai Campaign*, p.91.
8. Zur. Interview.
9. Zur. Interview.
10. Personal Account. Avshalom Adam. IDF Paratroopers History Site.
11. Personal Account. Muni Maroz. IDF Paratroopers History Site.
12. Dayan. *Diary of the Sinai Campaign*, p.102.
13. Lon Nordeen. *Fighters Over Israel* (London: Greenhill Books, 1990), p.46.
14. Dayan. *Diary of the Sinai Campaign*, p.102. Dayan did not punish Sharon for disobeying orders, and was forgiving in another case where the 7th Armored Brigade was ordered into action prematurely against his orders, about which he wrote: "I could not avoid a sympathetic feeling over the hastening of the brigade into combat even before they were required. Better to be engaged in restraining the noble stallion than in prodding the reluctant mule!" (Dayan. *Diary of the Sinai Campaign*, p.96) As for Sharon, this would not be the only occasion on which he would disregard orders. In the 1973 Yom Kippur War, while commanding an Armored Division operating by the Suez Canal, Sharon flagrantly violated orders by crossing the Canal into Egypt proper—a daring move that cut off the Egyptian Third Army and contributed to Egypt's defeat. A military tribunal later exonerated him on grounds that his actions were militarily effective.
15. Dayan. *Diary of the Sinai Campaign*, pp.101–2.
16. Dayan. *Diary of the Sinai Campaign*, p.102.
17. Nordeen. *Fighters Over Israel*, p.37.

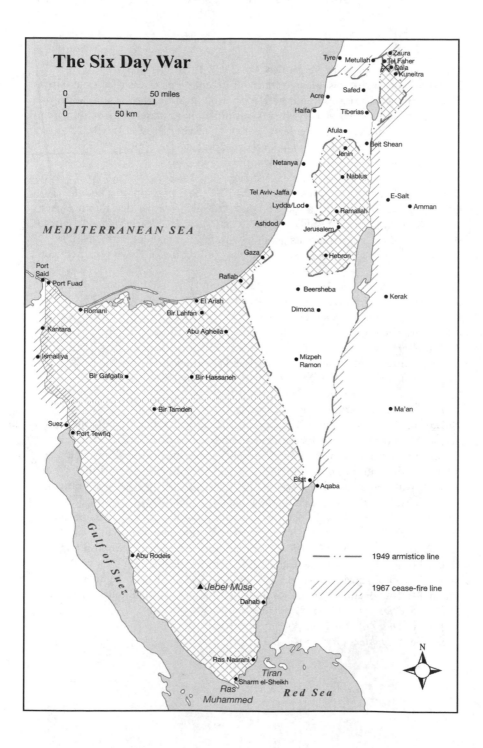

The Six Day War

0 50 miles
0 50 km

MEDITERRANEAN SEA

Tyre • • Metullah
Zaura •
• Tel Faher
✕ • Qala
• Kuneitra

• Acre
Safed •

Haifa • • Tiberias

Afula •
• Beit Shean

Jenin •

Netanya • • Nablus

Tel Aviv-Jaffa • • E-Salt
• Amman

Lydda/Lod •
• Ramallah

Ashdod • Jerusalem •

Gaza • • Hebron

Port • Kerak
Said • • Beersheba
• Port Fuad

Rafiah •
• El Arish
• Romani
Bir Lahfan •
Dimona •

Kantara •
Abu Agheila •

Ismailiya • Mizpeh
Ramon

Bir Gafgafa • • Bir Hassaneh

Ma'an •
• Bir Tamdeh

Suez •
• Port Tewfiq

Eilat • • Aqaba

Gulf of Suez

•••• 1949 armistice line

Abu Rodeis •

///// 1967 cease-fire line

▲ Jebel Mūsa

Dahab •

N

Ras Nasrani •
Tiran
Sharm el-Sheikh •
Ras
Muhammed Red Sea

CHAPTER 15

HOW THE HELL DID ANYONE GET UP THERE?

1967 SIX DAY WAR

Soldiers hugged and kissed one another. A few shed tears of joy. Some even joined in a festive folk dance. This celebration did not mark the end of a battle, but the beginning of one. It was Friday, June 9, 1967—the fifth day of the war that would become known as the Six Day War—and the IDF's Golani Infantry Brigade had just received orders authorizing operations against Syria.

Based in Israel's northern Galilee, the Golani troops felt a special responsibility for this sector. Yet for years its troops had watched helplessly while Syrian artillery randomly shelled Israeli fishermen on the Sea of Galilee, farmers in the Hula Valley, and the northern villages of Dan, Dafna, Shaar Yishuv, Beit-Hillel and HaGoshrim, destroying houses, setting crops alight and causing civilian casualties. Short of all-out war, there was little they could do. With the outbreak of war on June 5, 1967, Golani's soldiers were eager to settle the score. But as the IDF concentrated on the Egyptian and Jordanian fronts for four days, tension built up among the Golani as they waited to have their go. With international pressure for a cease-fire mounting, it was looking as if they might not get that chance.

Syria's efforts to make life miserable for Israel had even included a major engineering project to divert the Jordan River's headwaters and cut off northern Israel's water supply. Tensions along the border escalated until early April 1967, when Syrian artillery harassment increased in ferocity. In a subsequent dogfight, six Syrian Mikoyan-Gurevich MiG-21 fighters were shot down by Israel Air Force Dassault Mirage III fighters. At that point, Syria pressured Egypt into joining these latest efforts against Israel. Relatively isolated in the Arab world at the time, Egypt's President Gamal Abdel Nasser welcomed the opportunity. Calls for Israel's annihilation and other anti-Israel propaganda began radiating from Egypt. Nasser dispatched the bulk of his army, with hundreds of tanks and artillery pieces, to the Sinai Peninsula.

Israel closely monitored all developments but dismissed them as muscle-flexing on Nasser's part as long as the United Nations maintained its Sinai buffer force, installed following the 1956 Sinai Campaign as protection for Israel. When Syria accused Nasser of hiding behind the UN forces, however, he ordered them out on May 16, 1967. The evacuation of UN posts changed everything—Egypt and Israel were now eye to eye.

Nasser then upped the ante on May 22–23 by blockading the Straits of Tiran, the waterway leading into Israel's southern port of Eilat. That same action had contributed to Israel's Sinai invasion of 1956, and Israel still regarded it as an act of war. While Western powers and the UN scurried to find a diplomatic solution, the Arab world was unifying against Israel. Jordan's King Hussein flew to Cairo and concluded a mutual defense pact. Syria and Iraq reached similar agreements with Egypt. Nasser was on a high as these events catapulted him to center stage. Israel was on her own, with overwhelming forces arrayed against her on all fronts.

The war began on June 5, 1967, with Israel committing nearly its entire air force to a daring pre-emptive airstrike that surprised and virtually annihilated the Egyptian, Jordanian and Syrian air forces. IDF ground forces then swept across the vast expanse of the Egyptian Sinai Desert and Jordanian West Bank. East Jerusalem with the Old City was captured; Israel's capital was now united.

Despite ambitious plans to capture the eastern Galilee before advancing on Haifa, the Syrians—who had lost some 50 aircraft in the opening day's airstrike—largely sat out the war, except for three feeble attacks across the border, which amounted to little more than reconnaissance in force. That served Israel well while the IDF focused on the Egyptian and Jordanian fronts. Late in the week the Syrians stepped up their artillery barrages, as if goading Israel to attack. At that point, having defeated the Egyptian and Jordanian armies, Israel was able to reinforce the Golani force to where three armored brigades and five infantry brigades were poised to take on the Syrians.

Galilee residents implored the Israeli government to push the Syrians back to where their artillery could no longer torment them. However, with the Soviet Union threatening to intervene and the UN arranging a cease-fire, it seemed that the Syrians might retain their presence on the Golan Heights, symbolized by the ominous stone fortress of Tel Aziziat, which locals called "The Monster." But once it became clear the Soviets would stay out of the conflict, Israel's hands were freed. When the Syrians unleashed another round of shelling, violating the cease-fire, the Israeli GOC Northern Command, Major General David "Dado" Elazar, gave the go-ahead to launch the offensive. Given the background to that order, it was no wonder that there was such an outpouring of emotion among the Golani soldiers when told they would go into action against Syria.

Rising from the plains along almost the entire length of Israel's northern border with Syria, the Golan Heights themselves are a formidable natural barrier. The Golan Heights are made up of a 480 square mile (1,250 square km) volcanic (basalt) rock plateau perched above the Hula Valley to the west and Jordan Valley to the south. It rises gently from 600 feet (180m) in the south to 3,000 feet (915m) in the north, with abrupt escarpments dominating the valleys to the west and south. It is transected in some areas by impassable canyons, limiting the number of routes leading up from the valleys to the heights. The Syrians had established a network of heavily fortified positions along the border, and all possible routes of attack were mined, and well-covered by pre-ranged firing positions. Dug into the rough volcanic basalt was a Soviet-designed defensive network comprising level upon level of steel and concrete-reinforced bunkers, emplacements, pillboxes, and tunnels that were nearly impervious to air and artillery attack. One long-time resident of the area told of airstrikes against those positions that, judging by their intensity, seemed sufficient to silence them for good. But a few minutes after the smoke cleared, the Syrians would be back in action, firing at the Israeli communities below.

Manning the formidable defenses on what they called the "Palestine Front" were three Syrian brigades that in June 1967 received infantry, mechanized and armored reinforcements—some 56,000 troops in all. General Ahmed Sweidani's army fielded 300–550 tanks, mostly Soviet T-34s and T-54s, and more than 1,200 artillery pieces, including some of the most up-to-date Soviet mortars, howitzers and field guns, manned by Soviet-trained crews. Mobile and dug-in tanks, antitank guns, rocket launchers and antiaircraft guns added to the defenses.

As it turned its attention to the Golan Heights, the IDF had its work cut out for it—the Syrians seemed to have every military advantage except air superiority, which they made up for with some 200 antiaircraft guns. The Israelis would have to climb the Golan's steep rise in full view of well-entrenched Syrian troops. The IDF was taking on what appeared to be an impossible task.

Backed by artillery and close air support, the IDF attacked at multiple points along the border, with the main thrust directed against the Golan's northern fringe. The plan was to capture fortifications in that sector and to open the Banias–Mas'ada axis, the northernmost route leading to Kuneitra, capital of the Golan. The armored force was expected to overrun the Zaura area while the infantry was tasked with seizing the fortifications by Banias.

Before the assault, Israeli fighter-bombers streaked overhead dropping high-explosive ordnance and napalm onto the Syrian positions. While not that effective against the positions themselves, the airstrikes brought nearly all movement to a standstill. Syrian antiaircraft guns challenged the IAF, posing a threat that had to be eliminated before the IAF could provide effective close air support.

Just before noon, Colonel Abraham "Albert" Mandler's 8th Armored Brigade set out from Givat ha'Em, north of Kfar Szold. The terrain afforded little cover against observation from the Heights, and the Syrians began shelling the Israelis from the time they left their staging areas. The IAF put down a carpet of fire ahead of Mandler's armored columns, which included IDF-upgraded M-4 Sherman tanks known as Super Shermans, and infantry on M-3 halftracks, with specially improvised bulldozers leading the way. Combat engineers were at the forefront, clearing away mines and carving a path for the tanks while under heavy fire.

Syrian artillery took a heavy toll on the bulldozers and vulnerable halftracks, but in little more than an hour the Israelis had taken the Syrian positions at Gur-al-Aksar and Na'amush. The well-camouflaged Syrian bunkers were built deep into the rock and were immune to mortar fire, requiring the Israeli soldiers to take them out one by one with hand grenades.

So far, all was going according to plan, which called for Mandler's force to reach the Trans Arabian Pipeline (TAPline) route traversing the sector and then take the Zaura position at the base of Mount Hermon, securing a foothold on the northern Heights. There, however, the Israelis went astray. After taking their original objectives, an error in navigation left the vanguard Biro Battalion (named for its commander, Lieutenant Colonel Arye Biro) heading due south towards the Qala compound, a very heavily fortified Syrian position in a different sector. The Israelis realized their error when they found themselves attacking Sir-adib, below Qala. They took Sir-adib but were pinned down by heavy fire from Qala. The other armored forces continued according to plan and reached the TAPline route.

The Biro Battalion vainly looked for a way to bypass Qala and cut back towards Zaura, rather than advancing up the narrow, winding route to Qala, which was thought to be mined on the shoulders. Despite their efforts, the Israelis saw no option but to attack Qala head-on. The Israeli high command saw value in this deviation from the plan. A breakthrough at Qala would open the Nafakh–Kuneitra axis, allowing the IDF to advance much faster and deeper into the Golan than originally planned.

Many of Biro Battalion's tanks had already been knocked out by shells, damaged by mines, or hit during the initial breakthrough, and the rest made easy targets for the guns at Qala. Lieutenant Colonel Biro was injured and evacuated. Command of the 21 remaining tanks went to his executive officer—who was killed half an hour later.

Lieutenant Nethaniel "Nati" Hurwitz, a 25-year-old company commander, then took command of the battalion. A shell struck Hurwitz's
tank, injuring him and knocking out the tank's radio. Unable to
communicate with his force, Hurwitz had to switch tanks, only to
have to do so again when his second tank was also hit.

Large concrete antitank barricades known as "dragon's teeth,"
covered by Syrian antitank guns and machine-gun nests, blocked the
approach to Qala. Hurwitz called in artillery support that knocked
out the antitank guns, but not before they had disabled 11 Israeli
tanks. The damaged tanks provided cover fire while the 10 tanks still
in working order maneuvered through the dragon's teeth. Three tanks
were hit on the approach to Qala, and then several more were
knocked out by a hidden Syrian tank before it was spotted and
silenced by an armor-piercing round.

Word came in from Battalion Command that seven Syrian tanks
were en route to Qala. For Hurwitz's dwindling force, it was now a
race to reach Qala before the Syrian reinforcements arrived. One of
the three Israeli tanks that had made it into Qala was knocked out by
bazooka fire, and the remaining two hid among the town's houses.
Hurwitz called for assistance while crewmen from disabled tanks and
lightly injured soldiers secured the captured areas with Uzi submachine guns and grenades.

Meanwhile, most of the 8th Armored Brigade had found its way
to Zaura, as planned. Infantry accompanying the tanks crawled up
the steep terrain, cut through the barbed wire entanglements and
crossed the minefields to approach Zaura's defenses. A tank force
succeeded in breaking into the Syrian compound, though not without
first losing several tanks. After a brief struggle, Syrian resistance
broke. Isolated elements posed some problems, with Syrian soldiers
emerging from hidden positions and trying to disable tanks with
grenades or kill Israeli commanders. Mechanized infantry followed
the tanks and cleared out the Syrian positions. After securing Zaura,
the tanks hurriedly made their way 4 miles (6km) south to link up
with Hurwitz's force at Qala.

The remnants of the Biro Battalion at Qala waited in desperation
for the relief force. In response to their desperate calls for assistance,
air support arrived just minutes before nightfall, swooping down on

Syrian tanks as they arrived on scene, buying some time for the tiny force until elements of the 8th Brigade finally arrived from Zaura. Together, the combined Israeli armored forces completed the capture of Qala shortly after nightfall. Of the 21 tanks Hurwitz had when he assumed command earlier in the day, only two remained in working order. Hurwitz himself had gone through four. For his initiative and leadership, Hurwitz was awarded the *Itur haGvura*—Israel's highest military decoration.

Reporting on his ride with armored forces, British war correspondent Michael Bennett wrote: "Bunkers, gun emplacements, communication networks made to withstand any assault, were destroyed in hours. The bravery of the tank crews was beyond description, in the face of what looked like a suicidal frontal assault over a terrain not normally accepted as suitable for tanks. It was an honour to ride with such men."[1]

While the armored forces were fighting their way up the heights, a force from Colonel Yonah Efrat's Golani Brigade set out to take on the formidable company-sized Syrian border positions of Tel Aziziat and Tel Faher, just south of Banias. Tel Aziziat's concrete emplacements dominated the northeast Hula Valley. Tel Faher, situated 1,500 meters to the east on higher ground, commanded the approaches to Tel Aziziat. The Israeli attack plan called for both positions to be outflanked, which meant first overcoming the positions at Tel Faher and the adjacent position of Bourj Babil. Those two critical objectives fell on Golani's fully mechanized Barak Battalion, whose troops were mounted on M-3 halftracks, supported by a company of M-50 Super Shermans and AMX-13 light tanks. Led by Lieutenant Colonel Moshe "Musa" Klein, the Barak Battalion's *Aleph* and *Gimel* (akin to Alpha and Charlie) companies—about 125 officers and men with 19 halftracks and nine tanks—were to attack Tel Faher from the rear by means of a deep flanking maneuver to the TAPline road. Once Tel Faher was secured, *Bet* (Bravo) Company would attack Bourj Babil. After those two positions were in Israeli hands, a second Golani battalion, the "Boka'im HaRishon" would go into action against Tel Aziziat.

Of all the Syrian positions, Tel Faher was the largest and most strongly fortified. Situated on two hills, Tel Faher was commanded by the larger and higher northern position, where its main bunker was located. Secure behind layers of dense barbed wire entanglements and protective minefields, Tel Faher's reinforced bunkers and pillboxes, some cut into the rock, were connected via rows of concrete-lined communications trenches. Manning the positions and dugouts was a company from the Syrian 187th Infantry Battalion, including a unit armed with 57mm antitank guns, recoilless rifles, heavy machine guns and a battery of 82mm mortars.

At 13:00, following airstrikes and an artillery barrage on the Syrian positions and artillery, the Golani infantry crossed the Green Line, as the border was known, near Givat ha'Em. Following in the treads of Colonel Mandler's tanks, the Israeli force was immediately hit by a barrage of antitank and artillery fire from several Syrian positions. Tel Faher and Tel Aziziat were close enough for mutual fire support, and could also rely on the neighboring positions of Zaura and Ein Fit further up the heights, as well as Bourj Babil and Hirbat a-Suda.

Heavy, accurate Syrian fire and difficult terrain slowed the Israeli advance. A smoke screen failed to mask their approach, and as tanks and halftracks were stopped on the boulder-strewn path, the distance between the vehicles increased, and the force began suffering casualties. Communications became confused, and with the intense Syrian barrage contributing to the fog of war, the Israelis could not locate the intended attack route to the TAPline. Two hours had passed, and they were falling behind schedule, so Lieutenant Colonel Klein changed the plan. Instead of flanking Tel Faher and attacking from its more vulnerable eastern side, the men of the Barak Battalion would stage a direct, uphill assault.

From advantageous firing positions, the Syrian antitank fire targeted Israeli armor with great effectiveness. Not one of the Israeli tanks made it up to Tel Faher, and more than half the halftracks were damaged or stuck on the attack route. Klein's command halftrack took a hit, throwing off all on board. With the remaining halftracks drawing heavy fire, the Israelis decided to dismount and continue their assault on foot. Contact had been lost with much of the force, so orders had to be given verbally. Major Alex Krinsky, the battalion artillery officer, passed orders to Lieutenant Aharon Vardi's *Aleph*

Company. Four of *Aleph* Company's seven halftracks had been hit and 35 of Vardi's 60 men had been killed or wounded. Vardi and his men dismounted from their halftracks, and Krinsky divided the company. He would lead 12 men to attack Tel Faher's northern fortifications, while Vardi and the other 13 men would assault the southern positions.

Making their way up the twisting route to Tel Faher, Vardi's men faced a forest of barbed wire, just meters beyond which—across a minefield—lay their objective, Tel Faher's trenches and bunkers. They cut through the wire until heavy fire drove them back. Bangalore mines also failed to blast an opening through the wire, leaving the Israelis stranded and pinned down until infantryman David Shirazi came forward on his own initiative and lay across the barbed wire, becoming a human bridge. After the others had passed over him, Shirazi caught up with them and, as a "MAG'ist," as machine gunners were called after their FN MAG 7.62mm machine guns, he led the way into the outer trenches. Remaining cool under fire, Shirazi laid accurate suppressive fire that silenced several Syrian positions until he was killed by a sniper. Shirazi was posthumously awarded the *Itur haGvura* for his actions, which remain legendary to this day.

Syrian machine-gun nests continued spitting out murderous fire into the Golani infantrymen as they continued to advance uphill through the maze of trenches. When it became evident that the Barak Battalion would not quickly take Tel Faher according to plan, the Boka'im HaRishon battalion was ordered into action against its own assigned objectives. Moving into Syrian territory, the Boka'im reached the patrol road connecting the Syrian positions. Led by the battalion commander, Lieutenant Colonel Benny Inbar, *Bet* Company's seven halftracks and three tanks turned north, taking the fringe position at Bachrayat before assaulting heavily fortified Tel Aziziat from the rear.

The rows of barbed wire entanglements surrounding the position were only the beginning of Tel Aziziat's defenses. Crisscrossed with concrete and basalt stone bunkers, pillboxes, and deep, covered communication trenches, Tel Aziziat was topped by a concrete turret. Manning those formidable defenses was an infantry company of some 70 soldiers reinforced with small arms, machine guns, antitank guns and a World War II German Mark V Panther tank.

When a mine stopped one of *Bet* Company's tanks, combat engineers cleared the way under fire. Seeing the Israelis approaching, Tel Aziziat's defenders quickly mined the entrance to their position. When one of the Israeli halftracks set off a mine, the entrance was blocked. The original Israeli attack plan had called for the troops to ride their halftracks to the top of the position, but now the Golani troops had no choice but to dismount and go in by foot, clearing the trenches in a systematic fashion—working in pairs, one soldier provided suppressive fire while his partner threw grenades into each Syrian position.

The assault was proceeding like a well-rehearsed training exercise until fire from a concealed trench killed one Golani and injured others attempting to approach. Once the source of the fire was located, a rocket grenade silenced the sniper's nest. In the brief operation, the Golanis suffered only one soldier killed and seven wounded, while the Syrians lost 30 men dead and 26 captured; a handful managed to escape. By 17:05, the menacing Syrian position known as "The Monster" was in Israeli hands. The victorious soldiers raised the flags of Israel and of the Golani Brigade from a prominent tree over the newly captured position.

Up at Tel Faher, the battle was not going easily. What had been planned as a coordinated assault had deteriorated into engagements by small, dispersed groups. The Barak Battalion's *Aleph* Company was fighting a pitched battle against Tel Faher's stubborn defenders. Over the course of two hours, Vardi's group of 13 fought from bunker to bunker. In taking the trenches, all but three of the soldiers were killed or wounded, while the survivors ran out of ammunition.

Another force reached the southern positions after flanking Tel Faher, but while they knew that Vardi had gone in, they had no contact with him. After ramming through the gate, the Israelis cleared out trenches until they finally linked up with Vardi and his survivors and secured the southern positions.

In Tel Faher's northern sector, Krinsky and his dozen troops were clearing out the first trenches under deadly sniper fire from the stone fortification atop the position. By the time the Israelis approached the second tier of trenches, Krinsky had been hit and killed, and all but one of his men had been killed or wounded. Concerned about the battle's progress, battalion commander Moshe Klein followed the footsteps of "Force Krinsky," and learnt of its precarious state. To keep the battle's momentum going, Klein ordered the unwounded soldier to follow him as they charged into the trenches. The soldier yelled, "Battalion Commander—snipers!" Klein failed to heed the warning, and moments later he was shot dead.

At that point, Golani Brigade commander Colonel Efrat ordered in his reserve force—Captain Reuven "Ruvka" Eliaz's elite *sayeret* special reconnaissance unit, with its one tank, five halftracks and two jeeps—and sent in his deputy for an on-scene report. More Israeli troops also arrived, as men from Barak's *Gimel* Company—originally tasked as the assault force along with *Aleph* Company, reached the Syrian positions. Back after almost effortlessly taking the small fringe position of Bourj Babil between Tel Faher and Tel Aziziat, *Bet* Company and its four halftracks also joined the battle, arriving at the same time as the sayeret.

These reinforcements helped flush out the resilient defenders from the northern fortifications' trenches. The Golanis had to fight hard for every inch of ground. "We fought hand to hand with whatever we had," recounted one soldier. The Syrian defenders' determination and resolve was commendable, but by nightfall the Israelis finally secured Tel Faher.

Of the 13 positions taken by the Golani brigade on the Golan Heights, Tel Faher was the most difficult and costly to take. The battle site was renamed *Mitzpe Golani*, or Golani Lookout, as a memorial to the 34 Israeli soldiers killed and some 100 wounded there. The casualties included most of the Barak Battalion's command structure, from the battalion commander and his deputy down to company commanders. With so many of the senior officers killed at the outset of the battle, junior officers played a major role in leading the troops to victory.

Television producer Bill Cunningham, surveying a captured Syrian position, described the scene in amazement: "Tier upon tier of trenches and gun emplacements all commanding the plateau below. How the hell did anyone get up there?"[2] Chief of Staff Lieutenant General Yitzhak Rabin echoed those sentiments, saying, "Only when you see the enemy fortifications and bunkers up close can you understand what a difficult mission the Golani had . . ."[3]

Secondary attacks further south in the Heights also made inroads against the Syrian defenses. From Gonen, IDF troops fought their way up the Urfiya–Rawiye axis towards the TAPline route, opening the way for an armored force to advance into Syrian territory. Along the road running north of Bnot Yaakov Bridge, a combined force of tanks and infantry cracked the string of Syrian positions at Jelabina, Dardara, Tel Hilal and Darbashiya. On these and other attack points, IDF successes were straining the Syrians' ability to hold on.

By the end of the day, the entire Zaura–Qala region was in Israeli hands. While there was still a long way to go, the IDF was positioned to push towards Kuneitra from both the northern Banias–Mas'ada axis and the Nafakh–Kuneitra axis further south. Keeping alert for a possible counterattack, the Israelis spent the night fueling up their vehicles, replenishing provisions, bringing up reinforcements and regrouping in preparation for the next day's fighting.

On the morning of June 10, the IDF took Banias, Ein Fit, Mas'ada and Majdal Shams at the foot of Mount Hermon. The whole of the northern area along what until then had been the Syrian–Lebanese border was secured, clearing the northern approach to Kuneitra. From Qala, Israeli tank forces also pressed their attack eastward towards the Golan's capital.

When word reached them of the collapse of the northern Golan's defenses and of Israelis advancing towards Kuneitra from two directions, Syrians elsewhere in Golan knew their path of retreat was being cut off. Many Syrian officers, generally politically appointed Alawite religious sect officers, were quick to abandon their mostly Shiite Muslim soldiers for the safety of the rear.

Another front was opened on the morning of Saturday, June 10 by an Israeli advance southeast of the Sea of Galilee. Tanks and mounted infantry fought their way up the treacherous, winding mountain road from the lake's southern shores, breaking through the Syrian defenses at Tuwafik. IDF ground forces took the positions of Fiq, El Al and Boutmiya along the way to Rafid Junction, deep in the Golan. Some Israeli naval commandos, anxious to get in on the action, joined in this part of the operation. Ground forces cleared out areas on the southern axis into the Heights. Paratroopers were landed behind

Syrian lines by helicopter, but for the most part they found only isolated pockets of Syrian resistance. Other infantry units mopped up posts scattered throughout the sector, taking large numbers of prisoners.

The Syrian defenses had not collapsed completely. Earlier in the day, reinforcement convoys had headed towards what was becoming a rapidly receding front, and the situation was deteriorating. An IDF infantry and armored force had crossed the Jordan River and taken the lower and upper Customs House positions, and was now moving on Kuneitra from yet another direction. The Syrians tried to slow the Israeli advance by mining the roads, but there was no stopping the Israelis' momentum, and they arrived at Kuneitra's southern outskirts.

Within hours of the renewed Israeli operations that Saturday morning, the Syrians were fleeing the entire Golan. Speeding their retreat was a Radio Damascus report, meant either to motivate its soldiers to fight with greater resolve or to speed the UN into bringing about a cease-fire, announcing that Kuneitra had fallen—hours before the IDF arrived. The plan backfired as Syrian units still in Golan, fearing they would be encircled, beat a hasty retreat, leaving behind all sorts of weapons and equipment, down to boots and socks.

Kuneitra was surrounded and Mandler's 8th Armored Brigade moved in to complete its conquest. As a precautionary measure against Syrian snipers, only tanks entered at first. Finding the town all but deserted, Golani infantry went in to mop up and Kuneitra was securely in Israeli hands by 15:00.

Later, a force from the Golani's Gidon Battalion was flown by helicopter from Kuneitra to the southern face of Mount Hermon. Landing on the lower peak of the mountain, the Golani troops raised the national flag and determined Israel's new border. Perched high above the approaches from Damascus, that position would become a vital intelligence post for Israel.

The Golan Heights' 480 square miles had been captured in 27 hours, and the IDF was on the road to Damascus when a cease-fire went into effect at 18:00 on June 10. The Israelis then pulled back to a defensible line—a string of extinct volcanic cones commanding strategic views into Syria. For Syria, just as for Egypt and Jordan, the war was a humiliating defeat that left it seething for revenge. The final cease-fire was signed the following day in Kuneitra by Israeli and Syrian officers, overseen by UN military representatives.

The Battle for the Golan Heights had cost Israel 115 men killed and 306 wounded; Syrian casualties were estimated to be 10 times greater, along with about a third of its tank force and half its artillery. "Fortress Golan," as it was sometimes called, had been broken. While much of Israel was euphoric at the sudden end to its claustrophobia, with new borders far away from the Israeli heartland, the people of Israel's north finally had reason to be hopeful that after two decades of regular use, their protective shelters would become a thing of the past.

Notes

1. *Olei Britannia.*
2. William Stevenson. *Strike Zion!* (New York: Bantam Books, 1967), p.86.
3. Moty Har-Lev. *Golani Sheli [My Golani]* (Aviv Publishers), p.103.

CHAPTER 16

SACRIFICIAL STAND IN THE GOLAN HEIGHTS

1973 YOM KIPPUR WAR

Defeat seemed imminent. The Syrians' Soviet-style massive frontal assault was too much to bear, and the Israeli front lines had already collapsed. The Israeli general in charge of the entire front had abandoned his nearly surrounded headquarters and retired to a makeshift command post a few kilometers away. With two Syrian brigades advancing on the headquarters and no Israeli reserves in sight, defending the headquarters—left in the hands of infantrymen supported by only two trackless tanks mustered from the camp's repair depot—seemed almost futile.

On October 6, 1973, during Yom Kippur, the holiest day of the Jewish calendar, a Syrian armored force of 1,400 tanks backed by more than 1,000 artillery pieces and supporting air power began a coordinated assault along the Israeli–Syrian border in the Golan Heights in the north of Israel. The attack coincided with a similar onslaught by Egyptian forces along the Suez Canal, suddenly forcing Israel to fight a two-front war.

Israeli defense doctrine relies on the standing army to hold the line with air support while the reserves are mobilized. Therefore, the two

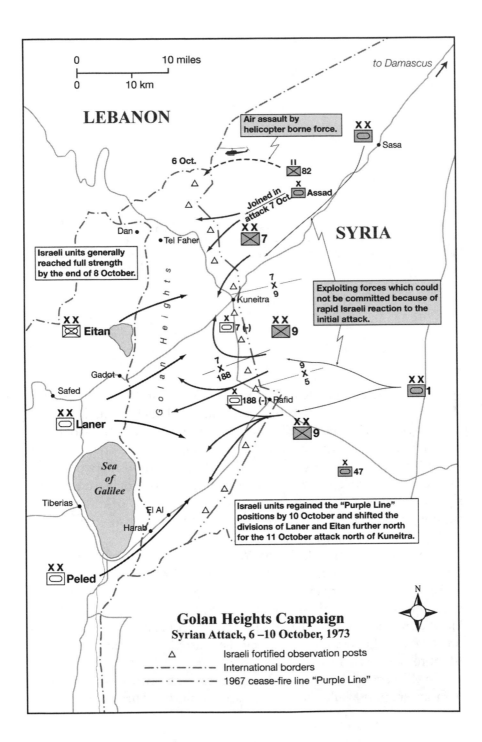

0 ─── 10 miles
0 ─── 10 km

to Damascus

LEBANON

Air assault by
helicopter borne force.

6 Oct.

SYRIA

Sasa

□□ XX

‖
⊠ 82

Joined in
attack 7 Oct.

X
☐ Assad

Dan

Tel Faher

XX
⊠ 7

Israeli units generally
reached full strength
by the end of 8 October.

Golan Heights

7
X
9

Kuneitra

Exploiting forces which could
not be committed because of
rapid Israeli reaction to the
initial attack.

XX
⊠ Eitan

X
☐ 7 (-)

XX
⊠ 9

Gadot

7
X
188

9
X
5

XX
☐ 1

Safed

X
☐ 188 (-) Rafid

XX
☐ Laner

XX
⊠ 9

*Sea
of
Galilee*

Tiberias

El Al

X
☐ 47

Harab

Israeli units regained the "Purple Line"
positions by 10 October and shifted the
divisions of Laner and Eitan further north
for the 11 October attack north of Kuneitra.

XX
☐ Peled

N

Golan Heights Campaign
Syrian Attack, 6–10 October, 1973

△   Israeli fortified observation posts
─ · ─ · ─   International borders
─ · · ─ · · ─ 1967 cease-fire line "Purple Line"

Israeli brigades that stood in the Syrians' way in the Golan had to hold off the onslaught long enough for Israel's reserve mobilization to kick in. The 7th Armored Brigade's epic defense of the northern Golan has come to be widely regarded as one of the finest defensive stands in military history. Less is known about the heroism of the shattered fragments of the 188th (Barak) Brigade in slowing the Syrian advance in the south. In some respects, however, the Barak Brigade's story is more incredible, considering the fact that hundreds of Syrian tanks had overrun its sector and were held off by only a handful of tanks.

The 1973 conflict was about honor. In the Six Day War of June 1967, Israel had seized the Golan Heights, sweeping out the Syrian defenders and putting an end to the harassment that the Syrians had inflicted on civilians in the Hula Valley and the villages of the north. The loss of the Golan Heights had been humiliating to Syria, and between 1967 and 1973, there had been frequent skirmishes along the cease-fire line. For months leading up to the attack, the Syrian army had been fully mobilized and on war alert. Since the Israelis were accustomed to seeing those forces at battle strength, the Syrians were able to make final attack preparations without sending noteworthy warning signals. Furthermore, with tensions escalating between the two countries, Israeli leadership feared that strengthening their defenses might be misconstrued as preparation for a pre-emptive strike, thus provoking the Syrians to attack.

Since the Golan Heights' geography restricted defensive mobility, Israel had continued its advance in 1967 until a defensible line was reached—a string of extinct volcano cones that commands strategic views into Syria. Post-1967, Israeli defenses were based on 17 fortified observation posts. The Purple Line, as the 1967 cease-fire line was known, marked the end of the no-man's land separating Syria from the Golan. Lacking a true defensive barrier, the Israelis had dug a 20-mile (30-km) antitank ditch along the border from Mount Hermon to Rafid, an obstacle Syrian armor would be forced to cross under fire from Israeli tanks positioned behind ramparts. At the outbreak of hostilities in 1973, the Golan Heights were defended by two armored brigades: the 7th, which had only been dispatched to the northern sector on October 4, and the 188th (Barak) Brigade, who were based in the area and intimately familiar with the local terrain, in the south. The modified Centurion and M-48 Patton tanks fielded by both brigades were fitted with the 105mm NATO gun and modern diesel engines.

Considering the faulty Israeli intelligence assessment suggested that, at most, armed skirmishes with the Syrians would break out, the 170 tanks and 70 artillery pieces in the Golan were thought to be enough to meet any Syrian threats, at least until the reserves arrived.

Against that comparatively small force, the Syrian army fielded five divisions for its attack: two armored and three mechanized infantry, including some 1,400 tanks. Approximately 400 of those tanks were T-62s, the most modern Soviet-bloc tank at the time, equipped with a 115mm smoothbore gun and infrared night-fighting capability. The balance of the tank force consisted of T-54s and T-55s armed with 100mm guns. The Syrian plan called for its 5th, 7th and 9th mechanized infantry divisions, in BTR-50 armored personnel carriers (APCs) supported by 900 tanks, to breach the Israeli lines, opening the way for the 1st and 3rd armored divisions to move in with their 500 tanks to capture the entire Golan Heights before Israel had a chance to mobilize.

At 14:00 on October 6, Syrian gunners opened up a tremendous barrage along the entire front as a prelude to their two-pronged attack—a northern one in the vicinity of the Kuneitra–Damascus road and one in the south where Rafid bulges into Syria.

7th Armored's Legendary Stand in the Northern Golan Heights

Facing Colonel Avigdor Ben-Gal's 7th Armored Brigade in the Golan's northern sector were the Syrian 3rd Armored Division under Brigadier General Mustapha Sharba, the 7th Mechanized Infantry Division and the Assad Republican Guard. When the Syrian assault began, mine-clearing tanks and bridge-layers led the way to overcome the Israeli obstacles. Naturally, those engineering vehicles were the 7th's first targets, but Syrian infantrymen, braving intense fire from the heights, rushed forward and used their entrenching tools to build up enough earthen causeways for their tanks to negotiate the Israeli antitank ditches.

While the Israelis took out every Syrian vehicle they could get in their sights, the sheer mass of some 500 enemy tanks and 700 APCs advancing toward their lines ensured that the defenses would be overwhelmed. The number of defenders dwindled as Israeli tanks were knocked out, yet the vastly outnumbered Israelis managed to take a heavy toll on Syrian armor. Despite heavy losses, the Syrians pressed their attack without let-up, yet the overexerted 7th managed to hold its ground, throwing stopgap blocking actions wherever the Syrians were on the verge of breaking through.

When darkness fell, the Israelis had nothing to match the Syrians' night-vision gear and the enemy armor were able to advance to ranges effective for night fighting. In the close fighting, the Syrians succeeded in seizing some of the high ground, but a counterattack by the small group of persistent defenders forced them back. When some Syrian tanks did overrun the Israeli lines, the 7th's gunners rotated their turrets to destroy them and then immediately turned their attention back to other oncoming tanks. It amounted to an armored version of hand-to-hand combat.

The battle raged for two more days as the Syrians, seemingly oblivious to their heavy losses, continued their assault. By the afternoon of October 9, the 7th Brigade was down to six tanks protecting what was otherwise, for all intents and purposes, a clear path into Israel's north.

Those last few tanks fought until they were down to their last rounds. Then, just as the 7th Brigade's tanks were finally starting to pull back, they were suddenly augmented by an impromptu force of some 15 tanks. The Syrians believed the clock had run out and that the first of the fresh Israeli reservists had arrived, and the Syrian offensive ran out of steam. In fact, it was a motley force of repaired tanks that had pulled back from Tel Faris, mustered by Lieutenant Colonel Yossi Ben-Hanan, a veteran commander who, upon hearing about the outbreak of war, had hurried home from his honeymoon overseas. By virtue of its timing, that force, now manned by injured and other crewmen, proved to be the 7th Brigade's saving grace. As individual tanks began to augment the Israeli forces, the Syrians, exhausted from three days of continuous fighting and unaware of how close to victory they actually were, turned in retreat. Hundreds of destroyed tanks and APCs scattered about the valley below the Israeli ramparts were testimony to the horrible destruction that had taken place there, leading an Israeli colonel to dub it the "Valley of Tears."

188th Stands Its Ground in the Southern Golan

Meanwhile, the Syrians, whose objectives included seizing the bridges spanning the Jordan River—most of which could be easily reached through the southern Golan, concentrated a large part of their attack in that sector on October 6. Up against hundreds of enemy tanks, arranged in a line of armor as far as the eye could see, the Barak Brigade crews had no choice but to try to hold fast, because the terrain did not allow for much defensive maneuvering. Retreat would give the Syrians nearly free rein to seize the entire heights and move on the Israeli villages in the valley below.

The Syrian advance was initially slowed by an Israeli minefield and by deadly, accurate cannon fire. With dozens of Syrian tanks destroyed, the first few hours of the war were encouraging for the Israeli crewmen, whose intense training was paying off. Knowing they would be outnumbered in any engagement, the Israeli tank gunners had focussed relentlessly in training on gunnery skills and rapid target acquisition to ensure kills on the first shot. But the Israeli defenses could not contend with so many Syrian tanks. The Syrians' losses did not deter them, and they kept coming.

When fighter aircraft were called in to help stem the flow of Syrian armor, many of the Douglas A-4 Skyhawks and McDonnell F-4E Phantoms that responded to the plea were shot down or damaged by the Syrians' dense antiaircraft umbrella. Aware that Israeli doctrine relied on air power to even the score against their enemies' numerical advantage, Syria had acquired massive quantities of the latest Soviet missile and antiaircraft systems. With the help of Soviet advisers, they created an air defense network over the Golan that was thicker than the one protecting Hanoi during the Vietnam War.

With their air support thus limited, the Israeli tanks on the Golan were on their own—and the fate of northern Israel was in their hands. The Israeli tanks stood their ground and were knocked out one by one. Pushed beyond their limits, the defenses in the southern sector broke.

Bypassing the Israeli fortifications and pouring through gaps in the defenses, Syrian tanks pushed through the Israeli lines onto the wide-open plain that was ideal for tanks. The Israelis defending the southern Golan knew that they had to hold on at all costs to allow time for the reserves to mobilize, and in many cases the tank crews sacrificed themselves rather than give ground. As the hours passed, fewer and fewer Israeli tanks were left to stem the tide of oncoming tanks. The Syrian force split into a two-pronged advance. Colonel Tewfik Jehani's 1st Armored Division moved northward toward the Golan command headquarters of Major General Rafael Eitan, situated on the road leading down to the Bnot Yaakov Bridge, over the Jordan River and into the Israeli hinterland. The second prong of the Syrian attack, spearheaded by the 46th Armored Brigade of the 5th Infantry Division, moved south from Rafid on the southern axis road toward El Al, with units breaking off toward the north in the direction of the Arik Bridge at the northern tip of the Sea of Galilee. Some 600 tanks were now engaged in the southern Golan, against which stood 12 tanks and isolated units that had been cut off near the various fortifications along the border.[1]

Night offered no respite from the Syrian advance as they capitalized on their advantage of sophisticated night-vision equipment. The Israeli crews' long-distance firing efficiency was hampered by their lack of adequate night-fighting equipment. They did their best to overcome this obstacle by ordering illumination rounds to light up the sky, in conjunction with the xenon light projectors mounted on their tanks. Those were no match for the Syrians' infrared searchlights, so the Israelis did what they do best—improvise. They directed small tank units to carry out stopgap blocking actions against the far superior enemy forces—a tactic that may have prevented the Syrians from overrunning the entire Golan.

One of those lethal holding actions that have become legend was led by a young lieutenant named Zvi Gringold, affectionately known as "Lieutenant Zvicka," whose nighttime hit-and-run attacks on October 6–7 are credited as single-handedly holding at bay a major thrust by almost 50 tanks. His guerrilla-style tactics on the route leading toward his brigade's HQ at Nafakh caused the Syrians to believe they were up against a sizable Israeli force. After more than ten of its tanks were destroyed, the Syrian column withdrew, its commander deciding to hold off and deal with the Israeli force in daylight. Gringold continued to engage the Syrians throughout the night and following day, destroying upward of 30 tanks, until injuries, burns, and exhaustion caught up with him and he was evacuated. Gringold recovered and was subsequently awarded the *Itur haGvura,* or Medal of Valor, for his heroic defense of Nafakh.

Another blocking force operating in the south, albeit attached to the 7th Brigade, was "Force Tiger" under Captain Meir Zamir. Force Tiger's seven tanks were sent to block a column of some 40 Syrian tanks that had broken through at Rafid and was heading north—a move that threatened to cut off and isolate the 7th Brigade. Force Tiger laid an ambush that succeeded in destroying half the Syrian tanks during the early hours of Sunday morning, October 7. When 20 tanks escaped, Zamir prepared a second ambush that succeeded in finishing off the Syrian battalion just after dawn the next morning.

Yet another Syrian thrust by two brigades was advancing rapidly on the southern access road in the wide-open southern sector and inexplicably stopped short in its tracks just before reaching El Al. While some of its units fanned off toward other objectives to the north, a large part of the Syrian force failed to press its advantage, meaning that in effect the Syrians just waited for the Israeli reserves to arrive and engage them. A number of theories abound as to why the Syrians would halt their advance in the midst of their momentum, including fear of an ambush on what certainly should have been a heavily defended route, lack of flexibility and initiative once their objectives had been achieved, overextended supply lines and the more far-fetched fear of an Israeli nuclear reprisal in that critical hour. Whatever the true reason, their lack of initiative at a critical moment robbed the Syrians of the chance to reach the Jordan River—and perhaps beyond—virtually unopposed.

In the morning of October 7, the Syrians pressed their attack yet again. The few remaining defenders of the Barak Brigade pleaded for air support, which again suffered heavy losses. Ironically, the Syrians helped solve the problem of the antiaircraft missile threat for the Israelis. After the Syrians fired rockets at Israeli civilian areas, the Israeli Air Force responded with reprisal attacks on Syrian infrastructure in Damascus and beyond. To defend against these attacks, the

Syrians pulled back some of their missile batteries from the Golan front. Overall, it took the IAF several days to develop tactics and gain experience in defeating Syrian air defense systems, and 27 Israeli aircraft were lost on the Golan front in ground-support missions, as well as scores of others suffering various degrees of damage.

On October 7, Minister of Defense Moshe Dayan toured the Golan front and recognized how critical the situation truly was. Not only were the access routes into the Golan threatened, but also the entire north of Israel. Grasping the very real prospect of a Syrian breakthrough into integral Israel, the minister of defense considered a retreat to a line just forward of the escarpment overlooking the Jordan Valley for a major defensive stand—in effect putting his forces' backs against a wall. Israel prepared to destroy the bridges over the Jordan River to prevent a Syrian breakthrough.

The Syrian 1st Armored Division was advancing up the route toward the Golan HQ at Nafakh. Colonel Yitzhak Ben-Shoham, commander of the Barak Brigade, realized his brigade was for all intents and purposes destroyed. He therefore organized and led a small group of surviving tanks in a holding action that slowed the Syrian advance on his HQ for several hours until he and the rest of the group were killed. With the brigade commander dead, no reserves in sight and two Syrian brigades advancing toward the Golan HQ—and with some units having bypassed the base on both flanks—the situation at Nakakh could only be described as grave. Lead elements of the Syrian brigades actually reached Nafakh and broke through the base's southern perimeter. One Syrian T-55 crashed into General Eitan's HQ, only to be knocked out by the last operational tank in Gringold's platoon.

At that point, Eitan evacuated his headquarters to an improvised location farther to the north. Those left to defend the base manned two trackless Centurions from the camp repair depot and fired bazookas in a final stand that knocked out several Syrian tanks until those last Israeli tanks were destroyed.

The 188th Barak Brigade was no more. The Syrians were poised to overrun the Golan headquarters at Nafakh and, seemingly, the entire Golan. That final stand, however, had been enough to buy a few crucial additional minutes. While the Syrians paused to regroup after their final opposition had been neutralized, the first Israeli reserve units began reaching what had become the front lines. Finding Syrian tanks milling about their command headquarters, the Israelis immediately opened fire and attacked, dispersing the Syrians.

The arrival of the Israeli reservists spelled the beginning of the end for Syria. For both sides, the war had been about time—the Israelis doing all they could to buy time until their reserves arrived, and the Syrians racing against the clock to achieve their objectives before the Israeli mobilization. While many more bloody battles would take place, those first reserve units coming up the Golan and engaging the Syrians at Nafakh meant that the tide had turned.

The reservists found the Syrians enjoying nearly free rein in the Golan's southern sector. With Syrian tanks advancing along the routes down toward the Jordan River, the critical situation allowed no time to organize divisions and brigades. Instead, platoons and companies of tanks and other units rushed off to battle as quickly as the forces were mustered, at times being thrown in against Syrian battalions and even brigades. The fresh Israeli reserve units halted the near—and, in some cases, actual—retreat and began to check the Syrian advance. By midnight on day two of the war, the reserves had managed to stabilize what had been a disintegrating front.

The Syrians had managed to penetrate to areas a mere 10-minute drive from the Jordan River and Sea of Galilee and to less than a kilometer from El Al on the southern access road. Those gains had not come easily. In spite of their superior numbers, the Syrians' supply lines, extending great distances from their rear areas to points deep into the Golan, had been decimated by the Israeli defenders, and they could no longer replenish and support their forces. Convoys of supplies and reinforcements were under constant attack by the IAF, as well as IDF armor and other ground forces, severely hampering the Syrian advance.

While the Syrians dug in to consolidate their gains, the Israelis went on the offensive. Brigadier General Moshe Peled led a division up the Ein Gev road into the center of the southern sector while Major General Dan Laner's division moved up the Yehudia road farther to the north—a parallel advance that boxed in the 1st Syrian Armored Division and effectively brought the Syrians' brief conquest to an end. The Syrians fought viciously to free themselves from that pincer movement. A major confrontation near Hushniya camp, which the Syrians had captured the previous night and turned into a forward supply base, ended with hundreds of wrecked, burning and smoldering Syrian tanks, armored vehicles, and other vehicles littering the landscape.

By October 10, the Israelis had forced the Syrians back to the antebellum cease-fire line in the southern sector. Well aware of the strong Syrian defensive preparations in the south, Israel chose the northern Golan, with its more difficult, less-defended terrain, as the launching area for its counterattack into Syria itself. Among the units joining the counterattack was the reincarnated Barak Brigade. Since 90 percent of its original commanders had been killed or wounded, Barak's remnants were joined by replacements, reorganized and returned to fighting strength for the counteroffensive that penetrated deep into Syria.

Syria clamored for assistance from ally Egypt to relieve pressure on its now embattled forces. After initial successes at the beginning of the war, when its forces crossed the formidable barrier of the Suez Canal, overcame Israeli defenses and secured a significant foothold, the Egyptians now ventured out from their defensive deployment at the behest of Syria. Massive tank battles of a scale not seen since World War II were fought in which Egyptian forces were decimated. The IDF had turned the tide, which they capitalized upon when Israeli forces crossed the Suez Canal into Egypt proper, trapping an entire Egyptian army in the Sinai Desert.

A United Nations-sanctioned cease-fire came into effect on October 23, officially ending hostilities. Although the war ended with Israeli forces on the move toward the Syrian capital and entrenched in Egypt proper, the Yom Kippur War—or Ramadan War, as it is known to the Arabs—shattered the myth of Israeli invincibility. The Syrians' success in maintaining the element of surprise and its forces' discipline in executing its attack helped that country regain much of the honor it had lost in the debacle of 1967. The victorious Israelis, on the other hand, had won a Pyrrhic victory. Horrible losses had been suffered, epitomized by the obliteration of the 188th Barak Brigade. While the war reaffirmed the Israeli defense doctrine of relying on the reserves to defeat a numerically superior enemy force, there was no time for celebration as the country buried the 2,222 soldiers who had paid the ultimate price for their country's survival, and attended to its 7,251 wounded.

Notes
1.Chaim Herzog. *The War of Atonement* (Jerusalem: Steimatzky's Agency, 1975), p.87.

CHAPTER 17

TURKEY SHOOT OVER THE BEKAA VALLEY

1982 Lebanon War

As Israeli Air Force (IAF) pilots flew their aircraft home and began to contemplate what they had been through, some were overcome with nervous excitement. It was not only isolated cases where pilots failed on their first landing attempts. Once the aircraft were safely back on the tarmac, ground crews saw that the launching rails, pylons and bomb racks were now largely empty. Mission tapes removed from the aircraft revealed the unprecedented feat the IAF had just pulled off—a mission nearly a decade in the making. Minister of Defense Ariel Sharon remarked that "the exemplary control, incredible accuracy, and precise planning displayed by Israel's pilots would be studied in military academies around the world."[1]

During the October 1973 Yom Kippur War, more than 40 Israeli aircraft, mostly McDonnell F-4E Phantoms and Douglas A-4 Skyhawks flying ground support and attack missions, had been shot down by Soviet-built Egyptian and Syrian surface-to-air missiles (SAMs). Stung by such heavy losses, Israel acted to ensure that its next contest against Arab SAMs would have a more successful outcome. The IAF's opportunity to implement plans based on the lessons learned from the 1973 war was Israel's 1982 invasion of Lebanon, called Operation *Peace for Galilee*.

In the spring of 1981, as part of the Israeli–Syrian power struggle over Lebanon, Syria moved SAM batteries into eastern Lebanon's Bekaa Valley, which stretches nearly 120 miles (200km) between the Lebanon Mountains and the Anti-Lebanon Mountains, from Mount Hermon in the south up to Zahla. Over the course of the next year, Syria built up an overlapping network of 19 SAM batteries, 15 of which were SA-6 sites, and a pair each of SA-2 and SA-3 for medium- and high-altitude aircraft, protected from attack by ZSU-23-4 radar-controlled antiaircraft artillery (AAA) and SA-7 Strela ("Arrow" in Russian) shoulder-launched missiles. With these capabilities, Syria could sweep the Bekaa Valley's airspace clean of Israeli aircraft.

Syrian involvement in Lebanon runs as long as Lebanon's history. As Lebanon's territory had been cut from Syria by European colonialists, Syria considered Lebanon part of its territory and never recognized its independence. Syrian troops entered the country in 1976 ostensibly in a peacekeeping role in the aftermath of Lebanon's 1975–76 civil war, their presence serving the dual purpose of blocking an exposed flank should Israel decide to invade Syria through Lebanon. Israel, however, felt equally threatened by Syria's apparent permanence in Lebanon.

Before the country erupted into civil war, Lebanon had been the "Paris of the Middle East"—a country rich and diverse both ethnically and culturally, yet held together in a delicate balancing act. Then, in 1970, when Palestinians became too cozy using Jordan as a base for terror operations against Israel and the West, King Hussein expelled them from his country. Weak and divided Lebanon became their refuge. Palestine Liberation Organization (PLO) terrorists established a state-within-a-state in Lebanon's mountainous territory. "Fatahland," as the area was known to Israel, became an armed PLO camp used to launch guerrilla infiltrations into Israel and to terrorize Israel's northern towns and villages with harassing rocket and artillery attacks.

In March 1978 the IDF launched a six-day ground incursion against the PLO in Lebanon called Operation *Litani*, but the PLO quickly recovered from that blow and continued its indiscriminate firing of Katyusha rockets and artillery salvos into Israel from south Lebanon. Overseas, an escalation in terror attacks against Israeli and Jewish sites culminated in the attempted assassination of the Israeli ambassador in London by a Palestinian terror group on June 3, 1982. In immediate retaliation for the assassination attempt, Israeli jets bombed PLO ammunition dumps and training bases in Lebanon. The PLO responded with a massive rocket and artillery bombardment against Israel's northern communities. Israel implemented its contingency plan to clear a 25-mile (40-km) security zone north of the Lebanon–Israel border that would push PLO artillery beyond range of Israel's northern settlements.

On June 6, 1982, Israeli units advanced into Lebanon along three axes, destroying PLO bases along the way. IAF fighters and attack helicopters bombed PLO strongholds, clearing the way for the ground forces. By the third day of the war, Israeli troops had achieved their goal of reaching a line 25 miles (40km) from the border. With its army in a favorable position vis-à-vis Syrian forces in Lebanon, Israel saw its chance to rid Lebanon of its Syrian foe as well. But support for its ground forces necessitated air superiority, and that was threatened by the Syrian missiles. The SAMs had to go.

Knowing that SAMs would remain a force to be dealt with in future warfare, over the years since the Yom Kippur War, Israel had developed special weapons and tactics to take them on. Syria's missile deployment in Lebanon posed a challenge to Israel, so Israel began piecing together its plan.

Since the SAM must track its target with its own radar, the key was taking out the radar. Radar is a pulse of electromagnetic energy in a concentrated beam. When a target is "illuminated" by this beam, some of the pulse is reflected back to the radar, giving the operator information on target bearing and range. The idea behind SEAD—suppression of enemy air defenses, as engaging and destroying SAMs is known in military lingo—is to entice the enemy to light up his search radars in order to destroy them. Doing so requires locating the mobile missile batteries with precise intelligence information, disrupting tracking and guidance radar systems and communications with electronic warfare, and diverting missiles by way of deception. To pull this off, Israel concocted an intricate plan involving drones, decoys, highly developed electronic counter-measures (ECM), anti-radiation (ARM) and precision-guided missiles, and other tactics which remain classified.

The first moves of the highly orchestrated operation against the Syrian air defense network in Lebanon were actually made long before the attack. Tasked with pinpointing the location of the SAMs, Israel Aircraft Industries (IAI) "Scout" and Tadiran "Mastiff" reconnaissance mini-UAVs (unmanned aerial vehicles, or pilot-less drones) flew over the area almost daily in the ELINT (Electronic Intelligence) role, scanning the area for emissions from radars and radios. In this way, Israel was able to locate the Syrian SAM batteries and identify their radar frequencies and operational sequences—information that was then used to develop appropriate electronic countermeasures. Several UAVs were downed, but the cost was negligible when compared with the risks of sending manned reconnaissance sorties over SAM-protected areas.

Electro-optical sensors on the UAVs relayed real-time intelligence data to operators controlling the aircraft from ground control stations. Their pictures revealed that the mobile SA-6s were deployed mostly in fixed positions. But since the SA-6 batteries could be easily redeployed, UAVs loitered in the air long before, during and after the attack, maintaining a vigil on them as the aircraft's cameras recorded a steady stream of intelligence information which was collected into an overall picture of the situation on the ground.

With all this intelligence information, Israel was able to put the finishing touch on its plans. Since the attack would reveal special weapons and tactics Israel had been developing over nearly a decade, Israeli leadership decided to attack on a grand scale, taking out the entire Syrian SAM network rather than a piecemeal approach concentrating on the most threatening sites.

On June 9, 1982, the fourth day of the war, at airbases throughout Israel, air crews suited up in their G suits and squadron leaders met in briefing rooms to review final preparations for the offensive. Even as the Cabinet discussed the plan submitted by Minister of Defense Ariel Sharon, Israeli pilots headed out to aircraft shelters where ground crews strapped pilots into their seats, shut them into cockpits and made final checks of the aircraft. Jet engines roared to life and aircraft rolled out to runways. When authorization to launch the attack came at 13:30 hours, an armada of aircraft howled into the sky and sped north on its brief flight to Lebanon. The attack aircraft—once the hunted—were now the hunters.

The Israeli attack force consisted of approximately 90 aircraft: McDonnell Douglas F-15 Eagles, General Dynamics F-16 Fighting Falcons (newcomers to the IAF, having arrived only in 1980), IAI Kfir C-2s, F-4E Phantoms and A-4 Skyhawks. The F-15s and F-16s flew top cover while the attack aircraft, coming from different bases, flew at different altitudes and intervals towards the batteries they were tasked with destroying. With so many aircraft involved, precise air traffic control was required. Here Israel had the luxury of running a war close to home, with full battlefield awareness. Grumman E-2C Hawkeye command aircraft, capable of automatically and simultaneously tracking hundreds of targets and controlling multiple airborne intercepts, assisted in providing continuous air control and coordination.

Flying outside of missile range, IAF Boeing 707s and other aircraft packed full of sophisticated electronic warfare equipment overlaid new data on the information previously collected by UAVs. The Electronic Warfare (EW) aircraft's highly sensitive receivers detected Syrian radars, ran their signals through computers to amplify and filter them and, by measuring frequencies of the signals, allowed the Israelis to pinpoint the locations of threatening sources. Jammers generated and returned incorrect signals to confuse the Syrian radar and disrupt communication channels. Supplemental stand-off jamming by the attack aircraft further "blinded" the radar sites, frustrating their ability to get a reliable fix on Israeli aircraft.

SAMs are most effective when operated in concert with long-range search radars which feed data on inbound aircraft to SAM batteries' targeting radars. This allows the SAM battery to activate its radar at the last moment and fire a missile with virtually no warning. Israel had done its homework to prevent such surprises by knowing the exact location of the missile batteries and by constantly monitoring for changes. The Syrians had also been helpful in this regard by deploying their missiles in visible locations, as if flaunting their presence to the Israelis. With their frequencies blocked or jammed, the

SAM batteries had minimal early warning and communication capabilities, crucial elements in an integrated air-defense network. The Israelis had also ensured that the Syrians would not have supplemental radar by launching attacks on radar installations, including an assault by a Bell AH-1G Cobra helicopter that destroyed a radar station south of Beirut with Hughes TOW (tube-launched, optically sighted, wire-guided) missiles.

The Israeli assault on the SAM sites began with a masterful feat of deception. Objects appearing on the Syrian radar as aircraft were not really aircraft. Meanwhile, the real IAF aircraft that were en route to attack the Syrians were not showing up on the radar. And the beams sent out by Syrian radar were used by some of the Israeli weapons to guide them to target. To confuse the radars still functioning, the Israelis saturated Lebanon's skies with simulated targets. The unpowered, air-launched Samson decoy, developed specifically for the IAF by Brunswick Defense, used special lenses or reflectors to enhance its radar signature, causing it to appear on radar screens as full-scale aircraft. The slew of decoys in the air forced Syrian SAM radar operators to light up their search radars, exposing themselves to ARM strikes, while they wasted their missiles on the decoys. After firing, missile launchers are extremely vulnerable as they reload, especially after publicizing their location by firing. To add to the confusion the jamming and the false images decoys were creating on Syrian radar screens, Israeli artillery unleashed a barrage of long-range shells and rockets against the SAM sites.

With all this going on, the waves of attack aircraft headed towards their targets in a massive simultaneous attack reminiscent of Israel's destruction of the Arab air forces in the 1967 Six Day War. The IAF strike force of Phantoms and F-16s went in for the kill at 14:00, descending on the Bekaa Valley trailing flares and chaff—bundles of thin metallic strips designed to confuse the guidance systems of any missiles the Syrians might succeed in launching. Following target acquisition and lock-on, the attack aircraft unleashed supersonic Shrike AGM-45 and AGM-78 ARMs to home in on the electromagnetic waves emitted by the activated SAM radar vans.

AGM-65 Mavericks and other precision-guided missiles were also fired at the SAM radars. Equipped with coordinates and aerial photographs of the sites they were tasked with destroying, Israeli airmen acquired targets visually, put radar vans between the crosshairs of their sights and launched their missiles. From the missile-eye view appearing on small cockpit screens, the Israeli aircrews could follow the missiles' progress as they raced in on "fire and forget" mode, seeing the entire missile battery coming into view in the distance, then focus on the central radar vehicle until only that vehicle could be seen, growing in size as the missile descended towards it, and then static on the screen as the missile hit.

Syria's command centers and radars were put out of action with high-explosive, fragmentation, and shaped-charge warheads, the latter designed to defeat heavy armor. The exploding vehicles were immediately engulfed in flames and thick gray smoke. The pilots pulled away, G forces pressing them back into their seats as they gained altitude and made for home.

Despite all their protective measures, the Israelis in the air still kept a wary eye out for missiles. The 20-foot (6-m) long SA-6 missiles looked like bright colored balls as they shot up from the ground. IAF pilots reported seeing some SAM launches, but they said that the missiles seemed to lack direction and did not actually threaten their aircraft. With the Syrian radars destroyed, there were no ground command links steering the missiles. With its semi-active homing radar, the SA-6 could still be lethal—until it has flown off course and its fuze times out, causing it to self-destruct.

Israeli aircraft were equipped with radar homing and warning receivers to alert pilots with a shrill alarm in their headsets if their aircraft were tracked. Small screens displaying alphanumeric figures reflected the type, angle of arrival, relative lethality and status of threats, with special warnings for missile launch. IAF pilots had been repeatedly drilled in the ways to avoid being targeted, from chaff and other countermeasures to jinking, or evasive flying. If a missile were launched against an aircraft, the pilot had to maintain incredible concentration to avoid it. In those critical moments, panic could result in death. Even if they could safely eject, the Israeli pilots did not know what type of reception they might receive below, especially after seeing televised images of the corpse of an Israeli airman downed by ground fire earlier in the war being dragged through the streets of

Beirut. But on June 9, 1982, the missiles—confused by Israeli jamming and electronic countermeasures—failed to hit a single Israeli aircraft.

Their radars destroyed, each SAM missile battery's armored Transporter Erector Launcher (TEL), with its complement of three missiles, was not only blinded, but vulnerable. Some batteries tried to protect themselves with smokescreens, but that only served to highlight their locations. Since they are mobile, SA-6s were not dug in, making them easier to spot from the air. Dozens of F-16s, Phantoms, Kfirs and Skyhawks, their hardpoints heavy-laden with general-purpose and cluster bombs, swooped in to bomb the missile batteries' defenseless launchers and AAA sites. Fused to detonate on impact, the general-purpose bombs' cast-steel cases shattered into thousands of destructive fragments. Cluster bombs, packed full of "bomblet" sub-munitions, proved particularly effective against each battery's dispersed area targets of command vehicles, generators and other support equipment. With their fuzes set to activate at a preset altitude, the bomblets dispersed and rained down on their targets in dense concentrations.

Although the SAMs were effectively blinded, bombing the launchers required aircraft to overfly the target, exposing themselves to AAA fire and optically aimed shoulder-launched SA-7 Strela missiles. To confuse the SA-7s' infra-red homing seekers, the Israeli pilots released pyrotechnic flares when going in to drop their ordnance.

Pilots knew when they had hit their mark. The ground shook from the force of explosions. Batteries went up in infernos of exploding ordnance combined with the SAMs' solid propellant and HE warheads, causing huge fireballs clearly visible from far away.

The entire attack lasted about two hours. In the opening minutes, 10 of the 19 SAM batteries were destroyed. When reconnaissance overflights revealed that not all the batteries attacked had been fully disabled, another wave of attack aircraft went in, knocking out seven more batteries. Some SA-6 batteries kept their radars off and managed to avoid destruction. The following day, however, another wave of Israeli jets destroyed the remaining sites. Syria's missile network in Lebanon had been reduced to a smoldering mass of twisted metal. The IAF had had the misfortune of being the first air force to face the

SA-6, but the hard lessons learned in the 1973 Yom Kippur War allowed Israel to make history in Operation *Peace for Galilee* with the first-ever direct, all-out attack on an integrated missile network. Israeli defense minister Ariel Sharon declared this, "one of the most brilliant, complicated and intricate operations ever carried out."[2]

Eagles and Falcons: Birds of Prey

Surprised as they were by the Israeli move, the Syrians did not idly sit by as the IAF ravaged their missile network in Lebanon. Dozens of Syrian Air Force fighters were scrambled from nearby bases to join Syrian patrol aircraft already airborne at the time of the attack. Brown and yellow-camouflaged Mikoyan-Gurevich MiG-21 Fishbeds, swept-wing MiG-23 Flogger fighters and some Sukhoi Su-22 Fitter fighters began filling the sky.

With Israel's E-2C Hawkeye airborne early warning command and control aircraft circling high in the sky, the Israelis had a comprehensive picture of the aerial battlefield. In IAF service for only a year, the propeller-driven Hawkeye, easily identified by the large radar dish on its back, was packed with powerful computers, situational displays and secure communications capable of detecting and assessing threats from approaching enemy aircraft over ranges of about 300 miles (480km). Operators sitting at consoles tracked Syrian aircraft as they took off from their bases and vectored F-15 and F-16 fighters to deal with them.

The Eagle and Falcon pilots, whose aircraft were equipped with advanced, on-board air-intercept radar, saw the dots on the radar screens representing Syrian aircraft and prepared to engage from afar. But in the limited airspace over Lebanon, where upward of 200 aircraft were operating that day, the IAF opted for a cautious approach, specifying that all aerial engagements were to take place within visual range. "We had to differentiate between our aircraft and those of the enemy," one pilot explained.[3]

With their Boeing 707s and other electronic warfare assets, the Israelis effectively jammed radio and data communications links to the Syrian pilots, who relied on ground controllers for situational awareness. The EW efforts were so successful that, in the words of the Syrians, "the entire Syrian air response was essentially disrupted . . ."[4]

Largely unaware that the missiles meant to ensure clear skies had been destroyed, the Syrians did not expect to find Israeli aircraft over the Bekaa Valley. Many a Syrian pilot first spotted the Israelis as they maneuvered to engage in air-to-air combat. In rapid dogfights lasting 30 to 40 seconds each, F-15s and F-16s downed the Syrians that came their way, most with Israel Weapons Development Authority (Rafael) Python 3 and American AIM-9 Sidewinder air-to-air missiles.

One Israeli pilot recounted how his four-man F-16 formation was on a routine patrol over the "safe zone" of central Lebanon—away from the dangers of the Syrian missile umbrella—when their controller instructed them to fly east, towards the Bekaa Valley. Since that heading would put them in what had until then been a no-fly zone for the IAF, the pilots asked for clarification. Their instructions confirmed, the pilots turned eastward and were warned of Syrian MiGs in the area. When a pair of MiGs was picked up on radar, the F-16s moved in for visual ID. Unaware that the Syrian missile batteries had already been attacked, the pilots kept a careful lookout for the bright flash indicating a SAM missile launch.

"I spotted them first: a pair of MiG-23s," the pilot recalled. "They saw us—they knew we were there. The MiGs turned sharply and broke away, trying to maneuver. I divvied them up with my partner." Hearing the tone in their headsets indicating lock-on, each pilot fired a missile at a MiG. The Sidewinder shot out from his F-16's wing, locked onto the MiG's hot engine exhaust, and flew the two nautical miles to slam into its engine. "The MiG was hit, caught on fire, lost control and came apart slowly—all before me, like in a movie. . . . The MiG managed to fly for about another 20 seconds. The pilot ejected and the MiG fell and exploded."[5]

At the Israeli ground control center, commanders watched in amazement as young soldiers keeping track of the action made wax pencil notations on transparent Plexiglas displays, showing twenty-two Syrian fighters shot down.[6] With so many aircraft taking part in such an intricate operation, losses and other complications were anticipated. Yet, thanks to meticulous planning and execution, those setbacks never materialized. Syria later admitted that Israel's superior airborne-control network gave it a clear advantage. While this certainly played an important role in the lopsided Israeli victory in the air battles, Israeli pilots simply found the Syrian pilots unremarkable. The IAF approached aerial combat with the Syrians considering them as equals, as a cavalier attitude of superiority can lead to carelessness. However, while some Syrian pilots fought valiantly and made maximum use of their aircraft, overall they proved no match for the skilled IAF pilots flying more agile American-built aircraft.[7]

Over the next few days, Syria continued challenging Israel's dominance of Lebanon's skies with combat air patrols and attack missions. On June 10, another 26 Syrian aircraft were destroyed, while all Israeli aircraft returned safely to base. On June 11, the Syrian air force took to the air once again and lost another 18 aircraft, again without a single Israeli aircraft lost. In all, between June 7 and 11, 1982, 81 Syrian aircraft were downed in aerial combat—with no Israeli losses. The Israelis had to suspend the customary air base fly-by after downing an enemy aircraft—simply too many Syrians were being shot down and the victory laps were interfering with air operations. The Syrian air force had been routed: not only did it lose billions of dollars' worth of aircraft, but half the Syrian pilots shot down were killed—a major blow. IAF F-15s were credited with 34 Syrian kills, while the F-16s surpassed them with 46. An F-4E Phantom is credited with one kill.

With the threat of the SAMs gone, Israeli aircraft controlled the skies over Lebanon; the IAF was free to provide ground support and otherwise operate at will. Syria abandoned Lebanon's skies to the IAF at that point, leaving its forces and those of its allies at the mercy of the IAF. The Israeli Air Force had achieved its mission: clear skies over Lebanon.

Israel's incursion into Lebanon, with its rapid successes in the air and on the ground, ultimately bogged down into an 18-year occupation of a security zone in southern Lebanon meant to protect Israel's north. Despite Israel's withdrawal in May 2000, the Islamic group Hezbollah, which had been battling Israel's presence in Lebanon, continued its armed resistance. Hezbollah's increasing audacity and provocations resulted in the 2006 Second Lebanon War.

Notes

1. Raful Eitan. *A Soldier's Story* (New York: Shapolsky Publishers, Inc., 1991), p.289.
2. Conor Cruise O'Brien. *The Siege* (New York: Touchstone, 1986), p.624.
3. Lon Nordeen. *Fighters Over Israel* (London: Greenhill Books, 1990), p.172.
4. Eliezer Cohen. *Israel's Best Defense* (London: Airlife Publishing Ltd., 1993), p.465.
5. Personal interview, January 1999.
6. IDF Spokesman's Office, www.idf.il.
7. While events proved this assessment true, it is nonetheless biased as it comes from an IAF F-16 pilot who became an ace during the conflict with five kills.

EPILOGUE

Holy Wars concludes with the 1982 invasion of Lebanon—a military operation that only ended eighteen years later, in 2000. Since that invasion, Israel has not undertaken all-out warfare, with aircraft dog-fighting or armored formations duking it out against peer adversaries. But that isn't to say Israel's infantry divisions, armored battalions and air force squadrons have been idle. Each has since taken part in operations, incursions and war. Instead of battling formal armies, the IDF has fought non- or quasi-state actors in asymmetric warfare. Lacking military equipment or capabilities anything remotely near those of the IDF, organizations such as Lebanon's Shiite Muslim militant group Hezbollah, or Party of God, which grew from resistance to Israel's occupation of Lebanon to become one of the most powerful actors in Lebanon, and the Palestinian Islamic fundamentalist group Hamas, an abbreviation for Islamic Resistance Movement, that seized control of the Gaza Strip, have targeted Israel's military or its civilian population, triggering IDF responses. Despite the gross disparity between the two sides, these militant groups have used clever manipulation, aided by an occasional errant Israeli artillery round, to win the battle for international public opinion, thus largely depriving the IDF of accolades for its military successes.

Operation Defensive Shield

On March 27, 2002, a man carrying a suitcase walked into Netanya's Park Hotel dining room, which was packed with some 250 people sharing a festive Passover holiday meal, known as a *seder*. The man was a Palestinian suicide bomber or, as some term it, a homicide bomber; he detonated his deadly load of explosives, killing 30 people and wounding more than 140. Palestinians had been resorting to terror attacks since the outbreak of the Second Intifada uprising in September 2000. The Passover Massacre, as it became known, was the eighth in a series of deadly suicide bombings that month alone in which some 33 Israelis had already been killed, and more than 260 injured. Palestinian militant group Hamas claimed responsibility for the Park Hotel bombing the aim of which—like the other attacks— had been simply to kill and maim.

Israel had had enough. The IDF launched Operation *Defensive Shield*—its largest military operation in the West Bank since the 1967 Six Day War—to root out the Palestinian terror infrastructure and stop the wave of suicide bombings. First order of business was moving into Ramallah, where the IDF besieged Palestinian Authority President Yasser Arafat in his headquarters compound. Arafat remained isolated and under siege until the end of 2004, when he was allowed out for medical treatment in Paris, where he died.

Operation *Defensive Shield* focused on the West Bank's cities and surrounding areas. Perhaps the best known aspect of the operation was the IDF's move on Jenin, the city from which a quarter of the Second Intifada's 100 suicide bombers were dispatched. Jenin's narrow streets were wired with booby traps and improvised explosive devices (IEDs) that slowed the Israeli advance. After an Israeli unit stumbled into a Palestinian ambush in which 13 soldiers were lost, the IDF relied heavily on D-9 armored bulldozers to clear the way for its troops. Some areas suffered extensive damage, which Palestinians highlighted to the media to propagate false accusations of Israeli atrocities.

During the three weeks of West Bank incursions, Palestinian casualty figures ranged from 240 to 500 (accounts vary), while Israel suffered 30 dead. The operation dealt a major blow to the Palestinian terror infrastructure, resulting in fewer subsequent attacks, although

Operation *Defensive Shield* did not bring an end to the Second Intifada.

2006 Lebanon War

The Second Lebanon War, as it is known in Israel, began on July 12, 2006 with an unprovoked Hezbollah cross-border attack and bombardment that resulted in the deaths of eight Israeli soldiers and the abduction of two.

Israel responded forcefully with punishing air strikes and artillery fire on Lebanese and Hezbollah targets. Even Hezbollah leader Sheikh Hassan Nasrallah admitted he did not expect such a strong Israeli response. The Shiite group answered with a barrage of rocket fire into cities and towns in the north of Israel—fire that continued throughout the war, paralyzing a huge part of Israel and forcing nearly one million Israeli citizens into bomb shelters.

Israel Defense Forces Chief of Staff Lieutenant General Dan Halutz, a former air force commander, believed that air power alone would bring about the return of the two abducted soldiers and punish Hezbollah for its actions. Israeli air strikes hit thousands of targets: Hezbollah command centers, weapon and ammunition stores and rocket launchers. Israel also struck Lebanese infrastructure—Lebanon's price for its symbiotic relationship with Hezbollah, which is part of Lebanon's government. As a deterrent, Israel has long practiced a policy of severe retribution to convey the message that attacks on its citizens or territory will not be tolerated.

The Israel Navy attacked Lebanese coastal targets and blockaded ports. Just two days into the war, Hezbollah fired a radar-guided antiship missile that hit and crippled INS *Hanit*, one of Israel's three advanced Saar 5 class corvettes. The Navy admitted not to have known this weapon was in Hezbollah's arsenal, meaning that the ship's extensive defensive systems had not been activated, an embarrassing and deadly intelligence failure.

Hezbollah continued firing rockets into Israel. Hezbollah's heavier rockets were largely destroyed, but the smaller launchers proved elusive. IAF unmanned aircraft (UAVs) and other air assets operating over Lebanon worked together to reduce the so-called sensor-to-shooter loop, meaning that when a rocket was launched, the IAF quickly responded to knock out its now-exposed launcher. Despite this, some 100 rockets were hitting Israel each day. Air power alone was not stopping Hezbollah.

When Israel unilaterally withdrew from southern Lebanon in May 2000—ending its 18-year occupation—Hezbollah moved in to fill the void. Established to resist Israel's occupation of Lebanon, Hezbollah did not limit its attacks to Israeli targets. Probably its most notorious action was its 1983 bombing of US Marine barracks in Beirut that killed 241 Americans, followed by an attack minutes later that killed 58 French troops. Both contingents were supporting a United Nations peacekeeping mission working to stabilize Lebanon.

After Israel's withdrawal from Lebanon, it was not long before Hezbollah began provocations. A particularly blatant one came after only five months, when Hezbollah fighters crossed into Israel where they abducted and killed three Israeli soldiers, revealing that their agenda was more than just expelling Israel from Lebanon. Exhausted from its 18-year Lebanese entanglement, Israel's response was lackluster, emboldening Hezbollah.

Israel and Hezbollah were now paying the price for their previous policies. Realizing that rooting out Hezbollah from southern Lebanon would require a ground invasion, IDF ground forces were sent into Lebanon, where they fought Hezbollah in villages throughout southern Lebanon's western, central and eastern sectors. IDF operations were hindered by blunders such as poor equipment, outdated maps and intelligence, and supplies not reaching the front. Unhappy with the way the war was being run, IDF leadership sidelined GOC Northern Command Major General Udi Adam.

In combat, Hezbollah proved a tenacious foe. These were not the Arab irregulars of yesteryear, but well-trained, equipped, and organized fighters who stood their ground. An illustrative example was the intense battle fought, beginning on July 24, in the central sector village of Bint Jbeil, a Hezbollah stronghold. It was here that Sheikh Hassan Nasrallah gave a famous victory speech just two weeks after Israel's May 2000 withdrawal from Lebanon where he called Israel "weaker than a spider's web." Israeli troops were now back, fighting in the town's mostly deserted streets and alleyways against a hardened core of Hezbollah fighters that resisted fiercely. Tens of

Israeli troops were killed or wounded, and Merkava Main Battle Tanks were knocked out by mines and antitank weapons. The battle caused extensive destruction to the village, which was later rebuilt with Iranian support.

Deployed along the Israeli border, Hezbollah had studied the ways of the Israeli army and devised tactics and strategies to overcome Israel's strengths. They employed modern communications and electronics equipment such as night vision goggles, and put antitank weapons to lethal use against both tanks and built-up structures, causing the bulk of Israeli military casualties. In one incident, nine paratroopers seeking shelter in a house in the village of Debel were killed by an antitank rocket. In another blow to the IDF, a dozen reservists were killed when a Hezbollah rocket struck their marshalling area near the Lebanese border.

As a United Nations cease-fire was being hammered out after nearly a month of fighting, the Israeli government decided to expand the military operation. In a final drive before the cease-fire was scheduled to go into effect on August 14, 2006, Israel suffered 33 casualties. Despite all the IDF efforts, Hezbollah continued launching rockets throughout the war; the last day before the cease-fire went into effect saw more than 250 rockets fired at Israel. In all, Hezbollah launched 3,970 rockets. The war ended with acceptance of UN Security Council Resolution 1701, in which wishful thinking called for the ineffectual Lebanese army and a United Nations force (UNIFIL) to eviscerate Hezbollah, which they failed to accomplish. The failure to disarm Hezbollah raises the question of how long the fragile cease-fire will last.

At 34 days, it was Israel's longest war, excepting the protracted War of Independence, and arguably the least conclusive. At best it can be considered a draw, an accomplishment on which Hezbollah prides itself, given that no Arab country had ever fared so well in war with the Jewish state. Israel claimed more than 500 Hezbollah fighters were killed; Hezbollah acknowledges only 65 deaths. One hundred and seventeen Israeli soldiers died in the war, as well as 39 civilians, with thousands injured. Both countries suffered losses to their infrastructure and economy. An Israeli commission of inquiry known as the Winograd Commission issued a report critical of the Israeli leadership's handling of the war, reproaching Prime Minister Ehud Olmert, hapless Defense Minister Amir Peretz, and Chief of Staff Dan Halutz.[1]

Israel had failed to destroy Hezbollah or free its two abducted soldiers; corpses of the two soldiers were returned to Israel in 2008. Hezbollah—its position strengthened by the war—has rearmed with Iranian and Syrian support.

Cast Lead Gaza Incursion

Israel reestablished some of its deterrence with its December 2008 incursion into the Gaza Strip. Operation *Cast Lead* was launched on December 27, 2008 in response to incessant rocket fire into Israel from Palestinian militant group Hamas-controlled Gaza. Israeli forces set about destroying Hamas' rocket and mortar launching capabilities and its supporting infrastructure. While Israel would be accused of overkill, the scale of the operation was perhaps a reaction to criticism from the 2006 Second Lebanon War that Israel failed to bring its might to bear. This time Israel used its power, sending a clear message that the country still knew how to fight—a message undoubtedly heard in Lebanon. In this part of the world, such a heavy-handed response to provocations is a sign of strength; restraint is for the weak. One must remember not to judge the Middle East using Western values, for very different rules are at play.

During the summer of 2005, Israel had unilaterally withdrawn from the Gaza Strip, which it had occupied since 1967. Areas in Israel bordering Gaza have been under rocket and mortar attack since 2001; some 8,000 have been fired at them, which even the UN called indiscriminate and deliberate attacks against civilians.[2] Replicating events in Lebanon, the Israeli withdrawal was followed by provocations, this time in the form of continued rocket fire. Hamas further escalated with a daring cross-border attack on an Israeli army base on June 25, 2006 during which IDF soldier Gilad Shalit was abducted and remains in Hamas custody. Hamas' next milestone came a year later when they seized control of the Gaza Strip in a June 2007 putsch. Israel declared the Gaza Strip "hostile territory" and imposed a blockade. The rocket and mortar fire continued.

Operation *Cast Lead* opened with a highly orchestrated air strike lasting three minutes and 40 seconds by tens of Israeli aircraft on more than 100 targets throughout Gaza. Undaunted, Hamas continued launching rockets against Israel. Over the course of a week, aerial operations continued against Hamas command posts, training camps, weapon stores, rocket and mortar launch sites, and smuggling tunnels.

Hamas launched rockets from among its own civilian population in urban areas, with little regard for casualties. Even the UN committee established to investigate the conflict, the Goldstone Commission, acknowledged that "Palestinian armed groups, where they launched attacks close to civilian or protected buildings, unnecessarily exposed the civilian population of Gaza to danger."[3] This was precisely Hamas' underdog strategy of getting its civilians killed, knowing that civilian casualties would turn international public opinion against Israel. To this end, Hamas is said to encourage Palestinian civilians to take risks in hopes of achieving martyrdom.

In an effort to avoid civilian casualties and minimize collateral damage, Israel employed laser-guided precision weapons, and various means including telephone calls and leaflets warning non-combatants to evacuate dangerous areas. Even special low-explosive rounds were dropped to warn civilians of impending attacks, a technique known as "knock on the roof." Despite these measures, the Goldstone Commission's report was highly critical of Israel. Even the "knock on the roof" warnings were criticized by the UN report as constituting a form of attack against the civilians in the building.

On January 3, 2009, IDF ground troops entered the Gaza Strip. Knowing Hamas would be ready with booby traps and IEDs, and would likely attempt to capture Israeli soldiers to gain leverage, the IDF ground forces took a careful approach, operating when possible with tanks and other armor.

Implementing lessons from the Second Lebanon War, Israel executed a precision air-land battle where infantry commanders on the ground directed dedicated air assets. Operating in Gaza's densely populated urban areas—a theater with limited situational awareness—ground commanders could rely on UAVs to provide over-the-hill, or next city block, view of where snipers or ambushes might be laying in wait. The IDF stopped short of a thrust into Gaza City out of concern for the potential for casualties on both sides. In all, ten

Israeli soldiers were killed during Operation *Cast Lead* versus well over a thousand Palestinians, a disproportionate outcome that led to UN accusations of Israeli war crimes such as the deliberate targeting of civilians—charges Israel rejects due to unsubstantiated claims, as well as an international diplomatic backlash epitomized by the deterioration in relations with Turkey. With the benefit of hindsight, the Goldstone Commission's chairman, Judge Richard Goldstone, reassessed the report's findings. "If I had known then what I know now," he wrote in the *Washington Post* on April 1, 2011, "the Goldstone Report would have been a different document." Goldstone noted that Israel did not intentionally target civilians, as originally claimed in the report, whereas Hamas "purposefully and indiscriminately aimed at civilian targets."

The operation ended on January 18, 2009, with Israel's unilateral ceasefire and IDF withdrawal from the Gaza Strip. Not long thereafter Hamas renewed its provocations against Israel, almost inviting Israel to respond yet again.

There seems to be no end in sight to the strife that has marred the Middle East since time immemorial. Turbulence and uncertainty continue on Israel's fronts near and far, making it appear that Isaiah's hopeful prayer will remain an elusive yearning. Only time will tell.

Notes

1. An English summary of the Committee's final report and links to the full (unclassified) report in Hebrew can be accessed via the Israel Ministry of Foreign Affairs website:
www.mfa.gov.il/MFA/MFAArchive/2000_2009/2008/Winograd%20Committee%20submits%20final%20report%2030-Jan-2008 (accessed March 16, 2011).
2. Human Rights In Palestine And Other Occupied Arab Territories. Report of the United Nations Fact Finding Mission on the Gaza Conflict.
3. Human Rights In Palestine And Other Occupied Arab Territories. Report of the United Nations Fact Finding Mission on the Gaza Conflict.

BIBLIOGRAPHY

Chapters 1 and 2

The Jewish Bible: Tanakh: The Holy Scriptures (Philadelphia: The Jewish Publication Society of America, 1985).

"Jericho," http://ccwf.cc.utexas.edu/~welli/archaeology/bible/jericho.html (accessed September 29, 1999).

"Was Joshua Justified in Exterminating the Whole Population of Jericho?" www.new-life.net/joshua.htm (accessed September 29, 1999).

Baretz, Julie. "Mount Tabor," *Gems in Israel* (August/September 2002), www.gemsinisrael.com/e_article000096511.htm (accessed March 14, 2011).

Dimont, Max. *Jews, God and History* (New York: Signet, 1962).

Duncan, Andrew and Opatowski, Michel. *War in the Holy Land. From Meggido to the West Bank* (Stroud, UK: Sutton Publishing Ltd., 1998).

Grayzel, Solomon. *A History of the Jews. From the Babylonian Exile to the Present 5728–1968* (New York: Mentor Books, 1968).

Herzog, Chaim and Mordechai Gichon. *Battles of the Bible* (London, UK: Greenhill Books, 1978).

Jackson, Wayne. "The Saga of Ancient Jericho," *Christian Courier,* www.christiancourier.com/archives/jericho.htm (accessed March 14, 2011).

Jaques, Don. "The Old Testament and the Ancient Near East. Jericho," www.georgefox.edu/academics/grad/wes/bst550/djaques/Jericho.html (accessed September 29, 1999).

Johnson, Paul. *A History of the Jews* (London, UK: Dent, 1911).

Josephus (translator William Whiston). *The Complete Works of Josephus* (Grand Rapids, MI: Kregel Publications, 1981).

Lemonick, Michael D. "Score one for the Bible," *TIME* (March 5, 1990), p.59.

Pearlman, Moshe. *In the Footsteps of Moses* (Tel Aviv: Nateev and Steimatzky, 1973).

Reviv, Hanoch. "The Canaanite and Israelite Periods (3200–332 BC)," in Michael Avi-Yonah (ed.) *A History of the Holy Land* (Jerusalem: Steimatzky's Agency Ltd. 1969).

Sanders, Michael. "Jericho Part II—The Biblical Account," *Mysteries of the Bible* (1998), www.biblemysteries.com/lectures/jericho2.htm (accessed March 14, 2011).

Wilson, Ralph F. "The Battle of Jericho," www.jesuswalk.com/joshua/lesson4-ex.htm (accessed March 14, 2011).

Wilson, Ralph F. "Why the Slaughter of Jericho? Devoted to Destruction—*Herem*," www.joyfulheart.com/joshua/herem.htm (accessed March 14, 2011).

Wood, Bryant. "Is the Bible accurate concerning the destruction of the walls of Jericho?" www.christiananswers.net/q-abr/abr-a011.html (accessed March 14, 2011).

Wood, Bryant. "The Walls of Jericho. Archaeology confirms: they really DID come a-tumblin' down," *Creation* (21:2, March 1999), pp.36–40.

Zaharoni, Menachem. "The Battle of Deborah and Barak Against Sisera," in Irit Zaharoni (ed.). *Israel Roots & Routes. A Nation Living in its Landscape* (Tel Aviv: MOD Publishing House, 1990).

Zaharoni, Menachem. "Gideon Fights the Midianites," in Irit

Zaharoni (ed.). *Israel Roots & Routes. A Nation Living in its Landscape* (Tel Aviv: MOD Publishing House, 1990).

Chapter 3

The Jewish Bible: Tanakh: The Holy Scriptures. (Philadelphia: The Jewish Publication Society of America, 1985).

Dagan, Yehuda. Interview: December 3, 2002.

Driscoll, J. F. "Philistines," *The Catholic Encyclopedia* (New York: Robert Appleton Company, 1911) http://www.newadvent.org/cathen/12021c.htm (accessed March 14, 2011).

Duncan, Andrew and Opatowski, Michel. *War in the Holy Land. From Meggido to the West Bank* (Stroud, UK: Sutton Publishing Ltd., 1998).

Gale, Richard, General Sir. *Great Battles of Biblical History* (London: Hutchinson & Co. 1968).

Garsiel, Moshe. "Ysodot shel historiah v'realiah b'tiur haMaaracha b'Emek HaElah v'krav David v'Goliat [Elements of History and Reality in the Description of the Ela Valley Warfare and the Combat Between David and Goliath]," *Beit Mikra* (Vol. 41, 1997), pp.293–316.

Grayzel, Solomon. *A History of the Jews. From the Babylonian Exile to the Present 5728–1968* (New York: Mentor Books, 1968).

Josephus (translator William Whiston). *The Complete Works of Josephus* (Grand Rapids, MI: Kregel Publications, 1981).

Reviv, Hanoch. "The Canaanite and Israelite Periods (3200–332 BC)," in Michael Avi-Yonah (ed.). *A History of the Holy Land* (Jerusalem: Steimatzky's Agency Ltd, 1969).

Roman, Yadin. "David v'Rehavam [David and Rehavam]," *Eretz v'Teva* (July–August 1998).

Zaharoni, Menachem. "Saul's Last Stand," in Irit Zaharoni (ed.). *Israel Roots & Routes. A Nation Living in its Landscape* (Tel Aviv: MOD Publishing House, 1990).

Chapter 4

The Jewish Bible: Tanakh: The Holy Scriptures (Philadelphia: The Jewish Publication Society of America, 1985).

"Accounts of the Campaign of Sennacherib, 701 BCE," in Oliver J. Thatcher (ed.) *The Library of Original Sources* (Milwaukee: University Research Extension Co., 1907), Vol. I: *The Ancient World*; *The Bible (Douai-Rheims Version)* (Baltimore: John Murphy Co., 1914). www.fordham.edu/halsall/ancient/701sennach.html (accessed March 14, 2011).

"Lachish: Royal City of the Kingdom of Judah," www.israel-mfa.gov.il.

"Sennacherib's Campaign (Iron Age, 8th century BCE)," http://staff.feldberg.brandeis.edu/...a/ANET/sennacherib_inscription.html (accessed August 18, 1999)

Borowski, Oded. "Hezekiah's Reforms and the Revolt against Assyria," www.asor.org/BA/Borowski.html (accessed August 30, 1999).

Halverson, Rob. "The Old Testment and the Ancient Near East—Lachish," www.georgefox.edu/academic...s/bst550/rhalverson/Lachish.html (accessed August 22, 1999).

Herzog, Chaim and Mordechai Gichon. *Battles of the Bible* (New York: Random House, 1978).

Rabinowitz, Allan. "The ghosts of Tel Lachish," *The Jerusalem Post* (May 6, 1999).

Reviv, Hanoch. "The Canaanite and Israelite Periods (3200–332 BC)," in Michael Avi-Yonah (ed.). *A History of the Holy Land* (Jerusalem: Steimatzky's Agency Ltd, 1969).

Ussishkin, David. *The Conquest of Lachish by Sennacherib* (Tel Aviv: Tel Aviv University Institute of Archaeology, 1982).

Chapter 5

The Apocrypha, or Deuterocanonical Books (New Revised Standard Version) (Cambridge, UK: Cambridge University Press, 1989).

Avi-Yonah, Michael. "The Second Temple (332 BC–AD 70)—Jews, Romans and Byzantines (70–640)," in Michael Avi-Yonah (ed.). *A History of the Holy Land* (Jerusalem: Steimatzky's Agency Ltd. 1969).

Bar-Kochva, Bezalel. *Judas Maccabaeus. The Jewish Struggle Against the Seleucids* (Cambridge, UK: Cambridge University Press, 1989).

Bar-Kochva, Bezalel. *The Seleucid Army. Organization and Tactics in the great Campaign* (Cambridge, UK: Cambridge University Press, 1979: reprinted with corrections).

Dimont, Max. *Jews, God and History* (New York: Signet Books, 1962).

Duncan, Andrew and Opatowski, Michel. *War in the Holy Land. From Meggido to the West Bank* (Stroud, UK: Sutton Publishing Ltd, 1998).

Gale, Richard, General Sir. *Great Battles of Biblical History* (London: Hutchinson & Co., 1968).

Grayzel, Solomon. *A History of the Jews. From the Babylonian Exile to the Present 5728–1968* (New York: Mentor Books, 1968).

Herzog, Chaim and Gichon, Mordechai. *Battles of the Bible* (London, UK: Greenhill Books, 1978).

Johnson, Paul. *A History of the Jews* (London, UK: Harper-Collins, 1988).

Josephus (translator William Whiston). *The Complete Works of Josephus* (Grand Rapids, MI: Kregel Publications, 1981).

Pearlman, Moshe. *The Maccabees* (New York: Macmillan Publishing Co. Inc., 1973).

Zaharoni, Menachem. "Early Scenes of Battle," in Irit Zaharoni (ed.). *Israel Roots & Routes. A Nation Living in its Landscape* (Tel Aviv: MOD Publishing House, 1990).

Chapter 6

Avi-Yonah, Michael. "The Second Temple (332 BC–AD 70)—Jews, Romans and Byzantines (70–640)," in Michael Avi-Yonah (ed.). *A History of the Holy Land* (Jerusalem: Steimatzky's Agency Ltd. 1969).

Biggs, Mark Wayne. "Forty Days at Jotapata," *Military History* (April 1999).

Dimont, Max. *Jews, God and History* (New York: Signet Books, 1962).

Duncan, Andrew and Opatowski, Michel. *War in the Holy Land. From Meggido to the West Bank* (Stroud, UK: Sutton Publishing Ltd, 1998).

'e, General Sir Richard. *Great Battles of Biblical History*
London: Hutchinson & Co., 1968).

Grayzel, Solomon. *A History of the Jews. From the Babylonian
Exile to the Present 5728–1968* (New York: Mentor Books,
1968).

Guttman, Shmaryahu. "Gamla—A Heroic Stand," in Irit Zaharoni
(ed.) *Israel Roots & Routes. A Nation Living in its Landscape*
(Tel Aviv: MOD Publishing House, 1990).

Johnson, Paul. *A History of the Jews* (London, UK: Harper-Collins,
1988).

Josephus (translator William Whiston). *The Complete Works of
Josephus* (Grand Rapids, MI: Kregel Publications, 1981).

Mattis, Richard L. "Holy City Under Siege," *Military History*
(December 1995).

Rappaport, Uriel. "How Anti-Roman Was the Galilee?" in Lee. I.
Levine (ed.). *The Galilee in Late Antiquity* (New York and
Jerusalem: Jewish Theological Seminary, 1992).

Rashba, Gary. "Masada—Israel," *Military History* (October 2007).

Schaalje, Jacqueline. "Gamla," *Jewish Magazine* (February 2001).
www.jewishmag.com/40mag/gamla/gamla.htm (accessed March
14, 2011).

Syon, Danny. "Gamla," (Israel Antiquities Authority)
www.antiquities.org.il (accessed March 14, 2011).

Syon, Danny. "Gamla—City of Refuge," in A. M. Berlin and J. A.
Overman (eds.). *The First Jewish Revolt. Archaeology, History
and Ideology* (London and New York: Routledge, 2002).

Syon, Danny. "Gamla: Portrait of a Rebellion," *Biblical
Archaeology Review* (January/February 1992, 18:01).

Tacitus (translators Alfred Church and William Brodribb). *Histories*
(London, UK: Macmillan, 1864–77) www.sacred-texts.com/
cla/tac/h05000.htm.

Chapter 7

Akram, A. I. *The Sword of Allah – Khaled bin Al-Waleed.* (October
1969). www.grandestrategy.com/2007/12/sword-of-allah-Khaled-
bin-al-waleed.html.

Antiochus Strategos (trans. F. Conybeare). "Antiochus Strategos'

Account of the Sack of Jerusalem (614)," *English Historical Review* (Issue 25, 1910), pp.506–508. www.fordham.edu/halsall/source/strategos1.html (accessed March 16, 2011).

Bischoff, Bernhard and Lapidge, Michael. *Biblical Commentaries from the Canterbury School of Theodore and Hadrian* (Cambridge, UK: Cambridge University Press, 1994).

Donner, Fred. *The Early Islamic Conquests* (Princeton: Princeton University Press, 1981).

Elton, Hugh. "Review of *Byzantium and the Early Islamic Conquests*, by Walter E. Kaegi," *The Medieval Review* (Ann Arbor: University of Michigan University Library, 1994).

Gibbon, Edward. *The History of the Decline and Fall of the Roman Empire* (London, UK: Strahan & Cadell, 1776–89). www.ccel.org/ccel/gibbon/decline.html (accessed March 16, 2011).

Gichon, Mordechai. *Carta's Atlas of Palestine From Bethther to Tel Hai* (Jerusalem: Carta, 1974).

Goldschmidt, Arthur Jr. *A Concise History of the Middle East* (Boulder: Westview Press, 1979).

Kaegi, Walter E. *Byzantium and the Early Islamic Conquests* (Cambridge, UK: Cambridge University Press, 1992).

Kaegi, Walter E. *Heraclius. Emperor of Byzantium* (Cambridge, UK: Cambridge University Press, 2003).

Kennedy, Hugh. *The Armies of the Caliphs* (New York: Routledge, 2001).

Lewis, Bernard. *The Arabs in History* (Harper Torchbooks, 1966).

Nicolle, David. *Armies of the Muslim Conquest* (Oxford, UK: Osprey Publishing, 1993).

Nicolle, David. *Yarmuk AD 636: The Muslim Conquest of Syria* (Oxford, UK: Osprey Publishing, 1994).

Norwich, John Julius. *Byzantium—The Early Centuries* (London: Viking Penguin Inc., 1988).

Ostrogorsky, George. *History of the Byzantine State* (New Brunswick: Rutgers University Press, 1957).

Sharon, Moshe. "The History of Palestine from the Arab Conquest until the Crusades (633–1099)," in Michael Avi-Yonah (ed.). *A History of the Holy Land* (Jerusalem: Steimatzky's Agency Ltd. 1969).

Vasiliev, A. A. *History of the Byzantine Empire, Volume 1, 324–1453* (Madison: University of Wisconsin Press, 1958).

Chapter 8
"The Horns of Hattin," www.web-site.co.uk/knights_templar/templar4_7.html (accessed March 3, 1998).

Czech, Kenneth P. "City Taken and Retaken," *Military History* (February 1994).

Dafoe, Stephen. "The Battle of Hattin—July 4th, 1187," (March 31, 2010) www.templarhistory.com/hattin.html (accessed March 14, 2011).

Ernoul, a Frank. "Battle of Hattin, 1187," www.hillsdale.edu (accessed April 6, 1998).

Goldschmidt, Arthur Jr. *A Concise History of the Middle East* (Boulder: Westview Press, 1979).

Hallam, Elizabeth (ed.). *Chronicles of the Crusades* (London: Weidenfeld & Nicolson, 1989).

Hamblin, William. "Saladin and Muslim Military Theory," in B. Z. Kedar (ed.). *The Horns of Hattin: Proceedings of the Second Conference of the Society of the Crusades and the Latin East* (London, UK: Variorum, 1992), pp.228–38. www.deremilitari.org/resources/pdfs/hamblin.pdf (accessed March 14, 2011).

Hildinger, Erik. "Mongol Invasion of Europe," *Military History* (June 1997).

Kedar, Benjamin Z. "The Battle of Hattin Revisited" in B. Z. Kedar (ed.). *The Horns of Hattin: Proceedings of the Second Conference of the Society of the Crusades and the Latin East* (London, UK: Variorum, 1992). www.deremilitari.org/resources/articles/kedar.htm (accessed March 14, 2011).

Prawer, Joshua. *The World of the Crusaders* (London: Weidenfeld & Nicolson, 1972).

Rabinowitz, Allan. "Twin peaks in the lower Galilee," *The Jerusalem Post* (May 17, 1998).

Riley-Smith, Jonathan. *The Crusaders. A Short History* (London: The Athlone Press, 1987).

Robinson, John J. *Born in Blood: The Lost Secrets of Freemasonry, Vol. I.* (M. Evans, 1989).

Rozenberg, Silvia (ed.). *Knights of the Holy Land. The Crusader Kingdom of Jerusalem* (Jerusalem: The Israel Museum, 1999).

Runciman, Steven. *A History of the Crusades. Volume II. The Kingdom of Jerusalem and the Frankish East 1100–1187* (Penguin Books, 1952).

Saunders, J. J. *A History of Medieval Islam* (Routledge and Kegan Paul Ltd, 1965).

Sivan, Emmanuel. "Palestine During the Crusades (1099–1291)," in Michael Avi-Yonah (ed.). *A History of the Holy Land* (Jerusalem: Steimatzky's Agency Ltd. 1969).

Stevenson, Joseph (ed.). *De Expugatione Terrae Sanctae per Saladinum*, [*The Capture of the Holy Land by Saladin*], Rolls Series (London: Longmans, 1875), translated by James Brundage, *The Crusades: A Documentary History*, (Milwaukee, WI: Marquette University Press, 1962), pp.153–159, at www.fordham.edu/halsall/source/1187hattin.html (accessed March 14, 2011).

Chapter 9

"Baybars," http://www.web-site.co.uk/knights_templar/templar4_9.html (accessed October 17, 1999).

"Islam and Islamic History in Arabia and The Middle East. The Mongols and the Mamluks." http://islam.org/mosque/ihame/Sec11.htm (accessed March 14, 2011).

"The Mamluk Empire," http://library.advanced.org/17137...History/Other_Empires/mamluk.html (accessed October 25, 1999).

"The Mamluk Period (1250–1517 CE)," http://jeru.huji.ac.il/eg1.htm (accessed September 21, 1999).

"The Mongol Hordes," www.armouries.com/mongols.htm (accessed October 17, 1999).

Amitai-Preiss, Reuven. "Ayn Jalut Revisited," *Tarih—Papers in Near Eastern Studies* (Vol. 2, 1992).

El-Halaby, Br. Muhammed. "The Battle of 'Ayn Jaloot', A Turning Point in History," *Nida'ul Islam* (December–January 1996–7).

Goldschmidt, Arthur Jr. *A Concise History of the Middle East* (Boulder: Westview Press, 1983).

Hallam, Elizabeth (ed.). *Chronicles of the Crusades* (London: Weidenfeld & Nicolson. 1989).

Hildinger, Erik. "Mongol Invasion of Europe," *Military History* (June 1997).

Housley, Norman. *The Later Crusades 1274–1580* (Oxford, UK: Oxford University Press, 1992).

Ludolph of Suchem (trans. Aubrey Stewart). *Description of the Holy Land and of the Way Thither* (London: Palestine Pilgrims' Text Society, 1895), XII, 54–61. www.fordham.edu/halsall/source/1291acre.html (accessed March 16, 2011).

Riley-Smith, Jonathan. *The Crusades* (London: The Athlone Press, 1987).

Saunders, J. J. *A History of Medieval Islam* (Routledge and Kegan Paul Ltd, 1965).

Sharon, Moshe. "Palestine under the Mameluks and the Ottoman Empire (1291–1918)," in Michael Avi-Yonah (ed.) *A History of the Holy Land* (Jerusalem: Steimatzky's Agency Ltd. 1969).

Smith, John Masson, Jr. "Ayn Jalut: Mamluk Success or Mongol Failure?" *Harvard Journal of Asiatic Studies* (Vol. 44: 2, December 1984).

Thorau, Peter. "The Battle of 'Ayn Jalut: a Re-examination," *Crusade and Settlement—Papers read at the First Conference of the Society for the Study of the Crusades and the Latin East and presented to R. C. Smail* (University College Cardiff Press, 1985), pp.236–241.

Tschanz, David W. "History's Hinge Ain Jalut" *Saudiaramco World* (Volume 58: 4).

Chapter 10

Ayalon, David. *Gunpowder and Firearms in the Mamluk Kingdom: A Challenge to Mediaeval Society* (London: 1956).

Cook, M. A. (ed.). *A History of the Ottoman Empire to 1730* (Cambridge: Cambridge University Press, 1976).

Gichon, Mordechai. *Carta's Atlas of Palestine From Bethther to Tel Hai (Military History)* (Jerusalem: Carta, 1969).

Goldschmidt, Arthur Jr. *A Concise History of the Middle East* (Boulder: Westview Press, 1979).

Housley, Norman. *The Later Crusades, From Lyons to Alcazar* (UK: Oxford University Press, 1952).

Petry, Carl. "The military institution and innovation in the late Mamluk period," in Carl Petry (ed.). *The Cambridge History of Egypt. Volume I: Islamic Egypt, 640–1517* (Cambridge: Cambridge University Press, 1998), pp.462–89.

Petry, Carl. *Protectors or Praetorians? The Last Mamluk Sultans and Egypt's Waning As a Great Power* (New York: State University of New York Press, 1994).

Petry, Carl. *Twilight of Majesty. The Reign of the Mamluk Sultans Al-Ashraf Qaytbay and Qansuh Al-Ghawri in Egypt* (Seattle: University of Washington Press, 1993).

Sharon, Moshe. "Palestine under the Mameluks and the Ottoman Empire (1291–1918)" in Michael Avi-Yonah (ed.). *A History of the Holy Land* (Jerusalem: Steimatzky's Agency Ltd. 1969).

Twain, Mark. *The Innocents Abroad* (Signet Classic, 1980).

Winter, Michael. "The Ottoman Occupation," in Carl Petry (ed.). *The Cambridge History of Egypt. Volume I: Islamic Egypt, 640–1517* (Cambridge, UK: Cambridge University Press, 1998), pp.490–516.

Winter, Michael. Interview: April 23, 2002. Tel Aviv, Israel.

Chapter 11

"Bonaparte's despatches from Egypt, parts IV and V," from *Pièces diverses et correspondance relatives aux opérations de l'armée d'Orient en Egypte* (Imprimée en exécution de l'arrêté du TRIBUNAT, en date du 7 Nivose an 9 de la République française. Paris, Baudouin . . . Messidor an IX). www.napoleon.org.

Berman, Ariel. Lecture on May 2, 1999 at the conference commemorating 200 years since Napoleon's Syrian Campaign (Akko, Israel).

Chandler, David. *Campaigns of Napoleon* (Weidenfeld & Nicolson, 1966).

Charles-Roux, F. *Bonaparte: Governor of Egypt* (London: Methuen & Co., Ltd. 1937).

Feinberg, Herb. "North to Palestine: Napoleon Marches Against the Turks," *Napoleonic Scholarship* (Vol. 1: 2, December 1998), pp.16–22.

Gichon, Mordechai. *Carta Atlas of Palestine From Bethther to Tel Hai* (Jerusalem: Carta Publishers, 1974).

Gichon, Mordechai. "Jaffa 1799," *Napoleonic Scholarship* (Volume 1: 2, December 1998), pp.23–32.

Godechot, Jacques. *Napoleon* (Paris: Editions Albin Michel. 1969).

Grant, A. T. *Europe in the Nineteenth Century (1789–1914)* (London: Longmans, Green & Co., 1929).

Klebanoff Allon Lecture on May 2, 1999 at the conference commemorating 200 years since Napoleon's Syrian Campaign (Akko, Israel).

Nafziger, George. "Bonaparte's Egyptian Campaign," *First Empire* (Issue 10) http://firstempire.net/samples/napegy.htm (accessed March 14, 2011).

Raveh, Kurt. Lecture on May 2, 1999 at the conference commemorating 200 years since Napoleon's Syrian Campaign (Akko, Israel).

Runyan, Cory. "Napoleon in Egypt or egomaniac on the loose," (1996) http://www.napoleon-series.org/military/battles/c_egypt.html (accessed March 14, 2011).

Shosenberg, James. "Napoleon Saves the Day at Mount Tabor," *Military History* (April 1999), pp.43–48.

Tulard, Jean. *Napoleon ou Le Mythe du Sauveur* (Fayard 1987).

Wachsmann, Shelly and Raveh, Kurt. *An Encounter at Tantura with Napoleon.* (Pamphlet, undated)

Chapter 12

Allan, Steven. "Gaza: The Unsurrendered City," *ERETZ Magazine* (Issue 49, November–December 1996), pp.36–41, 63.

Allenby, Sir Edmund. "The Fall of Jerusalem," in Charles F. Horne (ed.). *Source Records of the Great War, Vol. V* (National Alumni, 1923), www.firstworldwar.com/source/jerusalem_allenby1.htm (accessed March 14, 2011).

Allenby, Sir Edmund. "The Battle of Megiddo," in Charles F. Horne (ed.). *Source Records of the Great War, Vol. V* (National Alumni, 1923), www.firstworldwar.com/source/megiddo_allenby.htm (accessed March 14, 2011).

Bodart, Gaston. "Report on the Fall of Jerusalem, 9 December

1917," in Charles F. Horne (ed.). *Source Records of the Great War, Vol. V* (National Alumni, 1923), www.firstworldwar.com/source/jerusalem_bodart.htm (accessed March 14, 2011).

Bodart, Gaston. "The Fall of Turkey," in Charles F. Horne (ed.). *Source Records of the Great War, Vol. V* (National Alumni, 1923), www.firstworldwar.com/source/turkey_bodart.htm (accessed March 14, 2011).

Bowman-Manifold, Sir M. G. E. *An outline of the Egyptian and Palestine campaigns, 1914 to 1918* (Chatham: W. Y. J. Mackay & Co., 1922).

Brown, John. "Horsemen with Bayonets," *Military History* (April 1992).

Bullock, David L. *Allenby's War: The Palestine-Arabian Campaigns 1916–18* (Blandford Press, 1988).

Duncan, Andrew and Opatowski, Michel. *War in the Holy Land. From Meggido to the West Bank* (Stroud, UK: Sutton Publishing Ltd., 1998).

Grey, Jeffrey. *A Military History of Australia* (Cambridge: Cambridge University Press, 1990).

Gullet, H. S. *The Australian Imperial Force in Sinai and Palestine— 1914–1918.* (Queensland: University of Queensland Press, 1923).

Massey, W. T. "Allenby's Progress," in Charles F. Horne (ed.). *Source Records of the Great War, Vol. VI* (National Alumni, 1923), www.firstworldwar.com/source/allenby_massey.htm (accessed March 14, 2011).

Masterman E. W. G. "The Fall of Jerusalem," in Charles F. Horne (ed.). *Source Records of the Great War, Vol. V* (National Alumni, 1923), www.firstworldwar.com/source/jerusalem_masterman.htm (accessed March 14, 2011).

Meinertzhagen, Colonel R. *Middle East Diary* (London: The Cresset Press, 1959).

Hill, A. J. *Chauvel of the Light Horse* (Melbourne: Melbourne University Press, 1978).

Hughes, W. S. Kent. *Modern crusaders: an account of the campaign in Sinai and Palestine up to the capture of Jerusalem* (Melbourne: Melville & Mullen, 1919).

Jones, Ian. "Beersheeba: The light horse charge and the making of myths," *Journal of the Australian War Memorial* (No. 3, October 1983).

Lawrence, T. E. *Seven Pillars of Wisdom* (Penguin Books, 1926).

Spach, John Thom. "Allenby and the Last Crusade," *Military History* (March 1996).

Turnbull, Paul et al. *Pictures of health: War's Cruel Scythe: The Health of Australian Soldiers in the First World War* (Australian History WWW Project & Centre for Flexible Learning). http://nla.gov.au/nla.arc-13025 (accessed March 14, 2011).

Zakai, Abraham. "In the Footsteps of the ANZAC Warriors—The Battle for Beer Sheva During World War I." (Beer Sheva Municipality).

Zumbro, Ralph. *The Iron Cavalry* (New York: Pocket Books, 1998).

Chapter 13

"1948: The War of Independence," www.idf.il/English/UNITS/IAF/iaf2.htm (accessed April 6, 1999).

"The Battle for the Roads," www.idf.il/English/HISTORY/fiftyago.htm (accessed April 6, 1999).

Brandvein, Munio. Interviews on January 18, 2002 and September 24, 2002.

Brandvein, Munio (editor and compiler). *B'Mabat M'haHutz* [*A Look from the Outside. Listings of the Yad Mordechai Battles from May 19–23, 1948*] (Yad Mordechai: 1984).

Dupuy, Trevor. *Elusive Victory: The Arab-Israeli Wars 1947–1974* (Hero Books, Greenhill Books, 1984).

Elon, Amos. *The Israelis: Founders and Sons* (Holt, Rinehart and Winston, 1971).

Larkin, Margaret. *The Six Days of Yad Mordechai* (Yad Mordechai Museum, Israel, 1965).

Morse, Stan. *Modern Military Powers: Israel* (New York: The Military Press, 1984).

Nordeen, Lon. *Fighters Over Israel* (London: Greenhill Books, 1990).

O'Brien, Conor Cruise. *The Siege* (New York: Simon & Schuster, 1986).

Robinson, Donald. *Under Fire—Israel's 20-year Struggle for Survival* (New York: WW Norton & Co., 1968).

Rothwell, Steve. "Military Ally or Liability, The Egyptian Army 1936–1942," *Army Quarterly & Defence Journal* (Vol. 128: 2, April 1998).

Sachar, Howard. *A History of Israel* (New York: Alfred A. Knopf, 1985).

Transcript of interview with Grisha Zilberstein.

Chapter 14

Adam, Avshalom. Personal Account. IDF Paratroopers History Site. www.202.org.il/Pages/Footer/eduyot/avsha.php

Bar-Zohar, Michael (ed.). *Sefer haTzanchanim [The Book of the Paratroopers]* (Tel Aviv: Levine-Epstein, 1969).

Ben-Uziel, David. Interview: August 4, 2008.

Dayan, Moshe. *Diary of the Sinai Campaign* (New York: Schocken Books, 1965).

Dayan, Moshe. *Story of My Life* (Jerusalem: Steimatzky's Agency Ltd, 1976).

Duncan, Andrew and Opatowski Michel. *War in the Holy Land. From Meggido to the West Bank* (Stroud, UK: Sutton Publishing Ltd, 1998).

Eshel, Aharon. Interview: August 6, 2008.

Eshel, David. *Chariots of the Desert* (London: Brassey's Defence Publishers, 1989).

Gilai, Arieh. www.202.org.il/Pages/kadesh/sinai/jump.php

Katz, Samuel M. *Follow Me! A History of Israel's Military Elite* (London: Arms and Armour Press, 1989).

Maroz, Muni. Personal Account. IDF Paratroopers History Site. www.202.org.il/Pages/Footer/eduyot/muni.php

Milstein, Uri. *Milchamot haTzanchanim [The History of the Israel Paratroopers]*. Book 2 (Tel Aviv: Schalgi Ltd, 1985).

Morse, Stan. *Modern Military Powers: Israel* (NY: The Military Press, 1984).

Nordeen, Lon. *Fighters Over Israel* (London: Greenhill Books, 1990).

Oren, Amir. "38 soldiers killed. Who approved the action?" www.haaretz.com. (accessed October 29, 2006).

Oren, Michael B. "The Second War of Independence," *Azure Magazine* (Winter 2007).

Rapoport, Meron. "Into the valley of death," www.haaretz.com (accessed February 13, 2007).

Sachar, Howard M. *A History of Israel* (New York: Alfred A. Knopf, 1985).

Sharon, Ariel and David Chanoff. *Warrior: The Autobiography of Ariel Sharon* (New York: Simon & Schuster, 1989).

Shavitt, Matti. *On the Wings of Eagles: The Story of Arik Sharon, Commander of the Israel paratroopers* (Tel Aviv: Olive Books of Israel, 1970).

Zur, Avi. Interview with Micha Ben-Ari (Kapusta). www.inz.org.il/article.php?id=330 (accessed May 19, 2008)

Chapter 15

"The Six Day War—The Syrian Front," IDF Spokesperson's Office. http://www.idf.il/English/HISTORY/sixday5.htm (accessed June 25, 1998).

Armored Corps. *HaHativa Shelanu b'milchemet Sheshet Yamim* [*Our Brigade in the Six Day War*] (Israel Ministry of Defense Publishing House, 1969).

Associated Press. *Lightning Out of Israel: The Six Day War in the Middle East* (USA: The Associated Press, 1967).

Bashan, Raphael. *The Victory* (Chicago: Quadrangle Books, 1967).

Batelheim, Avi. *Golani—Mishpachat Lohemim* [*Golani—Family of Fighters*] (Golani Brigade Publishing, 1980).

Bennett, Michael. "From the Fighting Front," *Olei Britannia* (UJIA, July 1967).

Chesbiah, Arieh. *Hel haShirion. Tsahal b'Chilo. Encyclopedia l'Tsava u'l'bitachon.* [*The Armored Corps. Zahal and its Soldiers. Encyclopedia of the Army and Security*] (Rivivim Publishing, 1981).

Churchill, Randolph S. and Churchill, Winston S. *The Six Day War* (London: Heinemann, 1967).

Donovan, Robert. *Israel's Fight for Survival* (New York: Signet, 1967).

Duncan, Andrew and Opatowski, Michel. *War in the Holy Land.*

From Meggido to the West Bank (Stroud, UK: Sutton Publishing Ltd., 1998).

Eshel, David. *Chariots of the Desert* (London: Brassey's Defence Publishers, 1989).

Har-Lev, Moty. *Golani Sheli* [*My Golani*] (Aviv Publishers).

Herzog, Chaim. *Arab-Israeli Wars* (New York: Vintage Books, 1982).

IDF. *Anashei haPlada* [*Men of Steel*]. (IDF Armored Corps, Ministry of Defense Publishing House, 1983).

IDF. *Egrof haBarzel*. [*Iron Fist*] (IDF Armored Corps Command, 1969).

Katz, Samuel M. *Follow Me! A History of Israel's Military Elite* (London: Arms and Armour Press, 1989).

Marshall, S. L. A. *Swift Sword* (American Heritage Publishing Co., 1967).

Michelsohn, Benny. "A History of the IDF Through Four Decades. Part IV: Six Day War, June 5–10, 1967," www.idf.il/English/HISTORY/born4.htm (accessed June 4, 1999).

Morse, Stan. *Modern Military Powers: Israel* (New York: The Military Press, 1984).

Sachar, Howard M. *A History of Israel* (New York: Alfred A. Knopf, 1985).

Stevenson, William. *Strike Zion!* (New York: Bantam Books, 1967).

Chapter 16

Eshel, David. *The Yom Kippur War* (Israel: Eshel-Dramit Ltd, 1978).

Eshel, David. *Chariots of the Desert* (London: Brassey's Defence Publishers, 1989).

Herzog, Chaim. *The War of Atonement* (Jerusalem: Steimatzky's Agency, 1975).

Katz, Samuel M. *Fire and Steel* (New York: Pocket Books, 1996).

Katz, Samuel M. *Follow Me! A History of Israel's Military Elite* (London: Arms and Armour Press Ltd, 1989).

Nordeen, Lon. *Fighters Over Israel* (London: Greenhill Books, 1990).

Ostrinsky, David. Interviews: 1997.

Sachar, Howard. *A History of Israel* (New York: Alfred A. Knopf, 1985).
Zaharoni, Irit (ed.). *Israel—Roots & Routes* (Israel: MOD Publishing House, 1990).

Chapter 17
Barrie, Douglas. "The Future of Israeli Air Power," *Flight International* (supplement. 1998).
Braybrook, Roy. "Now you see me, Now you don't," *AIR International* (May 1998).
Clancy, Tom. *Fighter Wing* (New York: Berkley Books, 1995).
Cohen, Eliezer. *Israel's Best Defense* (London: Airlife Publishing Ltd., 1993).
Eitan, Raful. *A Soldier's Story* (New York: Shapolsky Publishers, Inc., 1991).
Elisra Electronic Systems Ltd. Product literature.
Eytan, Lieutenant Colonel, F-16 pilot. Interview: January 5, 1999.
Hewish, Mark, et al. *Air Forces of the World* (London: Peerage Books, 1979).
IDF Spokesman's Office (www.idf.il)
Janes' *All the World's Aircraft* (London: Jane's Information Group).
Morse, Stan. *Modern Military Powers: Israel* (New York: The Military Press, 1984).
Nordeen, Lon. *Fighters Over Israel* (London: Greenhill Books, 1990).
O'Brien, Conor Cruise. *The Siege* (New York: Touchstone, 1986).
Parmiter, James. "Israeli Air Force Tactical Development in the 1982 Bekaa Valley
Campaign," www.oocities.org/paris/LeftBank/7438/iaf.html (accessed March 23, 2011).
Sachar, Howard Morley. *A History of Israel. Volume II* (Oxford, UK: Oxford University Press, 1987).

Epilogue
Human Rights In Palestine And Other Occupied Arab Territories. Report of the United Nations Fact Finding Mission on the Gaza Conflict (United Nations, 2009)

www2.ohchr.org/english/bodies/hrcouncil/specialsession/9/docs/U
NFFMGC_Report.pdf (accessed March 14, 2011)

Goldstone, Richard. "Reconsidering the Goldstone Report on Israel
and War Crimes," *The Washington Post*. April 1, 2011.

"The Second Lebanon War (2006)" (Israel Ministry of Foreign
Affairs)
www.mfa.gov.il/MFA/History/Modern+History/Israel+wars/Hizbu
llah+attack+in+northern+Israel+and+Israels+response+12-Jul-
2006.htm (accessed March 14, 2011)

Zidoni, Ofer and Aloni, Shlomo. *Israel Air Force Yearbook. IAF At
War* (Israel: Wizard Publications, 2007).

INDEX